Bed&Breakfast
FRANCE

Thomas Cook

Published by Thomas Cook Publishing,
a division of Thomas Cook Tour Operations Limited
Company Registration No. 1450464 England
The Thomas Cook Business Park
9 Coningsby Road
Peterborough PE3 8SB
United Kingdom

Telephone: 01733 416477
email: sales@thomascook.com
www.thomascookpublishing.com

Text: © Bed & Breakfast France 2008

Maps: © Thomas Cook Publishing 2008

ISBN 978-1-84157-840-8

Production/DTP editor: Steven Collins

Text design, imagesetting and layout by
PDQ Digital Media Solutions, Bungay

Printed and bound in Spain by
GraphyCems

Photograph credits:

Front cover: Chateau de Chaumont sur Loire. © Fantuz
Olimpio/SIME-4Corners Images
Back cover: Top: 'Le Manoir Souhait', Gourvillette, p. 315;
Bottom: © Cristofori Marco/SIME-4Corners Images

Pages: 1, 3, 7, 8, 9, 11, 17 © AA World Travel Library
Pages: 6, 15 © Michael Hayward

About Bed & Breakfast France
Large enough to matter, small enough to care

During our 26 years' experience of recommending French B&Bs, our enthusiasm for this very special kind of hospitality has grown. For the past 9 years Thomas Cook Publishing has enjoyed a close working partnership with Bed & Breakfast France.

Having our own base in France allows us to offer a local knowledge and level of personal service that other organisations simply cannot match. We know all our hosts personally, we inspect and monitor their premises regularly, and we are very pleased to recommend them. As the French say, *'nous sommes passionnés de B&B.'*

Our Bed & Breakfast France team all love France, and work closely with our hosts. The team is mainly French, but we have some British members and other nationals too. The information listed in the guide is based on the wide range of needs, tastes and demands of our visitors from all over the world. This also helps us to keep our French hosts on their toes. Every establishment in the book is run by an independent owner, who is a qualifying member of the French Bed &

Breakfast Association (BAB France) and has been awarded a prestigious sun/*soleil* rating.

We work in partnership with our hosts to maintain and ensure the highest standard of welcome, to the benefit of clients and hosts alike. The ultimate test for our inspectors is, 'Would I be happy to stay here myself?' rather than slavishly working their way down a checklist of standard facilities. Low standards or a poor welcome are simply not tolerated. Each year applicants are weeded out by our inspections, and your comments are important in helping us maintain the level of hospitality of which we are so proud. Please let us know about your experiences using the form 'Le Feedback', at the back of the guide.

'Le B&B' is an internationally recognised term for accommodation in private homes, and our guide brings this uniquely French style of hospitality to a wider world. We urge you to try it! Language barriers will melt away, you will make many new friends, and our mission will be accomplished.

Contents

What makes *Bed & Breakfast France* so special?

France has thousands of B&Bs, and we are well aware that the quality can vary enormously. For *Bed & Breakfast France* we have picked out the *Grands Crus* from among the cellars of *vin de table*. Across the whole of France, our researchers and inspectors have tracked down the finest homes that offer the best in quality and style. Our approach is highly selective, but still broad enough that you're sure to find somewhere to suit your tastes, close to where you want to be. We aim for *Bed & Breakfast France* to cover the widest possible range, from Parisian apartments or simple farmhouses, up to the grandest, most luxurious châteaux.

Naturally, all of the homes in this guide provide comfortable, clean accommodation and excellent value for money, but they also offer that special, warm welcome that makes our guests feel truly at home.

- **Authentically French**
  We have French researchers, French inspectors, French staff and mostly French hosts, with a few truly Francophile exceptions.

- **We know all of our hosts personally**
  We have had a close relationship with the French Bed & Breakfast Association (BAB France) for the past 14 years and are in daily contact with our hosts.

- **All our hosts are vetted by BAB France**
  Our hosts have all signed up to their code of conduct. We continuously check and update their details and prices.

- **Unique sun/*soleil* rating**
  Our unique classification reflects as much the warmth of the welcome that radiates from our hosts as the quality of the accommodation.

- **Helpline**
  You are not on your own. Friendly, helpful English-speaking staff run our helpline, to assist with your booking and advise you of updates, new details about a property, or new listings in the area you want to visit.

- **Individually run establishments**
  All of our members are individual owners,

not part of large soulless chains or bureaucratic organisations.

- **Hobbies and activities**

  Specialist expertise, interests and activities that our hosts offer are listed in the guide. They include cordon bleu and medieval cookery courses, art classes and tours, hunting, shooting and fishing, golf, farming, truffle hunts, history trips, *grand cru* wine culture (of course) and many, many more.

This is where our hosts really score over those in lesser guides. Their local knowledge and connections can offer the traveller an entrée to golf courses, local artists' studios and galleries, vineyards and farms, giving you an inside track to the places and moments that can make your stay truly special and memorable. Whatever your tastes in a holiday, the best way to experience all that an area has to offer is to be guided and assisted by a local expert.

Bed & Breakfast France is perfect for single travellers who want a personally tailored holiday, but is also the ideal way to provide a unique family experience. There are endless opportunities for relaxation and discovery, just as if you were staying with friends abroad.

What to expect from our B&Bs
A warm, French welcome and superb value

Travel anywhere in France and you will pass forests of roadside signs advertising *Chambres d'hôtes*. Although many of these places may offer adequate accommodation, we will take you straight past all of them, directly to the bed and breakfast homes that we know to be the best. You will be taken to properties that our inspectors have visited: homes with comfortable rooms and hospitable owners, which have been awarded our unique and highly coveted 'Bed & Breakfast France Sun/*Soleil*' rating.

Whether you plan to stay in a rustic village, a rural town or a historic city, by the beautiful sandy coasts, up in the clear mountain air, or in the sun-dappled, rolling French countryside, you cannot fail to be charmed by the comfort and hospitality that we and our hosts strive to offer you.

You will be greeted with a generous, warm-hearted welcome by the owner of the house, and made to feel comfortable from the moment you arrive. If Madame offers you a drink on arrival, or some homemade pâté for your journey, it will be from the kindness of her heart and won't show up on a computerised bill when you are leaving. Our hosts are eager to introduce you to their local wines and regional specialities. Many sell their own produce and you may also find local arts and crafts on sale.

All of our bed and breakfast establishments offer excellent value for money, but we do not choose them for their price alone. You might well find cheaper accommodation in a 'pit stop' by a motorway or on a soulless industrial estate, but you won't be sure of waking up to:

- a delicious French breakfast, often prepared with homemade ingredients

- a comfortable bedroom, furnished and decorated with the host's individual style and character

- a home from home that is warm and cosy or chic and stylish, reflecting the taste of the host or the style of the region

- local knowledge and free personal advice on excursions or places to visit, where to buy good wine or how to avoid the traffic jams, from the experience of someone who has lived in the place for years and who really cares

- the warm welcome to the home of your French host, the reception that a friend of the family might expect, and an offer to join the family for dinner

This kind of true hospitality is the gold standard for bed and breakfast accommodation, and the key to a really memorable stay. We have chosen the hosts featured in this guide with meticulous care. With 26 years' experience of B&Bs, we have discovered what 'a warm welcome' can really mean.

French breakfast

The rates in this guide are inclusive of a real French breakfast (unless indicated otherwise). Breakfast consists of bread, usually a baguette, and sometimes croissants, brioches or crêpes will also be offered. Coffee is usually served, as is the French tradition, but tea and hot chocolate are also often available. Butter, jam (often homemade) and sometimes fruit juice are on offer. Some hosts will provide a cooked breakfast, which may include regional specialities.

Your host will usually serve your breakfast in the dining room, and this is always a good opportunity to discuss your plans for the day and glean advice. A few hosts will give you the option of preparing your own breakfast, and some may make a kitchen available to you.

Dinner

Many hosts offer dinner and, if they do, while you are not in any way obliged to do so, we suggest that you take full advantage. This is the ideal time to relax informally with your hosts and enjoy home cooking, often to French gastronomic standards. Over a superb dinner with a couple of glasses of wine, perhaps served outside on a warm summer evening, you can sink softly into the French way of life and get to know your hosts a little better. Some B&Bs offer barbecues for the use of guests. Hosts who do not provide dinner will be pleased to give you details of their favourite restaurants nearby.

If you wish to have dinner on the first night of your stay, please be sure to advise your host well in advance, and reconfirm on the day of your arrival, to avoid disappointment.

Rooms

Each room's facilities are listed in the host's entry in the guide. This enables you to reserve a particular room (they often have individual names). If you would like to get to know your hosts and the area really well, then make your choice from among the homes with fewer rooms, so that your host's time is less divided. If you stay outside the main tourist season, your host may be less busy, and able to spend more time with you.

Your hosts' hobbies and interests

This is a key distinction of the bed and breakfasts in our guide. Many hosts have special interests and local contacts which can open doors for the visitor. They may take you hunting or fishing, mushroom-hunting or hill-walking, or introduce you to their local golf club. The chef of the house may invite you to join them as they shop in the local markets, or Madame could offer to help you buy wine, foie gras, cheeses or charcuterie direct from the producers. Many hosts sell their own produce on the premises. We know all of our hosts well, and their entry in the guide indicates any specialist activities undertaken. They will be delighted to help you with any necessary arrangements, as they would for a friend. Their tips will provide vital keys to help you enjoy your stay. Don't hesitate to draw on their advice and years of experience.

How to use this book
Choosing a host

Homes are grouped by *région*, with a map of the *région* at the beginning of each section. *Régions* on the map are divided into *départements* (counties) with their postal code number. Major roads and railway lines are also included on the map, but it should be used in conjunction with a detailed road map for finding your way around.

Major towns and cities are indicated on the map by an orange dot and the page numbers of the entries for any local B&Bs are noted. Hosts' entries have two-part reference numbers. The first part is the *département* number, and the second part is the number for the host in that *département*.

Each host's entry includes the 'sun/*soleil*' rating (explained below), then usually a photograph of the property, the name of the host and their address and contact details. Distances are given to the nearest town, railway station and airport. Descriptions of the property and facilities are included, along with the host's specialities and interests. Information is given about dining arrangements, pets, and local amenities.

Brief directions are provided from the nearest main town but, again, a detailed road map should be used for navigation.

Prices
All prices are in euros

1 euro (€) = £ 0.70 (at the time of going to press)

The price per night is listed for each individual room and includes breakfast, along with the other facilities offered and the cost of extra beds or multiple occupancy. You will find beds from as little as €12 per person per night and up to €300 per person per night. The average price in the guide for a room for two persons with breakfast included is €50–€60. Note that prices in euros are written with a comma between the euros and centimes, e.g. €35,50.

Reductions/discounts

Reductions for a long stay Many hosts offer good discounts for stays of several nights. This is indicated in their entry.

Reductions for children Many hosts accommodate babies free of charge or offer reductions for children.

Off-peak discounts Some hosts offer good discounts for stays out of the main season. This is indicated in their entry.

Family rooms These are much cheaper where available.

Symbols and ratings

Our 'sun/soleil' ratings are unique, combining the warmth of the hosts' welcome with the quality of comfort of their accommodation. We are not bureaucrats who go around measuring mirrors, but we do insist that rooms are clean and beds are comfortable. Above all is that warmth of welcome is imparted to our guests.

What the 'sun/*soleil*' ratings mean:

☀	**1 sun** Warm and enthusiastic welcome. Simple, clean accommodation.
☀☀	**2 suns** Kind, welcoming hosts and a comfortable home, or one that is in a popular or attractive tourist area.
☀☀☀	**3 suns** High-quality welcome. Very comfortable home with charm and character.
☀☀☀☀	**4 suns** Top of the range, '*la crème de la crème*'. Luxury and charm, with a warm and first-class welcome in an attractive location.

 Bed & Breakfast France is recognised by the French Tourist Office as denoting excellent quality and was the first bed and breakfast organisation to be selected for their 'Bienvenue en France' campaign. Wherever you see this logo in France, you can be sure of a great welcome. Naturally, a large number of our B&B hosts have been selected to take part.

 Please use our 'Le Feedback' form at the back of this guide to send us your comments. These will be taken into account when we select the top 50 hosts who are awarded the Golden BAB sign. Look out for this sign in the guide, if you want to stay in one of the 50 best B&Bs in France.

Paris

Like all capital cities, Paris is more expensive than other cities or towns in the country. All of our B&Bs in Paris need to be booked through our Central Reservations Office (see page 13). We offer a range of private homes or apartments with shared or private bathrooms. Some of our Parisian hosts go out to work, so be sure to arrange an arrival time when they are able to be at home to greet you. Paris has excellent public transport and some places are only 10 minutes from the city centre by the RER (fast suburban train).

 The Paris HOTE QUALITE Charter guarantees quality accommodation in the main residence of a Parisian home-owner, who will serve a homemade French-style breakfast at the family table. It assures a warm Parisian welcome, in a Parisian home.

The charter can be seen in full online at: www.bedbreak.com

How to make a booking
Booking directly with the host

Bookings can be made directly with the host by telephone, fax or e-mail, or by letter. If you book direct, we recommend that you confirm in writing, sending any deposit the host may require, and re-confirm by telephone a day before your arrival.

Telephoning hosts in France

To dial from outside France, or on a non-French mobile, first dial the international dialling code, then the country code (33 for France) then the number in the guide, omitting the (0). So to call (0) 1 34 19 90 00 from a UK telephone, dial 00 33 134 19 90 00. To call from a French landline or mobile, dial the number as given in the guide, starting with the (0).

Book with Bed & Breakfast France

Bed & Breakfast France can make bookings for you, saving you time and preventing any problems with the language barrier or difficulties sending payments to France. You can book through Bed & Breakfast France by calling 0871 781 0834 (from outside the UK, call + 33 1 34 19 90 00) or e-mail bab@bedbreak.com, or book online at www.bedbreak.com. A booking fee applies. NB. For accommodation in Paris, booking through Bed & Breakfast France is essential.

1) Plan your trip

Decide the dates of your stay and the number of children and adults in your party, then choose where you would like to stay.

2) Contact us with your itinerary

Please give us a first and second choice, and quote the 4- or 5-digit host reference numbers. In the unlikely event that both your choices are full, we will offer the nearest match to your requirements. Hosts may have joined since the guide went to press, so you should never be located too far from your area of choice. Your trip will be more enjoyable and less tiring if you stay more than one night with each host, and you will have the opportunity to get to know them and the area better.

You can book by telephone or fax, e-mail to bab@bedbreak.com, or via the website www.bedbreak.com using a credit card, or by post enclosing a cheque.

Calling from the UK

dial 0871 781 0834

fax 0871 781 0835

Calling from outside the UK

dial + 33 1 34 19 90 00

fax + 33 1 39 94 89 72

Calling from France
(landline or French mobile)

dial 01 34 19 90 00

The reservations office is open Monday to Friday from 9am to 6pm French time (8am to 5pm GMT). Outside these hours, you may send in your reservation request by fax, e-mail or online.

3) We will send you a provisional booking

This will give brief details of your booking, the total balance to pay and the latest date by which the final payment should be received. Alterations can be made to your provisional booking until you confirm it.

4) Confirm your booking

To confirm your booking, pay the balance to Bed & Breakfast France no later than the date indicated.

5) Bed & Breakfast France will send you a confirmation voucher

When the full balance of your payment has been received, you will be sent a confirmation voucher (by post, fax or e-mail), giving full details of your accommodation and directions to find it.

- Once the confirmation voucher has been issued your booking cannot be changed.
- To make changes after this point a booking has to be cancelled and re-booked, and cancellation fees will apply. Booking fees are non-refundable. A booking is only confirmed and guaranteed when the final balance has been received before the payment date given. Last-minute reservations cannot be guaranteed if the final payment arrives late.

6) Payment

Bed & Breakfast France accepts both VISA and MasterCard, or you can send a sterling cheque payable to: Bed & Breakfast France.

bedbreak.com
Welcome to the Bed & Breakfast website

Bed & Breakfast France booking conditions

1. Role of Bed & Breakfast France

Bed & Breakfast France acts only as a booking agent. It makes the reservations as agent for the person(s) providing the accommodation and does not accept liability in connection with these reservations.

2. Deposit

No deposit is required.

3. Payment

All reservations must be pre-paid, and a reservation is not confirmed until full payment is received by Bed & Breakfast France. We do our best to rush through last-minute reservations, but cannot take any responsibility for problems arising due to reservations being confirmed at the last minute or payment not reaching us in time. If hosts have to collect payment from you (except for extras such as dinner), a €38 (£25) administration fee will be charged.

4. Recommended forms of payment

– Valid VISA or MasterCard

– Sterling cheque/draft on UK bank (sender to pay all charges)

– Sterling travellers' cheques (signed twice please)

– Cheque in euros on a French bank

For all other forms of payment there is a surcharge of €38 (£25) per booking.

5. Alterations

Alterations can be made to your provisional booking until you are happy with it and confirm it. No alteration can be made to confirmed bookings.

6. Re-instatement

If a booking is released because you have not paid the balance to us on time or delay your stay, a re-instatement fee of €38 (£25) will be charged for us to re-book the accommodation for you.

7. Cancellations

If you cancel a confirmed booking, notice must be received by Bed & Breakfast France by letter, fax or e-mail. The following charges apply to cancellations received as follows:

– 15 days or more before the first night booked: 30% or €50 (£30), whichever is the greater.

– 14 to 4 days before the first night booked: 97%.

– less than 4 days before the first night booked: 100%.

NB. The 'first night booked' is the earliest date on your confirmation voucher and applies to the whole itinerary and not individual stops. You must be covered by cancellation insurance to get these charges reimbursed.

8. Reservation fee

A reservation fee is charged by Bed & Breakfast France. This is 15% of the total cost of the accommodation.

9. Confirmation

Please check carefully that you are happy with your provisional booking before you confirm it, as confirmation of your reservation commits you to a firm booking that cannot be altered. You are advised to check the location of the hosts reserved in relation to your planned itinerary, especially if travelling by public transport.

10. Circumstances beyond our control

Bed & Breakfast France cannot be held liable for problems and delays resulting from circumstances beyond their control (force majeure), such as strikes, postal delays, transport delays, changes to the personal circumstances of the hosts, terrorism and war, etc.

11. Extra services

Bed & Breakfast France cannot be held liable for payment of additional charges for extra services and facilities not included in the basic price paid to Bed & Breakfast France. It is the client's responsibility to settle these charges before departing from the establishment.

12. Quality of hosts

Bed & Breakfast France has taken all reasonable care to ensure the quality of the hosts and accommodation reserved for clients and cannot be held liable for any dissatisfaction the clients may have with the hosts or the accommodation. All complaints must be registered with your hosts before departure to give them the opportunity to put matters right.

13. Errors and omissions

Every care has been taken in the production of the guide and all information is correct at the time of going to press. However Bed & Breakfast France cannot accept liability for errors or omissions it may inadvertently contain.

14. Telephone bookings

Bookings made by telephone are accepted on the clear understanding that Bed & Breakfast France cannot accept liability for errors or misunderstandings that may occur.

We advise you to leave sufficient time for written documents to reach you.

15. Responsibility

Bed & Breakfast France shall have no liability in contract, tort or otherwise for death, injury or loss to clients except to the extent that such liability is imposed by law and cannot be excluded or restricted.

16. Dispute

Any dispute or claim against Bed & Breakfast France or the person(s) providing accommodation shall be governed by English Law and subject to the exclusive jurisdiction of English Courts.

Cancellation insurance

Bed and breakfast hosts are small private homes. If you cancel a confirmed reservation they may not be able to re-let the room and will expect to be paid. For your protection, we strongly advise you to take out travel insurance when you travel to France that covers cancellations in order to be able to claim back any monies lost. See point 7 of the Conditions of Reservation.

Helpline

You are not on your own.

When in France our **HELPLINE** is available to you if you have a problem with a reservation.

Dial 01 34 19 90 00

From your mobile phone or outside of France: **+33 1 34 19 90 00**

Office hours only.

Unwind and recharge your batteries

There are so many ways that a holiday in France can make you feel so much better. You might choose a 'hyper active' holiday – a term very much in vogue in France today – where activities could include swimming or something more energetic like kite-surfing. Or perhaps a cultural holiday, enjoying the enormous range of festivals, exhibitions and historic sites available to visit. Themed stays are all the rage here now and a large number of our hosts offer them. Alternatively, many of our hosts also organise study holidays and courses. Whatever you'd like to do, a stay with our hosts opens the door to countless opportunities for getting away from your usual lifestyle.

If, however, you prefer to be pampered and looked after – especially if you never seem to find time to do so at home – then many of our hosts will have just the thing for you. Why not try massage, reflexology, essential oils, a sauna or hammam?

We have selected the hosts who will help you return revived and refreshed. You can find these located on the accompanying map and within the list that follows. Divided into three different categories, the first indicates those places offering massage and fitness services, the second will help you find places with spas, jacuzzis, saunas or hammams, while the third pinpoints hosts which offer delicious organic food.

So just relax and enjoy…

Relax and kick back

with our hosts offering you a great sense of wellbeing and the chance to unwind

NORD-PAS-DE-CALAIS

Cambrai

Dieppe
Cherbourg

NORMANDY

Deauville
Bayeux

PICARDIE

Rethel

Paris

Chartres

ILE DE FRANCE

CHAMPAGNE-ARDENNE

LORRAINE

ALSACE

Presqu'î le de Crozon

BRITTANY

Douarnenez

Le Mans

WESTERN LOIRE

Blois
Amboise

CENTRE-LOIRE VALLEY

Châteauroux

BURGUNDY

Pouilly-en-Auxois

Mulhouse

FRANCHE-COMTE

Beaune
Nevers
Autun

Nantes

Noirmoutier- en-l'île

POITOU-CHARENTES

St-Jean-d'Angély

LIMOUSIN

AUVERGNE

Roanne

RHONE-ALPES

Vienne

Chamonix

La Bourboule

Bordeaux
Arcachon

Sarlat-la-Canéda

Valence

AQUITAINE

Agen

Mont-de-Marsan

MIDI-PYRENEES

Alès

Avignon

PROVENCE-ALPES-COTE D'AZUR

LANGUEDOC-ROUSSILLON

Aix-en-Provence

Béziers
Montpellier

St-Gaudens

 Organic Food

 Spa/Hammam/Sauna

 Massage/Fitness

Organic Food

Region	Town	Host number	Host Page
Aquitaine	AGEN	47.06	79
Aquitaine	BORDEAUX	33.53	71
Brittany	PRESQU'ILE DE CROZON	29.44	129
Centre - Loire Valley	CHARTRES	28.16	149
Centre - Loire Valley	CHATEAUROUX	36.07	152
Champagne-Ardennes	RETHEL	08.01	181
Ile de France	PARIS	75.34	39
Languedoc-Roussillon	ALES	30.44	191
Midi-Pyrénées	ST-GAUDENS	31.11	208
Nord-Pas-de-Calais	CAMBRAI	59.11	216
Normandy	DEAUVILLE	14.015	257
Normandy	DEAUVILLE	14.001	261
Provence-Alpes-Côte d'Azur	AVIGNON	84.98	364
Rhône-Alpes	VALENCE	07.22	379
Rhône-Alpes	VALENCE	07.30	380
Western Loire	LE MANS	72.38	299
Western Loire	NANTES	44.20	289

Spa/Hammam/Sauna

Region	Town	Host number	Host Page
Alsace	MULHOUSE	68.05	54
Aquitaine	ARCACHON	40.10	68
Aquitaine	SARLAT-LA-CANEDA	24.76	67
Aquitaine	SARLAT-LA-CANEDA	24.68	62
Auvergne	LA BOURBOULE	63.12	92
Brittany	DOUARNENEZ	29.31	128
Brittany	PRESQU'ILE DE CROZON	29.44	129
Burgundy	AUTUN	71.19	114
Burgundy	POUILLY-EN-AUXOIS	21.52	110
Centre - Loire Valley	AMBOISE	37.68	152
Centre - Loire Valley	BLOIS	41.57	174
Ile de France	PARIS	75.23	38
Languedoc-Roussillon	BEZIERS	34.33	198
Languedoc-Roussillon	MONTPELLIER	34.36	200
Normandy	BAYEUX	14.24	238
Poitou-Charentes	ST-JEAN-D'ANGELY	17.54	315
Provence-Alpes-Côte d'Azur	AIX-EN-PROVENCE	13.18	339
Rhône-Alpes	CHAMONIX	74.32	385
Rhône-Alpes	ROANNE	42.19	381
Rhône-Alpes	ROANNE	42.18	381
Rhône-Alpes	VIENNE	38.21	380
Western Loire	NOIRMOUTIER-EN-L'ILE	85.21	301

Massage/Fitness

Region	Town	Host number	Host Page
Aquitaine	BORDEAUX	33.43	73
Aquitaine	MONT-DE-MARSAN	40.13	79
Aquitaine	SARLAT-LA-CANEDA	24.76	67
Auvergne	LA BOURBOULE	63.12	92
Brittany	PRESQU'ILE DE CROZON	29.44	129
Burgundy	NEVERS	58.13	112
Ile de France	PARIS	75.29	43
Normandy	CHERBOURG	50.61	277
Normandy	DIEPPE	76.39	283
Rhône-Alpes	ROANNE	42.19	381
Rhône-Alpes	VALENCE	07.30	380
Western Loire	NOIRMOUTIER-EN-L'ILE	85.21	301

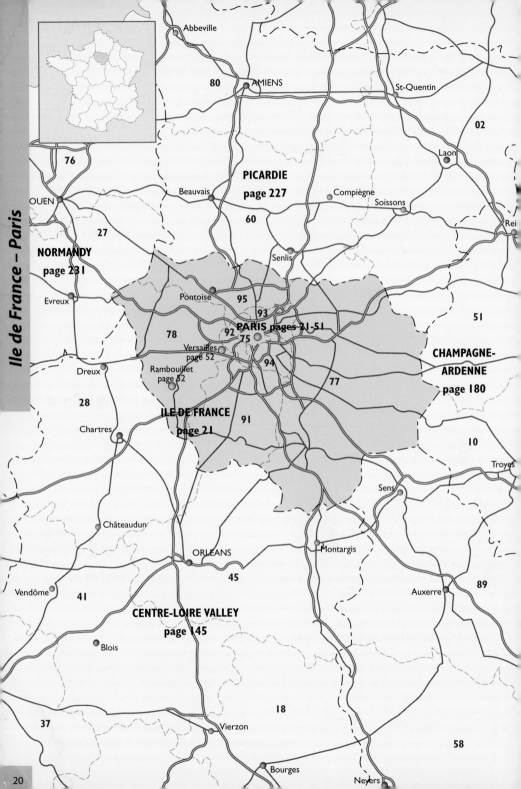

Abbeville

80   AMIENS   St-Quentin

02

Laon

76

PICARDIE
page 227

Beauvais   Compiègne

OUEN   Soissons   Rei

27   60

NORMANDY   Senlis   51
page 231

Evreux   Pontoise   95   93

78   92   **PARIS pages 21-51**   **CHAMPAGNE-**
ARDENNE
Dreux   Versailles   75   **page 180**
page 52   94

Rambouillet
page 52   77

28   **ILE DE FRANCE**   91   10
Chartres   **page 21**

Troyes

Sens

Châteaudun

ORLEANS   Montargis

Vendôme   45   Auxerre   89

41   **CENTRE-LOIRE VALLEY**
page 145

Blois

18

37   Vierzon

58

Bourges

Neyers

Location
Paris 1e
Châtelet — Hôtel de Ville — Marais
Nearest metro: Châtelet-Les-Halles
Airport: Paris-Orly 20km

hôtes
qualité
Paris

Apartment

Mona's place is warm and lively. A charming and pretty bedroom is furnished so as to give you maximum privacy. In a very quiet street in the centre of Paris. An excellent address.

Mona
Reservations:
Tel: +33 1 34 19 9000
Fax: +33 1 39 94 89 72
bab@bedbreak.com
www.bedbreak.com

Facilities: hosts have pets, pets not accepted, 2 nights minimum stay, closed: 01/07–10/09
Fluent English spoken

Price Structure – 1 Bedroom
bathroom, wc, twin beds: €93,50

Capacity: 2 people

Directions: Please contact the Central Reservations Office. Full address and directions will be provided on booking.

Location
Paris 1e
Châtelet — Hôtel de Ville — Marais
Nearest metro: Châtelet-Les-Halles
Airport: Paris-Orly 20km

Apartment

You are in the heart of the capital, an ideal location from which to explore the old parts of Paris on foot: le Louvre, les Tuileries, l'Ile de la Cité and la Sainte-Chapelle as well as the cathedral of Notre-Dame . . . If you cross the River Seine you arrive directly at St-Germain-des-Prés, a *quartier* loved by many an artist. Sabrina will welcome you to her apartment and show you her 'petit coin de paradis'. The guest bedroom is quiet, fairly spacious and comfortable.

Sabrina
Reservations:
Tel: +33 1 34 19 9000
Fax: +33 1 39 94 89 72
bab@bedbreak.com
www.bedbreak.com

Facilities: pets not accepted, kitchen, 100% no smoking, 1 shared bathroom, wc, 2 nights minimum stay
Fluent English spoken

Price Structure – 1 Bedroom
television, double bed: €78

Capacity: 2 people

Directions: Please contact the Central Reservations Office. Full address and directions will be provided on booking.

75.46 Paris

Apartment

Location
Paris 2e
Opéra
Nearest metro: Pyramides
Airport: Paris-Orly 20km

In the centre of Paris, this apartment offers comfort, space and peace and quiet. You can walk to the Louvre, to the Opéra and to Châtelet. Your hostess is a music lover. The kitchen is available, where you prepare your own breakfast.

Monique
Reservations:
Tel: +33 1 34 19 9000
Fax: +33 1 39 94 89 72
bab@bedbreak.com
www.bedbreak.com

Price Structure – 2 Bedrooms
television, along corridor shower room, wc, double bed: €90. Along corridor room: double bed: €80 – 2 people €170 – 4 people

Facilities: lounge, pets not accepted, kitchen, 100% no smoking, 10 years old minimum age, 2 nights minimum stay
Fluent English spoken

Capacity: 4 people

Directions: Please contact the Central Reservations Office. Full address and directions will be provided on booking.

75.59 Paris

Apartment

Location
Paris 3e
Marais — Beaubourg — République
Nearest metro: Temple
Airport: Paris-Orly 20km

This superb apartment is quietly situated in a beautiful Hausmann-designed building. It is very convenient for many sights as it's at the heart of the République area, near to Le Marais and five minutes from the Pompidou Centre (Centre Beaubourg). Your hostess is very kind.

Hélène
Reservations:
Tel: +33 1 34 19 9000
Fax: +33 1 39 94 89 72
bab@bedbreak.com
www.bedbreak.com

Price Structure – 1 Suite
bathroom, wc, double bed: €76
En-suite room double bed: €70

Facilities: pets not accepted, 100% no smoking, 7 years old minimum age, 3 nights minimum stay
Adequate English spoken

Extra Bed: €28
Capacity: 4 people

Directions: Please contact the Central Reservations Office. Full address and directions will be provided on booking.

Location
Paris 5e
Quartier Latin — Jardin des Plantes
Nearest metro: Austerlitz
Airport: Paris-Orly 20km

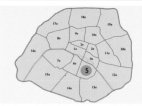

Apartment

A small, cosy apartment, quietly situated with an extensive view from the lounge. The nearby Jardin des Plantes is ideal for walking from the Grande Bibliothèque and Bercy. You can continue to the Rue Mouffetard via the typical small streets of the Latin Quarter.

Lélia
Reservations:
Tel: +33 1 34 19 9000
Fax: +33 1 39 94 89 72
bab@bedbreak.com
www.bedbreak.com

Facilities: pets not accepted, 3 nights minimum stay, closed: 01/08–31/08
Fluent English spoken

Price Structure – 1 Bedroom
television, shower room, wc, double bed, single bed: €100 – 2 people €123 – 3 people

Capacity: 3 people

Directions: Please contact the Central Reservations Office. Full address and directions will be provided on booking.

Location
Paris 5e
Quartier Latin — Notre Dame
Nearest metro: Maubert-Mutualité
Airport: Paris-Orly 20km

Apartment

A charming apartment located on the second floor of an 18th-century building. It is a stone's throw from Notre Dame de Paris and an ideal location from which to stroll around the Latin Quarter. The two bedrooms are independent, pleasant and quiet. One is on a mezzanine floor and has two extra beds for children. This is a good option for families or small groups of friends. On fine days you can enjoy the small enclosed garden, which is reached from the road. A secure parking space can be reserved here for a fee of €15 per 24 hours.

Brigitte
Reservations:
Tel: +33 1 34 19 9000
Fax: +33 1 39 94 89 72
bab@bedbreak.com
www.bedbreak.com

Facilities: garden, pets not accepted, babies welcome, free cot, 2 nights minimum stay
Fluent English spoken

Price Structure – 2 Bedrooms
'Bleue': lounge, television, along corridor bathroom, wc, double bed (queen-size), 2 single beds (child-size): €90 – 2 people €130 – 4 people.
'Rouge': shower room, wc, double bed: €75

Reduction: 4 nights
Capacity: 6 people

Directions: Please contact the Central Reservations Office. Full address and directions will be provided on booking.

Ile de France – Paris

75.45 Paris

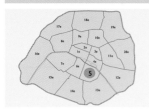

Apartment

Bienvenue en France

Location
Paris 5e
Quartier Latin — Jardin des Plantes
Nearest metro: Austerlitz
Airport: Paris-Orly 20km

Karen is a sculptress, and you may be able to watch her at work in her studio and admire some of her creations. Her apartment, which is very close to the Jardin des Plantes, is particularly quiet and relaxing and the atmosphere is easy-going and friendly.

Karen
Reservations:
Tel: +33 1 34 19 9000
Fax: +33 1 39 94 89 72
bab@bedbreak.com
www.bedbreak.com

Price Structure – 1 Bedroom
twin beds: €53,50

Capacity: 2 people

Facilities: hosts have pets, 1 shared bathroom, wc, 4 years old minimum age, 3 nights minimum stay
Fluent English spoken

Directions: Please contact the Central Reservations Office. Full address and directions will be provided on booking.

75.88 Paris

Apartment

Location
Paris 6e
Luxembourg — St-Germain-des-Prés — Quartier Latin
Nearest metro: Vavin
Airport: Paris-Orly 20km

This is a great location for getting about on foot as you are by the Jardin du Luxembourg and ten minutes on foot from St-Germain-des-Prés and not too far either from the Latin Quarter. Nonetheless, the area is also pretty well served by public transport, enabling you to quickly reach other principal sites of interest. With great warmth, Alain opens his doors to guests and he will rapidly put you at ease. As a former language teacher, he can easily offer advice or indulge you in longer conversations. His good humour comes through in several languages!

Alain
Reservations:
Tel: +33 1 34 19 9000
Fax: +33 1 39 94 89 72
bab@bedbreak.com
www.bedbreak.com

Price Structure – 2 Bedrooms
1 room: double bed: €80
1 room: single bed: €65 – 1 person

Capacity: 3 people

Facilities: tv lounge, pets not accepted, 100% no smoking, 1 shared bathroom, wc, 2 nights minimum stay
Fluent English spoken

Directions: Please contact the Central Reservations Office. Full address and directions will be provided on booking.

Location
Paris 7e
Musée d'Orsay — Jardin des
Tuileries
Nearest metro: Musée d'Orsay
Airport: Paris-Roissy 25km

Apartment

Just 50m from the famous Musée d'Orsay, Roselyne and Antoine welcome you as friends to their home. What's more, you are opposite the Jardin des Tuileries and can stroll along the River Seine. Your hosts can assist you with booking museum entry tickets and theatre tickets. After a long day's sightseeing, relax and put your feet up in their guest room with an adjoining lounge area, which together form a pleasant living space (the sofa bed is suitable for a child). Homemade jams are served at breakfast.

Roselyne & Antoine
Reservations:
Tel: +33 1 34 19 9000
Fax: +33 1 39 94 89 72
bab@bedbreak.com
www.bedbreak.com

Facilities: lounge, pets not accepted, babies welcome, free cot, 100% no smoking
Fluent English spoken

Price Structure – 1 Bedroom
lounge, shower room, wc, twin beds: €100

Extra Bed: €10
Reduction: 5 nights
Capacity: 2 people

Directions: Please contact the Central Reservations Office. Full address and directions will be provided on booking.

Location
Paris 8e
Etoile — Champs-Elysées
Nearest metro: Charles de Gaulle-Etoile
Airport: Paris-Roissy 20km

Apartment

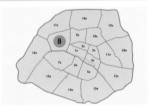

This B&B used to be in the 1st arrondissement, and has now moved to the 8th, just 300m from the famous Avenue des Champs-Elysées. This is the perfect place for exploring one of the most chic parts of the capital with its haute-couture fashion houses, antique dealers, art galleries and famous restaurants. The bedroom is pleasant and bright, comfortably furnished with a private bathroom and a dressing room.

Soisick
Reservations:
Tel: +33 1 34 19 9000
Fax: +33 1 39 94 89 72
bab@bedbreak.com
www.bedbreak.com

Facilities: tv lounge, pets not accepted, 100% no smoking, 2 nights minimum stay
Fluent English spoken

Price Structure – 1 Bedroom
shower room, wc, twin beds: €93,50

Capacity: 2 people

Directions: Please contact the Central Reservations Office. Full address and directions will be provided on booking.

Ile de France – Paris

75.82 Paris

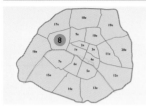

Apartment

Location
Paris 8e
Etoile — Champs-Elysées
Nearest metro: St-Augustin
Airport: Paris-Roissy 25km

hôtes
qualité
Paris

Françoise & Jean
Reservations:
Tel: +33 1 34 19 9000
Fax: +33 1 39 94 89 72
bab@bedbreak.com
www.bedbreak.com

Within easy reach of the Champs-Elysées, Opéra, and the area *les Grands Magasins*, is this Hausmann-style apartment, ideal for those of you who seek out green areas, it being just a few steps from Parc Monceau. The vast lounge is typical of the architecture during that *époque*. Your bedroom is spacious, of modest comfort, with twin beds and a private shower room which is a touch cramped. In the evening, you may be lucky enough to visit Paris 'by night' with M. le Vicomte himself as your chauffeur!

Price Structure – 1 Bedroom
shower room, wc, twin beds: €85

Capacity: 2 people

Facilities: lounge, hosts have pets, pets not accepted, dinner available, 100% no smoking, closed: 15/07 – 31/08
Basic English spoken

Directions: Please contact the Central Reservations Office. Full address and directions will be provided on booking.

75.99 Paris

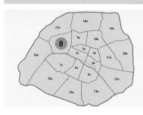

Residence of Outstanding Character

Location
Paris 8e
Concorde — Jardin des Tuileries
Nearest metro: Invalides
Airport: Paris-Orly 20km

hôtes
qualité
Paris

Rita & Alain
Reservations:
Tel: +33 1 34 19 9000
Fax: +33 1 39 94 89 72
bab@bedbreak.com
www.bedbreak.com

Fancy a stay in the centre of Paris but off the beaten track? Then this is the place for you as you are literally staying on the River Seine, on a barge, in the very centre of Paris just ten minutes on foot from the Champs-Elysées. A unique and original way to experience Paris!

Price Structure – 1 Bedroom
television, bathroom, wc, double bed (queen-size): €150

Reduction: 4 nights
Capacity: 2 people

Facilities: Off-street parking, lounge, pets not accepted, babies welcome, free cot, 100% no smoking, 18 years old minimum age
Fluent English spoken

Directions: Please contact the Central Reservations Office. Full address and directions will be provided on booking.

Location
Paris 9e
Grands Magasins
Nearest metro: Le Pelletier
Airport: Paris-Roissy 25km

Apartment

This apartment is quite basic, but right in the centre of Paris, between Gare du Nord and Boulevard Haussman and the *Grands Magasins* area with the large department stores. Convenient for the theatre district. Jacqueline loves music and art.

Jacqueline
Reservations:
Tel: +33 1 34 19 9000
Fax: +33 1 39 94 89 72
bab@bedbreak.com
www.bedbreak.com

Facilities: 100% no smoking, 2 nights minimum stay
Adequate English spoken

Price Structure – 1 Bedroom
shower, double bed, single bed: €78 – 2 people
€105 – 3 people

Capacity: 3 people

Directions: Please contact the Central Reservations Office. Full address and directions will be provided on booking.

Location
Paris 9e
Grands Magasins
Nearest metro: Pigalle
Airport: Paris-Roissy 25km

Apartment

An ideal location just ten minutes from Opéra and the *Grands Magasins* and 20 minutes from the Sacré Coeur. The *quartier* is lively, full of bustling restaurants and cafés being so close to the theatres and cabarets, leaving the prospect open for memorable evenings. The flat itself is quiet and pleasant with two lounges. The bright bedroom has its own bathroom and Emma provides lovely bed linen, making every effort for you to feel well received! NB. Her home is open from Thursday evening to Monday morning, perfect for long weekends!

Emma
Reservations:
Tel: +33 1 34 19 9000
Fax: +33 1 39 94 89 72
bab@bedbreak.com
www.bedbreak.com

Facilities: tv lounge, pets not accepted, 100% no smoking, 18 years old minimum age, 2 nights minimum stay
Fluent English spoken

Price Structure – 1 Bedroom
bathroom, wc, double bed: €78

Capacity: 2 people

Directions: Please contact the Central Reservations Office. Full address and directions will be provided on booking.

75.71 Paris

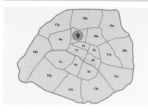

Apartment

Location
Paris 9e
Grands Magasins
Nearest metro: St-Lazare
Airport: Paris-Roissy 25km

hôtes
qualité
Paris

Myriam
Reservations:
Tel: +33 1 34 19 9000
Fax: +33 1 39 94 89 72
bab@bedbreak.com
www.bedbreak.com

Ten minutes on foot from Opéra and *Les Grands Magasins* in the area of St-Lazare, Myriam welcomes you to her splendid apartment that boasts a lovely enclosed garden, a rarity in Paris! A true gastronome, she has a hundred and one secret recipes for you to feast on in the garden, weather permitting. She knows Paris like the back of her hand and will happily accompany you on a stroll around the most charming parts of the capital. A lovely, spacious bedroom with garden access and a warm welcome to boot. A perfect combination.

Price Structure – 1 Bedroom
television, bathroom, wc, double bed: €80

Capacity: 2 people

Facilities: garden, lounge, hosts have pets, pets not accepted, dinner available, 100% no smoking
Fluent English spoken

Directions: Please contact the Central Reservations Office. Full address and directions will be provided on booking.

75.11 Paris

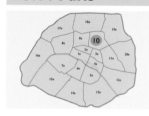

Apartment

Location
Paris 10e
Gare du Nord
Nearest metro: Gare du Nord
Airport: Paris-Roissy 20km

hôtes
qualité
Paris

Jeanine & Alain
Reservations:
Tel: +33 1 34 19 9000
Fax: +33 1 39 94 89 72
bab@bedbreak.com
www.bedbreak.com

You will be pampered by Jeanine and Alain. They are very nice and always pleased to help, and if necessary will also come and pick you up at the airport. They can help you buy theatre tickets, advise on transport, and should you prefer to eat out some evenings (Jeanine does dinner, and previously ran a traditional French restaurant) they can advise on the best restaurants anywhere in Paris. The room is spacious and inviting and has a shower fitted in the room.

Price Structure – 1 Bedroom
shower, washbasin, double bed: €80

Capacity: 2 people

Facilities: tv lounge, pets not accepted, dinner available, kitchen, 3 nights minimum stay
Fluent English spoken

Directions: Please contact the Central Reservations Office. Full address and directions will be provided on booking.

Location
Paris 10e
Gare du Nord
Nearest metro: Poissonnière
Airport: Paris-Orly 20km

Apartment

Marcelle, now retired, welcomes you to her apartment in the heart of Paris. The guest bedroom is furnished with taste. Here, you are close to the large department stores in the *quartier des Grands Magasins*, Montmartre and the theatre district. In short, a great location from which to explore this capital city. Marcelle will be more than happy to advise you and help you in any way she can.

Marcelle
Reservations:
Tel: +33 1 34 19 9000
Fax: +33 1 39 94 89 72
bab@bedbreak.com
www.bedbreak.com

Facilities: hosts have pets, pets not accepted, 100% no smoking, 3 nights minimum stay
Fluent English spoken

Price Structure – 1 Bedroom
bathroom, wc, double bed: €70

Capacity: 2 people

Directions: Please contact the Central Reservations Office. Full address and directions will be provided on booking.

Location
Paris 10e
Canal St-Martin
Nearest metro: Jacques Bonsergent
Airport: Paris-Roissy 20km

Apartment

This flat is in a great location beside the Canal St. Martin, great for walks and lazing in pavement cafés. Johanna is very friendly and has a charming home with bright and spacious reception rooms furnished with taste and harmony. It has a nice view over the canal. The room is spacious and has its own private bathroom that is reached by crossing the lounge. Johanna can advise you on the sights of Paris, and is happy to accompany you if she is free.

Johanna
Reservations:
Tel: +33 1 34 19 9000
Fax: +33 1 39 94 89 72
bab@bedbreak.com
www.bedbreak.com

Facilities: tv lounge
Fluent English spoken

Price Structure – 1 Bedroom
along corridor bathroom, wc, double bed: €80

Capacity: 2 people

Directions: Please contact the Central Reservations Office. Full address and directions will be provided on booking.

Ile de France – Paris

75.80 Paris

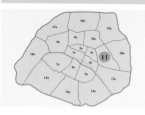

Apartment

Location
Paris 11e
Bastille
Nearest metro: Bréguet-Sabin
Airport: Paris-Orly 20km

Mado
Reservations:
Tel: +33 1 34 19 9000
Fax: +33 1 39 94 89 72
bab@bedbreak.com
www.bedbreak.com

Mado eagerly awaits your arrival to welcome you and swap tales of travels around the world. She loves markets and one day a week she devises a new route for a fresh look at Paris. Be sure to ask her for advice. Close by are the animated *quartiers* of Bastille, Le Marais and Place des Vosges. The guest bedroom is comfortable and spacious. French windows open onto a long balcony and during fair weather you can move a bistro table to sit out and enjoy the view over famous monuments. Very agreeable and *à la mode parisienne*!

Price Structure – 1 Bedroom
television, bathroom, twin beds: €70

Capacity: 2 people

Facilities: lounge, pets not accepted, 100% no smoking
Adequate English spoken

Directions: Please contact the Central Reservations Office. Full address and directions will be provided on booking.

75.04 Paris

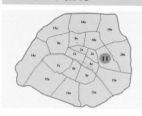

Private Home

Location
Paris 11e
République — Bastille
Nearest metro: Oberkampf
Airport: Paris-Orly 20km

Rebecca
Reservations:
Tel: +33 1 34 19 9000
Fax: +33 1 39 94 89 72
bab@bedbreak.com
www.bedbreak.com

Between the quartiers of République and Bastille, this attractive townhouse is in a quiet road near to local shops, restaurants and markets. Rebecca and her children welcome you to their family home which is warm and spacious. The large living room is tastefully decorated in warm colours and there is a garden too, full of flowers – a rarity in Paris! Rebecca is very interested in the arts in general including dance, painting and theatre and is a good source of advice for your cultural excursions. She can also lend you bicycles to explore Paris at a relaxed pace.

Price Structure – 5 Bedrooms
2 rooms: television, shower room, wc, double bed: €80
1 room: television, shower room, wc, four-poster double bed: €80
'suite': television, telephone, bathroom, wc, single bed. Along corridor room, television, single bed: €50
– 1 person €100 – 2 people

Extra Bed: €30
Reduction: 15 nights
Capacity: 8 people

Facilities: garden, lounge, pets not accepted, 100% no smoking, 3 nights minimum stay
Fluent English spoken

Directions: Please contact the Central Reservations Office. Full address and directions will be provided on booking.

Location
Paris 11e
République
Nearest metro: Parmentier
Airport: Paris-Orly 20km

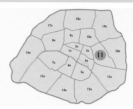

Apartment

Fabienne lives close to the lively *quartier* of République. The guest bedroom is very pretty, very spacious and decorated in warm colours. It was formerly part of an artist's studio and has been decorated with this in mind with paintings, sculptures and other objets d'art. Both of your hosts are artists and furniture makers. Their studio is next to your room, it is accessed from the road and is where you will find your hosts on arrival. Your bedroom also has its own independent entrance from the courtyard, and is very peaceful.

Facilities: babies welcome, free cot
Fluent English spoken

Directions: Please contact the Central Reservations Office. Full address and directions will be provided on booking.

Fabienne & Rodrigue
Reservations:
Tel: +33 1 34 19 9000
Fax: +33 1 39 94 89 72
bab@bedbreak.com
www.bedbreak.com

Price Structure – 1 Bedroom
shower room, wc, 2 double beds (super king-size):
€99 – 2 people €154 – 4 people

Capacity: 4 people

Location
Paris 11e
République
Nearest metro: Oberkampf
Airport: Paris-Roissy 25km

Apartment

A very animated *quartier* in constant change just a few steps from Place de la République and close to Bastille and Place des Vosges. Chez Sylvie the atmosphere is warm and sociable. The guest bedroom 'Senteurs d'Afrique' is fairly spacious and like its name suggests, has been inspired by her trips to Africa with her own paintings on the walls. Her apartment is also open to you and she readily helps you to explore the local shops and advises on cultural visits. Immerse yourself in the local daily *vie Parisienne*!

Facilities: Private parking, tv lounge, hosts have pets, dinner available, kitchen, babies welcome, free cot, 1 shared bathroom, wc
Fluent English spoken

Directions: Please contact the Central Reservations Office. Full address and directions will be provided on booking.

Sylvie
Reservations:
Tel: +33 1 34 19 9000
Fax: +33 1 39 94 89 72
bab@bedbreak.com
www.bedbreak.com

Price Structure – 2 Bedrooms
'Senteurs d'Afrique': television, double bed, single bed (child-size): €75 – 2 people €135 – 3 people
'Saveurs d'Asie': television, double bed: €75

Reduction: 01/09–30/11
Capacity: 5 people

Ile de France – Paris

75.83 Paris

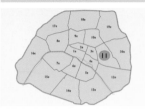

Apartment

Location
Paris 11e
République
Nearest metro: République
Airport: Paris-Orly 20km

A stone's throw from République, Elisabeth welcomes you with great warmth and enthusiasm. Her apartment is bright and quiet and there are two guest bedrooms, the yellow one being quite small but just as pleasant and comfortable as the other. You are welcome to use the lounge and play the piano or simply discuss your plans to visit Paris. She may even offer a guided tour of her *quartier* and advise you on the best places to visit nearby.

Elisabeth
Reservations:
Tel: +33 1 34 19 9000
Fax: +33 1 39 94 89 72
bab@bedbreak.com
www.bedbreak.com

Price Structure – 2 Bedrooms
'Bleue': bathroom, single bed: €50 – 1 person
'Jaune': single bed: €45 – 1 person

Capacity: 2 people

Facilities: tv lounge, dinner available, kitchen
Fluent English spoken

Directions: Please contact the Central Reservations Office. Full address and directions will be provided on booking.

75.92 Paris

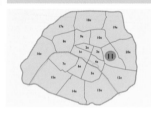

Apartment

Location
Paris 11e
République
Nearest metro: Goncourt
Airport: Paris-Orly 20km

A warm welcome awaits as does a welcome drink from Marguerite who will look after you well. The guest bedroom is spacious, simply furnished but equipped with a television, microwave, hi-fi and a kettle. The doors to her lounge are open to you if you wish to sit down, relax and have a chat. She also loves to cook and will prepare dinner if given notice.

Marguerite
Reservations:
Tel: +33 1 34 19 9000
Fax: +33 1 39 94 89 72
bab@bedbreak.com
www.bedbreak.com

Price Structure – 1 Bedroom
shower room, wc, single bed: €60 – 1 person

Reduction: 01/11–30/03, 10 nights
Capacity: 1 person

Facilities: lounge, dinner available, 100% no smoking, 2 nights minimum stay
Fluent English spoken

Directions: Please contact the Central Reservations Office. Full address and directions will be provided on booking.

Location
Paris 11e
Bastille — Nation — Père-Lachaise
Nearest metro: Charonne
Airport: Paris-Orly 20km

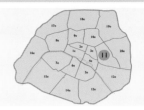

Private Home

By the Bastille quarter in a modern building is this studio flat with its own independent entrance. It adjoins Carine's townhouse and offers twin beds on a mezzanine floor and a comfortable sofa bed if needed. Enjoy this quiet location and sit out under the trees on the terrace, which is reserved just for you and very pleasant on sunny days. Carine serves you breakfast in her home or on the terrace, weather permitting.

Carine
Reservations:
Tel: +33 1 34 19 9000
Fax: +33 1 39 94 89 72
bab@bedbreak.com
www.bedbreak.com

Facilities: pets not accepted, 100% no smoking, 2 nights minimum stay
Adequate English spoken

Price Structure – 1 Apartment
lounge, television, kitchen, shower room, wc, twin beds: €78

Extra Bed: €22
Capacity: 2 people

Directions: Please contact the Central Reservations Office. Full address and directions will be provided on booking.

Location
Paris 12e
Gare de Lyon
Nearest metro: Gare de Lyon
Airport: Paris-Orly 20km

Apartment

This flat is in a Haussman designed building, a short walk from the Gare de Lyon. Beautiful parquet floors and plasterwork which your hosts have restored and redecorated with excellent taste. There are three comfortable bedrooms, of which two are very spacious. Each room has a theme and is personalised with objects they have collected on their travels. All the rooms share the one bathroom. A hearty buffet breakfast includes homemade bread and, as Peet is Dutch, he has added cheese and cold ham. An excellent address, ideal for small groups and with easy access to all transport.

Peet
Reservations:
Tel: +33 1 34 19 9000
Fax: +33 1 39 94 89 72
bab@bedbreak.com
www.bedbreak.com

Facilities: tv lounge, pets not accepted, internet access, dinner available, babies welcome, free cot, 100% no smoking, 1 shared bathroom, 2 wcs
Fluent English spoken

Price Structure – 3 Bedrooms
2 rooms: double bed (queen-size): €87,50
double bed (queen-size): €62

Extra Bed: €7,50
Capacity: 6 people

Directions: Please contact the Central Reservations Office. Full address and directions will be provided on booking.

Ile de France – Paris

75.55 Paris

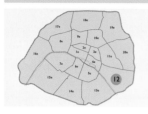

Apartment

hôtes
qualité
Paris

Location
Paris 12e
Bastille — Nation
Nearest metro: Faidherbe-Chaligny
Airport: Paris-Orly 20km

This flat is in the fashionable area between Nation and Bastille and has a bedroom with its own pretty sitting room. The atmosphere is quiet, warm, friendly and pleasant. Although you will be self-contained, your hostess is a lecturer and art lover and will be delighted to chat with you. She knows everything there is to know about Paris.

Patricia
Reservations:
Tel: +33 1 34 19 9000
Fax: +33 1 39 94 89 72
bab@bedbreak.com
www.bedbreak.com

Price Structure – 1 Bedroom
lounge, television, double bed: €55

Capacity: 2 people

Facilities: tv lounge, 1 shared bathroom, wc
Fluent English spoken

Directions: Please contact the Central Reservations Office. Full address and directions will be provided on booking.

75.56 Paris

Apartment

Location
Paris 12e
Bercy — Nation
Nearest metro: Bercy
Airport: Paris-Orly 20km

Jeannine's flat is in the recently rebuilt area of Bercy. The bedroom is basic but very quiet. Very practical for the Palais Omnisport (sports events and pop concerts).

Jeannine
Reservations:
Tel: +33 1 34 19 9000
Fax: +33 1 39 94 89 72
bab@bedbreak.com
www.bedbreak.com

Price Structure – 2 Bedrooms
double bed: €50,50
single bed: €38,50 – 1 person

Capacity: 3 people

Facilities: tv lounge, hosts have pets, pets not accepted, kitchen, 100% no smoking, 1 shared bathroom, wc
Adequate English spoken

Directions: Please contact the Central Reservations Office. Full address and directions will be provided on booking.

Location
Paris 12e
Bercy — Nation
Nearest metro: Bercy
Airport: Paris-Orly 20km

Apartment

Hélène's apartment is close to the Parc de Bercy. Her quiet ground floor flat also has access to a small garden which can be used in summer. The *quartier* is packed with a variety of different restaurants.

Hélène
Reservations:
Tel: +33 1 34 19 9000
Fax: +33 1 39 94 89 72
bab@bedbreak.com
www.bedbreak.com

Facilities: garden, tv lounge, hosts have pets, pets not accepted, dinner available, babies welcome, free cot, 1 shared shower room

Price Structure – 1 Bedroom
television, double bed: €50,50

Capacity: 2 people

Directions: Please contact the Central Reservations Office. Full address and directions will be provided on booking.

Location
Paris 13e
Grande Bibliothèque
Nearest metro: Bibliothèque-François Mitterrand
Airport: Paris-Orly 20km

Apartment

This place is in a quiet area, a short walk from the François Mitterrand Great Library and the Seine. Marie will welcome you to her flat, warmly decorated with objects and fabrics from Africa, as her husband is from Senegal. The bedroom and the bathroom are reached via the staircase and form a very pleasant ensemble, comfortable and nicely decorated. An unusual touch is the direct access to a small piece of private garden that is not overlooked. Take breakfast here, amongst the plants. Marie has had a long career in tourism, so knows what the word 'Welcome' means.

Marie
Reservations:
Tel: +33 1 34 19 9000
Fax: +33 1 39 94 89 72
bab@bedbreak.com
www.bedbreak.com

Facilities: garden, lounge, pets not accepted, 100% no smoking
Fluent English spoken

Price Structure – 1 Bedroom
bathroom, wc, double bed (queen-size): €89

Capacity: 2 people

Directions: Please contact the Central Reservations Office. Full address and directions will be provided on booking.

Ile de France – Paris

75.76 Paris

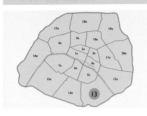

Apartment

Location
Paris 13e
Quartier chinois
Nearest metro: Place d'Italie
Airport: Paris-Orly 20km

Less than ten minutes on foot from La Butte aux Cailles and close to the *quartier chinois*, you can explore and compare these different *quartiers*. Danielle is very active and partakes in all sorts of sports plus singing and dancing. She is very welcoming and keen to meet foreign guests. Her flat is open to you as she aims to make you feel at home. The guest room can sleep up to three people with a double bed on a mezzanine floor and a single bed below. Enjoy a clear view of Paris, you can even see the Eiffel Tower!

Danielle
Reservations:
Tel: +33 1 34 19 9000
Fax: +33 1 39 94 89 72
bab@bedbreak.com
www.bedbreak.com

Price Structure – 1 Bedroom
double bed, single bed: €60 – 2 people
€75 – 3 people

Reduction: 7 nights
Capacity: 3 people

Facilities: private parking, tv lounge, dinner available, kitchen, 1 shared bathroom, wc
Fluent English spoken

Directions: Please contact the Central Reservations Office. Full address and directions will be provided on booking.

75.98 Paris

Apartment

Location
Paris 13e
Butte aux Cailles
Nearest metro: Glacière
Airport: Paris-Orly 20km

At the foot of La Butte aux Cailles, this former 1930s salt depository to the Mairie de Paris has been transformed into an artist's studio. Your hosts are artists, a *vidéaste* and Frédérique, whose welcome is unreservedly warm and friendly, is a sculptor. Charming, tastefully decorated living areas with a terrace where breakfast can be served. To make your stay in Paris even more special they host monthly art exhibitions, and dinners can also be enjoyed in this same space. An excellent address for an unforgettable experience.

Frédérique
Reservations:
Tel: +33 1 34 19 9000
Fax: +33 1 39 94 89 72
bab@bedbreak.com
www.bedbreak.com

Price Structure – 2 Bedrooms
along corridor bathroom, wc, double bed (super king-size). Along corridor room, double bed (queen-size): €80 – 2 people €150 – 4 people

Capacity: 4 people

Facilities: lounge, dinner available
Fluent English spoken

Directions: Please contact the Central Reservations Office. Full address and directions will be provided on booking.

Location
Paris 14e
Montparnasse
Nearest metro: Montparnasse
Airport: Paris-Orly 20km

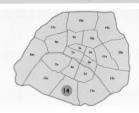

Apartment

A quiet and sunny guest room in an apartment on a shopping street at the foot of the Montparnasse tower. Cynthia and Christian have decorated their home with paintings in different styles and they would be delighted to chat with you about art or 'Paris by night', Christian's specialist subject! There is also a market, exclusively for paintings and ceramics, held opposite every Sunday, in addition to markets on Tuesdays and Fridays.

Cynthia & Christian
Reservations:
Tel: +33 1 34 19 9000
Fax: +33 1 39 94 89 72
bab@bedbreak.com
www.bedbreak.com

Facilities: pets not accepted, babies welcome, free cot, 100% no smoking, closed: 01/07–31/08
Fluent English spoken

Price Structure – 1 Bedroom
bathroom, wc, twin beds: €97

Capacity: 2 people

Directions: Please contact the Central Reservations Office. Full address and directions will be provided on booking.

Location
Paris 15e
Montparnasse
Nearest metro: Montparnasse
Airport: Paris-Orly 20km

Apartment

An ideal location in the centre of Montparnasse, a lively *quartier* with plenty of shops. Claudine and René have travelled a lot and enjoy meeting new people and the décor in their flat is a mix of modern and exotic furniture. They know Paris very well and are happy to accompany you out and about to show you the Paris that the locals know. They can advise you on cultural sightseeing and they even prepare packed lunches for day trips. Afterwards relax in the lounge or your own private seating area (extra sofa bed available).

Claudine & René
Reservations:
Tel: +33 1 34 19 9000
Fax: +33 1 39 94 89 72
bab@bedbreak.com
www.bedbreak.com

Facilities: private parking, lounge, pets not accepted, internet access, dinner available, 100% no smoking
Fluent English spoken

Price Structure – 1 Bedroom
lounge, bathroom, wc, double bed: €80

Extra Bed: €15
Capacity: 2 people

Directions: Please contact the Central Reservations Office. Full address and directions will be provided on booking.

Ile de France – Paris

75.23 Paris

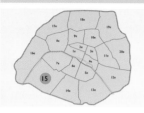

Apartment

Location
Paris 15e
Porte de Versailles
Nearest metro: Vaugirard
Airport: Paris-Orly 20km

Jean-Baptiste
Reservations:
Tel: +33 1 34 19 9000
Fax: +33 1 39 94 89 72
bab@bedbreak.com
www.bedbreak.com

Jean-Baptiste's flat is in a modern and quiet building, ideally situated midway between Montparnasse and the Porte de Versailles. The décor is both modern and unusual as Jean-Baptiste is a designer so it is done with taste but also includes a few unusual touches such as a swing hanging from the lounge window. A nice touch in the comfortable bedroom is the elevated bed that gives a different dimension to the room. Further down the corridor is a sauna; great after a hard day pounding the streets of Paris.

Price Structure – 1 Bedroom
double bed: €85

Capacity: 2 people

Facilities: tv lounge, internet access, kitchen, 1 shared bathroom, 3 nights minimum stay
Fluent English spoken

Directions: Please contact the Central Reservations Office. Full address and directions will be provided on booking.

75.36 Paris

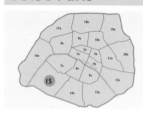

Apartment

Location
Paris 15e
Tour Eiffel
Nearest metro: La Motte Picquet Grenelle
Airport: Paris-Orly 20km

Huguette
Reservations:
Tel: +33 1 34 19 9000
Fax: +33 1 39 94 89 72
bab@bedbreak.com
www.bedbreak.com

This is a luxury apartment with modern furniture and beautiful décor. You will appreciate the quality and attention to detail, particularly the marble bathroom, or admire the view of the Eiffel Tower from your bed. As well as her great enthusiasm for interior decoration, your hostess will also share her knowledge of Parisian restaurants, so be sure to ask her to suggest the latest friendly little bistro that she has discovered.

Price Structure – 2 Bedrooms
television, bathroom, wc, twin beds: €89
shower room, wc, double bed: €89

Capacity: 4 people

Facilities: hosts have pets, pets not accepted, 100% no smoking, 18 years old minimum age, 3 nights minimum stay
Adequate English spoken

Directions: Please contact the Central Reservations Office. Full address and directions will be provided on booking.

Location
Paris 16e
Trocadéro
Nearest metro: La Muette
Airport: Paris-Orly 20km

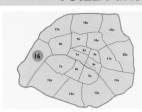

✦ ✦ ✦
Apartment

France is new to B&B and loves to meet new guests and chat. She will not fail to tell you about herself! Her large flat in the La Muette area is ten minutes' walk from the Trocadéro. The building is modern, in a quiet area full of little streets just waiting to be explored. The room has a large bed and you only share the bathroom with France's daughter. It is quite unusual for visitors to find accommodation in this exclusively residential area, but close to the tourist hot spots.

**France
Reservations:
Tel: +33 1 34 19 9000
Fax: +33 1 39 94 89 72
bab@bedbreak.com
www.bedbreak.com**

Facilities: tv lounge, dinner available, kitchen, babies welcome, free cot, 1 shared shower room, wc
Basic English spoken

Price Structure – 1 Bedroom
television, double bed (king-size): €60

Extra Bed: €55
Capacity: 2 people

Directions: Please contact the Central Reservations Office. Full address and directions will be provided on booking.

Location
Paris 16e
Etoile – Trocadéro
Nearest metro: Victor Hugo
Airport: Paris-Roissy 20km

✦ ✦ ✦
Apartment

From here you can walk to most of the chic parts of Paris, as this place is only ten minutes' walk from the Champs Elysées. Cédric welcomes you to his flat, which you reach via the adjoining listed shopping mall built by Gustave Eiffel. As your bedroom has a view of his tower, you can lie in bed and watch it sparkle. A bit clichéd but fascinating nonetheless. He loves Paris so will be delighted to give you the benefit of his historic knowledge and interesting anecdotes, as well as giving tips on the best places to shop and eat.

**Cédric
Reservations:
Tel: +33 1 34 19 9000
Fax: +33 1 39 94 89 72
bab@bedbreak.com
www.bedbreak.com**

Facilities: tv lounge, pets not accepted, internet access, 1 shared bathroom, wc

Price Structure – 1 Bedroom
double bed (queen-size): €90

Capacity: 2 people

Directions: Please contact the Central Reservations Office. Full address and directions will be provided on booking.

75.49 Paris

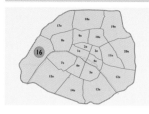

Apartment

hôtes
qualité
Paris

Location
Paris 16e
Bois de Boulogne — Auteuil
Nearest metro: Exelmans
Airport: Paris-Orly 20km

A classy, charming and typically Parisian apartment, furnished with antiques and only five minutes from the Bois de Boulogne. Nathalie is always on great form, and as a guide lecturer will be delighted to show you round Paris. Her passions are history and French cuisine.

Nathalie
Reservations:
Tel: +33 1 34 19 9000
Fax: +33 1 39 94 89 72
bab@bedbreak.com
www.bedbreak.com

Price Structure – 1 Suite
'Rose': television, bathroom, wc, shower, double bed: €63
En-suite room 'Jaune': single bed: €49,50 – 1 person

Capacity: 3 people

Facilities: lounge, pets not accepted, dinner available, kitchen, 15 years old minimum age, 3 nights minimum stay
Fluent English spoken

Directions: Please contact the Central Reservations Office. Full address and directions will be provided on booking.

75.09 Paris

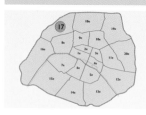

Apartment

Location
Paris 17e
Etoile — Champs Elysées
Nearest metro: Ternes
Airport: Paris-Roissy 25km

Fifth floor and no lift, but for those who can climb the steps, Rose's welcoming smile is worth it! What she loves is being able to meet and chat with people from all over the world. The guest room is pleasant with a wall draped in yellow fabric which creates the same intimate and calming effect of a draped four-poster bed. All her apartment is open to you including her pleasant lounge. You are less than ten minutes away from Etoile and the famous Champs Elysées. Excellent value for money in view of the location.

Rose
Reservations:
Tel: +33 1 34 19 9000
Fax: +33 1 39 94 89 72
bab@bedbreak.com
www.bedbreak.com

Price Structure – 1 Bedroom
bathroom, four-poster double bed (queen-size): €50

Capacity: 2 people

Facilities: tv lounge, pets not accepted, kitchen, 100% no smoking, 2 nights minimum stay
Adequate English spoken

Directions: Please contact the Central Reservations Office. Full address and directions will be provided on booking.

Location
Paris 17e
Montmartre — Marché aux Puces
Nearest metro: Guy Moquet
Airport: Paris-Roissy 25km

Apartment

Danielle and Franck welcome you to their flat in this well-to-do building, typical of Paris, opposite the metro. Montmartre is nearby. Be sure to visit the famous Montmartre cemetery where many famous artists and writers rest.

Danielle
Reservations:
Tel: +33 1 34 19 9000
Fax: +33 1 39 94 89 72
bab@bedbreak.com
www.bedbreak.com

Facilities: tv lounge, 100% no smoking, 1 shared bathroom, wc
Fluent English spoken

Price Structure – 1 Bedroom
double bed: €46

Capacity: 2 people

Directions: Please contact the Central Reservations Office. Full address and directions will be provided on booking.

Location
Paris 17e
Montmartre — Clichy
Nearest metro: Place de Clichy
Airport: Paris-Roissy 25km

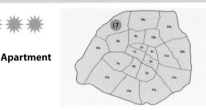

Apartment

Just five minutes from the Cimetière de Montmartre Marie-Anne welcomes you to her apartment, which is self-contained and very pleasant. You will enjoy a good level of comfort here with a bedroom and a separate lounge area with an extra sofa bed if needed. There is a well-equipped kitchenette too, with a fridge, oven, dishwasher etc. Your hostess lives in the apartment next door and is on hand for any advice or information you may need to plan your days. Breakfast can be served in your apartment or with Marie-Anne if you prefer.

Marie-Anne
Reservations:
Tel: +33 1 34 19 9000
Fax: +33 1 39 94 89 72
bab@bedbreak.com
www.bedbreak.com

Facilities: 2 nights minimum stay
Adequate English spoken

Price Structure – 1 Apartment
lounge, television, kitchen, shower room, wc, double bed: €90

Extra Bed: €20
Capacity: 2 people

Directions: Please contact the Central Reservations Office. Full address and directions will be provided on booking.

Ile de France – Paris

75.07 Paris

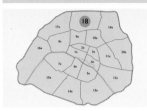

Apartment

Location
Paris 18e
Montmartre — Sacré Coeur — Place du Tertre
Nearest metro: Jules Joffrin
Airport: Paris-Roissy 25km

A good location in Montmartre near the lively 18th *arrondissement* with plenty of markets. Once a small apartment block, it is now one house on three floors. Your hosts' private quarters are on the first floor, then the guest rooms and then a lounge and a kitchen at the top. The main stairway has become their stairs! Ilhame is charming and kind and there is a warm family atmosphere with Patrice and their two children. The décor is inspired by Ilhame's Moroccan roots. For dinner enjoy French cuisine or tajines and couscous.

Ilhame & Patrice
Reservations:
Tel: +33 1 34 19 9000
Fax: +33 1 39 94 89 72
bab@bedbreak.com
www.bedbreak.com

Price Structure – 2 Bedrooms
'Joséphine': bathroom, wc, double bed: €85
'Marrakech': shower room, wc, double bed: €85

Capacity: 4 people

Facilities: tv lounge, pets not accepted, internet access, dinner available, kitchen, babies welcome, free cot, 100% no smoking, 2 nights minimum stay
Fluent English spoken

Directions: Please contact the Central Reservations Office. Full address and directions will be provided on booking.

75.18 Paris

Apartment

Location
Paris 18e
Place du Tertre — Sacré Cœur
Nearest metro: Abesses
Airport: Paris-Roissy 25km

You may have dreamed of the Place du Tertre, of a clear view over Paris and an open fire. Voilà! Geneviève's place offers all this. She is relaxed, loves art and culture, museums and animals. The flat reflects her character and has a soul.

Geneviève
Reservations:
Tel: +33 1 34 19 9000
Fax: +33 1 39 94 89 72
bab@bedbreak.com
www.bedbreak.com

Price Structure – 1 Bedroom
double bed: €67

Capacity: 2 people

Facilities: tv lounge, hosts have pets, dinner available, 1 shared bathroom, wc
Fluent English spoken

Directions: Please contact the Central Reservations Office. Full address and directions will be provided on booking.

Location
Paris 18e
Montmartre — Sacré Coeur — Place du Tertre
Nearest metro: Lamarck-Caulaincourt
Airport: Paris-Roissy 20km

Apartment

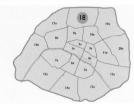

Patrice and Philippe will give you a good humoured welcome in their flat ideally situated at the foot of the Butte Montmartre. You can do the usual Montmartre tourist spots or let your hosts direct you to the less well known parts of this *quartier* with its local shops, bars and restaurants. All you need for a great stay in this comfortable flat, furnished and decorated with impeccable taste. The bedroom will take you back to the Seventies with its period décor. The lounge has a balcony where you can soak up the Parisian sun!

Patrice & Philippe
Reservations:
Tel: +33 1 34 19 9000
Fax: +33 1 39 94 89 72
bab@bedbreak.com
www.bedbreak.com

Facilities: tv lounge, pets not accepted, internet access, dinner available, 1 shared shower room, wc
Fluent English spoken

Price Structure – 1 Bedroom
telephone, 2 single beds: €75

Capacity: 2 people

Directions: Please contact the Central Reservations Office. Full address and directions will be provided on booking.

Location
Paris 18e
Montmartre — Sacré Coeur — Place du Tertre
Nearest metro: Lamarck-Caulaincourt
Airport: Paris-Roissy 20km

Bienvenue en France
hôtes qualité Paris

Residence of Outstanding Character

This is a very special place. This rare opportunity to be received by Morgane in her *hôtel particulier* in an inconspicuous passage, a haven of calm in Montmartre, is not to be missed. Pass through the gates and you enter an amazing oasis of lush vegetation. The inside of the house is equally charming and elegant. The bedrooms have each been decorated by different artists to create a unique ambiance. They are spacious and worthy of any luxury hotel. We have awarded this splendid place a *coup de coeur* as it guarantees a memorable stay. Well worth every penny.

Morgane
Reservations:
Tel: +33 1 34 19 9000
Fax: +33 1 39 94 89 72
bab@bedbreak.com
www.bedbreak.com

Facilities: private parking, garden, lounge, internet access, dinner available, babies welcome, free cot
Fluent English spoken

Price Structure – 5 Bedrooms
television, shower room, wc, double bed (super king-size): €430
television, bathroom, wc, double bed (super king-size): €430
2 rooms: lounge, television, bathroom, wc, shower, double bed (super king-size), single bed:
€430 – 2 people €450 – 3 people
'Apartment': lounge, television, bathroom, wc, shower, 2 double beds (super king-size):
€530 – 2 people €570 – 4 people

Capacity: 14 people

Directions: Please contact the Central Reservations Office. Full address and directions will be provided on booking.

75.50 Paris

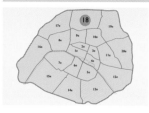

Apartment

Barbara
Reservations:
Tel: +33 1 34 19 9000
Fax: +33 1 39 94 89 72
bab@bedbreak.com
www.bedbreak.com

Price Structure – 2 Bedrooms
No 1 & 'Trône': double bed: €85

Extra Bed: €15
Capacity: 4 people

Location
Paris 18e
Montmartre — Sacré Coeur — Place
du Tertre
Nearest metro: Anvers
Airport: Paris-Roissy 25km

Barbara comes from the world of entertainment and she has decorated her apartment with great taste and original ideas. It is spacious, quiet and bright and very attractive. You are at the foot of the Sacré Coeur, almost in a village setting. As it is on the fifth floor with no lift, you need to be quite fit!

Facilities: hosts have pets, pets not accepted, 100% no smoking, 1 shared bathroom, wc, 10 years old minimum age, 2 nights minimum stay, closed: 26/12–02/01
Adequate English spoken

Directions: Please contact the Central Reservations Office. Full address and directions will be provided on booking.

75.47 Paris

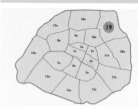

Apartment

Danièle
Reservations:
Tel: +33 1 34 19 9000
Fax: +33 1 39 94 89 72
bab@bedbreak.com
www.bedbreak.com

Price Structure – 1 Bedroom
shower room, wc, double bed: €77

Capacity: 2 people

Location
Paris 19e
Buttes Chaumont — Belleville
Nearest metro: Belleville
Airport: Paris-Roissy 25km

Bienvenue en France

hôtes
qualité
Paris

Danièle is Parisian and now retired. She welcomes you to her spacious apartment and can help you plan your visits. The comfortable guest room on the ninth floor has a view over Paris. This is a lively area with plenty of restaurants, near to the historic centre and behind the Parc des Buttes Chaumont.

Facilities: tv lounge, pets not accepted, 2 nights minimum stay
Basic English spoken

Directions: Please contact the Central Reservations Office. Full address and directions will be provided on booking.

Location
Paris 19e
Buttes Chaumont — Ménilmontant
Nearest metro: Pyrénées
Airport: Paris-Roissy 25km

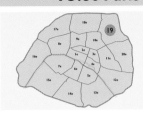

Apartment

This apartment is in a quiet street just 100m from the Parc des Buttes Chaumont, one of Paris's most beautiful parks, ideal for walks and loved by artists and joggers alike. Sylvie's kindness makes for a pleasant stay and you will appreciate the peaceful atmosphere in her apartment. The guest bedroom has a desk area and plenty of space for you to unpack as well as a hi-fi system and a television.

Sylvie
Reservations:
Tel: +33 1 34 19 9000
Fax: +33 1 39 94 89 72
bab@bedbreak.com
www.bedbreak.com

Facilities: lounge, kitchen, 1 shared bathroom, wc
Fluent English spoken

Price Structure – 1 Bedroom
double bed: €60

Extra Bed: €20
Capacity: 2 people

Directions: Please contact the Central Reservations Office. Full address and directions will be provided on booking.

Location
Paris 19e
Buttes Chaumont
Nearest metro: Botzaris
Airport: Paris-Roissy 20km

Apartment

Mireille is very charming and will quickly make you feel at home. Her flat is in a small building just 300m from les Buttes Chaumont. Your room is bright with a view of the garden without being overlooked. Take breakfast on the balcony, weather permitting. Mireille is keen for you to get the most out of your stay and will keep you informed by clipping the latest addresses from the press, and will even accompany you on your excursions if you wish. She loves to chat about her travels in Asia, and her hobbies of gardening and copper engraving.

Mireille
Reservations:
Tel: +33 1 34 19 9000
Fax: +33 1 39 94 89 72
bab@bedbreak.com
www.bedbreak.com

Facilities: private parking, garden, tv lounge, pets not accepted, kitchen, 100% no smoking, 1 shared bathroom, wc, 2 nights minimum stay
Fluent English spoken

Price Structure – 1 Bedroom
double bed: €50

Capacity: 2 people

Directions: Please contact the Central Reservations Office. Full address and directions will be provided on booking.

Ile de France – Paris

75.19 Paris

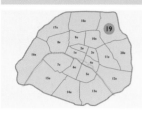

Residence of Outstanding Character

Location
Paris 19e
Buttes Chaumont
Nearest metro: Place des Fêtes
Airport: Paris-Roissy 20km

This really is a special address for an exceptional stay. Firstly, this 18th-century *hôtel particulier* is a beautiful residence, atypical of central Paris. The suite with its own lounge is a massive 60 square metres. The woodwork and parquet floors are all original, the linen is top quality, and the beautifully presented breakfast combines quantity and quality. A further bonus is your host Mary-Rose, who is charming and helpful and ready with advice on the latest trendy restaurants and boutiques.

Mary-Rose
Reservations:
Tel: +33 1 34 19 9000
Fax: +33 1 39 94 89 72
bab@bedbreak.com
www.bedbreak.com

Price Structure – 1 Bedroom
lounge, television, bathroom, wc, double bed (king-size): €145

Capacity: 2 people

Facilities: garden, hosts have pets, pets not accepted, 100% no smoking, 3 nights minimum stay
Fluent English spoken

Directions: Please contact the Central Reservations Office. Full address and directions will be provided on booking.

75.90 Paris

Apartment

Location
Paris 20e
Buttes Chaumont — Ménilmontant
Nearest metro: Jourdain
Airport: Paris-Roissy 25km

With an air of the country, this is Paris 'village life'. This triplex, a three-storey apartment, has two entrances onto quiet pedestrian cul-de-sacs. This area, more and more appreciated by Parisians, is close to the Père-Lachaise cemetery and the Parc des Buttes Chaumont. A little apartment, well designed with a small seating area and equipped kitchen with a washing machine and a spacious shower room. Enjoy breakfast on the terrace in the summer. Gwendaline lives just opposite, so don't hesitate to cross the terrace to ask her for advice.

Gwendaline
Reservations:
Tel: +33 1 34 19 9000
Fax: +33 1 39 94 89 72
bab@bedbreak.com
www.bedbreak.com

Price Structure – 1 Apartment
lounge, television, kitchen, shower room, wc, twin beds: €100

Capacity: 2 people

Facilities: tv lounge, dinner available, 2 nights minimum stay
Fluent English spoken

Directions: Please contact the Central Reservations Office. Full address and directions will be provided on booking.

Location
N W PARIS
in: Asnières, station pick-up on arrival/departure
Railway station: 100m
Airport: Paris-Orly 20km

Private Home

Cécilia will welcome you with great warmth and kindness and is full of smiles. Her house is quiet and next to the station (from where you can reach the Place de l'Opéra in ten minutes). She loves Italian culture, and also speaks Hebrew. You will appreciate the relaxing garden after a tiring day's sightseeing!

Cécilia
Reservations:
Tel: +33 1 34 19 9000
Fax: +33 1 39 94 89 72
bab@bedbreak.com
www.bedbreak.com

Facilities: off-street parking, garden, hosts have pets, pets not accepted, 100% no smoking, wheelchair access
Fluent English spoken

Directions: Please contact the Central Reservations Office. Full address and directions will be provided on booking.

Price Structure – 2 Bedrooms and 3 Apartments
rooms: television, Along corridor bathroom, wc, double bed. Along corridor room, television, single bed: €89 – 2 people €117 – 3 people
'Chasse' & 'Châlet': television, kitchen, shower room, wc, double bed: €89
'British': television, kitchen, along corridor shower room, wc, double bed: €89

Extra Bed: €28
Reduction: 01/10–31/01   **Capacity:** 9 people

Location
N W PARIS
in: Courbevoie
Nearest metro: Pont de Neuilly
Airport: Paris-Orly 20km

Apartment

Very practical if visiting Paris by car with two secure parking spaces on offer. Just 20–25 minutes from the centre by public transport and in a green and quiet residential area close to a pedestrianised centre with local shops. Friendly Marie-Alice and Patrice have lived abroad and know practically all of Europe! They love browsing in antique shops and flea markets and they have typical hand-painted Austrian furniture in their lovely lounge, which is bright with large bay windows. Your bathroom has a spacious shower.

Marie-Alice & Patrice
Reservations:
Tel: +33 1 34 19 9000
Fax: +33 1 39 94 89 72
bab@bedbreak.com
www.bedbreak.com

Facilities: private parking, tv lounge, hosts have pets, pets not accepted, dinner available, babies welcome, free cot
Adequate English spoken

Directions: Please contact the Central Reservations Office. Full address and directions will be provided on booking.

Price Structure – 1 Bedroom and 1 Apartment
television, shower room, wc, double bed (queen-size): €85
kitchen, shower room, wc, double bed (queen-size): €85

Capacity: 4 people

Ile de France – Paris

92.08 Paris

Apartment

Location
N W PARIS
in: Courbevoie
Nearest metro: La Défense-Grande Arche
Airport: Paris-Roissy 30km

Erika lives just 800m from the Grande Arche de la Défense in a quiet, residential part of Paris. From here, it is very quick and easy to access the very heart of Paris by public transport: Champs-Elysées, Opéra, le Louvre... Your bedroom is comfortable and you can opt to enjoy breakfast on the relatively spacious balcony, weather permitting. Your hostess speaks five languages fluently so you shouldn't have any trouble making yourself understood!

Erika
Reservations:
Tel: +33 1 34 19 9000
Fax: +33 1 39 94 89 72
bab@bedbreak.com
www.bedbreak.com

Price Structure – 1 Bedroom
double bed: €60

Capacity: 2 people

Facilities: tv lounge, dinner available, kitchen, 100% no smoking, 1 shared bathroom, wc, closed: 1/09 – 1/03
Fluent English spoken

Directions: Please contact the Central Reservations Office. Full address and directions will be provided on booking.

92.09 Paris

Apartment

Location
N W PARIS
in: Levallois-Perret
Nearest metro: Anatole France
Airport: Paris-Roissy 30km

Very convenient, just two stops away from Paris by metro and only 15 minutes to the *Grands Magasins*, Annouchka welcomes you to the centre of Levallois-Perret. Her flat is quiet and bright, close to local shops and just opposite the Parc de la Planchette which is ideal for jogging or a stroll. She offers two single bedrooms, one of which is a fairly small single. The lounge is pleasant and shows off Annouchka's own watercolours, as for several years she has dedicated herself to her art and would be delighted to show you her work.

Annouchka
Reservations:
Tel: +33 1 34 19 9000
Fax: +33 1 39 94 89 72
bab@bedbreak.com
www.bedbreak.com

Price Structure – 2 Bedrooms
2 rooms: single bed: €50 – 1 person

Extra Bed: €17
Capacity: 2 people

Facilities: lounge, pets not accepted, dinner available, kitchen, babies welcome, free cot, 100% no smoking, 1 shared bathroom, wc, 2 nights minimum stay
Basic English spoken

Directions: Please contact the Central Reservations Office. Full address and directions will be provided on booking.

Location
S PARIS
in: Malakoff
Nearest metro: Malakoff Plateau de Vanves
Airport: Paris-Orly 13km

Private Home

Renate is German and has lived in France for 30 years now. She loves meeting people, is interested in art so can give you excellent advice on the cultural scene in Paris. Her little townhouse with its flower garden is very pleasant. Although very quiet, it is only about ten minutes from Montparnasse by metro and 15 minutes from the Champs Elysées. The two rooms which are booked together provide a comfortable private space for a family.

Renate
Reservations:
Tel: +33 1 34 19 9000
Fax: +33 1 39 94 89 72
bab@bedbreak.com
www.bedbreak.com

Facilities: garden, tv lounge, pets not accepted, babies welcome, free cot, 100% no smoking, 2 nights minimum stay
Fluent English spoken

Directions: Please contact the Central Reservations Office. Full address and directions will be provided on booking.

Price Structure – 2 Bedrooms
along corridor bathroom, washbasin, double bed. along corridor room, 2 single beds: €60 – 2 people €110 – 4 people

Reduction: 7 nights, groups
Capacity: 4 people

Location
E PARIS
in: Vincennes
Nearest metro: Vincennes
Airport: Paris-Orly 20km

hôtes qualité Paris

Apartment

This apartment is one of the old buildings from the communes of the Château de Vincennes, where they used to keep horses in the courtyard. It is only a short walk from the Château and the Bois de Vincennes, in a busy shopping street. The two rooms, which can only be booked together, are spacious and bright. Your hostess is very friendly and likes meeting new people and telling them about the less well-known parts of Paris.

Ety
Reservations:
Tel: +33 1 34 19 9000
Fax: +33 1 39 94 89 72
bab@bedbreak.com
www.bedbreak.com

Facilities: dinner available, 100% no smoking
Fluent English spoken

Directions: Please contact the Central Reservations Office. Full address and directions will be provided on booking.

Price Structure – 2 Bedrooms
shower room, wc, double bed. Along corridor room, double bed: €65 – 2 people €115 – 4 people

Capacity: 4 people

Ile de France – Paris

92.10 Paris

Private Home

Françoise
Reservations:
Tel: +33 1 34 19 9000
Fax: +33 1 39 94 89 72
bab@bedbreak.com
www.bedbreak.com

Price Structure – 1 Bedroom
television, kitchen, double bed: €65

Extra Bed: €30
Reduction: children
Capacity: 2 people

Location
5km S W of PARIS
in: Sèvres, station pick-up on
arrival/departure
Nearest metro: Pont de Sèvres
Airport: Paris-Orly 20km

Françoise's house is in the upper part of Sèvres, in a quiet street surrounded by trees. A little green haven where you can relax, just ten minutes away from bustling Paris. The large bay window in the lounge has a clear view over the lower part of Sèvres. The guest bedroom is on the first floor, which is reserved exclusively for guests. You also have your own independent access to your room which includes many facilities such as a television, fridge, microwave and electric hob.

Facilities: private parking, garden, tv lounge, babies welcome, free cot, 1 shared bathroom, wc, 2 nights minimum stay
Fluent English spoken

Directions: Please contact the Central Reservations Office. Full address and directions will be provided on booking.

93.05 Paris

Private Home

Hélène BALLAND
28 rue Lucien Berneux, 93250 VILLEMOMBLE
Tel: (0) 1 48 54 19 91 / (0) 671 72 55 32
bahelene@wanadoo.fr

Price Structure – 2 Bedrooms
'Bleu': double bed: €55
'Rouge': twin beds: €55

Reduction: 3 nights
Capacity: 4 people

Location
10km E of PARIS
in: Villemomble
Nearest metro: RER E Le Raincy-
Villemomble
Airport: Paris-Roissy 10km

Bienvenue
en
France

Fifteen minutes from the centre of the capital, in the peace and quiet of a charming residential area, Hélène welcomes you with a lovely smile. Although it is just 15 minutes on foot to the train station, she will offer to drop and collect you from the station. All your needs will be taken care of during your stay in one of her two guest bedrooms. Hélène will be delighted to guide you around some of the most beautiful parts of Paris, so do not hesitate to ask! Direct access to Disneyland Paris and the Villepinte Exhibition Centre.

Facilities: garden, tv lounge, pets not accepted, babies welcome, free cot, 100% no smoking, 1 shared shower room
Adequate English spoken

Directions: Please contact your host in advance for detailed directions.

Private Home

Location
15km N W of PARIS
in: Maisons-Lafitte, station pick-up
on arrival/departure
Nearest metro: RER A Maisons-Lafitte
Airport: Paris-Roissy 38km

This house is in the grounds of the château at Maisons-Lafitte at the edge of the St-Germain-en-Laye forest. It is only 15 minutes from the Champs-Elysées by the RER (fast suburban metro) and is also close to St-Germain and Versailles. This part of west Paris is very pleasant.

Irène & Jacques JAMES
'Les Colombes', 21 avenue Béranger,
78600 MAISONS-LAFITTE
Tel: (0) 1 39 62 82 48 / (0) 671 13 51 05
jacques.james@wanadoo.fr
http://perso.orange.fr/les-colombes

Facilities: private parking, garden, tv lounge, pets not accepted, dinner available, babies welcome, free cot, 100% no smoking, cycling
Adequate English spoken

Directions: By public transport: RER A Maisons-Lafitte. By car: From the Porte Maillot go towards La Défense then towards Cergy-Pontoise.

Price Structure – 3 Bedrooms
'Jaune': television, shower room, wc, double bed: €73
'Rose': television, bathroom, wc, twin beds: €80
'Normande': television, shower room, wc, double bed: €75

Extra Bed: €25
Reduction: 8 nights
Capacity: 6 people

Location
35km W of PARIS
in: Vaux-sur-Seine, station pick-up
on arrival/departure
Railway station: 1km
Airport: Paris-Roissy 30km
car essential

Residence of Outstanding Character

Two hours from Calais and 30 minutes from Paris, this beautiful, spacious villa is in a residential area, only ten minutes' walk from the station. They have a swimming pool, a boules pitch and a billiard table, to help you relax after serious sightseeing in Paris, Versailles, Auvers-sur-Oise, Giverny. . .

Jean & Françoise BULOT
'La Cascade', 30 chemin des Valences,
78740 VAUX-SUR-SEINE
Tel: (0) 1 34 74 84 91 / (0) 607 04 31 59
Fax: (0) 1 34 92 02 33
bulotlacascade@wanadoo.fr
http://la-cascade.monsite.wanadoo.fr

Facilities: off-street parking, garden, tv lounge, dinner available, private swimming pool, hiking, cycling 1km, fishing 1km, mushroom-picking 1km, lake watersports 5km, golf course 12km
Basic English spoken

Directions: A13, Exit 9. At Meulan, follow Vaux-sur-Seine (D190) towards St-Germain-en-Laye. Pass the station (on right) and the railway bridge. After 150m, 2nd on the right (hairpin bend). The road undulates, ending in a cul-de-sac on the left.

Price Structure – 1 Bedroom and 2 Suites
'Myosotis': bathroom, wc, twin beds. Along corridor room, single bed: €65 – 2 people €85 – 3 people
'Familiale': shower room, wc, twin beds. En-suite room, 2 single beds: €65 – 2 people
€105 – 4 people
'Lilas': shower room, wc, double bed: €65

Extra Bed: €18
Reduction: 01/11–31/12, 10 nights
Capacity: 9 people

Ile de France – Paris

28.11 Rambouillet

Private Home

Catherine & Jean-Marc SIMON
'Les Chandelles', 19 rue des Sablons, Chandelles,
28130 VILLIERS-LE-MORHIER
Tel: (0) 2 37 82 71 59 / (0) 609 80 55 07
Fax: (0) 2 37 82 71 59
info@chandelles-golf.com
www.chandelles-golf.com

Price Structure – 5 Bedrooms
'Les Fleurs': television, bathroom, wc, double bed:
€75
'Oiseaux' & 'Chevaux': television, bathroom, wc, twin
beds: €75
'Le Golf': television, bathroom, wc, double bed (queen-
size), single bed: €90 – 2 people €110 – 3 people
'La Ferme': television, bathroom, wc, double bed
(queen-size), 2 single beds: €100 – 2 people
€140 – 4 people
Extra Bed: €25
Reduction: 2 nights   **Capacity:** 13 people

Location
28km S W of RAMBOUILLET
in: Chandelles, station pick-up on
arrival/departure
Railway station: 5km
Airport: Paris-Orly 70km
car essential

This restored old farmhouse, far from the stress of the
big city, will enable you to make the most of its
beautiful, peaceful location surrounded by woods,
although watch out for the steep staircase. The 'Golf'
and 'Ferme' rooms are really very pleasant and
spacious. Jean-Marc is a professional golf instructor
and will be delighted to give you some coaching.
Convenient for playing golf and visiting Rambouillet,
Versailles and Paris.

Facilities: private parking, extensive grounds,
lounge, hosts have pets, pets not accepted, hiking,
cycling, fishing, mushroom-picking, golf course 5km,
lake watersports 5km, riversports 5km
Fluent English spoken

Directions: At Rambouillet, take the D906 towards
Chartres to Maintenon. Then take the D116 towards
Villiers-le-Morhier and Chandelles is the next village.
The Rue des Sablons is the main high street of
Chandelles.

78.09 Versailles

Private Home

Corinne & Denis LAVENANT
'La Ferme du Château', 5 route de Boissy,
Le Breuil, 78890 GARANCIERES
Tel: (0) 1 34 86 53 94 / (0) 612 68 57 90
Fax: (0) 1 34 86 53 77
info@la-ferme-du-chateau.com
www.la-ferme-du-chateau.com

Price Structure – 3 Bedrooms
'Garance': lounge, television, bathroom, wc, four-
poster double bed (queen-size): €140
'Hortensia': television, shower room, wc, washbasin,
double bed (queen-size), cot: €120
'Pavot': television, bathroom, wc, washbasin, double
bed (queen-size): €120

Capacity: 6 people

Location
25km W of VERSAILLES
in: Garancières
Railway station: 2km
Airport: Paris-Orly 50km
car essential

Corinne has thought of everything, she really has. You
could have practically forgotten all your toiletries or
even the baby's comfort blanket, or 'doudou' as it is
known here, and she will have what you need. An
excellent welcome can be expected here as well as
charming guest rooms with safes, internet access and
cakes. It is a former 17th-century farm to the château
and has been in the family for eight generations! There
is a dovecote and a press in the garden and a seating
area for relaxation. Bicycles are also at your disposal.

Facilities: private parking, garden, tv lounge, hosts
have pets, pets not accepted, internet access, babies
welcome, free cot, 100% no smoking, closed:
15/01–15/02, hiking, cycling, golf course 3km,
mushroom-picking 5km, interesting flora 5km,
gliding 15km
Adequate English spoken

Directions: Please contact your hosts in advance for
detailed directions.

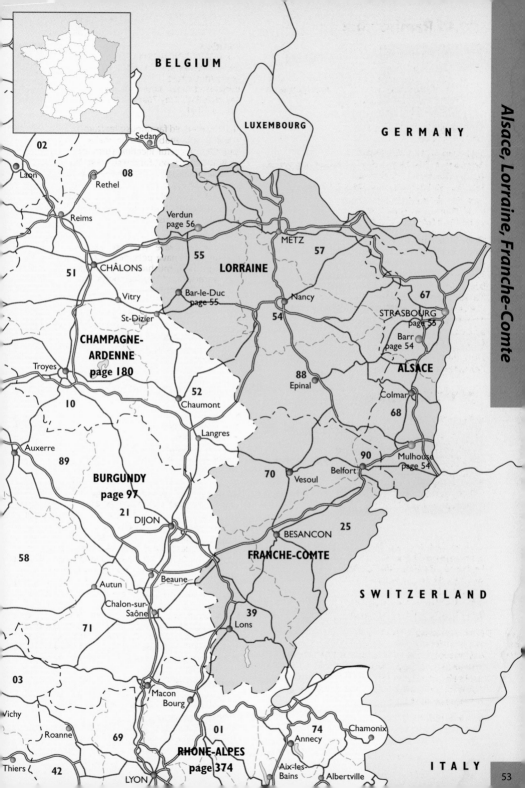

BELGIUM

LUXEMBOURG

GERMANY

02

Laon

08

Rethel

Sedan

Reims

Verdun
page 56

55

METZ

57

LORRAINE

51

CHÂLONS

Vitry

Bar-le-Duc
page 55

Nancy

67

St-Dizier

54

STRASBOURG
page 55

CHAMPAGNE-
ARDENNE
page 180

52

Chaumont

88
Epinal

Barr
page 54

ALSACE

Troyes

10

Langres

Colmar

68

Auxerre

89

70

Vesoul

90

Belfort

Mulhouse
page 54

BURGUNDY
page 97

21

DIJON

25

BESANCON

58

Beaune

FRANCHE-COMTE

Autun

Chalon-sur-
Saône

71

39

Lons

SWITZERLAND

03

Macon
Bourg

Vichy

01

74

Chamonix

Roanne

69

Annecy

Thiers

42

LYON

RHONE-ALPES
page 374

Aix-les-
Bains

Albertville

ITALY

67.02 Barr

Private Home

Tilly & Gérard HAZEMANN
'Tilly's Bed & Breakfast', 28 rue Principale, 67140
LE HOHWALD
Tel: (0) 3 88 08 33 34 Fax: (0) 3 88 08 30 17
gerard.hazemann@wanadoo.fr

Price Structure – 1 Bedroom
and 2 Apartments
first room: television, kitchen, bathroom, wc, double
bed: €70
second room: television, kitchen, bathroom, wc, twin
beds: €70
third room: television, along corridor bathroom, wc,
twin beds: €70

Reduction: 01/09–30/06, 3 nights, groups
Capacity: 6 people

Location
15km W of BARR
in: Le Hohwald
Railway station: 14km
Airport: Strasbourg 35km
car essential

Quite an experience. Of course this area is magnificent, but you will also breathe in deeply the pure air and go for unforgettable walks. In the heart of Alsace, this area is steeped in European culture. The bedrooms are spacious with beautiful bathrooms.

Facilities: private parking, pets not accepted, dinner available, kitchen, babies welcome, free cot, hiking, cycling, fishing, hunting, interesting flora, mushroom-picking, bird-watching, winter sports
Fluent English spoken

Directions: On the A35 from Strasbourg towards Colmar take the Barr exit. Follow Andiau. Le Hohwald is on the D425.

68.05 Mulhouse

Private Home

Annie & Alain LANDWERLIN
'La Faïencière', 59 rue de Bellevue,
68350 BRUNSTATT
Tel: (0) 3 89 06 17 71
a.landwerlin@evhr.net
www.la-faienciere.com

Price Structure – 2 Bedrooms and 1 Suite
'Clairefontaine': television, telephone, shower room, wc, double bed: €86
'Limoges': television, telephone, bathroom, wc, shower, double bed: €105
'Luneville': television, telephone, bathroom, wc, double bed. En-suite room, single bed:
€108 – 2 people €134 – 3 people

Extra Bed: €26
Capacity: 7 people

Location
4km S of MULHOUSE
in: Brunstatt, station pick-up on arrival/departure
Railway station: 1km
Airport: Bâle 25km

A *maison bourgeoise* from 1929 situated high up in Mulhouse surrounded by small formal gardens which you cross to reach the spa and the hammam. A 19th-century interior, with period furniture and a beautiful collection of Sarreguemines faience earthenware. Alain is a passionate collector and an expert (lectures possible). Moreover, each room is named after well-known faience which form part of the décor and the crockery at breakfast. Your hosts, with their roots and heart firmly planted in the region, offer a good cuisine of regional specialities and a warm and enlightening welcome. Unmissable for collectors!

Facilities: off-street parking, garden, lounge, pets not accepted, dinner available, hiking, cycling, interesting flora, vineyard 20km, winter sports 30km
Adequate English spoken

Directions: From Mulhouse, A36 towards Belfort, exit 16, Les Côteaux. Head towards Brunstatt. Continue to the roundabout by McDonalds, and head for Brunstatt. After the railway line, turn right and then left in front of Pizza Hut. Ahead at the next roundabout and up the hill, then right into Rue de Bellevue.

Location
34km S W of STRASBOURG
in: Boersch, station pick-up on arrival/departure
Railway station: 5km
Airport: Strasbourg 27km
car essential

Private Home

Alsace, Lorraine – Strasbourg, Bar-le-Duc

As you will see, Micheline is lovely. She loves hiking in the nearby Vosges and is fascinated by heritage. At present she has only two suns', until all the final finishing work is done in the adjoining building where the bedrooms are located, which should be good. The interior courtyard full of flowers and a sunny lawn, and the simply furnished rooms are very pleasant. Breakfast is Alsace style, of course.

Micheline MANNY
'La Parpaillotte', 25 rue du Rempart,
67530 BOERSCH
Tel: (0) 3 88 95 89 83 / (0) 682 66 91 63
kestubois@parpaillotte.fr
www.parpaillotte.fr

Facilities: garden, hosts have pets, internet access, dinner available, babies welcome, free cot, 100% no smoking
Adequate English spoken

Price Structure – 1 Bedroom and 1 Apartment
'Le Nid': kitchen, shower room, wc, double bed: €50
'Le Dortoir': double bed, 3 single beds:
€50 – 2 people €125 – 5 people

Reduction: children
Capacity: 7 people

Directions: Please contact your hosts for detailed directions.

Location
44km S E of BAR-LE-DUC
in: Bonnet
Railway station: 40km
car essential

Private Home

As we go to press, this host has not yet been classified, but will be shortly. Michèle and Gérard's place is in the heart of Joan of Arc country, in a listed building, formerly a presbytery, with its old stone walls, large flagstones and priest's garden. Then you will realise that it is also a modern art museum, reflecting the talent of Gérard the artist and Michèle's love of art in general. They team up with another artist, the neighbouring landlord, to offer Art and Gastronomy stays. Art, good food and good company are the watchwords here.

Michèle & Gérard LARGUIER
'Ancien Presbytère', 1 rue de Ribeaucourt,
55130 BONNET
Tel: (0) 3 29 89 77 58 / (0) 688 90 58 06
Fax: (0) 3 29 89 77 58
gerard.larguier@wanadoo.fr
www.larguier-residence.com

Facilities: garden, lounge, hosts have pets, pets not accepted, dinner available, 100% no smoking, 12 years old minimum age
Fluent English spoken

Price Structure – 2 Bedrooms
'Oratoire': shower room, wc, twin beds: €80
'Chambre à Pains': bathroom, wc, double bed: €80

Capacity: 4 people

Directions: On the Bar-le-Duc to Neufchâteau route, take the N135 then the D966. At Houdelaincourt take the D960 on the right towards Bonnet.

55.02 Verdun

Residence of Outstanding Character

Marie-Jeanne CHRISTIAENS
'Villa les roses', La Vignette, 55120 LES ISLETTES
Tel: (0) 3 26 60 81 91 Fax: (0) 3 26 60 23 09
gites-christiaens@wanadoo.fr

Price Structure – 5 Bedrooms and 1 Apartment
'Agnès' (our favourite room): television, bathroom, wc, double bed: €65
'Martine': television, shower room, wc, twin beds: €50
'Familiale': television, bathroom, wc, shower, twin beds, 2 single beds: €75 – 2 people €115 – 4 people
'Grand-Mère' & 'Rose': television, shower room, wc, double bed: €50
'Séraphin': wheelchair access, television, kitchen, shower room, wc, twin beds: €55

Extra Bed: €15
Reduction: 3 nights, groups
Capacity: 14 people

Location
34km W of VERDUN
in: Les Islettes, station pick-up on arrival/departure
Railway station: Les Islettes
car essential

Deep in the Argonne forest is this impressive *Maison de Maître* in extensive wooded grounds with games for children and a swimming pool. Ignore the entrance hall (due to be restored) and pass directly to the redecorated, comfortable bedrooms (some with exposed beams). The rooms have sloping ceilings but are spacious and we particularly liked 'Agnès' and its bathroom. The family room has a multi-jet shower and a corner bathtub. Breakfasts of *pâtisseries* and homemade jam with dandelion flower syrup! A charming welcome.

Facilities: off-street parking, garden, babies welcome, free cot, wheelchair access, hunting, fishing, mushroom-picking, bird-watching, hiking, golf course 30km

Directions: A4 between Châlons-en-Champagne and Verdun. Exit 29 to Ste-Ménéhould, then N3 towards Verdun for 9km. The house is 300m before Les Islettes on the left (signposted).

55.03 Verdun

Private Home;

Bénédicte & Denis HEBRARD
'La Scholastique', 3 rue de l'Eglise,
55120 LE NEUFOUR
Tel: (0) 3 29 88 29 19 / (0) 673 33 54 92
d.hebrard.argonne@wanadoo.fr
www.lascholastique.fr

Price Structure – 1 Bedroom and 1 Suite
'Béatrice': wheelchair access, shower room, wc, double bed (queen-size): €55
'Thérèse': bathroom, wc, double bed (king-size). En-suite room, single bed: €60 – 2 people €75 – 3 people

Extra Bed: €15
Capacity: 5 people

Location
35km W of VERDUN
in: Le Neufour, station pick-up on arrival/departure
Railway station: 3km
car essential

This family was made for meeting and greeting as they, Bénédicte, Denis and their daughters, love to welcome guests. Former employees of Air France they have grasped the concept of a *Maison d'Hôtes* and true hospitality. Denis will guide you over the battlefields of Argonne and perhaps you'll be lucky enough to taste a *tarte aux fraises* made by Bénédicte. The guest bedrooms are fairly spacious and very comfortable with some interesting features. The little extra touches make you feel very welcome.

Facilities: off-street parking, garden, lounge, hosts have pets, pets not accepted, babies welcome, free cot, 100% no smoking, hiking
Fluent English spoken

Directions: Motorway A4 Paris-Metz, exit Ste-Ménéhould direction N3 Verdun. At Les Islettes, direction Le Neufour. 'La Scholastique' is in the first road on the right (From Metz, exit Clermont-en-Argonne direction Les Islettes).

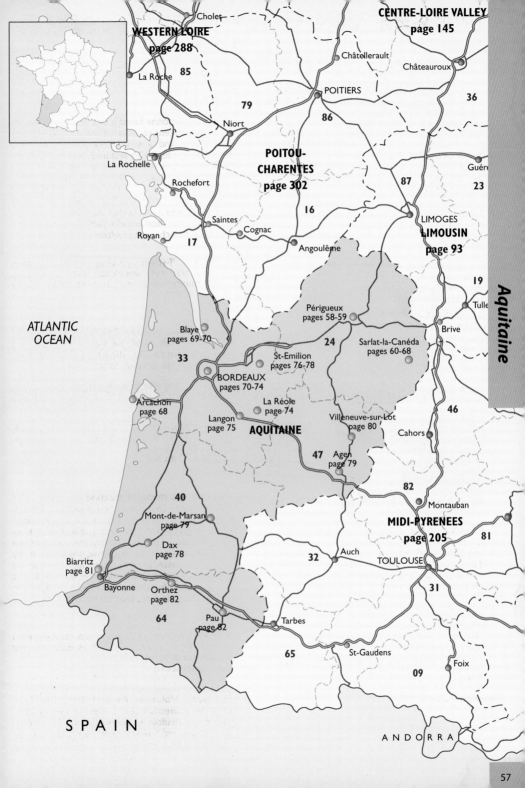

WESTERN LOIRE
page 288

CENTRE-LOIRE VALLEY
page 145

POITOU-CHARENTES
page 302

LIMOUSIN
page 93

Blaye
pages 69-70

Périgueux
pages 58-59

Sarlat-la-Canéda
pages 60-68

St-Emilion
pages 76-78

BORDEAUX
pages 70-74

Arcachon
page 68

La Réole
page 74

Villeneuve-sur-Lot
page 80

Langon
page 75

AQUITAINE

Agen
page 79

Mont-de-Marsan
page 79

MIDI-PYRENEES
page 205

Dax
page 78

Biarritz
page 81

Orthez
page 82

Pau
page 82

Cholet

La Roche

Niort

La Rochelle

Rochefort

Saintes

Cognac

Royan

Angoulême

POITIERS

Châtellerault

Châteauroux

Guéro

LIMOGES

Tulle

Brive

Cahors

Auch

TOULOUSE

Montauban

Tarbes

St-Gaudens

Foix

Bayonne

ATLANTIC
OCEAN

85

79

86

36

87

23

16

17

19

24

46

33

47

82

81

40

32

31

64

65

09

SPAIN

ANDORRA

Aquitaine

24.74 Périgueux

Château/Manor House

Geneviève & Christian FLEURY
'Château de Monciaux',
Monciaux, 24110 BOURROU
Tel: (0) 5 53 80 75 48 Fax: (0) 5 53 80 75 48
contact@chateau-de-monciaux.com
www.chateau-de-monciaux.com

Price Structure – 4 Bedrooms
'Cuvier': bathroom, wc, double bed (queen-size): €98
'Lamarck': shower room, wc, double bed (queen-size): €98
'Jussieu': bathroom, wc, twin beds: €98
'Buffon': shower room, wc, twin beds: €98

Extra Bed: €20
Reduction: 1/10–30/04
Capacity: 8 people

Location
27km S of PERIGUEUX
in: Bourrou
Railway station: 13km
Airport: Bergerac 25km
car essential

In the heart of the Dordogne, halfway between Bergerac and Périgueux is this tucked away elegant little family château. Dating back to the 18th century it stands in 16 hectares of wooded grounds and is equally delightful inside. The pleasant, opulent-looking bedrooms are spacious with period furniture and for some, a bathroom in a turret. The rooms have internet access. A plentiful breakfast is served in the dining room with an impressive fireplace. An ideal location for walks or to simply relax by the pool or play some tennis.

Facilities: off-street parking, extensive grounds, lounge, hosts have pets, pets not accepted, internet access, dinner available, babies welcome, free cot, 100% no smoking, closed: 22/12–29/12, private swimming pool, private tennis court, bird-watching, hiking, cycling
Fluent English spoken

Directions: At Bergerac N21 direction Périgueux for 23km to the hamlet Les Trois Frères. D42 direction Villamblard/Bourrou and then follow signs to 'Château de Monciaux'.

24.64 Périgueux

Private Home

Patricia & Laurent DUVERNEUIL
Champlebout, 24380 CHALAGNAC
Tel: (0) 5 53 46 68 96 / (0) 670 95 27 19
Fax: (0) 5 53 46 68 66
lduverneuil@wanadoo.fr
www.chambres-dhotes-champlebout.com

Price Structure – 2 Bedrooms
2 rooms: shower room, wc, double bed (queen-size): €59

Extra Bed: €15
Reduction: 1/09–30/06, 6 nights
Capacity: 4 people

Location
12km S of PERIGUEUX
in: Chalagnac
Railway station: 12km
Airport: Bergerac 35km
car essential

Perfect for lovers of the great outdoors: 14 hectares close to the touristic sites of the Périgord Noir! The guest bedrooms are on the ground floor with their own exterior entrance, a garden seating area and an uninterrupted view of the valley down to the lake. The open-plan lounge and breakfast room lie under the original framework. Young couple Patricia and Laurent are from the region and readily advise on the local produce. They organise weekend trips: fishing and shooting for woodcock. Dogs accepted and kennels available.

Facilities: private parking, extensive grounds, hosts have pets, babies welcome, free cot, 3 nights minimum stay: 1/07–31/08, private swimming pool, fishing, hunting, mushroom-picking, hiking, cycling, interesting flora, lake watersports, golf course 12km, vineyard 30km
Basic English spoken

Directions: From Périgueux N21 towards Bergerac for 11km then turn right onto the D44 towards Chalagnac. Continue for 3km, pass the village on your left and take the small road on the right towards Champlebout. Follow the signs.

Location
30km N of PERIGUEUX
in: Champagnac-de-Belair, station
pick-up on arrival/departure
Railway station: 50km
Airport: Périgueux 30km
car essential

Château/Manor House

A totally authentic ancient 13th-century fortress, restored and furnished with period furniture. Spend your day visiting the caves and the Abbey of Brantôme and, on summer evenings, dine under the stars in the inner courtyard of the château.

Claude & Michel DUSEAU
'Château de La Borie-Saulnier',
24530 CHAMPAGNAC-DE-BELAIR
Tel: (0) 5 53 54 22 99 Fax: (0) 5 53 08 53 78
chateau-de-la-borie-saulnier@wanadoo.fr

Facilities: private parking, extensive grounds, lounge, hosts have pets, dinner available, babies welcome, free cot, closed: 01/01–01/02, private swimming pool, cycling, fishing, riversports, golf course 30km
Fluent English spoken

Price Structure – 4 Bedrooms and 1 Suite
'Jaune': bathroom, wc, double bed, single bed:
€79 – 2 people €90 – 3 people
'Verte': bathroom, wc, double bed: €79
'Turquoise' & 'Grise': bathroom, wc, twin beds: €75
suite 'Bleue': shower room, wc, double bed. En-suite room, double bed, single bed: €79 – 2 people
€120 – 5 people

Extra Bed: €22
Reduction: 6 nights, children
Capacity: 14 people

Directions: In Périgueux, take the D939 towards Angoulême. In Brantôme, go in the direction of Angoulême, Nontron. Before the cycle shop, take the road 'chez Ravailles' (VC3) for 3.5km.

Location
18km S E of PERIGUEUX
in: Ladouze, station pick-up on
arrival/departure
Railway station: 18km
Airport: Périgueux 14km
car essential

Working Farm

Jean-Claude and Claudine will give you a hearty welcome to their livestock farm surrounded by fields and woods. There are caves and medieval towns to visit, and after a hard day's sightseeing, you will enjoy unwinding beside the swimming pool.

Jean-Claude SALIVES
'Peyssut', 24330 LADOUZE
Tel: (0) 5 53 06 72 92
lafermedugroschene@wanadoo.fr
http://perso-wanadoo.fr/peyssut/

Facilities: off-street parking, garden, tv lounge, hosts have pets, pets not accepted, kitchen, babies welcome, free cot, 100% no smoking, wheelchair access, private swimming pool, hiking, cycling, interesting flora, mushroom-picking, golf course 10km, riversports 20km

Price Structure – 6 Bedrooms
5 rooms: shower room, wc, washbasin, double bed, single bed: €44 – 2 people €57 – 3 people
shower room, wc, washbasin, double bed: €47

Extra Bed: €13
Capacity: 17 people

Directions: At Périgueux head towards Cahors (N89) then turn right to Le Bugue, Sarlat (D710). 'Peyssut' is on the D710.

Aquitaine – Périgueux

24.15 Sarlat-la-Canéda

Private Home

Françoise HERPIN FORGET
'Le Verseau', 49 route des Pechs,
24200 SARLAT-LA-CANEDA
Tel: (0) 5 53 31 02 63 Fax: (0) 5 53 31 02 63
verseau-sarlat@wanadoo.fr
www.verseau-sarlat.com

Price Structure – 3 Bedrooms and 1 Suite
television, shower room, wc, double bed, single bed.
En-suite room, single bed: €45 – 2 people
€75 – 4 people
shower room, wc, double bed, single bed:
€39 – 2 people €48 – 3 people
shower room, wc, double bed, single bed:
€46 – 2 people €55 – 3 people
television, shower room, wc, double bed: €46

Extra Bed: €9
Capacity: 12 people

Location
SARLAT-LA-CANEDA
in: Sarlat-la-Canéda, station pick-up on arrival/departure
Railway station: 2km
Airport: Bergerac 70km

Sarlat is a great place to live, and Françoise will help you enjoy every minute of it during your stay. Her house, in typical Périgord style, is set in grounds with magnificent trees and views over the valley of Sarlat. Be sure to try a trip in a horse-drawn carriage and visit the Dordogne, the châteaux, the prehistoric caves and the medieval villages.

Facilities: off-street parking, extensive grounds, hosts have pets, pets not accepted, babies welcome, free cot, 100% no smoking, 1 shared shower room, wc, cycling 3km, lake watersports 6km, golf course 10km, riversports 10km
Basic English spoken

Directions: From the centre of Sarlat, go to the railway station, continue for 300m and turn left towards Les Flèches. Continue for 1.2km. The house is on the right (B&B France sign).

24.59 Sarlat-la-Canéda

Private Home

Monique & Paul MATHIEU
'Aux Trois Sources', Pech Lafaille,
24200 SARLAT-LA-CANEDA
Tel: (0) 5 53 59 08 19 Fax: (0) 5 53 59 08 19
mathieu@hebergement-sarlat.com
www.hebergement-sarlat.com

Price Structure – 5 Bedrooms
and 1 Apartment
television, kitchen, shower room, wc, double bed: €53
2 rooms: shower room, wc, double bed, single bed:
€43 – 2 people €55 – 3 people
2 rooms: shower room, wc, double bed: €43
television, bathroom, wc, double bed: €48

Extra Bed: €12
Capacity: 14 people

Location
SARLAT-LA-CANEDA
in: Sarlat-la-Canéda
Railway station: 3km
Airport: Bergerac 70km
car essential

Deep in the countryside on the edge of Sarlat, this typical 17th-century Périgord residence is in two parts, separated by one of three springs nearby that supply drinking water. Sloping terraced grounds surround you with charming areas like the barbecue corner close to the pond, shaded by a small grove of banana trees. The bedrooms are located in the annex each with their own independent entrance. Besides being comfortable, you will appreciate the extras, e.g. fridge, kettle, magazines. Paul is a former cabinetmaker.

Facilities: private parking, extensive grounds, tv lounge, hosts have pets, 100% no smoking, wheelchair access, closed: 15/11–15/02, hiking, golf course 6km, fishing 6km, riversports 6km

Directions: In Sarlat head for Ste-Nathalène for 3km, then turn right and follow the 'Chambres d'Hôtes' signs to 'Les Trois Sources'.

Location
30km S W of SARLAT-LA-CANEDA
in: Belvès
car essential

Private Home

A warm, amiable and genuine welcome awaits you in the heart of Belvès, a protected classified medieval village. Award yourself a stop in this former hunting lodge from the 16th century set in a shady park of age-old trees. The guest bedrooms are on the first floor whilst breakfast is served in the large living room which has a beautiful chimney. There is also a sitting room for your comfort. Their gîte can also be booked on a bed and breakfast basis depending on the season.

Alain GIRAUDET
'Manoir de la Moissie', 24170 BELVES
Tel: (0) 5 53 30 25 19 / (0) 680 95 43 89
moissie@tiscali.fr
www.moissie.com

Facilities: off-street parking, extensive grounds, lounge, hosts have pets, pets not accepted, babies welcome, free cot, cycling
Adequate English spoken

Price Structure – 1 Bedroom and 1 Suite
'Venise': television, shower room, wc, double bed, single bed: €50 – 2 people €70 – 3 people
suite 'Asie': television, bathroom, wc, double bed, single bed. En-suite room, single bed:
€60 – 2 people €90 – 4 people
Capacity: 7 people

Directions: At Sarlat, take the D57 and then the D703 for Bergerac. At Siorac, take the D770 on the left as far as Belvès. Head towards Monpazier. Turn right immediately after the municipal swimming pool, and it is the first lane on the left in front of a small wall. Go up this lane (following signs to 'La Moissie').

Location
31km N W of SARLAT-LA-CANEDA
in: Fleurac
Railway station: 10km
car essential

Bienvenue en France

Private Home

Alain has come from the Camargue to breathe new life into this former little farm, set by meadows, woods and orchards. The renovated bedrooms, independent from the main house, are around a small courtyard in the old *bergerie*. Although a little cramped and with modest bathrooms, in their favour is an uninterrupted view from a private terrace or exotic decor, take your pick! The pool also has panoramic views. Alain, full of energy, sees to your every need and earns three 'suns' all on his own. He may even sing you a song!

Annie & Alain SCHIMICCI
'Les Audies', 24580 FLEURAC
Tel: (0) 5 53 08 04 98 / (0) 631 79 03 02
Fax: (0) 5 53 08 04 98
gites-les-audies.2@wanadoo.fr
www.perigord-gites.net

Facilities: off-street parking, extensive grounds, lounge, hosts have pets, pets not accepted, kitchen, babies welcome, free cot, 100% no smoking, 2 nights minimum stay, private swimming pool, hiking, cycling, riversports 8km, golf course 10km, vineyard 40km
Adequate English spoken

Price Structure – 3 Bedrooms
'Verte' & 'Jaune': shower room, wc, double bed: €42
'Orientale': shower room, wc, twin beds: €42

Extra Bed: €5
Reduction: 01/10–31/05, groups
Capacity: 6 people

Directions: From Sarlat D47 towards Périgueux. After Les Eysies, at Manaurie take the D31 on the right towards Rouffignac then turn left down a small road following signs to 'Les Audies'.

24.68 Sarlat-la-Canéda

Residence of Outstanding Character

Catharine & Gert-Jan VAN WIJK
'Le Noyer Résidence', Le Reclaud,
24260 LE BUGUE
Tel: (0) 5 53 04 40 02 Fax: (0) 5 53 04 46 65
info@le-noyer.com
www.lenoyerresidence.com

Price Structure – 5 Bedrooms
'Beach': bathroom, wc, shower, 2 single beds: €85
'Siena': bathroom, wc, twin beds: €85
'Nature': bathroom, wc, double bed: €85
'Lucca' & 'Como': bathroom, wc, 2 single beds: €85

Extra Bed: €25
Reduction: 3 nights
Capacity: 10 people

Location
31km W of SARLAT-LA-CANEDA
in: Le Bugue, station pick-up on arrival/departure
Railway station: 5km
Airport: Bergerac 30km
car essential

Not far from Sarlat and Bugue is this typical Périgord house encircled by absolutely charming grounds and woods. A farm transformed into an *auberge* with a restaurant that has known great acclaim. Inside, whether it be in the bedrooms, the large lounge or the breakfast room, everything is well laid out for you to rest, relax and converse in good company. The terrace, swimming pool and a well-kept lawn are perfect as is the magical view. An attentive, warm welcome from Catharine and Gert-Jan in a relaxed and serene setting.

Facilities: off-street parking, extensive grounds, tv lounge, hosts have pets, pets not accepted, dinner available, 100% no smoking, 3 nights minimum stay: 01/06–31/08, private swimming pool, hiking, interesting flora, cycling 4km, vineyard 4km, fishing 5km, riversports 5km
Fluent English spoken

Directions: From Sarlat take the D703 to Bugue, then once in the village head for St-Alvère staying on the D703 for 4km. The house is on the left on a turning. Signposted 'Le Noyer'.

24.70 Sarlat-la-Canéda

Private Home

Christine & Jean-Louis BIGAROLI
Le Pecheychus, 24480 LE BUISSON-DE-CADOUIN
Tel: (0) 5 53 22 93 97 / (0) 603 91 12 97
jean-louis.bigaroli@wanadoo.fr

Price Structure – 3 Bedrooms and 1 Suite
'Rouge': shower room, wc, double bed. En-suite room, shower room, wc, single bed: €46 – 2 people €55 – 3 people
'Le Peyral' & 'Le Maine': shower room, wc, double bed: €48
'Gavernot': shower room, wc, double bed (queen-size): €48

Extra Bed: €9
Capacity: 9 people

Location
39km W of SARLAT-LA-CANEDA
in: Le Buisson-de-Cadouin, station pick-up on arrival/departure
Railway station: 4km
Airport: Bergerac 35km
car essential

In the countryside is this contemporary house in the regional style, easily accessible from the Bergerac–Sarlat axis. Stay in a modest ground level bedroom in the main house, or for more independence, in the small house where the rooms are bright with their own entrance and terrace. Christine, who has honed her skills over 23 years in the hotel-catering trade, prepares recipes with produce from the vegetable plot: pâtés, *confits*, homemade foie gras, jams. Smiling and energetic, she hosts themed evenings and mushroom-hunting.

Facilities: off-street parking, garden, lounge, dinner available, babies welcome, free cot, mushroom-picking, cycling, hiking, fishing 4km, riversports 4km, golf course 16km, vineyard 35km
Fluent English spoken

Directions: On the D29, halfway between Bergerac and Sarlat. Coming from Sarlat pass Le Buisson-de-Cadouin and continue for 4km. The house is on this road on the right.

Location
25km S W of SARLAT-LA-CANEDA
in: Le Coux-et-Bigaroque, station
pick-up on arrival/departure
Railway station: 7km
Airport: Bergerac 40km
car essential

✹ ✹ ✹ ✹

Château/Manor House

An authentic 15th-century *maison forte* transformed over centuries into a comfortable manor house, ideally situated in the Périgord Noir. Encompassed by three hectares of ground, it dominates the Dordogne valley. Inside is a sociable atmosphere where musical soirées are held in the living room. The comfortable bedrooms boast high ceilings and have wooden floors. Be sure to book dinner as Henriette, your actual hostess, is an excellent cook and loves to share her talent. A welcome of great warmth and kindness. On site: cookery courses.

Facilities: off-street parking, extensive grounds, tv lounge, pets not accepted, dinner available, babies welcome, free cot, 100% no smoking, private swimming pool, hiking, cycling, fishing 2km, riversports 2km, golf course 3km, mushroom-picking 5km
Adequate English spoken

Directions: From Sarlat, D57 and D703 towards Bergerac for 29km to Siorac-en-Périgord, then turn right onto the D703 until you reach Coux-et-Bigaroque. Take the first turn on the left after the town hall 'la Mairie'. Follow the signs.

Joyce VILLEMUR
**'Manoir de la Brunie',
24220 LE COUX-ET-BIGAROQUE**
Tel: (0) 5 53 31 95 62 **Fax:** (0) 5 53 31 95 62
manoirdelabrunie@wanadoo.fr
www.manoirdelabrunie.com

Price Structure – 4 Bedrooms and 1 Suite
'Castelnaud': bathroom, wc, shower, double bed (queen-size). En-suite room, 2 single beds (child-size): €99 – 2 people €133 – 4 people
'Comarque' & 'Fayrac': bathroom, wc, shower, double bed (queen-size): €109
'Puymentin': bathroom, wc, shower, double bed: €94
'Beynac': bathroom, wc, double bed: €84

Extra Bed: €17
Reduction: 01/09–30/06
Capacity: 12 people

Location
20km N W of SARLAT-LA-CANEDA
in: Les Eyzies-de-Tayac
Railway station: Les Eyzies-de-Tayac
Airport: Bergerac 50km
car essential

✹ ✹

Private Home

Uncover this region's historic treasures from a base a few hundred metres away from the famous caves at Eyzies, once inhabited by Cro-Magnon man. From the garden with a swimming pool shielded by a thick bamboo hedge, is a superb view of chalk cliffs and carved gorges. The fairly basic rooms are being renovated bit by bit in this house which was the annex to the nearby hotel. At the bottom of the garden, canoe or kayak on the river. You can also arrive by train at the nearby station. Book well in advance for this busy summer destination.

Facilities: private parking, extensive grounds, pets not accepted, kitchen, closed: 15/11–15/03, private swimming pool, fishing, mushroom-picking, hiking, cycling, interesting flora, riversports, golf course 15km, lake watersports 20km, vineyard 40km
Adequate English spoken

Directions: Les Eyzies is on the D47 between Sarlat and Périgueux. 'Le Ménestrel' is on this road, between the railway line and the river.

Christiane & Jean-Pierre PLATEL
**'Le Ménestrel', 1 rue de Laugerie,
24620 LES EYZIES-DE-TAYAC**
Tel: (0) 5 53 04 58 94 **Fax:** (0) 5 53 08 16 59
contact@menestrel-perigord.com
www.menestrel-perigord.com

Price Structure – 5 Bedrooms
2 rooms: television, bathroom, wc, double bed: €75
wheelchair access, television, bathroom, wc, twin beds: €75
2 rooms: bathroom, wc, twin beds: €75

Extra Bed: €15
Reduction: 15/03–14/07 & 30/08–15/11, 4 nights
Capacity: 10 people

Aquitaine – Sarlat-la-Canéda

24.66 Sarlat-la-Canéda

Residence of Outstanding Character

Monique & Roger BALTZER
'Domaine la Bélie', Lieu-dit l'Abeille,
24200 MEYRALS
Tel: (0) 5 53 59 55 82 / (0) 686 13 37 70
contacter@perigord-labelie.com
www.perigord-labelie.com

Price Structure – 2 Bedrooms and 1 Suite
'La Petite Maison': wheelchair access, shower room, wc, twin beds: €100
'La Suite': lounge, shower room, wc, double bed (queen-size). En-suite room, single bed: €120 – 2 people €140 – 3 people
'La Chambre Bleue': shower room, wc, double bed (queen-size): €80

Reduction: 7 nights
Capacity: 7 people

Location
14km W of SARLAT-LA-CANEDA
in: Meyrals
Railway station: 15km
Airport: Périgueux 50km
car essential

This former 16th-century farm is now a sophisticated and ecological home. Old stones contrast with the modern in this beautiful, bright and pleasant space. Before sailing off together on their catamaran, Monique and Roger were journalists, television directors and cinema producers. The large lounge (heated by a *canton*, a traditional Périgord fireplace), the living rooms and the three lovely bedrooms all hint at their love of travel. A haven of peace. a sanctuary for birds, wild boar and roe deer. Not to be missed!

Facilities: off-street parking, extensive grounds, tv lounge, hosts have pets, pets not accepted, babies welcome, free cot, 100% no smoking, 2 nights minimum stay, closed: 01/10–1/04, hiking, cycling, vineyard, fishing 5km, riversports 7km, golf course 15km
Fluent English spoken

Directions: From Sarlat, D47 towards Périgueux for 12km, then at 'Bénivet', turn left towards Meyrals for about 3km and then turn left down a small road towards 'l'Abeille'. Look for signs on a wooden gate on the left.

24.69 Sarlat-la-Canéda

Château/Manor House

Françoise & Claude GAZEL de TORRENTE
'Domaine des Farguettes', 24480 PALEYRAC
Tel: (0) 5 53 23 48 23 Fax: (0) 5 53 23 48 23
clagazel@wanadoo.fr
www.farguettes.fr

Price Structure – 5 Bedrooms and 1 Suite
bathroom, wc, double bed (queen-size), single bed: €85 – 2 people €115 – 3 people
along corridor bathroom, wc, double bed: €70
along corridor bathroom, wc, double bed. En-suite room, single bed: €70 – 2 people €100 – 3 people
bathroom, wc, twin beds: €110
bathroom, wc, double bed (queen-size): €110
shower room, wc, twin beds: €110

Extra Bed: €10
Reduction: groups
Capacity: 14 people

Location
32km W of SARLAT-LA-CANEDA
in: Paleyrac
Railway station: 8km
Airport: Bergerac 40km
car essential

An authentically restored manor house, built in 1664, with a fabulous panorama of rolling meadows, cypress, linden and plane trees and forests of chestnut trees. Continuing the tradition here of good hospitality, convivial Claude and Françoise are passionate about theatre and poetry. Three bedrooms are upstairs under beautiful beams, with four others in a converted barn. The latter have either ground floor access or a small kitchen area. A captivating atmosphere where animated dinner conversations are punctuated with laughter.

Facilities: off-street parking, extensive grounds, tv lounge, dinner available, kitchen, babies welcome, free cot, private swimming pool, hunting, mushroom-picking, hiking, fishing 3km, golf course 7km, cycling 7km, riversports 7km, interesting flora 10km, vineyard 40km
Adequate English spoken

Directions: Halfway between Bergerac and Sarlat. Coming from Sarlat pass Siorac-en-Périgord on the D25, continue for 5km and turn left to Paleyrac. From the village church, follows the signs 'La Farguette' for 1.5km to the woods. On the left, the two pillars mark the entrance to the grounds.

Location
20km S of SARLAT-LA-CANEDA
in: Poudens
Railway station: 6km
car essential

Residence of
Outstanding
Character

Your Dutch hosts, Occo and Carin, welcome you to their 18th-century residence, which they have completely restored. The bedrooms are spacious, comfortable and tastefully decorated and a varied combination of French, Dutch and English breakfast is served on the terrace with a splendid view over the lovely Céou Valley. The setting is quiet and rural with a large swimming pool and extensive grounds.

Carin & Occo BINNENDIJK
'La Cabane', Poudens, 46340 DEGAGNAC
Tel: (0) 5 65 41 49 74 / (0) 689 64 06 54
Fax: (0) 5 65 41 49 74
lacabane@wanadoo.fr
www.lacabane.com

Facilities: off-street parking, extensive grounds, hosts have pets, pets not accepted, babies welcome, free cot, 100% no smoking, closed: 01/11–01/04, private swimming pool, hiking, cycling, fishing, bird-watching, riversports 12km, golf course 20km, vineyard 20km
Fluent English spoken

Price Structure – 3 Bedrooms
first room: lounge, bathroom, wc, shower, double bed (queen-size): €68
second room: shower room, wc, double bed (queen-size): €58
third room: lounge, shower room, wc, twin beds: €68

Extra Bed: €18
Reduction: children
Capacity: 6 people

Directions: On the N20 Brive-Gourdon road, take exit Gourdon. Head towards Cahors on the D12, and, after 6km, at the bridge over the river, look for the sign 'La Cabane'.

Location
30km S W of SARLAT-LA-CANEDA
in: Siorac-en-Périgord, station pick-up on arrival/departure
Railway station: 2km
Airport: Bergerac 50km
car essential

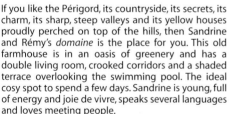

Private Home

If you like the Périgord, its countryside, its secrets, its charm, its sharp, steep valleys and its yellow houses proudly perched on top of the hills, then Sandrine and Rémy's *domaine* is the place for you. This old farmhouse is in an oasis of greenery and has a double living room, crooked corridors and a shaded terrace overlooking the swimming pool. The ideal cosy spot to spend a few days. Sandrine is young, full of energy and joie de vivre, speaks several languages and loves meeting people.

Sandrine & Rémy BRUNETEAU LORENZO
'Domaine de la Dame Blanche', Rispe,
24170 SIORAC-EN-PERIGORD
Tel: (0) 5 53 28 19 21 / (0) 612 48 50 34
bruneteau.lorenzo@wanadoo.fr
www.perigord.com/ladameblanche

Facilities: off-street parking, garden, tv lounge, hosts have pets, pets not accepted, babies welcome, free cot, 100% no smoking, 2 nights minimum stay: 01/07–31/08, private swimming pool, hiking, fishing 2km, riversports 2km, golf course 3km, gliding 5km
Fluent English spoken

Directions: Siorac is between Sarlat and Bergerac on the left bank of the Dordogne river. When you reach the village, cross the railway line towards Urval (there are small signs). Continue for 2km up the valley and at the junction, take the small road, which is a dead end, to the right of the iron cross and follow the signs. The house is the one with red shutters.

Price Structure – 4 Bedrooms and 1 Suite
'Au petit nid douillet', 'Paradis d'Azur' & 'Fleur d'O': shower room, wc, double bed: €65
'Puits d'Amour': shower room, wc, double bed, single bed. En-suite room, twin beds:
  €75 – 2 people €90 – 5 people
'Océane': shower room, wc, double bed, single bed:
  €65 – 2 people €80 – 3 people

Extra Bed: €15
Reduction: 4 nights
Capacity: 14 people

Aquitaine – Sarlat-la-Canéda

24.44 Sarlat-la-Canéda

Residence of Outstanding Character

Location
9km N of SARLAT-LA-CANEDA
in: St-Crépin-et-Carlucet
Railway station: 10km
Airport: Périgueux 50km
car essential

Béatrice & Jean-Yves FAUSTE
'Les Granges Hautes', St-Crépin,
24590 ST-CREPIN-ET-CARLUCET
Tel: (0) 5 53 29 35 60
fauste@netcourrier.com
www.les-granges-hautes.fr

This beautiful Périgord house is at the centre of superb grounds. Each room is different, and has its own individual style which will transport you to Italy or the Orient. A delicious breakfast, an excellent swimming pool and the warm welcome of your hosts all add up to an enchanting place.

Price Structure – 5 Bedrooms
'Toscane': bathroom, wc, double bed, single bed:
€102 – 2 people €133 – 3 people
'Virginie': bathroom, wc, twin beds: €102
'Irina': shower room, wc, double bed, single bed:
€94 – 2 people €117 – 3 people
'Oiseaux': shower room, wc, double bed, twin beds:
€122 – 2 people €154 – 4 people
'Pamela': shower room, wc, twin beds: €102

Facilities: off-street parking, extensive grounds, tv lounge, pets not accepted, dinner available, babies welcome, free cot, 100% no smoking, wheelchair access, 5 years old minimum age, closed: 15/11–15/03, private swimming pool, hiking, cycling, golf course 15km
Adequate English spoken

Extra Bed: €25
Reduction: 15/03–15/07 & 25/08–15/11, 10 nights
Capacity: 14 people

Directions: At Sarlat, take the D704 towards Montignac. After 9km, turn right and take the D60 towards St-Crépin-et-Carlucet. In the village, follow the signs to 'Les Granges Hautes'.

24.67 Sarlat-la-Canéda

Residence of Outstanding Character

Location
12km N of SARLAT-LA-CANEDA
in: St-Crépin-et-Carlucet
Railway station: 12km
Airport: Périgueux 50km
car essential

Helen & Eric EDGAR
'Les Charmes de Carlucet', Carlucet,
24590 ST-CREPIN-ET-CARLUCET
Tel: (0) 5 53 31 22 60
lescharmes@carlucet.com
www.carlucet.com

Helen and Eric have opened up their magnificent character house. In this tranquil spot, the bedrooms are comfortable with tasteful furniture and quality bedding and facilities. A full breakfast can be served by the pool. Explore the two hectares of grounds where you find gardens framed with dry-stone walls, shaded picnic areas and a children's playground. Restaurants are five minutes away on foot. Also available is a quality gîte with a private pool. An impeccable welcome and a family atmosphere–the children are charming!

Price Structure – 4 Bedrooms
'Monet': television, shower room, wc, double bed:
€75
'Volny': television, bathroom, wc, double bed: €89
'Lavande': television, shower room, wc, double bed (queen-size), 2 single beds: €99 – 2 people
€139 – 4 people
'Le Pigeonnier': television, bathroom, wc, double bed (queen-size), 2 single beds: €99 – 2 people
€139 – 4 people

Facilities: off-street parking, extensive grounds, tv lounge, hosts have pets, pets not accepted, babies welcome, free cot, 100% no smoking, wheelchair access, 2 nights minimum stay, private swimming pool, hiking, cycling, riversports 15km, golf course 20km
Fluent English spoken

Extra Bed: €20
Reduction: 1/09–30/06
Capacity: 12 people

Directions: At Sarlat D704 towards Montignac for 9km then D60 on the right to Salignac. Cross through St-Crépin-et-Carlucet and continue for 3km. Pass the stadium and then after 500m, turn right towards Carlucet. Continue for 1.5km, and the house is on the left.

Location
18km W of SARLAT-LA-CANEDA
in: St-Cyprien, station pick-up on arrival/departure
Railway station: 2km
Airport: Bergerac 50km

Residence of Outstanding Character

A charming 12th-century house with plenty of character in the heart of a picturesque medieval village, high up with panoramic views. Monique loves beautiful old objects and has hunted out furniture at antique fairs from the 17th and 18th centuries. Rest and relaxation are de rigueur and massages are available as is a hot-tub on the terrace, available all year round. All the rooms have a TV, CD/DVD player and air-conditioning and some have multi-jet showers, hammams and jacuzzi baths. The welcome here is warm and sincere.

Facilities: garden, tv lounge, babies welcome, free cot, 100% no smoking, private swimming pool, mushroom-picking 1km, hiking 1km, hunting 2km, fishing 2km, cycling 2km, riversports 3km, vineyard 3km, golf course 8km, gliding 15km
Adequate English spoken

Directions: Please contact your host in advance for detailed directions.

Monique DUBOIS
'Demeure du Coeur de Lion', 6 rue du Lion, 24220 ST-CYPRIEN
Tel: (0) 5 53 31 13 85 / (0) 633 74 07 71
Fax: (0) 5 53 31 13 85
romaneix24@voila.fr
www.perigord-gites-de-charmes.com

Price Structure – 5 Apartments
'Marie-Louise' & 'Joséphine': television, kitchen, bathroom, wc, washbasin, twin beds: €132
'Aliénor': television, kitchen, bathroom, wc, washbasin, double bed (queen-size), single bed: €132 – 2 people €144 – 3 people
'Coeur de Lion': television, kitchen, bathroom, wc, double bed: €112
'Coeur de Lion-petite': television, kitchen, bathroom, twin beds: €92

Extra Bed: €15   **Reduction:** 01/10–30/04, groups
Capacity: 11 people

Location
8km E of SARLAT-LA-CANEDA
in: Ste-Nathalène, station pick-up on arrival/departure
Railway station: 7km
Airport: Bergerac 75km
car essential

Private Home

Ten minutes from Sarlat, on the edge of a forest and fields perfect for lovely country walks, is this pretty little contemporary house, built in *périgourdine* style, where you can unwind on the terrace and in the salt-water swimming pool. The bright bedrooms are upstairs with a view over the wooded garden and have their own independent entrance. Dinner is available if booked in advance and is inspired by local traditional dishes and Theresa's Indian roots. A tranquil haven with a warm and relaxed welcome.

Facilities: off-street parking, extensive grounds, tv lounge, 100% no smoking, private swimming pool, hiking, fishing 2km, riversports 4km, interesting flora 5km, golf course 8km
Fluent English spoken

Directions: From Sarlat D47 towards Carlux until Ste-Nathalène. On arrival at the village, turn left towards Salignac, Le Manoir d'Eyrignac. Continue for 800m. 'Les Petites Charmilles' is signed on the right.

Theresa & James COGGER
'Les Petites Charmilles', La Croix d'Esteil, 24200 STE-NATHALENE
Tel: (0) 5 53 29 13 13 / (0) 689 46 17 87
info@lespetitescharmilles.com
www.lespetitescharmilles.com

Price Structure – 4 Bedrooms
shower, wc, double bed: €50
along corridor shower room, wc, double bed: €50
along corridor shower room, wc, twin beds: €50
shower room, wc, double bed: €50

Extra Bed: €14
Reduction: 01/10–31/05, 7 nights
Capacity: 8 people

Aquitaine – Sarlat-la-Canéda

24.72 Sarlat-la-Canéda

Residence of Outstanding Character

Location
8km E of SARLAT-LA-CANEDA
in: Ste-Nathalène, station pick-up on arrival/departure
Railway station: 7km
Airport: Bergerac 75km
car essential

Bienvenue en France

This former 18th-century farm is set in vast wooded grounds, 8km from Sarlat. It is restored true to Périgord traditions but with great pains to make it comfortable whilst preserving its authenticity. The character bedrooms are independent; 'Tilleul', a former bread oven with a monumental fireplace; 'Hortensia', on the ground floor in the main house and 'Chêne' on two levels with exposed beams. A full breakfast and traditional cooking are served in the dining room or the garden. A youthful, attentive welcome.

Sandrine & Marc AUDOUARD
'La Roche d'Esteil', La Croix d'Esteil,
24200 STE-NATHALENE
Tel: (0) 5 53 29 14 42 / (0) 687 72 19 80
contact@perigord-hotes.com
www.perigord-hotes.com

Price Structure – 5 Bedrooms
'Tilleul': shower room, wc, double bed: €98
'Hortensia': shower, double bed, single bed:
€80 – 2 people €99 – 3 people
'Chêne': shower room, wc, double bed, twin beds:
€90 – 2 people €150 – 4 people
'Charme': shower, double bed (queen-size): €90
'Lilas': shower, twin beds: €90

Extra Bed: €22
Reduction: 01/09–30/06, 3 nights, children
Capacity: 13 people

Facilities: off-street parking, extensive grounds, hosts have pets, pets not accepted, dinner available, babies welcome, free cot, 100% no smoking, closed: 15/11–15/03, private swimming pool, hiking, fishing 2km, riversports 4km, interesting flora 5km, golf course 8km
Adequate English spoken

Directions: From Sarlat D47 towards Carlux until Ste-Nathalène. On arrival at the village, turn left towards Salignac, Le Manoir d'Eyrignac. Continue for 900m. 'La Roche d'Esteil' is signposted on the right.

40.10 Arcachon

Private Home

Location
40km S E of ARCACHON
in: Le Muret
Railway station: 20km
Airport: Bordeaux-Mérignac 75km
car essential

Bienvenue en France

Pascal wanted to create a certain ambience and he has certainly succeeded! You will be agreeably surprised as you cross the threshold of his home. Everything is in perfect taste and the welcome is warm. There is a swimming pool, jacuzzi and sauna. This is the essence of real B&B.

Pascal & Catherine LANDAIS-HART
'La Maranne', Le Muret,
40410 SAUGNACQ-ET-MURET
Tel: (0) 5 58 09 61 71 / (0) 684 63 05 11
Fax: (0) 5 58 09 61 51
la-maranne@wanadoo.fr

Price Structure – 5 Bedrooms
'Favori': television, shower room, wc, double bed, single bed: €66 – 2 people €75 – 3 people
'Hildalgo': television, shower room, wc, twin beds, single bed: €66 – 2 people €75 – 3 people
'Eclair', 'Jap' & 'Ucarios': television, shower room, wc, double bed: €60

Extra Bed: €15
Reduction: 3 nights
Capacity: 12 people

Facilities: private parking, extensive grounds, tv lounge, hosts have pets, pets not accepted, dinner available, babies welcome, free cot, closed: 01/11–31/03, private swimming pool, cycling, hunting, mushroom-picking, riversports 5km, golf course 10km, sea watersports 35km
Fluent English spoken

Directions: From Arcachon, N250 then D5, then N10 towards the south. (From Bordeaux, A63 exit 18 towards Le Muret). The property is on the D20E.

Location
39km N E of BLAYE
in: Montlieu-la-Garde
Railway station: 10km
Airport: Bordeaux-Mérignac 55km
car essential

★★★

Residence of Outstanding Character

This residence has been passed down in the family for an unbelievable four centuries and is now under Pascal's helm. Slowly letting go of the farming, he dedicates his time to his guests and provides a good welcome and service. The bedrooms are in the house or the outbuildings at ground level and hark back to the era of beautiful parquet floors. The part-wooded 40 hectares around the house include a private lake with a pedal boat. Stabling for horses available. 800m from the Maison de la Forêt. On sale: local produce.

Pascal MENANTEAU
'Domaine les Galards', Les Galards,
17210 MONTLIEU-LA-GARDE
Tel: (0) 5 46 04 53 62 / (0) 615 42 95 25
Fax: (0) 5 46 04 32 33
lesgalards@orange.fr
http://www.lesgalards.com

Facilities: off-street parking, extensive grounds, lounge, hosts have pets, babies welcome, free cot, 100% no smoking, wheelchair access, hunting, fishing, hiking, interesting flora, vineyard 3km, golf course 10km, riversports 30km
Adequate English spoken

Price Structure – 4 Bedrooms
'Erable': bathroom, wc, twin beds: €54
'Art-Déco': bathroom, wc, double bed: €54
'Poulailler': wheelchair access, shower room, wc, twin beds: €59
'Charles Vigen': wheelchair access, bathroom, wc, four-poster double bed (queen-size): €59

Extra Bed: €20
Reduction: 3 nights
Capacity: 8 people

Directions: Montlieu-la-Garde is on the N10 halfway between Angoulême and Bordeaux. From this road on arrival at the village take the D730 towards Montendre. The house is a bit further on, on the left (signposted).

Location
10km S E of BLAYE
in: St-Ciers-de-Canesse
Railway station: 7km
Airport: Bordeaux-Mérignac 40km
car essential

★★★

Château/Manor House

In family hands for a century and a half, this château is in a prestigious Côtes de Bourg vineyard. The bedrooms, authentically renovated, have family antiques and marble fireplaces (the 'Mirandole' is very spacious with a lovely balcony). From the windows, look out over the vines that cover the bank of the Gironde River. Dynamic Marie-Agnès serves breakfast in the large traditional dining room. Jean-François, a former geologist turned winegrower, shows you his vineyard, awards and wine stores. A sincere, enlightening welcome.

Marie-Agnès & Jean-François BRETON
'Château les Tours Seguy',
33710 ST-CIERS-DE-CANESSE
Tel: (0) 5 57 64 99 57 / (0) 672 70 59 32
Fax: (0) 5 57 64 99 57
chateau-les-tours-seguy@wanadoo.fr
www.chateau-les-tours-seguy.com

Facilities: private parking, garden, lounge, pets not accepted, babies welcome, free cot, 100% no smoking, hiking, vineyard, riversports 3km, cycling 7km, lake watersports 10km
Fluent English spoken

Price Structure – 4 Bedrooms
'Grimoire', 'Likerlis' & 'Echauguette': shower room, wc, double bed: €55
'Mirandole': shower room, wc, double bed, single bed: €62 – 2 people €77 – 3 people

Extra Bed: €15
Reduction: 4 nights
Capacity: 9 people

Directions: From Bordeaux, A10 towards Paris exit 40a to St-André-de-Cubzac. D669 towards Bourg-sur-Gironde. At the exit to Bourg, D251 towards Berson for 7km until Baillou, then turn left towards St-Ciers-de-Canesse and follow signs to the Château.

Aquitaine – Blaye

33.37 Blaye

Château/Manor House

Vincent LEMAITRE
'Château Rousselle',
33710 ST-CIERS-DE-CANESSE
Tel: (0) 5 57 42 16 62 / (0) 681 82 14 87
Fax: (0) 5 57 42 19 51
chateau@chateaurousselle.com
www.chateaurousselle.com

Price Structure – 3 Bedrooms
'Merlot': television, bathroom, wc, double bed
(queen-size): €82
'Cabernet': television, bathroom, wc, double bed
(queen-size): €82
'Malbec': television, bathroom, wc, double bed
(queen-size), twin beds: €82 – 2 people
€112 – 4 people

Extra Bed: €15
Reduction: 01/10–31/05, 7 nights
Capacity: 8 people

Location
10km S E of BLAYE
in: St-Ciers-de-Canesse
Railway station: 40km
Airport: Bordeaux-Mérignac 50km
car essential

Nathalie and Vincent have quite recently taken over this winegrowing property, located not far from the Gironde estuary, between the famous vineyards of Côtes de Blaye and Côtes de Bourg. Their enthusiasm, dynamism and hospitality skills not only attract wine lovers but also visitors who are looking for a charming place to stay in this unique region. The bedrooms are a short distance from the villa.

Facilities: private parking, extensive grounds, hosts have pets, kitchen, babies welcome, free cot, closed: 20/12–15/01, vineyard, cycling 2km, fishing 5km, bird-watching 20km, sea watersports 50km
Fluent English spoken

Directions: From the A10, Exit 38 or 40 and then take the N137 towards Blaye. At Blaye, head to the Centre-Ville and go along by the river towards Bourg. On the D669, turn left onto the D250, turn left before Villeneuve and continue for 1km until you reach the 'Stop' sign, where you turn right.

33.27 Bordeaux

Private Home

Alice BONDONNY
61 rue Leberthon, 33000 BORDEAUX
Tel: (0) 5 56 94 59 11 Fax: (0) 5 56 94 59 11
malicejg@free.fr

Price Structure – 3 Bedrooms
3 rooms: television, along corridor shower, bathroom, wc, double bed: €70

Reduction: 5 nights
Capacity: 6 people

Location
BORDEAUX
in: Bordeaux
Railway station: Bordeaux
Airport: Bordeaux-Mérignac 8km

Alice is a retired anaesthetist and welcomes you to her house right in the centre of Bordeaux. After days of serious sightseeing and wine tasting, you will appreciate relaxing in her attractive garden.

Facilities: private parking, garden, tv lounge, hosts have pets, pets not accepted, kitchen, 1 shared bathroom, 1 shared shower room, 2 years old minimum age, interesting flora 3km, golf course 8km, cycling 10km, sea watersports 60km
Fluent English spoken

Directions: In Bordeaux, head towards Place de la Victoire, Cours Aristide Briand and then take the second street on the left, then first street on the right and first right again.

Location
BORDEAUX
in: Bordeaux
Railway station: 4km
Airport: Bordeaux-Mérignac 10km

Private Home

'When I go to Bordeaux I shall always stay with Sabine and Patrick' is how a visitor summed up these hosts. Sabine is very welcoming and likes to see her house 'overrun' as she says. No need to panic as she only has one room and it is very spacious. The house is a typical *maison bourgeoise* in the Bordeaux style with lots of charm. It is on a boulevard but is well insulated and faces a quiet garden. It is easy to find by car and a bus passes the door for the town centre.

Sabine & Patrick BROUSSE
241 boulevard du Maréchal Leclerc,
33000 BORDEAUX
Tel: (0) 5 56 51 23 55 / (0) 609 24 24 72
Fax: (0) 5 56 51 23 55
patrick.brousse@fr.ey.com

Facilities: garden, lounge, babies welcome, free cot, 100% no smoking, closed: 01/08–31/08, hiking, cycling, vineyard, golf course 5km, bird-watching 50km, sea watersports 50km
Fluent English spoken

Price Structure – 1 Bedroom
bathroom, wc, shower, double bed (queen-size): €100

Capacity: 2 people

Directions: Please contact your hosts for detailed directions.

Location
30km N of BORDEAUX
in: Bourg-sur-Gironde
Railway station: 15km
Airport: Bordeaux-Mérignac 45km
car essential

Château/Manor House

Refreshed by a good night's sleep, your breakfast will be served in the large, white-stone dining room. You will then be ready to go walking through the maze of vines and then cool off beside the pool and take in the superb view over the valleys covered in vines. You will certainly leave with a few bottles of their own wine as a souvenir. Its superb location earns this place four 'suns'. Excellent value for money. On sale: their own wine.

Facilities: private parking, extensive grounds, tv lounge, hosts have pets, pets not accepted, babies welcome, free cot, closed: 15/08–01/09 & 01/02–01/03, private swimming pool, hiking, vineyard, cycling 2km, fishing 5km, bird-watching 20km, golf course 35km
Fluent English spoken

Valérie & Philippe BASSEREAU
'Château de la Grave',
33710 BOURG-SUR-GIRONDE
Tel: (0) 5 57 68 41 49 Fax: (0) 5 57 68 49 26
chateau.de.la.grave@wanadoo.fr
www.chateaudelagrave.com

Price Structure – 3 Bedrooms
'Coté Jardin': shower room, wc, double bed: €70
'Coté Vigne': shower room, wc, twin beds, single bed: €70 – 2 people €85 – 3 people
'La Tour': shower room, wc, double bed, 2 single beds: €85 – 2 people €120 – 4 people

Capacity: 9 people

Directions: From Bordeaux on the A10, exit Bourg-sur-Gironde. At Bourg, head towards Blaye, and then turn right towards Berson. Then take the second on the right and follow the signs to 'Château de la Grave'.

Aquitaine – Bordeaux

33.51 Bordeaux

Château/Manor House

Murielle GINEBRE
'Château de Lantic', 10 route de Lartigue,
33650 MARTILLAC
Tel: (0) 5 56 72 58 68 / (0) 683 03 27 87
Fax: (0) 5 56 72 58 67
mginebre@wanadoo.fr
www.chateau-de-lantic.com
Price Structure – 5 Bedrooms
and 5 Apartments
'Roméo et Juliette' (our favourite room): television,
kitchen, bathroom, wc, double bed: €159
'Roxane': television, kitchen, shower room, wc, twin
beds: €99
'Mauriac': television, kitchen, bathroom, wc, twin beds,
single bed: €109 – 2 people €125 – 3 people
'Sonneville': television, telephone, bathroom, wc,
double bed, twin beds: €99 – 2 people
€150 – 4 people
'La Boetie': bathroom, wc, double bed: €80
plus 3 rooms, 2 apart.

Reduction: 01/10–01/05, 5 nights, groups
Capacity: 24 people

Location
20km S of BORDEAUX
in: Martillac
Railway station: 22km
Airport: Bordeaux-Mérignac 25km
car essential

A great stop on the Bordeaux Route des Vins. This *Maison de Maître* from the 18th century, surrounded by vines, offers comfortable accommodation in a magnificent setting just 15 minutes away from Bordeaux. Among the many bedrooms on offer you can choose between two types of room: either ones with a discreet kitchenette in the corner of the room or more traditional bedrooms which tend to be more spacious. We especially liked the room 'Roméo et Juliette'. Wine tours and day trips are on offer. What is more there is a large swimming pool amid the vines. Magical!

Facilities: off-street parking, extensive grounds, lounge, hosts have pets, private swimming pool, hiking, cycling, vineyard, sea watersports 45km
Fluent English spoken

Directions: From Bordeaux, A62 towards Toulouse, exit 1 Martillac and head for Martillac. The château is behind the church; third gate on the left.

33.08 Bordeaux

Residence of Outstanding Character

Alain GENESTINE
'Domaine les Sapins', Bouqueyran,
33480 MOULIS-EN-MEDOC
Tel: (0) 5 56 58 18 26 / (0) 680 22 45 07
Fax: (0) 5 56 58 28 45
domaine-les-sapins@wanadoo.fr
domaine-les-sapins.com

Price Structure – 7 Bedrooms, 1 Suite
and 1 Apartment
Suite 'Margaux': bathroom, wc, double bed (super king-size). En-suite room: double bed, single bed:
€148 – 5 people
'Petrus', 'Lafite' & 'Yquem': shower room, wc, double bed (super king-size): €78
'Cheval Blanc': shower room, wc, double bed (super king-size): €68
'Léoville': shower room, wc, double bed, single bed:
€58
kitchen, shower room, wc, washbasin, 2 single beds:
€46
plus 2 rooms

Extra Bed: €25
Reduction: 21/11–19/03, 3 nights, groups
Capacity: 22 people

Location
25km N W of BORDEAUX
in: Moulis-en-Médoc
Railway station: 4km
Airport: Bordeaux-Mérignac 24km

Bienvenue
en France

Here the atmosphere is cosy and you feel like one of the family. The large house dates from the beginning of the 19th century and is set amongst vines, surrounded by beautiful grounds. Nathalie, who is a *cordon bleu* cook, will serve you her specialities, and Alain will share his expertise in wine with you.

Facilities: off-street parking, extensive grounds, lounge, hosts have pets, dinner available, babies welcome, free cot, 100% no smoking, wheelchair access, private swimming pool, hiking, vineyard, cycling 1km, hunting 1km, golf course 12km, fishing 20km, sea watersports 25km
Fluent English spoken

Directions: At Bordeaux, on the A630 take exit 7 and the D1 towards Le Verdon-sur-Soulac. In Castelnau, take the N215 in the same direction, for 3km. In Bouqueyran, turn left (large sign).

Private Home

Location
40km S of BORDEAUX
in: Origne, station pick-up on arrival/departure
Railway station: 50km
Airport: Bordeaux-Mérignac 45km
car essential

A warm welcome from Corinne and Gérard in a renovated former vicarage, in a charming village in the heart of the Parc Régional des Landes de Gascogne and very close to the Sauternes vineyards. The spot is so quiet that rabbits bask out in the sun by the swimming pool! The tastefully decorated bedrooms are in a recent extension and lead onto a large living room. A breakfast of homemade jam and *pâtisseries* is served in the dining room or by the pool (enclosed).

Corinne & Gérard de ROCHEFORT
'La Maison Rose', 33113 ORIGNE
Tel: (0) 5 56 25 79 83 / (0) 624 83 55 54
Fax: (0) 5 56 02 34 25
cdrorigne@free.fr
http://cdrorigne.free.fr

Facilities: off-street parking, garden, lounge, pets not accepted, dinner available, 2 nights minimum stay, closed: 31/12–01/01, private swimming pool, private tennis court, hunting, hiking, cycling, riversports 12km, vineyard 15km, sea watersports 50km, golf course 50km
Fluent English spoken

Price Structure – 5 Bedrooms
1 room: bathroom, wc, double bed (queen-size), single bed: €60 – 2 people €80 – 3 people
1 room: shower room, wc, double bed: €60
1 room: bathroom, wc, double bed, single bed: €60 – 2 people €80 – 3 people
1 room: bathroom, wc, twin beds: €60
along corridor bathroom, wc, single bed: €55

Extra Bed: €20
Reduction: 01/10–30/04
Capacity: 11 people

Directions: From the A62 between Bordeaux and Agen, take exit 2. Head towards Landiras then Balizac on the D11. Turn right onto the D110 to Origne. 'La Maison Rose' is opposite the entrance to the church on the other side of the road.

Private Home

Location
15km S E of BORDEAUX
in: Sadirac, station pick-up on arrival/departure
Railway station: 15km
Airport: Bordeaux-Mérignac 30km
car essential

The gentle hills of the 'Entre-Deux-Mers' region, an abundant patchwork of vineyards, woods and cultural heritage is where, in the middle of a pine forest, Sylvette opens her doors to you. The guest bedrooms are quite basic but be sure to take advantage of Sylvette's knowledge of relaxation techniques and beauty treatment skills. Algae bath treatments, thermal mud wraps, massages and reflexology.

Sylvette BON
4 route départementale 14, 33670 SADIRAC
Tel: (0) 5 56 30 63 96 / (0) 689 33 94 41

Facilities: off-street parking, garden, tv lounge, babies welcome, free cot, 100% no smoking, wc, hiking 2km, cycling 2km, vineyard 2km, bird-watching 80km
Basic English spoken

Price Structure – 3 Bedrooms
No 1: bathroom, double bed: €44
No 2: along corridor bathroom, twin beds: €44
No 3: along corridor shower room, wc, double bed: €44

Extra Bed: €8
Capacity: 6 people

Directions: On the Bordeaux ring road, exit 22. Then head to Cadillac on the D113 for 5km to Camblanes then the D14 towards Créon for 7km. It is the first house on the left after the sawmill.

Aquitaine – Bordeaux

33.54 Bordeaux

Residence of Outstanding Character

Location
20km S of BORDEAUX
in: St-Médard-d'Eyrans
Railway station: 15km
Airport: Bordeaux-Mérignac 25km
car essential

Marie-Cécile GRAMONT
'Domaine de Larchey', 28-30 route de Larchey,
33650 ST-MEDARD-D'EYRANS
Tel: (0) 5 56 72 19 59 / (0) 686 51 55 63
Fax: (0) 5 56 72 20 35
contact@domainedelarchey.com
www.domainedelarchey.com

Marie-Cécile spent her childhood in this substantial winegrower's house which belonged to her grandfather. She loves this place with its 3 hectares of grounds, the old wine vats now restored as a welcome lobby, a chapel, a tennis court to be renovated, all surrounded by the famous wine châteaux of Graves. Add to this the warm welcome from your hostess who has lived and worked abroad including in Germany, Britain and Cambodia. Breakfast is either served in the dining room or under the veranda. You will feel at home here.

Price Structure – 4 Bedrooms
'Cambodgienne': shower room, wc, double bed.
along corridor room 'Vigneronne': shower room, wc, double bed: €80 – 2 people €160 – 4 people
'Suite': lounge, bathroom, wc, double bed, twin beds: €120 – 2 people €140 – 4 people
'Basque': bathroom, wc, shower, double bed: €100

Extra Bed: €20
Reduction: 01/10–31/03
Capacity: 10 people

Facilities: private parking, extensive grounds, tv lounge, hosts have pets, pets not accepted, internet access, babies welcome, free cot, 100% no smoking, closed: 06/01–12/01 & 01/11–07/11, private tennis court, fishing, hiking, cycling, riversports, vineyard, golf course 15km
Fluent English spoken

Directions: Please contact your hosts for detailed directions.

47.23 La Réole

Château/Manor House

Location
10km S E of LA REOLE
in: Meilhan-sur-Garonne
Airport: Bordeaux-Mérignac 80km
car essential

Frédérique & Anthony QUILICO
'La Maison Noble', Labeyrie,
47180 MEILHAN-SUR-GARONNE
Tel: (0) 5 53 89 58 07 / (0) 618 41 26 35
lamaisonnoble@mac.com
www.lamaisonnoblefr.com

A truly noble house. Anthony is American and Frédérique is French. Not only are they warm and welcoming but their home has character and class. It is a longhouse, a former barn from 1782. The garden reaches as far as the eye can see, with roses and an old-style swimming pool. The lounge is charming and the breakfast table comes with tablecloth, napkins and porcelain. Quality bed linen and each room has a style and name to match. You really are the queen in 'La Reine'! Access for persons of limited mobility, even the first floor.

Price Structure – 1 Bedroom and 1 Suite
'La Reine': bathroom, wc, double bed (queen-size): €90
'Jardin': wheelchair access, bathroom, wc, double bed (queen-size). En-suite room, double bed: €90 – 2 people €150 – 4 people

Extra Bed: €20
Capacity: 6 people

Facilities: private parking, extensive grounds, tv lounge, hosts have pets, dinner available, babies welcome, free cot, wheelchair access, closed: 15/01–30/03, private swimming pool, fishing, mushroom-picking, bird-watching, hiking, riversports 10km, lake watersports 10km, golf course 15km
Fluent English spoken

Directions: Please contact your hosts in advance for detailed directions.

Location
22km S of LANGON
in: Bernos-Beaulac, station pick-up on arrival/departure
Railway station: 22km
Airport: Bordeaux-Mérignac 65km car essential

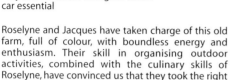

✸ ✸ ✸

Residence of Outstanding Character

Roselyne and Jacques have taken charge of this old farm, full of colour, with boundless energy and enthusiasm. Their skill in organising outdoor activities, combined with the culinary skills of Roselyne, have convinced us that they took the right decision to move from Normandy to this enchanting place.

Roselyne & Jacques CHAPDELAINE
'Dousud', 33430 BERNOS-BEAULAC
Tel: (0) 5 56 25 43 23 / (0) 686 73 81 76
Fax: (0) 5 56 25 42 75
info@dousud.fr
www.dousud.fr

Facilities: private parking, extensive grounds, tv lounge, hosts have pets, dinner available, kitchen, babies welcome, free cot, 100% no smoking, wheelchair access, private swimming pool, hiking, cycling, fishing, hunting, mushroom-picking, riversports 3km, vineyard 20km, golf course 25km
Adequate English spoken

Price Structure – 5 Bedrooms
'Bleu Roi': television, telephone, bathroom, wc, twin beds: €80 – 2 people
'Vol Bleu': wheelchair access, television, telephone, bathroom, wc, twin beds: €80
'Coeur Bleu': television, telephone, bathroom, wc, twin beds: €80
'Terre Bleu': wheelchair access, television, telephone, bathroom, wc, double bed: €80
'Bleu Claire': wheelchair access, lounge, television, telephone, bathroom, wc, double bed: €80

Extra Bed: €15
Reduction: 01/09–30/06, 7 nights
Capacity: 10 people

Directions: From the A62, exit 3 and take the D932 towards Pau for about 20km. In Bernos-Beaulac turn right towards Pompejac and follow the signs to 'Dousud'.

Location
44km S W of LANGON
in: Mano, station pick-up on arrival/departure
Railway station: 50km
Airport: Bordeaux-Mérignac 50km car essential

✸ ✸ ✸

Residence of Outstanding Character

Here you are 100% in the heart of the countryside yet less than an hour from Bordeaux, the Bassin d'Arcachon, the beaches and vineyards! This house is nestled in the Parc Naturel des Landes where there is space and peace and quiet. Its long triangular roof shelters two comfortable, brightly-coloured bedrooms and a living room with large bay windows. From the terrace, enjoy breakfast with a view of the line of oak trees by the lake with birds and goats. There is a jacuzzi and a swimming pool with an original shower.

Eliane COUZAN-ELMALIH
'Aux Vieux Chênes', Lieu-dit Odoy, 40410 MANO
Tel: (0) 5 58 07 73 79
auxvieuxchenes@free.fr
http://auxvieuxchenes.free.fr

Facilities: private parking, extensive grounds, tv lounge, hosts have pets, pets not accepted, dinner available, babies welcome, free cot, private swimming pool, hunting, mushroom-picking, hiking, cycling, interesting flora, sea watersports 10km, vineyard 30km
Basic English spoken

Price Structure – 4 Bedrooms
'Bruyere', 'Lilas' & 'Coquelicot': shower room, wc, double bed: €55
'Myosotis': shower room, wc, double bed, 2 single beds: €65 – 2 people €95 – 4 people

Extra Bed: €15
Reduction: 7 nights
Capacity: 10 people

Directions: From Bordeaux A63 towards Bayonne exit 21 Salles, direction Belin Beliet, then D3 on the left until Hostens. D651 direction Sore, to Mano then D348 direction Biganon for 300m. After the little bridge take the road on the left, the house is 500m on the right.

Aquitaine – Langon

33.52 St-Emilion

Private Home

Brigitte & Yves JEAN-JOSEPH
'La Chênaie', 16 route de Fonsegrède,
33500 ARVEYRES
Tel: (0) 5 57 24 80 93 / (0) 687 15 91 79
Fax: (0) 5 57 24 80 93
bordesbr@wanadoo.fr

Price Structure – 2 Bedrooms
'Louis Philippe': television, shower room, wc, twin
beds, single bed: €57 – 2 people €76 – 3 people
'Bleue': television, shower room, wc, double bed:
€57

Capacity: 5 people

Location
14km W of ST-EMILION
in: Arveyres, station pick-up on
arrival/departure
Railway station: 4km
Airport: Bordeaux-Mérignac 43km
car essential

The location and the very warm welcome alone
deserve three 'suns'. In the pleasant grounds, Brigitte
and Yves have transformed the outbuildings into
their own home, and restored the nearby main house
for their guests. They love ferreting out antiques and
the décor reflects the fruits of their travels. The vast
living room and lounge is available to you. The
bedrooms are pleasant with a high level of bathroom
equipment, such as hydro-jet showers. The ground
floor room leads directly on to the garden.

Facilities: private parking, extensive grounds, pets
not accepted, internet access, babies welcome, free
cot, 100% no smoking, mushroom-picking, hiking,
cycling, vineyard, lake watersports 7km, golf course
10km
Basic English spoken

Directions: Please contact your hosts for detailed
directions.

33.48 St-Emilion

**Château/Manor
House**

Grégoire JAMES
'Château de la Rivière', 33126 LA RIVIERE
Tel: (0) 5 57 55 56 51 Fax: (0) 5 57 55 56 54
reception@chateau-de-la-riviere.com
www.chateau-de-la-riviere.com

Price Structure – 5 Bedrooms
'Charlemagne': television, telephone, shower room,
wc, washbasin, twin beds: €170
'Gaston de l'Isle' & 'Aliénor': television, telephone,
shower room, wc, washbasin, double bed
(queen-size): €150
'Viollet-le-Duc': television, telephone, bathroom, wc,
shower, washbasin, double bed (queen-size): €190
'Marie-Charlotte': television, telephone, shower
room, wc, washbasin, double bed, single bed: €180

Extra Bed: €20
Reduction: 01/11–31/03
Capacity: 11 people

Location
16km W of ST-EMILION
in: La Rivière
Railway station: 8km
Airport: Bordeaux-Mérignac 49km
car essential

Bienvenue en France

On the vestiges of a defensive site under Charlemagne,
this château was built in 1577 by Gaston de l'Isle and
later rebuilt by Viollet-le-Duc. West of Libourne,
dominating the Dordogne Valley with 60 hectares of
vines, it produces a renowned AOC Fronsac wine. Five
rooms in the 'Renaissance' wing allow you to
experience its unique, authentic charm. The owners
live in the central part and are on hand to welcome you
but, if they are absent, Mélanie looks after you and
shows you the wine cellars. Enjoy the pool, tennis court
and tranquil grounds. Enchanting!

Facilities: private parking, extensive grounds,
lounge, pets not accepted, kitchen, babies welcome,
free cot, 100% no smoking, closed: 15/12–15/01,
private swimming pool, private tennis court, fishing,
mushroom-picking, bird-watching, hiking, vineyard,
cycling 1km, golf course 20km
Fluent English spoken

Directions: From Bordeaux, A9 towards Paris, exit
40A at St-André-de-Cubzac and then the D670
towards Libourne for 16km. The château is on the left
in La Rivière.

Location
19km W of ST-EMILION
in: St-Germain-du-Puch
Railway station: 10km
Airport: Bordeaux-Mérignac 30km
car essential

Château/Manor House

An agreeable stop on the Bordeaux wine route. Wine enthusiasts are in their element at this historic 14th- and 15th-century château. Marvel with Bruno at the vines, vaulted cellars and wine-tasting stores of this award-winning vineyard. The bedrooms, carefully redecorated, are in one wing, off an enclosed garden. Breakfast can be served in the Romanesque vaulted room from the 15th century. The absence of a family lounge justifies their rating but the rest is worthy of more! A courteous, charming welcome at moderate prices.

Marie-Paule & Bruno DE LA RIVIERE
'Château du petit Puch',
33750 ST-GERMAIN-DU-PUCH
Tel: (0) 5 57 24 52 36 / (0) 607 36 57 97
Fax: (0) 5 57 24 01 82
chateaupetitpuch@yahoo.fr
www.chateaupetitpuch.com

Facilities: off-street parking, extensive grounds, lounge, pets not accepted, kitchen, hiking, cycling, vineyard, golf course 10km
Fluent English spoken

Price Structure – 4 Bedrooms
'Ocre': bathroom, wc, double bed: €80
'Rose': shower room, wc, double bed: €80
'Bleue': along corridor shower room, wc, double bed: €80
'Verte': shower room, wc, twin beds: €80

Capacity: 8 people

Directions: From the Bordeaux ring-road, exit 26, N89 towards Libourne. Leave the N89 at exit 8 heading for St-Germain-du-Puch. Cross the village. The château is on this road on the right after 600m.

Location
5km S E of ST-EMILION
in: St-Hippolyte
Railway station: 10km
Airport: Bordeaux-Mérignac 50km
car essential

Residence of Outstanding Character

A must for all lovers of *Grand Cru* fine wines! In a fantastic location in the middle of the vineyards of St-Emilion is this beautiful 18th-century residence. Above all, you can discover the prize-winning wines produced on the property, visit the wine cellars, the vineyards and sample the wines with Bernard, a real character! He is at once inexhaustible, enthusiastic, cheerful and professional. The guest bedrooms are spacious and traditionally furnished. Breakfast is served in a room built from St-Emilion stone, with noteworthy tables made with the lids of prestigious wine boxes. Receptions are possible here.

Bernard RIVALS
'Musset Rivals', Château Monlot,
33330 ST-HIPPOLYTE
Tel: (0) 5 57 74 49 47 / (0) 687 14 00 75
Fax: (0) 5 57 24 62 33
MussetRivals@BelAir-Monlot.com
www.belair-monlot.com

Facilities: off-street parking, extensive grounds, lounge, kitchen, babies welcome, free cot, hunting, mushroom-picking, hiking, vineyard, cycling 3km, sea watersports 15km, riversports 20km, golf course 30km, fishing 30km, gliding 60km
Fluent English spoken

Price Structure – 5 Bedrooms and 1 Suite
'Merlot': television, bathroom, shower, wc, double bed: €77,20
'Cabernet': television, bathroom, shower, wc, twin beds: €85,20
'Malbec': television, bathroom, shower, wc, double bed: €92,20
'Sauvignon': television, bathroom, shower, wc, double bed: €102,20
'Sémillon': lounge, television, bathroom, shower, wc, double bed: €102,20
'Suite d'Aliénor': lounge, television, bathroom, shower, wc, four-poster double bed. En-suite room, 2 single beds: €154,40 – 4 people

Extra Bed: €15   **Capacity:** 14 people

Directions: On the D670 between Libourne and Castillon-La-Bataille, take the D243 towards St-Laurent-des-Combes and St-Hippolyte then turn right to 'Château Monlot Capet'.

Aquitaine – St-Emilion

33.28 St-Emilion

Château/Manor House

Michel MORTEYROL
'Château de Courtebotte',
33420 ST-JEAN-DE-BLAIGNAC
Tel: (0) 5 57 84 61 61 / (0) 683 07 18 25
Fax: (0) 5 57 84 68 68
michel.morteyrol@wanadoo.fr
www.chateaudecourtebotte.com

Price Structure – 6 Bedrooms
'Suite Mathilde' (our favourite room): lounge, bathroom, wc, double bed (queen-size): €220
'Sylvia': shower room, wc, double bed: €120
'Marianne': bathroom, wc, shower, double bed (queen-size): €180
'Melissa': shower room, wc, twin beds: €150
'Bali': bathroom, wc, shower, four-poster double bed (queen-size): €160
'Suite Maria Grazia': lounge, shower room, wc, four-poster double bed (queen-size): €180

Extra Bed: €32
Capacity: 12 people

Location
9km S of ST-EMILION
in: St-Jean-de-Blaignac
Railway station: 12km
Airport: Bordeaux-Mérignac 45km
car essential

In the region of St-Emilion, this château with the evocative name of 'Courtebotte' was built beside the Dordogne in the reign of Henri IV. The views are outstanding and Michel, who is a photographer and landscape gardener, pulls out all the stops to make you feel at home. Nothing is boring here, and there is always something new to discover about his cooking, the style and originality of the bedrooms, the gardens, swimming pool or relaxing walks in the forest.

Facilities: private parking, extensive grounds, tv lounge, pets not accepted, dinner available, babies welcome, free cot, private swimming pool, fishing, mushroom-picking, bird-watching, vineyard, cycling 5km, riversports 15km, golf course 20km
Adequate English spoken

Directions: At St-Emilion, take the D670 towards La Réole. At St-Jean-de-Blaignac, follow the D119 towards Civrac.

40.12 Dax

Private Home

Jacqueline & Christian VIVES
'Le Petit Pedebosq', 402 chemin de Pedebosq,
40180 SORT-EN-CHALOSSE
Tel: (0) 5 58 89 59 31
lepetitpedebosq@club-internet.fr
http://cvives.club.fr/index.htm

Price Structure – 4 Bedrooms
'Junior suite': television, wc, washbasin, double bed (queen-size), single bed: €63 – 2 people
€77 – 3 people
'Rose': television, double bed, single bed:
€61 – 2 people €75 – 3 people
'Bleue': lounge, television, double bed: €61
'Master suite': lounge, television, bathroom, wc, along corridor shower, double bed (super king-size), single bed: €83 – 2 people €83 – 3 people

Extra Bed: €13
Reduction: 30/09–30/04
Capacity: 11 people

Location
11km E of DAX
in: Sort-en-Chalosse
Railway station: 8km
Airport: Biarritz 60km
car essential

In Gascony, by paths to St-Jacques-de-Compostelle, is this 18th-century farmhouse with a large roof, typical of the area. It has been renovated by Jacqueline and Christian, a Franco-British couple for whom conversation comes easily. Surrounded by fields, the garden has a swimming pool and is crossed by a small stream. Enjoy complete calm here, in the knowledge that within easy reach are Dax, the beaches of Biarritz (30 minutes by car), the Pyrenees and Spain! Jacqueline makes adorable tea cosies. Dinner must be booked in advance.

Facilities: off-street parking, extensive grounds, tv lounge, dinner available, babies welcome, free cot, 100% no smoking, 7 nights minimum stay: 1/08–31/08, private swimming pool, mushroom-picking, bird-watching, hiking, cycling, interesting flora, fishing 2km, sea watersports 10km
Fluent English spoken

Directions: From Dax D947 towards Orthez then when exiting the town, D32 on the left towards Montfort-en-Chalosse for 10km. D324 on the right to Sort-en-Chalosse. Continue on this road towards Clermont, cross the river, and the house is on the right after about 1km.

40.13 Mont-de-Marsan

Private Home

Location
26km S of MONT-DE-MARSAN
in: Ste-Colombe, station pick-up on arrival/departure
Railway station: 35km
Airport: Pau-Pyrénées 55km
car essential

Under an hour to the ocean and Pyrenees, Caroline and Marc welcome you with great kindness to their old house in the woods. You are met by aromas of bouquets, simmering cooking and *pâtisserie* straight from the oven. The comfortable bedrooms have their own entrance and terrace. Caroline loves to spoil her guests and serves a full sweet and savoury breakfast. For dinner local produce and the vegetable garden serve to create local, Alsace and internationally inspired dishes. She also holds cookery classes. Marc loves classic cars. You can try your hand at *trinquet* (pelota). Rest and relaxation guaranteed!

Facilities: private parking, extensive grounds, tv lounge, hosts have pets, dinner available, babies welcome, free cot, wheelchair access, hunting, fishing, mushroom-picking, bird-watching, hiking, cycling, interesting flora 10km, riversports 20km, sea watersports 80km, winter sports 90km
Fluent English spoken

Caroline & Marc DELUNSCH
'Le Puyo', 591 chemin de Couloumine,
40700 STE-COLOMBE
Tel: (0) 5 58 79 38 46 / (0) 622 74 15 01
lepuyo@free.fr

Price Structure – 2 Bedrooms
'Cottage': wheelchair access, bathroom, wc, double bed: €50
'Belle Epoque': shower room, wc, double bed: €50

Reduction: 3 nights, children
Capacity: 4 people

Directions: From Mont-de-Marsan D933 towards Orthez. 8km after St-Sever take the D350 on the left to Ste-Colombe. In the village pass in front of the church and the car park and take the small road on the right (Route de Serre Gaston) and then right and right again. The house is on the left on a road that heads back down towards the village.

47.06 Agen

Location
22km W of AGEN
in: Bazens, station pick-up on arrival/departure
Railway station: 4km
Airport: Agen 22km
car essential

Private Home

Maria and Henri welcome you with a real fire. They try to cater for everybody's individual tastes. Organic and vegetarian dishes and excellent wine, some homemade, can be provided. This region is rich in caves and châteaux. Henri is a sculptor.

Facilities: off-street parking, extensive grounds, tv lounge, hosts have pets, dinner available, 100% no smoking, 1 shared shower room, wc, closed: 01/11–01/02, hiking, cycling
Fluent English spoken

Maria VAN STRAATEN
'Le Marchon', 47130 BAZENS
Tel: (0) 5 53 87 22 26 / (0) 662 71 22 26
Fax: (0) 5 53 87 22 26
0662712226@orange.fr
www.francebandb.com

Price Structure – 2 Bedrooms
bathroom, wc, double bed, single bed:
€47 – 2 people €53 – 3 people
bathroom, wc, double bed: €47

Extra Bed: €10
Reduction: 01/09–30/06, 2 nights
Capacity: 5 people

Directions: In Agen take the N113 towards Bordeaux for 20km. Turn right towards Bazens (D118) and then the D231 towards Galapian until you reach the sign.

47.20 Villeneuve-sur-Lot

✳ ✳ ✳

Residence of Outstanding Character

Henri REGEER & Yuphin JAEMKRAJANG
'Rebel Haut', Ste-Radegonde,
47300 VILLENEUVE-SUR-LOT
Tel: (0) 5 53 70 11 14 / (0) 670 32 69 07
Fax: (0) 5 53 70 11 55
info@rebelhaut.com
www.rebelhaut.com

Price Structure – 2 Bedrooms
'Venus': television, shower room, wc, double bed: €80
'Serena': television, bathroom, wc, twin beds: €70

Extra Bed: €10
Capacity: 4 people

Location
VILLENEUVE-SUR-LOT
in: Villeneuve-sur-Lot
Railway station: 30km
Airport: Bergerac 50km
car essential

On top of a hill is this beautiful 19th-century *Maison de Maître* in two hectares of grounds with mature trees. The bright air-conditioned rooms with spacious bathrooms have sloping ceilings and are a touch minimalist in style. The pleasant living area is graced by five languid cats. A discreet and relaxed welcome from Henri, a translator and Yuphin, who are Dutch and Thai respectively. Enjoy Yuphin's cooking and make use of the pool, solarium and summer kitchen and barbecue. Excellent for walks and cycling (bikes for rent).

Facilities: off-street parking, extensive grounds, tv lounge, hosts have pets, pets not accepted, dinner available, 100% no smoking, private swimming pool, private tennis court, hiking, cycling, riversports 5km, golf course 10km, vineyard 20km
Fluent English spoken

Directions: North of Villeneuve-sur-Lot on the N21 towards Bergerac, take the D676 from the roundabout towards Montflanquin for 1km, and then turn right towards Rebel (small sign) for 2km. Rebel Haut is on the left after Rebel Bas (signposted).

47.22 Villeneuve-sur-Lot

✳ ✳

Residence of Outstanding Character

Raymond SALLE
'L'Orée du Bois', route de Loubejac,
47500 SAUVETERRE-LA-LEMANCE
Tel: (0) 5 53 49 37 69

Price Structure – 2 Bedrooms
telephone, wc, washbasin, four-poster double bed: €50
washbasin, twin beds, single bed: €50 – 2 people
€65 – 3 people

Extra Bed: €10
Capacity: 5 people

Location
41km N E of VILLENEUVE-SUR-LOT
in: Sauveterre-la-Lemance
Airport: Bergerac 60km
car essential

A beautiful location for this large *maison bourgeoise* in the shadow of the Château de Sauveterre. The atmosphere is relaxed as you can laze in the grounds by a stream or on the terrace. Raymond, a former hotelier, concocts delicious cuisine, and homemade *pâtisseries* for breakfast. The décor is in places a little dated but the bedrooms are pleasant and there is a lounge with a piano. The bathroom installations are quite basic: small wc, and a shared bathroom. A friendly welcome from Raymond (and dog Wendy), who can take you to visit local winegrowers. Bargain prices.

Facilities: private parking, extensive grounds, lounge, hosts have pets, dinner available, babies welcome, free cot, 1 shared bathroom, closed: 15/12–15/01, fishing, mushroom-picking, hiking, cycling, vineyard, riversports 12km
Fluent English spoken

Directions: From Villeneuve-sur-Lot, D911 to Fumel (24km) then the D710 to Sauveterre-la-Lemance (13km). In the centre of the village take the high street towards Loubejac on the left.

Location
6km S of BIARRITZ
in: Ahetze, station pick-up on arrival/departure
Railway station: 5km
Airport: Biarritz 8km
car essential

Private Home

The welcome is very warm and the view over the valley and the village is uninterrupted! We did not hesitate in giving this place three 'suns' as it is a very relaxing spot near the beach. The shower is in the room in the 'Jaune', 'Bleue' and 'Verte' bedrooms. In the little neighbouring restaurants you can try *piperade*. Basque pelota, traditional dances and surfing are worth seeing.

Bernadette & Pierre MENDIONDO
'Villa Arrosen-Artean', 171 chemin d'Ithulrraldia,
64210 AHETZE
Tel: (0) 5 59 41 93 03 / (0) 672 67 40 09
Fax: (0) 5 59 41 93 03
bmend@tele2.fr
http://chambre-en-pays-basque.chez-alice.fr/

Facilities: private parking, garden, tv lounge, kitchen, babies welcome, free cot, 100% no smoking, 1 shared bathroom, 1 shared shower room, 3 wcs, 2 nights minimum stay, cycling, fishing, hunting, mushroom-picking 2km, hiking 3km, sea watersports 4km

Price Structure – 5 Bedrooms
'Rose': shower room, wc, double bed, single bed: €60 – 2 people €80 – 3 people
'Saumon': shower, double bed, single bed: €54 – 2 people €64 – 3 people
'Jaune', 'Bleue' & 'Verte': shower, washbasin, double bed: €56

Reduction: 01/09–30/06, 2 nights, groups
Capacity: 12 people

Directions: On the A63, exit Biarritz. N10 towards Bidart for 3km. At the roundabout by the shop 'Monsieur Bricolage', turn left towards Ahetze for 4km. At the church, go towards St-Pée-sur-Nivelle for 300m. After the small roundabout, turn right onto Chemin d'Ithulrraldia then take the 2nd lane on the left. The house is at the end.

Location
2km S of BIARRITZ
in: Arbonne, station pick-up on arrival/departure
Railway station: 2km
Airport: Biarritz 4km
car essential

Bienvenue en **France**

Residence of Outstanding Character

In a little green oasis, five minutes from the centre of Biarritz, is this charming house of Basque style from the turn of the 20th century. Arcades surround a patio by a garden with ponds and arbours. Two comfortable guest rooms are on offer, with décor in soft greens and yellows, creating a relaxing environment. The bedroom in the house has a private terrace surrounded by a hedge of hydrangeas and camellias. The other guest room is perfect for those that prefer to be a bit more independent. Breakfast is served on the terrace. A good address.

Colette de PUYMORIN
'Villa de Pouy', chemin de Kastilua,
64210 ARBONNE
Tel: (0) 5 59 23 77 02 / (0) 686 26 40 77
colette.hotes@cegetel.net

Facilities: private parking, extensive grounds, tv lounge, pets not accepted, dinner available, 2 nights minimum stay, closed: 15/10–1/04, golf course 2km, sea watersports 5km, gliding 15km, hiking 15km, cycling 15km, riversports 15km
Fluent English spoken

Price Structure – 2 Bedrooms
'La Gazelle': shower room, wc, double bed: €105
'Les Arômes': shower room, wc, double bed: €95

Reduction: 15/05–15/06 & 15/09–15/10, 7 nights
Capacity: 4 people

Directions: South of Biarritz A63 exit 4 direction Biarritz then D255 on the right towards Arbonne. Pass over the motorway bridge and take the first road on the left. It's the first house on the left.

Aquitaine – Biarritz

64.33 Orthez

Château/Manor House

Location
15km W of ORTHEZ
in: Salies-en-Béarn
Railway station: 7km
Airport: Biarritz 60km

This impressive former gothic presbytery has a grand façade and long arched windows. The interior is warm and inviting, largely due to Patricia's artistic talents. She has a gentle and obliging nature and projects an atmosphere of wellbeing, so it is no surprise that she is a naturopath and holds consultations on the premises. The bedrooms with views over the grounds are brightly coloured and space has been conserved by shielding the showers from view with high curtains. On sale: oneiric paintings, jewellery.

Patricia TARNUS
'La demeure St Martin', 42 rue St Martin,
64270 SALIES-EN-BEARN
Tel: (0) 5 59 38 07 01 / (0) 662 82 47 29
lademeure.stmartin@neuf.fr
www.lademeuresaintmartin.com

Price Structure – 3 Bedrooms and 1 Suite
'Rose d'Hispashan' & 'Lys de France': shower, double bed, single bed: €87 – 2 people €127 – 3 people
'Reine des Primevères': shower, twin beds: €76
'Pivoine d'Himalaya': along corridor shower, double bed. En-suite room, 2 single beds: €109 – 2 people €169 – 4 people

Extra Bed: €20
Reduction: groups, children
Capacity: 12 people

Facilities: garden, tv lounge, hosts have pets, pets not accepted, dinner available, babies welcome, free cot, 2 wcs, closed: 15/11–15/03, riversports, hunting, fishing, mushroom-picking, interesting flora, bird-watching, hiking, cycling, vineyard, winter sports 50km
Adequate English spoken

Directions: A64 between Pau and Bayonne, exit 7. D430 towards Salies-en-Béarn. In the town, follow signs to 'Eglise St Martin'. The house is next to the church.

64.31 Pau

Private Home

Location
14km E of PAU
in: Angaïs
Railway station: 13km
Airport: Pau-Pyrénées 25km
car essential

Bienvenue en France

Marie and François, native to the village, have enlarged this old house with a contemporary extension. From the lounge bay windows you have a vast panoramic view of the Pyrenees. This property, on the edge of woods, opens onto orchards and pastures where your hosts' lambs graze. François is a keen fisherman and hunter (he uses a bow), and a lover of the great outdoors, making him an excellent guide. Breakfast can be served on the terrace or by the old fireplace. Their two young children readily play with young visitors.

François BONNEMAIZON
6 rue du Lac, 64510 ANGAIS
Tel: (0) 5 59 53 11 17 / (0) 615 95 15 67
f.bonnemaizon@wanadoo.fr

Price Structure – 1 Bedroom
wheelchair access, bathroom, wc, shower, double bed: €50

Reduction: 3 nights
Capacity: 2 people

Facilities: off-street parking, extensive grounds, tv lounge, hosts have pets, dinner available, babies welcome, free cot, wheelchair access, hunting, mushroom-picking, bird-watching, hiking, cycling, interesting flora, fishing 5km, riversports 5km, vineyard 10km, golf course 13km
Fluent English spoken

Directions: From Pau, D938 towards Lourdes for 10km then the D212 on the left to Angaïs. Follow signs 'Stade, Salle des Sports'. The house is behind the multi-use hall. Pass in front of the château, second house on the right.

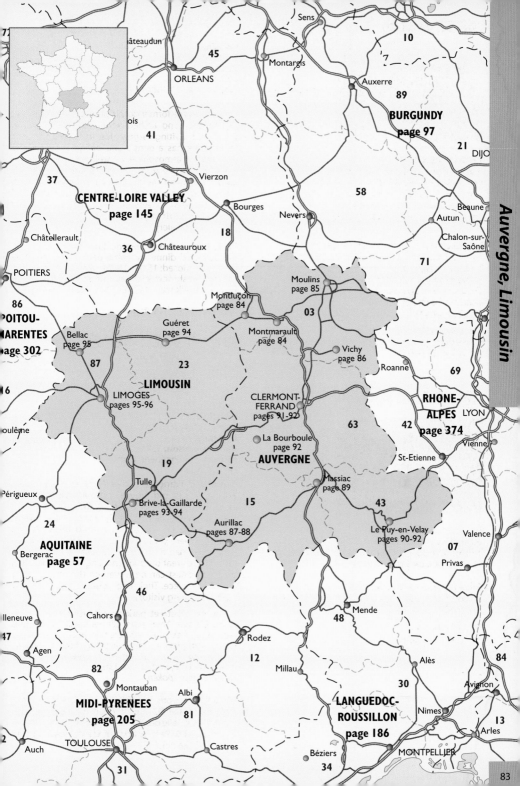

Châteaudun

Sens

10

45

ORLEANS

Montargis

Auxerre

BURGUNDY
page 97

89

21

DIJO

37

CENTRE-LOIRE VALLEY
page 145

Vierzon

58

Beaune

Autun

Chalon-sur-Saône

Châtellerault

Bourges

Nevers

POITIERS

36

Châteauroux

18

Moulins
page 85

71

86
POITOU-
HARENTES
age 302

Bellac
page 95

Guéret
page 94

Montluçon
page 84

03

Montmarault
page 84

Vichy
page 86

Roanne

69

87

23

LIMOUSIN

LIMOGES
pages 95-96

CLERMONT-
FERRAND
pages 91-92

63

RHONE-
ALPES
page 374

LYON

oulême

42

Vienne

19

La Bourboule
page 92

AUVERGNE

St-Etienne

Périgueux

Tulle

Brive-la-Gaillarde
pages 93-94

15

Massiac
page 89

43

Le Puy-en-Velay
pages 90-92

Valence

24

AQUITAINE
page 57

Bergerac

Aurillac
pages 87-88

07

Privas

46

lleneuve

Cahors

48

Mende

84

47

Agen

12

Rodez

Millau

Alès

82

MIDI-PYRENEES
page 205

Montauban

Albi

81

30

LANGUEDOC-
ROUSSILLON
page 186

Avignon

Nimes

13

Arles

2

TOULOUSE

Auch

Castres

31

Béziers

34

MONTPELLIER

03.22 Montluçon

Château/Manor House

Location
30km N of MONTLUÇON
in: Meaulne
car essential

Catherine GRENINGER
'Manoir du Mortier', 03360 MEAULNE
Tel: (0) 4 70 06 99 87 / (0) 662 21 08 82
manoirdumortier@yahoo.fr
www.manoirdumortier.com

Catherine spends the winter in Belgium, but in the summer she is here to welcome you to her superb family residence overlooking the Massif Central. Surrounded by wildlife to the point that deer and wild boar often eat her lettuces, she also has horses, cats and dogs that delight her children and grandchildren, who are often there. The superb bedrooms are in a separate building with spacious bathrooms. The atmosphere is warm and friendly, the food good and the whole house is open to you. You can even share their babysitter. This is just a lovely family home.

Price Structure – 2 Bedrooms and 1 Suite
'Tour Ronde': television, shower room, wc, double bed (queen-size): €115
'Suite': television, bathroom, wc, double bed (king-size). En-suite room, twin beds. En-suite room, single bed: €160 – 2 people €220 – 5 people
'Tour Carrée': television, bathroom, wc, twin beds: €125

Extra Bed: €25
Capacity: 8 people

Facilities: private parking, extensive grounds, lounge, hosts have pets, pets not accepted, dinner available, kitchen, babies welcome, free cot, closed: 01/12–01/04, private swimming pool, hunting, fishing, mushroom-picking, hiking, cycling, vineyard, golf course 12km
Adequate English spoken

Directions: Please contact your hosts for detailed directions.

03.01 Montmarault

Château/Manor House

Location
10km N E of MONTMARAULT
in: Deux-Chaises
Railway station: 35km
Airport: Clermont-Ferrand 100km
car essential

A real château embracing our desire for refinement and rural retreats. The interior décor is revisited bit by bit and furnished to preserve the character and uniqueness of the place (the fake marble, however, is in parts a bit kitsch.). A large stairway leads to the guest bedrooms furnished with four-poster beds and period furniture. Geneviève and Rodolphe make every effort to create a good ambience with candlelit dinners in the dining room, ideal for savouring their traditional and regional cuisine. Billiards and chess are available to play in the sitting room.

Geneviève MARCHAND
'Château de Longeville', 03240 DEUX-CHAISES
Tel: (0) 4 70 47 32 91 / (0) 683 74 95 13
Fax: (0) 4 70 47 32 91
chateaudelongeville@hotmail.com
http://chateaudelongeville.com

Price Structure – 3 Bedrooms and 1 Suite
'Jaune' & 'Fleurie': bathroom, wc, four-poster double bed: €75
'Rouge': bathroom, wc, four-poster double bed, single bed: €75 – 2 people €90 – 3 people
'Bleue': along corridor bathroom, wc, four-poster double bed. En-suite room, twin beds: €75 – 2 people €110 – 4 people

Extra Bed: €15
Capacity: 11 people

Facilities: off-street parking, extensive grounds, tv lounge, hosts have pets, dinner available, babies welcome, free cot, fishing, hiking, cycling, mushroom-picking 8km, lake watersports 20km, vineyard 22km, riversports 30km, golf course 32km
Basic English spoken

Directions: On the A71, take the Exit 'Montmarault' and the N145 towards Moulins. Exit Deux-Chaises and follow the signs 'Chambres d'hôtes'.

Location
7km N of MOULINS
in: Gennetines, station pick-up on
arrival/departure
Railway station: 7km

Working Farm

You will get a really warm welcome from Valérie and her farmhouse has a friendly atmosphere. This is a working farm, with lots of land and farm animals (cows, donkeys and goats) so children will love it. Very much a family holiday place with games in the garden. The bedrooms are simply furnished with no great pretentions in the style department. They serve dinner at a large table in the dining room with its wood fire in winter, so be sure to book. Good value for money. Their own produce is on sale.

Facilities: off-street parking, extensive grounds, tv lounge, hosts have pets, dinner available, babies welcome, free cot, private swimming pool, hiking, cycling, mushroom-picking 4km, fishing 10km, bird-watching 15km, golf course 20km
Basic English spoken

Directions: On the N7 take the Moulins diversion and then exit 45 towards St-Ennemond. Head towards Decize on the D979a and take the second lane on the left after the petrol station (which is closed). Follow the signs.

Valérie BESSIERE
'Domaine des Parisses', Les Parisses,
03400 GENNETINES
Tel: (0) 4 70 44 38 19 / (0) 630 44 12 51
Fax: (0) 4 70 34 01 68

Price Structure – 3 Bedrooms, 1 Suite and 2 Apartments
'Family Suite': television, shower room, wc, double bed. En-suite room, 2 single beds: €38 – 2 people €55 – 4 people
2 rooms: television, shower room, wc, 2 single beds: €38
television, shower room, wc, washbasin, double bed: €38
'Gîte 1': lounge, television, kitchen, shower room, wc, double bed, single bed: €55 – 3 people
'Gîte 2': lounge, television, kitchen, shower room, wc, double bed, 2 single beds: €65 – 4 people

Extra Bed: €8   **Capacity:** 17 people

Location
14km N W of MOULINS
in: Villeneuve-sur-Allier
car essential

Château/Manor House

Dating back to the 18th century, this château, set back from the main road, has been given a new lease of life by its new owner who until recently ran one of the restaurants in the village. She has brought to the château a personal touch whereby styles from different eras are presented from room to room; Louis XV, Napoléon III, Rococo. Slowly but surely the château relives as rooms are transformed into beautiful spaces including the lounge and the dining room decorated with antique dolls and earthenware. A practical and easy stopover at bargain prices.

Facilities: private parking, extensive grounds, tv lounge, hosts have pets, dinner available, babies welcome, free cot, closed: 01/10–31/03, fishing, hiking, interesting flora
Adequate English spoken

Directions: From Moulins take the N7 towards Nevers for 13km. The château is on this road, in the village on the left.

Béatrice COLLIN
'Château les 3 Roys', 34 route de Moulins,
03460 VILLENEUVE-SUR-ALLIER
Tel: (0) 4 70 43 33 29 Fax: (0) 4 70 43 36 45
anne.mollet@wanadoo.fr

Price Structure – 5 Bedrooms
'Louis XV': bathroom, wc, double bed: €50
'Napoléon III': television, shower room, wc, double bed: €50
'Contemporaine': television, bathroom, wc, double bed: €50
'Henri II': television, bathroom, wc, double bed, twin beds, single bed: €50 – 2 people €90 – 5 people
'Louis Philippe': television, bathroom, wc, double bed, single bed: €50 – 2 people €70 – 3 people

Extra Bed: €15
Reduction: 3 nights
Capacity: 14 people

03.11 Vichy

Apartment

Marie-Claude MARTIN
'Les Printanières', 23 rue Harpet, 03200 VICHY
Tel: (0) 4 70 98 03 26 Fax: (0) 4 70 98 20 04
mcmb@ifrance.com
www.accueil-MCMB.com

Price Structure – 1 Bedroom and 3 Suites
'Les Myrtilles': lounge, television, kitchen, along corridor bathroom, wc, double bed. En-suite room, bathroom, wc, 2 single beds: €80 – 2 people €130 – 4 people
'Les Véroniques': lounge, television, kitchen, bathroom, wc, double bed: €80
'Les Myosotis': double bed. En-suite room, bathroom, wc, single bed: €100 – 3 people
'Les Muguets': lounge, bathroom, wc, double bed. En-suite room, lounge, double bed, single bed: €150 – 5 people

Extra Bed: €23
Reduction: groups   **Capacity:** 14 people

Location
VICHY
in: Vichy, station pick-up on arrival/departure
Railway station: Vichy
Airport: Clermont-Ferrand 50km

Bienvenue en France

You may think that you know Vichy well, but Marie-Claude will surprise you. She was born here, and loves her native town, famous for its spa waters, so passionately that she will be sure to show you something that is new to you. She has a talent for entertaining, and throws open her house with great enthusiasm. You will always feel at home here, and if you wish to discuss flying, she holds a pilot's licence.

Facilities: off-street parking, hosts have pets, kitchen, babies welcome, free cot, 2 nights minimum stay, hiking, cycling, lake watersports, riversports, golf course 3km, gliding 5km, vineyard 30km, interesting flora 60km
Basic English spoken

Directions: Please contact your host in advance for detailed directions.

03.20 Vichy

Private Home

Jacques KAPPS
'Les Jardins du Valençon', Le Bourg, 03220 CINDRE
Tel: (0) 4 70 55 74 20
rooms4u@laposte.net
http://dadon.club.fr/jarval.html

Price Structure – 2 Bedrooms
'La Tonkinoise': lounge, shower room, wc, double bed: €45
'La Bourbonnaise': lounge, shower room, wc, twin beds: €50

Extra Bed: €20
Capacity: 4 people

Location
30km N of VICHY
in: Cindré
Airport: Clermont-Ferrand 90km
car essential

Jacques has taken on this former farmhouse that he is restoring. Breakfast is served in Jacques' lounge. Whilst modest, his home is clean and Jacques is a discreet gentleman who has worked in the tourism industry before retiring to this beautiful region near to the famous thermal spa-town of Vichy.

Facilities: private parking, extensive grounds, lounge, hosts have pets, 100% no smoking, 5 years old minimum age, hiking, fishing 2km, riversports 6km, gliding 12km, cycling 12km, bird-watching 20km, interesting flora 20km, golf course 30km, winter sports 40km
Fluent English spoken

Directions: Please contact your host in advance for detailed directions.

Location
30km S of AURILLAC
in: Aubespeyre
Railway station: 40km
Airport: Aurillac 40km
car essential

✸ ✸

Private Home

Claude will welcome you as a friend to his house situated 750m up in the heart of the country between Auvergne and Rouergue. He will be delighted to guide and advise you on your trips throughout this region, which he knows particularly well. The house is simple and very well designed. Do not miss Conques.

Claude BRUEL
Aubespeyre de Junhac, 15120 MONTSALVY
Tel: (0) 4 71 49 22 70 / (0) 670 79 80 11

Facilities: off-street parking, extensive grounds, tv lounge, pets not accepted, closed: 30/11–01/03, hiking, fishing, hunting, interesting flora, mushroom-picking, golf course 4km, lake watersports 4km

Price Structure – 5 Bedrooms
2 rooms: shower room, wc, double bed, single bed: €46 – 2 people €56 – 3 people
2 rooms: shower room, wc, washbasin, double bed: €46
shower room, wc, 2 double beds: €46 – 2 people €65 – 4 people

Directions: At Aurillac, take the D920 as far as Montsalvy, and then the D341 on the right towards Aubespeyre. In Aubespeyre, follow the signs.

Reduction: 01/09–30/06, 3 nights, groups
Capacity: 14 people

Auvergne – Aurillac

Location
7km E of AURILLAC
in: Giou-de-Mamou, station pick-up on arrival/departure
Railway station: 8km
Airport: Aurillac 8km
car essential

✸ ✸ ✸

Residence of Outstanding Character

This charming 19th-century house with lots of character is near to the Cantal Mountains. There is a nice contrast between the rugged exterior stone walls and the bright pastel shades inside. The charm of the interior décor, the warm welcome and the mass of tourist information available give you all you need for an excellent stay.

Michèle & Alain LAFON
'La Maison', Le Bourg, 15130 GIOU-DE-MAMOU
Tel: (0) 4 71 64 51 55 / (0) 609 75 23 95
lafonalain@voila.fr
http://site.voila.fr/chlaf

Facilities: off-street parking, garden, pets not accepted, dinner available, 100% no smoking, private swimming pool, hiking, cycling, fishing, hunting, interesting flora, golf course 4km, lake watersports 20km, winter sports 25km
Basic English spoken

Price Structure – 4 Bedrooms
'Campagne': bathroom, wc, double bed: €52
'Tilleul': shower room, wc, twin beds: €55
2 rooms: shower room, wc, double bed, single bed: €54 – 2 people €72 – 3 people

Extra Bed: €18
Reduction: groups
Capacity: 10 people

Directions: At Aurillac, take the N122 towards Murat. After 7km, turn left towards Giou-de-Mamou. The house is located just as you enter the village (look for the B&B France sign).

15.13 Aurillac

Château/Manor House

Location
15km N of AURILLAC
in: Marmanhac, station pick-up on arrival/departure
Railway station: 15km
Airport: Aurillac 15km
car essential

Bab & Patrice de VARAX
'Château de Sédaiges', 15250 MARMANHAC
Tel: (0) 4 71 47 30 01 / (0) 688 98 18 20
Fax: (0) 4 71 47 30 01
bdevarax@netcourrier.com
www.chateausedaiges.com

What luck to come across this gem set in this quiet valley, where 19 generations of the same family have lived. This château is straight out of a fairytale, with its spectacular oak staircase, Flanders tapestries (a present from King Louis XVI), a collection of antique toys and dolls and the remarkable copperware in the 12th-century kitchen, where Bab will join you for breakfast. Also be sure to explore the grounds. If you miss this place, you will certainly regret it. Excellent value for money.

Price Structure – 3 Bedrooms and 2 Suites
suite 'Perse': bathroom, wc, double bed. En-suite room, single bed: €120 – 2 people €130 – 3 people
suite 'du Midi': shower room, wc, double bed. En-suite room, double bed: €120 – 2 people €140 – 4 people
'Jaune': shower, wc, double bed: €100
'Bleue' & 'Verte': shower room, wc, double bed (super king-size): €120

Capacity: 13 people

Facilities: off-street parking, extensive grounds, tv lounge, pets not accepted, babies welcome, free cot, closed: 01/10–01/05, private swimming pool, cycling, fishing, golf course 15km, lake watersports 15km, riversports 30km
Fluent English spoken

Directions: At Aurillac, take the D922 towards Mauriac, as far as Jussac. Then take the D59 on the right for Marmanhac and follow signs to the 'Château de Sédaiges'.

15.20 Aurillac

Château/Manor House

Location
31km W of AURILLAC
in: Glénat
Railway station: 10km
Airport: Aurillac 30km
car essential

Claude-Marie BERGON
'Château de La Grillère', Le Bourg, 15150 GLENAT
Tel: (0) 4 71 62 28 14 Fax: (0) 4 71 62 28 70
chateaudelagrillere@free.fr

Real luxury in the heart of the countryside. This place has not yet been classified, but we really could not leave it out! This château from the 13th century, revamped in the 17th, oozes charm and elegance from its ancient walls. The two impressive towers with their machicolations, the four-poster beds, the original beams, the 16th-century painted ceiling in the 'Temple' bedroom, the beautiful staircase...all with a view over the Cantal hills. You will love the spacious bedrooms with their pleasant bathrooms with all modern comforts. For dinner they serve the best of local gastronomy.

Price Structure – 5 Bedrooms
'Temple': television, shower room, wc, double bed (queen-size): €150
'Donjon': television, bathroom, wc, double bed, single bed (child-size): €130 – 2 people €160 – 3 people
'Mâchicoulis': television, bathroom, wc, twin beds, single bed: €130 – 2 people €160 – 3 people
'Roses': shower room, wc, twin beds: €100
'Reine': television, bathroom, wc, double bed (queen-size): €150

Reduction: 10/05–30/06 & 1/09–25/09, 3 nights
Capacity: 12 people

Facilities: off-street parking, extensive grounds, tv lounge, pets not accepted, internet access, dinner available, 6 years old minimum age, closed: 25/09–10/05, private swimming pool
Adequate English spoken

Directions: Please contact your host in advance for detailed directions.

Location
MASSIAC
in: Massiac
Railway station: 2km
Airport: Clermont-Ferrand 70km
car essential

Working Farm

On the main north-south route of the pleasant A75, this 'green stop' is off the beaten track, yet conveniently close to the *autoroute*. This Flemish couple, a designer and an architect, recently took over this place, and the pleasant rooms are in a separate building. They can lend you bikes to work up an appetite. As this was formerly a farmhouse-inn, they continue the tradition by serving dinner.

Victoor KURT & Els RUMMENS
'Ferme de Vazerat', 15500 MASSIAC
Tel: (0) 4 71 23 03 05 / (0) 683 55 84 33
Fax: (0) 4 71 23 03 05
info@ferme-de-vazerat.com
www.ferme-de-vazerat.com

Facilities: off-street parking, garden, lounge, hosts have pets, dinner available, babies welcome, free cot
Fluent English spoken

Price Structure – 5 Bedrooms
shower room, wc, double bed, twin beds, single bed (child-size): €55 – 2 people €85 – 5 people
shower room, wc, twin beds, single bed (child-size): €55 – 2 people €70 – 3 people
shower room, wc, double bed, cot: €55
shower room, wc, double bed, single bed: €55 – 2 people €70 – 3 people
double bed, twin beds, 2 single beds (child-size): €58 – 2 people €100 – 6 people

Directions: From the A75, take exit 23 or 24 towards Massiac. Follow the arrows from the church.

Extra Bed: €10   **Reduction:** 3 nights, children
Capacity: 9 people

Location
48km N W of MASSIAC
in: Montgreleix
Airport: Clermont-Ferrand 80km
car essential

Private Home

Get back to nature and stay by a wild lake, a fly fishing reserve in the Parc Naturel des Volcans d'Auvergne. You are upriver from Montgreleix, the highest town in the Cantal area at 1238m. The hamlet is like a little holiday village with chalets and caravans (rented weekly). The bedrooms here are pleasant with wooden floors and a communal room with a small kitchen area. Breakfast and dinner are served chez Ghislaine and Alain in their adjoining house. Complete calm and a swimming pool: a good dose of fresh air at bargain prices.

Ghislaine & Alain CHAMBON
'Le Lac des Estives', 15190 MONTGRELEIX
Tel: (0) 4 71 78 84 65 Fax: (0) 4 71 78 84 65
lac.estives@free.fr
www.lac-estives.com

Facilities: extensive grounds, lounge, hosts have pets, pets not accepted, dinner available, kitchen, 100% no smoking, fishing, mushroom-picking, hiking, winter sports, cycling 3km
Basic English spoken

Price Structure – 4 Bedrooms
'Rouge': shower room, wc, double bed, twin beds, single bed: €49,50 – 2 people €108,00 – 5 people
'Bleue' & 'Verte': shower room, wc, double bed, twin beds: €49,50 – 2 people €88,50 – 4 people
'Jaune': shower room, wc, double bed, single bed: €49,50 – 2 people €69,00 – 3 people

Directions: A75 exit 23 or 24. Head for Massiac and when on the N122, take the D21 on the right towards Allanche and continue on the D679 towards Condat for 13.5km. Then take the D104 on the right to Montgreleix. Continue towards Le Lac. Signposted 'Chambres d'hôtes'.

Extra Bed: €15
Reduction: groups
Capacity: 16 people

Auvergne – Massiac

43.17 Le Puy-en-Velay

Château/Manor House

Françoise & Jean-Nicolas CHAMBON du GARAY
'Maison Forte de Durianne', 43700 LE MONTEIL
Tel: (0) 4 71 02 90 36 / (0) 680 70 59 32
info@chateaudedurianne
chateaudedurianne.com

Price Structure – 2 Bedrooms and 1 Suite
'Simone de Murel': bathroom, wc, double bed, single bed: €60 – 2 people €75 – 3 people
'Emile Chassagne': shower room, wc, double bed, 2 single beds: €60 – 2 people €90 – 4 people
'Eugénie du Garay': along corridor shower room, wc, double bed, single bed. En-suite room, twin beds: €55 – 2 people €130 – 5 people

Extra Bed: €15
Reduction: 22/09–15/06, 3 nights
Capacity: 12 people

Location
4km N E of LE PUY-EN-VELAY
in: Le Monteil
Railway station: 5km
Airport: Le Puy-en-Velay-Loudes 10km
car essential

A *maison forte* dating back to the end of the 15th century. It is near the Gorges de la Loire by Puy-en-Velay and its cathedral is a world heritage site. Steeped in family history, it is typical of its kind. The sequoia tree in the courtyard, the towers, thick stone walls, vaulted dining room and large fireplace hint at its heritage. The three huge bedrooms are bright and furnished with antiques. Françoise, Jean-Nicolas and their four children welcome you. Their family cares for the environment and champions renewable energy.

Facilities: off-street parking, extensive grounds, lounge, dinner available, babies welcome, free cot, 100% no smoking, fishing, mushroom-picking, cycling, golf course 5km, interesting flora 5km, bird-watching 10km, riversports 20km, winter sports 25km, lake watersports 30km
Fluent English spoken

Directions: North of Puy-en-Velay, D103 towards Lavoute-sur-Loire (Vallée de la Loire). After 4km to Durianne take the first road up the hill on the right until you reach the fortress at the end.

43.19 Le Puy-en-Velay

Residence of Outstanding Character

Carry & Lucas RETERA
'Le Marconnès', 43420 ST-ARCONS-DE-BARGES
Tel: (0) 4 71 01 01 16 Fax: (0) 4 71 01 01 16
lemarconnes@wanadoo.fr
www.lemarconnes.com

Price Structure – 6 Bedrooms
'Jaune', 'Terra', 'Bleue' & 'Blanc cassé': shower room, wc, double bed, 2 single beds: €43 – 2 people €75 – 4 people
'Orange': shower room, wc, twin beds: €43
'Azur': shower room, wc, double bed, 3 single beds: €43 – 2 people €89 – 5 people

Extra Bed: €25
Capacity: 23 people

Location
25km S of LE PUY-EN-VELAY
in: St-Arcons-de-Barges
Railway station: 25km
Airport: Lyon-St Exupéry 180km
car essential

This B&B with a small campsite has a superb panoramic view of the Auvergne mountains. There is an easy-going, family atmosphere, thanks to its Dutch owners. You lodge in a 16th-century *capitainerie*. The thick stone walls of the stables now house the restaurant where breakfast is served, as well as simple cuisine. Upstairs are six bedrooms of adequate comfort (untidy pipes!). The pool, up the hill, is open to everyone but there are not crowds of people thanks to the spacious modest set-up. A grocery sells essential items.

Facilities: off-street parking, extensive grounds, lounge, hosts have pets, dinner available, babies welcome, free cot, wheelchair access, closed: 01/11–31/03, private swimming pool, hunting, hiking, cycling, fishing 8km, golf course 17km, riversports 25km, winter sports 25km
Fluent English spoken

Directions: From Puy-en-Velay, N88 towards Mende, Aubenas until La Sauvetat (24km) then the D53 on the left towards Barges. Then follow the signs on your right to 'Le Marconnès, camping'.

Location
17km N of LE PUY-EN-VELAY
in: St-Vincent, station pick-up on arrival/departure
Railway station: 2km
Airport: Le Puy-en-Velay-Loudes 15km

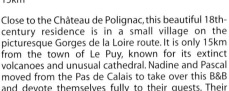

☀ ☀ ☀

Residence of Outstanding Character

Close to the Château de Polignac, this beautiful 18th-century residence is in a small village on the picturesque Gorges de la Loire route. It is only 15km from the town of Le Puy, known for its extinct volcanoes and unusual cathedral. Nadine and Pascal moved from the Pas de Calais to take over this B&B and devote themselves fully to their guests. Their meals use seasonal produce from local suppliers.

Pascal MONCHIET & Nadine VAN DURME
'La Buissonnière', Chalignac, 43800 ST-VINCENT
Tel: (0) 4 71 08 54 41 / (0) 682 21 36 22
Fax: (0) 4 71 08 54 41
buiss@free.fr
www.buissonniere-auvergne.com

Facilities: private parking, extensive grounds, tv lounge, hosts have pets, pets not accepted, internet access, dinner available, babies welcome, free cot, 100% no smoking, hiking, interesting flora, riversports 1km, cycling 4km, golf course 20km, winter sports 25km
Adequate English spoken

Price Structure – 4 Bedrooms and 1 Apartment
'Provençale': shower room, wc, double bed: €53
'Bleue': television, shower room, wc, double bed, single bed: €60 – 2 people €78 – 3 people
'Vanille': bathroom, wc, double bed, single bed: €60 – 2 people €78 – 3 people
'Romantique': shower room, wc, twin beds: €57
apartment: kitchen, shower room, wc, double bed, twin beds: €75 – 2 people €100 – 4 people

Extra Bed: €18   **Reduction:** groups
Capacity: 14 people

Directions: From Le Puy-en-Velay take the D103 towards Les Gorges de la Loire for about 15km. At St-Vincent, turn left towards the station. Continue straight on for about 250m following signs to 'La Buissonnière' which is a large house on the right.

Location
25km N of CLERMONT-FERRAND
in: Chaptes
Railway station: 9km
Airport: Clermont-Ferrand 25km
car essential

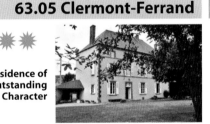

☀ ☀ ☀

Residence of Outstanding Character

This 18th-century home is only a few kilometres from the gentle, volcanic countryside of the Auvergne. It is surrounded by attractive buildings and a walled garden. Inside, a refined atmosphere is created by the antique furniture, paintings and artefacts on display. Your hosts ensure a dynamic and lively welcome. During the winter months, it is essential to phone in advance.

Elisabeth BEAUJEARD
8 rue de la Limagne, Chaptes,
63460 BEAUREGARD-VENDON
Tel: (0) 4 73 63 35 62

Facilities: private parking, extensive grounds, lounge, pets not accepted, 100% no smoking, hiking, interesting flora, mushroom-picking, fishing 6km, cycling 10km, riversports 15km, golf course 25km, bird-watching 25km, gliding 25km, winter sports 70km
Adequate English spoken

Price Structure – 3 Bedrooms
first room: shower room, wc, double bed: €75
second room: shower room, wc, double bed: €70
third room: shower room, wc, double bed: €65

Extra Bed: €22
Capacity: 6 people

Directions: A71, exit Riom. After the *autoroute* 'péage', when you reach the first roundabout follow the sign 'Toutes Directions'. At the second roundabout, take the D2144 towards Montluçon, and 2.5km after Davayat take the D122 on the right for Chaptes and follow the signs in the village.

Auvergne – Le Puy, Clermont-Ferrand

63.10 Clermont-Ferrand

Private Home

Gillian DEGNAN
'Les Chênes', 15 rue Guy de Maupassant,
63140 CHATELGUYON
Tel: (0) 4 73 86 02 88
gillian.degnan@wanadoo.fr
http://leschenes.monsite.orange.fr

Price Structure – 3 Bedrooms and 2 Suites
'Romain': television, telephone, shower room, wc,
twin beds: €46
suite 'Alexia': television, telephone, shower room, wc,
double bed. En-suite room, 2 single beds:
€70 – 4 people
'Carla': television, telephone, shower room, wc, double
bed. En-suite room, 2 single beds: €70 – 4 people
'Léo' & 'Marius': television, telephone, shower room,
wc, double bed: €46

Extra Bed: €15   **Reduction:** 2 nights, groups,
children   **Capacity:** 14 people

Location
20km N of CLERMONT-FERRAND
in: Châtelguyon, station pick-up on
arrival/departure
Railway station: 5km
Airport: Clermont-Ferrand 20km
car essential

Although this old family guesthouse is right in the
centre of Châtelguyon, a famous little spa town with
a park and a casino, their garden is a haven of peace
with an aviary, shaded terrace and a conservatory.
This is a good base for visiting Parc Vulcania or to
take the hiking routes to the volcanoes (there are
organised excursions).

Facilities: off-street parking, garden, tv lounge, hosts
have pets, kitchen, babies welcome, free cot, 100% no
smoking, hiking, cycling, fishing, mushroom-picking,
vineyard, lake watersports 10km, golf course 20km,
riversports 20km, winter sports 50km
Fluent English spoken

Directions: This place is 20km north of Clermont-
Ferrand near to Riom. Continue to the centre of
Châtelguyon as far as the church and then follow the
signs (about 100m from the church).

63.12 La Bourboule

Private Home

Martine & Jean-Claude GOIGOUX
'La Lauzeraie', 577 chemin de la Suchère,
63150 LA BOURBOULE
Tel: (0) 4 73 81 15 70 / (0) 678 14 37 74
goigoux.martine@wanadoo.fr
www.lalauzeraie.net

Price Structure – 4 Bedrooms
'Tenon': television, bathroom, wc, shower, double
bed: €90
'Puy Gros' & 'Banne d'Ordanche': lounge, television,
bathroom, wc, shower, double bed (queen-size):
€105
'Charlannes': lounge, television, bathroom, wc,
shower, twin beds: €125

Capacity: 8 people

Location
LA BOURBOULE
in: La Bourboule
Railway station: La Bourboule
Airport: Clermont-Ferrand 60km

A 'zen' area with an armchair that massages you while
you relax, anti-stress music and perfumes wafting
through the house is just to get you in the mood. Add
to this a superb covered pool with a jacuzzi, a sports
room, a hammam and a relaxing lounge and you get
the picture. They want you to chill out here. The
bedrooms are beautifully decorated with spacious
bathrooms. Enjoy a sun-lounger in the garden with
magnificent views, play billiards or relax in the main
lounge. We fell in love with this place.

Facilities: private parking, extensive grounds, tv
lounge, hosts have pets, pets not accepted, 100% no
smoking, 15 years old minimum age, closed:
1/11–30/11, private swimming pool, fishing,
mushroom-picking, hiking, cycling, winter sports, golf
course 7km
Basic English spoken

Directions: As you enter la Bourboule, take the exit
off the bridge on the right towards Charlannes, then
after about 200m when you see the sign 'Sortie
Bourboule', turn left. La Lauzeraie is 200m further on,
on your right.

Location
10km S W of BRIVE-LA-GAILLARDE
in: Lissac-sur-Couze
Railway station: 10km
Airport: Limoges 80km
car essential

Château/Manor House

This superb château has been constantly modified ever since the feudal days of the 12th century. The location, overlooking the Lac du Causse, is worth a detour in itself. Inside there are white walls, contemporary objects and large rooms contrasting with the enclosed corridors linking the bedrooms to the bathrooms. It has been tastefully decorated to great effect. The sitting room was a former staff room and breakfast is served in the vaulted kitchen or on the terrace with a superb view over the lake. Magical!

Facilities: private parking, extensive grounds, lounge, pets not accepted, babies welcome, free cot, hiking, cycling, riversports, lake watersports, golf course 2km, fishing 2km
Basic English spoken

Directions: From Brive-la-Gaillarde take the N89 direction Périgueux and then straight away the D59 on the left towards Lac du Causse, Lissac-sur-Couze. The château is in the part of the village that backs onto the lake.

Catherine MEYJONADE & Julien HENRIQUES
'Château de Lissac', Le Bourg,
19600 LISSAC-SUR-COUZE
Tel: (0) 5 55 85 14 19 / (0) 675 24 06 31
chateaudelissac@wanadoo.fr
www.chateaudelissac.com

Price Structure – 5 Bedrooms and 1 Suite
'Tulipe': television, shower room, wc, double bed: €130
'Jacinthe': lounge, television, bathroom, shower, wc, double bed (queen-size): €170
'Pivoine': lounge, television, shower room, wc, four-poster double bed: €160
'Rose': lounge, television, shower room, wc, washbasin, double bed. En-suite room, double bed (queen-size): €240 – 2 people €275 – 4 people
'Arum': television, bathroom, shower, wc, double bed: €170
plus 1 room

Extra Bed: €25   **Reduction:** 15/03–1/05, 5 nights
Capacity: 14 people

Location
41km E of BRIVE-LA-GAILLARDE
in: Monceaux-sur-Dordogne, station pick-up on arrival/departure
Railway station: 45km
Airport: Brive 45km

Residence of Outstanding Character

In the Dordogne valley, overhanging a pretty village 300m from the river, is this 18th-century Corrèze house, converted into a farmhouse. Encircled by hills, this tranquil setting is perfect for nature lovers but convenient too for Rocamadour and the Gouffre de Padirac. Here, Cathy treats all at her table like guests of honour. She spoils you with the best produce from the farm and garden – a mouthwatering menu! The bedrooms are air-conditioned with a seating area and mezzanine floor which, in some cases, is a touch cramped.

Facilities: private parking, extensive grounds, tv lounge, hosts have pets, dinner available, babies welcome, free cot, 100% no smoking, fishing, mushroom-picking, hiking, cycling, riversports, vineyard 20km, golf course 30km, lake watersports 30km, winter sports 90km
Adequate English spoken

Directions: From Brive-la-Gaillarde take the D921 towards Beynat then rejoin the N120 to Argentat. From there take the D12 towards Beaulieu for about 3km and then turn right to Monceaux. From the village head to Neuville then Champeaux for 300m. It is on the left-hand side.

Cathy & Daniel LHERM
'Ferme du Chassang', Le Chassang,
19400 MONCEAUX-SUR-DORDOGNE
Tel: (0) 5 55 28 04 75 / (0) 665 33 33 22
Fax: (0) 5 55 28 52 53
d.lherm@19.sideral.fr
http://pro.sideral.fr/ferme_auberge_chassang

Price Structure – 3 Bedrooms and 2 Apartments
'Narcisse': lounge, television, bathroom, wc, twin beds, 2 single beds: €50 – 2 people €88 – 4 people
'Camomille': lounge, television, shower room, wc, twin beds, 2 single beds: €48 – 2 people €88 – 4 people
'Anis': lounge, television, bathroom, wc, double bed, single bed: €55 – 2 people €83 – 3 people
2 apartments: lounge, television, kitchen, bathroom, wc, double bed, twin beds: €80 – 4 people

Extra Bed: €20   **Reduction:** 4 nights, groups
Capacity: 19 people

Limousin – Brive-la-Gaillarde

19.16 Brive-la-Gaillarde

Château/Manor House

Jacqueline & Pierre APPERT
'Manoir de la Brunie', La Brunie,
19500 ST-BAZILE-DE-MEYSSAC
Tel: (0) 5 55 84 23 07 / (0) 618 95 13 81
Fax: (0) 5 55 84 23 07
appierre@wanadoo.fr
www.manoirlabrunie.com

Price Structure – 2 Bedrooms and 2 Suites
'Coeur': lounge, bathroom, wc, double bed (queen-size): €100
'Pampilles': bathroom, wc, double bed (queen-size): €80
'Angelots': lounge, television, telephone, bathroom, wc, double bed (queen-size). En-suite room, single bed: €100 – 2 people €130 – 3 people
'Suite familiale': shower room, wc, double bed. En-suite room, 2 single beds: €70 – 2 people €110 – 4 people

Extra Bed: €30   **Reduction:** 3 nights
Capacity: 11 people

Location
27km S E of BRIVE-LA-GAILLARDE
in: St-Bazile-de-Meyssac
Railway station: 28km
Airport: Brive 18km
car essential

Jacqueline and Pierre retired to La Corrèze to this 18th-century manor house that was 'just waiting for them'! They really enjoy receiving guests. At the crossroads of the Dordogne valley, the Auvergne and Quercy, the house and the bedrooms have views over the village and the region. It is a super property with 15 hectares of land. The bedrooms have tasteful décor and furnishings. A large fireplace in the lounge adds to the warm atmosphere. At breakfast Jacqueline spoils you with homemade cakes, fruit jellies and fruit compotes.

Facilities: off-street parking, extensive grounds, tv lounge, hosts have pets, pets not accepted, internet access, babies welcome, free cot, 100% no smoking, mushroom-picking, hiking, fishing 1km, vineyard 4km, riversports 10km, golf course 20km
Fluent English spoken

Directions: Please contact your hosts in advance for detailed directions.

23.02 Guéret

Working Farm

Monique & Hans JACOBS
'La Ferme de Montenon', Montenon,
23240 LE GRAND-BOURG
Tel: (0) 5 55 81 30 00
montenon@wanadoo.fr
www.ferme-de-montenon.com

Price Structure – 6 Bedrooms
rooms 1 & 4: shower room, wc, double bed, 3 single beds: €47,50 – 2 people €89,50 – 5 people
room 2: shower room, wc, twin beds: €47,50
room 3: shower room, wc, double bed: €47,50
'Anzeme': shower room, wc, double bed, 3 single beds (2 child-size): €45,00 – 2 people €83,50 – 5 people
'St-Pardoux': shower room, wc, single bed: €37,50 – 1 person

Reduction: 7 nights, groups, children
Capacity: 20 people

Location
20km W of GUERET
in: Le Grand-Bourg
Railway station: 25km
Airport: Limoges 50km
car essential

In the heart of the countryside, this farm stands on a hillside with a great view over the Gartempe Valley. Here you can really enjoy the peace and tranquillity on long walks or relax by the pool and savour homemade regional specialities on the large veranda. Meanwhile, games, ponies, a donkey and rabbits will delight the children. Monique and Hans offer produce from the farm, and there is also a campsite. A good address to recharge batteries on holiday and take advantage of the great outdoors in an area that is enjoying renewed popularity.

Facilities: extensive grounds, tv lounge, hosts have pets, pets not accepted, dinner available, babies welcome, free cot, private swimming pool, riding, hiking, cycling, fishing 5km, lake watersports 18km, interesting flora 20km, riversports 20km, golf course 25km
Fluent English spoken

Directions: From Guéret take the fast road N145 towards La Souterraine for 17km, then the D912 on the left towards Le Grand-Bourg until the crossroads with the D4 (9km). Follow the D4 for 2.5km heading for La Brionne then the D96 on the right for 2.5km, and finally left to Montenon.

Location
12km W of BELLAC
in: Mézières-sur-Issoire, station pick-up on arrival/departure
Railway station: 15km
Airport: Limoges 40km

Private Home

In a region where even bison are reared, sheep welcome you to this home (don't worry, they aren't real!). Judith and Robin have found happiness here in their large bourgeois house in the centre of the village. Their lounge opens out onto a large garden. The guest bedrooms are spacious and well equipped with a kettle and a fridge. A real B&B, comfortable, pleasant, relaxed and great value. Recommended.

Judith & Robin CHATFIELD
'Aux Champs des Cloches', 26 avenue de Seltz,
87330 MEZIERES-SUR-ISSOIRE
Tel: (0) 5 55 60 44 79 / (0) 676 31 21 98
Fax: (0) 5 55 60 44 79
robin.chatfield@wanadoo.fr
www.aux-champs-des-cloches.com

Facilities: off-street parking, extensive grounds, lounge, hosts have pets, dinner available, babies welcome, free cot, hunting, fishing, mushroom-picking, bird-watching, hiking, cycling, golf course 25km, riversports 25km, lake watersports 25km, interesting flora 40km
Fluent English spoken

Price Structure – 4 Bedrooms
'Violette': along corridor bathroom, wc, double bed, cot: €45
'Jaune': television, shower room, wc, double bed, single bed (child-size): €45 – 2 people
€55 – 3 people
'Bleue': shower room, wc, double bed: €45
'Verte': shower, wc, twin beds: €45

Extra Bed: €10
Reduction: groups
Capacity: 9 people

Directions: A20, exit 23. N145 towards Angoulême, Bellac. Pass through Bellac. Then take the N147 for 5km and then the D951 towards Angoulême. In Mézières-sur-Issoire, the house is opposite the chemist (*pharmacie*).

Location
LIMOGES
in: Limoges, station pick-up on arrival/departure
Railway station: 5km
Airport: Limoges 8km

Private Home

In a quiet *quartier* of Limoges, this newly-built house is situated at the end of a cul-de-sac. The house is modern and bright and looks out onto a lovely garden with a terrace and a pretty pond surrounded by flowers. The garden slopes down gently to a wooded area perfect for walks with plenty for the children to see and do. The comfortable bedrooms are spotlessly clean and have their own independent entrance. Viviane is full of enthusiasm and eager to help in any way she can.

Viviane & Pascal MORQUIN
'Le Moulin de l'Aurence', 7 allée Robert Chapatte,
87100 LIMOGES
Tel: (0) 5 55 35 28 58 Fax: (0) 5 55 35 28 38
v.morquin@gmail.com
www.morquin.com

Facilities: off-street parking, garden, tv lounge, hosts have pets, babies welcome, free cot, 100% no smoking, closed: 25/10—05/11, fishing, bird-watching, hiking, interesting flora 4km, riversports 7km, golf course 8km, lake watersports 20km

Price Structure – 2 Bedrooms and 1 Suite
'Jaune': television, shower room, wc, twin beds: €45
'Verte': television, shower room, wc, double bed (queen-size): €45
'Bleue': television, shower room, wc, double bed (queen-size). En-suite room, twin beds: €45 – 2 people €65 – 4 people

Extra Bed: €8
Reduction: 2 nights
Capacity: 8 people

Directions: A20 exit 30, Limoges-Nord, towards ZI Nord. Pass in front of the shopping centre 'Leclerc'. Turn left into Rue F. Coferrer and then turn left by the car-part shop 'JM'. Head down the hill and take the 1st left turn into Rue St. Jean de Perse. At the roundabout turn right and right again.

Limousin – Bellac, Limoges

Residence of Outstanding Character

Galina & Peter FENTON
'La Croix du Reh', avenue Amédée Tarrade,
Châteauneuf-la-Forêt, 87130 LIMOGES
Tel: (0) 5 55 69 75 37 / (0) 689 76 43 08
Lacroixdureh3@aol.com
www.lacroixdureh.com

Price Structure – 4 Bedrooms and 1 Suite
'Rose': bathroom, wc, double bed: €70
'Yellow': shower room, wc, washbasin, double bed.
En-suite room, 3 single beds (1 child-size):
€70 – 2 people €95 – 5 people
'Blue': wheelchair access, bathroom, wc, double bed:
€70
'Gold': shower room, wc, double bed, single bed:
€70 – 2 people €80 – 3 people
'Lavender': shower room, wc, double bed, 3 single
beds: €70 – 2 people €98 – 5 people

Extra Bed: €12   **Reduction:** 20/09–1/06, 5 nights
Capacity: 17 people

Location
40km S E of LIMOGES
in: Châteauneuf-la-Forêt
Railway station: 12km
Airport: Limoges 45km
car essential

Peter and Galina have taken over this old house full of character. Their home is easy to find and ideally situated for a convenient stopover as it is placed between Limoges (famous for its porcelain) and the Lac de Vassivière, one of the largest man-made lakes in France, as well as the martyrs' village of Oradour-sur-Glane. Although it's on the main road, it has a beautiful, quiet landscaped garden, lit up at night, where you can enjoy a drink during the warm summer evenings.

Facilities: private parking, extensive grounds, tv lounge, hosts have pets, dinner available, babies welcome, free cot, wheelchair access, hiking, cycling, fishing, mushroom-picking, riversports 12km, lake watersports 20km, golf course 25km, winter sports 35km
Fluent English spoken

Directions: From Limoges, head east on the D979 towards Masléon, Eymoutiers. 5km from Masléon, at Lattée, turn right towards Châteauneuf-la-Forêt, which is 2km further on. 'La Croix du Reh' is right by the junction, opposite the school.

Limousin – Limoges

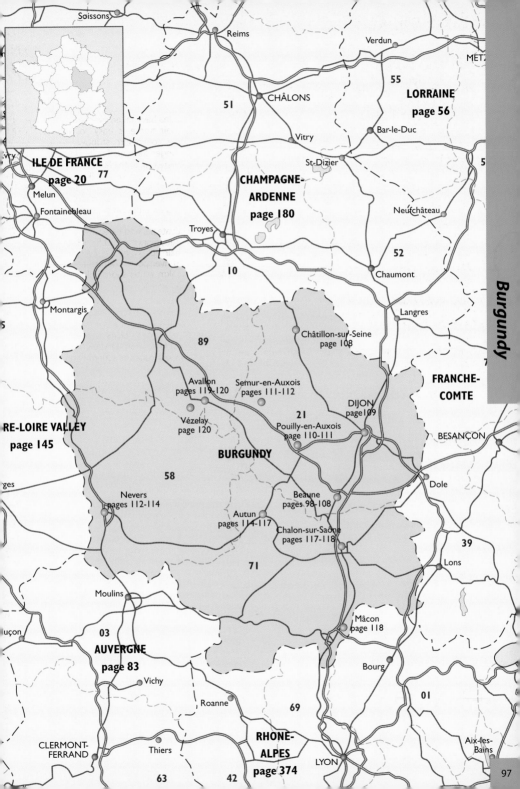

Soissons

Reims

Verdun

METZ

51

55

LORRAINE
page 56

CHÂLONS

Vitry

Bar-le-Duc

5

ILE DE FRANCE
page 20 77

St-Dizier

Melun

Fontainebleau

Neufchâteau

CHAMPAGNE-
ARDENNE
page 180

Troyes

52

Chaumont

10

Montargis

Langres

89

Châtillon-sur-Seine
page 108

7

Avallon
pages 119-120

Semur-en-Auxois
pages 111-112

FRANCHE-
COMTE

Vézelay
page 120

21

DIJON
page109

BESANÇON

Pouilly-en-Auxois
page 110-111

RE-LOIRE VALLEY
page 145

BURGUNDY

ges

58

Dole

Nevers
pages 112-114

Beaune
pages 98-108

Autun
pages 114-117

Chalon-sur-Saône
pages 117-118

39

Lons

71

Moulins

çon

03

AUVERGNE
page 83

Mâcon
page 118

Bourg

01

Vichy

Roanne

69

CLERMONT-
FERRAND

Thiers

RHONE-
ALPES
page 374

LYON

Aix-les-
Bains

63

42

21.02 Beaune

Private Home

Christine & Jean-Louis MARTIN
'La Terre d'Or', rue Izembart, La Montagne,
21200 BEAUNE
Tel: (0) 3 80 25 90 90 / (0) 685 08 61 49
Fax: (0) 8 21 47 99 67
jlmartin@laterredor.com
www.laterredor.com

Price Structure – 5 Bedrooms
and 1 Apartment
'Chèvrefeuille' & 'Orchidées Sauvages': bathroom,
wc, shower, double bed (queen-size): €235
'Aubépines': shower room, wc, twin beds: €190
'Liserons': bathroom, wc, shower, double bed
(queen-size): €205
'Campanules': bathroom, wc, shower, double bed
(queen-size), single bed: €205 – 2 people
€235 – 3 people
'Lupins': shower room, wc, double bed (queen-size),
2 single beds (child-size). En-suite room, shower
room, wc, double bed (queen-size): €480 – 6 people
Capacity: 17 people

Location
BEAUNE
in: Beaune, station pick-up on
arrival/departure
Railway station: 2km

Jean-Louis welcomes you to his two houses next to each other, just 100m from where he lives. However, he is always around during the day. The first house is large, attractive, and overlooks the centre of Beaune and its surrounding vineyards. The view is magnificent. The second house was formerly a wine-grower's. The charming, spacious rooms have been decorated with taste by your host. A must see, is Jean-Louis' personal wine cellar, installed in a cave that was formerly a riverbed. Top of the range services are provided, such as an English speaking baby-sitter.

Facilities: off-street parking, garden, pets not accepted, internet access, kitchen, babies welcome, free cot, 100% no smoking, private swimming pool, cycling, vineyard
Fluent English spoken

Directions: In Beaune, follow signs to Auxerre and take the D970 for 1.9km. Then turn right into the road that goes upwards and follow signs to "La Terre d'Or".

21.49 Beaune

Private Home

Nathalie & Williams LACOMBE
'L'Octroi Saint-Jacques', 15 rue de l'Hôtel-Dieu,
21200 BEAUNE
Tel: (0) 3 80 22 59 29 / (0) 675 03 03 76
Fax: (0) 3 80 22 59 29
loctroisaintjacques@wanadoo.fr
www.loctroisaintjacques.com

Price Structure – 2 Bedrooms and 1 Suite
'Hortensia' & 'Sophora': television, bathroom, wc,
double bed (queen-size): €180
'Gingko': television, bathroom, wc, shower, double
bed (king-size). En-suite room, double bed:
€215 – 2 people €230 – 4 people

Capacity: 8 people

Location
BEAUNE
in: Beaune, station pick-up on
arrival/departure
Railway station: 2km
Airport: Dijon 35km

A sought-after address – a 19th-century toll-house on the ramparts of the city. An ideal base to explore without a car. Parisian antique dealers, Nathalie and Williams, welcome you openly to the authentic, refined atmosphere of their home. The luxurious well-equipped bedrooms are across the garden and have made to measure furniture, large LCD TVs, air-con, WIFI, flowers and candles. Taste and purchase wine in the cellar and sample treats served by Nathalie. Homemade jams for breakfast include dandelion honey and poppy jelly!

Facilities: private parking, garden, pets not accepted, babies welcome, free cot, 100% no smoking, hiking, interesting flora, mushroom-picking 3km, lake watersports 4km, golf course 5km, hunting 10km, fishing 15km
Adequate English spoken

Directions: Please contact your hosts in advance for detailed directions.

Location
18km W of BEAUNE
in: Bligny-sur-Ouche
Railway station: 18km
Airport: Dijon 48km
car essential

✳ ✳ ✳
Working Farm

Just 15 minutes from Beaune is this former 16th-century hunting lodge hidden in the woods. The spacious bedrooms are air-conditioned, with DVD facilities, but true to the character of an old fortified farm. (Avoid the 'Poule' bathroom if you are tall.) Frédéric has worked for 18 years in top restaurants and cooks with a passion from authentic produce. The poultry, lambs and pigs, born and raised here, are bred from old pure breeds. So too are the more exotic llamas and rhea birds. Donkey rides possible. On site: cookery courses.

Eva & Frédéric MENAGER
'La Ruchotte', 21360 BLIGNY-SUR-OUCHE
Tel: (0) 3 80 20 04 79 / (0) 608 68 61 53
laruchotte@wanadoo.fr
www.laruchotte.com

Facilities: off-street parking, extensive grounds, hosts have pets, pets not accepted, dinner available, babies welcome, free cot, closed: 15/12–15/02, riding, mushroom-picking, hiking, cycling, fishing 4km
Basic English spoken

Price Structure – 1 Bedroom
'Poule': television, bathroom, wc, double bed (queen-size), single bed: €100

Capacity: 3 people

Directions: From Beaune take the D970 towards Bligny-sur-Ouche for 11.5km to the crossroads with the D111a. Turn right towards Bessey-en-Chaume. By the belvedere, turn left towards Bligny-sur-Ouche for about 5km and then turn right and follow the signs to 'La Ruchotte'.

Burgundy – Beaune

Location
4km N E of BEAUNE
in: Chorey-lès-Beaune
Railway station: 3km
car essential

✳ ✳ ✳ ✳
Château/Manor House

This splendid, romantic 17th-century château still retains its moat and two towers. The large bedrooms with their spacious bathrooms are beautifully furnished (one has a four-poster bed) with views over the grounds. The property has a vineyard and François is a retired winegrower. He will naturally invite you to visit his cellar under the house and try some of his wines and those of this region.

François GERMAIN
'Château de Chorey', 2 rue J. Germain,
21200 CHOREY-LES-BEAUNE
Tel: (0) 3 80 22 06 05 / (0) 610 84 34 34
Fax: (0) 3 80 24 03 93
chateau-de-chorey@wanadoo.fr
www.chateau-de-chorey-les-beaune.fr

Facilities: off-street parking, extensive grounds, tv lounge, hosts have pets, internet access, kitchen, babies welcome, free cot, 100% no smoking, closed: 1/11–31/03, hiking, cycling, vineyard, golf course 5km
Fluent English spoken

Price Structure – 4 Bedrooms and 1 Suite
'Les Teurons': bathroom, wc, shower, four-poster double bed, single bed: €195 – 2 people
€225 – 3 people
'Les Crus': bathroom, wc, shower, four-poster double bed: €195
'Les Vignes Franches': bathroom, wc, shower, four-poster double bed: €185
'Les Pelands': lounge, bathroom, wc, shower, double bed: €220
'Les Bons Ores': bathroom, wc, shower, double bed. En-suite room, 2 single beds: €220 – 2 people
€260 – 4 people

Extra Bed: €30   **Reduction:** 5 nights
Capacity: 13 people

Directions: Please contact your hosts for detailed directions.

21.42 Beaune

Private Home

Huguette GIBOULOT
16 Grande Rue, Changey, 21420 ECHEVRONNE
Tel: (0) 3 80 21 59 87 / (0) 680 73 79 80
Fax: (0) 3 80 21 59 87
huguette.giboulot@wanadoo.fr

Price Structure – 2 Bedrooms
first room: lounge, double bed: €39
second room: double bed, single bed:
€39 – 2 people €54 – 3 people

Extra Bed: €10
Capacity: 5 people

Location
10km N of BEAUNE
in: Echevronne, station pick-up on arrival/departure
Railway station: 9km
Airport: Dijon 40km
car essential

In a small picturesque village on the hillside, between vineyards and woodland, Huguette has reserved part of her small house for guests. It is like having your own independent flat although the kitchen area is used exclusively by Huguette to prepare breakfast. Huguette (a sewing machine representative) has brightened the decor with embroidery and patchworks. To appreciate the full extent of her talent, visit her workshop, crammed full with swathes of coloured fabrics, or enjoy a walk on the pathway leading off from the little garden into the wooded undergrowth by the hillside.

Facilities: private parking, garden, tv lounge, hosts have pets, babies welcome, free cot, 100% no smoking, hunting, mushroom-picking, hiking, vineyard, cycling 9km
Basic English spoken

Directions: North of Beaune, take the D18 to Changey (10km). In the village head for Echevronne. The house is on the left after 200m.

21.25 Beaune

Residence of Outstanding Character

Françoise & Alain BERTHAUD
'La Saura', route de Beaune,
21360 LUSIGNY-SUR-OUCHE
Tel: (0) 3 80 20 17 46 / (0) 610 32 68 87
la-saura@wanadoo.fr
www.douix.com/la-saura

Price Structure – 6 Bedrooms
ground floor 'Botanique' (our favourite room): lounge, shower room, wc, double bed (queen-size), 2 single beds: €87 – 2 people €127 – 4 people
ground floor 'Aux Fleurs': wheelchair access, shower room, wc, double bed (queen-size): €77
first floor 'Bleue' & 'Orientale': shower room, wc, double bed (queen-size): €77
first floor 'Aux Chinois': along corridor bathroom, double bed: €67
first floor 'Romantique': shower room, wc, twin beds: €77

Extra Bed: €15   **Reduction:** 4 nights
Capacity: 14 people

Location
17km N W of BEAUNE
in: Lusigny-sur-Ouche
Railway station: 17km
Airport: Lyon-St Exupéry 160km
car essential

Françoise and Alain will give you a warm welcome to their large and impressive house. The bedrooms are quiet, comfortable, spacious and decorated in excellent taste. This is the ideal spot for staying several days and getting to know the vintage wines of this area.

Facilities: private parking, garden, tv lounge, dinner available, babies welcome, free cot, 100% no smoking, wheelchair access, private swimming pool, hiking, fishing, cycling 2km, vineyard 10km, golf course 15km, lake watersports 20km
Adequate English spoken

Directions: When coming from Bligny-sur-Ouche on the D970, it is the first house on the right by the church. If coming from Beaune, it is the last house on the left.

Location
10km N E of BEAUNE
in: Magny-les-Villers
Railway station: 10km
Airport: Dijon 30km
car essential

✴ ✴ ✴

Private Home

This one-time *café-épicerie* is now guest accommodation on the other side of the road to where your hosts live but Marie-Paule is always on hand and returns home only at night! The pleasant bedrooms include lots of little extras. The house was empty for a long time but is now restored with stone walls on show in the wine cellar, now a lounge, and typical Corton stone laid on the floor. As active members of the tourist organisation for Nuits-St-Georges they accompany tours, their interests being walking and gastronomy.

Facilities: off-street parking, garden, tv lounge, pets not accepted, babies welcome, free cot, 100% no smoking, closed: 01/12–15/01, mushroom-picking, hiking, cycling, vineyard, golf course 10km, fishing 15km, interesting flora 30km, riversports 30km

Marie-Paule & Serge MARCILLET
'Logis St Martin', rue de l'Aye,
21700 MAGNY-LES-VILLERS
Tel: (0) 3 80 62 70 82 Fax: (0) 3 80 62 70 82
logissaintmartin@free.fr
http://logissaintmartin.free.fr

Price Structure – 2 Bedrooms and 1 Suite
'Bully' & 'La Flie': shower room, wc, double bed: €70
'Foigery': shower room, wc, double bed. En-suite room, 2 single beds: €70 – 2 people
€120 – 4 people

Reduction: 01/10–31/03, 3 nights
Capacity: 8 people

Directions: A6, exit Beaune-St-Nicolas. D974 direction Dijon for 6km. In Ladoix-Serrigny D115c on the left by the pharmacy for 3km until Magny-les-Villers. The Place St-Martin is close to the town hall (*la mairie*).

Location
10km N E of BEAUNE
in: Magny-les-Villers
Railway station: 9km
Airport: Dijon 30km
car essential

✴ ✴

Private Home

A friendly welcome from Jocelyne at the heart of prestigious vineyards. The guest bedrooms here are in a separate independent building. Some of the guest rooms have been redecorated and are pleasant. It is Jocelyne's husband who has renovated the bedrooms and the bathrooms and installed walk-in showers. The remaining rooms are also due for a makeover. In the large dining room, where light streams through the plants, is a sizeable family dining table where breakfast is served. On fine days you can also sit out in the garden.

Facilities: off-street parking, extensive grounds, hosts have pets, pets not accepted, dinner available, kitchen, mushroom-picking, interesting flora, hiking, vineyard, cycling, golf course 12km
Adequate English spoken

Jocelyne GAUGEY
'La Maison des Abeilles', rue de Pernand,
21700 MAGNY-LES-VILLERS
Tel: (0) 3 80 62 95 42
joel.gaugey@wanadoo.fr
perso.wanadoo.fr/maison-des-abeilles/

Price Structure – 6 Bedrooms
'Meursault': shower room, wc, twin beds: €53
'Volnay': shower room, wc, double bed (queen-size): €53
'Pomme': shower room, wc, twin beds: €53
'Beaune': shower room, wc, double bed (queen-size), twin beds: €47 – 2 people €90 – 4 people
'Chamboll': bathroom, wc, double bed, 2 single beds: €47 – 2 people €80 – 4 people
'Clos': bathroom, wc, 2 double beds: €53 – 2 people €80 – 4 people

Capacity: 18 people

Directions: Please contact your host in advance for detailed directions.

Burgundy – Beaune

21.50 Beaune

Private Home

Bienvenue en France

Location
33km W of BEAUNE
in: Maligny
car essential

Véronique & Gérald PAILLARD
21230 MALIGNY
Tel: (0) 3 80 84 26 39 / (0) 614 01 08 07

A small village house with comfortable rooms in a quiet and peaceful village not far from the famous vineyards. Your host Gérald can advise on where to buy Burgundy wine. Enjoy the large garden and orchard where Véronique will serve you an excellent breakfast. A very hospitable couple and Gérald knows everybody in the village – he is the mayor, after all!

Price Structure – 3 Bedrooms
'Lilas': television, bathroom, wc, double bed: €50
'Bouton d'or': television, bathroom, wc, twin beds: €50
'L'herbier': television, shower room, wc, double bed: €50

Extra Bed: €10
Capacity: 6 people

Facilities: extensive grounds, tv lounge, dinner available, babies welcome, free cot, 100% no smoking, fishing 6km, bird-watching 6km, cycling 6km, gliding 20km, golf course 30km, vineyard 30km
Adequate English spoken

Directions: Please contact your host in advance for detailed directions.

21.46 Beaune

Château/Manor House

Location
12km E of BEAUNE
in: Meursanges
Railway station: 10km
Airport: Lyon-St Exupéry 160km
car essential

Mandy & Hervé KERLANN
'Château de Laborde', Hameau de Laborde-au-Château, 21200 MEURSANGES
Tel: (0) 3 80 26 54 44 **Fax:** (0) 3 80 26 59 69
info@labordeauchateau.com
www.labordeauchateau.com

By famous vines and close to Beaune, this imposing château is one of the most impressive buildings in the area. It dates back to the 11th century and the Ducs de Bourgogne. The guest rooms are in renovated former outbuildings. There are two large suites decorated in a chic rustic style with a kitchen area. Luxurious hand-embroidered sheets are testament to Mandy's artistic talents and she also has a passion for cooking. Sample the wine produced by this French-Canadian couple who welcome you as friends. Breakfast is served at your convenience.

Price Structure – 2 Apartments
'Chardonnay': lounge, television, kitchen, bathroom, wc, double bed. En-suite room, twin beds:
€180 – 2 people €280 – 4 people
'Pinot Noir': wheelchair access, lounge, television, kitchen, bathroom, wc, double bed (queen-size): €180

Reduction: 7 nights
Capacity: 6 people

Facilities: private parking, extensive grounds, hosts have pets, dinner available, babies welcome, free cot, 100% no smoking, 2 nights minimum stay, cycling, vineyard, mushroom-picking 2km, bird-watching 2km, golf course 5km
Fluent English spoken

Directions: A6, exit 24.1, Beaune Sud. D970 direction Ste-Marie-la-Blanche, then just after the village D25c on the left to the hamlet Laborde-au-Château. The Kerlann home is the large red brick building in the centre of the hamlet.

Location
4km S of BEAUNE
in: Montagny-lès-Beaune
Railway station: 4km
Airport: Dijon 30km
car essential

Private Home

Very easy access to this restored, former farm, in a small, quiet, rural town very near to Beaune. The interior décor, inspired by Brigitte and Lucien's long trips to Polynesia, marries succesfully the bright and cheerful colours and influences of the islands with the authentic character of the farm. Genuine wooden farm equipment mixes together with model ships, ethnic objects and musical instruments. The guest bedrooms are spacious and generous portions of Burgundy cuisine are served up for dinner. Ample secure parking.

Brigitte & Lucien MOREL
4 rue des Gravières,
21200 MONTAGNY-LES-BEAUNE
Tel: (0) 3 80 24 02 11 Fax: (0) 3 80 22 65 70

Price Structure – 5 Bedrooms
4 rooms: shower room, wc, double bed, single bed:
€76 – 2 people €96 – 3 people
shower room, wc, twin beds: €76

Reduction: 3 nights
Capacity: 14 people

Facilities: private parking, tv lounge, pets not accepted, dinner available, closed: 24/12–31/01, fishing, hiking, vineyard 3km, golf course 3km

Directions: From Beaune, A31 exit sud 24.1. At the roundabout, turn right heading to Montagny-lès-Beaune. In the village, head towards Bligny and the house is straightaway on the right. Enter and park inside the large closed courtyard.

Burgundy – Beaune

21.43 Beaune

Location
8km W of BEAUNE
in: Nantoux
Railway station: 8km
Airport: Dijon 49km
car essential

Private Home

Close to the prestigious Beaune vineyards is this recent purpose-built building. Set just below the main house you enjoy wonderful panoramic views from the terrace and swimming pool. The bedrooms are spacious (some with walk-in showers) and dotted with unusual objects. The communal room has high beams, a large open fireplace and a big rustic table. Although away from the main house, this doesn't diminish the attention from Nathalie and Denis who help you discover their region, the wines and, in season, fresh Bourgogne truffles.

Facilities: off-street parking, garden, tv lounge, hosts have pets, babies welcome, free cot, wheelchair access, private swimming pool, hiking, interesting flora, vineyard, cycling 8km, golf course 12km
Adequate English spoken

Directions: From Beaune, D973 towards Autun, Pommard. At Pommard turn right heading towards Nantoux (D17 then the D23). In the village, take the 3rd road on the left and continue to the end of the road.

Nathalie & Denis CHARLES
'Domaine de la Combotte', La Combotte,
21190 NANTOUX
Tel: (0) 3 80 26 02 66 Fax: (0) 3 80 26 07 84
info@lacombotte.com
www.lacombotte.com

Price Structure – 5 Bedrooms and 1 Suite
'Les Coucous': television, bathroom, wc, shower, double bed (queen-size). En-suite room, twin beds:
€118 – 2 people €158 – 4 people
'Les Meurgers': wheelchair access, television, bathroom, wc, twin beds: €113
'La Planche Pinson': television, shower room, wc, double bed (queen-size), twin beds, single bed.
along corridor room 'La Meurette': television, shower room, wc, double bed: €113 – 2 people
€168 – 7 people
plus 2 rooms

Extra Bed: €20   **Reduction:** 01/10–30/04, 4 nights
Capacity: 20 people

21.51 Beaune

Private Home

Location
20km S W of BEAUNE
in: Nolay, station pick-up on arrival/departure
Railway station: 20km

In a medieval village, Jill has restored this former tannery in her own inimitable style with an interesting eclectic array of antiques. Pascal is a professional artist and you enter the house via his studio. The atmosphere here is warm and relaxed and Jill and Pascal are very approachable, as are their two little redheads that welcome you all smiles! Breakfast is served in the 18th-century gallery overlooking the interior courtyard. The guest bedrooms are spacious and comfortable with brand new bathrooms. Internet access – WIFI.

Jill & Pascal LABRANCHE
'Esprit d'un moment', 16 rue Sadi Carnot, 21340 NOLAY
Tel: (0) 3 80 21 79 41 / (0) 687 73 24 99
Fax: (0) 3 80 21 83 12
espritdun@wanadoo.fr
espritdunmoment.com

Price Structure – 1 Bedroom and 1 Suite
'Tomette': shower room, wc, double bed, single bed: €50 – 2 people €57 – 3 people
'Bois': bathroom, wc, double bed, single bed. En-suite room, washbasin, double bed: €50 – 2 people €80 – 5 people

Extra Bed: €10
Reduction: children
Capacity: 8 people

Facilities: garden, lounge, hosts have pets, pets not accepted, internet access, kitchen, babies welcome, free cot, 100% no smoking, gliding, hiking, cycling, vineyard
Fluent English spoken

Directions: A6, exit 24.1 Beaune, Chagny. Follow Chagny to the N74, turn left onto the D973 via La Rochepot to Nolay. Once at the Place Sadi Carnot, when facing the bronze statue, the road is on the left, one minute on foot.

21.05 Beaune

Residence of Outstanding Character

Location
16km N E of BEAUNE
in: Nuits-St-Georges
Railway station: 1km
Airport: Dijon 20km

The Countess de Loisy, Master of Wine and a registered guide, welcomes you to her wonderful home with comfortable rooms, furnished with antiques. The splendid salon and the dining room on the ground floor open on to indoor gardens. Please book ahead and do not arrive before 5pm.

Christiane de LOISY
'Domaine Comtesse Michel de Loisy', 28 rue du Gal de Gaulle, 21700 NUITS-ST-GEORGES
Tel: (0) 3 80 61 02 72 / (0) 684 82 53 98
Fax: (0) 3 80 61 36 14
domaine.loisy@wanadoo.fr
www.domaine-de-loisy.com

Price Structure – 3 Bedrooms and 2 Suites
'Madame': bathroom, wc, double bed (king-size): €132
'Monsieur': along corridor bathroom, wc, double bed: €92
'Boudoir': bathroom, wc, twin beds: €112
suite 'Children's room bleus': bathroom, wc, double bed. En-suite room, 2 single beds: €132 – 2 people €182 – 4 people
suite 'Mademoiselle': shower room, wc, double bed. En-suite room, 2 single beds: €132 – 2 people €182 – 4 people

Extra Bed: €25 **Reduction:** 12/11–14/03, 3 nights, groups, children
Capacity: 14 people

Facilities: private parking, extensive grounds, tv lounge, hosts have pets, babies welcome, free cot, 100% no smoking, 2 wcs, golf course 16km
Fluent English spoken

Directions: In Beaune, take the A31 towards Dijon. Take exit Nuits-St-Georges. After the fourth roundabout, follow the signs to Beaune (N74). The street starts at the second set of traffic lights. Continue for 120m towards Beaune.

Working Farm

Location
6km S of BEAUNE
in: Puligny-Montrachet, station pick-up on arrival/departure
Railway station: 4km
car essential

Encircled by the famous vineyards of Puligny-Montrachet, which produce some of the world's most renowned white wines, stands this house on 5 hectares of land. Corinne, born into a family of wine producers, is also a professor of oenology. Passionate about her trade, she will with great enthusiasm and joie de vivre advise you on where to visit and buy wine in the area. The small bedrooms are in the annex, once the sleeping quarters for grape-pickers, but now renovated with care to preserve their charm and stone walls.

Facilities: private parking, garden, hosts have pets, pets not accepted, kitchen, babies welcome, free cot, 100% no smoking, hiking, hunting, vineyard, mushroom-picking 5km, golf course 15km, gliding 15km, fishing 25km
Fluent English spoken

Directions: From Beaune, N74 towards Chagny for 12km to Puligny-Montrachet. From the centre of the village head towards Meursault. Last house in the village on the right.

Corinne GUILLEMARD
'Nuits de Bacchus', 19 rue Drouhin,
21190 PULIGNY-MONTRACHET
Tel: (0) 3 80 21 34 22
guillemard-clerc.domaine@wanadoo.fr
www.guillemard-clerc.com

Price Structure – 3 Bedrooms
'Chambre à secret': television, shower room, wc, double bed, single bed: €55 – 2 people
€70 – 3 people
'Chambre basse': television, shower room, wc, double bed, 2 single beds: €55 – 2 people
€90 – 4 people
'Chambre à four': television, along corridor shower room, wc, double bed: €55

Extra Bed: €15
Reduction: 2 nights
Capacity: 9 people

Private Home

Location
20km N E of BEAUNE
in: St-Bernard, station pick-up on arrival/departure
Railway station
car essential

A very warm and welcoming couple and an impeccably clean house. You are just 7km from the motorway exit in a completely tranquil and quiet location close to the vines of Nuits-St-Georges (and 5km from Clos Vougeot), so the perfect choice for a stopover or short wine break. A magical location for connoisseurs of the big "*Grand Crus*".

Facilities: private parking, garden, tv lounge, hosts have pets, dinner available, fishing, interesting flora, mushroom-picking, vineyard 5km, hunting 5km, golf course 20km, lake watersports 20km
Adequate English spoken

Directions: From the A31, exit Nuits-St-Georges and then take the D8 as far as Boncourt-le-Bois. In the village take the first road on the left which is the D116b towards St-Bernard. Follow the signs.

Jeanne ESMONIN
Paquis de Rolanges, 21700 ST-BERNARD
Tel: (0) 3 80 62 81 60 / (0) 620 52 69 19
les-rolanges@wanadoo.fr

Price Structure – 3 Bedrooms
'Bleuet': shower room, wc, double bed: €57
'Orchidée': shower room, wc, double bed: €55
'Hortensia': shower room, wc, twin beds: €57

Extra Bed: €25
Capacity: 6 people

Burgundy – Beaune

21.54 Beaune

Private Home

**Fiore MANCUSO & Stéphanie JONES
'Aux Quatre Saisons', 35 rue de la Fontaine,
21700 ST-NICOLAS-LES-CITEAUX
Tel: (0) 3 80 61 29 61 / (0) 661 12 60 03
Fax: (0) 3 80 61 29 61
aux4saisons35@aol.com
www.aux-quatre-saisons.net**

Location
16km N E of BEAUNE
in: St-Nicolas-lès-Citeaux
Railway station: 7km
Airport: Dijon 25km
car essential

This Anglo-Italian couple now live in France. Your hostess runs a wine cellar and will be delighted to share her passion for wine with you. Fiore's speciality is pizza, as you might expect, and he organises pizza parties around his oven in the large garden. The spacious bedrooms are in a separate building and there will also be a room with a lounge and kitchen just for guests and a pool is planned for 2008. The welcome is warm from very friendly hosts and you have the run of the entire house.

Price Structure – 2 Bedrooms
'Hiver': bathroom, wc, double bed (queen-size), single bed: €55 – 2 people €65 – 3 people
'Printemps': shower room, wc, double bed (queen-size), single bed: €55 – 2 people €65 – 3 people

Extra Bed: €10
Capacity: 6 people

Facilities: private parking, garden, tv lounge, hosts have pets, babies welcome, free cot, 100% no smoking, hiking, cycling, vineyard 7km
Fluent English spoken

Directions: A31 exit 1 Nuit-St-Georges. D8 towards St-Nicolas-lès-Citeaux. As you enter the village, continue for 400m and turn left in to Rue de la Fontaine.

21.18 Beaune

Residence of Outstanding Character

**Françoise MOINE
'La Monastille', 21360 THOMIREY
Tel: (0) 3 80 20 00 80 Fax: (0) 3 80 20 00 80
moine.francoise@wanadoo.fr
www.monastille.com**

Location
27km N W of BEAUNE
in: Thomirey, station pick-up on arrival/departure
Railway station: 25km
Airport: Lyon-St Exupéry 170km

Françoise is completely refurbishing this old farm building, typical of the area, with comfortable, rustic bedrooms. The old dining room centres around a large farmhouse table and a beautiful fireplace. Genuine atmosphere and a sincere welcome.

Price Structure – 4 Bedrooms
'Bleue': shower room, wc, double bed: €65
'Beige': shower room, wc, twin beds: €65
'Verte': shower room, wc, double bed, 2 single beds: €105 – 4 people
'Jaune': shower room, wc, double bed, single bed: €65 – 2 people €85 – 3 people

Extra Bed: €20
Reduction: groups
Capacity: 11 people

Facilities: off-street parking, garden, hosts have pets, dinner available, babies welcome, free cot, 100% no smoking, hiking, mushroom-picking, bird-watching 1km, fishing 10km, hunting 10km, golf course 25km
Adequate English spoken

Directions: On the A6 from Paris, exit Pouilly-en-Auxois. Take the N81 towards Arnay-le-Duc and then the N6 towards La Rochepot, Chagny for 10km. Turn left towards Thomirey. The house is situated just as you leave the village, towards Ecutigny.

Location
20km N of BEAUNE
in: Villars-Fontaine
Railway station: 5km
Airport: 25km
car essential

Private Home

This place is at the centre of a little village, on the slopes of Les Hautes Côtes de Nuits-St-Georges vineyards. A find that will really get you excited. Start with the jovial welcome from Philippe, followed by breakfast in the cellar. He is very well versed in wine-making, particularly the *Grands Crus*, but can also talk about New York amongst other things. Be sure to ask him to demonstrate the workings of the amazing 'Robocop' shutters on the bedroom windows.

Andrée & Philippe JEANJEAN
rue de Vergy, 21700 VILLARS-FONTAINE
Tel: (0) 3 80 61 29 59 Fax: (0) 3 80 61 33 34
jeanjean.philippe@wanadoo.fr
http://chambres.ifrance.com

Facilities: off-street parking, lounge, hosts have pets, kitchen, closed: 01/12–31/01, hiking, cycling, bird-watching, vineyard, fishing 1km, interesting flora 1km, mushroom-picking 1km, lake watersports 5km, golf course 20km
Basic English spoken

Price Structure – 4 Bedrooms
2 rooms: shower room, wc, washbasin, double bed: €38
shower room, wc, washbasin, double bed, single bed: €38 – 2 people €44 – 3 people
lounge, shower room, wc, double bed, twin beds: €38 – 2 people €55 – 4 people

Directions: A31 towards Beaune, exit Nuits-St-Georges. Then head towards Dijon as far as the traffic lights and take the D25 for Villars-Fontaine. You will find the house as you enter the village, 20m after the restaurant.

Extra Bed: €13
Reduction: 2 nights
Capacity: 11 people

Location
9km S E of BEAUNE
in: St-Loup-Géanges, station pick-up on arrival/departure
Railway station: 10km
Airport: Lyon-St Exupéry 130km
car essential

Residence of Outstanding Character

Relax completely in this beautiful old bourgeois mansion house dating from the 18th century, just a few kilometres from Beaune and seductive wines. It is surrounded by age-old trees in grounds where a few sheep graze. Pascale is a doctor and while she looks after her patients, Patrick slowly restores the house. There is a spacious suite with curved lines and two recently refurbished bedrooms, as well as a large lounge.

Pascale & Patrick MOUTON
'Château Georges', 1 rue Claude,
71350 ST-LOUP-GEANGES
Tel: (0) 3 85 49 94 01 Fax: (0) 3 85 49 94 01
chateau.georges@free.fr
http://chateau.georges.free.fr

Facilities: private parking, extensive grounds, lounge, hosts have pets, pets not accepted, dinner available, babies welcome, free cot, 100% no smoking, hiking, cycling, hunting, mushroom-picking, riversports 10km, vineyard 10km, golf course 20km
Basic English spoken

Price Structure – 2 Bedrooms and 1 Suite
suite: bathroom, wc, double bed (queen-size). En-suite room, single bed: €70 – 2 people
€85 – 3 people
1 room: shower room, wc, double bed (queen-size): €70
1 room: shower room, wc, bathroom, twin beds: €70

Directions: From Beaune take the D970 towards Verdun-sur-le-Doubs for 9km to St-Loup-Géanges. Take the road on the right just after the *pharmacie*. The house is on the left at the next crossroads.

Extra Bed: €15
Capacity: 7 people

Burgundy – Beaune

71.27 Beaune

Residence of Outstanding Character

Mireille MARQUET
'La Messalière', 29 rue du 8 mai 1945,
71510 ST-LEGER-SUR-DHEUNE
Tel: (0) 3 85 45 35 75 / (0) 686 83 02 49
Fax: (0) 3 85 45 40 96
reservations@saintlegersurdheune.com
www.saintlegersurdheune.com

Price Structure – 3 Bedrooms and 1 Suite
'Catherine de France': shower room, wc, double bed: €65
'Guigone de Salins': shower room, wc, double bed: €85
'Isabelle de Portugal': lounge, shower room, wc, four-poster double bed: €100
'Marguerite de Flandres': lounge, shower room, wc, double bed (queen-size). En-suite room, single bed: €110 – 2 people €130 – 3 people

Extra Bed: €20   **Capacity:** 9 people

Location
26km S of BEAUNE
in: St-Léger-sur-Dheune
Railway station: 15km
Airport: Lyon-St Exupéry 120km
car essential

This is a charming 17th-century residence in enclosed grounds by a small tranquil canal (a stretch greatly appreciated by canal boat enthusiasts), equidistant from Beaune and Chalon. During the summer season, breakfast and dinner are served on the terrace. Mireille pays special attention at dinner time to promoting Burgundy traditions and wines, sometimes inviting local wine producers for dinner. The bedrooms have been decorated stylishly with period furniture and we particularly liked the romantic feel of the 'Isabelle de Portugal' bedroom using toile de Jouy fabrics.

Facilities: private parking, extensive grounds, tv lounge, pets not accepted, dinner available, babies welcome, free cot, 100% no smoking, wheelchair access, 2 nights minimum stay: 01/07–31/08, closed: 01/12–01/03, fishing, hiking, cycling, vineyard, golf course 15km, riversports 15km
Basic English spoken

Directions: From Beaune on the N74 take the D974 towards Le Creusot as far as St-Léger-sur-Dheune (26km). 'La Messalière' is on this road in the centre of the village on the right.

21.20 Châtillon-sur-Seine

Private Home

Pierre BAEHLER
'L'Oasis', porte de Châtillon, 21400 POTHIERES
Tel: (0) 3 80 81 94 44 Fax: (0) 3 80 81 94 44
info@oasis-21.com
www.oasis-21.com

Price Structure – 3 Bedrooms
'Coccinelle' & ' Papillon': television, double bed, single bed: €51 – 2 people €57 – 3 people
'Orchidée': television, shower room, wc, double bed, single bed: €56 – 2 people €67 – 3 people

Extra Bed: €9
Reduction: 7 nights, groups
Capacity: 9 people

Location
6km N W of CHATILLON-SUR-SEINE
in: Pothières
Railway station: 28km
Airport: Dijon 85km
car essential

Pierre is Swiss, and his place near the main Troyes–Dijon road is a paradise for nature lovers. Particularly well known for shooting and fishing (this is an excellent area for fly-fishing). The wildlife in the forest is exceptional: stags, hinds, birds. Ideal for eco-tourists.

Facilities: private parking, extensive grounds, hosts have pets, dinner available, 1 shared shower room, wc, closed: 15/12–15/01, hiking, fishing, bird-watching, hunting 1km, mushroom-picking 2km, cycling 6km, lake watersports 6km

Directions: At Tonnere, head for Châtillon-sur-Seine on the D965 and the N71 towards Troyes. Cross Montliot and turn left towards Vix, then head towards Pothières. It is the first house on the right in the village.

Location
40km N E of DIJON
in: St-Seine-sur-Vingeanne
Railway station: 40km
Airport: Dijon 40km
car essential

Château/Manor House

This fortress, situated on the edge of Bourgogne, Champagne and Franche-Comté, is tastefully furnished. We did not hesitate in giving this place four 'suns' as it has so much character, and dominates the Vingeanne valley in the heart of an area steeped in history. Excellent for walking, cycling and horse-riding.

Facilities: private parking, extensive grounds, pets not accepted, dinner available, babies welcome, free cot, hiking, fishing, cycling
Basic English spoken

Bertrand BERGEROT
'Château de Rosières', St-Seine-sur-Vingeanne, 21610 FONTAINE-FRANÇAISE
Tel: (0) 3 80 75 96 24 Fax: (0) 3 80 75 96 24
rosieresbb@aol.com
www.chateauderosieres.com

Directions: On the A31 Dijon–Chaumont, exit 5 Til-Chatel. Turn right towards Fontaine-Française. In Orville turn right towards Fontaine-Française. At Fontaine-Française head for St-Seine-sur-Vingeanne. Turn right in front of the church, go through the village and the 'Château de Rosières' is 3km further on after the village.

Price Structure – 4 Bedrooms and 1 Apartment
'Chambre du Puits': along corridor shower room, wc, twin beds: €50
first floor: bathroom, wc, double bed: €80
apartment: lounge, television, kitchen, bathroom, wc, double bed. En-suite room, double bed: €110 – 2 people €140 – 4 people
'Cour': bathroom, wc, double bed: €60
'Chambre de la cour': bathroom, wc, double bed: €60

Extra Bed: €15
Capacity: 12 people

Burgundy – Dijon

Location
30km N E of DIJON
in: Véronnes
Railway station: 30km
Airport: Dijon 30km
car essential

Private Home

Françoise and Marcel will welcome you to their old farmhouse, which has been completely restored and modernised to a high level of comfort. If you like Burgundy, Marcel can advise you, because he is a *Chevalier du Tastevin*, and therefore an expert. If you wish, he will be delighted to accompany you to visit wine cellars and assist you in your choice.

Facilities: private parking, garden, tv lounge, hosts have pets, pets not accepted, dinner available, babies welcome, free cot, 100% no smoking, wheelchair access, hiking, fishing, hunting, mushroom-picking, gliding 5km, golf course 20km, vineyard 40km
Basic English spoken

Françoise & Marcel VEY
'Aux Iris', route d'Orville, 27 rue de Petigny, 21260 VERONNES
Tel: (0) 3 80 75 39 55 / (0) 630 77 69 92
Francoise.BEGRAND@wanadoo.fr
http://perso.wanadoo.fr/aux-iris/

Directions: On the A31 Dijon–Chaumont, exit 5 to Til-Chatel. Head towards Langres. In Orville, take the first on the right towards Véronnes on the D120. The house is at the entrance of the village, on the right. Look for the stone pillar and the red gate.

Price Structure – 4 Bedrooms and 1 Suite
ground floor-room 1: wheelchair access, along corridor bathroom, shower & wc, double bed. Along corridor room 2, wheelchair access, double bed: €120 – 4 people
rooms 3 & 5: shower room, wc, double bed: €60
room 4: bathroom, wc, double bed: €60
room 6: shower room, wc, twin beds: €65

Extra Bed: €20
Capacity: 12 people

21.35 Pouilly-en-Auxois

Private Home

Location
16km S of POUILLY-EN-AUXOIS
in: Arnay-le-Duc, station pick-up on
arrival/departure
Railway station: 35km
Airport: Dijon 50km
car essential

Viviane POMPON
'Echoppe-St-Honoré', 18 rue St Honoré,
21230 ARNAY-LE-DUC
Tel: (0) 3 80 90 12 87 / (0) 611 09 05 73
echoppesthonore@aol.com
www.echoppe-saint-honore.com

This very original B&B is in the heart of the medieval citadel, clinging onto the walls of the Château des Princes de Condé, which dates from the 16th century. It was originally part of the outbuildings of the former residence of the Dauphin (Crown Prince) of France. As you take a cup of tea in the courtyard at the foot of the château, you will soak up the heritage of this place.

Price Structure – 4 Bedrooms
'Océane': television, bathroom, wc, shower, double bed: €50
'Soleil' & 'Nature' : television, bathroom, wc, shower, double bed, single bed: €50,00 – 2 people €61,50 – 3 people
'Saumon': television, bathroom, wc, shower, twin beds: €53

Extra Bed: €10
Reduction: 4 nights
Capacity: 10 people

Facilities: off-street parking, hosts have pets, dinner available, hiking, cycling, fishing, golf course 15km, lake watersports 15km, riversports 15km, vineyard 20km

Directions: From the A38 exit 24, then take the N81 in the direction Autun as far as Arnay-le-Duc. The Rue St. Honoré is in the centre of the town, near to the château.

21.52 Pouilly-en-Auxois

Private Home

Location
16km S of POUILLY-EN-AUXOIS
in: Arnay-le-Duc
Railway station: 30km
Airport: Dijon 50km
car essential

Brigitte & Laurent SCHMITT
'La Bourgeoise', 6 rue des 3 Tourelles,
21230 ARNAY-LE-DUC
Tel: (0) 3 80 84 00 81 / (0) 698 95 61 29
la.bourgeoise21@wanadoo.fr
www.la-bourgeoise.com

Brigitte and Laurent are from Haute-Savoie and have recently moved to this area. You get a warm and genuine welcome in this grand residence that they have called 'La Bourgeoise', after the mountain where they used to live. The two rooms are large and decorated in the theme 'Sea and Mountains' using old skis and paintings from their grandparents. The rooms are well equipped and there is a large garden. It would be a pity not to take dinner here, as they offer a selection of regional dishes using seasonal produce. Just hearing them talk about it made our mouths water.

Price Structure – 2 Bedrooms
'Montagne': television, bathroom, wc, shower, twin beds, single bed: €70 – 2 people €90 – 3 people
'Mer': television, bathroom, wc, double bed: €60

Reduction: 4 nights, children
Capacity: 5 people

Facilities: private parking, garden, lounge, pets not accepted, dinner available, 100% no smoking, hunting, mushroom-picking, hiking, cycling, lake watersports, vineyard 20km, golf course 25km
Fluent English spoken

Directions: Exit 24 Pouilly-en-Auxois from the A6. Then take the D981 to Arnay-le-Duc. As you enter the village, turn left into the Rue de l'Arquebuse and continue straight on into the Rue Claude Guyot, then turn right into the Rue des 3 Tourelles.

21.12 Pouilly-en-Auxois

Location
8km N W of POUILLY-EN-AUXOIS
in: Eguilly, station pick-up on arrival/departure
Railway station: 50km
Airport: Dijon 50km
car essential

Working Farm

Here you will find absolute peace and quiet, not far from the exit from the A6 *autoroute*, at this beautiful farmhouse in the middle of the countryside and with pleasant surroundings. Chantal and Michel offer a warm welcome and, having stopped here once, theirs is an address you will want to hang on to.

Chantal & Michel RANCE
'La Rente d'Eguilly', Eguilly,
21320 POUILLY-EN-AUXOIS
Tel: (0) 3 80 90 83 48 / (0) 615 50 43 35
Fax: (0) 3 80 90 83 48

Facilities: off-street parking, garden, lounge, hosts have pets, pets not accepted, dinner available, 100% no smoking, wheelchair access, closed: 15/11–15/02

Price Structure – 3 Bedrooms and 1 Suite
'Four': shower room, wc, twin beds: €54
ground floor-room 1: along corridor bathroom, wc, washbasin, twin beds: €54
room 2: bathroom, wc, double bed, twin beds: €58 – 2 people €102 – 4 people
suite: lounge, bathroom, wc, washbasin, 2 single beds. En-suite room, double bed: €77 – 2 people €162 – 4 people

Directions: From the A6, exit Pouilly-en-Auxois. Back to Pouilly and cross the village on the D970. After 4.5km, turn left towards Eguilly. Cross the A6 and turn left, then right towards Blancey. The farm is on the left.

Extra Bed: €15
Reduction: 4 nights
Capacity: 12 people

21.03 Semur-en-Auxois

Location
17km E of SEMUR-EN-AUXOIS
in: Flavigny-sur-Ozerain
Railway station: 8km
Airport: Dijon 70km
car essential

Private Home

A superb location. Judith is English and a great cook. You will be surprised to find yourself going downstairs to the bedrooms. They are in a 17th-century convent in the centre of what is considered to be one of the most beautiful medieval villages in France. The view of L'Auxois and the Valley of Alésia is also superb.

Judith LEMOINE
'Couvent des Castafours',
21150 FLAVIGNY-SUR-OZERAIN
Tel: (0) 3 80 96 24 92 / (0) 675 99 45 37
judith.lemoine@wanadoo.fr
http://perso.wanadoo.fr/judith.lemoine/
chambres_d_hotes.htm

Facilities: off-street parking, garden, tv lounge, pets not accepted, babies welcome, free cot, hiking, cycling, fishing
Fluent English spoken

Price Structure – 2 Bedrooms
'Beige': along corridor shower room, wc, double bed: €52,20
'Rose': shower room, wc, twin beds: €54,20

Directions: On the A6, take the exit Bierre-lès-Semur towards Semur. Take the D9 towards Pouillenay and Flavigny. Go to the church and you can see the house below in the courtyard.

Extra Bed: €16,60
Reduction: 7 nights
Capacity: 4 people

21.40 Semur-en-Auxois

Private Home

Location
19km N of SEMUR-EN-AUXOIS
in: Montbard, station pick-up on arrival/departure
Railway station: 1km

A house in a narrow street amid the old houses and walls of the Montbard *quartier*. Guests are lodged in an apartment, independent of Flore's home. A living room with a fireplace, a small kitchen area, a small courtyard and a private garden are all at your disposal. You can choose to have breakfast served in the small kitchen area or in the main house with your host. Cyclists can store their bikes in the basement. There are numerous places to visit within 20km: Fontenay Abbey, Château de Bussy and medieval Semur-en-Auxois.

Flore HUET
20 rue de la Fontaine, 21500 MONTBARD
Tel: (0) 3 80 92 47 77 / (0) 661 13 47 77
Fax: (0) 3 80 92 47 77
flore.huet@wanadoo.fr

Price Structure – 1 Apartment
'Studio': lounge, kitchen, shower room, wc, double bed, single bed (child-size): €50

Extra Bed: €8
Reduction: 2 nights
Capacity: 3 people

Facilities: off-street parking, garden, pets not accepted, babies welcome, free cot, 100% no smoking, closed: 15/11–15/03, hiking, cycling, interesting flora, mushroom-picking 3km, golf course 13km, vineyard 60km
Fluent English spoken

Directions: From Dijon, D905 to Montbard (62km). On reaching the town, at the first set of traffic lights take a sharp right turn up the hill and then the first left turn into Rue de la Fontaine.

58.13 Nevers

Residence of Outstanding Character

Location
30km E of NEVERS
in: Rouy-Osseux, station pick-up on arrival/departure
Railway station: 30km car essential

A superbly restored mill from the 19th century that straddles a river by hillsides and woods. Spacious rooms decorated with Helena's paintings look out over the landscaped garden and grounds. The romantic bedrooms have shower rooms with a separated-off toilet. Breakfast is served in the lounge or on the covered terrace overlooking the river. Helena offers ayurvedic massages and reflexology for the ladies as well as vegetarian meals if desired. A boat is at your disposal too. A great address pushing towards four 'suns'.

Helena SCHRODER
'Moulin des Prés', 58110 ROUY-OSSEUX
Tel: (0) 3 86 60 29 63 Fax: (0) 3 86 60 29 63
nataschaschroder@yahoo.com

Price Structure – 3 Bedrooms
'Bleue': lounge, shower room, wc, double bed: €58
'Rose': lounge, shower room, wc, double bed: €65
'Jaune': lounge, shower room, wc, four-poster double bed: €70

Extra Bed: €15
Reduction: 3 nights
Capacity: 6 people

Facilities: private parking, garden, lounge, hosts have pets, pets not accepted, dinner available, 100% no smoking, closed: 01/11–31/03, fishing, bird-watching, hiking, interesting flora, riversports, lake watersports 20km, golf course 35km
Fluent English spoken

Directions: From Nevers D978 towards Château-Chinon for 26km to Rouy. In the village, follow the signs 'Ferme Fromagerie', Osseux. Pass in front of the farm and take the first lane on the left.

Location
17km W of NEVERS
in: St-Benin-d'Azy
Railway station: 17km
car essential

**Château/Manor
House**

If you are looking to escape from the hustle and bustle of everyday life, look no further than the Château du Vieil Azy. Here the scream of racing engines at the Magny-Cours circuit (only 17km away) becomes a vague memory. This place has all the style of *la belle France*, whether you are walking beside the lake in the grounds full of ancient trees or relaxing in the library. Be sure to visit Le Palais des Ducs at Nevers.

Facilities: off-street parking, extensive grounds, tv lounge, hosts have pets, dinner available, babies welcome, free cot, closed: 02/11–15/04, hiking, fishing, mushroom-picking, vineyard, golf course 25km
Fluent English spoken

Directions: From Nevers take the D978 towards Autun for about 17km. At St-Benin-d'Azy head towards La Machine and the château is on your left.

**Anne-Elisabeth BENOIST d'AZY
'Château du Vieil Azy', 58270 ST-BENIN-D'AZY
Tel: (0) 3 86 58 47 93 Fax: (0) 3 86 58 50 82**

Price Structure – 5 Bedrooms
'Suite Brière': shower, bathroom, wc, double bed, twin beds: €92,40 – 2 people €184,80 – 4 people
'Suite Vogué': telephone, shower, bathroom, wc, double bed, single bed: €92,40 – 2 people €139,70 – 3 people
'Suite Surville': telephone, bathroom, wc, shower, double bed, twin beds: €92,40 – 2 people €184,80 – 4 people
'Jallerange': telephone, bathroom, wc, twin beds: €88
'Germiny': telephone, bathroom, wc, twin beds: €88

Extra Bed: €25
Reduction: 4 nights, children
Capacity: 15 people

Location
25km N E of NEVERS
in: St-Saulge
Railway station: 25km
Airport: 35km
car essential

Private Home

Marie-France is a writer who opens her spacious country house to you, overlooking woodland gardens. She spares no effort to ensure you feel good and relax. Only 40km from the Magny-Cours motor-racing circuit. Well worth the detour.

Facilities: private parking, extensive grounds, tv lounge, pets not accepted, dinner available, wheelchair access, 2 nights minimum stay: 1/07–31/08, closed: 01/01–31/01, hiking, cycling, lake watersports 5km, fishing 12km
Fluent English spoken

Directions: In Nevers, take the D978 towards Autun, Dijon, for 10km. Turn left onto the D958 towards St-Saulge where you go towards Jailly. Exit St-Saulge. Follow the signs 'Le Beauvais'.

**Marie-France O'LEARY
'Le Beauvais', 58330 ST-SAULGE
Tel: (0) 3 86 58 29 98 / (0) 611 99 55 42
Fax: (0) 3 86 58 29 97
oleary.mariefrance@orange.fr
www.nomade-de-la-terre.com**

Price Structure – 4 Bedrooms
'Verte': telephone, shower room, wc, double bed: €79
'Bleue': lounge, telephone, bathroom, wc, double bed: €79
'Pêche': along corridor shower room, wc, washbasin, 2 single beds: €52
'Jaune': television, telephone, shower, wc, double bed: €65

Extra Bed: €15
Reduction: 2 nights, groups, children
Capacity: 8 people

Burgundy – Nevers

58.12 Nevers

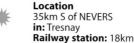

Private Home

Location
35km S of NEVERS
in: Tresnay
Railway station: 18km
Airport: Moulins 18km
car essential

A small peaceful village, a church, meadows and a small lake bordered with bamboo form the backdrop to this farmhouse that once served a château. Jean-Pierre, a retired brewer, spoils you with good seasonal cooking using local produce, notably Charolais beef and lamb. He will even cook your catch from a day's fishing on their small lake (small boat at your disposal). Canal boat trips and walks in the nearby arboretum are possible. Be sure to sample the local apple juice. Magny-Cours racing circuit is 22km away and Moulins 15km.

Martine & Jean-Pierre VERGNE
'La Ferme du Château', 58240 TRESNAY
Tel: (0) 3 86 38 67 74 / (0) 616 17 02 18
JPMGITE@aol.com
http://perso.wanadoo.fr/fermeduchateau

Price Structure – 3 Bedrooms
shower room, wc, double bed, 2 single beds:
€47 – 2 people €87 – 4 people
2 rooms: shower room, wc, twin beds: €47

Extra Bed: €20
Reduction: 4 nights, groups
Capacity: 8 people

Facilities: off-street parking, extensive grounds, tv lounge, dinner available, babies welcome, free cot, wheelchair access, closed: 01–31/01, hiking, cycling, fishing, mushroom-picking, interesting flora 5km, riversports 11km, golf course 22km
Basic English spoken

Directions: From Nevers, take the N7 to Moulins. At approximately 10km after St-Pierre-de-Moutier, turn right and continue to Tresnay. The farm is 100m further on from the church.

71.19 Autun

Residence of Outstanding Character

Location
AUTUN
in: Autun
Railway station: 35km
Airport: Lyon-St Exupéry 190km
car essential

Nadine and Jean-Baptiste both teach at the military high school and have one self-contained room in their 19th-century house, in the heart of the medieval town of Autun, which was also a Roman city. It is in a very quiet street, so you will enjoy breakfast in the garden before setting off on excursions to the Roman churches or the vineyards. On sale: Morvan honey and homemade jam.

Nadine & Jean-Baptiste BRUN
9 rue Aux Raz, 71400 AUTUN
Tel: (0) 3 85 52 36 97 Fax: (0) 3 85 52 36 97
brun.nadine@wanadoo.fr

Price Structure – 1 Bedroom
shower room, wc, double bed, cot: €50

Capacity: 2 people

Facilities: private parking, garden, pets not accepted, dinner available, babies welcome, free cot, 100% no smoking, closed: 10/07–14/08
Adequate English spoken

Directions: At Autun, follow signs to the Centre-Ville and Place du Champ de Mars. The house is in the street behind the 'Lycée Bonaparte' (the building with a large iron gate). As their street is a cul-de-sac, parking is easy.

71.34 Autun

Location
20km E of AUTUN
in: Epinac
Railway station: 40km
Airport: Dijon 70km
car essential

Private Home

A kind couple who have used their savoir faire and good taste to restore this 18th-century farmhouse offering spacious guest rooms. They delight in antique fairs and flea markets to hone the décor which is elegant and romantic (period furniture, toile de Jouy, *tommette* tiles, canopies.). Cooking is also one of Françoise's favourite pastimes! She serves a 'terroir' menu of regional dishes or her 'comme chez soi' menu based on the the best buys from the market that day. They can also accompany you to sample local wines.

Facilities: private parking, extensive grounds, tv lounge, pets not accepted, internet access, dinner available, babies welcome, free cot, 100% no smoking, wheelchair access, closed: 01/11–01/04, hunting, fishing, mushroom-picking, hiking, cycling, vineyard 15km, golf course 18km
Basic English spoken

Directions: Please contact your host in advance for detailed directions.

Françoise CORNILLE
'Le Pré du Monestoy', 7 rue de la Fontaine
Bonhomme, Grandvaux, 71360 EPINAC
Tel: (0) 3 85 82 94 40 / (0) 624 83 58 15
Fax: (0) 3 85 82 94 40
contact@le-pre-du-monestoy.com
www.le-pre-du-monestoy.com

Price Structure – 2 Bedrooms and 1 Suite
'Adelaïde': bathroom, wc, double bed. En-suite room, wc, single bed: €70 – 2 people €115 – 3 people
'Eugénie': wheelchair access, lounge, television, shower room, wc, double bed (queen-size): €95
'Hortense': shower room, wc, double bed (queen-size), single bed: €80 – 2 people €95 – 3 people

Capacity: 8 people

Burgundy – Autun

71.31 Autun

Location
45km S W of AUTUN
in: Issy-l'Evêque, station pick-up on arrival/departure
Railway station: 12km
car essential

Residence of Outstanding Character

An attractive 18th-century residence with its façade reflected in the waters of a lake, by the Parc Naturel du Morvan, in a region known for quality beef and Roman sites. The three independent bedrooms are in the far end of the house with a contemporary feel, attractive wooden floors, reclining beds and spacious bathrooms. A delicious breakfast, with a selection of *viennoiseries* and different types of bread, satisfies even the most greedy. There is a swimming pool by a quiet terrace and a summer kitchen. A friendly welcome.

Facilities: private parking, extensive grounds, lounge, hosts have pets, pets not accepted, dinner available, kitchen, babies welcome, free cot, 100% no smoking, private swimming pool, fishing, mushroom-picking, hiking, cycling
Adequate English spoken

Directions: From Autun N81 towards Moulins for 34km to Luzy. 3km after Luzy take the D25 on the left to Issy-l'Evêque. The house is on the right at the exit to the village, direction Geugnon.

Dominique & Léon-Michel SESTER
'Les Grandes Taupières', 71760 ISSY-L'EVEQUE
Tel: (0) 3 85 24 97 20 Fax: (0) 3 85 24 97 20
dominique.sester@tiscali.fr

Price Structure – 3 Bedrooms
lounge, shower room, wc, twin beds, single bed (child-size), cot: €55 – 2 people €75 – 3 people
lounge, bathroom, wc, twin beds: €55
lounge, bathroom, wc, double bed (queen-size), single bed (child-size): €55 – 2 people
€75 – 3 people

Extra Bed: €20
Reduction: 5 nights, groups
Capacity: 8 people

71.37 Autun

Private Home

Location
16km N of AUTUN
in: Lucenay-l'Evêque
Railway station: 15km
Airport: Dijon 70km
car essential

Marion & Jérôme NIERKENS
'La Mortaise', Mortaise,
71540 LUCENAY-L'EVEQUE
Tel: (0) 3 85 82 61 86
contact@mortaise.com
www.mortaise.com

Price Structure – 3 Bedrooms
and 1 Apartment
'La Rose': shower room, wc, twin beds: €55
'La Tulipe': shower room, wc, double bed (queen-size), single bed: €55 – 2 people €65 – 3 people
'L'Iris': bathroom, wc, shower, double bed (queen-size): €55
'Villa Paulette': kitchen, bathroom, wc, shower, double bed, twin beds: €100 – 2 people
€120 – 4 people

Capacity: 11 people

Marion, Jérôme and their two young boys left the Netherlands to settle in France and then decided to welcome guests to their home in their new region. The bedrooms are in a separate building, surrounded by a superb garden with a pool and games for the children. You hosts are keen cyclists and walkers so can advise on that or other matters over a chat in their lounge. The plentiful breakfast includes Dutch cheese, and as Jérôme is a *cordon bleu* cook he combines local produce and a Dutch influence in his dinners, so be sure to book.

Facilities: off-street parking, extensive grounds, lounge, pets not accepted, dinner available, babies welcome, free cot, 100% no smoking, 3 nights minimum stay: 1/07–31/08, closed: 1/11–30/03, private swimming pool, fishing, hiking, cycling, golf course 15km, vineyard 30km
Fluent English spoken

Directions: Please contact your hosts for detailed directions.

21.45 Autun

Jacques GRENEU

Location
45km S of AUTUN
in: Monceau-les-Mines
car essential

'Au Fil de l'Eau', 71300 MONTCEAU-LES-MINES
Tel: (0) 672 51 62 91
jacques.greneu@wanadoo.fr
www.penichevoyage.fr

Price Structure – 4 Bedrooms
4 rooms: shower room, wc, twin beds, single bed:
€73 – 2 people €108 – 3 people

Reduction: groups
Capacity: 12 people

A fantastic opportunity. . . B&B on a barge! A particularly original and exciting way to discover the charms of the Canal du Centre. A unique opportunity to gently experience the tranquillity of the countryside. Inside, the boat has been carefully organised and offers four comfortable, cosy cabins (all standard boat sizes but the ones at the stern are more spacious), equipped with two sailor bunkbeds (120 and 90cm). There is also a pleasant lounge with a bookcase, a piano and a dining area decorated with fluvial frescos. An especially pleasant welcome for a stay quite literally off the beaten track!

Facilities: lounge, dinner available, kitchen, 10 years old minimum age
Basic English spoken

Directions: Telephone your hosts to find out in which port they are moored when you plan to stay.

58.10 Autun

Location
28km S W of AUTUN
in: Poil-Luzy
Railway station: 15km
car essential

Working Farm

Well worth the many detours to get there, you will finally discover this château lost in the heart of the Morvan National Park. It nestles amongst the trees, almost forgotten by time. Here, life runs at the rhythm of the seasons, and is determined by rearing the ewes and grazing the cows. You may find the interior of the château and the bedrooms a little basic, but this is more than offset by the charm of this place and the even more enchanting welcome of Marina and Olivier, a Belgian couple, whose kindness and welcome are just so genuine.

Marina & Olivier NEERMAN
'Château de Pierrefitte', Pierrefitte,
58170 POIL-LUZY
Tel: (0) 3 86 30 48 37 / (0) 698 87 48 37
Fax: (0) 3 86 30 45 42
neerman.o@wanadoo.fr
www.pierrefitte.net

Facilities: private parking, extensive grounds, lounge, hosts have pets, dinner available, babies welcome, free cot, wheelchair access, private swimming pool, hiking, fishing, hunting, mushroom-picking, lake watersports 10km, cycling 20km, winter sports 20km, vineyard 30km, riversports 40km
Adequate English spoken

Price Structure – 3 Bedrooms
'Terrasse': shower room, wc, double bed: €69
'Bleue': shower room, wc, double bed, single bed, cot: €72 – 2 people €82 – 3 people
'Blanche': shower room, wc, double bed: €59

Extra Bed: €8
Reduction: 7 nights, groups, children
Capacity: 7 people

Directions: From Autun, take the N81 towards Luzy, then as you leave Maison de Bourgogne, take the D192 on the right. At Poil, keep following signs to 'Pierrefitte–fromages fermiers' for 6km.

71.18 Chalon-sur-Saône

Location
20km S of CHALON-SUR-SAONE
in: La Chapelle-de-Bragny
Railway station: 27km
car essential

Private Home

In this sleepy old village, between the church and the château, you will receive a friendly welcome from France, Jean-Pierre and their two small dogs. They are interesting hosts: France is Canadian and they both taught languages, largely overseas, before they retired. They have a large flat ideal for families. You also have the use of a room which serves as a laundry and gym. If you wish to listen to music, watch TV or read, their lounge is also available. In the summer, breakfast is served in the walled garden, a haven of shade and calm.

France & Jean-Pierre JOUVIN
'L'Arcane', 71240 LA CHAPELLE-DE-BRAGNY
Tel: (0) 3 85 92 25 31 / (0) 689 96 75 51
jpf.jouvin@wanadoo.fr
www.larcane.com

Facilities: garden, tv lounge, hosts have pets, babies welcome, free cot, 100% no smoking, cycling, riversports, fishing, mushroom-picking, hiking, lake watersports, vineyard
Fluent English spoken

Price Structure – 1 Apartment
'Apartment': television, kitchen, shower room, wc, double bed. Along corridor room, bathroom, wc, twin beds. Along corridor room, double bed: €50 – 2 people €150 – 6 people

Capacity: 6 people

Directions: Exit 26 Chalon-Sud from the A6. Take the N6 towards Mâcon and then the D6 on the right for Chapelle-de-Bragny. The house is 200m from the church.

71.36 Chalon-sur-Saône

Château/Manor House

Bernard PETITJEAN
'Le Clos des Tourelles', rue de la République,
71240 SENNECEY-LE-GRAND
Tel: (0) 3 85 44 83 95 Fax: (0) 3 85 44 90 18
info@leclosdestourelles.fr
www.leclosdestourelles.fr

Price Structure – 7 Bedrooms and 1 Suite
'Georgina' & 'Victoria': lounge, bathroom, wc, four-poster double bed: €156
'Emily': telephone, bathroom, wc, double bed: €96
'Elisabeth': telephone, bathroom, wc, double bed. En-suite room, bathroom, 3 single beds: €255 – 5 people
'Natasha': telephone, bathroom, wc, double bed (king-size): €166
'Alexandra': lounge, telephone, bathroom, wc, twin beds: €156
plus 2 rooms

Extra Bed: €10
Reduction: 1/10–1/04   **Capacity:** 19 people

Location
17km S of CHALON-SUR-SAONE
in: Sennecey-le-Grand, station pick-up on arrival/departure
Railway station: 15km
Airport: Lyon-St Exupéry 130km

This property consists of several elements: an 18th-century château where guests reside, a 15th-century manor house where the owners currently live and an impressive 11th-century tower which occasionally serves as a reception area for small groups. The furniture dates largely back to the 19th century, some of it recovered from the cellars and lofts of the château. The vast sitting room is pleasant and bright. Breakfast can be served in several locations including the notable semi-circular veranda. The bedrooms are spacious and nicely laid-out.

Facilities: off-street parking, extensive grounds, tv lounge, hosts have pets, internet access, babies welcome, free cot, closed: 1/01–31/01, hunting, fishing, mushroom-picking, bird-watching, hiking, interesting flora, vineyard, golf course 15km, riversports 15km
Adequate English spoken

Directions: Please contact your host in advance for detailed directions.

71.33 Mâcon

Private Home

Christine & Grahame TAYLOR
'La Grange Fleurie', Le Bourg, 71520 TRAMAYES
Tel: (0) 3 85 50 59 36 Fax: (0) 3 85 50 59 36
grangefleurie@wanadoo.fr
www.lagrangefleurie.fr

Price Structure – 6 Bedrooms and 1 Apartment
'Coquelicot' & 'Delphinium': shower room, wc, double bed: €65
'Anémone': shower room, wc, four-poster double bed: €65
'Lys': shower room, wc, 2 single beds: €65
'Tournesol': shower room, wc, double bed, 2 single beds: €95 – 4 people
'Tulipe': shower room, wc, double bed, single bed: €80 – 3 people
apartment 'Rose': wheelchair access, lounge, kitchen, shower room, wc, double bed, 2 single beds: €100 – 4 people

Extra Bed: €15   **Reduction:** 1/11–29/02, 3 nights, groups   **Capacity:** 19 people

Location
35km W of MACON
in: Tramayes
Railway station: 20km
Airport: Lyon-St Exupéry 85km
car essential

Christine and Grahame, a British couple with a background in floral arts, undertook the renovation of this large house dating back to 1837. They have not diminished its character and rustic charm. Choose from six pretty, floral-themed bedrooms. The apartment on the ground floor has been designed for persons of limited mobility. Breakfast is served in the vast lounge with a beautiful panorama of the valley. Discover Roman churches and Cluny or simply enjoy the peaceful countryside. Or, better still, one of Christine's painting courses!

Facilities: private parking, garden, tv lounge, hosts have pets, dinner available, babies welcome, free cot, 100% no smoking, wheelchair access, hiking, cycling, fishing 3km, lake watersports 3km, vineyard 5km, interesting flora 10km, golf course 18km
Fluent English spoken

Directions: A6, exit 29 Mâcon-Sud, direction Cluny. N79, for 22km. D95 on the right to Tramayes (11km). The house is near to the town on the right in the direction of Brandon.

Location
40km N of AVALLON
in: Annay-sur-Serein
Railway station: 17km
car essential

Residence of Outstanding Character

A medieval style *maison bourgeoise* dating back to the 16th century, in a quiet village between the vines and the valley. The bedrooms, in a wing of the house with an independent entrance, all differ but have exposed beams, wooden floors and flagstones from Burgundy. Relax by the fireplace or on the terrace in the enclosed courtyard. The ambience is relaxed, pleasant and a touch bohemian. Pascal and Rose-Marie offer gastronomic menus from regional produce and more exotic flavours. The dog Léon is a hit with guests!

Rose-Marie & Pascal GASTEBOIS
'Chambres et Tables d'Hôtes de la Vallée', 35 Grande Rue, 89310 ANNAY-SUR-SEREIN
Tel: (0) 3 86 82 63 98 Fax: (0) 3 86 82 63 98
valleeduserein@yahoo.fr
http://valleeduserein.free.fr

Facilities: private parking, garden, lounge, hosts have pets, dinner available, babies welcome, free cot, closed: 15/11–31/03, fishing, hiking, vineyard 17km
Adequate English spoken

Price Structure – 4 Bedrooms
'Camel': shower room, wc, double bed, 2 single beds: €45 – 2 people €75 – 4 people
'Bleue': shower room, wc, double bed, single bed: €45 – 2 people €60 – 3 people
'Capri': shower room, wc, washbasin, double bed: €45
'Verte': shower room, wc, washbasin, double bed, single bed: €45 – 2 people €60 – 3 people

Capacity: 12 people

Directions: From Auxerre, A6 motorway to Lyon, first exit 21 to Nitry. Then the D944 and the D49 direction Noyers to Puits-de-Bon followed by a small road on the left, direction Annay. The house is on the high street that crosses the village.

Location
18km S E of AVALLON
in: Bussières, station pick-up on arrival/departure
Railway station: 37km
car essential

Château/Manor House

Your hosts are full of enthusiasm! They have bought this pretty longhouse and they have renovated the barn which boasts a lounge with exposed beams, internet access and a lovely terrace – very cute and comfortable. Watch your head entering the bedrooms which are a little small but offer everything you need. They have two horses that roam freely in the field opposite. Plenty of walks and bridle paths to explore. A great welcome from hosts who are always available and on hand to make your stay as pleasurable as possible.

Martine GOICHON
'Les Champs Cordois', 46 route de Rouvray, 89630 BUSSIERES
Tel: (0) 3 86 33 01 31 / (0) 620 42 89 63
Fax: (0) 3 86 33 15 66
les.champs.cordois@wanadoo.fr
www.les-champs-cordois.com

Facilities: off-street parking, extensive grounds, tv lounge, hosts have pets, pets not accepted, internet access, dinner available, babies welcome, free cot, 100% no smoking, mushroom-picking, hiking, fishing 1km, riversports 20km, lake watersports 20km, vineyard 20km
Fluent English spoken

Price Structure – 2 Suites
'Sully': bathroom, wc, shower, double bed. En-suite room, 2 single beds: €65 – 2 people €95 – 4 people
'Beauvilliers': shower room, wc, double bed. En-suite room, 2 single beds: €65 – 2 people €95 – 4 people

Extra Bed: €15
Reduction: groups
Capacity: 8 people

Directions: Please contact your host in advance for detailed directions.

Burgundy – Avallon

89.04 Avallon

✺ ✺ ✺ ✺

Château/Manor House

Location
13km E of AVALLON
in: Ste-Magnance
Railway station: 35km

Bienvenue en France

Martine COSTAILLE
'Château Jaquot', 2 rue d'Avallon,
89420 STE-MAGNANCE
Tel: (0) 3 86 33 00 22

Price Structure – 1 Bedroom
lounge, shower room, wc, double bed, 2 single beds:
€120 – 2 people €200 – 4 people

Extra Bed: €15
Capacity: 4 people

Impressive. Be ready to step back in time to the 14th century. Martine has restored her home down to the smallest detail. She doesn't go as far as meeting you in period dress but we wouldn't rule it out. The garden full of spices feels authentic and in the large fireplace in the living room, chickens are roasted on a spit as they were seven centuries ago. The comfortable bedroom is well laid out with low lighting in keeping with the ambience. A real treat for history lovers. Dinner is also anything but ordinary.

Facilities: private parking, extensive grounds, lounge, hosts have pets, dinner available, 100% no smoking, hiking, interesting flora, mushroom-picking, fishing 25km, hunting 25km, riversports 25km, vineyard 35km
Adequate English spoken

Directions: From the A6, take the exit to Avallon. Then join the N6 and turn left towards Saulieu. You can see the château as you arrive at Ste-Magnance.

89.17 Vézelay

✺ ✺ ✺

Château/Manor House

Location
1km E of VEZELAY
in: St-Père-sous-Vézelay, station pick-up on arrival/departure
Railway station: 10km
car essential

Bienvenue en France

Dominique ARMENGAUD-CARREZ
'Val en Sel', 1 chemin de la Fontaine,
89450 ST PERE-SOUS-VEZELAY
Tel: (0) 3 86 33 26 95 / (0) 680 33 33 01
Fax: (0) 3 86 33 26 95
valensel@aol.com
valensel.vezelay.free.fr

Price Structure – 2 Bedrooms, 1 Suite and 1 Apartment
'Bleue': shower room, wc, double bed: €80
'Jaune': bathroom, wc, twin beds: €80
'Rouge': lounge, television, kitchen, bathroom, wc, double bed: €80
suite 'Aux Voûtes': shower room, wc, double bed. En-suite room, twin beds: €80 – 2 people €130 – 4 people

Reduction: 5 nights   **Capacity:** 10 people

Down below the town of Vézelay, this charming 18th-century house has been in the same family for generations. A stream runs around the edge of the property, which is surrounded by enclosed gardens where the scent of roses, hydrangeas and lavender mingle. The rooms are beautifully decorated and contain prints and antique furniture. St-Père is renowned for its gastronomic restaurant. On sale: Vézelay wine and locally produced walnut oil.

Facilities: off-street parking, extensive grounds, tv lounge, hosts have pets, kitchen, babies welcome, free cot, closed: 12/11–15/04, hiking, cycling, riversports, vineyard, mushroom-picking 2km, lake watersports 20km, golf course 40km
Fluent English spoken

Directions: At Vézelay, take the D958 towards St-Père for 1km. Go through St-Père and at the first junction, turn right towards Cerbigny. Pass in front of the church, continuing until the last house on the right, alongside which runs a street. 'Val en Sel' is in this sreet, on the left with a white gate.

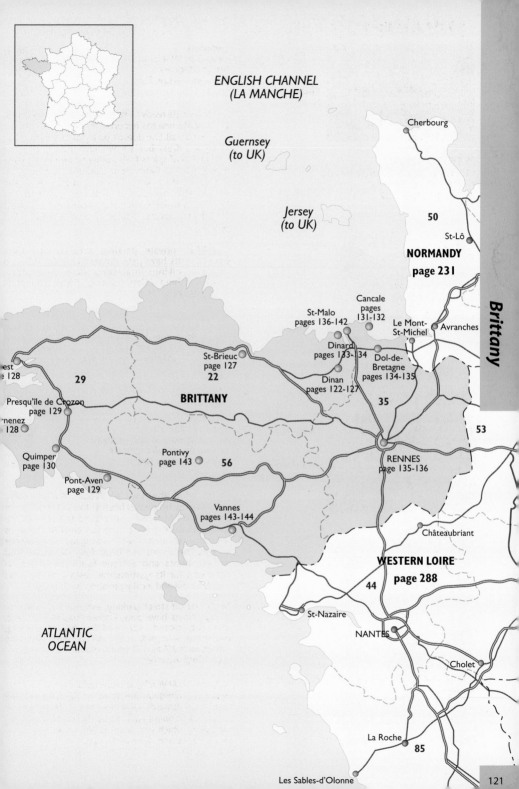

ENGLISH CHANNEL
(LA MANCHE)

Guernsey
(to UK)

Jersey
(to UK)

Cherbourg

50

St-Lô

NORMANDY
page 231

Avranches

Cancale
pages
131-132

St-Malo
pages 136-142

Le Mont-
St-Michel

Dinard
pages 133-34

Dol-de-
Bretagne
pages 134-135

St-Brieuc
page 127

Dinan
pages 122-127

29

22

35

53

BRITTANY

Presqu'île de Crozon
page 129

est
e 128

nenez
128

Quimper
page 130

Pontivy
page 143

56

RENNES
page 135-136

Pont-Aven
page 129

Vannes
pages 143-144

Châteaubriant

WESTERN LOIRE
page 288

44

St-Nazaire

NANTES

Cholet

ATLANTIC
OCEAN

La Roche

85

Les Sables-d'Olonne

22.02 Dinan

Residence of Outstanding Character

Sylvie RONSSERAY
'Le Logis du Jerzual', 25-27 rue du Petit Fort,
22100 DINAN
Tel: (0) 2 96 85 46 54 Fax: (0) 2 96 39 46 94
ronsseray@wanadoo.fr
www.logis-du-jerzual.com

Price Structure – 4 Bedrooms
and 1 Apartment
room 1: shower room, wc, four-poster double bed:
€85
'Husbeck': shower room, wc, double bed, twin beds:
€85 – 2 people €125 – 4 people
'Perse': shower room, wc, double bed: €75
'Pastorale': bathroom, wc, shower, double bed: €75
'La Halte': kitchen, shower room, wc, double bed
(king-size): €85

Extra Bed: €20
Capacity: 12 people

Location
DINAN
in: Dinan
Railway station: 1km
Airport: Dinard St-Malo 12km

A real gem. This house has been featured in many magazines. Although the architecture is impressive and rooted in local history, your hosts, who work for the Ministry of Historic Monuments, are even more interesting and welcoming. The house is near the yacht harbour, in the heart of the old town, which is a protected site. There are 5,000m^2 of terraced gardens, with an outstanding view over the old harbour. Credit cards accepted.

Facilities: garden, tv lounge, hosts have pets, kitchen, golf course 15km, sea watersports 15km
Fluent English spoken

Directions: From the port of Dinan, the street is opposite the old bridge. The car park is 150m higher up on the right. The Rue du Petit Fort is accessible by car in both directions. Stop by the sign, in front of the steps.

22.53 Dinan

Residence of Outstanding Character

Béatrice LEBOULANGER
'La Villa Côté Cour', 10 rue Lord Kitchener,
22100 DINAN
Tel: (0) 2 96 39 30 07
contact@villa-cote-cour-dinan.com
http://www.villa-cote-cour.fr

Price Structure – 4 Bedrooms
'Harmonie' & 'Vitalité': television, shower room, wc,
double bed (king-size): €95
'Evasion': television, bathroom, wc, double bed
(king-size): €140
'Suite Renaissance': lounge, television, bathroom, wc,
double bed (queen-size), single bed (child-size):
€180 – 2 people €200 – 3 people

Extra Bed: €20
Reduction: 1/10–31/03, 4 nights, groups
Capacity: 9 people

Location
DINAN
in: Dinan, station pick-up on
arrival/departure
Railway station: Dinan
Airport: Dinard St-Malo 12km

In the heart of Dinan, this *Maison de Maître* offers impeccable facilities. The spacious bedrooms are reached by an attractive wooden staircase. The beautiful bathrooms have jacuzzi-style baths or showers (two-person bath in the suite). Quality spa products and your own internet point too. Beatrice, native to the region, serves a healthy breakfast and offers a carefully selected collection of teas and coffees. Breakfast is taken in the conservatory, once an artist's workshop. A smiling and discreet welcome

Facilities: private parking, garden, tv lounge, hosts have pets, pets not accepted, internet access, babies welcome, free cot, 100% no smoking, 2 nights minimum stay, cycling, sea watersports, hiking 1km golf course 20km
Fluent English spoken

Directions: From Dinan town centre, head towards 'la Gare', and then take the road opposite the station. The house is in this road, 200m further on, on the left-hand side.

Location
22km S E of DINAN
in: Jugon-les-Lacs
Railway station: 15km
Airport: Dinard St-Malo 27km

Private Home

Jugon is a little character settlement with houses in granite and a central square that hints at its past defensive history. By a natural lake, it is one of the most engaging places in Brittany. This house stands on the site of a former mill on the edge of the village, facing woodland. The stream still passes under the house and down the small garden of flowers to the village. The pastel bedrooms boast large beds. Justin, a former chef in top restaurants, strives with Louise to make you welcome. Babysitting possible.

Louise & Justin HIGGENS
'Le Val de l'Arguenon', 1 rue de la Petite Chaussée, 22270 JUGON-LES-LACS
Tel: (0) 2 96 31 71 47
jlhiggens@aol.com

Facilities: off-street parking, garden, lounge, hosts have pets, pets not accepted, dinner available, kitchen, babies welcome, free cot, 2 nights minimum stay: 01/07–31/08, closed: 01/10–01/04, fishing, bird-watching, cycling, riversports, golf course 5km, sea watersports 20km
Fluent English spoken

Price Structure – 4 Bedrooms
2 rooms: shower room, wc, double bed: €62
shower room, wc, 2 single beds: €62
bathroom, wc, shower, double bed: €62

Extra Bed: €13
Reduction: 3 nights, groups
Capacity: 8 people

Directions: Jugon-les-Lacs is on the fast road between Lamballe (17km) and Dinan (22km). At Jugon, take the D792 towards Plénée-Jugon. The house is on the left at the last crossroads just before the end of the village.

Brittany – Dinan

Location
10km W of DINAN
in: La Landec
Airport: Dinard St-Malo 20km
car essential

Working Farm

On the way from Dinan to St-Brieuc, this is an old stone farmhouse with lots of character, near a lake. Quiet and rural but handy for Dinan. Beautifully decorated with hanging flower baskets. There is a riding centre nearby. A great place to relax, and less than half an hour from Le Mont-St-Michel and St-Malo.

Pierre & Yvonne JOUFFE
'Le Chesnay-Chel', 22980 LA LANDEC
Tel: (0) 2 96 27 65 89

Facilities: off-street parking, garden, tv lounge, hosts have pets, dinner available, kitchen, hiking, cycling, fishing, golf course 5km, sea watersports 15km

Price Structure – 3 Bedrooms
first room: shower room, wc, double bed, single bed: €40 – 2 people €48 – 3 people
second room: shower room, wc, double bed: €40
third room: bathroom, wc, double bed, single bed: €40 – 2 people €48 – 3 people

Extra Bed: €8
Capacity: 8 people

Directions: In Dinan take the N176 towards St-Brieuc. At the crossroads, do not follow the sign for La Landec, but take the opposite direction. After 1km you will see a sign to the farm.

22.09 Dinan

Private Home

Jean POMMERET
'La Gravelle', 22690 PLEUDIHEN-SUR-RANCE
Tel: (0) 2 96 83 20 82 / (0) 678 97 74 69
www.chambres-gravelle-saint-malo.com

Location
10km N E of DINAN
in: Pleudihen-sur-Rance, station
pick-up on arrival/departure
Railway station: 10km
Airport: Dinard St-Malo 18km
car essential

A stone farmhouse in a pretty hamlet, in pleasant surroundings with lots of flowers. Friendly Madame Pommeret will give you an excellent, warm welcome and ensure you are well looked after in her clean rooms. Ideal for an overnight stop or a longer stay to explore this part of Brittany.

Price Structure – 5 Bedrooms
3 rooms: washbasin, double bed: €45
shower room, wc, double bed, 2 single beds:
€45 – 2 people €65 – 4 people
shower room, wc, double bed: €45

Extra Bed: €8
Capacity: 12 people

Facilities: off-street parking, garden, pets not accepted, 100% no smoking, 2 shared bathrooms, wc, 2 years old minimum age, golf course 5km, sea watersports 15km

Directions: Go through the centre of Dinan following the signs Rennes, Caen. Continue for 6km, then turn left onto the D29 towards Pleudihen. Go past the church and the cemetery. Turn right at the crossroads and follow the signs for 'Camping La Vilger'.

22.45 Dinan

Private Home

Isabelle & Patrick PALHIERE-NORIS
'La Chataigneraie', Les Rouchiviers,
22690 PLEUDIHEN-SUR-RANCE
Tel: (0) 2 96 88 29 64 / (0) 603 77 03 74
lachataigneraie@hotmail.com
www.bretagne-hebergement.com

Location
10km N E of DINAN
in: Pleudihen-sur-Rance, station
pick-up on arrival/departure
Ferry port: 19km
Airport: Dinard St-Malo 20km
car essential

This old farmhouse dating from the 19th century happily combines the rural atmosphere of a typical Breton hamlet with the pleasures of the sea. Stroll on the beaches of St-Malo or follow the footpaths beside the River Rance. Sometimes Isabelle organises themed weekends, or tempts you with her delicious local specialities.

Price Structure – 3 Bedrooms
'Oxica': shower room, wc, double bed, twin beds,
single bed (child-size): €64 – 2 people
€105 – 5 people
'Oregane': shower room, wc, double bed (king-size),
single bed (child-size): €64 – 2 people
€78 – 3 people
'Osara': shower room, wc, 4 single beds:
€64 – 2 people €93 – 4 people

Reduction: 4 nights, groups
Capacity: 12 people

Facilities: private parking, extensive grounds, tv lounge, pets not accepted, dinner available, 100% no smoking, 2 nights minimum stay, hiking, cycling, fishing, interesting flora, mushroom-picking, golf course 8km, sea watersports 20km
Fluent English spoken

Directions: At St-Malo, N137 as far as Châteauneuf-d'Ille-et-Vilaine. Then D29 to Pleudihen-sur-Rance. When you are facing the church, follow signs to 'Val Hervelin'. Straight on for 2km. Continue towards Les Rouchiviers, turning left at the second fork. 'La Chataigneraie' is the first house on the left as you enter the village.

Location
10km N E of DINAN
In: Pleudihen-sur-Rance, station
pick-up on arrival/departure
Railway station: 4km
Airport: Dinard St-Malo 20km

Bienvenue en France

Private Home

Halfway between two towns full of character, Dinan and Dol-de-Bretagne, is this authentic Breton longhouse dating back to 1881. The large aloe plants in front of the house testify to the mildness of the climate in this part of Brittany. Annick and Jacques have retired from farming to devote themselves to their guests. The garden has a lawn and tables with parasols where you can picnic or make use of the barbecue and the small kitchen area. A washing machine and a tumble dryer are also at your disposal and there are games for the children.

Annick & Jacques DUVAL
'Le Grand Gain', Launay-Mousson, Le Val
Hervelin, 22690 PLEUDIHEN-SUR-RANCE
Tel: (0) 2 96 83 21 63 / (0) 619 04 86 86
Fax: (0) 2 96 83 21 63
dbparty@free.fr
www.legrandgain.com

Facilities: private parking, extensive grounds, tv lounge, kitchen, babies welcome, free cot, hunting 2km, fishing 2km, mushroom-picking 2km, hiking 2km, sea watersports 3km, golf course 6km
Basic English spoken

Price Structure – 4 Bedrooms
2 rooms: shower room, wc, double bed, single bed:
€48 – 2 people €60 – 3 people
along corridor bathroom, wc, double bed: €48
wheelchair access, shower room, wc, double bed:
€48

Directions: Travel through the centre of Dinan following the signs to Rennes and Caen. Continue straight ahead for 6km then left towards Le Val Hervelin and then right straight away. Signed 'Le Grand Gain'.

Extra Bed: €12
Reduction: 01/01–01/03
Capacity: 10 people

Location
10km N E of DINAN
In: Pleudihen-sur-Rance, station
pick-up on arrival/departure
Railway station: 20km
Airport: Dinard St-Malo 20km
Car essential

Bienvenue en France

Private Home

Between St-Malo and Dinan, tucked away in a peaceful town on the River Rance, is this house on a small courtyard with several other local-style granite buildings dating back to the 19th century. Inside, the traditional rustic Breton furnishings are in keeping with the style of the house. Behind is a maze of cobbled streets that lead to a large park on the hillside with a lovely scenic viewpoint of the Rance estuary and the countryside. For breakfast enjoy homemade jams, cheese and the local speciality: *craquelinantes*.

Thérèse HUE
'La Cour es Meuniers', 6 rue des Camélias,
22690 PLEUDIHEN-SUR-RANCE
Tel: (0) 2 96 83 34 23 / (0) 667 78 69 03
Fax: (0) 2 96 83 34 23
therese.hue@wanadoo.fr
www.lacouresmeuniers.com

Facilities: off-street parking, extensive grounds, tv lounge, hosts have pets, pets not accepted, babies welcome, free cot, fishing 2km, hiking 2km, sea watersports 7km, golf course 10km, cycling 10km, riversports 10km
Fluent English spoken

Price Structure – 3 Bedrooms and 3 Suites
'Suite 1': shower room, wc, double bed. En-suite room, single bed: €48 – 2 people €65 – 3 people
'Suite 2': bathroom, wc, double bed. En-suite room, twin beds: €48 – 2 people €82 – 4 people
1 & 2: shower room, wc, double bed: €48
shower room, wc, twin beds: €48
'Suite 3': shower room, wc, twin beds. En-suite room, single bed: €48 – 2 people €72 – 3 people

Directions: From St-Malo, take the fast road N137 towards Rennes, exit at Châteauneuf-d'Ille-et-Vilaine, then follow the D29 towards Pleudihen-sur-Rance. In the village turn right heading for the town hall (*la mairie*) behind the church and head up Rue des Camélias.

Extra Bed: €14
Reduction: 30/09–30/03, 3 nights, groups
Capacity: 16 people

Brittany – Dinan

22.04 Dinan

Private Home

Bienvenue en France

Location
8km N of DINAN
in: Plouër-sur-Rance, station pick-up
on arrival/departure
Railway station: 10km
Airport: Dinard St-Malo 10km
car essential

Suzanne & John ROBINSON
'La Renardais', Le Repos,
22490 PLOUER-SUR-RANCE
Tel: (0) 2 96 86 89 81 Fax: (0) 2 96 86 99 22
suzanne.robinson@wanadoo.fr
http://perso.orange.fr/suzanne.robinson.bnb/

Price Structure – 3 Bedrooms and 1 Suite
shower room, wc, double bed, single bed:
€75 – 2 people €95 – 3 people
shower room, wc, double bed, single bed. En-suite
room, 2 single beds: €75 – 2 people
€150 – 5 people
shower room, wc, twin beds: €75
shower room, wc, double bed, 2 single beds:
€75 – 2 people €115 – 4 people

Extra Bed: €20
Reduction: 01/11–28/02
Capacity: 14 people

This British couple have merged the best of both worlds. Their house and the garden full of flowers is open to you and is really very charming with good comforts and bathrooms. Suzanne and John are very welcoming and have been settled here for 15 years now. They are truly mindful of what a good welcome in a *Maison d'Hôtes* represents. Their passions include watercolour painting, decorating, cuisine and sports. A perfect place from which to visit the Mont-St-Michel, St-Malo, Dinard and the medieval town of Dinan.

Facilities: off-street parking, garden, tv lounge, pets not accepted, 100% no smoking, hunting 1km, fishing 1km, mushroom-picking 1km, hiking 1km, cycling 1km, bird-watching 1km, interesting flora 8km, golf course 8km, gliding 10km
Fluent English spoken

Directions: On the N17b, exit Plouer. D12 direction La Hisse. 'La Renardais' is on the right after 3km.

35.52 Dinan

Residence of Outstanding Character

Bienvenue en France

Location
10km E of DINAN
in: St-Pierre-de-Plesguen
Railway station: 15km
Airport: Rennes St-Jacques 60km
car essential

Régis MAILLARD
'Le Petit Moulin du Rouvre',
35720 ST-PIERRE-DE-PLESGUEN
Tel: (0) 2 99 73 85 84 / (0) 668 80 59 09
maillard.regis@aumoulindurouvre.com
www.aumoulindurouvre.com

Price Structure – 5 Bedrooms
'Meunier' & 'Aurore': television, bathroom, wc,
double bed, single bed: €65 – 2 people
€80 – 3 people
'Romantique' & 'Marine': television, bathroom, wc,
double bed: €65
'Marichal': television, shower room, wc, double bed
(queen-size): €65

Extra Bed: €18
Reduction: 15/10–15/04, 4 nights, groups
Capacity: 12 people

This old watermill dating from the 17th century is surrounded by forest, lakes and fields typical of romantic Brittany, and guarantees total peace and quiet. Régis took over the business from his grandmother and welcomes you as an old friend. As a trained chef he is able to use his skill in the traditional dinners he serves, complemented by skilfully chosen wines. A large living room, a rustic salon and the Breton furniture in the bedrooms all contribute to the unique ambience of this place.

Facilities: off-street parking, extensive grounds, tv lounge, hosts have pets, pets not accepted, dinner available, 100% no smoking, wheelchair access, hiking, cycling, fishing, hunting, mushroom-picking, interesting flora 5km, golf course 15km, sea watersports 30km
Fluent English spoken

Directions: Take the N137 dual carriageway Rennes–St-Malo road and exit at St-Pierre-de-Plesguen. In front of the church at St-Pierre, take the D10 towards Lanhelin and follow the signs for 3 km. From Dinan take the D794 towards Rennes.

Location
10km N of DINAN
In: Trémereuc
Railway station: 15km
Airport: Dinard St-Malo 5km
Car essential

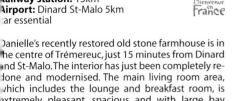

✸ ✸ ✸

Private Home

Danielle's recently restored old stone farmhouse is in the centre of Trémereuc, just 15 minutes from Dinard and St-Malo. The interior has just been completely re-done and modernised. The main living room area, which includes the lounge and breakfast room, is extremely pleasant, spacious and with large bay windows. It is on quite a busy road but inside the house is quiet and a bypass is currently under construction. Your hosts are dedicated to ensuring you have an enjoyable stay, which we are sure they will achieve.

Facilities: private parking, garden, tv lounge, hosts have pets, kitchen, babies welcome, free cot, hiking, golf course, fishing, hunting, sea watersports 8km
Basic English spoken

Danielle CADOT
'Les Colverts', 12 rue de Bel Air,
22490 TREMEREUC
Tel: (0) 2 96 27 17 65 Fax: (0) 2 96 27 17 65
chambres.hotes.cadot@wanadoo.fr

Price Structure – 4 Bedrooms
first room: shower, bathroom, wc, double bed, twin beds: €52 – 2 people €76 – 4 people
2 rooms: along corridor shower room, wc, twin beds: €42
fourth room: bathroom, wc, double bed: €46

Reduction: 4 nights
Capacity: 10 people

Directions: At Dinan, take the D766 towards Dinard. The house is in the centre of Trémereuc.

Location
2km S W of ST-BRIEUC
In: Ploufragan, station pick-up on arrival/departure
Railway station: 3km
Airport: St-Brieuc 8km
Car essential

✸ ✸

Private Home

Marie-Hélène and Lucien, both retired, are always on hand to greet you and welcome you into their contemporary house with a large garden where they will be sure to make you feel at home. Open to you is the lounge, terrace, barbecue and a microwave. Marie-Hélène practises yoga. From this base in the centre of Côtes d'Armor you can easily tour around, visiting the Côte de Granit Rose at Brehat and continuing on to St-Malo and the Mont-St-Michel.

Facilities: off-street parking, extensive grounds, tv lounge, pets not accepted, kitchen, babies welcome, free cot, 100% no smoking, wc, closed: 01/09–30/06, hiking, cycling, fishing 2km, sea watersports 2km, riversports 2km
Adequate English spoken

Marie-Hélène & Lucien CHOUPAUX
11 rue du Tertre de la Motte,
22440 PLOUFRAGAN
Tel: (0) 2 96 78 65 81
choupaux.lucien@wanadoo.fr

Price Structure – 5 Bedrooms
'Diamant': shower room, wc, washbasin, double bed: €49
'Cristal' & 'Rubis': along corridor shower room, wc, washbasin, twin beds: €48
'Saphir': bathroom, wc, double bed: €49
ground floor 'l'Oasis': television, shower room, wc, double bed (queen-size): €52

Extra Bed: €18
Reduction: 4 nights, groups, children
Capacity: 10 people

Directions: In the suburbs of St-Brieuc, head for the centre of Ploufragan then follow signs to 'Zoopole, ZI des Chatelets'. After 500m at the first roundabout follow signs to 'Zoopole, Beaucemaine'. Pass in front of the 'Relais de Beaucemaine' and after 600m take the first road on the left. Signed 'Clévacances'.

29.43 Brest

✸ ✸ ✸ ✸

Residence of Outstanding Character

Stéphane PECOT
'Domaine de Moulin Mer', 34 route de Moulin Mer, 29460 LOGONNA-DAOULAS
Tel: (0) 2 98 07 24 45 / (0) 680 53 62 13
stephane@domaine-moulin-mer.com
www.domaine-moulin-mer.com

Price Structure – 5 Bedrooms
'Suite Rosmorduc': lounge, shower room, wc, double bed (queen-size): €110
'Suite du Roz': lounge, shower room, wc, twin beds: €110
'St-Monna': shower room, wc, double bed (queen-size): €80
'Kersanton': shower room, wc, twin beds: €80
'Ruliver': shower room, wc, double bed: €65

Extra Bed: €30
Reduction: 2 nights
Capacity: 10 people

Location
20km E of BREST
in: Logonna-Daoulas
Railway station: 25km
Airport: Brest 25km

This residence, full of character, was built in the 1920s by an important family in the shellfish fishing business and there are still the remains of the fish store in the grounds. The garden is full of palm trees and an 'island' of bamboo adds an exotic flavour. This place is a haven of peace so close to the sea. Stéphane has renovated the interior, keeping the charm and elegance of the building intact. The bedrooms are pleasant and have been decorated and furnished with care. This is an unusual place with a warm welcome for a relaxing stay.

Facilities: private parking, extensive grounds, tv lounge, hosts have pets, pets not accepted, internet access, dinner available, babies welcome, free cot 100% no smoking, fishing, hiking, sea watersports, golf course 15km, gliding 20km
Fluent English spoken

Directions: From Brest, N165 towards Quimper and turn off to Daoulas. D770 for Daoulas. Cross the village and take the first street on the right after the lights. Continue for 50m. D333 on the left towards Logonna-Daoulas. When you see the village sign, continue for another 500m, turn left and immediately right towards Port-de-Moulin Mer. At the end of this road turn left. The domain is about 600m further on, on a bend.

29.31 Douarnenez

✸ ✸ ✸

Residence of Outstanding Character

Josy & René GUEGUEN GONIDEC
Lanevry, 29100 KERLAZ
Tel: (0) 2 98 92 14 87 / (0) 675 79 63 63
info@lanevry.com
www.lanevry.com

Price Structure – 5 Bedrooms
'Ville d'Ys', 'Yseult', 'Gradlon' & 'Korrigan': shower room, wc, double bed: €56
'Tristan': shower room, wc, 2 single beds: €56

Capacity: 10 people

Location
4km E of DOUARNENEZ
in: Kerlaz
Airport: Quimper 17km
car essential

Several generations live in this attractive family farmhouse although they no longer work the land. You will feel at home in this spacious house. The old farm buildings have been attractively modernised and the courtyard is full of flowers. Regional specialities for breakfast. Your hosts have created a leisure area with hammam, spa etc. (supplement payable).

Facilities: off-street parking, garden, tv lounge, hosts have pets, kitchen
Fluent English spoken

Directions: In Douarnenez, take the D7 towards Châteaulin. Just before Kerlaz take the first road on the left and follow the signs 'chambre d'hôtes'. It is the first farm on the left.

29.41 Pont-Aven

Private Home

Location
18km N of PONT-AVEN
in: Scaër, station pick-up on arrival/departure
Railway station: 40km
Airport: Lorient 40km
car essential

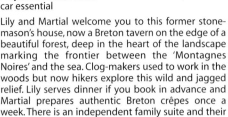
Bienvenue en France

Lily and Martial welcome you to this former stonemason's house, now a Breton tavern on the edge of a beautiful forest, deep in the heart of the landscape marking the frontier between the 'Montagnes Noires' and the sea. Clog-makers used to work in the woods but now hikers explore this wild and jagged relief. Lily serves dinner if you book in advance and Martial prepares authentic Breton crêpes once a week. There is an independent family suite and their friendly bar, frequented by local characters, is open from 11am to 8pm.

Facilities: private parking, tv lounge, pets not accepted, dinner available, babies welcome, free cot, closed: 15/10–31/10, hiking, cycling, fishing, hunting, mushroom-picking, golf course 25km, sea watersports 25km
Basic English spoken

Directions: On the fast road between Quimperlé and Quimper, exit Bannalec. Then head for Scaër on the D4. 2km before Scaër turn left towards 'La forêt de Coat Loach' and follow signs to 'Bar étape de Toul arc'Hoat'.

Lily & Martial LE GALL
'Le Toul arc'Hoat', Forêt de Coat Loch, 29390 SCAER
Tel: (0) 2 98 59 00 77 Fax: (0) 2 98 59 00 77
TOUL.ARCHOAT@wanadoo.fr
www.etape-bretagne.com

Price Structure – 6 Bedrooms
'Amérique','Asie' & 'Afrique': shower room, wc, double bed, single bed: €66 – 2 people €82 – 3 people
'Europe' & 'Océanie': shower room, wc, double bed: €66
'Amérique du Sud': shower room, wc, 2 double beds, single bed: €66 – 2 people €150 – 5 people

Extra Bed: €18
Reduction: 01/09–31/06, 7 nights
Capacity: 18 people

29.44 Presqu'île de Crozon

Private Home

Location
PRESQU'-ILE DE CROZON
in: Camaret-sur-Mer, station pick-up on arrival/departure
Railway station: 55km
Airport: Brest 55km

As we go to press this home has not yet been classified, but will be shortly. Bring your slippers if you decide to stay here. Fill your lungs with the freshest of air from the open sea, which is quite a sight, as this place is at the extremity of the furthest point in Britanny, a place rich in Celtic culture. Or try catamaran sailing, diving or windsurfing. After that there is yoga, a sauna, keep-fit... and for those with slippers, a relaxing evening round the fire. Your hosts are lively, smiling happy people.

Facilities: Off-street parking, garden, tv lounge, hosts have pets, pets not accepted, internet access, dinner available, kitchen, 100% no smoking, 1 shared bathroom, 1 shared shower room, 2wc, 2 nights minimum stay: 15/06-1/10
Fluent English spoken

Directions: Camaret is at the end of the Crozon peninsula.

Karen & Frédéric BAUDRY
'Villa Trouz Ar Mor', B.P.20 Kerloc'h, 29570 CAMARET-SUR-MER
Tel: (0) 2 98 27 83 57 / (0) 609 97 99 87
lesondelamer@trouzarmor.com
www.trouzarmor.com

Price Structure – 5 Bedrooms
1 room: television, bathroom, wc, double bed (queen-size): €70,60
2 rooms: double bed: €55,60
2 rooms: double bed: €60,60

Extra Bed: €18
Reduction: 1/10–15/06, groups, children
Capacity: 10 people

29.11 Quimper

Private Home

Location
12km S of QUIMPER
in: Clohars-Fouesnant-Bénodet,
station pick-up on arrival/departure
Railway station: 13km
Airport: Quimper 14km

Annick QUILFEN
'Kerjaouen', 23 route de Kerouter, Clohars Fouesnant, 29950 BENODET
Tel: (0) 2 98 57 01 86 / (0) 680 93 29 72

Dynamic, generous, happy, pleasant, natural: this is the way in which past guests have described Annick. Two very comfortable rooms in a large modern house. This place is situated 2km from Bénodet, a charming fishing port with many restaurants.

Price Structure – 2 Bedrooms
shower room, wc, double bed: €46
bathroom, wc, double bed: €46

Extra Bed: €16
Capacity: 4 people

Facilities: off-street parking, garden, tv lounge, hiking, cycling, sea watersports 2km

Directions: In Quimper, take the D34 towards Bénodet. Take the second road on the right towards Gouesnac'h (by Bénéteau boats), then left into Route de Kerouter and twice left.

29.42 Quimper

Private Home

Location
15km S E of QUIMPER
in: La Forêt-Fouesnant, station pick-up on arrival/departure
Railway station: 15km
Airport: Quimper 20km

Mesmine & Jean-Charles LE TORTOREC
2 allée du Mesmeur,
29940 LA FORET-FOUESNANT
Tel: (0) 2 98 56 96 95 / (0) 662 05 80 72
jcm.letortorec@wanadoo.fr
www.residences-mimosa.com

A beautiful, peaceful and green setting for this large house that benefits from the charm of an authentic Breton village by the sea. The guest bedroom is spacious, bright and comfortable with a private entrance and a terrace with a view over the bay, where breakfast can be served. By taking the path that runs by the house, you can walk along the coast, past an attractive golf course, yachting marina and a beautiful beach of fine sand. Jean-Charles, a keen navigator, advises on boat trips and how to reach the Iles du Glénant.

Price Structure – 1 Suite
lounge, television, shower room, wc, double bed. En-suite room, single bed: €65 – 2 people
€85 – 3 people

Extra Bed: €15
Reduction: 01/09–30/06, 7 nights
Capacity: 3 people

Facilities: off-street parking, garden, tv lounge, pets not accepted, babies welcome, free cot, 100% no smoking, 2 nights minimum stay, golf course, fishing, hiking, cycling, sea watersports, bird-watching 5km
Fluent English spoken

Directions: Fast road between Lorient and Quimper, exit D44 towards Concarneau, La Forêt-Fouesnant. On arrival at La Forêt-Fouesnant, at the roundabout facing the bay, turn left and then immediately turn right into a small street towards the golf course. First house on the left.

Location
CANCALE
in: Cancale
Railway station: 12km
Airport: Rennes St-Jacques 60km
car essential

Château/Manor House

Myriam and Etienne, who fish for local shellfish, happily welcome you to their Breton manor house of chiselled granite. The bedrooms are reached via a small winding staircase but there is also a lift. They are attractively furnished with typical rustic Cancale wardrobes and Italian marble in the bathrooms. We especially liked the room on the first floor with its impressive fireplace and coat of arms. You will be charmed by the idyllic flower garden and the ducks on the pond. Good local Breton produce is served for breakfast.

Myriam & Etienne CERASY
'Manoir des Douets Fleuris', Les Douets Fleuris, 35260 CANCALE
Tel: (0) 2 23 15 13 81 / (0) 620 07 16 80
Fax: (0) 2 23 15 13 81
manoirdesdouetsfleuris@wanadoo.fr
www.manoirdesdouetsfleuris.com

Facilities: off-street parking, garden, lounge, hosts have pets, babies welcome, free cot, wheelchair access, hiking, cycling, sea watersports 1km, interesting flora 10km, fishing 12km, golf course 30km
Fluent English spoken

Price Structure – 5 Bedrooms
ground floor: wheelchair access, television, bathroom, wc, shower, twin beds: €114
first & second floor: wheelchair access, television, bathroom, wc, shower, double bed (queen-size): €144
'Suite ground floor' & 'Suite first floor': lounge, television, bathroom, wc, shower, double bed (queen-size): €174

Directions: At Cancale take the D355 towards St-Malo for approximately 1km. Just after the hotel 'Le Chatellier' take the road on the right and follow signs to 'Les Douets Fleuris'.

Extra Bed: €17,20
Capacity: 10 people

Location
CANCALE
in: Cancale
Airport: Rennes St-Jacques 50km

Private Home

A perfect stopover, easy to find, on the road that leads to Rennes on the edge of town, yet five minutes on foot from the port via a small lane. Marie-Christine welcomes you to this former oyster farm, now reorganised into gîtes and a B&B. Screened behind hydrangeas, the bedrooms are on the ground floor of an outbuilding. A living room with a kitchen area at your disposal is where breakfast is served. Sit and chat with Marie-Christine in the garden who happily recounts nostalgic tales of family life fishing for oysters.

Marie-Christine MASSON
'La Ville es Gris', 67 rue des Français Libres, 35260 CANCALE
Tel: (0) 8 75 76 12 42 / (0) 660 43 45 05
Fax: (0) 2 99 89 67 27
villeesgris@club-internet.fr
www.gitesetchambresdemer.com

Facilities: off-street parking, garden, tv lounge, hosts have pets, pets not accepted, kitchen, babies welcome, free cot, 100% no smoking, fishing, bird-watching, hiking, sea watersports 5km, golf course 20km
Basic English spoken

Price Structure – 5 Bedrooms
'Le Herpin' & 'Taumain': shower room, wc, double bed: €55
'Rogonde': bathroom, wc, double bed, single bed: €57 – 2 people €67 – 3 people
'Les Landes': shower room, wc, twin beds: €55
'Les Ruets': shower room, wc, double bed, 2 single beds: €57 – 2 people €80 – 4 people

Capacity: 13 people

Directions: Head for the port of Cancale. Continue along the port with the sea on your left.

Brittany – Cancale

35.80 Cancale

Residence of Outstanding Character

Françoise & Michel BUSSON
'La Seigneurie', 35114 ST-BENOIT-DES-ONDES
Tel: (0) 2 99 58 62 96 / (0) 672 43 06 97
contact@la-seigneurie-des-ondes.net
la-seigneurie-des-ondes.net

Price Structure – 1 Suite
and 2 Apartments
'Côté Cour': television, kitchen, bathroom, wc,
double bed. En-suite room, single bed:
€90 – 2 people €100 – 3 people
'Côté Jardin': television, kitchen, shower room, wc,
double bed. En-suite room, 2 single beds:
€110 – 2 people €130 – 4 people
'Grande Cour': television, bathroom, wc, double bed
(queen-size), single bed. En-suite room, double bed:
€130 – 2 people €150 – 5 people

Extra Bed: €10
Reduction: 1/11–28/02
Capacity: 12 people

Location
9km S of CANCALE
in: St-Benoit-des-Ondes, station
pick-up on arrival/departure
Railway station: 10km
Airport: Dinard St-Malo 25km
car essential

Bienvenue en France

In the bay of the Mont-St-Michel, Françoise and Michel will give you a great welcome to their old priory that dates from the 12th century, and whose history is linked to the town of St-Malo. They have one suite and two charming flats. The wood and tasteful décor show real class. Françoise is an antique dealer and has chosen Louis XV and XVI furniture, old embroidered linen sheets and lots of other objects that blend in perfect harmony with the décor. You are welcome to join your hosts in the lounge around the open fire in winter.

Facilities: off-street parking, garden, tv lounge, hosts have pets, pets not accepted, internet access, babies welcome, free cot, 100% no smoking, hunting, fishing, hiking, cycling, gliding 3km, sea watersports 3km, golf course 15km
Fluent English spoken

Directions: From Cancale take the D76 to Les Portes Rouges, then the D155 to St-Benoît-des-Ondes. In the village, make for the church and La Seigneurie is right next to it.

35.79 Cancale

Private Home

René THOMAS
'Rod an Avel', La Haute-Ville Enoux, 13 rue Anse
Duguesclin, 35350 ST-COULOMB
Tel: (0) 2 99 89 04 79 / (0) 679 50 29 26
Fax: (0) 2 99 89 04 78
renethomas@hotmail.fr
www.rod-an-avel.com

Price Structure – 4 Bedrooms
'Surcouf' & 'Chateaubriand': shower room, wc,
double bed, single bed: €47 – 2 people
€57 – 3 people
'Jacques Cartier': shower room, wc, double bed: €47
'Duguay Trouin': shower room, wc, double bed,
single bed: €47 – 2 people €57 – 3 people

Extra Bed: €17
Reduction: 1/11–31/03, 7 nights
Capacity: 11 people

Location
4km W of CANCALE
in: St-Coulomb, station pick-up on
arrival/departure
Railway station: 10km
Airport: Dinard St-Malo 17km
car essential

Bienvenue en France

Chez René you get a warm and sincere welcome. He is a real Breton sailor who has been welcoming guests to his home for years. He can also organise a trip inland to the calm of the countryside if you wish. The sea is definitely the theme here; from the famous seagull that everybody photographs that regularly descends on the house, via the rooms with their maritime names, to the crockery and linen with their nautical motifs. Ship ahoy!

Facilities: off-street parking, garden, tv lounge, hosts have pets, babies welcome, free cot, hiking, fishing 4km, sea watersports 4km, golf course 30km
Fluent English spoken

Directions: From Cancale take the D355 for St-Malo. In the village of St-Coulomb, opposite the church, take the narrow lane that goes up on the left (rue du Pont de la Teurtre) and continue for 1.4 km. At the 'Stop' sign turn left. It is the fourth house on the right, after you have passed the road that leads to the village of Tannée.

Location
4km S of DINARD
in: Pleurtuit, station pick-up on arrival/departure
Ferry port: 10km
Airport: Dinard St-Malo 6km
car essential

Private Home

You will be welcomed to this modern house with a large garden, situated in the village of Pleurtuit. It is an ideal base for visiting this part of Brittany, renowned for its tourist towns: Dinard (4km), St-Malo (8km) and Cancale (20km). The 'Bleue' and 'Verte' rooms are self-contained. Do not miss the Breton crêpes and *galettes*, served by Marie-Christine in her pleasant flower-filled conservatory.

Marie-Christine & Hugues BARBERE
'La Sauvageais', 35730 PLEURTUIT
Tel: (0) 2 99 88 82 47
barberemariechristine@yahoo.fr
http://monsite.orange.fr/chambredhote.barbere

Facilities: private parking, garden, lounge, hosts have pets, pets not accepted, dinner available, babies welcome, free cot, 100% no smoking, closed: 01/11–01/04, hiking, cycling, fishing 2km, interesting flora 2km, sea watersports 2km, golf course 8km, riversports 15km
Adequate English spoken

Price Structure – 4 Bedrooms
'Rose': bathroom, wc, double bed: €53
'Jaune': shower room, wc, washbasin, double bed, 2 single beds (child-size): €53 – 2 people
€93 – 4 people
'Bleue': shower room, wc, twin beds, 2 single beds (child-size): €53 – 2 people €93 – 4 people
'Verte': shower room, wc, double bed, 2 single beds (child-size): €53 – 2 people €93 – 4 people

Extra Bed: €20
Capacity: 14 people

Directions: From Dinard, take the D266 as far as Pleurtuit, then turn left and continue as far as the edge of the village towards 'La Sauvageais'. Continue for another 800m, as far as the 'Stop' sign, and turn right. Then continue for another 50m.

Location
4km S of DINARD
in: Pleurtuit, station pick-up on arrival/departure
Ferry port: 7km
Airport: Dinard St-Malo 3km

Private Home

This 19th-century mill with its private grounds is the perfect spot for lovers of sea and countryside. It backs onto woods and is surrounded by water at high tide, a really unusual location. As the ebb and flow of the estuary passes beneath your feet, the large windows of the salon offer a unique view. The décor is a bit outdated but the warm and relaxed welcome from your hosts means that we recommend this place without hesitation.

Jacqueline & François LEFEVRE
Le Moulin Neuf, 35730 PLEURTUIT
Tel: (0) 2 99 88 61 25 / (0) 607 22 08 95
lemoulinpleurtuit@free.fr
http://lemoulinpleurtuit.free.fr

Facilities: off-street parking, extensive grounds, tv lounge, hosts have pets, pets not accepted, babies welcome, free cot, 2 nights minimum stay: 01/07–31/08, private tennis court, hiking, cycling, fishing, interesting flora, sea watersports, riversports, golf course 7km
Fluent English spoken

Price Structure – 1 Bedroom
and 1 Apartment
lounge, television, bathroom, wc, double bed (queen-size): €90
apartment: lounge, television, kitchen, bathroom, wc, double bed. En-suite room, television, double bed: €100 – 2 people €130 – 4 people

Extra Bed: €20
Reduction: 01/10–30/06, 3 nights
Capacity: 6 people

Directions: From St-Malo, cross the dam over the River Rance towards Dinard and then take the first on the left at the traffic lights towards La Richardais (D114) as far as the hamlet of Le Moulin Neuf. The mill sits on a tributary of the River Rance.

Brittany – Dinard

22.23 Dinard

Château/Manor House

Location
20km S W of DINARD
in: St-Lormel
Railway station: 30km
Airport: Dinard St-Malo 18km
car essential

Yvonnick LE MIRE
'Château de la Villerobert', 22130 ST-LORMEL
Tel: (0) 2 96 84 12 88 Fax: (0) 2 96 84 03 27

Monsieur and Madame Le Mire will receive you like old friends in their 17th-century château, quietly situated in its own grounds. It is furnished with antiques and only 5km from the sea. An ideal base for the 'Emerald Coast', it is also very practical to visit Dinan, Dinard and St-Malo.

Price Structure – 3 Bedrooms
'Bleue': shower, wc, double bed, single bed:
€73 – 2 people €87 – 3 people
'Rose': along corridor bathroom, wc, twin beds: €73
'Jaune': shower room, wc, double bed, single bed:
€73 – 2 people €87 – 3 people

Extra Bed: €16
Capacity: 8 people

Facilities: private parking, extensive grounds, tv lounge, golf course 8km, sea watersports 8km
Adequate English spoken

Directions: From Dinan, take the D794 towards Plancoët. There, head to St-Lormel. Go through St-Lormel then 50m after the sign as you exit the village, the château is on the left. (Coming from Dinard, go towards Ploubalay and Plancoët. After Crehen, turn right towards St-Lormel.)

35.82 Dol-de-Bretagne

Private Home

Location
DOL-DE-BRETAGNE
in: Dol-de-Bretagne
Railway station: 3km
car essential

Colette POIDEVIN
Cardequin, 35120 DOL-DE-BRETAGNE
Tel: (0) 2 99 48 28 90

This is a great base from which to discover the Dol area and, of course, the bay of the Mont-St-Michel. Collette gives you a warm welcome in her restored farmhouse. She has recently restored some outbuildings, separate from the main house, and the four bedrooms are quite large and immaculately clean. They are simply furnished with comfortable beds and private bathrooms. There is a kitchen exclusively for these rooms in the building opposite, and in summer she puts out chairs and tables in the garden.

Price Structure – 4 Bedrooms
4 rooms: shower room, wc, double bed: €40

Extra Bed: €12
Capacity: 8 people

Facilities: off-street parking, garden, hosts have pets, pets not accepted, kitchen, babies welcome, free cot, 100% no smoking, closed: 1/11–31/01, hiking, cycling, fishing 5km, sea watersports 7km, golf course 10km

Directions: At Dol-de-Bretagne, take the D676 towards Dinan and after about 1.7km turn right towards Cardequin. Then follow the signs.

Location
7km N of DOL-DE-BRETAGNE
in: Le Vivier-sur-Mer
Railway station: 7km
Airport: Dinard St-Malo 25km
car essential

Residence of Outstanding Character

This house is just beside the sea, facing the bay between the Mont-St-Michel and Cancale (famous for its oysters). 'The peace and quiet of the country, beside the sea' is the slogan of Monique and Alain who bought this place specially to start a B&B. It was originally a small hotel, but Monique has made it more welcoming and cosy, plus there is her and Alain's sincere and courteous welcome. A great location, with three rooms with a sea view and lots to do close by.

Monique & Alain RIETZ
'Le Manoir de la Salmonière', 40 rue Grève,
35960 LE VIVIER-SUR-MER
Tel: (0) 2 99 48 85 02 / (0) 680 41 24 06
Fax: (0) 2 99 89 79 03
alain.rietz@wanadoo.fr
www.manoir-de-la-salmoniere.com

Facilities: private parking, garden, hosts have pets, internet access, babies welcome, free cot, hiking, cycling, sea watersports, golf course 9km
Fluent English spoken

Price Structure – 5 Bedrooms
2 rooms: television, bathroom, wc, double bed,
2 single beds: €60 – 2 people €90 – 4 people
television, bathroom, wc, 2 double beds:
€60 – 2 people €90 – 4 people
television, washbasin, double bed, single bed:
€60 – 2 people €75 – 3 people
television, bathroom, wc, double bed: €60

Reduction: 1/01–31/03
Capacity: 17 people

Directions: From Dol, take the D155 for 7km as far as Vivier-sur-Mer. At the end of the Rue de Dol, turn left into Rue Grève (which runs along by the sea). Le Manoir is about 700m along on the left. Look for the signs.

Location
32km N of RENNES
in: La Haye-d'Irée
Railway station: 30km
Airport: Rennes St-Jacques 40km
car essential

Château/Manor House

This old manor house, situated near many of the principal tourist attractions of Haute Bretagne, also housed a royal glass-making factory for almost 500 years. All of this property, which overlooks the surrounding countryside, has that delightful charm of old family houses, full of souvenirs and warm nostalgia, but also offers a high standard of comfort. Micheline is in the process of creating a botanical garden and is a mine of information on the gardens of Brittany.

Micheline & Jean-Louis LESCHEVIN de PREVOISIN
La Haye-d'Irée, 35560 ST-REMY-DU-PLAIN
Tel: (0) 2 99 73 62 07
m.deprevoisin@wanadoo.fr
www.chateaubreton.com

Facilities: off-street parking, extensive grounds, tv lounge, dinner available, babies welcome, free cot, closed: 01/11–01/04, private swimming pool, hiking, cycling, fishing, interesting flora, mushroom-picking, sea watersports 5km, golf course 20km, riversports 20km
Fluent English spoken

Price Structure – 2 Bedrooms, 2 Suites and 1 Apartment
'Chambre du Marquis': shower room, wc, four-poster double bed: €110
'Rouge': lounge, television, bathroom, wc, twin beds: €110
'Chouette': bathroom, wc, double bed. En-suite room, washbasin, twin beds: €80 – 2 people €125 – 4 people
'Bleue': shower room, wc, double bed. En-suite room, single bed: €80 – 2 people €95 – 3 people
Apartment: television, kitchen, shower room, wc, double bed: €125

Extra Bed: €15
Capacity: 13 people

Directions: At Rennes, take the D175 as far as Sens-de-Bretagne for 26km, then take the D794 as far as St-Remy-du-Plain. In the village, follow the D90 road along by the church and then after 1.5km, turn right onto the D12 towards Feins. The house is 30m further on, on the right.

35.83 Rennes

Château/Manor House

Laure BERTHELEME
'Château du Bois Glaume', Le Bois Glaume, 35320 POLIGNE
Tel: (0) 2 99 43 83 05 / (0) 607 22 40 18
Fax: (0) 2 99 43 79 40
bertheleme_laure@lilly.com

Price Structure – 4 Bedrooms
2 rooms: lounge, television, bathroom, wc, four-poster double bed: €130
1 room: shower room, wc, four-poster double bed, 2 single beds, cot: €95 – 2 people
1 room: bathroom, wc, double bed: €95

Capacity: 10 people

Location
26Km S of RENNES
in: Poligné, station pick-up on arrival/departure
Railway station: 25km
Airport: Rennes St-Jacques 15km
car essential

As we go to press this home has not yet been classified, but will be shortly. Twenty years ago, this place was very dilapidated and had not been lived in for a century. Laura's restoration of it has been a labour of love and a success in bringing these old stones to life again. She is keen on the fine arts and the result is fantastic. You can even fish in the lake. Her dinners are pretty good too and her specialities are Tournedos Rossini or, as you are in Brittany, fish and coquilles St Jacques. Enjoy.

Facilities: private parking, extensive grounds, tv lounge, hosts have pets, dinner available, babies welcome, free cot, 100% no smoking
Basic English spoken

Directions: When coming from Rennes, Poligné is near to the N137 Rennes to Nantes dual carriageway, 15km from Rennes and 6km before Bain-de-Bretagne.

35.12 St-Malo

Residence of Outstanding Character

Maryline BASLÉ
'Les Croix Gibouins', Paramé, 35400 ST-MALO 2402
Tel: (0) 2 99 81 12 41
contact@les-croix-gibouins.com

Price Structure – 2 Bedrooms and 1 Suite
shower room, wc, double bed, single bed:
€57 – 2 people €64 – 3 people
bathroom, wc, double bed: €55
shower room, wc, double bed. En-suite room, single bed: €50 – 2 people €62 – 3 people

Extra Bed: €20
Reduction: 2 nights, groups
Capacity: 8 people

Location
ST-MALO
in: St-Malo, station pick-up on arrival/departure
Airport: Dinard St-Malo 10km
car essential

Maryline has been welcoming guests for 15 years to her character home in St-Malo. Set back from the road in the tranquil countryside, this *gentilhommière* was a former 16th-century hunting lodge and is a real family home. Enjoy life at a tranquil pace as lived out here on the terrace opposite the orchard and the old press, or in the dining room which once served as a seed bed for potatoes! The large fireplace and the long convivial tables are of note, as are the *craquelins* served at breakfast. Extra facilities include a fridge and a garage.

Facilities: off-street parking, garden, tv lounge, hosts have pets, pets not accepted, 100% no smoking, 2 nights minimum stay, closed: 13/11–31/03, birdwatching 8km
Adequate English spoken

Directions: From St-Malo Paramé (the last roundabout) take the D155 towards Pontorson, Dol-de-Bretagne for 2.5km. The house is at the end of the lane on the left.

Location
ST-MALO
in: St-Malo, station pick-up on arrival/departure
Railway station: 2km
Airport: Dinard St-Malo 10km

Private Home

Marithé is a retired teacher, and she fled Paris with her son to recharge her batteries in the old town of St-Malo. 'I am neither French, nor Breton, but from St-Malo' she declares, and this strong attachment to the town is quite typical. It is a vibrant, lively town with its centre enclosed by ramparts and a yacht harbour. Marithé's house is in a quiet area, with a walled garden and a terrace, but only a few minutes' drive from the centre.

Facilities: private parking, garden, pets not accepted, internet access, kitchen, babies welcome, free cot, 100% no smoking, cycling, hiking 2km, fishing 2km, sea watersports 2km, golf course 15km
Adequate English spoken

Directions: Please contact your hosts for detailed directions.

Marithé PERTHUISOT
'Rozven', 16 rue du Revenant, 35400 ST-MALO
Tel: (0) 2 99 82 30 29 / (0) 670 00 90 51
mtperthuisot@wanadoo.fr
http://site.voila.fr/bab-rozven

Price Structure – 3 Bedrooms
'Marine': along corridor bathroom, wc, twin beds: €50
'Sable': shower room, wc, double bed, single bed: €50 – 2 people €67 – 3 people
'1900': shower room, wc, double bed: €50

Extra Bed: €17
Capacity: 7 people

Location
ST-MALO
in: St-Malo, station pick-up on arrival/departure
Railway station: 4km
Airport: Dinard St-Malo 6km
car essential

Private Home

After a life travelling the world as a sailor and putting down roots in a few places, including five years in Germany, Gilbert is ending his career working at the dockyard at St-Malo. He and his wife are now settled in a residential area high up above the River Rance less than a kilometre from this famous tidal dam. This is a lovely, quiet area with a view over the estuary which is easily reached. You can measure the generosity of their welcome by the size of their breakfasts, Breton style. *Bon appétit!*

Facilities: off-street parking, garden, tv lounge, hosts have pets, dinner available, babies welcome, free cot, 100% no smoking, 2 shared shower rooms, 3 wcs, hiking, fishing, sea watersports, golf course 15km
Basic English spoken

Directions: On the dual carriageway from Rennes towards St-Malo and Dinard, turn right about 1km before the tidal dam (Barrage de la Rance) towards Château Le Bos and go under the dual carriageway, continuing as far as the 'Manoir de la Goëletterie'. The house is opposite, at number 15.

Marie & Gilbert FIEURGANT
15 rue de la Goëletterie, 35400 ST-MALO
Tel: (0) 2 99 81 97 27 / (0) 682 00 20 61
Fax: (0) 2 99 81 97 27
phareouest35@aol.com

Price Structure – 5 Bedrooms
'Solidor': twin beds: €38
2 rooms: double bed: €45
'Cézembre': double bed, single bed: €45 – 2 people €55 – 3 people
'Le Grand Bé': double bed, 2 single beds: €45 – 2 people €60 – 4 people

Extra Bed: €7
Reduction: 4 nights, children
Capacity: 13 people

Brittany – St-Malo

35.67 St-Malo

Private Home

Location
ST-MALO
in: St-Malo
Railway station: 3km
Airport: Dinard St-Malo 10km
car essential

An agreeable Breton-style house in a quiet cul-de-sac in the residential area of St-Malo, just seven minutes from the walled centre and 400m from La Rance. Despite the fact that the three guest bedrooms share one bathroom, the bedrooms are spacious, well-decorated and uplifting and would deserve three 'suns'. You will see that Sophie's artistic talents do not stop at decorating – she also makes frames and lamps from driftwood.

Sophie CALONI
15 impasse de la Léonore, 35400 ST-MALO
Tel: (0) 2 99 40 36 13 / (0) 662 36 36 13
Fax: (0) 2 99 20 17 74
jp.caloni@wanadoo.fr

Price Structure – 3 Bedrooms
'Cézembre': bathroom, wc, twin beds: €55
'La Varde': television, bathroom, wc, double bed: €55
'Conché': double bed: €50

Extra Bed: €15
Capacity: 6 people

Facilities: private parking, garden, tv lounge, hosts have pets, dinner available, babies welcome, free cot, 100% no smoking, 2 nights minimum stay: 01/07–31/08, hiking, cycling 3km, sea watersports 3km, golf course 10km
Fluent English spoken

Directions: From Rennes, when arriving at St-Malo on the N137, head in the direction of Dinard and then turn right to St-Malo, St-Servan. Then take the second turn on the right and the first left.

35.71 St-Malo

Private Home

Location
ST-MALO
in: St-Malo
Railway station: 5km
Airport:
car essential

A large, white Breton-style house on the walking route of the Château du Colombier and Malouinières and just 3km from the sea in large, landscaped grounds, 7500M² in size. Anita and Jean-Paul offer well looked after, bright, spacious rooms with marine-themed bathrooms. In the garden you'll find an arbour and a barbecue at your disposal. A friendly welcome.

Anita & Jean-Paul LEVEN
'La Chesnaie', 35400 ST-MALO
Tel: (0) 2 99 81 73 52 / (0) 674 45 01 45
contact@lachesnaie.org
www.lachesnaie.org

Price Structure – 4 Bedrooms
'Chateaubriand': bathroom, wc, shower, double bed, single bed: €53 – 2 people €68 – 3 people
'Mahé de la Bourdonnais': shower room, wc, double bed: €53
'Cartier' & 'Duguay-Trouin': along corridor shower room, wc, double bed: €53

Extra Bed: €15
Capacity: 9 people

Facilities: off-street parking, extensive grounds, tv lounge, pets not accepted, 100% no smoking, closed: 1/10–1/05, hiking, fishing 3km, sea watersports 3km, bird-watching 5km, golf course 10km
Adequate English spoken

Directions: On arrival at Rennes via the dual carriageway, head for Paramé Cancale. At the fifth roundabout, turn right and right again towards La Buzardière, then turn left at the 'Stop' sign. Follow the arrow to the house (1.5km from the ring-road).

Location
ST-MALO
in: St-Malo
car essential

Château/Manor House

Josette is a sailor's wife and proud to be a 'malouine' and an officer's wife! Her house is a *malouinière*, a manor house, or, in French, a *gentilhommière*, from the 17th century. The house is fairly simple but you will appreciate the breakfast room and its stone walls. It is here in the mornings that you can enjoy fresh fruit juice and homemade jam. You are 2km from the walls of St-Malo and 1km from the beaches. There is a barbecue at your disposal and games including table tennis, table football and billiards.

Josette FERET
'La Ville Auray', 35400 ST-MALO
Tel: (0) 2 99 81 64 37 / (0) 680 35 83 94
daniel.feret@9online.fr
www.ville-auray.com

Facilities: off-street parking, extensive grounds, hosts have pets, babies welcome, free cot, hunting, fishing, cycling, sea watersports, hiking 3km, gliding 10km, golf course 20km, mushroom-picking 20km, bird-watching 35km
Fluent English spoken

Directions: Please contact your host in advance for detailed directions.

Price Structure – 3 Bedrooms
'Angelique': television, shower room, wc, four-poster double bed: €50
'Adelaïde': television, shower room, wc, double bed, 2 single beds (child-size): €50 – 2 people €70 – 4 people
'Clarisse': television, along corridor bathroom, wc, washbasin, double bed: €50

Extra Bed: €10
Capacity: 8 people

Location
16km S of ST-MALO
in: La Ville-es-Nonais, station pick-up on arrival/departure
Railway station: 15km
Airport: Rennes St-Jacques 60km
car essential

Private Home

This house is located between St-Malo and Dinard in a tranquil little hamlet surrounded by fields and only 300m from the River Rance and the village beach. The traditional interior has a lounge with exposed stone walls, lots of plants, a beautiful fireplace and an open plan kitchen that all create a warm and friendly atmosphere. A wooden staircase leads to the bedrooms, which are not very large but comfortable and with parquet floors. Jacqueline is a former shopkeeper and her welcome is warm. They do not serve dinner, but you are welcome to share the family kitchen with them.

Jacqueline & Michel LE PEN
7 rue de la Fontaine, 35430 LA-VILLE-ES-NONAIS
Tel: (0) 2 99 58 38 76 / (0) 607 76 98 11

Facilities: off-street parking, garden, tv lounge, hosts have pets, pets not accepted, kitchen, babies welcome, free cot, 100% no smoking, hiking 1km, bird-watching 7km, fishing 10km, sea watersports 15km, golf course 18km
Adequate English spoken

Price Structure – 1 Bedroom and 1 Suite
room: along corridor bathroom, wc, along corridor shower, double bed: €40
suite: shower room, wc, double bed. En-suite room, single bed: €40 – 2 people €50 – 3 people

Reduction: 22/09–22/04, 7 nights
Capacity: 5 people

Directions: From St-Malo take the fast road towards Rennes for 10km, exit at Châteauneuf, direction La Ville-es-Nonais. In the village pass in front of the bar and take the first turn on the left towards Pleudihen for 800m. Turn left into Rue de la Fontaine. Continue to the end of the road, staying on the left.

35.45 St-Malo

Private Home

Location
15km S of ST-MALO
in: Miniac-Morvan, station pick-up
on arrival/departure
Railway station: 12km
Airport: Dinard St-Malo 20km
car essential

Tina & Malcom KINZETT
'Estival', La Ville Blanche,
35540 MINIAC-MORVAN
Tel: (0) 2 96 83 33 30 / (0) 670 11 48 40
Fax: (0) 2 96 88 26 56
estival@tiscali.fr
www.estivalbrittany.com

Price Structure – 4 Bedrooms and 1 Suite
suite: shower room, wc, double bed. En-suite room,
twin beds: €58 – 2 people €104 – 4 people
3 rooms: shower room, wc, double bed: €58
along corridor shower room, wc, double bed: €58

Extra Bed: €16
Reduction: 01/09–30/06
Capacity: 12 people

You will find 'Estival' in spacious grounds, full of flowers, at the crossroads of St-Malo, Dinan and Le Mont-St-Michel. This renovated old farmhouse is run with great joie de vivre by Tina and Malcolm, a British couple. Breakfast is served in the living room, which was formerly a restaurant, and the menu has been expertly devised by Tina, who was trained by a famous chef.

Facilities: off-street parking, garden, tv lounge, pets not accepted, dinner available, babies welcome, free cot, 100% no smoking, closed: 15/11–28/02, hiking, cycling, bird-watching, golf course 8km, fishing 8km, riversports 10km, sea watersports 20km
Fluent English spoken

Directions: From St-Malo, take the N137 towards Rennes, as far as the exit to Miniac-Morvan. Do not go into Miniac, but continue on the D337 as far as Vieux Bourg. Go through Vieux Bourg and at the crossroads turn right onto the D676 towards Dinan. 'Estival' is 2km further on, on the right.

35.65 St-Malo

**Residence of
Outstanding
Character**

Location
3km S E of ST-MALO
in: St-Jouan-des-Guérets
Railway station: 3km
Airport: Dinard St-Malo 10km
car essential

Five minutes from the walls of St-Malo is this pretty little manor house built by a Scot in the 19th century. It sits in the centre of a large wooded parkland by the fast road nearby. Although the road noise is noticeable from the outside it is inaudible once inside. An impressive oak staircase leads you up to the guest bedrooms, which although unexceptional are comfortable. The bright dining room, the terrace and the garden, together with the welcome from Nicole, makes this *manoir* a pleasant and practical base from which to explore the area.

Nicole BERTIN
'Manoir de Blanche Roche',
35430 ST-JOUAN-DES-GUERETS
Tel: (0) 2 99 19 11 11 / (0) 670 98 54 25
Fax: (0) 2 99 19 11 11
manoirdeblancheroche@orange.fr

Price Structure – 6 Bedrooms
3 rooms: bathroom, wc, double bed: €58
2 rooms: bathroom, wc, double bed,
single bed: €58 – 2 people €78 – 3 people
shower room, wc, double bed: €58

Extra Bed: €20
Reduction: 2 nights, groups
Capacity: 14 people

Facilities: off-street parking, extensive grounds, tv lounge, pets not accepted, dinner available, babies welcome, free cot, 100% no smoking, wheelchair access, hiking 3km, fishing 4km, sea watersports 4km, golf course 12km
Basic English spoken

Directions: From St-Malo take the N137 towards Rennes, exit at St-Jouan, then head in the direction of St-Malo to join the fast road in the opposite direction. Continue for just 150m. The entrance to the 'Manoir' is signposted on the right.

Brittany – St-Malo

35.24 St-Malo

Location
7km E of ST-MALO
in: St-Méloir-des-Ondes
Airport: Dinard St-Malo 16km
car essential

Private Home

Martine is a charming person. Her house is very well situated, 5km from Cancale and 7km from St-Malo. The barbecue, dishwasher and fridge are available for your use. There are many restaurants and *crêperies* nearby, and of course you are in the land of oysters and mussels.

Martine MONSIMET
'La Rimbaudais', 35350 ST-MELOIR-DES-ONDES
Tel: (0) 2 99 89 19 75 / (0) 662 29 70 31
Fax: (0) 2 99 89 19 75
yama35@wanadoo.fr

Facilities: private parking, garden, hosts have pets, pets not accepted, babies welcome, free cot, hiking, cycling 5km, fishing 5km, bird-watching 5km, sea watersports 5km, riversports 5km, golf course 10km, gliding 10km
Basic English spoken

Price Structure – 2 Bedrooms
first room: shower room, wc, double bed, single bed: €62 – 2 people €70 – 3 people
second room: along corridor shower room, wc, double bed: €62

Extra Bed: €20
Capacity: 5 people

Directions: At St-Malo, head in the direction of Le Mont-St-Michel via the D155, and then turn right towards St-Méloir. At the town hall (*la mairie*), take the D2 towards St-Servan for 1.5km as far as 'La Rimbaudais'.

35.48 St-Malo

Location
7km E of ST-MALO
in: St-Méloir-des-Ondes, station pick-up on arrival/departure
Ferry port: 5km
Airport: Dinard St-Malo 15km
car essential

Private Home

Midway between Le Mont-St-Michel and Cancale, this Breton mansion has splendid views from its windows over the bay and Le Mont-St-Michel. Micheline and Francis run this place in a professional and well-organised way. They have thought of everything to make your stay enjoyable: pretty rooms, varied breakfasts, morning delivery of seafood and oysters, a relaxing garden and a lockable garage for motorbikes – all served with a smile. Be sure to dine with them and enjoy the local produce such as fish and meat cooked in cider.

Micheline & Francis RAVENAUX
'La Pastourelle', Les Nielles, 35350
ST-MELOIR-DES-ONDES
Tel: (0) 2 99 89 10 09 Fax: (0) 2 99 89 10 09
pastourelle@baie-saintmichel.com
www.baie-saintmichel.com/hebergements/
pastourelle.php

Facilities: private parking, garden, tv lounge, hosts have pets, dinner available, babies welcome, free cot, 2 nights minimum stay, closed: 15/12–15/01, hiking, sea watersports 5km, riversports 5km, golf course 15km
Basic English spoken

Price Structure – 7 Bedrooms
5 rooms: shower room, wc, double bed: €60
2 rooms: lounge, shower room, wc, double bed, single bed (child-size): €74 – 2 people €85 – 3 people

Reduction: 01/09–30/06, 2 nights
Capacity: 16 people

Directions: From Cancale or St-Malo take the D155, following the bay of Le Mont-St-Michel. 'La Pastourelle' is on this road after the karting track and about 1km before St-Benoît-des-Ondes.

Brittany – St-Malo

35.60 St-Malo

Private Home

Location
5km S E of ST-MALO
in: St-Père-Marc-en-Poulet
Railway station: 7km
Airport: Dinard St-Malo 10km
car essential

On the Emerald Coast, near the sea and only 10 minutes from St-Malo, discover this beautiful property standing in 2 hectares of land. It was the former residence of the Lords of St-Père and the bread oven that once served the hamlet is still in use today. Marcel-Auguste is fanatical about local history and can explain all about the Lords of St-Père and where to visit nearby. Marie-Claude, for her part, prides herself on serving you a hearty breakfast. The bedrooms are modern and are in the converted barn.

Marie-Claude & Marcel-Auguste LEBIHAN
'Manoir de la Ville-Hermessan', la Ville-Hermessan, 35430 ST-PERE-MARC-EN-POULET
Tel: (0) 2 99 58 22 02 / (0) 687 94 89 14
Fax: (0) 2 99 58 22 02
laville.hermessan@free.fr
laville.hermessan.free.fr

Facilities: private parking, extensive grounds, lounge, pets not accepted, 100% no smoking, 2 nights minimum stay, closed: 30/09–31/03, hiking, cycling, sea watersports 4km, fishing 5km, golf course 10km
Adequate English spoken

Price Structure – 4 Bedrooms
'Golf' & 'Fleurs': shower room, wc, double bed, single bed: €55 – 2 people €67 – 3 people
'Marine' & 'Le Pain': shower room, wc, double bed: €50

Capacity: 10 people

Directions: From St-Malo take the N137 towards Rennes for 2km then the D4 on the left towards La Gouesnière. At the second intersection turn right to St-Père. 'La Ville-Hermessan' is signed on this road on your right.

35.27 St-Malo

Residence of Outstanding Character

Location
10km S of ST-MALO
in: St-Suliac, station pick-up on arrival/departure
Ferry port: 10km
Airport: Dinard St-Malo 20km

Bienvenue en France

This Franco-German couple will welcome you to their 17th-century stone house, in the heart of one of the most beautiful fishing villages in Brittany. The bedrooms have been tastefully modernised and you will love the courtyard and the garden. The breakfast is substantial and there is parking space for one car in the courtyard.

Peter SOBEK
'La Goëlette', 2 rue Besnier, 35430 ST-SULIAC
Tel: (0) 2 99 58 47 03 Fax: (0) 2 99 58 47 03
www.cosybnb.com

Facilities: garden, tv lounge, pets not accepted, dinner available, 5 years old minimum age, hiking, cycling, fishing, sea watersports, bird-watching 2km, golf course 15km
Fluent English spoken

Price Structure – 3 Bedrooms
bathroom, wc, double bed (queen-size): €60
shower room, wc, double bed (queen-size), 3 single beds: €85 – 2 people €115 – 5 people
shower room, wc, double bed (queen-size), single bed: €60 – 2 people €70 – 3 people

Extra Bed: €10
Reduction: 01/09–30/06, 3 nights
Capacity: 10 people

Directions: At St-Malo, take the N137 towards Rennes. Come off at St-Suliac and 50m before the church, on Place de la Poste, towards the street that goes up on the left, you will see their large white gates on the left.

Location
18km N of PONTIVY
in: St-Caradec
car essential

Private Home

Christian has opened up his family home for the first time to welcome B&B guests. Returning from a career as a caterer in the USA with his American wife, they have thrown themselves into local life and know the region and walks very well. The comfortable bedrooms have been thoughtfully decorated with imported USA mattresses. Plenty of attention to detail. The rooms overlook a tranquil avenue or the garden with fruit trees watered from the well. Enjoy a welcome drink in the lounge. Muffins and other homemade cakes for breakfast.

Facilities: off-street parking, garden, tv lounge, hosts have pets, pets not accepted, babies welcome, free cot, 100% no smoking, closed: 01/11–15/01, hiking 2km, cycling 2km, mushroom-picking 10km, interesting flora 10km, riversports 24km, sea watersports 75km
Fluent English spoken

Directions: Please contact your hosts in advance for detailed directions.

Christian CAILLE & Christiana ADAMS
'La Prévenchère', 11 place du Champ de Foire,
22600 ST-CARADEC
Tel: (0) 2 96 25 17 55
laprevenchere@wanadoo.fr
www.beautifulbrittany.com

Price Structure – 6 Bedrooms
'Chinoise': bathroom, wc, double bed: €39
'Coquelicot': shower room, wc, double bed: €37
'Louis XV': along corridor shower room, wc, double bed (€39). Along corridor room 'Régence': double bed: €35 – 2 people €74 – 4 people
'St Anne': along corridor shower room, wc, twin beds: €35. Along corridor room 'Bleue': double bed, 2 single beds:(child size): €35 - 2 people €70 - 6 people

Extra Bed: €15
Capacity: 14 people

Location
40km E of VANNES
in: Castellan
car essential

Château/Manor House

This 18th-century château is in superb surroundings, and one bedroom is listed as an historic monument. It is a farmhouse inn, run by the family, famous for their *pâté en croûte*, as well as other excellent traditional Breton dishes. On sale: jam, gingerbread, terrines, local produce.

Facilities: off-street parking, extensive grounds, pets not accepted, dinner available, babies welcome, free cot, 2 nights minimum stay: 01/08–31/08, hiking, cycling, fishing 2km, interesting flora 18km, sea watersports 40km, bird-watching 45km

Directions: At Vannes, take the N166 towards Rennes, then the D776 towards Malestroit. In Malestroit, take the D764 towards St-Congard, then the D149 towards St-Martin. Follow the sign 'Auberge', on the left before you reach St-Martin.

Marie & Patrick COSSÉ
'Auberge du Château de Castellan', Castellan,
56200 ST-MARTIN-SUR-OUST
Tel: (0) 2 99 91 51 69 / (0) 603 47 69 05
Fax: (0) 2 99 91 57 41
auberge@club-internet.fr
www.castellan.fr.st

Price Structure – 6 Bedrooms
'Saumon': television, shower room, wc, double bed, single bed: €85 – 2 people €104 – 3 people
'Bateaux': television, shower room, wc, twin beds: €85
'Médaillon': television, bathroom, wc, double bed, twin beds: €110 – 2 people €149 – 4 people
'Roland': television, bathroom, wc, double bed: €85
'Dortoir': television, shower room, wc, double bed, twin beds: €142 – 4 people
'Laverdure': television, bathroom, wc, double bed, 4 single beds: €164 – 6 people

Extra Bed: €25   **Capacity:** 21 people

Brittany – Pontivy, Vannes

56.05 Vannes

Working Farm

Location
15km W of VANNES
in: Guerlan
Railway station: 10km
Airport: 40km
car essential

Monique and Daniel, a friendly young farming couple, welcome you with a smile into their imposing house. Much of the typical Breton furniture has been restored by Monique as a labour of love. 10km from the Bay of Morbihan.

Monique & Daniel le DOUARAN
Guerlan, Plougoumelen, 56400 AURAY
Tel: (0) 2 97 57 65 50 / (0) 615 71 19 49
Fax: (0) 2 97 57 65 50
ledouaran@aol.com

Price Structure – 5 Bedrooms and 1 Suite
'Chambre au balcon': shower room, wc, double bed: €50
'Verte': shower room, wc, twin beds: €38
ground floor 'Berder': shower room, wc, double bed: €50
'Gaur'Iwiz': shower room, wc, double bed. En-suite room, double bed: €50 – 2 people €84 – 4 people
first floor 'Logodew': shower room, wc, double bed, single bed: €50 – 2 people €64 – 3 people
first floor 'Irus': shower, wc, 3 single beds: €50 – 2 people €64 – 3 people

Extra Bed: €10
Reduction: 01/09-30/06 **Capacity:** 16 people

Facilities: off-street parking, garden, tv lounge, hosts have pets, kitchen, babies welcome, free cot, wheelchair access, 2 nights minimum stay, sea watersports 30km
Adequate English spoken

Directions: In Vannes, take the N165 towards Lorient. After Vannes, take the first exit Ploeren, Meriadec and take the D127 towards Meriadec for 3.5km. It is the second farm on the left (after the level-crossing).

56.38 Vannes

Private Home

Location
13km W of VANNES
in: Plougoumelen, station pick-up on arrival/departure
Railway station: 10km
car essential

In a listed hamlet on the edge of a forest, Marie-Aline, a former restaurateur, spoils you with seafood and other delicacies. She holds *galette* evenings and serves such a copious breakfast of crêpes and *viennoiseries* that she'll save what you can't finish for your lunch! You'll also be won over by the quality décor in the bedrooms and a pleasant garden. Aside from the railway line that passes at the foot of the garden, this is a really welcoming address at good value prices that would otherwise be worthy of three 'suns'.

Marie-Aline KERVADEC
'Chez Marie-Aline', 31 rue du Pont Tiret,
Trémodec, 56400 PLOUGOUMELEN
Tel: (0) 2 97 50 80 97 / (0) 610 13 89 81

Price Structure – 3 Bedrooms
2 rooms: wc, double bed, single bed: €40 – 2 people
€55 – 3 people
wheelchair access, television, bathroom, wc, double bed: €45

Extra Bed: €15
Reduction: 7 nights, groups
Capacity: 8 people

Facilities: private parking, garden, tv lounge, hosts have pets, dinner available, babies welcome, free cot, shared bathroom, wc, 3 nights minimum stay: 01/07–31/08, mushroom-picking, hiking, fishing 1km, bird-watching 6km, sea watersports 7km, golf course 8km

Directions: Halfway on the fast road between Vannes and Auray, exit Plougoumelen, D101 direction Trémodec on the right. The house is 1.5km from the restaurant.

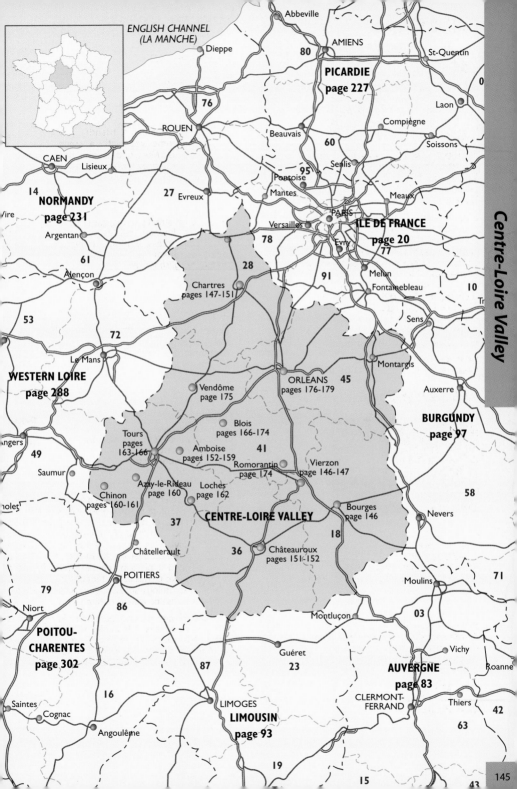

ENGLISH CHANNEL
(LA MANCHE)

Abbeville

AMIENS
80

St-Quentin

PICARDIE
page 227

0

Laon

Compiègne

Soissons

Dieppe

ROUEN

Beauvais

60

Senlis

Meaux

76

95
Pontoise

Mantes

CAEN

Lisieux

14

27

Evreux

Versailles

PARIS

ILE DE FRANCE
page 20

NORMANDY
page 231

78

Evny

77

Argentan

28

91

Melun

Fontainebleau

10

Chartres
pages 147-151

Sens

61

Alençon

Tr

53

72

Montargis

Le Mans

ORLEANS
pages 176-179

45

Auxerre

WESTERN LOIRE
page 288

Vendôme
page 175

BURGUNDY
page 97

Blois
pages 166-174

ngers

49

Tours
pages
163-166

Amboise
pages 152-159

41

Romorantin
page 174

Vierzon
page 146-147

58

Saumur

Azay-le-Rideau
page 160

Loches
page 162

Nevers

olet

Chinon
pages 160-161

Bourges
page 146

CENTRE-LOIRE VALLEY

37

18

Châtellerault

36

Châteauroux
pages 151-152

Moulins

71

POITIERS

79

86

03

Niort

Montluçon

POITOU-
CHARENTES
page 302

Guéret

Vichy

Roanne

87

23

AUVERGNE
page 83

16

Saintes

Cognac

LIMOGES

LIMOUSIN
page 93

CLERMONT-
FERRAND

Thiers

42

Angoulême

63

19

15

43

18.19 Bourges

Private Home

Location
16km S W of BOURGES
in: St-Florent-sur-Cher
Railway station: 16km
car essential

Laure MEDINA
'La Faisanderie', 18400 ST-FLORENT-SUR-CHER
Tel: (0) 2 48 26 46 04 / (0) 677 77 85 92
lafaisanderie@tiscali.fr
http://monsite.wanadoo.fr/lafaisanderie/

Price Structure – 2 Bedrooms
shower room, wc, double bed, 2 single beds
(child-size): €49 – 2 people €85 – 4 people
along corridor bathroom, wc, double bed: €49

Reduction: 4 nights, children
Capacity: 6 people

In the Berry, this beautiful residence is situated in pretty wooded grounds. It is somewhat isolated from the rest of the village, so delightfully quiet and relaxing. You have unrestricted access to the pool, and your rooms are in separate outbuildings that have been modernised, with your own kitchen. The rooms are comfortable with a pleasant décor, and the two rooms together are ideal for families or a group of friends. As the main house has a lot of character, you can take breakfast or dinner in the dining room if you wish.

Facilities: private parking, extensive grounds, tv lounge, hosts have pets, pets not accepted, dinner available, kitchen, babies welcome, free cot, private swimming pool
Fluent English spoken

Directions: Exit 7 Bourges from the A71. Then take the N151 towards Châteauroux. At St-Florent, cross the level-crossing and turn right immediately beside the railway line. Continue straight on and take the unmade road on the left that leads to the wood.

36.11 Vierzon

Private Home

Location
35km S W of VIERZON
in: Bouges-le-Château, station pick-up on arrival/departure
Railway station: 28km
Airport: Tours 90km

Bienvenue en France

Mary PETULA
'Le Grand Verdenay', 36110
BOUGES-LE-CHATEAU
Tel: (0) 2 54 35 77 05 / (0) 680 63 92 37
Fax: (0) 2 54 35 77 05
julian.armitage@wanadoo.fr

Price Structure – 3 Bedrooms
2 rooms: shower room, wc, washbasin, double bed, single bed (child-size): €50
'Romantique': wheelchair access, shower room, wc, washbasin, double bed: €50

Extra Bed: €15
Capacity: 8 people

This former little farm in the Berrichonne countryside is a few minutes away from the Château de Bouges and its attractive grounds. Pady can easily chat to you about the château as he is involved with its security! The bedrooms are at ground level, each with its own exterior entrance. Modest but prettily decorated, the 'Romantique' is the most pleasant with a four-poster bed and wrought-iron furniture. Breakfast is served inside or in the lovely garden open to surrounding fields. Table tennis, badminton and mini-golf on site.

Facilities: off-street parking, garden, tv lounge, hosts have pets, pets not accepted, dinner available, wheelchair access, closed: 01/12–14/02, hiking, cycling, fishing 3km, vineyard 14km, bird-watching 25km
Adequate English spoken

Directions: From Châteauroux, D956 towards Valençay to Levroux (13km), then when exiting the village take the D2 on the right towards Bouges-le-Château. The house is 500m before the village entrance on the left (signposted).

Location
2km S of VIERZON
in: Méreau, station pick-up on arrival/departure
Railway station: 2km
Airport: Bourges 55km
car essential

Private Home

Pierre is a pastry cook, and you will enjoy the delicious results of his skills at breakfast. Each bedroom has its own personality: one with soft pastel colours, a rustic room with a piano and another with a gaming table. The family welcome is warm and relaxing. On sale: honey, wine.

Colette & Pierre PARENT
'Les Caillotières', 54 chemin Blanc,
18120 MEREAU
Tel: (0) 2 48 71 11 56

Facilities: private parking, garden, tv lounge, hosts have pets, dinner available, kitchen, 1 shared bathroom, wc, fishing, riversports 2km, hiking 4km, cycling 4km, golf course 5km, mushroom-picking 5km, lake watersports 10km, interesting flora 20km, hunting 30km
Basic English spoken

Price Structure – 4 Bedrooms
'Rouge-Gorge': single bed: €34 – 1 person
'Mésange': double bed, 2 single beds (child-size): €38 – 2 people €53 – 4 people
'Pivert': double bed, single bed (child-size): €38 – 2 people €49 – 3 people
'Serin': double bed: €38

Extra Bed: €10
Capacity: 10 people

Directions: On the A20, exit 7 to Vierzon heading towards Méreau, Issoudun via the D320. On this road, look out on the right for the signs 'Chambres d'Hôtes' (do not go as far as Méreau, as the house is nearer to the *autoroute* exit at Vierzon).

Location
35km N W of CHARTRES
in: Blévy, station pick-up on arrival/departure
Railway station: 20km
car essential

Private Home

Dagmar is adorable and our clients can't praise her highly enough. She is German and has been living in France for many years; a warm welcome is guaranteed. The bedrooms are very pretty, and the breakfast plentiful. Well worth a detour.

Dagmar PARMENTIER
2 rue des Champarts, 28170 BLEVY
Tel: (0) 2 37 48 01 21 Fax: (0) 2 37 48 01 21
parti@club-internet.fr
www.bab-blevy.com

Facilities: private parking, garden, tv lounge, kitchen, closed: 01/01–28/02, hiking, cycling, golf course 8km
Fluent English spoken

Price Structure – 1 Bedroom and 1 Suite
'Blévy': television, along corridor bathroom, wc, double bed: €46
'Paris': shower room, wc, double bed. En-suite room, television, double bed: €54 – 2 people
€82 – 4 people

Extra Bed: €24
Capacity: 6 people

Directions: Exit Chartres on the A11. In Chartres, take the D939 towards Verneuil-sur-Avre. In Maillebois, turn right onto the D20 towards Blévy and Dreux. In Blévy go towards Laons and as you leave the village, the house is the first on the right.

Centre-Loire Valley – Vierzon, Chartres

28.08 Chartres

Working Farm

Location
15km S of CHARTRES
in: La Bourdinière-St-Loup
car essential

Marguerite and Marcel are a farming couple who welcome you to their farmhouse, formerly an 18th-century coaching inn. It is conveniently situated near Chartres and on the Route des Châteaux. The bedrooms are basic, practical and quiet at night, despite the house's proximity to the main road. There is a nice green area in the farm courtyard with a swing. Marcel has a passion for tomatoes! He will often invite you to sample them and you may find yourself leaving with some too, if you show an interest in his garden. They pride themselves in making their guests welcome.

Marguerite & Marcel GUIARD
3 Route Nationale 10, Le Temple,
28360 LA BOURDINIERE-ST-LOUP
Tel: (0) 2 37 26 61 90 Fax: (0) 2 37 26 61 90
contact@labourdiniere.com
www.labourdiniere.com

Price Structure – 5 Bedrooms
2 rooms: shower room, wc, double bed, single bed: €45 – 2 people €60 – 3 people
2 rooms: shower room, wc, double bed: €45
shower room, wc, 2 double beds: €45 – 2 people €75 – 4 people

Extra Bed: €15
Reduction: 3 nights
Capacity: 14 people

Facilities: private parking, garden, lounge, hosts have pets, kitchen, babies welcome, free cot, 100% no smoking
Fluent English spoken

Directions: From the A11, take exit 3 (or if coming from Chartres, take the N10 towards Tours). 'Le Temple' is 4km from motorway exit 3, on the right.

28.15 Chartres

Private Home

Location
23km N W of CHARTRES
in: Le Boullay-Thierry
car essential

Between Chartres and its cathedral and the royal chapel at Dreux is this 17th-century house set in a tranquil, charming village complete with château and ancient church. The enclosed garden, full of flowers and fruit trees, has a terrace with teak furniture. Of note is an underground chapel built during the Revolution. The guest rooms are tastefully decorated by Guy, an amateur painter and a car enthusiast. We loved the spacious suite with half-timbered partitions. Breakfasts at your leisure. Be sure to visit all the nearby châteaux.

Claire CHARLIOT-POINCELET
'La Musardière', 7 rue du Marchis,
28210 LE BOULLAY-THIERRY
Tel: (0) 2 37 38 32 72 / (0) 612 05 49 56
cyril.moreau4@wanadoo.fr
www.france.bonjour.com/la-musardiere/

Price Structure – 2 Bedrooms
'La Suite Rose' (our favourite room): television, bathroom, wc, double bed, 2 single beds: €58 – 2 people €98 – 4 people
'Jaune': lounge, television, bathroom, wc, double bed: €53

Extra Bed: €20
Capacity: 6 people

Facilities: private parking, garden, tv lounge, hosts have pets, dinner available, babies welcome, free cot, 100% no smoking, fishing, hiking, cycling, mushroom-picking 2km, lake watersports 10km, golf course 12km, interesting flora 12km, gliding 22km
Fluent English spoken

Directions: From Chartres N154 towards Dreux for 22km, then turn right onto the D26 towards Nogent-le-Roi, then first left turn to Le Boullay-Thierry. In the village, head for Villemeux. The house is on the left just before the château.

Centre-Loire Valley – Chartres

Working Farm

This is a really handy stop on the way south, spotlessly clean and quiet. You can park your car in the interior courtyard in complete safety. They have earned their three 'suns' because of their meticulously high standards of cleanliness and security. On sale: homemade jam, eggs, fruit and vegetables. One self-catering apartment for five persons available to rent weekly.

Géraldine NIVET
8 rue de Chanzy, 28140 LOIGNY-LA-BATAILLE
Tel: (0) 2 37 99 70 71 Fax: (0) 2 37 99 70 71

Location
40km S E of CHARTRES
in: Loigny-La-Bataille
car essential

Facilities: private parking, garden, tv lounge, hosts have pets, dinner available, hiking 5km, cycling 5km, fishing 5km

Price Structure – 4 Bedrooms
ground floor–2 rooms: shower room, wc, double bed, single bed: €43 – 2 people €50 – 3 people first floor: shower room, wc, double bed. Along corridor room, single bed: €43 – 2 people €50 – 3 people

Directions: From the A10, exit Artenay, then the D10 towards Poupry and then the D3-9 towards Loigny-la-Bataille.

Extra Bed: €10
Capacity: 9 people

Centre-Loire Valley – Chartres

Location
23km N of CHARTRES
in: Néron
Railway station: 6km
Airport: Paris-Roissy 100km
car essential

Working Farm

This residence, like the village Néron, reflects its rich past on the route of pilgrims, soldiers and builders. Around a large courtyard stand a dovecote, a medieval tower, barns and the guest room with a sloping ceiling accessed via an external staircase. Your hosts have taken to organic farming and offer produce including flours used to make the bread for breakfast as well as eggs, honey, walnuts, lentils, flax. Françoise is an actress with a theatre company and breeds horses for competitions. A truly charming address.

Françoise & François LHOPITEAU
'La Ferme au Colombier', 2 rue d'Ormoy,
28210 NERON
Tel: (0) 2 37 82 74 85 / (0) 673 50 06 42
Fax: (0) 2 37 82 59 88
francoislhopiteau@wanadoo.fr
www.ferme-au-colombier.com

Facilities: private parking, extensive grounds, hosts have pets, kitchen, babies welcome, free cot, 100% no smoking, riding, hunting, mushroom-picking, bird-watching, hiking, cycling, interesting flora, golf course 6km, lake watersports 10km, gliding 15km, riversports 18km
Fluent English spoken

Price Structure – 1 Bedroom
'Cyprien': shower room, wc, twin beds, single bed: €55 – 2 people €65 – 3 people

Extra Bed: €10
Capacity: 3 people

Directions: On the N154 between Dreux and Chartres, D26 towards Nogent-le-Roi to Ormoy then the D136 on the right to Néron. The house is on this road, in the village, on your left (signposted).

28.19 Chartres

Private Home

Location
26km W of CHARTRES
in: Pontgouin, station pick-up on arrival/departure
Railway station: 2km

This old thatched cottage dating from the 19th century, on the edge of the forest in the Eure valley, is a dream of a place to recharge your batteries and explore this area. It is in the Perche Regional Nature Park, known for its forests, hills and hedges, horses and delightful little villages. Katrien left her native Belgium to open her B&B in France and welcomes you with great warmth. You have the run of the house, so you can relax in the lounge or play a few notes on the piano if the mood takes you.

Katrien VAN DAELE
'La Grange du Bois', 34 la Grange du Bois,
28190 PONTGOUIN
Tel: (0) 2 37 37 47 69 / (0) 689 83 19 89
lagrange-du-bois@orange.fr
www.lagrangedubois.fr

Price Structure – 2 Bedrooms
'Le Rosier': television, bathroom, wc, shower, double bed, single bed: €55 – 2 people €65 – 3 people
'La Glycine': wheelchair access, television, shower room, wc, twin beds: €55

Reduction: groups
Capacity: 5 people

Facilities: private parking, garden, hosts have pets, dinner available, babies welcome, free cot, wheelchair access
Fluent English spoken

Directions: From Chartres, take the N23 towards Le Mans for 19km. At Courville-sur-Eure, take the D920 towards La Loupe. Then at Pontgouin take the D155 towards Senonches for 3km.

28.07 Chartres

Private Home

Location
8km N of CHARTRES
in: St-Prest
Railway station: 2km
Airport: Paris-Orly 80km
car essential

An old thatched-roof farm with a fireplace and warm atmosphere. In summer, breakfast will be served in the garden. It is 8km from Chartres (cathedral, old town, cultural activities, music festivals) and 10km from Maintenon (castle), golf course, horse-riding, cycling, hiking, gliding, hot air balloon flights.

Claire & Etienne BROSSOLLET
49 rue des Fontaines, 28300 ST-PREST
Tel: (0) 2 37 22 25 31
claire.etienne.brossollet@gmail.com

Price Structure – 2 Suites
suite 1: lounge, bathroom, wc, double bed, single bed. En-suite room, 3 single beds. En-suite room, single bed: €55 – 2 people €155 – 7 people
suite 2: shower room, wc, double bed, single bed. En-suite room, 2 single beds: €55 – 2 people €130 – 5 people

Extra Bed: €25
Reduction: 3 nights, children
Capacity: 12 people

Facilities: private parking, garden, tv lounge, hosts have pets, pets not accepted, dinner available, babies welcome, free cot, 100% no smoking, private tennis court
Adequate English spoken

Directions: At Chartres, take the D6 towards Maintenon (Vallée de l'Eure). The house is 1km after the church of St-Prest in the direction of Jouy.

Location
34km N of CHARTRES
in: Vernouillet, station pick-up on arrival/departure
Railway station: 2km

Private Home

Sylvie and Gérard welcome you with great sincerity. From their newly built house enjoy a 180-degree view of Dreux and Vernouillet. There is internet access in each of the guest rooms. If you would like to spend some quality time with your hosts they offer to accompany you on visits to Chartres, Versailles, Giverny and Maintenon with a picnic basket. A lovely day out in good company!

Sylvie & Gérard SIMEON
83 rue Nicolas Robert, 28500 VERNOUILLET
Tel: (0) 2 37 46 63 67 / (0) 610 71 99 17
simeon.gerard@neuf.fr

Facilities: private parking, garden, tv lounge, internet access, babies welcome, free cot, closed: 01/06–10/08 & 09/09–30/10, cycling, riversports 5km
Adequate English spoken

Price Structure – 1 Suite
television, along corridor shower room, wc, double bed, single bed. En-suite room, double bed:
€45 – 2 people €75 – 5 people

Reduction: 2 nights
Capacity: 5 people

Directions: Please contact your hosts in advance for detailed directions.

Location
5km S E of CHATEAUROUX
in: Etrechet, station pick-up on arrival/departure
Railway station: 5km
Airport: Châteauroux 8km
car essential

Residence of Outstanding Character

Easy to find, close to Châteauroux but benefitting from the peace and quiet of the countryside, this former hunting lodge, an outbuilding of an arable farm, has been the home of Scottish couple Nicole and Hugues for more than 15 years. The property has high ceilings, a large circular staircase and comfortable, unfussy bedrooms. One of the meadows on the property leads down to the River Indre and a small lake where you can enjoy a spot of fishing.

Nicole & Hugues LYSTER
'Les Menas', 36120 ETRECHET
Tel: (0) 2 54 22 63 85 Fax: (0) 2 54 22 63 85
menas@wanadoo.fr

Facilities: off-street parking, extensive grounds, tv lounge, hosts have pets, dinner available, babies welcome, free cot, fishing, mushroom-picking, hiking, cycling, bird-watching 10km, golf course 10km, lake watersports 25km
Fluent English spoken

Price Structure – 5 Bedrooms
'Pan': television, bathroom, wc, double bed: €45
'Bleue' & 'Marron': television, shower room, wc, double bed: €45
'Fleurs': television, bathroom, wc, double bed, single bed: €45 – 2 people €59 – 3 people
'Parc': television, shower room, wc, twin beds: €45

Extra Bed: €14
Reduction: 3 nights
Capacity: 11 people

Directions: A20 exit 12 towards Montluçon, La Châtre. At the 3rd roundabout, D67 towards La Châtre and then first lane on the left.

36.07 Châteauroux

Château/Manor House

Anne-Marie & Gabriel FABIAN-SCHAUL
'Château de Bois Robert', 36500 NEUILLAY-LES-BOIS
Tel: (0) 2 54 39 46 18 Fax: (0) 2 54 39 46 18
www.chateaudeboisrobert.fr

Price Structure – 4 Bedrooms
'Christelle': shower room, wc, double bed: €75
'Laetitia': lounge, shower room, wc, double bed: €85
'Aurélie': shower room, wc, double bed, 2 single beds: €75 – 2 people €120 – 4 people
'Alexandre': shower room, wc, four-poster double bed: €75

Extra Bed: €20
Reduction: 4 nights, groups
Capacity: 10 people

Location
18km S W of CHATEAUROUX
in: Neuillay-les-Bois, station pick-up on arrival/departure
Railway station: 18km
car essential

This couple from Luxembourg and their four children have restored this large house, dating from the end of the 19th century, situated in the land of a thousand lakes. There is a friendly, family atmosphere here. The large lake is surrounded by ancient woodland, including some very rare trees, and good fishing is guaranteed. Their dinners make use of their own produce, which is completely organic. It is difficult to choose between the many excursions available to markets and châteaux. Enjoy!

Facilities: private parking, extensive grounds, tv lounge, hosts have pets, dinner available, babies welcome, free cot, closed: 01/10–30/03, private tennis court, hiking, cycling, fishing, interesting flora, mushroom-picking, golf course 11km, riversports 12km
Fluent English spoken

Directions: From the A20, exit 13.1. Take the D925 towards Châtellerault for 4km, then left onto the D80, then right onto the D21 towards Neuillay-les-Bois. The château is signposted on the right.

37.68 Amboise

Residence of Outstanding Character

Odile & Frédéric RENARD
'Manoir du Parc', 8 avenue Léonard de Vinci,
37400 AMBOISE
Tel: (0) 2 47 30 13 96 / (0) 673 98 01 29
Fax: (0) 2 47 30 13 96
info@manoirparc.com
www.manoirparc.com

Price Structure – 4 Bedrooms
shower room, wc, twin beds: €85
shower room, wc, double bed: €95
bathroom, wc, double bed: €105
bathroom, wc, shower, double bed, single bed: €115 – 2 people €135 – 3 people

Extra Bed: €20
Reduction: 01/11–31/03
Capacity: 9 people

Location
AMBOISE
in: Amboise
Railway station: 2km
Airport: Tours 25km

Bienvenue en **France**

This 19th-century *Maison de Maître* stands proudly above Amboise, with a unique view from the bedrooms over the château and Clos Lucé. Visit easily these historic sites but profit too from the tranquil grounds. The garden with a pool extends out to woods, a vegetable plot and an orchard. Inside are spacious bedrooms with fireplaces and annexes containing a sports room (sauna, jacuzzi), a meeting room hosting oenological events and two apartments, rented weekly. A relaxed, professional welcome in a renowned town.

Facilities: private parking, extensive grounds, tv lounge, hosts have pets, pets not accepted, 100% no smoking, 6 years old minimum age, private swimming pool, hiking, riversports, fishing 1km, hunting 5km, mushroom-picking 5km, golf course 25km
Adequate English spoken

Directions: A10 exit 18. Cross the Loire River and continue to the centre of Amboise. D61, towards Montrichard. The house is on this road just after the square, Place Richelieu.

Location
AMBOISE
in: Amboise, station pick-up on
arrival/departure
Railway station: 2km
Airport: Tours 25km

Private Home

Arrive in Amboise and enter through Yveline's big red gate to her converted barn in the heart of the town. The terrace and the small flower garden add to the intimate atmosphere here. Leave your car behind and take the time to explore the town on foot and taste some good wines. Don't be surprised if on your return, you find paintings and sculptures in the garden, as it often serves as an exhibition space for local artists. Yveline is very friendly and cheerful and serves homemade jams, cakes and fruit compotes at breakfast. An excellent address.

Facilities: garden, lounge, kitchen, babies welcome, free cot, 100% no smoking, 2 nights minimum stay: 1/06–15/09, fishing, hiking, cycling, riversports, vineyard, hunting 5km, mushroom-picking 5km, gliding 10km, golf course 20km
Adequate English spoken

Directions: Please contact your host in advance for detailed directions.

Yveline SAVIN
'La Grange', 18 rue Chaptal, 37400 AMBOISE
Tel: (0) 2 47 57 57 22 / (0) 689 35 14 29
yvelinesavin-lagrange@wanadoo.fr
www.la-grange-amboise.com

Price Structure – 4 Bedrooms
'Jaune': shower room, wc, double bed (queen-size): €68
'1930': shower room, wc, double bed, 2 single beds: €68 – 2 people €104 – 4 people
'Familiale': bathroom, wc, double bed (queen-size), 2 single beds: €75 – 2 people €111 – 4 people
wheelchair access, shower room, wc, twin beds: €68

Extra Bed: €18
Reduction: 4 nights
Capacity: 12 people

Location
10km S of AMBOISE
in: Athée-sur-Cher
Railway station: 20km
Airport: Tours 22km
car essential

**Residence of
Outstanding
Character**

This delightful 17th-century villa is in a very beautiful spot on the banks of the River Cher in the middle of grounds and fields facing the Forest of Amboise. You are in rowing distance of Chenonceau in this peaceful spot. Enjoy the cool patio shaded by the wisteria or the royal delights of the four-poster bedroom. Breakfast on the terrace in the summer is fantastic. This is a wonderful spot.

Facilities: off-street parking, extensive grounds, tv lounge, hosts have pets, pets not accepted, 100% no smoking, 12 years old minimum age
Adequate English spoken

Directions: From Amboise take the D31 as far as Bléré, then the N76 towards Tours and at Granlay turn right towards 'Vallet'. (If coming from Tours, take the N76 towards Bléré, Chenonceaux and at Granlay turn left towards 'Vallet'.)

Astrid & Christian LANGE
'Le Pavillon de Vallet', 4 rue de l'Acqueduc,
37270 ATHEE-SUR-CHER
Tel: (0) 2 47 50 67 83 / (0) 687 00 51 27
Fax: (0) 2 47 50 68 31
pavillon.vallet@wanadoo.fr
http://lepavillondevallet.site.voila.fr

Price Structure – 3 Bedrooms
'King Size': television, bathroom, wc, four-poster double bed (super king-size), single bed: €80 – 2 people €100 – 3 people
'Claire': television, bathroom, wc, double bed, single bed: €70 – 2 people €90 – 3 people
'Four à Pain': wheelchair access, television, bathroom, wc, double bed: €65

Extra Bed: €15
Capacity: 8 people

Centre-Loire Valley – Amboise

37.41 Amboise

Residence of Outstanding Character

Florence & François-Xavier HEURTEBISE
'Le Moulin du Fief Gentil', 3 rue de Culoison,
37150 BLERE
Tel: (0) 2 47 30 32 51 / (0) 664 82 37 18
contact@fiefgentil.com
www.fiefgentil.com

Price Structure – 4 Bedrooms and 1 Suite
'Camélia': bathroom, wc, double bed: €95
'Clémentine': bathroom, wc, double bed: €95
'Séraphine': bathroom, wc, twin beds: €90
'Primevère': shower room, wc, twin beds: €75
'Suite du Meunier': bathroom, wc, washbasin, twin beds. En-suite room, wc, 2 single beds:
€125 – 2 people €161 – 4 people

Extra Bed: €18
Capacity: 12 people

Location
10km S of AMBOISE
in: Bléré
Railway station: 30km
Airport: Tours 30km
car essential

Near Chenonceaux, a superb 16th-century mill in lovely grounds with a small lake. The large lounge and notably the dining room with its large bay window and breathtaking view over the mill's waterway, deserve a special mention. A pleasant address with plenty of charm.

Facilities: off-street parking, extensive grounds, lounge, hosts have pets, pets not accepted, dinner available, 10 years old minimum age, fishing, hiking, cycling, riversports, gliding 8km, golf course 30km
Fluent English spoken

Directions: At Amboise, D31 to Bléré (From Tours N76 towards Bléré, Chenonceaux). At Bléré, D52 heading towards Luzillé. The mill is on this road, 700m from the centre on the right.

37.47 Amboise

Château/Manor House

Dominique & Jean-Renaud GUILLEMOT
24 rue des Déportés, 37150 BLERE
Tel: (0) 2 47 30 30 25 Fax: (0) 2 47 30 30 25
jr.guillemot@wanadoo.fr
http://thebelvedere.free.fr

Price Structure – 2 Bedrooms and 1 Suite
'Chambre des Dames': shower room, wc, double bed: €90
'Bleue': shower room, wc, twin beds. En-suite room, double bed: €90 – 2 people €140 – 4 people
'Villa Bébé': bathroom, wc, double bed, single bed: €90 – 2 people €110 – 3 people

Extra Bed: €20
Reduction: 4 nights
Capacity: 9 people

Location
10km S of AMBOISE
in: Bléré, station pick-up on arrival/departure
Railway station: 2km
Airport: Tours 30km
car essential

Dominique and Jean-Renaud, a former air-hostess and airline pilot, welcome you to their listed house near the châteaux of Amboise and Chenonceau. Their welcome is kind and courteous and they are antiques' collectors, as reflected in the excellent décor of their home. Breakfast is served under a charming arbour.

Facilities: private parking, extensive grounds, lounge, hosts have pets, pets not accepted, 100% no smoking, 10 years old minimum age, hiking, cycling, fishing, riversports, hunting 8km, interesting flora 15km, bird-watching 15km
Fluent English spoken

Directions: At Amboise, take the D31 as far as Bléré. (From Tours, take the N76 towards Bléré, Chenonceaux.) The house is in the centre of Bléré, in the street opposite the bridge over the River Cher.

Location
15km N E of AMBOISE
in: Cangey
Railway station: 15km
Airport: Tours 40km
car essential

✺ ✺ ✺
Private Home

Katia and Mark are a Franco-English couple who welcome you to their home in a green and quiet setting, 15 minutes from Amboise. Their old longhouse has been restored with excellent taste to a high level of comfort and is located on a private 9-hole golf course designed by your hosts. Breakfast is served on the terrace overlooking the golf course, in the middle of fields surrounded by woods, where you may spot a deer or a wild boar. It is easily reached from the *autoroute*.

Facilities: private parking, garden, lounge, pets not accepted, dinner available, 100% no smoking, wheelchair access, closed: 01/12–01/02, private swimming pool, hiking, golf course, vineyard 2km, cycling 5km, fishing 5km, interesting flora 10km, riversports 20km, lake watersports 30km
Fluent English spoken

Directions: From the A10, exit 18. Then take the D31 towards Amboise. At Autrèche, take the D55 as far as Dame-Marie-les-Bois, then the D74 towards Cangey for 2km. 'Le Clos du Golf' is on the left.

Katia & Mark FOSTER
'Le Clos du Golf', route de Dame-Marie-les-Bois,
Fleuray, 37530 CANGEY-AMBOISE
Tel: (0) 2 47 56 07 07
closdugolf@wanadoo.fr
www.bonadresse.com/val-de-loire/cangey-amboise.htm

Price Structure – 4 Bedrooms
'La Mare': bathroom, wc, shower, double bed (queen-size): €80
'Les Biches': shower room, wc, twin beds: €70
'Lavande': wheelchair access, shower room, wc, double bed: €65
'Le Jardin': shower room, wc, single bed: €50

Extra Bed: €18
Capacity: 7 people

Location
27km S E of AMBOISE
in: Céré-la-Ronde, station pick-up on arrival/departure
car essential

✺ ✺ ✺ ✺
Château/Manor House

Even though this is quite a big place, those who already know Michèle and her animal kingdom will be even more enthusiastic about her new property. This is set in 40 hectares of beautiful grounds with a swimming pool and tennis court and a menagerie as delightful as ever, with llamas, alpacas, ostriches, peacocks and deer – and she intends to get even more! The bedrooms are top of the range, in keeping with the property, and she also has buildings that can take groups, with a seminar room and a games room.

Facilities: private parking, extensive grounds, tv lounge, hosts have pets, kitchen, wheelchair access, private swimming pool, private tennis court, hiking, fishing, hunting, vineyard, cycling 10km, riversports 15km, golf course 30km
Basic English spoken

Directions: From Amboise via the D31, head to Bléré and the N76. Take the N76 as far as Chenonceaux, then turn right onto the D81, go through Francueil and Epeigné-les-Bois to Monpoupon. There, head towards Céré-la-Ronde for about 2km and Razay is on the right.

Michèle DUVIVIER
'Château de Razay', Razay,
37460 CERE-LA-RONDE
Tel: (0) 2 47 94 38 33 Fax: (0) 2 47 94 35 70
chateauderazay@wanadoo.fr

Price Structure – 29 Bedrooms and 1 Suite
'Cheverny' (our favourite room): television, bathroom, wc, shower, double bed: €130
'Chambord' (our other favourite room): bathroom, wc, double bed, twin beds: €130 – 4 people
Suite 'Amboise': television, bathroom, wc, double bed, twin beds, 4 single beds: €308 – 8 people
'Beaugency': television, bathroom, wc, double bed, twin beds: €95 – 2 people €130 – 4 people
'Villandry': television, bathroom, shower, wc, double bed, single bed: €115 – 3 people
plus 25 rooms

Reduction: groups
Capacity: 73 people

37.38 Amboise

Residence of Outstanding Character

Caroline MANIE
'Auberge Forestière Marcheroux', route de Chenonceaux D81, 37400 FORET-D'AMBOISE
Tel: (0) 2 47 57 27 57 / (0) 607 68 17 48
aubergemarcheroux@wanadoo.fr

Price Structure – 5 Bedrooms
no 1 & no 2 : television, shower room, wc, washbasin, double bed: €65
no 3 & no 4: television, shower room, wc, washbasin, double bed, single bed: €65 – 2 people
€75 – 3 people
no 5: television, shower room, wc, washbasin, double bed, twin beds: €65 – 2 people
€85 – 4 people

Reduction: 15/10–30/03, 3 nights, groups
Capacity: 14 people

Location
2km S of AMBOISE
in: Forêt-d'Amboise
Railway station: 5km
Airport: Tours 30km
car essential

A former 17th-century hunting lodge, this inn, in the heart of the Amboise forest, is an ideal base for day trips (2km from Amboise and 4km from Chenonceaux). Simple rooms, off the beaten track. Try some classic old-fashioned dishes in the restaurant. Helicopter trips over the châteaux can be arranged. Special rate for accommodation + dinner + helicopter ride over the chateaux.

Facilities: private parking, extensive grounds, tv lounge, hosts have pets, dinner available, babies welcome, free cot, private swimming pool, hiking, mushroom-picking, cycling, hunting 1km, fishing 4km, riversports 4km, golf course 10km
Adequate English spoken

Directions: From Paris, take the A10, then the N18 exit to Amboise. Near Amboise, on the D751, head towards Chenonceaux (D81). Take the first right after 2km. Follow the signs.

37.55 Amboise

Château/Manor House

Jean-Claude JOYEZ
'Le Moulin de Francueil', 28 rue du Moulin, 37150 FRANCUEIL
Tel: (0) 2 47 23 93 44
moulinfrancueil@aol.com
www.moulinfrancueil.com

Price Structure – 5 Bedrooms and 1 Suite
'Le Notre': bathroom, wc, double bed (queen-size).
En-suite room, wc, twin beds: €110 – 2 people
€150 – 4 people
'Royale': bathroom, shower, wc, four-poster double bed (king-size), single bed: €130 – 2 people
€146 – 3 people
'Choiseul': bathroom, wc, double bed (queen-size), single bed: €126 – 3 people
'Marie-Antoinette' & 'La Valière': bathroom, wc, double bed: €110
'Lully': bathroom, wc, 2 double beds: €140 – 4 people

Extra Bed: €16
Reduction: 5 nights, groups, children
Capacity: 18 people

Location
15km S of AMBOISE
in: Francueil, station pick-up on arrival/departure
Railway station: 7km
Airport: Tours 35km
car essential

Nature lovers and fans of peace and tranquillity will appreciate this 19th-century watermill in the heart of the Loire Valley on the edge of a river, with grounds crossed by streams and a waterfall. There is a family atmosphere here, and the bedrooms are comfortable and decorated with pretty fabrics. Enjoy the particularly delightful view over the grounds as you sit for breakfast or dinner. This is the ideal base for visiting the famous sites of Touraine, the Loire Valley and the Château de Chenonceau (3km).

Facilities: private parking, extensive grounds, lounge, pets not accepted, dinner available, babies welcome, free cot, 100% no smoking, private swimming pool, hiking, cycling, fishing, hunting, mushroom-picking, vineyard, riversports 5km, golf course 20km
Fluent English spoken

Directions: From Tours take the N76 towards Vierzon. 5km after Bléré turn right as far as Francueil. In this village head towards Loches for about 300m and 'Le Moulin' is on the right. (From Amboise, rejoin Bléré and continue on the N76 towards Vierzon.)

Location
10km S of AMBOISE
in: La Croix-en-Touraine
Railway station: 3km
car essential

Private Home

This modernised farm has all modern comforts, an enclosed garden full of flowers and animals to entertain the kids. It is situated on the edge of the Amboise forest. Ideal for ramblers and anglers, as well as for visits to the châteaux de Touraine.

Martine ALEKSIC
'La Chevalerie', 37150 LA CROIX-EN-TOURAINE
Tel: (0) 2 47 57 83 64
lyoubisa.aleksic@orange.fr

Facilities: off-street parking, garden, lounge, hosts have pets, pets not accepted, kitchen, babies welcome, free cot, hiking, fishing 2km, riversports 4km, cycling 5km, gliding 6km, lake watersports 10km, golf course 20km, interesting flora 20km
Adequate English spoken

Price Structure – 4 Bedrooms
2 rooms: shower room, wc, double bed, single bed:
€43 – 2 people €58 – 3 people
shower room, wc, double bed: €45
shower room, wc, 2 single beds: €45

Directions: In Amboise, take the D31 towards La Croix-en-Touraine. The farm is on this road, 3km before the village. Follow the signs.

Reduction: groups
Capacity: 10 people

Location
10km S of AMBOISE
in: La Croix-en-Touraine, station pick-up on arrival/departure
Railway station: 3km
Airport: Tours 30km
car essential

Château/Manor House

In the heart of the châteaux of the Loire Valley, on the edge of the Amboise forest, this large property offers total tranquillity. Its landscaped grounds are the work of a world famous 19th-century landscape designer. The beautiful floral displays have been done by Bénédicte and Laurent. The simple, basic rooms, some of which are in the main château and some in the former stables, are ideal for a group of friends or families.

Bénédicte & Laurent DUJARDIN
'La Herserie', 37150 LA CROIX-EN-TOURAINE
Tel: (0) 2 47 23 54 36 Fax: (0) 2 47 23 54 36
contact@la-herserie.com
www.la-herserie.com

Facilities: off-street parking, extensive grounds, tv lounge, pets not accepted, kitchen, babies welcome, free cot, 100% no smoking, 2 shared shower rooms, 4 wcs, hiking, cycling 5km, fishing 10km, lake watersports 25km
Fluent English spoken

Price Structure – 19 Bedrooms
château 4 rooms: shower room, wc, washbasin, double bed: €55
château 3 rooms: shower, wc, washbasin, double bed: €55
communs 7 rooms: shower room, wc, double bed: €55
communs 3 rooms: along corridor shower room, wc, washbasin, double bed: €50
communs 2 rooms: shower, washbasin, double bed: €45

Directions: At Amboise take the D31 towards La Croix-en-Touraine (if coming from Tours take the D140 towards Chenonceaux). From the centre of La Croix-en-Touraine head towards Chenonceaux then take the second road on the left. The château is 700m further on, on the right.

Extra Bed: €23
Reduction: groups
Capacity: 38 people

Centre-Loire Valley – Amboise

37.48 Amboise

Private Home

Location
10km S of AMBOISE
in: La Croix-en-Touraine, station pick-up on arrival/departure
Railway station: 3km
Airport: Tours 25km
car essential

This modern, comfortable detached house is situated in its own grounds, on the edge of the Forest of Amboise, 6km from the Château de Chenonceaux. It is quiet and relaxing and there is a play area for children. Suzanne and Jean ensure that you are well looked after, and are happy to advise you on how to get the best out of this fabulous region.

Suzanne & Jean FLOURIOT
'La Chauvinière', 37150 LA CROIX-EN-TOURAINE
Tel: (0) 2 47 57 86 72 Fax: (0) 2 47 57 86 72

Price Structure – 1 Bedroom and 1 Suite
'Rose': lounge, television, shower room, wc, double bed: €45
'Verte': television, shower room, wc, double bed: €40 En-suite room 'Bleu': twin beds: €31

Extra Bed: €12
Reduction: 3 nights
Capacity: 6 people

Facilities: private parking, extensive grounds, tv lounge, hosts have pets, babies welcome, free cot, hiking, cycling, hunting, mushroom-picking, vineyard 3km, fishing 4km, lake watersports 4km, riversports 4km, golf course 5km

Directions: At Amboise, take the D31 towards La Croix-en-Touraine (if coming from Tours, take the D140 towards Chenonceaux). From the centre of La Croix-en-Touraine, head towards Chenonceaux on the D40, then take the third road on the left.

37.72 Amboise

Residence of Outstanding Character

Location
10km W of AMBOISE
in: Noizay, station pick-up on arrival/departure
Railway station: 12km
Airport: Tours 15km
car essential

This 19th-century house is at the heart of an apple orchard on an estate of 4 hectares. If travelling on horseback this is also a stopover (*point étape équestre*) and Isabelle and François can accommodate up to four horses, and their riders of course! They are located on a GR route (Grande Randonnée), and the Touraine Wine Route. The guest rooms are attractive and tastefully decorated in warm colours. Despite there not being a family lounge, François is always on hand and the welcome here is sincere and warm.

Isabelle & François GUILBERT
'Demeure de l'Hommelaye', L'Hommelaye, 37210 NOIZAY
Tel: (0) 2 47 52 12 29 / (0) 687 68 14 99
demeurehommelaye@wanadoo.fr
www.demeurehommelaye.fr

Price Structure – 2 Bedrooms and 1 Suite
'Coquelicot': television, bathroom, wc, double bed (queen-size): €59
lounge, television, shower room, wc, double bed (queen-size): €65
'Fleur de Lys': television, shower room, wc, double bed (queen-size). En-suite room, 2 single beds: €59 – 2 people €83 – 4 people

Extra Bed: €15
Capacity: 8 people

Facilities: off-street parking, extensive grounds, hosts have pets, babies welcome, free cot, 100% no smoking, fishing, mushroom-picking, hiking, cycling, riversports 2km, vineyard 2km, lake watersports 15km, golf course 20km, gliding 25km
Fluent English spoken

Directions: Please contact your hosts in advance for detailed directions.

Location
18km S E of AMBOISE
in: Montrichard, station pick-up on arrival/departure
Railway station: 35km
car essential

Residence of Outstanding Character

As we go to press this home has not yet been classified, but will be shortly. After 20 years in Parisian haute couture, Bernard and Jean-Marie have given it all up to settle in this beautiful residence on the banks of the river Cher. As they love interior decoration and old buildings they have now put on show in their B&B all the objects that they have collected over the years. The result is a warm and refined atmosphere. If you fancy a cup of tea, they will serve it in the gazebo with a view over the river.

Facilities: garden, tv lounge, hosts have pets, dinner available, babies welcome, free cot
Fluent English spoken

Directions: From Amboise, take the D61 for Montrichard.

Bernard BARDIOT & Jean-Marie BATAILLE
'La Villa Marguerite', 8 quai de la République,
41400 MONTRICHARD
Tel: (0) 684 06 74 19
lavillamarguerite@free.fr
www.lavillamarguerite.fr

Price Structure – 6 Bedrooms
'Pivoine': shower room, wc, double bed: €90
'Iris': bathroom, wc, double bed: €70
'Hortensia': bathroom, wc, double bed: €80
'Orchidée': bathroom, wc, shower, twin beds, 2 single beds: €120 – 2 people €150 – 4 people
'Lys': bathroom, wc, shower, double bed (queen-size), single bed: €120 – 2 people €138 – 3 people
'Cyclamen': shower room, wc, double bed: €100

Extra Bed: €18
Reduction: 15/11–15/03, 5 nights, groups
Capacity: 15 people

Location
18km S E of AMBOISE
in: St-Georges-sur-Cher
Railway station: 5km
Airport: Tours 35km
car essential

Residence of Outstanding Character

A warm, genuine welcome awaits at this mill dating back to 1883 on the edge of the River Cher. It is a superb property which was once a retirement home and still has a lift in service up to the bedrooms! Admire the mill-wheel through the bay windows in the lounge or from the little balcony above. The rooms have a superb view over the river as does the veranda where breakfast is served by Isabelle and Thierry. They have excellent contacts with local producers, so stay for dinner and sample the local fare and traditional recipes.

Facilities: private parking, extensive grounds, tv lounge, hosts have pets, pets not accepted, dinner available, babies welcome, free cot, 100% no smoking, wheelchair access, private swimming pool, fishing, hiking, cycling, vineyard 2km, lake water-sports 5km, riversports 5km
Adequate English spoken

Directions: Please contact your hosts in advance for detailed directions.

Isabelle & Thierry MOREAU
'Le Moulin du Port', 26 rue du gué de l'Arche,
41400 ST-GEORGES-SUR-CHER
Tel: (0) 2 54 32 01 37 / (0) 663 06 71 25
Fax: (0) 2 54 32 01 37
bandbf@lemoulinduport.com
www.lemoulinduport.com

Price Structure – 5 Bedrooms
'Arabesque' & 'Romance': bathroom, wc, double bed (queen-size): €115
'Orangerie': shower room, wc, double bed (queen-size): €115
'Pivoine': shower room, wc, four-poster double bed (queen-size): €110
'Côté Jardin': shower room, wc, twin beds: €95

Extra Bed: €25
Reduction: 7 nights, groups, children
Capacity: 10 people

Centre-Loire Valley – Amboise

37.03 Azay-le-Rideau

✳ ✳ ✳ ✳

Château/Manor House

Bienvenue en France

Location
AZAY-LE-RIDEAU
in: Azay-le-Rideau
Railway station: 4km
Airport: Tours 30km
car essential

This was a hunting lodge of the former kings of France, particularly favoured by Louis XI for falconry. The château was built at the beginning of the 20th century. The rooms are rather sober, but the location is wonderful. Deer roam in the grounds.

Sophie DE CHENERILLES
'Château du Gerfaut', Le Gerfaut,
37190 AZAY-LE-RIDEAU
Tel: (0) 2 47 45 40 16 / (0) 662 20 81 06
Fax: (0) 2 47 45 20 15
contact@legerfaut.com
www.legerfaut.com

Facilities: off-street parking, extensive grounds, lounge, hosts have pets, pets not accepted, dinner available, babies welcome, free cot, 100% non smoking, closed: 01/11–01/04, private tennis court, hiking, cycling, golf course 12km
Basic English spoken

Price Structure – 4 Bedrooms
'Verte': bathroom, wc, double bed,
single bed: €105 – 2 people €130 – 3 people
'Rouge': bathroom, wc, shower, twin beds: €95
'Rose': bathroom, wc, double bed,
single bed: €92 – 2 people €115 – 3 people
'Blanche': shower, wc, double bed: €85

Extra Bed: €25
Reduction: 4 nights, children
Capacity: 10 people

Directions: In Azay-le-Rideau, take the D751 towards Tours. At the roundabout turn left towards Villandry, then take the first road on the right.

37.69 Chinon

✳ ✳ ✳

Private Home

Location
17km N of CHINON
in: La Chapelle-sur-Loire
Railway station: 3km
Airport: Tours 40km
car essential

Near the banks of the Loire, this former *tourangelle* longhouse in *tuffeau* stone offers an agreeable and practical stop (near the N152) on the Route des Châteaux. The independent rooms are like small flats with (except 'Pivoines' upstairs) an equipped kitchen area. The enclosed landscaped garden with a large terrace and a heated pool (in season) serves as a backdrop for breakfast. Regular wine-tastings on site (Bourgueil, Saumur) with local winegrowers. Table tennis, barbecue and bicycles at your disposal.

Julie & Jean-Marc DUCHATELLE
'Le Clos de la Chapelle', 2 rue des Rochereaux,
37140 LA CHAPELLE-SUR-LOIRE
Tel: (0) 2 47 97 31 72 / (0) 603 90 46 90
Fax: (0) 2 47 97 85 35
closdelachapelle@free.fr
www.closdelachapelle.com

Price Structure – 1 Suite
and 3 Apartments
'Magnolias': lounge, television, kitchen, shower room, wc, four-poster double bed (queen-size): €90
'Hibiscus': lounge, television, kitchen, bathroom, wc, double bed: €100
'Pivoines': bathroom, wc, double bed: €80
'Glycines': lounge, television, kitchen, bathroom, wc, double bed (queen-size). En-suite room, double bed (queen-size): €110 – 2 people €130 – 4 people

Facilities: off-street parking, garden, tv lounge, hosts have pets, babies welcome, free cot, private swimming pool, fishing, bird-watching, hiking, cycling, mushroom-picking 10km, interesting flora 15km
Adequate English spoken

Extra Bed: €15
Reduction: 01/09–30/06, 3 nights, groups
Capacity: 10 people

Directions: From Tours head towards Saumur on the A85, until Langeais. Continue on the N152 towards Saumur. The house is on a small road on the right, 3km before La Chapelle-sur-Loire.

Location
5km S E of CHINON
in: Ligré
Railway station: 7km
Airport: Tours 50km
car essential

**Château/
Manor House**

A great choice for all the family. Near to the prestigious châteaux is this 17th-century manor house, a legendary refuge of the Chouans. A stairway in the listed turret leads up to the guest rooms. The rooms on the second floor are spacious and well decorated. Of note are 'Bambous' and 'Elfes'. Homemade bread and jams are served at breakfast. There is a play area and an enclosed swimming pool in the garden and two horses to visit in the pastures or stables. If the weather is cold, the *apéritif* is served by the fire. On site: stabling.

Facilities: private parking, extensive grounds, tv lounge, hosts have pets, dinner available, babies welcome, free cot, 100% no smoking, private swimming pool, hunting, fishing, mushroom-picking, hiking, vineyard, cycling 7km, riversports 7km, golf course 15km
Adequate English spoken

**Anne & Jean-Jacques GEAIX
'Au Prince Grenouille', Le Manoir de Beauvais,
37500 LIGRE
Tel: (0) 2 47 93 49 97 Fax: (0) 2 47 98 08 89
info@auprincegrenouille.fr
www.auprincegrenouille.fr**

Price Structure – 3 Bedrooms and 1 Suite
'Libellules': bathroom, wc, double bed, single bed:
€90 – 2 people €115 – 3 people
'Nénuphars': bathroom, wc, double bed. En-suite room, double bed, single bed:
€90 – 2 people €165 – 5 people
'Elfes': shower room, wc, twin beds, single bed:
€110 – 2 people €135 – 3 people
'Bambous': shower room, wc, four-poster double bed: €110

Extra Bed: €25
Reduction: 3 nights, groups, children
Capacity: 13 people

Directions: At Chinon cross La Vienne direction Richelieu. D749 for 5km then D26 on the right towards Ligré. The *manoir* is 2km on your right.

Location
19km S of CHINON
in: Sammarçolles
Railway station: 20km
car essential

Bienvenue en France

Private Home

Andrea and Simon are from the West of England, and left their home country to settle in this area that they loved so much as tourists. Their old stone long-house, close to the châteaux of the Loire, offers total peace and quiet. There is a lovely, warm and friendly family atmosphere – you will feel at home here. Andrea is a *Cordon Bleu* cook and for dinner she makes delicious Anglo-French dishes of which she alone knows the recipe. Desserts are her speciality, so be sure to leave some room! The rooms are large and well furnished.

Facilities: private parking, garden, tv lounge, hosts have pets, dinner available, babies welcome, free cot, 100% no smoking
Fluent English spoken

**Andrea MULHOLLAND
'Les Doinets', Estrepieds, 86200 SAMMARCOLLES
Tel: (0) 5 49 98 39 56
holidays@lesdoinets.com
www.lesdoinets.com**

Price Structure – 2 Bedrooms and 1 Apartment
shower room, wc, double bed, single bed (child-size): €55 – 2 people €65 – 3 people
shower room, wc, double bed: €55
lounge, kitchen, shower room, wc, double bed, 2 single beds (child-size): €55 – 2 people
€75 – 4 people

Extra Bed: €10
Reduction: 1/11–28/02, 3 nights
Capacity: 9 people

Directions: At Chinon, take the D751 then the D759 towards Loudun. Before Loudun, go into Sammarçolles and take the D23. Then go into Estrepieds and follow the 'Chambre d'hôte' signs.

Centre-Loire Valley – Chinon

37.74 Loches

Private Home

Claude REBEN
'Demeure Saint-Ours', 11 rue du Château,
37600 LOCHES
Tel: (0) 2 47 59 56 69 / (0) 633 74 54 82
saintours@orange.fr
www.saintours.eu

Price Structure – 3 Bedrooms
'Jeanne': shower room, wc, double bed: €75
'Agnès': shower room, wc, 2 single beds: €65
'Isabelle': shower room, wc, double bed, single bed:
€75 – 2 people €90 – 3 people

Extra Bed: €15
Reduction: groups
Capacity: 7 people

Location
LOCHES
in: Loches, station pick-up on
arrival/departure
Railway station: Loches
Airport: Tours 35km

Expect a warm welcome at Claude's place in the heart of the royal town of Loches, right by the château and at the foot of the medieval citadel. Claude is keen on history so let him give you a quick run-down on the town he loves so much. The ground floor of this 16th-century townhouse is an art gallery. The splendid listed wooden staircase gives an extra cachet to the heart of this place. The plentiful breakfast is served in the delightful, bright and airy lounge, which you are welcome to use at any time.

Facilities: lounge, pets not accepted, babies welcome, free cot, 100% no smoking, hiking, cycling, vineyard, fishing 1km, hunting 5km, mushroom-picking 5km, golf course 10km, lake watersports 15km, gliding 30km
Adequate English spoken

Directions: In Loches, head for the railway station and take the street opposite the station, Rue de la République, towards the town centre. The Rue du Château is in the heart of the town, unsurprisingly next to the château.

37.61 Loches

Private Home

Anne-Fabienne BOUVIER
'La Ferme Blanche', route de la Chaume-
Brangerie, 37240 CUSSAY
Tel: (0) 2 47 91 94 43 / (0) 661 72 68 30
contact@la-ferme-blanche.com
www.la-ferme-blanche.com

Price Structure – 1 Bedroom and 2 Suites
first floor: bathroom, wc, double bed (queen-size).
En-suite room, twin beds: €95 – 2 people €223 – 6 people
'Rez-de-Jardin': shower room, wc, washbasin, double bed. En-suite room, twin beds: €95 – 2 people
€159 – 4 people
'Four à Pain': lounge, shower room, wc, double bed (queen-size): €115

Extra Bed: €20
Capacity: 12 people

Location
21km S W of LOCHES
in: Cussay
Railway station: 20km
Airport: Tours 45km

A B&B with real character, situated 20km from the famous medieval fortress of Loches, in a tranquil natural setting. The warmth of the interior, with its large living room and light parquet floor, elegant décor and unusual ornaments underline the authentic and homely feel to this former farm. It is obvious that Anne-Fabienne loves her home. She is very attentive and kind and welcomes you as a friend with great enthusiasm. She is very talented at arts and crafts and also organises themed stays (gastronomic, cultural). Hearty breakfasts can be served in the garden.

Facilities: private parking, garden, lounge, pets not accepted, dinner available, 100% no smoking, 2 nights minimum stay: 01/07–31/08, private swimming pool, hunting, mushroom-picking, hiking, cycling, fishing 3km, riversports 8km, gliding 14km, golf course 18km, vineyard 20km
Adequate English spoken

Directions: From Tours take the A10 towards Poitiers, exit 25 towards Ste-Maure-de-Touraine and then the D59 as far as Ligueil. Cussay is 3.5km on the D31 towards Descartes. In the village, turn left behind the church, signed 'La Chaume-Brangerie' and then the first road on the right. The house is on the left-hand side.

Private Home

Location
14km W of TOURS
in: Berthenay
Railway station: 17km
car essential

In her restored farmhouse Danielle has three bedrooms, all with garden view. Her piano is available if you are musical, but cycling tours and organised trips to vineyards are the things to do here. She is happy to let you use the pool as long as any children are supervised.

Danielle GRANDENSCHWILLER
'La Fouacière', La Grange aux Moines,
37510 BERTHENAY
Tel: (0) 2 47 43 50 82
lafouaciere@aol.com
http://lafouaciere.site.voila.fr

Facilities: private parking, garden, tv lounge, hosts have pets, pets not accepted, kitchen, private swimming pool
Adequate English spoken

Price Structure – 3 Bedrooms
lounge, shower room, wc, four-poster double bed, single bed: €60 – 2 people €70 – 3 people
lounge, shower room, wc, double bed: €60
lounge, bathroom, wc, double bed, single bed: €60 – 2 people €70 – 3 people

Extra Bed: €10
Capacity: 8 people

Directions: Please contact your hosts for detailed directions.

Bienvenue en France

Private Home

Location
15km E of TOURS
in: Chançay
Railway station: 15km
Airport: Tours 15km
car essential

We wrote that this farm, dating back to the 14th and 18th centuries, when it belonged to Jean-Pierre, the former owner, was at the heart of the Loire Valley amid the Vouvray vineyards and would seduce you from the very first moment. This holds true today under new owners, Sophie and her family. The bedrooms have been changed around, the welcome is warm and the children are lovely. It is a peaceful setting with grounds of two hectares full of trees and a small lake. Having stopped working to raise her children, Sophie is always on hand.

Sophie LEBRETON
'Ferme de Launay', 37210 CHANÇAY
Tel: (0) 2 47 52 28 21 / (0) 612 08 58 18
Fax: (0) 2 47 52 28 51
fermedelaunay2@wanadoo.fr
www.fermedelaunay.com

Facilities: private parking, extensive grounds, tv lounge, hosts have pets, babies welcome, free cot, 100% no smoking, fishing, hunting, interesting flora, mushroom-picking, bird-watching, vineyard, cycling, riversports, golf course, gliding
Basic English spoken

Price Structure – 2 Bedrooms
'Rose': bathroom, wc, twin beds,
2 single beds: €60 – 2 people €90 – 4 people
'Jaune': shower room, wc, double bed: €60

Extra Bed: €15
Capacity: 6 people

Directions: When coming from Tours, take the N152 as far as Vouvray. Turn left at the traffic lights in the direction of Château-Renault and the D46 (third on the right). Pass Vernou and 2km further on the house is on the left on a big bend.

37.70 Tours

Château/Manor House

Anne & Sean DIGNAM
'Domaine de la Guillotière',
37320 ESVRES-SUR-INDRE
Tel: (0) 2 47 34 80 53 / (0) 663 38 61 96
Fax: (0) 2 47 34 80 53
dignam@wanadoo.fr
www.frenchguesthouse.com

Price Structure – 4 Bedrooms
'Joyce': bathroom, wc, shower, double bed: €90
'Yeats': bathroom, wc, shower, double bed (queen-size): €90
'Oscar Wilde' (our favourite room): shower room, wc, double bed (queen-size): €90
'Beckett': shower room, wc, twin beds: €90

Extra Bed: €15
Reduction: 1/09–30/06, 3 nights
Capacity: 8 people

Location
18km S of TOURS
in: Esvres-sur-Indre
car essential

Bienvenue en France

In 6 hectares of magnificent wooded parkland dominating the Indre is this truly romantic manor house from the 18th century. A turret stands by the edge of the swimming pool by an impressive sequoia tree. The interior is classically styled and there is a piano in the sitting room. The bedrooms, named after Irish writers, are on the first floor. Like Sean and Bailey the Labrador, Anne is Irish and may serve her delicious scones at breakfast. Sean is a helicopter pilot. Delightful!

Facilities: private parking, extensive grounds, hosts have pets, kitchen, private swimming pool, fishing, mushroom-picking, bird-watching, riversports, hiking, cycling, vineyard 3km, interesting flora 7km, golf course 15km, hunting 15km
Fluent English spoken

Directions: From Tours N143 towards Loches for approximately 6km then turn right and continue to Esvres. In the village, D85 direction St-Branchs, turn left before the level-crossing and then left again. Follow signs for 'La Guillotière'; the property is on the left.

37.30 Tours

Private Home

Anne-Marie LARIE
'Le Clos du Paradis', 46 rue Descartes,
37130 LANGEAIS
Tel: (0) 2 47 96 65 37 / (0) 666 03 97 04
Fax: (0) 2 47 96 65 37
aml@leclosduparadis.fr
www.leclosduparadis.fr

Price Structure – 4 Bedrooms and 1 Suite
'Peintre' & '2 Parcs': washbasin, double bed, cot: €47
'Vue': twin beds: €47
third room: twin beds: €47
ground floor suite: shower room, wc, twin beds.
En-suite room, shower room, wc, twin beds:
€52 – 2 people €73 – 4 people

Extra Bed: €11
Capacity: 12 people

Location
25km W of TOURS
in: Langeais
Railway station: 25km
Airport: Tours 30km
car essential

Bienvenue en France

This house is in quiet grounds in the centre of the town, with a view over the Château de Langeais, where Charles VIII and Anne de Bretagne were married. Many artists come to Le Clos in order to paint the view of the château from the bedroom called 'Peintre'.

Facilities: private parking, extensive grounds, tv lounge, pets not accepted, babies welcome, free cot, 100% no smoking, wheelchair access, 1 shared bathroom, 1 shared shower room, wc, hiking, cycling, fishing, bird-watching, golf course 10km, riversports 10km
Basic English spoken

Directions: At Tours, take the N152 towards Saumur. In the town, turn right at the château. The street is immediately on the left after the church.

Location
3km N E of TOURS
in: Rochecorbon, station pick-up on arrival/departure
Railway station: 7km
Airport: Tours 8km
car essential

Private Home

A modern Touraine-style house, on the hillside overlooking the village. All the rooms are spotlessly clean and have a beautiful view. You will be able to taste the Vouvray wine as Jacqueline lives beside a vineyard.

Jacqueline GAY
'Les Hautes Gatinières', 7 chemin de Bois Soleil,
37210 ROCHECORBON
Tel: (0) 2 47 52 88 08
gatinieres@wanadoo.fr
www.gatinieres.eu.ki

Facilities: private parking, garden, lounge, hosts have pets, internet access, babies welcome, free cot, 100% no smoking, closed: 01/11–15/11, hiking, cycling, fishing, riversports, vineyard, mushroom-picking 4km, interesting flora 6km, golf course 10km, hunting 10km
Adequate English spoken

Price Structure – 2 Bedrooms and 1 Suite
suite: television, bathroom, wc, double bed. En-suite room, 2 single beds: €55 – 2 people €89 – 4 people
television, bathroom, wc, double bed, single bed: €55 – 2 people €71 – 3 people
television, bathroom, wc, double bed: €55

Extra Bed: €16
Reduction: 6 nights
Capacity: 9 people

Directions: In Tours, take the D952 towards Vouvray. At the traffic lights, just after the information point 'l'Observatoire', turn left into Rue des Clouets, then follow the signs 'Chambres d'Hôtes'.

Location
4km N W of TOURS
in: St-Cyr-sur-Loire
Railway station: 2km
Airport: Tours 4km

Private Home

As we go to press, this host has not yet been classified, but will be shortly. Angela's place dates from the 19th century, beside the Loire yet only five minutes walk from the historic centre of Tours, heart of Touraine, much loved by the kings of France. Angela has five bedrooms which have been modernised. She serves a hearty breakfast to see you through a hard day's march of visiting the magical Loire Valley châteaux, unless you prefer to just sit on the banks of the Loire in Tours, a beautiful town well worth devoting some time to.

Angela WESLEY
'La Maison Bohème', 19 quai Portillon,
37540 ST-CYR-SUR-LOIRE
Tel: (0) 2 47 61 73 40 / (0) 628 32 13 42
Fax: (0) 2 47 51 25 58
contact@lamaisonboheme.com
www.lamaisonboheme.com

Facilities: private parking, garden, tv lounge, pets not accepted, dinner available, babies welcome, free cot, 100% no smoking, 12 years old minimum age
Fluent English spoken

Price Structure – 5 Bedrooms
1 room: television, shower room, wc, twin beds: €85
2 rooms: television, shower room, wc, twin beds: €90
1 room: television, bathroom, wc, double bed: €100
1 room: television, bathroom, wc, double bed: €115

Extra Bed: €25
Reduction: 4 nights, groups
Capacity: 10 people

Directions: From the A10, exit 21 towards Amboise. At the roundabout, take the 2nd right (Av. André Malraux) and at the fourth set of lights turn right over the bridge across the Loire (Pont Wilson). At the first lights as you come off the bridge, turn left on to the Quai Portillon beside the river. The house is on the right after about 100m.

Centre-Loire Valley – Tours

37.62 Tours

Private Home

Madeleine FAUQUET
11 rue Dorothée de Dino, 37130 ST-PATRICE
Tel: (0) 2 47 96 90 09 Fax: (0) 2 47 96 90 09

Price Structure – 1 Bedroom
and 1 Apartment
along corridor bathroom, wc, double bed, twin beds:
€40 – 2 people €66 – 4 people
lounge, kitchen, along corridor shower room, wc,
double bed, cot: €52

Extra Bed: €13
Capacity: 6 people

Location
30km W of TOURS
in: St-Patrice
Railway station: St-Patrice
Airport: Tours 30km
car essential

You may already know Madeleine and Pierre from their former home in Normandy. They now live on a former *tourangelle* vineyard on a hillside by the edge of the forest of Rochecotte. The original wine press and troglodyte cellar carved into the *tuffeau* rock are still intact. The house sits above the Loire River 1km away and is accessible on foot via numerous walking trails. In the village, you can stock up on a supply of Bourgueil wine (150m away is a local winegrower with a small private Gallo-Roman museum).

Facilities: private parking, extensive grounds, hosts have pets, pets not accepted, dinner available, fishing, hiking, vineyard
Adequate English spoken

Directions: From Tours take the N152 towards Angers as far as St-Patrice. When you reach the village via the D35, cross the railway line and the house is just after the bend, on the right.

41.44 Blois

Residence of Outstanding Character

Michelle & Michel LESCURE
'La Petite Fugue', 9 quai du Foix, 41000 BLOIS
Tel: (0) 2 54 78 42 95
lapetitefugue@wanadoo.fr
www.lapetitefugue.com

Price Structure – 4 Bedrooms
'Jardin secret': shower room, wc, double bed: €95
'L'Alcove': bathroom, wc, shower, double bed: €105
'Clair obscur': shower room, wc, twin beds: €115
'Au fil de l'eau': bathroom, wc, shower, twin beds, single bed: €135 – 2 people €160 – 3 people

Extra Bed: €25
Capacity: 9 people

Location
BLOIS
in: Blois
Railway station: Blois
Airport: Tours 60km

This house sits on the bank of the Loire River, near to the town centre of Blois and its château. The interior, tastefully decorated with restraint in light grey colours, is enhanced with period furniture and beautiful paintings. Comfortable bedrooms with refined décor boast views over the Loire. A full plentiful breakfast is served, as are delicious dinners, perfected by Michelle/Michel after many years in the restaurant business. Unwind in the lounge by the fireplace or in the intimate little courtyard. Secure parking. A peaceful atmosphere and a warm welcome.

Facilities: private parking, garden, lounge, pets not accepted, dinner available, babies welcome, free cot, 100% no smoking, 2 nights minimum stay: 1/04–30/09, fishing, bird-watching, hiking, cycling, mushroom-picking 3km, hunting 5km, golf course 10km
Fluent English spoken

Directions: From the centre of Blois, from the château, take the Rue des Fossés du Château, and then the Rue des Trois Marchands to the Loire River. At the traffic lights, turn right, and pass a small car park. It is the fourth house.

Location
BLOIS
in: Blois, station pick-up on arrival/departure
Railway station: 2km
Airport: Tours 50km

Bienvenue en France

Residence of Outstanding Character

By the state forest of Blois, the town centre and the château, is this former winegrowers' house surrounded by trees. The bedrooms are in a separate building, all tastefully decorated, with period furniture and air-conditioning. There is a romantic feel to the two larger rooms on the first floor under a sloping ceiling. There is a heated swimming pool too, in the courtyard, and a former orangery with seating and games. Breakfasts are varied and plentiful, true to Patricia and Michel who open their doors with obvious enjoyment.

Facilities: private parking, extensive grounds, lounge, hosts have pets, babies welcome, free cot, 100% no smoking, wheelchair access, private swimming pool, hiking, cycling 2km, riversports 5km, lake watersports 5km, vineyard 10km, golf course 15km
Adequate English spoken

Patricia & Michel COFFART
Le Plessis, 195 rue Albert 1er, 41000 BLOIS
Tel: (0) 2 54 43 80 08 Fax: (0) 2 54 43 95 24
leplessisblois@wanadoo.fr
www.leplessisblois.com

Price Structure – 5 Bedrooms
'Rose' & 'Bleue': shower room, wc, twin beds: €105
'Violette': shower room, wc, double bed (queen-size): €105
'Rouge' & 'Jaune': bathroom, wc, double bed (queen-size): €125

Extra Bed: €25
Capacity: 10 people

Directions: At the centre of Blois, head for the station, and follow signs to 'Lycée Hôtelier' (well signposted). The house is just opposite the 'Lycée'.

Location
10km S W of BLOIS
in: Chouzy-sur-Cisse
Railway station: 5km
car essential

Private Home

This solid 70s house, between Blois, Chaumont-sur-Loire and Amboise is an ideal stopover. Appreciate the tranquillity and the birdlife of the Cisse Valley. Early risers may spot rabbits and roe deer that graze at the edge of the forest. The house is spacious with a bucolic living room with a fireplace, exposed beams and a billiard table. It is just the 'Orange' room that shares a bathroom. Try a spot of archery in the garden, by the swimming pool. Evelyne and Michel happily advise where best to visit in the area over breakfast.

Facilities: off-street parking, garden, tv lounge, hosts have pets, pets not accepted, babies welcome, free cot, 100% no smoking, 1 shared bathroom, wc, private swimming pool, fishing, cycling, vineyard, hiking 1km, golf course 3km, interesting flora 5km
Adequate English spoken

Evelyne & Michel MARECHAL
'La Dame de Cisse', 48 route d'Onzain,
41150 CHOUZY-SUR-CISSE
Tel: (0) 2 54 20 49 64 / (0) 610 35 72 05
ladamedecisse@wanadoo.fr
ladamedecisse.free.fr

Price Structure – 3 Bedrooms
and 1 Apartment
'Verte' & 'Bleue': lounge, shower room, wc, double bed: €45
'Orange': wc, double bed: €40
'Apartment': lounge, kitchen, shower room, wc, double bed, 2 single beds (child-size): €80 – 4 people

Extra Bed: €10
Reduction: 1/10–1/03, 3 nights
Capacity: 10 people

Directions: From Blois, N152 direction Tours for 9km then turn right direction Chouzy-sur-Cisse and follow the main road across the village heading for Onzain to the exit of Chouzy-sur-Cisse. The house is on the right.

41.42 Blois

Private Home

Location
29km S of BLOIS
in: Couddes
Airport: Tours 60km
car essential

It won't be Julie and David, a British couple, that welcome you, but the two mascots: Beeky the goose and Bliss the dog! A relaxed family atmosphere at this newly built house, set in 2.5 hectares of woodland with walking trails and a small lake. There is a wooden hut where you can pour yourself a cold drink. Inside, each bedroom has a separated-off shower area and there is a dining room and a classic-style lounge with a lovely fireplace. The eggs served for breakfast are supplied by the 'Spice Girls', their hens!

Julie BURKE
'Le Gros Chêne B&B', 41700 COUDDES
Tel: (0) 2 54 71 42 76
info@legroschenebb.com
www.legroschenebb.com

Price Structure – 3 Bedrooms
'Pêche' & 'Verte': shower room, wc, double bed, single bed: €46 – 2 people €58 – 3 people
'Bleue': shower room, wc, double bed: €42

Extra Bed: €12
Reduction: 4 nights, children
Capacity: 8 people

Facilities: private parking, extensive grounds, lounge, hosts have pets, pets not accepted, dinner available, babies welcome, free cot, 100% no smoking, cycling, hiking, interesting flora, vineyard 3km, golf course 15km
Fluent English spoken

Directions: From Blois, D956 to Contres, then the D675 towards St-Aignan to Couddes. In the village take the D11 on the right to Thésée. Le 'Gros Chêne' is 2km ahead on the right (B&B France sign).

41.33 Blois

Working Farm

Location
29km E of BLOIS
in: Dhuizon
Railway station: 25km
Airport: Paris-Orly 180km

'And just one more thing,' says Claude, because he always has something interesting to tell you. He is a retired goat farmer, and will explain all about goat's milk and cheese, as well as the Château de Chambord and all the walks and hiking routes through the forest. The welcome here is sincere, down to earth and full of local colour. The bedrooms overlook the lake and the land of châteaux and goats.

Claude MOREAU
'Le Patis des Bouleaux', 41220 DHUIZON
Tel: (0) 2 54 98 30 32 / (0) 689 56 24 77

Price Structure – 2 Bedrooms
first room: shower room, wc, double bed, single bed: €46 – 2 people €58 – 3 people
second room: shower room, wc, 3 single beds: €46 – 2 people €58 – 3 people

Extra Bed: €12
Reduction: 3 nights
Capacity: 6 people

Facilities: private parking, garden, lounge, hosts have pets, pets not accepted, babies welcome, free cot, wheelchair access, hiking, cycling, fishing 3km, hunting 4km, golf course 20km, vineyard 25km, lake watersports 30km, riversports 30km

Directions: Leave Blois on the D765 towards Romorantin, and then take the D923 as far as Neuvy, then the D18 as far as Dhuizon. In this village, head towards Villeny for 3km. 'Le Patis des Bouleaux' is on the right. Go through the gates, and if no one is about, continue as far as the *fromagerie*.

Location
10km E of BLOIS
in: Mont-Près-Chambord, station
pick-up on arrival/departure
Railway station: 12km
car essential

Residence of Outstanding Character

This watermill was originally built in the 11th century. It then evolved and grew to become the B&B that now welcomes you. This residence, so full of character, beside the river in the heart of the Loire châteaux, will enchant you. It is also on the 'Châteaux by Bike' route. Frédérique and Ulysse will give you a great welcome to their home, where they have renovated the interior into five comfortable apartments decorated with excellent taste, and furnished with antique period furniture. There are 5 hectares of grounds for you to enjoy, where donkeys, goats, sheep and ducks roam peacefully.

Facilities: off-street parking, extensive grounds, tv lounge, hosts have pets, kitchen, babies welcome, free cot
Fluent English spoken

Ulysse BRUNET & Frédérique JUQUIER
'Moulin à Eau du Bas-Pesé', 275 rue du Moulin,
41250 MONT-PRES-CHAMBORD
Tel: (0) 2 54 46 10 42 / (0) 687 93 67 99
fjuquier@yahoo.fr
sejour-chambord.com

Price Structure – 5 Apartments
'Iris': lounge, television, kitchen, bathroom, wc, double bed: €50
'Pivoine': lounge, television, kitchen, bathroom, wc, double bed, single bed: €75 – 3 people
'Nénuphars': lounge, television, kitchen, shower room, wc, double bed, single bed: €75 – 3 people
lounge, television, kitchen, shower room, wc, double bed, 2 single beds: €100 – 4 people
lounge, television, kitchen, bathroom, shower, wc, double bed, 3 single beds: €125 – 5 people

Reduction: 1/11–31/03, groups
Capacity: 17 people

Directions: Please contact your hosts for detailed directions.

Location
32km S of BLOIS
in: Monthou-sur-Cher, station pick-up on arrival/departure
Railway station: 9km
Airport: Tours 60km
car essential

Private Home

Cheerful Lydie dedicates herself to looking after her B&B guests and her gîte. This is an old property, built in the Touraine tradition, which has been renovated preserving the architectural style. The garden is large with a picnic and children's play area. The bedrooms are springlike and Lydie's daughter has added paintings and furniture decoration in keeping with each room's flower theme. Her husband, for his part, organises wine tastings with the local winegrowers followed by a picnic among the vines in the Cher valley.

Facilities: private parking, extensive grounds, lounge, pets not accepted, dinner available, babies welcome, free cot, 100% no smoking, wheelchair access, fishing, hiking, cycling, vineyard, riversports 10km, golf course 20km, interesting flora 20km, gliding 30km

Lydie SOUADET
'La Varenne', 1 route de Blois,
41400 MONTHOU-SUR-CHER
Tel: (0) 2 54 71 11 64
souadet.lavarenne@free.fr
http://souadet.lavarenne.free.fr

Price Structure – 4 Bedrooms and 1 Suite
'Lilas': shower room, wc, double bed. En-suite room, 3 single beds: €55 – 2 people €96 – 5 people
'Fuchsia': shower room, wc, double bed, cot: €53
'Bleuet': shower room, wc, double bed: €50
'Coquelicot': shower room, wc, double bed, 2 single beds (1 = child-size): €55 – 2 people €82 – 4 people
'Tournesol': bathroom, wc, twin beds, cot: €55

Extra Bed: €15
Reduction: groups
Capacity: 15 people

Directions: Motorway A10 exit 17, Blois then direction Châteauroux, Vierzon. Just after the bridge crossing the Loire River take direction Blois Sud, then Montrichard. At the exit of Pontlevoy, turn left direction Monthou-sur-Cher. At Monthou-sur-Cher, at the 'Stop' sign, turn left, follow signs to 'La Varenne'. After 450m, the entrance is on the left on the bend.

Centre-Loire Valley – Blois

41.52 Blois

Private Home

Location
32km S of BLOIS
in: Monthou-sur-Cher, station pick-up on arrival/departure
Railway station: 7km
Airport: Tours 40km
car essential

Arlene is British but has been living in France for 30 years. She is a former potter who now dedicates herself to her B&B guests and making jewellery, and from time to time she puts on show her jewellery and pottery creations. Arlene and her husband are warm and always on hand to be of assistance. From the garden is a lovely view of the valley and it is on the terrace here that Arlene serves dinner and organises barbecues. The guest bedrooms are comfortable and bright.

Arlene BESSON
'Les Iris', 66 route du Château,
41400 MONTHOU-SUR-CHER
Tel: (0) 2 54 71 01 33 / (0) 671 54 14 88
arlene.besson@wanadoo.fr
http://lesiris-.monsite.orange.fr

Price Structure – 3 Bedrooms
'Hortensia': shower room, wc, double bed, single bed: €55 – 2 people €70 – 3 people
'Tilleul': shower room, wc, double bed, 2 single beds (child-size): €55 – 2 people €85 – 4 people
'St Martin': shower room, wc, double bed, 2 single beds: €55 – 2 people €85 – 4 people

Extra Bed: €15
Capacity: 11 people

Facilities: off-street parking, garden, lounge, dinner available, babies welcome, free cot, private swimming pool, fishing, hiking, vineyard, mushroom-picking 10km, riversports 12km, golf course 18km
Fluent English spoken

Directions: Please contact your host in advance for detailed directions.

41.47 Blois

Private Home

Location
23km S of BLOIS
in: Pontlevoy, station pick-up on arrival/departure
Railway station: 7km
Airport: Tours 45km
car essential

Cécile and Alain have taken on a real challenge, restoring this former farmhouse dating back to 1860 that they fell in love with. They are only using original materials to enhance and remain true to the building's stone walls, beams and framework. Numerous activities are due to be available to guests, including: cookery courses, tastings, guided historic and garden tours. Be sure to check if these are available when you book. A spa offering massages and treatments is also part of their future plans. In the meantime, the welcome here is very pleasant and friendly.

Cécile & Alain DELMAS
'La ferme d'O', 10 rue de Paradis,
41400 PONTLEVOY
Tel: (0) 2 54 32 58 07 / (0) 699 01 39 95
Fax: (0) 2 54 32 58 07
contact@ferme-do.com
www.ferme-do.com

Price Structure – 3 Bedrooms
and 2 Apartments
'Fraise' & 'Cassis': telephone, shower room, wc, washbasin, double bed: €65
'Pomme': telephone, shower room, wc, washbasin, double bed: €75
'Rose': wheelchair access, telephone, kitchen, shower room, wc, washbasin, double bed, single bed: €85 – 2 people €100 – 3 people
'Bambou': wheelchair access, telephone, kitchen, shower room, wc, washbasin, double bed, 2 single beds: €85 – 2 people €100 – 4 people

Extra Bed: €15
Reduction: 01/01–30/04, 2 nights, groups
Capacity: 13 people

Facilities: private parking, garden, lounge, dinner available, babies welcome, free cot, 100% no smoking, wheelchair access, 3 nights minimum stay, closed: 01–15/02 & 01–15/12, bird-watching, hiking, cycling, interesting flora, riversports, fishing 2km, golf course 15km
Fluent English spoken

Directions: In Blois, take the D764 towards Pontlevoy-Montrichard. In Pontlevoy, opposite the town hall (*la mairie*), turn right towards Chaumont-sur-Loire, Vallières and then take the first road on the left (Rue de Paradis). The farm is on the right.

Location
23km S of BLOIS
in: Pontlevoy
Railway station: 15km
car essential

Château/Manor House

This beautiful property has 5 hectares of grounds full of pheasants, rabbits and squirrels, surrounded by an ancient wall. Vines also cover another hectare. Trips they recommend are hot air balloon flights or a visit to the vineyard, where you can taste and buy. In fact the accommodation is in the old wine-making buildings with the wine press, and the lounge is the room where the grapes were pressed. The rooms are pleasant and spacious and Patrick's international roots – German father, Brazilian mother, and brought up in Britain – result in a very warm welcome. We loved this place.

Facilities: private parking, garden, lounge, pets not accepted, kitchen, babies welcome, free cot, 100% no smoking, closed: 15/10–1/04
Fluent English spoken

Patrick RECCHIA
'Le Pressoir', Les Grandes Vignes,
41400 PONTLEVOY
Tel: (0) 2 54 32 83 39 Fax: (0) 2 54 32 83 45
brecchia@compuserve.com
www.lesgrandesvignes.com

Price Structure – 4 Bedrooms
and 1 Apartment
'Cheverny': lounge, bathroom, wc, double bed: €100
'Chenonceau': lounge, bathroom, wc, twin beds: €100
'Amboise': bathroom, wc, double bed: €85
'Chaumont': bathroom, wc, double bed: €75
apartment: wheelchair access, kitchen, shower room, wc, double bed, 4 single beds: €75 – 2 people €120 – 6 people

Extra Bed: €15
Reduction: 2 nights, groups
Capacity: 14 people

Directions: From the A10, exit 17, Blois. At the second roundabout head for Châteauroux. Cross the River Loire and at the roundabout, take the D765 as far as Contres. After the petrol station, take the D30 towards Thenay, Pontlevoy. After Thenay, continue for 1km and turn left at the sign 'Les Grandes Vignes'. Enter through the third gate on the left.

Location
13km S of BLOIS
in: Seur
Railway station: 10km
car essential

Private Home

Madeleine throws open all of her grand *maison bourgeoise* dating from the 18th century, with its French-style garden. The bedrooms are on the first floor and are comfortable, quite spacious and spotlessly clean. There is also a guest lounge. Breakfast is taken in the large ground floor room, and the kitchen is also available to you. There is also a corner with information on this region, especially its châteaux and vineyards, although it may be simpler to ask your hosts as they have lived here for 20 years. Madeleine's breakfast is massive. *Bon appétit!*

Facilities: private parking, garden, lounge, pets not accepted, kitchen, babies welcome, free cot, 100% no smoking, hunting, fishing, mushroom-picking, hiking, cycling, interesting flora, vineyard, golf course 10km, gliding 10km, lake watersports 10km
Fluent English spoken

Madeleine & Jean-Pierre D'ELIA
10 route de Cellettes, 41120 SEUR
Tel: (0) 2 54 44 03 85
la.valiniere@laposte.net
http://lavaliniere.free.fr

Price Structure – 3 Bedrooms
'Royale': shower room, wc, 2 double beds: €65,50 – 2 people €90,00 – 4 people
'Côté Cour': bathroom, wc, double bed (queen-size): €61,50
'Côté Jardin': bathroom, wc, twin beds: €61,50

Reduction: 2 nights, children
Capacity: 8 people

Directions: Exit 17 Blois from the A10. At Blois, take the D956 towards Châteauroux. At Cellettes, take the D77 on the right to Seur. It is the third house on the right as you enter the village.

41.31 Blois

Private Home

Marie-Thérèse & Rémi BELLETESTE
'Les Fondières', 20 route de Muides,
41220 THOURY-EN-SOLOGNE
Tel: (0) 2 54 87 08 62
lesfondieres@wanadoo.fr
www.lesfondieres.com

Price Structure – 3 Bedrooms
'Erable': shower room, wc, double bed: €81,60
'Napoléon': shower room, wc, double bed: €77,20
'Chinoise': along corridor shower room, wc, double bed: €70,60

Reduction: 3 nights
Capacity: 6 people

Location
23km E of BLOIS
in: Thoury-en-Sologne, station pick-up on arrival/departure
Railway station: 12km
car essential

In the heart of Sologne,1.5km from the Château de Chambord in this former 100-year-old hunting lodge, Marie-Thérèse and Rémi will be expecting you. There is a warm and relaxed atmosphere here, whether you are sitting around the dinner table or outside by the barbecue in the shade of the age-old maple tree that has watched over hunters throughout the century. Your hosts still organise hunting trips in the forests of Sologne. An extra spare room is available. They accept only small pets.

Facilities: private parking, garden, tv lounge, hosts have pets, pets not accepted, dinner available, 2 nights minimum stay, closed: 15/12–15/01, hiking, cycling, mushroom-picking 2km, golf course 10km, hunting 20km, lake watersports 20km, gliding 40km
Fluent English spoken

Directions: From Blois take the D951 as far as Muides. Then turn right onto the D103 towards Crouy-sur-Cosson. After 4km turn right onto the D22 towards Thoury. 'Les Fondières' is on the left, 150m further on after the village sign for Thoury.

41.48 Blois

Private Home

Michèle SANGLIER
'L'Oiseau de Paradis', 4 route de Dhuizon,
41220 THOURY-EN-SOLOGNE
Tel: (0) 2 54 87 04 01 Fax: (0) 2 54 87 58 46
sangliermichele@free.fr

Price Structure – 2 Bedrooms and 1 Suite
'L'Orient': lounge, bathroom, wc, double bed, single bed: €67 – 2 people €79 – 3 people
'Chambord': lounge, shower room, wc, double bed, 2 single beds: €67 – 2 people €89 – 4 people
'Londres': lounge, television, shower room, wc, double bed. En-suite room, 3 single beds: €67 – 2 people €100 – 5 people

Capacity: 12 people

Location
23km E of BLOIS
in: Thoury-en-Sologne
Railway station: 12km
Airport: Paris-Orly 125km
car essential

Michèle and Pierre live in the centre of a little village on the edge of the Chambord estate and forest, a mountain bike ride away. They offer three carefully decorated bedrooms, each one with its own theme. A few improvements to the exterior are yet to be completed but the garden is pleasant and there are also aviaries of exotic birds (toucans, parakeets). Plentiful breakfasts and good-value home-cooked dinners are served (special child rates). A seating and kitchen area are being improved for guests' use.

Facilities: garden, hosts have pets, pets not accepted, dinner available, kitchen, babies welcome, free cot, 100% no smoking, private swimming pool, hunting, fishing, mushroom-picking, hiking, cycling, vineyard, lake watersports 5km, riversports 10km, golf course 20km
Basic English spoken

Directions: A10 between Blois and Orléans, exit 16 to Mer, direction Mer, then D112 towards Chambord. Just after Muides-sur-Loire, D103 on the left towards Crouy-sur-Cosson, then D22 on the right to Thoury. In Thoury, park in the church car park. The house is a few metres away on the Route de Dhuizon.

Centre-Loire Valley – Blois

Location
18km S of BLOIS
in: Valaire
Railway station: 18km
car essential

Private Home

The exterior of this 11th-century priory gives no idea of the pleasant surprise that awaits you inside. The décor is rich in fabrics, local religious objects, antique furniture and Asian knick-knacks. The magic is continued in the bedrooms, with four-poster beds and stained-glass windows. It continues in the grounds, with a lake with an island on which you will spot a Thai-style house on stilts. You will enjoy breakfast in the beautiful conservatory. You will have some great times here, in excellent company.

Facilities: private parking, garden, tv lounge, hosts have pets, pets not accepted, dinner available, 100% no smoking, 8 years old minimum age, hiking, cycling, fishing, hunting, mushroom-picking, golf course 10km, lake watersports 18km, riversports 18km
Fluent English spoken

Marie-France & François LE GALL GALLOU
'Les Métamorphozes', Domaine du Prieuré,
41120 VALAIRE
Tel: (0) 2 54 44 14 62
contact@les-metamorphozes.com
www.au-domaine-du-prieure.com

Price Structure – 4 Bedrooms and 1 Suite
'Prestige': lounge, shower room, wc, four-poster double bed: €75
'Okita Zen': shower room, wc, double bed (queen-size), single bed: €105 – 3 people
'Manoir': bathroom, wc, shower, double bed (queen-size), single bed: €110 – 3 people
'Kessel Safari': shower room, wc, double bed (queen-size), single bed: €105 – 3 people
'Suite Wishumpur': lounge, shower room, wc, double bed (queen-size). En-suite room, double bed (queen-size): €130 – 4 people

Extra Bed: €30
Reduction: 2 nights   **Capacity:** 15 people

Directions: From Blois, D764 towards Montrichard for 18km, as far as Monthou-sur-Bièvre, then turn right onto the D169 as far as Valaire.'Le Domaine du Prieuré' adjoins the church.

Location
25km S W of BLOIS
in: Vallières-les-Grandes, station pick-up on arrival/departure
Railway station: 12km
car essential

Private Home

A former winegrower's house built right up against a rock face (visible from the inside!) with a large garden. The comfortable bedrooms have been renovated and decorated with care, inspired by marine, oriental and romantic themes. There is also a large, charming sitting room with a fireplace and exposed beams. Lydia and René, a kind couple, offer dinner and serve beautifully presented dishes. René is a connoisseur of fine wines and will obligingly dust off a few bottles from his cellar dug deep into the *tuffeau* rock.

Facilities: off-street parking, garden, tv lounge, hosts have pets, dinner available, 100% no smoking, hiking, cycling, vineyard 8km, golf course 15km
Adequate English spoken

Lydia & René HIRONDART
'Sainte Fripette', Bout,
41400 VALLIERES-LES-GRANDES
Tel: (0) 2 54 20 94 47 / (0) 672 39 14 13
hirondart@aol.com
www.chambrehotes.fr.tc

Price Structure – 3 Bedrooms and 1 Apartment
'Marine': shower, wc, double bed: €58
'Cosy': shower room, wc, double bed: €58
'Romance': bathroom, wc, twin beds: €65
'Orientale': lounge, kitchen, shower room, wc, twin beds: €65

Reduction: groups
Capacity: 8 people

Directions: Bypass Amboise via the D31. At the roundabout by the supermarket 'Leclerc', take the D23 to Souvigny-de-Touraine and then the D30 towards Vallières-les-Grandes. 1km before the entrance to the village, turn right towards Bout and follow signs to 'Ste-Fripette'.

Centre-Loire Valley – Blois

41.57 Blois

✳ ✳ ✳ ✳

Private Home

Location
45km S of BLOIS
in: Couffy
Railway station: 6km
Airport: Tours 40km
car essential

Christine and Jean-Michel welcome you to their spacious, charming home surrounded by vines. There are organised tours to the châteaux and you are only 5km from one of the largest zoo-parks in Europe. They are very safety conscious as the magnificent pool and spa have an electronic alarm, and there are fire alarms in the bedrooms. There is even one in the bedroom in the converted laundry room, now converted into a love nest, which we particularly liked. Each bedroom has a different décor, all under the eaves but spacious and with high ceilings. The staircase is very attractive.

Christine & Jean-Michel DURAND
'La Ferme de Couffy', 25 rue de la Ferme,
41110 COUFFY
Tel: (0) 2 54 75 23 07
chambres-d-hotes41@orange.fr
www.lafermedecouffy.com

Price Structure – 4 Bedrooms
'Ronde' & 'Suspendue': shower room, wc, double bed: €55
'Buanderie': lounge, shower room, wc, double bed: €90
'Ecurie': shower room, wc, double bed, 2 single beds (child-size): €70 – 2 people €100 – 4 people

Extra Bed: €15
Reduction: groups
Capacity: 10 people

Facilities: off-street parking, garden, lounge, internet access, dinner available, babies welcome, free cot, 100% no smoking, private swimming pool
Adequate English spoken

Directions: From either the A85 or the A10 when you reach the bridge at St-Aignan-sur-Cher, turn left and go along the 'quais' beside the river Cher. Keep going straight on for 6km as far as Couffy. Just as you enter this village, turn right towards Châteauvieux. Follow signs to 'La Ferme de Couffy'.

41.55 Romorantin

✳ ✳ ✳

Private Home

Location
21km N of ROMORANTIN
in: Neung-sur-Beuvron, station pick-up on arrival/departure
Railway station: 16km
car essential

Bienvenue en France

At Colette and Michel's place they serve good, hearty breakfasts including local specialities like *sablés* and, of course, homemade jam. They are also into serious fishing, with a lake, hire of tackle and a host who organises competitions. Why not have a go, although they will not let you eat your catch! There is a covered, heated pool and they organise guided tours and cycle rides. The house is decorated with taste and has a very attractive guest lounge.

Colette & Michel DUMONT
'Le Grand Soupeau', route de Chaumont-sur-Tharonne, 41210 NEUNG-SUR-BEUVRON
Tel: (0) 2 54 83 64 92 / (0) 684 94 96 55
Fax: (0) 2 54 83 64 92
dumont-michel@orange.fr
www.sologne-naturel.com

Price Structure – 5 Bedrooms
'Tournesol': shower room, wc, double bed: €65
'Lilas': shower room, wc, double bed: €75
'Rose': bathroom, wc, double bed: €85
'Pivoine': shower room, wc, double bed, single bed: €110 – 2 people €110 – 3 people
'Eglantine': shower room, wc, double bed, 3 single beds: €120 – 2 people €120 – 5 people

Extra Bed: €10
Reduction: groups
Capacity: 14 people

Facilities: private parking, extensive grounds, tv lounge, hosts have pets, kitchen, babies welcome, free cot, 100% no smoking, private swimming pool
Adequate English spoken

Directions: On the A71 exit 3, Lamotte-Beuvron, and then head towards la Ferté-Beauharnais, Romorantin. In la Ferté-Beauharnais at the 'Stop' sign, take the D922 on the right towards Orléans. Le Grand Soupeau is about 2km further on, on the right.

Location
29km N of VENDOME
in: Bouffry, station pick-up on arrival/departure
Railway station: 29km
car essential

Private Home

A superb location for this house, between Châteaudun and Vendôme and surrounding woodland. Not surprising then that the bedrooms with views over the fields are named 'La Clef des Champs' or 'Le Soleil Couchant'. Breakfast is served in the winter garden from which there is a lovely view of the lawn, framed by fir trees and extending down to a private lake. An ideal place to recharge your batteries and enjoy walks and a spot of fishing. Take home regional products and visit the troglodyte caves. An attentive welcome.

Elisabeth & Jean-Luc GRATIEN
'La Pacquerie', route de la Chapelle Vicomtesse,
41270 BOUFFRY
Tel: (0) 2 54 80 19 79 / (0) 681 68 58 08
Fax: (0) 2 54 80 19 79
jean-luc-gratien@wanadoo.fr
www.lapacquerie.fr

Facilities: private parking, extensive grounds, tv lounge, hosts have pets, babies welcome, free cot, 100% no smoking, hunting, fishing, hiking, cycling, lake watersports 11km, vineyard 35km
Basic English spoken

Price Structure – 2 Bedrooms and 1 Suite
'La Clef des Champs': shower, wc, double bed: €59
'L'Ocrerie': bathroom, wc, double bed: €69
'Le Soleil Couchant': wheelchair access, bathroom, wc, double bed. En-suite room, 2 single beds: €69 – 2 people €90 – 4 people

Reduction: 4 nights
Capacity: 8 people

Directions: From Vendôme take the N10 towards Châteaudun for 7km, then at St-Firmin-des-Prés, take the D111 on the left and then the D141 to La Ville-aux-Clercs, Chauvigny-du-Perche and Bouffry. The house is on the road of 'La Chapelle Vicomtesse' on the right-hand side.

Location
7km E of VENDOME
in: Coulommiers-la-Tour, station pick-up on arrival/departure
Railway station: 10km
car essential

Private Home

Not far from the châteaux of the Loire Valley, in a small village close to Vendôme, is this old farm with real character boasting a square tower and an interior courtyard. Inside, the guest bedrooms are of standard comfort and have their own entrance. Breakfast is served in a small dining room reserved for guests or on the terrace overlooking the garden. Patricia would be delighted to show you around the troglodyte cave dwellings and walk with you down by the Loire River. Patricia is a musician and loves music.

Patricia LESOURD
15 rue Vendômoise,
41100 COULOMMIERS-LA-TOUR
Tel: (0) 2 54 77 00 33
patriciabluet@wanadoo.fr

Facilities: private parking, garden, lounge, pets not accepted, dinner available, babies welcome, free cot, fishing, hiking, cycling, gliding 10km, hunting 10km, lake watersports 10km, vineyard 10km, golf course 20km, riversports 30km
Fluent English spoken

Price Structure – 2 Bedrooms and 1 Suite
shower room, wc, twin beds: €46
shower room, wc, double bed: €46
shower room, wc, double bed. En-suite room, 3 single beds: €46 – 2 people €94 – 5 people

Extra Bed: €16
Capacity: 9 people

Directions: From Vendôme, D917 towards Beaugency to Coulommiers-la-Tour (7km). The house is on this road, at the entrance to the village on the left.

Centre-Loire Valley – Vendôme

45.08 Orléans

Working Farm

Location
15km E of ORLEANS
in: Donnery, station pick-up on arrival/departure
Railway station: 20km
Airport: Paris-Orly 120km

Marie-Claude CHARLES
'La Poterie', 45450 DONNERY
Tel: (0) 2 38 59 20 03
lapoteriecharles@wanadoo.fr
http://perso.orange.fr/lapoterie.charles

Marie-Claude kindly welcomes you to her working farm with homemade cakes. The guest bedrooms here have independent entrances, are comfortable but are simply furnished. There are plenty of activities on offer nearby, notably strolls along the long canal built in the 17th century to transport wood, or the banks of the Loire if you prefer. The largest state-owned forest in France is 10km away and for golfers there is an 18-hole course a stone's throw away.

Price Structure – 3 Bedrooms
'Verte' & 'Rose': shower room, wc, double bed:
€53,90
'Bleue': shower room, wc, 3 single beds:
€53,90 – 2 people €64,90 – 3 people

Extra Bed: €10
Reduction: 4 nights
Capacity: 7 people

Facilities: off-street parking, lounge, hosts have pets, pets not accepted, kitchen, hiking, cycling 1km, riversports 1km, golf course 2km
Adequate English spoken

Directions: At Orléans (exit Orléans-Nord from A11), take the N60 towards Montargis for 20km. Turn off at La Fay-aux-Loges. In Fay-aux-Loges take the first on the left after the church and follow the D709 towards Donnery. The farm is 2.5km further on, on the right.

45.14 Orléans

Private Home

Location
15km E of ORLEANS
in: Donnery
Railway station: 17km
Airport: Paris-Orly 100km
car essential

Marie & Pierre DULAC
50 rue de Boisgault, 45450 DONNERY
Tel: (0) 2 38 59 22 34 / (0) 610 89 45 79
pdulac@neuf.fr
www.chambres-donnery.fr

This house is in a quiet location, surrounded by green fields, and can easily be reached from Orléans, the châteaux of the Loire Valley or Sologne. The bedrooms are comfortable, tastefully decorated and promise a good night's sleep. Your hosts are former restaurateurs and Marie, who is of Italian origin, will be delighted to knock up a few Italian specialities for dinner.

Facilities: private parking, extensive grounds, tv lounge, pets not accepted, babies welcome, free cot, golf course, riversports, hiking 1km, cycling 1km, fishing 1km, mushroom-picking 1km, hunting 3km, gliding 5km, interesting flora 15km

Price Structure – 2 Bedrooms
'Bleue': shower room, wc, double bed, single bed, cot: €45 – 2 people €60 – 3 people
'Rose': shower room, wc, twin beds, single bed, cot: €45 – 2 people €60 – 3 people

Extra Bed: €10
Reduction: 4 nights
Capacity: 6 people

Directions: On the N60 (the dual carriageway from Orléans), head towards Montargis. Exit at La Fay-aux-Loges and take the D709 for Donnery. In this village turn right by the post office and after the town hall (*la mairie*), take the first street on the left. The house is about 1.2km from the village.

Location
35km S E of ORLEANS
in: Isdes
Railway station: 20km
car essential

✸✸✸
Residence of Outstanding Character

A romantic atmosphere fills this manor house. Relax and chat in the lounge, or enjoy the cool of the garden. On summer evenings you will dine under the arbour, with its attractive coloured lights. Your hostess is distinguished, charming and cultured. There is also a semi-detached lodge, independent from the main house. Special reduced green fees can be arranged.

Muguette BERNARD
'Grand'Maison', 4 route de Clémont, 45620 ISDES
Tel: (0) 2 38 29 12 10/10 89 / (0) 678 45 16 04
Fax: (0) 2 38 29 10 00
bernard.muguette@orange.fr

Facilities: private parking, garden, tv lounge, pets not accepted, dinner available, 100% no smoking, hiking, fishing, golf course 12km, hunting 12km, lake watersports 12km
Fluent English spoken

Price Structure – 2 Bedrooms and 1 Apartment
'Jaune': bathroom, wc, double bed: €55
'Rose': along corridor bathroom, wc, washbasin, double bed: €55
'Petit Pavillon': kitchen, shower room, wc, double bed: €55

Capacity: 6 people

Directions: Exit 3 on the A71 (Lamotte-Beuvron). Head towards Vouzon, Souvigny, Isdes on the D101. The house is in the centre of the village.

Location
35km S E of ORLEANS
in: Isdes
Railway station: 20km
car essential

✸✸✸
Private Home

Renée and Gilbert are a retired couple and have two separate studio rooms on the ground floor of their home in this delightful, quiet Sologne village full of flowers. Your rooms open onto a large garden where several hens peck about freely. In the evening their next-door neighbour Muguette serves dinner at her place and is great company. Alternatively there is one of the best restaurants in the region nearby. This is a small corner of real France and well worth three 'suns'.

Renée & Gilbert HATTE
'La Grand'Maison', 30 route de Clémont, 45620 ISDES
Tel: (0) 2 38 29 10 89 / (0) 678 45 16 04
Fax: (0) 2 38 29 10 00

Facilities: extensive grounds, dinner available, hiking, fishing, golf course 12km, hunting 12km, lake watersports 12km
Adequate English spoken

Price Structure – 2 Apartments
'Licou': lounge, kitchen, bathroom, wc, double bed, single bed: €60 – 2 people €75 – 3 people
'Harnais': lounge, kitchen, bathroom, wc, double bed: €60

Capacity: 5 people

Directions: From the A71 exit 3, Lamotte-Beuvron. From the town centre head towards Vouzon, Souvigny and Isdes via the D101. The house is in the centre of the village.

Centre-Loire Valley – Orléans

45.09 Orléans

Residence of Outstanding Character

Bienvenue en France

Location
30km S E of ORLEANS
in: St-Benoît-sur-Loire
Railway station: 25km
Airport: Paris-Orly 150km
car essential

This couple took early retirement and have put their hearts into renovating this farmhouse without it losing any of its character. You may think you are going to stay for just one night but by the time Denise has served you your delicious meals you will certainly extend your stay much longer. On sale: watercolour courses.

Denise & Pierre DURIN
9 chemin du Pleu, 45730 ST-BENOIT-SUR-LOIRE
Tel: (0) 2 38 35 72 68 / (0) 680 68 05 76
Fax: (0) 2 38 35 72 68
durin.pierre@wanadoo.fr

Price Structure – 1 Bedroom and 1 Suite
suite: along corridor bathroom, wc, shower, double bed. En-suite room, twin beds: €52 – 2 people €94 – 4 people
'Mansardée': shower, wc, double bed, 2 single beds: €52 – 2 people €84 – 4 people

Extra Bed: €16
Reduction: 3 nights
Capacity: 8 people

Facilities: off-street parking, garden, tv lounge, hosts have pets, pets not accepted, dinner available, kitchen, babies welcome, free cot, closed: 01/10–01/04, cycling, fishing, riversports, hiking 5km, golf course 10km, interesting flora 10km, lake watersports 20km
Fluent English spoken

Directions: On the A10, exit Orléans-Nord. Take the N60 towards Montargis. At St-Martin-d'Abbat turn right towards Germiny and follow signs towards St-Benoît. The house is midway between St-Benoît and St-Père in the hamlet of Les Places (head towards ULM and enter on the side of the garden).

45.12 Orléans

Private Home

Bienvenue en France

Location
30km S of ORLEANS
in: Vannes-sur-Cosson
Railway station: 35km
Airport: Paris-Orly 140km
car essential

This French couple, with Swedish ancestry, welcome you like long-lost friends to their large, red-brick house in the heart of La Sologne. Their English-style breakfasts will set you up for the day. Perhaps you will try your luck at fishing in the neighbouring lake, or just crash out on the large terrace beside the pool.

James FALCK
'Bagatelle', 40 rue de Bagatelle,
45510 VANNES-SUR-COSSON
Tel: (0) 2 38 58 15 10 / (0) 672 23 18 67
Fax: (0) 2 38 58 15 10

Price Structure – 3 Bedrooms
'Bleue': along corridor bathroom, wc, double bed: €55
'Rose': shower room, wc, double bed, 2 single beds: €57 – 2 people €97 – 4 people
'Blanche': single bed: €45 – 1 person

Extra Bed: €18
Reduction: 7 nights
Capacity: 7 people

Facilities: private parking, extensive grounds, tv lounge, hosts have pets, dinner available, babies welcome, free cot, 100% no smoking, 3 shared bathrooms, wc, 1 shared shower room, private swimming pool, fishing, golf course 10km
Adequate English spoken

Directions: From Orléans, take the Voie Express N60 towards Gien. At Châteauneuf-sur-Loire, take the D11 as far as Vannes. When you are in the village, it is the first street on the right.

Location
35km E of ORLEANS
in: Vitry-aux-Loges
Railway station: 30km
car essential

Working Farm

Brigitte and Hervé live on this former farm in vast meadows, on the edge of the forest of Orléans, where they continue to rear horses. The property consists of three independent buildings, one of which is dedicated to guests and has a communal room. The bedrooms are fairly simple and share a large bathroom but are clean and sufficiently comfortable. Outside, a pergola of vines shades a table by the barbecue. The surrounding countryside is the main attraction here, where you get a lot of space for your money! Horses can be accommodated in stables or in the meadow.

Facilities: off-street parking, extensive grounds, tv lounge, hosts have pets, kitchen, babies welcome, free cot, 1 shared bathroom, wc, closed: 25/12, mushroom-picking, hiking, fishing 5km, riversports 5km, gliding 15km, golf course 20km
Adequate English spoken

Directions: From Orléans take the N60 towards Montargis as far as Châteauneuf-sur-Loire, then the D10 towards Vitry-aux-Loges. When you reach the village 'Les Quatre Routes' turn right towards Combreux. Continue for 1.5km and then turn down a little road on your right and follow the signs to 'Le Petit Houssat'.

Brigitte & Hervé AGARD-FARRUGIA
'Le Petit Houssat', 168 route de Nombrun,
45530 VITRY-AUX-LOGES
Tel: (0) 2 38 59 34 72 / (0) 617 06 77 99
hfarru@free.fr
http://lepetithoussat.free.fr

Price Structure – 4 Bedrooms
3 rooms: washbasin, twin beds: €38,50
washbasin, twin beds, single bed: €38,50 – 2 people
€49,50 – 3 people

Extra Bed: €10
Reduction: 2 nights
Capacity: 9 people

Centre-Loire Valley – Orléans

179

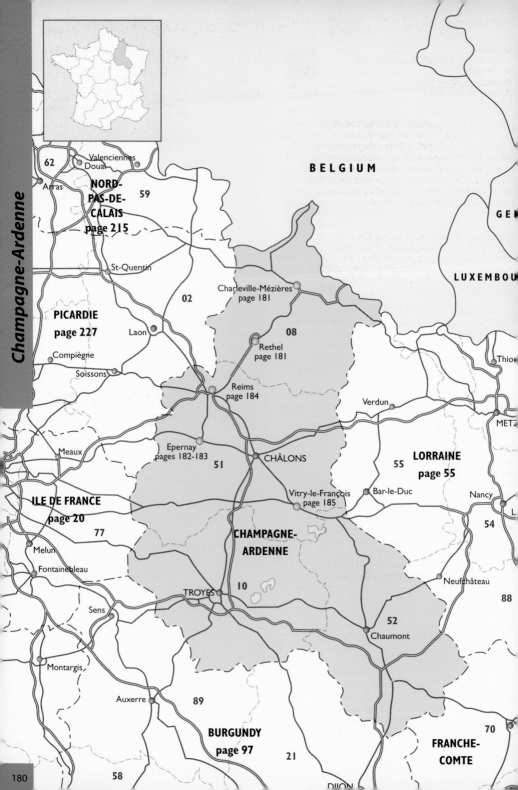

BELGIUM

GE

LUXEMBOU

62

Valenciennes
Douai

Arras

NORD-
PAS-DE-
CALAIS
page 215

59

St-Quentin

Charleville-Mézières
page 181

02

08

PICARDIE
page 227

Laon

Rethel
page 181

Compiègne

Soissons

Reims
page 184

Verdun

Thio

MET

Meaux

Epernay
pages 182-183

51

CHÂLONS

LORRAINE
page 55

55

ILE DE FRANCE
page 20

77

Vitry-le-François
page 185

Bar-le-Duc

Nancy

L

54

Melun

Fontainebleau

CHAMPAGNE-
ARDENNE

Neufchâteau

88

TROYES

10

Sens

52

Chaumont

Montargis

Auxerre

89

70

BURGUNDY
page 97

21

FRANCHE-
COMTE

58

DIJON

Location
30km N E of CHARLEVILLE-MEZIERES
in: Girondelle
Railway station: 35km
Airport: Reims 80km
car essential

Working Farm

This is an old woodcutter's house converted into a farm and B&B. It is on the 'Route of Fortified Churches' in a charming little village nestling in the valley. The setting is rural and wooded and ideal for some wonderful walks. Pierrette serves delicious regional dishes made with farm produce and this is a great opportunity to try her milk-jam, rhubarb wine, homemade charcuterie or even nettle jelly on the terrace!

Facilities: off-street parking, garden, tv lounge, hosts have pets, pets not accepted, dinner available, 100% no smoking, cycling, fishing, hiking 5km, mushroom-picking 5km, lake watersports 15km, winter sports 15km, riversports 20km, golf course 25km
Basic English spoken

Pierrette & Pascal BROSSE
08260 GIRONDELLE
Tel: (0) 3 24 54 31 32 / (0) 685 49 98 06
Fax: (0) 3 24 54 31 32
pierrette.brosse@wanadoo.fr
http://perso.orange.fr/pierrette.brosse/

Price Structure – 3 Bedrooms
'Cheval': shower room, wc, double bed: €45
'Oiseau': shower room, wc, double bed, single bed:
€45 – 2 people €63 – 3 people
'Chat': shower room, wc, double bed, 2 single beds:
€45 – 2 people €81 – 4 people

Extra Bed: €18
Capacity: 9 people

Directions: At Charleville-Mézières take the N43 towards Hirson as far as Maubert-Fontaine, then turn left onto the D36 towards Girondelle. (If you are coming from Hirson, follow the signs from d'Auvillers-les-Forges.) In the village follow the signs to 'Chambres d'Hôtes'.

Location
12km N E of RETHEL
in: Saulces-Monclin, station pick-up on arrival/departure
Railway station: 12km
Airport: Reims 55km
car essential

Private Home

This place is set in extensive grounds, with a river, a lake where you can fish and a waterfall. Sylvie is very friendly and you will enjoy just relaxing and enjoying the countryside. Be sure to try her excellent homemade apple juice. Dinner is also great fun and the conversation will be sure to turn to organic food, yoga and the internet. Sylvie also paints on wood and silk. Private fishing.

Facilities: off-street parking, extensive grounds, tv lounge, hosts have pets, dinner available, 100% no smoking, 1 shared bathroom, 2 wcs, fishing
Adequate English spoken

Sylvie GOULDEN
'Les Sources', 1 rue du Moulin d'en Haut,
08270 SAULCES-MONCLIN
Tel: (0) 3 24 38 59 71 Fax: (0) 3 24 72 74 60
contact@les-sources.info
www.les-sources.info

Price Structure – 8 Bedrooms
3 rooms: bathroom, wc, washbasin, 3 single beds:
€50 – 2 people €62 – 3 people
'Anémone' & 'Rose': bathroom, wc, washbasin,
4 single beds: €50 – 2 people €74 – 4 people
3 rooms: shower, washbasin, 2 single beds: €50

Reduction: 3 nights
Capacity: 23 people

Directions: *Autoroute* A34 E17, Reims to Charleville-Mézières, take exit 14 Faissault and Saulces-Monclin. At Saulces-Monclin, follow signs to 'Les Sources'.

51.18 Epernay

Working Farm

Sophie & Philippe BRUN
'Logis des Pressureurs', 1 rue Henri IV, 51160 AY
Tel: (0) 3 26 54 56 37 Fax: (0) 3 26 54 09 40
info@champagne-roger-brun.com
www.champagne-roger-brun.com

Price Structure – 7 Bedrooms
1, 2 & 3: shower room, wc, double bed: €50
shower room, wc, 4 single beds:
€50 – 2 people €70 – 4 people
wheelchair access, shower room, wc,
double bed: €50
6 & 7: shower room, wc, double bed,
single bed: €50 – 2 people €60 – 3 people

Extra Bed: €12
Capacity: 18 people

Location
3km N E of EPERNAY
in: Ay-Champagne, station pick-up
on arrival/departure
Railway station: 1km
Airport: Reims 30km
car essential

As well as being well known to French crossword puzzle fanatics, Ay is also famous for its prestigious champagne. Except during the wine harvest, Sophie and Philippe welcome you to their house near to the cellars of Champagne Roger Brun, a delicious *Grand Cru*. Their house is in the centre of the village in a quiet spot near to the 15th-century church and 500m from the vineyards. Surprisingly, the bedrooms are rather sober, but comfortable. They will be delighted for you to taste their champagne and visit the cellars.

Facilities: private parking, tv lounge, hosts have pets, pets not accepted, kitchen, 100% no smoking, wheelchair access, closed: 15/12–01/02 & 15/09–15/10, riding, hiking, fishing, vineyard, golf course 30km
Fluent English spoken

Directions: Ay is 3km to the east of Epernay. The house is just behind the church (near to the champagne house Roger Brun).

51.21 Epernay

Private Home

Virginie PHILIZOT
'L'Arbanne', 49 Grande Rue, 51480 REUIL
Tel: (0) 3 26 51 02 96 / (0) 670 42 11 50
Fax: (0) 3 26 57 76 69
champagne.philizot.fils@wanadoo.fr
www.champagne.philizot.fr

Price Structure – 2 Bedrooms
'Chambre du Château': lounge, television, bathroom, wc, four-poster double bed: €150
'Chambre de la Vallée': lounge, television, shower room, wc, double bed, 2 single beds (child-size): €150 – 2 people €150 – 4 people

Capacity: 6 people

Location
14km W of EPERNAY
in: Reuil
Railway station: 15km
car essential

As we go to press this host has not yet been classified, but will be shortly. It is on the threshold of the Champagne area, as you leave the *autoroute* at Dormans for Epernay, a famous Champagne town. Here the River Marne meanders through the valley and the vines on its slopes stretch to the horizon. By now you should be looking forward to your arrival at Virginie's place and the bottle of champagne that she will offer you, as she is a producer. Your hosts have prepared a handy guide on all that this region offers, in addition to visiting champagne cellars.

Facilities: off-street parking, tv lounge, pets not accepted, internet access, dinner available, babies welcome, free cot, 100% no smoking, closed: 21/12–5/01, private swimming pool
Adequate English spoken

Directions: From the A4 exit 21 Dormans. Head towards Epernay to the N3.

Location
25km W of EPERNAY
in: Verneuil
car essential

**Residence of
Outstanding
Character**

In the heart of the village, with a river at the bottom of the garden, is this *maison bourgeoise*, once a farm breeding work horses. Inscribed in history, it was a command post during WW2 and deeply involved in WW1, shown by the fragments of shells encrusted here and there. Today, wild ducks have made it their home. Relax by the river, the bowling pitch or the former pigeon lofts and stables, now a summer kitchen. Sabine put her heart and soul into decorating the house and with Simon, together they run a champagne vineyard.

Sabine & Simon BLIN
'Le Havre du Percheron',
22 rue de la Tour, 51700 VERNEUIL
Tel: (0) 3 26 51 92 29 / (0) 664 09 62 92
Fax: (0) 3 26 51 92 29
setsblin@aol.com
www.havredupercheron.com

Facilities: Private parking, extensive grounds, tv lounge, hosts have pets, kitchen, babies welcome, free cot, 100% no smoking, fishing, hiking, cycling, vineyard, mushroom-picking 3km, golf course 7km, hunting 7km
Fluent English spoken

Price Structure – 2 Bedrooms
shower room, wc, double bed (queen-size): €80
shower room, wc, twin beds, 2 single beds:
€80 – 2 people €100 – 4 people

Extra Bed: €10
Reduction: 2 nights
Capacity: 6 people

Directions: Take the A4 motorway Paris — Reims, exit 21 Dormans. D980 towards Dormans to Verneuil. The house is on this main road in the centre of the village on the right.

Location
27km W of EPERNAY
in: Vincelles
Railway station: 3km
Airport: Paris-Roissy 90km
car essential

Private Home

A house in a superb spot, high up in a peaceful village by vines, overhanging the Marne Valley. The bedrooms have views over the river or the hillsides. For a little more room, opt for the suite (access to a fridge, too). Charles' work often takes him abroad but he is from the region and can guide and advise you on the best vineyards. Sandra, with Haitian roots, hosts you with great kindness and offers a traditional or savoury breakfast. Champagne producers and the Bataille de la Marne memorial nearby. Boat trips possible.

Sandra & Charles SIMON
'L'Escale Fleurie', 3 rue Paul Chapelle,
51700 VINCELLES
Tel: (0) 3 26 58 87 94 / (0) 684 43 52 32
Fax: (0) 3 26 58 87 94
simonsandra@club-internet.fr
www.simonsandra.club.fr

Facilities: private parking, garden, tv lounge, pets not accepted, babies welcome, free cot, 100% no smoking, fishing, hiking, cycling, vineyard, riversports 3km, lake watersports 5km, golf course 8km, hunting 10km, bird-watching 10km
Fluent English spoken

Price Structure – 2 Bedrooms and 1 Suite
'N°1 Verte': shower room, wc, double bed: €58
'N°2 Rose': along corridor shower room, wc, double bed: €58
'N°3 Suite': lounge, along corridor shower, 2 double beds. En-suite room, double bed: €85 – 2 people
€185 – 6 people

Extra Bed: €25
Reduction: 1/01–28/02, 2 nights
Capacity: 10 people

Directions: From Reims, A4 motorway direction Paris exit 21. D980 direction Dormans to Verneuil (9km) then right on the D1 to Vincelles. The house is down a lane on the left from the main road close to the village church (signposted).

51.06 Reims

Working Farm

Location
10km S of REIMS
in: Mailly-Champagne
Railway station: 10km
car essential

A simple home, but to champagne lovers this is a real find. Annie-France produces her own, to *Grand Cru* standards, so it's worth ordering some if you have room. This old house in the centre of the village is comfortably furnished with family furniture and heirlooms and Annie-France loves to chat. Her two large dogs are very docile once you have been introduced. If you park in her drive, watch your exhaust. On sale: their own champagne (*Grand Cru classé* 100%).

Annie-France MALISSART
9 rue Thiers, 51500 MAILLY-CHAMPAGNE
Tel: (0) 3 26 49 43 47 / (0) 683 13 97 87
Fax: (0) 3 26 49 43 47
afmalissart@infonie.fr

Price Structure – 2 Bedrooms
2 rooms: washbasin, double bed: €38,50

Extra Bed: €15
Capacity: 4 people

Facilities: garden, tv lounge, hosts have pets, 100% no smoking, 1 shared bathroom, wc, hiking, vineyard
Fluent English spoken

Directions: At Reims, on the A4, take exit 26 to Cormentreuil. In Cormentreuil, take the D9 towards Louvois. There, turn left onto the D26 towards Mailly-Champagne.

51.22 Reims

Private Home

Location
10km S of REIMS
in: Mailly-Champagne
Railway station: 10km
car essential

As we go to press this home has not yet been classified, but will be shortly. It is in a really quiet village, like an island surrounded by an ocean of vines. Not only is it in the Champagne region, but it is also a *Grand Cru*, the very best. There are famous villages to visit on the Montagne de Reims and the weird 'Faux de Verzy'. Andy's house is comfortable and although he does not speak much French yet, he adores his new home region. The new station of the TGV-Est is only ten minutes away.

Andy WADE
8 rue de la Libération,
51500 MAILLY-CHAMPAGNE
Tel: (0) 3 26 91 11 14 / (0) 667 17 71 99
andy.wade@orange.fr

Price Structure – 1 Suite
Suite: shower room, wc, double bed. En-suite room, single bed: €55 – 2 people €70 – 3 people

Extra Bed: €15
Capacity: 3 people

Facilities: garden, tv lounge, hosts have pets, internet access, 100% no smoking, hiking, cycling, vineyard, fishing 5km, riversports 5km
Fluent English spoken

Directions: At Reims, on the A4, take exit 26 to Cormentreuil. In Cormentreuil, take the D9 towards Louvois. There, turn left onto the D26 towards Mailly-Champagne.

Location
20km S of VITRY-LE-FRANÇOIS
in: Margerie-Hancourt, station pick-up on arrival/departure
Railway station: 20km
car essential

✳ ✳ ✳

Working Farm

This working farm, with pigeons everywhere, makes an excellent overnight stop with a warm and friendly welcome. It's only 15km from the 'Lac du Der', famous for its migratory birds and fishing. Do not miss the unusual wooden churches.

Michelle & Denis GEOFFROY
16 rue de Hancourt,
51290 MARGERIE-HANCOURT
Tel: (0) 3 26 72 48 47 / (0) 663 16 39 09
Fax: (0) 3 26 72 48 47
denis.geoffroy@wanadoo.fr

Facilities: off-street parking, garden, tv lounge, hosts have pets, dinner available, kitchen, babies welcome, free cot, closed: 15/12–15/01, fishing, bird-watching 15km, lake watersports 15km

Price Structure – 3 Bedrooms
ground floor: shower room, wc, washbasin, double bed: €36
first floor – first room: shower room, wc, 2 double beds: €36 – 2 people €48 – 4 people
first floor – second room: shower room, wc, double bed, single bed: €36 – 2 people €44 – 3 people

Extra Bed: €8
Reduction: 4 nights
Capacity: 9 people

Directions: In Vitry, take the D396 towards Brienne-le-Château. Just before Margerie-Hancourt, turn left, then right. Follow the sign 'Ferme de Hancourt'.

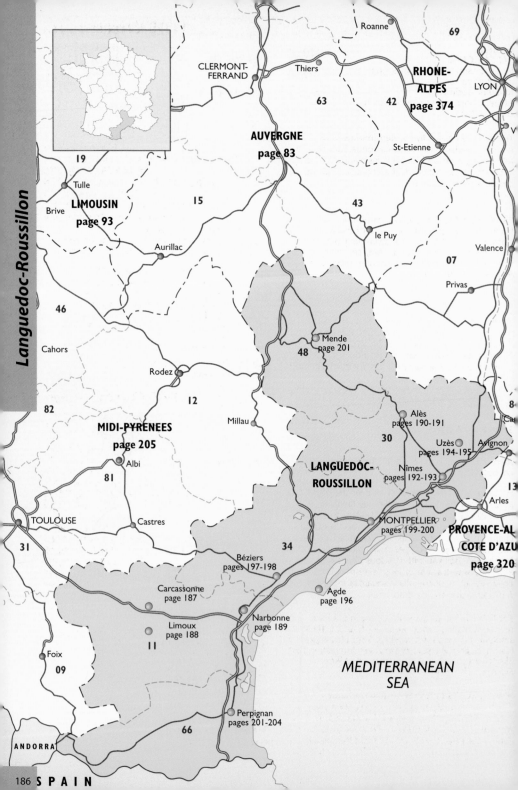

Roanne

69

CLERMONT-
FERRAND

Thiers

**RHONE-
ALPES
page 374**

LYON

V

63

42

**AUVERGNE
page 83**

St-Etienne

19

Tulle

Brive

**LIMOUSIN
page 93**

15

43

le Puy

Valence

Aurillac

07

Privas

46

Cahors

Mende
page 201

48

Rodez

12

Millau

Alès
pages 190-191

30

Uzès
pages 194-195

Avignon

82

**MIDI-PYRENEES
page 205**

Albi

81

Castres

**LANGUEDOC-
ROUSSILLON**

Nîmes
pages 192-193

13

Arles

TOULOUSE

31

34

Béziers
pages 197-198

MONTPELLIER
pages 199-200

**PROVENCE-AL
COTE D'AZU
page 320**

Carcassonne
page 187

Agde
page 196

Limoux
page 188

11

Narbonne
page 189

Foix

09

**MEDITERRANEAN
SEA**

Perpignan
pages 201-204

66

ANDORRA

S P A I N

Location
CARCASSONNE
in: Carcassonne, station pick-up on arrival/departure
Railway station: 3km
Airport: Carcassonne-Salvaza 6km
car essential

✹ ✹ ✹

Private Home

This house is peacefully situated amongst vines, 1.8km from the medieval city of Carcassonne. Your hosts are retired gardeners and Nicole loves plants. The interior of the house has a great deal of character and you will be well looked after here.

Nicole GALINIER
'La Maison sur la Colline', Mas de Ste Croix,
11000 CARCASSONNE
Tel: (0) 4 68 47 57 94 / (0) 685 90 70 58
Fax: (0) 4 68 47 57 94
contact@lamaisonsurlacolline.com
www.lamaisonsurlacolline.com

Facilities: off-street parking, garden, lounge, hosts have pets, dinner available, 2 nights minimum stay, closed: 15/12–14/02, private swimming pool, hiking, cycling, fishing, interesting flora, sea watersports, vineyard, golf course 3km, mushroom-picking 15km
Adequate English spoken

Price Structure – 6 Bedrooms
'Bleue' (our favourite room): television, bathroom, wc, shower, double bed, single bed: €90 – 2 people €115 – 3 people
'Jaune': shower room, wc, double bed: €70
'Beige': television, along corridor shower room, wc, double bed, single bed: €105 – 3 people
'Rez de jardin-Blanche': television, shower room, wc, double bed: €75
'Tonnelle': lounge, shower room, wc, 2 double beds: €140 – 4 people
'Rose': lounge, shower room, wc, double bed: €70

Directions: In Carcassonne, head for the cemetery which is on the left of the entrance to Place du Prado. Follow it round and keep to the left. DO NOT take Chemin des Anglais, which descends. The house is 1km further on, after you have gone under the bridge.

Extra Bed: €25   **Reduction:** 4 nights
Capacity: 16 people

Location
31km E of CARCASSONNE
in: Azille
Railway station: 20km
Airport: Carcassonne-Salvaza 35km
car essential

✹ ✹ ✹

Private Home

Having left America, travelled all over the world and lived in Italy for a time, Natalie has finally found 'La Dolce Vita' in the heart of this little village tucked away amongst the vines. Inspired by her travels, the quiet and charming guest bedrooms are decorated by theme with exotic objects, drapes and coloured cushions. Natalie will spoil you with delicious dishes from home and away as well as sumptuous desserts which you can enjoy sitting out on the village square facing the house. A relaxed and convivial atmosphere.

Natalie TRENT
'La Dolce Vita', 19 Grand Rue, 11700 AZILLE
Tel: (0) 4 68 91 83 92 / (0) 630 01 50 10
Fax: (0) 4 68 91 83 92
thesweetlife@wanadoo.fr
www.dolcevita-azille.com

Facilities: off-street parking, lounge, hosts have pets, dinner available, babies welcome, free cot, 100% no smoking, hunting, mushroom-picking, bird-watching, hiking, cycling, vineyard, fishing 3km, interesting flora 3km, riversports 3km, sea watersports 35km
Fluent English spoken

Price Structure – 3 Bedrooms and 1 Apartment
'Marocaine': shower room, wc, double bed, single bed: €60 – 2 people €75 – 3 people
'Minervois': double bed: €55
'Safari': double bed: €55
'Mosaïque': lounge, kitchen, shower room, wc, double bed, single bed: €75 – 2 people €100 – 3 people

Directions: Motorway A61 between Narbonne and Toulouse exit 24, direction Trèbes then head to Béziers for 21km. D11 on the left towards Laredorte then the D72, small road on the right to Azille. 'La Dolce Vita' awaits you in the centre of the village.

Extra Bed: €15
Reduction: 15/10–15/04, 7 nights, groups
Capacity: 10 people

11.44 Limoux

Private Home

Bienvenue en **France**

Pat & Chris KENWAY
'Les Eaux Tranquilles', 9 quartier de la Condamine, 11500 BELVIANES-ET-CAVIRAC
Tel: (0) 4 68 20 82 79
info@chambresdhote.com
www.chambresdhote.com

Location
31km S of LIMOUX
in: Belvianes-et-Cavirac, station pick-up on arrival/departure
Railway station: 4km
Airport: Carcassonne-Salvaza 60km
car essential

Pat and Chris are a pleasant British couple who left their stressful London lives to retreat here to revitalise themselves at the foot of the Pyrenees, in wooded parkland by the fast waters of the Aude River. In good weather, life is played out on the wooden terrace where copious breakfasts are served. The bedrooms, some with mountain and river views, are harmoniously decorated and have multi-jet showers. Chris is a model railway nut and can show you his best engines at work in the garden. Internet access, garage for cars and motorbikes.

Price Structure – 4 Bedrooms
'Lavender' & 'Sauge': wheelchair access, bathroom, wc, shower, double bed (queen-size): €60
'Fontainebleau': wheelchair access, shower room, wc, washbasin, double bed: €50
'Aude': shower room, wc, twin beds: €40

Reduction: 7 nights
Capacity: 8 people

Facilities: private parking, extensive grounds, lounge, hosts have pets, pets not accepted, internet access, dinner available, wheelchair access, 14 years old minimum age, fishing, hiking, riversports, cycling 4km, winter sports 50km
Fluent English spoken

Directions: From Carcassonne take the D118 until Quillian then the D117 towards Perpignan for 5km to Belvianes-et-Cavirac. Cross the village. The house is just at the end of the village on the left (signposted).

11.48 Limoux

Private Home

Tilly & William HOWARD
'Le Trésor', 20 place de l'Eglise,
11230 SONNAC-SUR-L'HERS
Tel: (0) 4 68 69 37 94 Fax: (0) 4 68 69 37 94
contact@le-tresor.com
www.le-tresor.com

Location
25km S E of LIMOUX
in: Sonnac-sur-l'Hers
Airport: Carcassonne-Salvaza 40km

This British couple are full of enthusiasm at opening their own B&B! Tilly is charming and William is working up to learning French. Here, you are in the depths of l'Aude but just 40km from a direct flight to London. Their guest bedrooms are cosy and of a high standard with plenty of finesse: bathrobes, quality linens, flowers. Internet access is available in the house and they have a lovely garden with isolated corners for the hammock or the table-tennis table.

Price Structure – 4 Bedrooms
lounge, television, bathroom, wc, washbasin, double bed (queen-size), 2 single beds: €95 – 2 people
€135 – 4 people
lounge, television, shower room, wc, double bed: €70
lounge, television, shower room, wc, twin beds: €75
lounge, television, shower room, wc, double bed (queen-size): €80

Extra Bed: €60
Reduction: 01/10–01/04
Capacity: 10 people

Facilities: off-street parking, garden, lounge, hosts have pets, pets not accepted, internet access, dinner available, babies welcome, free cot, 100% no smoking, mushroom-picking, hiking, fishing 1km, lake watersports 8km, vineyard 15km, winter sports 40km
Fluent English spoken

Directions: From Carcassonne, take the D118 as far as Limoux, then the D620 as far as Chalabre and the D16 as far as Sonnac. The house is just opposite the church, number 20.

Location
NARBONNE
in: Narbonne
Railway station: 5km
Airport: Carcassonne-Salvaza 30km
car essential

Bienvenue en France

Private Home

This is an old winegrower's house in the process of being restored. Serge and Marie offer a warm welcome, and you must try their delicious cooking in the magnificent dining room decorated with wine vats. This place really has the atmosphere of a typical old farmhouse.

Serge MAYEN
'Domaine du Petit Fidèle', ancienne route de Coursan, 11100 NARBONNE
Tel: (0) 4 68 32 18 12 / (0) 676 51 78 09
info@petitfidele.com
www.petitfidele.com

Facilities: off-street parking, garden, lounge, pets not accepted, dinner available, fishing, golf course 2km, hiking 15km, interesting flora 15km, mushroom-picking 15km, sea watersports 15km
Basic English spoken

Price Structure – 3 Bedrooms and 1 Suite
2 rooms: shower room, wc, double bed: €53
shower room, wc, 2 single beds: €53
suite: shower room, wc, double bed. En-suite room, 2 single beds: €72 – 2 people €90 – 4 people

Extra Bed: €10
Reduction: 7 nights
Capacity: 10 people

Directions: Take the exit Narbonne-Sud from the A9. Go straight on along the bypass. At the fourth roundabout turn right, turn left immediately and left again (the old road to Coursan). Continue for 2.5km. The house is a reddish-ochre colour.

Location
11km N W of NARBONNE
in: Ginestas, station pick-up on arrival/departure
Railway station: 16km
Airport: Carcassonne-Salvaza 60km
car essential

Château/Manor House

In a typical Minervois village, between the Montagnes Noires and the Mediterranean Sea, is this superb property in the style of Napoléon III, set in peaceful countryside. The spacious bedrooms boast large, comfortable beds and are carefully decorated complete with paintings by your hosts, who are talented artists. Sasha and Timothy can count chef, painter and professional photographer among their talents and propose a delightful range of services including gastronomic lunches and dinners and cookery or photography lessons including tours to vineyards. However, this is also a good spot just to relax and enjoy the heated swimming pool.

Sasha & Timothy HAZAEL
'Go Holiday France', Domaine du Puits Es Pratx, 40 avenue du Minervois, 11120 GINESTAS
Tel: (0) 4 68 46 58 33 Fax: (0) 4 68 33 90 76
sasha@goholidayfrance.com
www.goholidayfrance.com

Facilities: private parking, garden, tv lounge, pets not accepted, dinner available, babies welcome, free cot, 100% no smoking, private swimming pool, hiking, cycling, vineyard, fishing 4km, gliding 15km, golf course 20km, sea watersports 37km, riversports 38km
Fluent English spoken

Price Structure – 5 Bedrooms and 1 Apartment
'Triumph': television, shower room, wc, double bed: €114
'Artilleur' & 'Fantassin': television, shower room, wc, double bed (super king-size), single bed: €144 – 2 people €144 – 3 people
'Cartagene': television, along corridor shower room, wc, twin beds: €114
'Turco': television, shower room, wc, twin beds: €90
'Suite d'été': lounge, television, kitchen, shower room, wc, double bed. En-suite room, shower room, wc, twin beds: €211 – 4 people

Reduction: 1/10–30/04   **Capacity:** 16 people

Directions: From Narbonne ring road north, D607 to Ginestas (18km). In the village, D26 direction Bize-Minervois. The house is on the right, about 100m before the end of the village.

30.59 Alès

Residence of Outstanding Character

Bienvenue en France

Stéphane DIAZ
'La Magnanerie', 909 route du Mas Miger,
30140 ANDUZE-BAGARD
Tel: (0) 4 66 61 60 33 / (0) 607 10 93 02
Fax: (0) 4 66 61 60 33
lamagnaneriebagard@wanadoo.fr
www.la-magnanerie.com

Price Structure – 5 Bedrooms and 1 Suite
'Provence' & 'Bambouseraie': shower room, wc,
double bed: €71
'Camargue' & 'Cévenol': shower room, wc,
twin beds: €71
'Méditerranée': shower room, wc, twin beds,
2 single beds: €91 – 2 people €106 – 4 people
'Familiale': shower room, wc, double bed. En-suite
room, twin beds. En-suite room, 2 single beds:
€111 – 6 people

Extra Bed: €20
Reduction: 1/09–30/09, 3 nights
Capacity: 18 people

Location
15km S W of ALES
in: Bagard, station pick-up on
arrival/departure
Railway station: 10km
Airport: Montpellier-Méditerranée 80km
car essential

This former 17th-century silkworm farm is in
Piedmont Cévenol. The guest rooms are independent
in a wing of the house. Fresco paintings on the doors
hint at the themes of the rooms. There are plenty of
places to sit and read in the garden, including a Berber
tent or in the shade on the terrace where breakfast is
served. Dinner is prepared by Stéphane, a former cook,
who serves typical Cévenol and Mediterranean dishes
from fresh farm produce. At your disposal: a fridge,
local produce, children's games and a 12x6m
swimming pool.

Facilities: off-street parking, garden, tv lounge, hosts
have pets, pets not accepted, dinner available, babies
welcome, free cot, 100% no smoking, private
swimming pool, hunting, hiking, cycling, fishing 5km,
riversports 5km, vineyard 5km, interesting flora 10km
Adequate English spoken

Directions: From Alès N110 towards Montpellier for
2km, then at St-Christol-lès-Alès, D910 on the right
towards Anduze. Pass Bagard, direction Boisset-et-
Gaujac for 2km then turn left and continue for 900m
to 'Mas Miger'.

30.57 Alès

Residence of Outstanding Character

Irena TYMRUK
'Domaine de la Cledette', Le Grand Bois,
30460 COLOGNAC-SUR-LASALLE
Tel: (0) 4 66 85 46 93 / (0) 674 56 22 19
contact@domaine-de-la-cledette.com
www.domaine-de-la-cledette.com

Price Structure – 3 Bedrooms
'Rose' : bathroom, wc, double bed: €70
'Mimosa': shower room, wc, double bed: €55
'Iris': shower room, wc, twin beds,
single bed: €65 – 2 people €80 – 3 people

Reduction: 7 nights
Capacity: 7 people

Location
38km S W of ALES
in: Colognac-sur-Lasalle
Airport: Nîmes-Arles-Camargue
50km
car essential

Irena and Bernard, a Franco-British couple, were
seduced by this large 18th-century *maison bourgeoise*
which they have restored with a great deal of love and
care. The guest rooms are a good size and tastefully
decorated with antique furniture and authentic floor
tiles. From the large terrace you look out over 3 hectares
of streams and wooded hillsides. Take to the wild paths
and on your return rest under the shade of the lime
trees or on the lawn. Irena, an international guide, is well
placed to answer your requests.

Facilities: extensive grounds, hosts have pets, pets
not accepted, kitchen, babies welcome, free cot,
100% no smoking, hiking, cycling, fishing 3km,
mushroom-picking 3km, vineyard 10km, interesting
flora 12km, winter sports 20km, riversports 20km
Fluent English spoken

Directions: From Alès head towards Anduze on the
N110 and D910, then the D907 and D57 towards
Lasalle. Do not enter Lasalle but continue to St-
Hippolyte-du-Fort on the D39 for about 3km. Take
the lane on the right and follow the signs to 'Domaine
de la Cledette' (watch out for the second turning on
the right which is a hairpin bend).

Location
28km S E of ALES
in: Durfort-et-St-Martin-de-Sossenac,
station pick-up on arrival/departure
Railway station: 46km
Airport: Montpellier-Méditerranée 60km

Discover this renovated former silkworm farm, deep in the countryside facing the imposing Cévenoles mountains. Of note: a remarkable stone archway leading into the interior courtyard covered with wisteria, where nature and art are entwined. Helmut owns an art gallery and has adorned his house with contemporary paintings and sculptures which sit with a profusion of plants and cascading water features. An oriental-style tea room, simple bedrooms, choice of supper, trout farming, vegetable plots and a full organic German-style breakfast.

Facilities: private parking, garden, lounge, hosts have pets, dinner available, kitchen, babies welcome, free cot, 1 shared shower room, wc, private swimming pool, hiking, cycling, vineyard 2km, golf course 30km, riversports 30km
Fluent English spoken

Directions: At Alès, N110 towards Montpellier then right onto the D910 to Anduze. D907 towards Nîmes and right onto the D982 for Durfort. Before the roundabout on the D149, turn right towards Baruel, then right heading for Valensole. Once in the 'mini' hamlet, it is the third house on the right in a cul-de-sac.

**Residence of
Outstanding
Character**

**Helmut ARETZ
'La Vieille Maison', Hameau de Valensole,
30170 DURFORT-ET-ST-MARTIN-DE-SOSSENAC
Tel: (0) 4 66 77 06 46 / (0) 608 26 72 85
Fax: (0) 4 66 77 06 46
vieillemaison@turquoise.fr
www.turquoise.fr/vieillemaison**

Price Structure – 2 Bedrooms and 1 Suite
'Balcon' & 'Bleue': along corridor shower room, wc,
double bed: €85
suite 'Jaune': along corridor shower room, wc,
double bed. En-suite room, twin beds:
€65 – 2 people €95 – 4 people

Extra Bed: €20
Reduction: 08/01–31/03 & 01/05–30/06 &
01/09–20/12, 7 nights, groups, children
Capacity: 8 people

Location
9km E of ALES
in: Mons
Railway station: 6km
car essential

Bienvenue en **France**

Private Home

Quiet and easy to reach, this old *mas* stands high up on a wooded hillside. The swimming pool is surrounded by typical Mediterranean *garrigue* with holm oaks and pine trees which give off wonderful aromas. The area is equally rich in fauna. Bernard rears a few horses and can offer stabling. The guest bedroom on the ground floor, under the arcade, has its own independent entrance. The facilities are basic and functional (a washing machine is at your disposal). Nearby and away from the beaten track are the wild Gorges de l'Aiguillon. Ideal for nature lovers.

Facilities: off-street parking, extensive grounds, hosts have pets, dinner available, private swimming pool, cycling, interesting flora, vineyard 5km, riversports 10km
Adequate English spoken

Directions: From Alès, D6 towards Bagnols-sur-Cèze for 6km. After the roundabout (pharmacy on the right) continue on this road and then straight away take the first road on the right. The house is at the end of the lane.

**Bernard LAISSUS
'Mas de Font Sadoulé',
92 chemin de Bel Air, 30340 MONS
Tel: (0) 4 66 25 66 50
dlaissus@wanadoo.fr**

Price Structure – 1 Suite
wheelchair access, shower room, wc, washbasin,
double bed. En-suite room, 2 single beds:
€55 – 2 people €90 – 4 people

Reduction: children
Capacity: 4 people

Languedoc-Roussillon – Alès

30.66 Nîmes

Private Home

Josyane PIERSON
'La Magne', 296 D impasse des Troènes,
30900 NIMES
Tel: (0) 4 66 23 70 86 / (0) 612 58 43 57
Fax: (0) 4 66 23 70 86
josyane.pierson@club-internet.fr
www.chambres-la-magne.com

Price Structure – 3 Bedrooms
'Lavande': television, shower room, wc,
twin beds: €80
'Chevrefeuille': television, shower room,
wc, double bed (queen-size): €90
'Venitienne': television, shower room,
wc, double bed (queen-size): €95

Extra Bed: €20
Reduction: 01/10–30/04
Capacity: 6 people

Location
NIMES
in: Nîmes, station pick-up on
arrival/departure
Railway station: 4km
Airport: Nîmes-Arles-Camargue 6km
car essential

Ten minutes from the city on the hills above Nîmes you come to the land of olive trees and Mediterranean plants. Josyane is a 'naturologist', charming and full of energy, so take full advantage of her advice to stay on top form. Two bedrooms lead off the garden and are very attractive, comfortable and air-conditioned and the third bedroom on the first floor is reached by a spiral staircase. Great décor and a pool. A summer kitchen is to be added later. This is the south in style.

Facilities: private parking, extensive grounds, hosts have pets, pets not accepted, internet access, dinner available, kitchen, private swimming pool, fishing, golf course 1km, hunting 5km, vineyard 10km, riversports 15km, sea watersports 40km
Basic English spoken

Directions: Exit Nîmes-Ouest from the A9. Then take the N106 to Alès. At the third set of lights peel off on the right to cross the main road on the right to Chemin du Mas de Lauze and then the Impasse des Troênes opposite on the left.

30.39 Nîmes

Private Home

Graziella & Gérard PONGE
'Les Oliviers', 200 chemin de Sernhac,
30320 BEZOUCE
Tel: (0) 4 66 75 15 90 / (0) 618 83 74 22
www.sous-l-olivier.com

Price Structure – 3 Bedrooms
'L'Olivier': television, shower room, wc, washbasin,
double bed, single bed: €55 – 2 people
€70 – 3 people
'La Vigne': television, shower room, wc, washbasin,
2 double beds: €55 – 2 people €85 – 4 people
'Les Lavandes': television, along corridor shower
room, wc, washbasin, double bed, cot: €55

Extra Bed: €15
Reduction: 01/10–31/03, 5 nights, groups
Capacity: 9 people

Location
10km N E of NIMES
in: Bezouce
Railway station: 15km
Airport: Nîmes-Arles-Camargue 20km
car essential

After many years on the road as a commercial traveller, Graziella has now retired and is getting her breath back in her small corner of paradise in the centre of a quiet little village between Nîmes and the Pont du Gard. Graziella will give you a warm welcome and Gérard, who is a farmer, will be delighted to show you his olive groves. Breakfast, served under the olive tree, will include jam from the fruits of their orchard. On sale: olive oil.

Facilities: private parking, garden, lounge, hosts have pets, pets not accepted, babies welcome, free cot, 100% no smoking, private swimming pool, hiking, cycling, riversports 10km, golf course 15km, lake watersports 50km
Basic English spoken

Directions: Bezouce is on the N86 Nîmes to Avignon road, about 10km from either the exit Nîmes-Est or the exit Remoulins from the A9. If you are coming from Nîmes, turn right at the second set of traffic lights. If coming from Remoulins, turn left at the first set of traffic lights. It is 200m after the town hall (*la mairie*).

Location
21km E of NIMES
in: Comps, station pick-up on arrival/departure
Railway station: 4km
Airport: Montpellier-Méditerranée 60km
car essential

Private Home

In a beautiful touristic area, France welcomes you to her idyllic restored village house. Inside the stone walls and stained-glass windows, France displays earthenwares alongside finds picked up over time. The guest bedrooms on the first floor have a balcony and are air-conditioned. The bathrooms have been modernised but could be narrow and awkward for some. On fine days, breakfast and dinner are served on the patio by an illuminated water feature and the jacuzzi. Quality facilities, a sincere welcome and joie de vivre!

Facilities: off-street parking, garden, tv lounge, hosts have pets, dinner available, wheelchair access, fishing, hiking, riversports, vineyard, cycling 2km, interesting flora 5km, golf course 10km, bird-watching 20km
Basic English spoken

France LOMBARD
'Douce France', 30 place Carnot, 30300 COMPS
Tel: (0) 4 66 74 37 87 / (0) 613 06 14 29
gite.douce.france@wanadoo.fr
http://www.gite-douce-france.com

Price Structure – 5 Bedrooms
'Lapins': television, shower room, wc, 2 sets of twin beds: €58 – 2 people €65 – 4 people
'Oies': shower room, wc, double bed, single bed: €55 – 2 people €60 – 3 people
'Anes': television, shower, double bed: €58
'Coq': television, shower room, wc, twin beds, single bed (child-size): €55 – 2 people €60 – 3 people
'Cochons': shower room, wc, twin beds: €55

Extra Bed: €10
Reduction: 1/10–30/03, 3 nights
Capacity: 14 people

Directions: Motorway A9 between Nîmes and Avignon exit 23. At Remoulins, head to Pont du Gard then the D986 towards Beaucaire, Tarascon to Comps (11km). The Place Carnot is in the centre of the village.

Location
25km S W of NIMES
in: Villevieille
car essential

Residence of Outstanding Character

Sophie and Thierry's home is alongside the château with a common courtyard in a medieval village with superb views of vines, olive groves and Pic St-Loup. One of the guest bedrooms is a converted stone vaulted cellar (the manger still exists) with a kitchenette. Both rooms have their own entrances. Share their passion for wine, olive growing and horse-riding and book a carriage ride. At the end of September assist in a traditional morning of grape-picking, when beautiful horses replace tractors. A genuine, down to earth welcome.

Facilities: private parking, garden, hosts have pets, closed: 15/07–15/08, hiking, cycling, vineyard, golf course 28km, gliding 28km, fishing 28km, lake watersports 28km
Basic English spoken

Sophie & Thierry DE CRAENE
'Chambres d'Hôtes de la Migrane', 1 impasse de la Migrane, 30250 VILLEVIEILLE
Tel: (0) 4 66 77 74 48
thierry.de-craene@wanadoo.fr
www.la-migrane.com

Price Structure – 2 Bedrooms
'Haut': television, shower room, wc, double bed: €54
'Bas': shower room, wc, double bed, single bed: €68 – 2 people €68 – 3 people

Extra Bed: €13
Reduction: 7 nights
Capacity: 5 people

Directions: From Nîmes, D40 to Villevieille or from the A9 Montpellier-Nîmes, exit 27. D34 to Sommières and on towards the Château de Villevieille. Pass in front of the château and continue straight ahead for 100m. The house is on the left (signed).

Languedoc-Roussillon – Nîmes

30.27 Uzès

Private Home

Michèle DELCOR
'Les Pins de Jol', St-Quentin-la-Poterie,
30700 UZES
Tel: (0) 4 66 03 16 84 / (0) 616 28 92 88
Fax: (0) 4 66 03 16 84
lespinsdejol@orange.fr
http://lespinsdejol.free.fr

Price Structure – 1 Bedroom, 1 Suite
and 2 Apartments
'l'Olivier': kitchen, shower room, wc, double bed: €65
'Le Chêne': kitchen, shower room, wc, double bed,
single bed: €70 – 2 people €85 – 3 people
'Le Phénix': shower room, wc, double bed. En-suite
room, twin beds: €70 – 2 people €100 – 4 people
'l'Eucalyptus': shower room, wc, double bed, single
bed: €70 – 2 people €85 – 3 people

Extra Bed: €15
Reduction: 01/09–30/06, 7 nights
Capacity: 12 people

Location
UZES
in: Uzès
Railway station: 30km
Airport: Nîmes-Arles-Camargue 35km
car essential

If you are visiting the Gard area, you really must stop
at Michèle's place. You will fall in love with her
hospitality, her house, so calm in the heart of a pine
forest, and her swimming pool. Michèle is more than
happy to talk about the local pottery as well as the
superb Roman sites nearby.

Facilities: private parking, extensive grounds, tv
lounge, hosts have pets, pets not accepted, internet
access, 100% no smoking, wheelchair access, 2 nights
minimum stay, private swimming pool, hiking, cycling
2km, golf course 5km, fishing 15km, lake watersports
15km
Adequate English spoken

Directions: From Nîmes, take the D979 to Uzès.
Continue towards Lussan then turn right on to the
D125 in the direction of St Quentin-la-Poterie for 700
metres. Turn right to 'Les Pins de Jol'.

30.65 Uzès

Private Home

Francette DUVAL
'Sucette et Abricot', Mas des 3 Pins, route de
Marignac, 30700 AIGALIERS
Tel: (0) 4 66 22 11 78 / (0) 622 20 14 93
Fax: (0) 4 66 22 11 78
gilbert.duval@club-internet.fr
gites-uzes.com

Price Structure – 2 Bedrooms
and 2 Apartments
'Agathe': television, shower room, wc, double bed
(queen-size): €100
'Velours': television, bathroom, wc, double bed: €80
'Bleu-cerise': lounge, television, kitchen, shower
room, wc, 2 double beds (queen-size):
€100 – 2 people €200 – 4 people
'La Belle': lounge, television, kitchen, shower room,
wc, double bed (queen-size): €120

Extra Bed: €20
Reduction: 1/10–31/03, groups
Capacity: 10 people

Location
10km N W of UZES
in: Aigaliers
Railway station: 25km
Airport: Montpellier-Méditerranée
50km
car essential

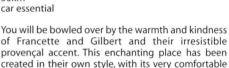

You will be bowled over by the warmth and kindness
of Francette and Gilbert and their irresistible
provençal accent. This enchanting place has been
created in their own style, with its very comfortable
bedrooms and bathrooms and décor worthy of the
glossy magazines. You will be hooked on Francette's
personality and Gilbert's wonderful cooking and will
be sure to come back. This is a very special place for
an unforgettable stay.

Facilities: private parking, garden, lounge, hosts
have pets, pets not accepted, dinner available, 100%
no smoking, 16 years old minimum age, 2 nights
minimum stay, private swimming pool, cycling,
vineyard, hiking 4km, golf course 12km, riversports
20km

Directions: Exit 23 from the A9 towards Remoulins,
Uzès and Alès. On the D981, 6km after Uzès, take the
D115 on the right to Aigaliers. The house is at the
bottom of the village on the left.

Location
4km W of UZES
in: Arpaillargues
Railway station: 40km
Airport: Nîmes-Arles-Camargue 30km
car essential

Private Home

Diane and Clive are English and love living in France, so expect a good British welcome to their charming home with its warm ambience. The spacious rooms are all furnished in the Louis Philippe style. This very attractive area has so much to offer. Uzès will captivate you, the potteries at Anduze (whose products are reputed to resist freezing temperatures) will amaze you, and the famous Bamboo Forest (Bambouseraie) is well worth a visit. This area of *garrigues* is characterised by its dry-stone built *cabanes* and its châteaux. So there is plenty to see here.

Diane & Clive NORWOOD
'Mas du Moulin', route d'Uzès,
30700 ARPAILLARGUES
Tel: (0) 4 66 58 46 42 / (0) 632 47 15 91
Fax: (0) 4 66 58 46 42
diane.norwood@wanadoo.fr
www.lemasdumoulin.com

Facilities: private parking, garden, tv lounge, hosts have pets, pets not accepted, kitchen, 100% no smoking, 15 years old minimum age, 2 nights minimum stay: 1/07–31/08, closed: 30/10–15/03, private swimming pool, hiking, cycling, vineyard, golf course 4km
Fluent English spoken

Price Structure – 4 Bedrooms
and 1 Apartment
'Cerisier', 'Olivier', 'Murier' & 'Mimosa': shower room, wc, twin beds: €90
'Figuier': kitchen, shower room, wc, twin beds: €100

Extra Bed: €20
Reduction: 15/03–1/07 & 1/09–30/10, 3 nights
Capacity: 10 people

Directions: Exit 23 Remoulins from the A9. Take the D981 towards Alès and Uzès. At Uzès head towards Anduze for 3km on the D982. It is on the right, just before the bridge 'Les Seynes'.

Location
13km N of UZES
in: La Bruguière
Railway station: 39km
Airport: Nîmes-Arles-Camargue 50km
car essential

Residence of
Outstanding
Character

This large and imposing 19th-century house with well-decorated, comfortable rooms is situated near Uzès. This is the Midi, with its little villages, vineyards and châteaux. You will stay on for the beauty of the surroundings as well as the genuine welcome of your hosts, Michel and John.

John KARAVIAS
'Les Marronniers', place de la Mairie,
30580 LA BRUGUIERE
Tel: (0) 4 66 72 84 77 / (0) 614 98 76 93
info@lesmarronniers.biz
www.lesmarronniers.biz

Facilities: garden, lounge, pets not accepted, dinner available, 100% no smoking, 15 years old minimum age, 3 nights minimum stay, private swimming pool, hiking, cycling, mushroom-picking, vineyard, golf course 11km, riversports 15km
Fluent English spoken

Price Structure – 4 Bedrooms
2 rooms: television, shower room, wc,
double bed: €100
television, shower room, wc, twin beds: €100
television, bathroom, wc, shower, twin beds: €115

Capacity: 8 people

Directions: From Nîmes, take the D979 to Uzès. Continue towards Lussan for 8km. Turn right onto the D238 as far as La Bruguière. The house is in the main village square, next to the town hall and the château.

Languedoc-Roussillon – Uzès

34.13 Agde

Private Home

Jeanne & André CRISIAS
'Résidence Le Clôt', 111-113 quai Cornu, La
Tamarissière, 34300 AGDE
Tel: (0) 4 67 94 21 78 Fax: (0) 4 67 94 19 32
crisias@residence-leclot.com
www.residence-leclot.com

Price Structure – 3 Apartments
3 rooms: kitchen, shower room, wc, double bed, 2
single beds (child-size): €45 – 2 people €59 – 4
people

Capacity: 12 people

Location
AGDE
in: Agde, station pick-up on
arrival/departure
Railway station: 3km
Airport: Béziers-Vias 6km
car essential

Here the accommodation is in basic studio-cabins
which are 100m from the River Hérault and 1km from
the sea. You are free to explore the 10-hectare wooded
estate and there are many games provided for
children.

Facilities: off-street parking, garden, pets not
accepted, 7 nights minimum stay: 01/07–31/08,
closed: 01/10–31/03, private swimming pool, hiking,
fishing, sea watersports, golf course 4km, bird-
watching 6km
Basic English spoken

Directions: In Agde take the N32 towards Sète, then
right towards La Tamarissière. 'Le Clôt' is on the right-
hand side of the road.

34.38 Agde

Residence of
Outstanding
Character

Alix & Richard GUY
'Villa St Germain', 13 route de la Grange,
34120 CAZOULS-D'HERAULT
Tel: (0) 4 67 25 28 06 / (0) 620 19 82 34
aetrguy@tiscali.fr
www.villa-saint-germain.com

Price Structure – 1 Bedroom and 2 Suites
'Henriette': shower room, wc, 2 single beds: €75
'Oscar': along corridor bathroom, wc, double bed.
En-suite room, twin beds: €75 – 2 people
€120 – 4 people
'Comtesse': bathroom, wc, double bed. En-suite
room, single bed: €75 – 2 people €90 – 3 people

Extra Bed: €15
Reduction: 7 nights
Capacity: 9 people

Location
28km N of AGDE
in: Cazouls-d'Herault
Railway station: 25km
Airport: Montpellier-Méditerranée 50km
car essential
This is a beautiful, grand old house from the 19th
century set in grounds full of age-old trees. It has
recently received overdue attention after a period of
inactivity whilst in the care of the family. The renovated
guest rooms are on the first floor off an enormous
hallway. They are spacious and furnished with period
furniture and high dressed windows. The 'Henriette'
room is smaller but boasts a pretty ornamental ceiling.
Languedoc pottery adorns the kitchen which is where
breakfast is served and from where you can step out to
the swimming pool.

Facilities: private parking, extensive grounds, tv
lounge, hosts have pets, babies welcome, free cot,
private swimming pool, fishing, hiking, vineyard,
gliding 4km, riversports 15km, golf course 20km, sea
watersports 25km, bird-watching 70km, mushroom-
picking 80km
Adequate English spoken

Directions: A9 between Montpellier and Béziers, exit
34 towards Pézenas. D13 around Pézenas direction
Lodève. N9 exit 58 Paulhan, Adissan, D128 direction
Cazouls-d'Hérault. The house is on the left just at the
entrance to the village.

Location
25km N E of BEZIERS
in: Montagnac
Railway station: 20km
Airport: Montpellier-Méditerranée 35km
car essential

Residence of Outstanding Character

Margaret and Martin (a lively rugby player) have filled this house with wooden masks and sculptures brought back from their travels in Africa. Here there is an irrestible joie de vivre, and you will have great evenings in the charming interior courtyard with its informal Mediterranean-style garden, where breakfast is also served.

Margaret & Martin HASKINS
'La Vigneronne', 15 avenue Pierre Sirven,
34530 MONTAGNAC
Tel: (0) 4 67 24 14 36 Fax: (0) 4 67 24 03 59
mhaskins@wanadoo.fr

Facilities: private parking, garden, tv lounge, hosts have pets, pets not accepted, dinner available, 100% no smoking, cycling, fishing 3km, golf course 12km, riversports 20km, sea watersports 36km
Fluent English spoken

Price Structure – 4 Bedrooms
2 rooms: shower room, wc, double bed: €55
shower room, wc, double bed, single bed:
€55 – 2 people €70 – 3 people
bathroom, wc, twin beds: €70

Extra Bed: €15
Capacity: 9 people

Directions: From Béziers, take the N9 towards Pézenas, which you bypass, and then turn right onto the N113 towards Montagnac. 'La Vigneronne' is on this road in the centre of the village, on the right.

Location
7km S W of BEZIERS
in: Nissan-lez-Enserune, station pick-up on arrival/departure
Railway station: 7km
Airport: Béziers-Vias 20km
car essential

Residence of Outstanding Character

Jacqueline and her son, Laurent, will give you a really warm welcome to their impressive house, typical of the Languedoc region, surrounded by pines and the vineyards of their *domaine*. It is so relaxing here, but you are still close to Béziers, Narbonne and the beaches. There is a large enclosed courtyard, usually bathed in sunlight, where they organise barbecues. On sale: wine, foie gras. Two self-catering apartments rented weekly.

Jacqueline & Laurent ROUSSELON
'Domaine Salabert',
34440 NISSAN-LEZ-ENSERUNE
Tel: (0) 4 67 37 00 27 / (0) 662 74 36 29
Fax: (0) 4 67 37 00 27

Facilities: private parking, extensive grounds, tv lounge, hosts have pets, dinner available, kitchen, babies welcome, free cot, 1 shared shower room, 3 wcs, private swimming pool, hiking, cycling, vineyard, sea watersports 15km, riversports 25km
Fluent English spoken

Price Structure – 3 Bedrooms and 1 Suite
suite 'Raisin': shower room, wc, washbasin, double bed (queen-size), single bed (child-size): €45
en-suite room 'Lune': washbasin, double bed: €45
'Eugène': shower room, wc, double bed (king-size), single bed (child-size): €45
'Egypte': telephone, shower room, wc, double bed (queen-size): €45
shower room, wc, double bed, single bed:
€45 – 2 people €50 – 3 people

Extra Bed: €9
Reduction: groups, children
Capacity: 13 people

Directions: Leave Béziers and head towards Narbonne on the N9. After 6km, by the tractor garage 'Matha', take the lane on the left and follow signs to 'Domaine Salabert'. Drive into the *domaine*, and look for the 'Bed & Breakfast France' sign.

34.33 Béziers

Private Home

Location
18km N of BEZIERS
in: Pouzolles, station pick-up on arrival/departure
Railway station: 25km
car essential

Imagine the feat undertaken by Gilles and Sabine who have built their house with their own hands! It is purpose-built to maximise your comfort: spacious bedrooms with independent entrances, spa, multi-jet showers, terracotta tiles, art deco features, antiques. There is an open living room with a mezzanine lounge. Add a pool under a timber frame, a summer kitchen, badminton and a jacuzzi. Everything is in place to guarantee a great stay. A very warm welcome from your hosts who play the saxophone and enjoy dancing.

Sabine & Gilles BOYE
8 chemin de Cassan, 34480 POUZOLLES
Tel: (0) 4 67 24 71 48 Fax: (0) 4 67 24 71 48
sabine.boye@wanadoo.fr
http://monsite.wanadoo.fr/chambrespouzolles34/

Price Structure – 3 Bedrooms
'Campagnarde' & 'Louis XIV': television, bathroom, wc, shower, double bed: €90
'Louis Philippe': television, bathroom, wc, shower, double bed, single bed: €80 – 2 people
€100 – 3 people

Extra Bed: €20
Reduction: 3 nights
Capacity: 7 people

Facilities: private parking, garden, tv lounge, hosts have pets, dinner available, kitchen, babies welcome, free cot, 100% no smoking, closed: 01/10–31/03, private swimming pool, cycling, hiking, sea watersports 30km
Basic English spoken

Directions: From Béziers-Nord, take the D909 towards Bédarieux then the D15 on the right towards Raujan to Pouzolles. In the village, head for Gabian and then at the end of the road, right turn into Chemin de Cassan.

34.26 Béziers

Residence of Outstanding Character

Location
10km S of BEZIERS
in: Villeneuve-lès-Béziers
Railway station: 10km
Airport: Béziers-Vias 10km
car essential

The whole concept of this place is quite unique. It is a former wine cellar dating from 1890, which has been completely restored by the skilful hand of Bruno. He has created a modern, spacious and comfortable home and provides top-quality accommodation in a quiet and gentle manner, reflecting the lifestyle of the Languedoc region. Bruno is also a sophisticated cook, with emphasis on local flavours, accompanied by regional wines. There is a tropical patio, where you can take breakfast or just relax. On sale: regional wines.

Bruno SAUREL
'La Chamberte', rue de la Source,
34420 VILLENEUVE-LES-BEZIERS
Tel: (0) 4 67 39 84 83
contact@lachamberte.com
www.lachamberte.com

Price Structure – 5 Bedrooms
shower room, wc, double bed (queen-size): €96
2 rooms: shower room, wc, twin beds: €96
2 rooms: shower room, wc, double bed: €96

Reduction: 3 nights
Capacity: 10 people

Facilities: off-street parking, garden, tv lounge, hosts have pets, pets not accepted, dinner available, 100% no smoking, 12 years old minimum age, closed: 1/03–15/03, cycling, vineyard, hiking 1km, sea watersports 5km, golf course 10km, riversports 10km
Fluent English spoken

Directions: At Béziers, take the N112 towards Valras Plage for 6km. Then turn left towards Villeneuve. Head for the Centre-Ville and at the supermarket turn left and then right. Rue de la Source is the third on the left. 'La Chamberte' is on the right with a large green gate.

Location
MONTPELLIER
in: Montpellier, station pick-up on arrival/departure
Railway station: Montpellier
Airport: Montpellier-Méditerranée 10km

Apartment

A rare opportunity to stay in Montpellier's old town in 14th-century listed buildings. Your host Alexandre, a cultured individual, knows Montpellier extremely well. Peace and quiet is disturbed only by the rustling of the birds in the aviary and the purring of the three resident cats. The suite with its warm and charming ambiance is all yours. Gourmet dinners and secure parking are also noteworthy here. An unusual location with a good-natured and genuine welcome.

Alexandre GUMBAU
1 rue Germain, 34000 MONTPELLIER
Tel: (0) 4 34 50 33 51 / (0) 662 07 33 52
alexandre.gumbau@club-internet.fr
www.alexandre-gumbau.fr

Facilities: private parking, tv lounge, hosts have pets, pets not accepted, dinner available, 10 years old minimum age, interesting flora, cycling 10km, sea watersports 10km, vineyard 10km, golf course 30km, riversports 30km
Adequate English spoken

Price Structure – 1 Bedroom
lounge, television, along corridor bathroom, wc, double bed (queen-size): €95

Extra Bed: €25
Reduction: 7 nights
Capacity: 2 people

Directions: In Montpellier head for the Centre Historique and park on arrival in the Parking de la Préfecture or the Parking Comédie car parks. (Vehicles are not permitted in the old town without a permit, which your host will provide on arrival. Garage available.)

Location
20km N W of MONTPELLIER
in: Murles
Railway station: 20km
Airport: Montpellier-Méditerranée 35km
car essential

Residence of Outstanding Character

North of Montpellier, amid pine trees and holm oaks is this vineyard, passed down the family since the 17th century. Inside, a large stone stairway leads up to the bedrooms and the drawing room. Furnished with family heirlooms, they are fairly spacious, depending on the bathrooms built within the existing space. In the garden are seats, a barbecue and a swimming pool. Waffles, *pâtisseries* and homemade *brioches* are served at breakfast. Be sure to taste their *Cru* wine (AOC *coteaux du Languedoc*) produced by the children.

Geneviève PONSON
'Mas de Perry', 34980 MURLES
Tel: (0) 4 67 84 40 89 Fax: (0) 4 67 84 01 79
masdeperry@wanadoo.fr
www.masdeperry.com

Facilities: off-street parking, extensive grounds, lounge, pets not accepted, babies welcome, free cot, 100% no smoking, private swimming pool, hiking, vineyard, golf course 8km, gliding 12km, riversports 15km, sea watersports 20km
Basic English spoken

Price Structure – 3 Bedrooms and 1 Suite
suite 'Les Vignes': shower room, wc, four-poster double bed (queen-size). En-suite room, 2 single beds: €80 – 2 people €110 – 4 people
'Jardin': shower room, wc, twin beds: €70
'Les Pins' & 'Les Acacias': shower room, wc, double bed: €70

Extra Bed: €20
Reduction: 5 nights
Capacity: 10 people

Directions: At Montpellier N109 direction Millau, exit 62 and D111 direction Vailhauquès. With the village on your left continue straight ahead on the D127 towards Murles. The *mas* is before the village.

Languedoc-Roussillon – Montpellier

34.25 Montpellier

Private Home

Christine & Xavier JEANROY
'L'Auberge Campagnarde de la Vallée du Salagou', route du Mas Canet, 34800 SALASC
Tel: (0) 4 67 88 13 39 Fax: (0) 4 67 96 15 62
xavier@aubergedusalagou.fr
www.aubergedusalagou.fr

Price Structure – 6 Bedrooms
2 rooms: shower room, wc, double bed, single bed: €49 – 2 people €66 – 3 people
shower room, wc, twin beds: €49
3 rooms: shower room, wc, double bed: €49

Reduction: 3 nights, children
Capacity: 14 people

Location
40km W of MONTPELLIER
in: Salsac
Airport: Montpellier-Méditerranée 40km
car essential

Paradise is not easy to find, but if you like wild places away from it all, with panoramic views over magnificent countryside, then be sure to stay at l'Auberge. Here you dominate the valley and the lake from the private patio of your room. You are well away from the main roads and can easily imagine that this area belongs to you alone, as so far, only nature lovers know this address.

Facilities: off-street parking, extensive grounds, lounge, hosts have pets, dinner available, babies welcome, free cot, closed: 1/11–31/03, mushroom-picking, vineyard, hiking, cycling, fishing, sea watersports, riversports, interesting flora
Adequate English spoken

Directions: From Montpellier, take the N109 as far as Clermont-l'Hérault, then the D908 as far as Bédarieux and continue for 12km. Then turn right on to the D148, as far as Salasc. In the village, take the road to Le Mas Canet, which goes downhill, and l'Auberge is then signposted.

34.36 Montpellier

Private Home

Christine & Frédéric PREVOST
'Les Chênes de Babara', 34270 VACQUIERES
Tel: (0) 4 67 55 25 90 / (0) 678 08 67 01
chenesbabara@wanadoo.fr
www.chenesbabara.com

Price Structure – 2 Bedrooms
and 1 Apartment
'Billardière' & 'Cabane du Trappeur': television, shower room, wc, double bed (queen-size): €70
'Suite Provençale': lounge, television, kitchen, bathroom, wc, double bed, twin beds:
€70 – 2 people €140 – 4 people

Reduction: 15/09–30/04, 3 nights
Capacity: 8 people

Location
26km N of MONTPELLIER
in: Vacquières, station pick-up on arrival/departure
Railway station: 27km
Airport: Montpellier-Méditerranée 28km
car essential

The guest rooms are spread around a superb swimming pool by holm oaks. The 'Billardière' has two entrances: to the billiards room and to the garage. The screened-off wooden chalet is a little love nest, with air-conditioning for cool summers or cosy winters. An apartment with a kitchen and a seating area is also available. Breakfast is served by the pool-house or inside. The pool is 15x6m with a jacuzzi and jets or in winter opt for a sauna or the hammam! Christine and Frédéric also host themed evenings during the summer months.

Facilities: private parking, extensive grounds, tv lounge, hosts have pets, pets not accepted, 100% no smoking, private swimming pool, hunting, mushroom-picking, hiking, cycling, vineyard, fishing 6km, golf course 15km, gliding 17km, interesting flora 20km, sea watersports 32km
Adequate English spoken

Directions: A9 motorway between Nîmes and Montpellier exit 28 Vendargues direction Castries. At the roundabout, D68 opposite for 8km and D109 in the direction towards Ste-Croix-de-Quintillargues and then turn right and then left to Fontanès. After leaving Fontanès, continue for 4km. The house is at the junction on the right (signposted).

48.08 Mende

Location
47km N E of MENDE
in: Langogne
Railway station: 2km
Airport: Lyon-St Exupéry 188km
car essential

Private Home

In an extremely picturesque spot, perched on a rocky outcrop, this house dominates the valley of the Langouyrou river. Find peace and tranquillity here with magnificent views, especially from the verandas. With a talent for interior decoration, Christine has decorated her rooms with flair. A visit to the nearby Naussac Lake is a must, as too are walks through spectacular scenic river gorges. Christine also organises creative holidays (on-site studio: painting, arts & crafts). An assured warm welcome and simple, good taste.

Christine COOPER
'Villa les Roches', 48300 LANGOGNE
Tel: (0) 4 66 46 69 53 / (0) 633 58 08 91
info@villa-les-roches.com
www.villa-les-roches.com

Facilities: off-street parking, garden, lounge, hosts have pets, pets not accepted, dinner available, 100% no smoking, 3 years old minimum age, closed: 1/11–31/03, golf course, fishing, hiking, cycling, interesting flora, lake watersports, winter sports 40km
Fluent English spoken

Price Structure – 5 Bedrooms
'Myrtille': bathroom, wc, shower, double bed (king-size): €55
'Sureau': along corridor bathroom, wc, along corridor shower, double bed: €48
'Chanterelle': bathroom, wc, shower, four-poster double bed: €50
'Prunelle': bathroom, wc, shower, twin beds: €55
'Framboise': shower room, wc, twin beds: €55

Directions: Langogne is at the crossroads between Aubenas, Le Puy-en-Velay and Mende. 'Villa les Roches' is at the exit of Langogne, heading to Mende (signposted).

Extra Bed: €15
Reduction: 7 nights
Capacity: 10 people

66.11 Perpignan

Location
9km S E of PERPIGNAN
in: Aiénya, station pick-up on arrival/departure
Railway station: 10km
Airport: Perpignan 15km
car essential

Residence of Outstanding Character

This imposing Catalan *mas* is set amongst the vineyards and orchards of Le Roussillon, a short distance from the beaches. Set on this wine-growing property, the house is covered with wisteria, climbing roses and jasmine. Ancient trees provide the shade for the vast courtyard, which is almost like a second living room. Everything contributes to the holiday mood: the spacious living room, the large swimming pool and the enthusiastic welcome of Myriam and Idéal.

Myriam & Idéal GARNIER
'Domaine du Mas Bazan', 66200 ALENYA
Tel: (0) 4 68 22 98 26 / (0) 683 51 51 13
Fax: (0) 4 68 22 98 26
masbazan@wanadoo.fr
www.masbazan.com

Facilities: off-street parking, extensive grounds, lounge, dinner available, kitchen, babies welcome, free cot, private swimming pool, hiking, vineyard, golf course 3km, sea watersports 4km
Adequate English spoken

Price Structure – 4 Bedrooms
and 1 Apartment
'Bleue': television, shower room, wc, bathroom, double bed: €62
'Verte', 'Jaune' & 'Pêche': shower room, wc, bathroom, double bed, single bed: €62 – 2 people
€69 – 3 people
suite 'Campagnarde': lounge, kitchen, shower room, wc, bathroom, double bed. En-suite room, 2 single beds: €120 – 4 people

Capacity: 15 people

Directions: At Perpignan (exit Perpignan-Sud from the A9), take the N114 towards Argelès-sur-Mer. Take exit 3 towards Saleille, then the D22 towards Alénya. The 'Domaine du Mas Bazan' is situated before the village. Turn on the left into a road through the vines and continue to the end.

66.23 Perpignan

Residence of Outstanding Character

Claire & Gregor PENFOLD
'Mas d'en Bach', 66480 MAUREILLAS
Tel: (0) 4 68 83 04 10 Fax: (0) 4 68 83 07 69
masdenbach@hotmail.co.uk
www.masdenbach-ceret.net

Price Structure – 4 Bedrooms and 1 Suite
'Mûrier': bathroom, wc, double bed (queen-size): €60
'Bambou': bathroom, wc, double bed: €65
'Palmier': lounge, bathroom, wc, double bed (super king-size): €75
'Olivier': shower room, wc, double bed, 2 single beds: €75 – 2 people €115 – 4 people
'Laurier Sauce 1': shower room, wc, washbasin, twin beds. En-suite room, twin beds: €115 – 4 people

Extra Bed: €20
Capacity: 14 people

Location
29km S of PERPIGNAN
in: Maureillas
Railway station: 26km
Airport: Perpignan 30km
car essential

By the Vallespir Valley, this 18th-century Catalan *mas* has a privileged position on a wooded hillside that descends to the river. The grounds with a thicket, a freshwater fountain and an esplanade by the swimming pool also include four semi-wild hectares being tamed by Gregor, a former landscape designer. Claire and Gregor champion local produce at breakfast (apple juice, honey) and regional cuisine and wines for dinner. Expect a dry sense of humour and a pleasant welcome here. Ceret and its Modern Art Museum is nearby.

Facilities: off-street parking, extensive grounds, tv lounge, hosts have pets, pets not accepted, dinner available, 100% no smoking, 5 years old minimum age, private swimming pool, hiking, cycling, vineyard 3km, fishing 6km, sea watersports 26km
Fluent English spoken

Directions: From Perpignan on the A9 towards Spain, exit 43 Le Boulou, then the N9 towards Spain for 2km, then right onto the D618 until the centre of Maureillas and then head for Ceret. At the exit of Maureillas turn left and follow the arrows and signs 'Chambres d'Hôtes'.

66.12 Perpignan

Working Farm

Rose-Marie & André TUBERT
'Mas du Tech', rue des Jardins, 66560 ORTAFFA
Tel: (0) 4 68 22 03 18 / (0) 683 35 83 23
Fax: (0) 4 68 22 03 18
mas-du-tech@wanadoo.fr
www.mas-du-tech.ifrance.com

Price Structure – 6 Bedrooms
5 rooms: wheelchair access, shower room, wc, double bed, single bed: €43 – 2 people
€53 – 3 people
wheelchair access, shower room, wc, double bed: €43

Capacity: 17 people

Location
14km S of PERPIGNAN
in: Ortaffa
Railway station: 10km
Airport: Perpignan 30km
car essential

It is worth a detour just to enjoy Rose-Marie's cooking and André's charm. They welcome you warmly to this quiet place, with simply furnished yet comfortable rooms. Their large garden is a cool oasis, where it is easy to chill out amongst the fruit trees, far away from the crowded beaches.

Facilities: private parking, extensive grounds, tv lounge, hosts have pets, pets not accepted, dinner available, babies welcome, free cot, 100% no smoking, wheelchair access, 3 nights minimum stay: 1/07–31/08, private swimming pool, hiking, vineyard 4km, sea watersports 9km

Directions: From Perpignan, N114 towards Argelès-sur-Mer. At Elne, turn right onto the D40 towards Ortaffa. In the village, go past the *boulangerie*, left just after the *boucherie*. After 300m, turn right following the sign 'passage à gué'. It is immediately on the right.

Location
38km N of PERPIGNAN
in: Paziols
Railway station: 45km
Airport: Perpignan 30km
car essential

Private Home

On the Cathar route and near the Fitou vineyard and Château d'Aguilar, in a pretty village set in the *garrigue* and vines, is Chantal and Philippe's home. Step inside, and their maisonette is a cosy refuge with white stone walls, typical red *tommette* floors and a traditional kitchen. The bedrooms are comfortable with multi-jet showers. A friendly, relaxed atmosphere as Philippe serves a bottle of local Fitou, made from his own vines. Chantal, active in village life, advises on the Citadelles du Vertige and Tautavel caves.

Chantal & Philippe FABREGA
'Le Fitoun', 11350 PAZIOLS
Tel: (0) 4 68 45 43 49 / (0) 661 36 55 81
Fax: (0) 4 68 45 43 49
le.fitoun@wanadoo.fr
www.lefitoun.com

Facilities: off-street parking, garden, lounge, hosts have pets, pets not accepted, babies welcome, free cot, 100% no smoking, hunting, fishing, mushroom-picking, hiking, vineyard, riversports 30km
Basic English spoken

Directions: From Narbonne take the N9 towards Perpignan for 12km, then the D611 on the right to Durban, Tuchan et Paziols. As you enter the village, pass the bridge and take the first road on the right. Continue for 300m and then fork left. The house is 50m further on, on the left.

Price Structure – 3 Bedrooms
'Peyrepertuse' (our favourite room): shower room, wc, washbasin, 3 single beds: €49 – 2 people €66 – 3 people
'Quéribus': bathroom, wc, shower, 3 single beds: €49 – 2 people €66 – 3 people
'Aguilar': shower room, wc, washbasin, double bed: €49

Capacity: 8 people

Location
26km S of PERPIGNAN
in: Sorède
Railway station: 25km
Airport: Perpignan 30km
car essential

Private Home

At just 10km from the beaches at Collioure, this contemporary house has a lovely open plan living room and kitchen. Inside the quality decoration and furnishings and the numerous framed pictures lends a charm to the interior that you wouldn't necessarily expect from the outside. The most spacious bedroom is the 'Petite Suite' with a seating area and a lovely white marble fireplace. Gilberte, a former proofreader, provides a natural and warm welcome.

Gilberte TENA
'L'Oasis', 25 rue de l'Oasis, 66690 SOREDE
Tel: (0) 4 68 95 57 60 / (0) 631 91 10 13
sorede.bb@gmail.com
sorede.bb.free.fr

Facilities: garden, lounge, internet access, babies welcome, free cot, 100% no smoking, 1 shared bathroom, 2 wcs, 2 nights minimum stay: 01/07–15/09, mushroom-picking, hiking, fishing 10km, sea watersports 10km, vineyard 10km, golf course 15km
Fluent English spoken

Directions: From Perpignan, A9 towards Spain, exit 43 at Le Boulou, then the D618 towards Argelès for 11km. D11 on the right to Sorède and then from the centre take the D2 towards Argelès, cross the bridge and take the second road on the right.

Price Structure – 4 Bedrooms
'Café' & 'Rose': shower, double bed: €65
'Petite Suite': lounge, television, shower, double bed: €75
'Bleue': shower room, wc, double bed: €65

Extra Bed: €20
Capacity: 8 people

66.22 Perpignan

Residence of Outstanding Character

Mario DE SOUSA
'L'Hospitalité la Fauvelle', 60 avenue Fauvelle, 66300 THUIR
Tel: (0) 4 68 50 50 50 Fax: (0) 4 68 53 38 23
mario.rego@lafauvelle.com
www.lafauvelle.com

Price Structure – 16 Bedrooms
14 rooms: wheelchair access, shower room, wc, twin beds: €90
2 rooms: shower room, wc, double bed: €90

Extra Bed: €15
Reduction: 01/10–31/03, 3 nights
Capacity: 32 people

Location
15km S W of PERPIGNAN
in: Thuir
car essential

Near medieval Castelnou in Catalan country, between sea and mountains, Mario welcomes you to his 19th-century pottery. It is surrounded by fabulous half-wild grounds with a salt-water pool. Totally reorganised, it consists of three buildings and terraces amid plants, vines, stone arches and shaded areas under pine and palm trees. Enjoy the spacious interior decorated with paintings by local artists. The bedrooms are air-conditioned and minimalist in style. Mario offers a very professional, attentive welcome. Trips possible.

Facilities: private parking, extensive grounds, lounge, dinner available, wheelchair access, private swimming pool, cycling, hiking 2km, vineyard 3km, golf course 18km, winter sports 50km
Fluent English spoken

Directions: A9 exit Perpignan-Sud, towards Thuir. Head for the centre of Thuir and then head for Castelnou. The house is on this road just before exiting the town.

66.24 Perpignan

Private Home

Marie-Christine CLAUZIER
'Les Mandariniers', 8 rue des Mésanges, 66300 THUIR
Tel: (0) 4 68 53 06 77 / (0) 620 87 54 94
mandariniers@yahoo.fr
www.mandariniers.fr.st

Price Structure – 4 Bedrooms
'Mimosa': wheelchair access, shower, bathroom, double bed: €53
'Tournesol': wheelchair access, television, shower, twin beds: €50
'Lavande': wheelchair access, shower room, wc, double bed: €53
'Grenade': wheelchair access, shower room, wc, double bed: €56

Extra Bed: €10
Reduction: 5 nights
Capacity: 8 people

Location
15km S W of PERPIGNAN
in: Thuir, station pick-up on arrival/departure
Railway station: 13km
Airport: Perpignan 13km
car essential

At the foot of the Canigou, in a quiet, residential part of Thuir, are three guest rooms in the wing of a pleasant family house. The independent rooms in spring colours are named after flowers. Soak up the Mediterranean atmosphere and taste traditional Catalan delights on the terrace by mandarin, fig and grapefruit trees. Be sure to visit Cave Byrrh with the largest oak vat in the world! Of note: secure parking and a summer kitchen with a fridge and washing machine. Good value prices for quality and facilities just pushing three 'suns'.

Facilities: private parking, garden, hosts have pets, pets not accepted, dinner available, kitchen, babies welcome, free cot, 100% no smoking, wheelchair access, wc, hiking, vineyard, riversports 20km, golf course 25km, fishing 25km, sea watersports 25km
Fluent English spoken

Directions: From Perpignan-Sud, A9 exit 42. D612 to Thuir. Pass around Thuir towards Iles-sur-Têt, Millas. When the stadium is on your left, turn left as if you are entering the stadium and continue along the road (Avenue des Sports). Take the fourth road on the right into Rue des Mésanges.

Languedoc-Roussillon – Perpignan

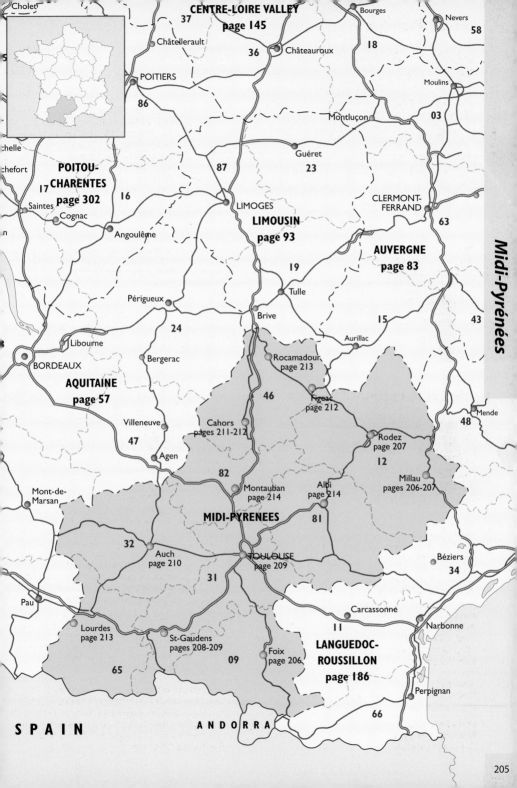

CENTRE-LOIRE VALLEY
page 145

Cholet

37

Châtellerault

Bourges

Nevers

58

36

Châteauroux

18

POITIERS

Moulins

86

Montluçon

03

chelle

Guéret

23

POITOU-
CHARENTES
page 302

chefort

87

17

CLERMONT-
FERRAND

Saintes

16

LIMOGES

63

Cognac

LIMOUSIN
page 93

Angoulême

AUVERGNE
page 83

19

Tulle

15

43

Périgueux

Brive

24

Aurillac

Libourne

Rocamadour
page 213

Mende

BORDEAUX

Bergerac

46

Figeac
page 212

48

AQUITAINE
page 57

Cahors
pages 211-212

Rodez
page 207

Villeneuve

12

47

Agen

Millau
pages 206-207

82

Mont-de-
Marsan

Montauban
page 214

Albi
page 214

MIDI-PYRENEES

81

32

Auch
page 210

TOULOUSE
page 209

Béziers

34

31

Pau

Carcassonne

Lourdes
page 213

11

Narbonne

St-Gaudens
pages 208-209

Foix
page 206

**LANGUEDOC-
ROUSSILLON**
page 186

65

09

Perpignan

S P A I N

A N D O R R A

66

Midi-Pyrénées

205

09.07 Foix

Private Home

Location
30km N E of FOIX
in: Coutens
Airport: Carcassonne-Salvaza 50km
car essential

Harriet and Robert are Americans, happy to have found their piece of paradise, to open the doors to their longhouse and welcome you over a drink. Soon you'll feel you have known them for years. Children are king here and the welcoming family lounge is open to you, as is a swimming pool, large bedrooms, large wardrobes – everything to make you feel at home. Harriet and Robert join you for dinner prepared from farm produce. They love France and living here and this is the true concept of B&B. On site: gîte, rented weekly.

Harriet & Robert STOW
'La Ferme de Boyer', 09500 COUTENS
Tel: (0) 5 61 68 93 41 / (0) 622 04 05 84
Fax: (0) 5 61 69 33 84
ferme.boyer@wanadoo.fr
www.fermeboyer.iowners.net

Price Structure – 2 Bedrooms and 1 Apartment
bathroom, wc, shower, double bed: €80
bathroom, wc, shower, twin beds: €80
kitchen, along corridor bathroom, wc, shower, twin beds. En-suite room, double bed. En-suite room, 3 single beds: €70 – 2 people €140 – 7 people

Capacity: 11 people

Facilities: private parking, garden, tv lounge, hosts have pets, pets not accepted, dinner available, kitchen, babies welcome, free cot, private swimming pool, mushroom-picking, hiking, fishing 2km, cycling 10km, riversports 10km, vineyard 20km, winter sports 50km
Fluent English spoken

Directions: A61 Toulouse-Montpellier then A66 direction Foix, Andorre. Exit Pamiers Sud. D119 towards Mirepoix for 17km. Go through Coutens. 'La Ferme de Boyer' is on the right.

12.10 Millau

Château/Manor House

Location
50km S of MILLAU
in: Camarès
Railway station: 80km
Airport: Montpellier-Méditerranée 110km
car essential

Friendly Eliane and Jean-Louis welcome you to this attractive building. Children are welcome and the family lounge has a library and games area. They are always on hand to help, and with a passion for walking they will happily join you on walks. The bedrooms are not big but are well-maintained and have a lovely view of windmills! Creative cuisine from local produce and crêpes, cake and homemade jam for breakfast. A real find lies behind a door; open it and see – a lovely chapel, all original, with beautiful stained glass windows. It's *magnifique*!

Eliane & Jean-Louis BACHELET
'Prieuré St Jean', Rigols, 12360 CAMARES
Tel: (0) 5 65 99 56 10 / (0) 683 29 24 96
Fax: (0) 5 65 99 56 10
jbachelet@hotmail.com
www.prieuresaintjean.com

Price Structure – 4 Bedrooms and 1 Suite
'Gauguin' & 'Vénus': shower room, wc, double bed: €48
'Eole': shower room, wc, double bed. Along corridor room 'Océane': wheelchair access, shower room, wc, 3 single beds: €48 – 2 people €112 – 5 people
'Van Gogh': shower room, wc, 3 single beds: €48
'Toulouse Lautrec': shower room, wc, 3 single beds: €48 – 2 people €80 – 3 people

Extra Bed: €16
Reduction: 7 nights, groups
Capacity: 14 people

Facilities: off-street parking, extensive grounds, lounge, hosts have pets, dinner available, babies welcome, free cot, hunting, fishing, mushroom-picking, bird-watching, hiking, cycling, interesting flora, winter sports, gliding 14km, riversports 20km
Adequate English spoken

Directions: Please contact your hosts in advance for detailed directions.

Location
25km S of MILLAU
in: Cornus, station pick-up on arrival/departure
Railway station: 40km
car essential

Château/Manor House

As we go to press this host has not yet been classified, but will be shortly. Yvonne and Patrick's place is on the mystical Plateau de Larzac. It is a large building, dating from the 11th century, which then became a château in the 13th century. It is majestic; its stones are steeped in history which you feel all around you. The bedrooms have been sensitively modernised to today's standards. Yvonne is very artistic and has managed to retain the soul and history of this place. It is a haven of comfort not far from the Millau Viaduct.

Yvonne & Patrick GIANSILY
'Château de Sorgues', 12540 CORNUS
Tel: (0) 5 65 97 50 21 Fax: (0) 5 65 97 50 21
contact@chateaudesorgues.fr
www.chateaudesorgues.fr

Facilities: extensive grounds, tv lounge, pets not accepted, internet access, dinner available, babies welcome, free cot, private swimming pool
Adequate English spoken

Price Structure – 5 Bedrooms
'Micropolis': shower room, wc, twin beds, single bed: €100 – 2 people €123 – 3 people
'Hospitalier': shower room, wc, four-poster double bed (queen-size): €95
'Templiers': shower room, wc, four-poster double bed (queen-size): €140
'Noria': shower room, wc, double bed (queen-size), single bed: €122 – 2 people €214 – 3 people
'Pastoralia': lounge, shower room, wc, double bed (queen-size): €134

Directions: From the A75, exit 48 Cornus, south of Millau, and go to the village of Cornus, about 6km. Go through the village and after 1.5km, turn left on a bend towards Sorgues. The château is 5km further on, on the left.

Extra Bed: €23 **Reduction:** 4 nights, children
Capacity: 12 people

Location
4km N of RODEZ
in: Onet-le-Château, station pick-up on arrival/departure
Railway station: 5km
Airport: Rodez 7km

Château/Manor House

On a tranquil estate, this refined 16th-century château offers seven bedrooms. The renovated rooms, decorated mixing romanticism and modernity, are in different parts of the château, some on the ground floor with an independent entrance and larger ones above. Jean, the owner, is passionate about antiques and his appreciation for beautiful things can be seen all around. We loved the harpsichord in 'De Créato'. But it is Gisèle and Jean-Pierre who greet you here. The vast swimming pool is set by fruit trees and vines. Wonderful!

Gisèle & Jean-Pierre RIVIERE
'Château de Labro', 12850 ONET-LE-CHATEAU
Tel: (0) 5 65 67 90 62 / (0) 684 19 81 94
Fax: (0) 5 65 67 45 79
chateau.labro@wanadoo.fr
www.chateaulabro.fr

Facilities: off-street parking, extensive grounds, hosts have pets, pets not accepted, dinner available, babies welcome, free cot, private swimming pool, hiking, cycling, golf course 3km, vineyard 15km, fishing 25km, riversports 25km, winter sports 35km
Adequate English spoken

Price Structure – 6 Bedrooms and 1 Suite
'Margot' & 'Violette': bathroom, wc, double bed (queen-size): €90
'Polonaise' & 'Cardinale': shower room, wc, four-poster double bed (queen-size): €130
'Rouquetière': lounge, bathroom, wc, double bed (queen-size), single bed: €130
'De Créato': lounge, shower room, wc, double bed (queen-size): €150
'De Nattes': lounge, bathroom, wc, double bed. En-suite room, twin beds: €150

Directions: From Rodez, ring road North direction Marcillac, Conques. D901 for 5km. Keep the Parc de Vabre on your right and turn left to the village Onet-le-Château. The Château de Labro is indicated on the right.

Capacity: 17 people

Midi-Pyrénées – Millau, Rodez

31.13 St-Gaudens

Private Home

Sylvie DUFOUR
'La Maison du Village d'en Bas', 31 Haute-
Garonne, Le Village d'en Bas, 31230 BOISSEDE
Tel: (0) 5 61 95 42 56 / (0) 603 98 80 70
sylduf20@yahoo.fr
www.e-monsite.com/maisonvillageenbas/

Price Structure – 1 Bedroom
bathroom, wc, twin beds: €55

Reduction: 2 nights
Capacity: 2 people

Location
44km N of ST-GAUDENS
in: Boissède
Airport: Toulouse-Blagnac 60km
car essential

Sylvie's little farmhouse dates from 1750 and she has renovated it with great charm. She has just one very pleasant and comfortable room, so you will get her undivided attention. They still catch crayfish here in this calm and peaceful spot, just one hour from the low cost flights at Toulouse or Carcassonne. Do not miss the Samatan market on Mondays, as this isolated village of 60 souls in deepest rural France is renowned for its foie gras.

Facilities: off-street parking, garden, tv lounge, hosts have pets, pets not accepted, internet access, dinner available, babies welcome, free cot, 100% no smoking, hunting, fishing, mushroom-picking, cycling, hiking 10km
Adequate English spoken

Directions: From Toulouse, N124 dual carriageway towards Auch. Turn off at Samatan, Lombez. Straight on for about 20km. As you enter Samatan, left to Lombez, follow signs to L'Isle-en-Dodon. In a small wood, Boissède is signed to the right. Cross the wood. At the crossroads right towards Boissède. The house is in the first group of houses on the left, near to the small lake with weeping willows.

31.11 St-Gaudens

Private Home

Monique & Ton VAN DER LIST
'Au Palmier de Barran', 31230 MONTBERNARD
Tel: (0) 5 61 94 19 04
info@palmierdebarran.com
www.palmierdebarran.com

Price Structure – 3 Bedrooms
'Au Soleil du Midi': shower room, wc, double bed: €60
'Suite Nocturne en Vert': 2 sets of twin beds: €50 – 2 people €95 – 4 people
'Au Vent du Large': shower room, wc, double bed, single bed: €60 – 2 people €75 – 3 people

Extra Bed: €15
Reduction: 7 nights
Capacity: 9 people

Location
30km N of ST-GAUDENS
in: Montbernard, station pick-up on arrival/departure
Railway station: 30km
Airport: Toulouse-Blagnac 70km
car essential

Monique and Ton, from Holland, have found here in the superb undulating Gascony landscape a haven of peace and the great outdoors. This large 18th-century building stands on a hill, presiding over a beautiful panoramic view of the Pyrenees. Bedrooms boast decorative fireplaces, antique furniture, canopies, chandeliers and a semi-open bathroom for the 'Au Soleil du Midi' room, but more modest for the 'Suite'. A full, delicious, organic-based breakfast is served on the large sheltered terrace with views. Monique serves a mix of regional and international dishes from homegrown and local farm produce. Child meals on offer.

Facilities: private parking, garden, tv lounge, hosts have pets, dinner available, closed: 01/10–22/12 & 06/01–01/05, hiking, cycling 2km, riversports 7km, fishing 8km, lake watersports 8km, interesting flora 10km, winter sports 40km
Fluent English spoken

Directions: From Toulouse, N124 towards Auch until L'Isle-Jourdain then the D634 on the left and the D17 towards Lannemezan. 10km after L'Isle-en-Dodon, pass Montbernard, then the D55d, third small road on the right towards Mondilhan. After 1km, the house is on the left.

Location
15km N E of ST-GAUDENS
in: Sepx
Airport: Toulouse-Blagnac 80km
car essential

Private Home

This dynamic couple left Paris for a stone ruin on the route to Compostella, 55km from Spain. Wait until you see the result! Comfort and lots of charm, and a superb view of the Pyrenees as you sit by the pool. This is a great area for walking and mountain biking and there is also a spa resort 10km away. Unsurprisingly Alexandre is a keen marathon runner yet is happy to advise on less demanding walks. Sylvie is lively and justly proud of her impeccable home. She serves a good, hearty breakfast.

Sylvie & Alexandre LECLERCQ
'La Grangette', 31360 SEPX
Tel: (0) 5 61 90 69 92 / (0) 680 74 32 80

Facilities: off-street parking, garden, tv lounge, hosts have pets, pets not accepted, babies welcome, free cot, 100% no smoking, private swimming pool, hunting, fishing, mushroom-picking, hiking, cycling, golf course 18km, riversports 40km, winter sports 50km
Basic English spoken

Price Structure – 4 Bedrooms
'Mathieu': television, shower room, wc, double bed, single bed: €80 – 2 people €95 – 3 people
'Princesse', 'Xavier' & 'Sandra': shower room, wc, double bed: €80

Capacity: 9 people

Directions: From the A64, EITHER take exit 18 St-Gaudens then the N117 towards St-Gaudens and Lestelle OR take exit 19 and the N117 to Lestelle-de-St-Martory. At Lestelle-de-St-Martory, D69 towards Les Assivets, Castillon-de-St-Martory then Sepx. The house is on the right between Castillon and Sepx.

31.12 Toulouse

Location
17km S E of TOULOUSE
in: Ste-Foy d'Aigrefeuille
Railway station: 14km
Airport: Toulouse-Blagnac 19km
car essential

Bienvenue en France

Château/Manor House

This magnificent manor full of character, typical of the architectural style of Toulouse, has been in the family for six generations. The young grandson Nicolas will look after you. He has given up his job to run his grandparents' property with great enthusiasm. Family heirlooms sit side by side with broadband and vast modernised bathrooms. The large pool surrounded by 150 hectares is heated from April onwards and the views over the golf course all contribute to your dream holiday. We are sure that it will not be long before Nicolas earns four 'suns'.

Nicolas MONTSARRAT
'Domaine de St-Martin de Ronsac', route de la Saune D18, 31570 STE-FOY D'AIGREFEUILLE
Tel: (0) 5 61 83 61 02 / (0) 613 63 78 71
francoise.montsarrat@orange.fr
www.domainesaintmartinderonsac.com

Facilities: off-street parking, extensive grounds, tv lounge, internet access, babies welcome, free cot, 100% no smoking, private swimming pool, hunting, fishing, golf course 1km, gliding 9km
Fluent English spoken

Price Structure – 4 Bedrooms
'Orchidée': lounge, television, bathroom, wc, shower, twin beds: €110
'Marguerite': lounge, bathroom, wc, shower, double bed: €110
'Rose': lounge, shower room, wc, double bed: €110
'Fleur de Lys': lounge, television, bathroom, wc, double bed: €110

Capacity: 8 people

Directions: Exit 17 from the A61. Then take the N126 Castres road for 3km, then the D18 on the right for 3km. Between Aigrefeuille and Ste-Foy-d'Aigrefeuille at the little white bridge, turn left and continue for 2km as far as the statue on the left. Turn left here.

32.13 Auch

Château/Manor House

Brigitte & Pierre SALVAGE
'Domaine d'Izaute', Château d'Izaute, route de Laujuzan, 32110 CAUPENNE-D'ARMAGNAC
Tel: (0) 5 62 08 89 46 / (0) 686 16 03 54
Fax: (0) 5 62 08 89 47
izaute@wanadoo.fr
www.visitorama.com/32/Izaute

Price Structure – 8 Bedrooms
3 rooms: lounge, television, bathroom, wc, double bed: €95
Room 2: lounge, television, shower room, wc, four-poster double bed, single bed: €95
'Indonésie': lounge, television, shower room, wc, twin beds: €95
3 rooms: lounge, television, shower room, wc, twin beds: €95

Extra Bed: €25   **Capacity:** 17 people

Location
66km N W of AUCH
in: Caupenne-d'Armagnac
Railway station: 60km
Airport: Pau-Pyrénées 50km
car essential

In Gascony, 5km from the Nogaro racing circuit, are these former outbuildings to the château (which is undergoing restoration). Brigitte and Pierre's good taste, competence and their meticulous attention to detail have created magnificent rooms. Whether on the ground floor, or upstairs in the interlinked balcony rooms, each bedroom boasts quality Asiatic and Oriental furnishings and sumptuous fabrics. Moreover, the bathrooms, the large living areas, the garden, the shell-shaped swimming pool and the pool-house are not upstaged.

Facilities: off-street parking, extensive grounds, lounge, pets not accepted, kitchen, wheelchair access, closed: 01/10–01/06, private swimming pool, vineyard, hiking 3km, gliding 5km, golf course 20km
Fluent English spoken

Directions: Between Auch on the N124 (62km) and Mont-de-Marsan (39km), continue as far as Nogaro, then in the centre take the D43 towards Laujuzan for 4.5km. The château is on the left.

32.14 Auch

Residence of Outstanding Character

Christine & Francis BOSSEAUX
'Le Bourda', 11 rue St Jean,
32160 PRECHAC-SUR-ADOUR
Tel: (0) 5 62 69 16 65 / (0) 670 77 83 19
frabo@wanadoo.fr
http://halte-au-bourdat.monsite.wanadoo.fr

Price Structure – 1 Suite
'Les Oiseaux': lounge, bathroom, wc, twin beds. En-suite room, twin beds: €56 – 2 people €112 – 4 people

Extra Bed: €18
Reduction: 7 nights
Capacity: 4 people

Location
55km W of AUCH
in: Préchac-sur-Adour
Railway station: 45km
car essential

This 18th-century house is in a peaceful little village close to a fishing lake. The bedrooms are pleasant (and can only be booked together by the same party). The lush garden boasts four palm trees. Breakfast is served in the lounge by the fireplace. Your hosts are part of a local organisation striving to maintain and promote the local heritage and are excellent sources of information. They know where to savour the best of this well-known cuisine and receive the best Gascony welcome!

Facilities: private parking, extensive grounds, tv lounge, pets not accepted, 100% no smoking, fishing, cycling 4km, lake watersports 4km, vineyard 10km, golf course 28km, winter sports 60km
Fluent English spoken

Directions: From Tarbes D935 towards Aire-sur-Adour for 42km then D946 on the right to Plaisance until Préchac-sur-Adour (1.5km). 'Le Bourda' is on the road behind the *mairie*.

Location
35km N W of CAHORS
in: Frayssinet-Le-Gelat
Railway station: 35km
Airport: 150km
car essential

Working Farm

You are sure of a friendly, family welcome from Annick and Marie-France in this 18th-century *ferme-auberge*, typical of Le Quercy, in the middle of the country, full of flowers. Admire their beautiful old dovecote and taste the local produce.

'Aux Délices de La Serpt', Ferme Auberge,
46250 FRAYSSINET-LE-GELAT
Tel: (0) 5 65 36 66 15 Fax: (0) 5 65 36 60 34

Facilities: off-street parking, garden, lounge, hosts have pets, dinner available, closed: 1/10–31/03, hiking, cycling, mushroom-picking, fishing 4km, riversports 30km
Adequate English spoken

Price Structure – 1 Bedroom
shower room, wc, double bed: €35

Extra Bed: €8
Capacity: 2 people

Directions: At Cahors, take the D911 towards Villeneuve-sur-Lot for 15.5km as far as Rostassac. Turn right onto the D660 towards Frayssinet. At the roundabout, go towards Villefranche, Périgueux. Follow the signs.

Location
28km S of CAHORS
in: Montpezat-de-Quercy, station pick-up on arrival/departure
Railway station: 12km
Airport: Toulouse-Blagnac 80km

Residence of Outstanding Character

From the narrow lanes of this authentic historic village, it is hard to envisage what lies behind the gates to this property. The dimensions of the rooms are impressive and the décor restrained and harmonious. The bedrooms are contemporary with period furniture adding unique character, notably 'La Chapelle' with an original bathroom. Quality extras include safes and dressing gowns. Discover the view from three terraces out over the garden and a 14th-century collegiate church. A refined environment with a sincere, relaxed welcome.

Patricia & Philippe DIEUDONNE
'Les trois terrasses', rue de la Libération,
82270 MONTPEZAT-DE-QUERCY
Tel: (0) 5 63 02 66 21 / (0) 674 50 26 66
Fax: (0) 5 63 64 01 62
infos@trois-terrasses.com
www.trois-terrasses.com

Facilities: private parking, garden, lounge, hosts have pets, pets not accepted, dinner available, kitchen, 100% no smoking, fishing, mushroom-picking, bird-watching, hiking, cycling, vineyard, golf course 90km
Fluent English spoken

Price Structure – 5 Bedrooms
'La Chapelle': television, bathroom, wc, shower, washbasin, double bed (queen-size): €165
'La Collégiale' & 'L'Anglaise': bathroom, wc, washbasin, double bed (queen-size): €145
'l'Alcove': shower room, wc, washbasin, double bed (queen-size): €100
'La Galerie': television, bathroom, wc, shower, washbasin, double bed, 2 single beds:
€165 – 2 people €215 – 4 people

Extra Bed: €25   **Reduction:** 4 nights
Capacity: 12 people

Directions: From Cahors take the N20 towards Montauban, Caussade, for 24km. Then take the D20 on the right to Montpezat-de-Quercy. Head to the centre of the village and take the road just opposite the *mairie* (town hall), into Rue de la Libération. Fourth house on the right.

46.33 Cahors

Private Home

Location
28km W of CAHORS
in: Prayssac
Railway station: 25km
Airport: Bergerac 80km
car essential

Amidst the orchards and vineyards of Cahors is this contemporary house on the edge of a small Lot town. The pleasant garden and terrace sit in a peaceful and rural setting on the edge of a wooded hillside, ideal for walks. Breakfast is served on the terrace or in the lovely large kitchen. The bedrooms, decorated in soft colours, are upstairs, except the 'Lavande' which is at garden level with its own independent entrance. Ian is passionate about jazz music and Linda is an excellent cook. Uncover the region from this tranquil spot.

Linda WEBSTER
'Les Cèdres', La Figueyrade, route du Théron,
46220 PRAYSSAC
Tel: (0) 5 65 30 04 94
webster2@wanadoo.fr
www.lotchambres.com

Price Structure – 4 Bedrooms
'Lavande' & 'Glycines': shower room, wc, double bed: €50
'Tournesol': along corridor shower room, wc, single bed: €47 – 1 person
'Cerise': along corridor shower room, wc, twin beds: €50

Reduction: 01/07–30/06, 7 nights
Capacity: 7 people

Facilities: off-street parking, garden, tv lounge, hosts have pets, pets not accepted, dinner available, 100% no smoking, 2 nights minimum stay: 01/07–31/08, closed: 25/12, interesting flora, hunting, hiking, vineyard, cycling 2km, riversports 8km, golf course 40km
Fluent English spoken

Directions: From Cahors D811 (former D911) towards Villeneuve-sur-Lot for 15km until Prayssac. Pass around the church and head for Le Théron for about 2km. It is the house with the blue shutters after the bridge on the right.

46.34 Figeac

Château/Manor House

Location
FIGEAC
in: Figeac
Railway station: 3km
Airport: Rodez 60km
car essential

Above Figeac, overlooking the valley, this grand 16th- and 18th-century house has a swimming pool with a terrace, a summer kitchen and stunning views. The original architecture has been respected and the thick walls keep you cool in summer and retain the heat from the fires in winter. The bedrooms are impeccably maintained and there is a jacuzzi. The apartment on the ground floor has a terrace. Homemade bread is served at breakfast by the pool. A pleasant welcome from Hubert, a keen astronomer. On site: a self-contained cottage.

Agnès & Hubert EVRARD
'Manoir de Conjat', 46100 FIGEAC
Tel: (0) 5 65 34 37 95 / (0) 672 72 63 79
manoirdeconjat@free.fr
http://monsite.wanadoo.fr/manoirdeconjat/

Price Structure – 3 Bedrooms
and 1 Apartment
'Tour': television, bathroom, wc, double bed (king-size), single bed: €90 – 2 people €120 – 3 people
'Magnolia': shower room, wc, double bed, single bed: €70 – 2 people €100 – 3 people
'Cyprès': shower room, wc, double bed: €80
'Cottage Tilleuls': kitchen, shower room, wc, double bed. En-suite room, single bed: €106 – 2 people €106 – 3 people

Extra Bed: €30
Capacity: 11 people

Facilities: off-street parking, extensive grounds, tv lounge, hosts have pets, dinner available, private swimming pool, mushroom-picking, hiking, cycling, fishing 3km, riversports 3km, vineyard 3km, golf course 30km, winter sports 70km
Fluent English spoken

Directions: From Figeac N140 direction Rodez for 2km then the D2 on the left towards Montredon. At the crossroads, turn left and head down the lane to the gate (signposted).

Location
23km N E of ROCAMADOUR
in: Carennac, station pick-up on
arrival/departure
Railway station: 12km
Airport: Brive 40km

Private Home

The instant you arrive you are blown away by the panoramic view over the valley and a medieval village. The five guest bedrooms here are bright and sunny and tastefully furnished (we loved 'Tournesol'). Colette offers good advice, in part due to her time in the diplomatic corps, as she is a proficient organiser with links to local businesses. A continental self-service breakfast is taken on the terrace or in the basement where a kitchen area and drinks are available. A large lounge with a fireplace is also open to guests.

Facilities: private parking, extensive grounds, tv lounge, pets not accepted, kitchen, babies welcome, free cot, 100% no smoking, wheelchair access, hunting, fishing, mushroom-picking, bird-watching, hiking, cycling, interesting flora, riversports, golf course 13km, vineyard 15km
Fluent English spoken

Directions: From Brive A20 direction Cahors, Montauban, exit 55. D703 Souillac, then to Martel and Vayrac. 3km after Vayrac at Bétaille, D20 on the right to Carennac. Stay in the top part of the village and take the the little road opposite the 'Hôtel du Quercy' and follow signs for the 'parking municipal'. The house is on the right, signed Bed & Breakfast France.

Colette LEMANT
'L'Oustal Nau', Les Combes, 46110 CARENNAC
Tel: (0) 5 65 10 94 09 / (0) 688 18 13 43
Fax: (0) 5 65 50 27 49
lemant@club-internet.fr
www.oustalnau-carennac.com

Price Structure – 5 Bedrooms
'Tournesol' (our favourite room): lounge, television, bathroom, wc, shower, twin beds, single bed:
€101 – 2 people €121 – 3 people
'Ajonc': television, bathroom, wc, shower, double bed (queen-size), single bed: €91 – 2 people
€101 – 3 people
'Dahlia': television, bathroom, wc, shower, twin beds, single bed: €101 – 3 people
'Myosotis': wheelchair access, television, bathroom, wc, shower, twin beds: €91
plus 1 room

Extra Bed: €10 **Reduction:** 21/08–12/07, 2 nights, groups **Capacity:** 13 people

Location
10km N W of LOURDES
in: Pontacq
Railway station: 10km
Airport: Tarbes-Lourdes-Pyrénées 10km
car essential

Private Home

Situated 10km from Lourdes, at the gateway to the Pyrenees and just 30km from the ski slopes, is this large longhouse with spacious rooms. This includes the lounge, the dining room and the bedroom at garden level. This bedroom is classically decorated with a wooden floor and furniture, a period-style bed and a bathroom decorated with a collection of perfume bottles. The bedroom upstairs has a sloping ceiling. At your disposal is an enclosed garden and secure parking. Coralie, a nurse, offers a sincere and friendly welcome.

Facilities: private parking, garden, hosts have pets, dinner available, babies welcome, free cot, wheelchair access, cycling, golf course 10km, sea watersports 10km, winter sports 30km
Adequate English spoken

Directions: A9 Pau-Tarbes, exit 11. D940 towards Lourdes to Pontacq. In the village pass the war memorial and the 'Hôtel du Commerce'. The house is 100m ahead on the left.

Coralie DONNET
'Laxara', 3 rue des Pyrénées, 64530 PONTACQ
Tel: (0) 5 59 53 69 15 / (0) 681 09 44 38
Fax: (0) 5 59 53 69 15
laxara64@gmail.com

Price Structure – 2 Bedrooms and 1 Suite
wheelchair access, shower room, wc, double bed:
€48
twin beds: €45
'Suite': washbasin, double bed. En-suite room, single bed: €50 – 2 people €70 – 3 people

Extra Bed: €15
Capacity: 7 people

Midi-Pyrénées – Rocamadour, Lourdes

81.16 Albi

Residence of Outstanding Character

Monique GOUPIL
'Domaine d'en Rigou', 81500 GIROUSSENS
Tel: (0) 5 63 41 69 25 / (0) 611 11 81 56
Fax: (0) 5 63 41 68 16
monique.goupil@wanadoo.fr
http://domainerigou.com

Price Structure – 5 Bedrooms and 1 Suite
'Carmen': lounge, television, bathroom, wc, twin beds: €80
'Manon' & 'Salomé': lounge, television, shower room, wc, twin beds: €80
'Aïda': lounge, television, bathroom, wc, shower, twin beds: €80
'Tosca': lounge, television, shower room, wc, 2 double beds: €80 – 2 people €150 – 4 people
'Butterfly': lounge, television, kitchen, bathroom, wc, shower, 2 double beds. En-suite room, twin beds, 2 single beds (child-size): €196 – 8 people

Extra Bed: €30   **Reduction:** 7 nights
Capacity: 20 people

Location
41km S W of ALBI
in: Giroussens
Railway station: 8km
Airport: Toulouse-Blagnac 40km
car essential

Bienvenue en France

Between Toulouse and Albi, in a potter's village, is this big *maison bourgeoise* of local stone in a plain of orchards. A pleasant atmosphere and an affable, courteous welcome from smiling Monique. A large corridor leads to a lounge, a bar and a vast dining room. The bedrooms are upstairs. The romantic 'Butterfly' suite can be rented with other rooms on the floor. There is an outside kitchen with barbecue and a curved pool to tempt you! Free tickets to the Martel gardens for weekly stays. On sale: their own fruit juice and poultry.

Facilities: off-street parking, extensive grounds, tv lounge, hosts have pets, dinner available, kitchen, babies welcome, free cot, 100% no smoking, 2 nights minimum stay, private swimming pool, private tennis court, hiking, cycling, riversports 3km, golf course 7km
Adequate English spoken

Directions: From the A68 Toulouse to Albi, take exit 7. Then the D12 to Giroussens. Take the small road that runs down in front of the post office (*La Poste*). Follow the signs 'Domaine d'en Rigou' for 1km.

81.25 Montauban

Private Home

Jean-Luc VIEILLARD
'Presbytère de St Pierre', 81630 SALVAGNAC
Tel: (0) 607 10 29 99
Fax: (0) 5 63 33 58 72
contact@toscaneenfrance.com
www.toscaneenfrance.com

Price Structure – 4 Bedrooms
'Suite': lounge, television, shower room, wc, double bed (king-size), single bed: €165 – 3 people
'Rouge': television, bathroom, wc, shower, washbasin, double bed: €80
'Bleue': television, bathroom, wc, shower, double bed (queen-size): €100
'Acajou': television, along corridor bathroom, wc, shower, double bed (queen-size): €120

Extra Bed: €20
Reduction: 8 nights
Capacity: 9 people

Location
32kmE of MONTAUBAN
in: Salvagnac, station pick-up on arrival/departure
Airport: Toulouse-Blagnac 50km
car essential

A real gem! Jean-Luc, your host, is absolutely charming. He is an interior designer who loves art and design and it shows. Charm, sophistication, refinement, a beautiful garden, a superb swimming pool and a family sitting room – all this for you to enjoy. The facilities are in fact very up to date with flat screen TVs, DVD players, glossy magazines and big dressing rooms to name but a few. Porcelain and silver of course for your breakfast, which includes fresh fruit and eggs. A superb base from which to visit the notable nearby villages known as 'Bastides Albigeoises'.

Facilities: off-street parking, garden, tv lounge, hosts have pets, 100% no smoking, 3 nights minimum stay: 01/07–31/08, private swimming pool, cycling, fishing 2km, mushroom-picking 5km, hiking 5km, vineyard 12km, golf course 25km, riversports 30km
Fluent English spoken

Directions: Please contact your host in advance for detailed directions.

NETHERLANDS

BELGIUM

Calais
pages 220-224

Dunkerque

St-Omer
page 226

Boulogne-sur-Mer
page 220

NORD-PAS-DE-CALAIS

LILLE
page 217

Le Touquet-Paris-Plage
page 225

Béthune
page 219

59

ENGLISH CHANNEL
(LA MANCHE)

Hesdin
page 224

62

Abbeville
pages 230

Arras
pages 218-219

Cambrai
page 216

Dieppe

80

AMIENS

Charleville-Mézières

Sedan

PICARDIE

02

76

08

Rethel

ROUEN

Compiègne
page 229

Beauvais
pages 227-228

60

Soissons
page 227

Reims

eux

27

Evreux

95

Pontoise

Mantes

Meaux

51

CHÂLONS

55

ANDY
e 231

92

92

Versailles

PARIS

75

94

77

ILE DE FRANCE
page 20

Bar-le-Duc

Vitry

St-Dizier

61

Dreux

78

Evry

CHAMPAGNE-
ARDENNE
page 180

52

28

Chartres

91

Melun

Fontainebleau

Troyes

on

CENTRE-LOIRE VALLEY
page 145

Sens

Chaumont

72

Châteaudun

10

Vendôme

ORLEANS

45

Montargis

Auxerre

89

BURGUNDY
page 97

21

59.08 Cambrai

Residence of Outstanding Character

Elisabeth & Roger QUERO
'Le Clos St Jacques', 9 rue St Jacques,
59400 CAMBRAI
Tel: (0) 3 27 74 37 61 / (0) 679 84 31 98
leclosstjacques@orange.fr
www.leclosstjacques.com

Price Structure – 4 Bedrooms and 1 Suite
'Soleil': bathroom, wc, twin beds: €86
'Régence': telephone, bathroom, wc, double bed: €82
'Nature': bathroom, wc, double bed: €86
'Campagne': lounge, wc, double bed (queen-size): €89
suite 'des Anges': bathroom, wc, four-poster double bed (king-size). En-suite room, lounge, bathroom, wc, shower, single bed: €154 – 2 people
€169 – 3 people

Extra Bed: €21,50
Capacity: 11 people

Location
CAMBRAI
in: Cambrai
Railway station: Cambrai
Airport: Lille-Lesquin 60km
car essential

In the heart of Cambrai, a town rich in history and art, Babeth and Roger have wonderfully restored this beautiful old house, whose façade and décor date from 1890. In the Middle Ages it was a favourite stop for the pilgrims en route for St-Jacques-de-Compostelle. In the 21st century, your hosts continue this tradition, offering modern travellers five beautiful cosy and quiet bedrooms. Both your hosts are past-masters in the art of hospitality and entertaining.

Facilities: off-street parking, tv lounge, hosts have pets, pets not accepted, dinner available, babies welcome, free cot, 100% no smoking, closed: 11/08–23/08, hiking, cycling, riversports 2km
Fluent English spoken

Directions: In Cambrai, head towards the town centre and the 'Hôtel de Ville'. Take the Rue du Général de Gaulle on the right, which runs alongside the town hall (*Hôtel de Ville*), and then the second on the right, Rue St Jacques.

59.11 Cambrai

Private Home

Dominique BEGAR-ROGEE
'Ferme de l'Ostrevent', 26 rue du Mont,
59151 ESTREES
Tel: (0) 3 27 90 65 24 / (0) 675 62 05 26
Fax: (0) 3 27 96 96 34
ferme-ostrevent@wanadoo.fr
http://ferme.ostrevent.free.fr

Price Structure – 4 Bedrooms
'Sensée' & 'Madras': bathroom, wc, double bed: €55
'Ostrevent' & 'De Staël': shower room, wc, double bed: €55

Extra Bed: €20
Reduction: 2 nights, groups
Capacity: 8 people

Location
23km N W of CAMBRAI
in: Estrées, station pick-up on arrival/departure
Railway station: 10km
Airport: Lille-Lesquin 40km
car essential

This former farm from the late 19th century once served as a butchers. Dominique has completely restored it whilst maintaining its charm but with a certain originality! She loves nature and cares about the environment. If this is your passion too, she has reading material to recommend. Naturally, breakfast is organic. Trust her to advise you on the best walks and routes to take. The farm's emblem is at the bottom of the garden: her donkey!

Facilities: garden, tv lounge, hosts have pets, babies welcome, free cot, 100% no smoking, mushroom-picking, hiking, cycling, interesting flora, fishing 5km, bird-watching 5km, riversports 10km
Adequate English spoken

Directions: From Cambrai head in the direction of Douai. At Bugnicourt, turn left towards Arleux then follow signs for Estrées.

Location
3km N W of LILLE
in: Lambersart, station pick-up on
arrival/departure
Railway station: 4km
Airport: Lille-Lesquin 10km
car essential

Château/Manor House

As we go to press this home has not yet been classified, but will be shortly. Only 3.5km from the centre of Lille, this beautiful 19th-century residence, full of character, is set in 2 hectares of grounds. The building has retained the authentic design of this part of France and inside Isabelle and Jacques have installed all modern comforts in their five bedrooms. The lounge is an inviting place to relax, much appreciated after a day visiting the beautiful city of Lille.

Isabelle & Jacques MARTIN
**'Le Château des Ormes', 1 allée des Ormes,
59130 LAMBERSART**
Tel: (0) 3 20 09 61 99 / (0) 660 69 61 99
Fax: (0) 3 20 42 26 25
bienvenue@lechateaudesormes.com
www.lechateaudesormes.com

Facilities: private parking, extensive grounds, tv lounge, hosts have pets, pets not accepted, internet access, babies welcome, free cot, 100% no smoking
Adequate English spoken

Price Structure – 5 Bedrooms
'Catalane' & 'Orientale': television, telephone, bathroom, wc, shower, double bed (queen-size): €90
'Dagobert': television, telephone, bathroom, wc, shower, double bed (king-size): €130
'Boticelli': television, telephone, bathroom, wc, shower, double bed (king-size): €120
'Arômes': television, telephone, bathroom, wc, shower, double bed (king-size): €80

Directions: Please contact your hosts for detailed directions.

Extra Bed: €20
Reduction: 1/01–28/02, groups
Capacity: 10 people

Nord-Pas-de-Calais – Lille

Location
15km S W of LILLE
in: Wavrin
Railway station: 11km
Airport: Lille-Lesquin 17km
car essential

Bienvenue en France

✻ ✻

Private Home

Her sociable personality and an appreciation of cultural exchanges incited Marie-Paule (who once lived in Italy) to open the doors to one of her out-buildings. She offers a ground floor bedroom, basic but with its own entrance and a small kitchen area. It is a short hop across the garden to her dining room with a large brick fireplace where breakfast is served. Marie-Paule can advise on the floral gardens, mining history, museums and flea markets in the area. Lille train station is close by, so it's easy to reach by train.

Marie-Paule PITAU
36 rue Sadi Carnot, 59136 WAVRIN
Tel: (0) 3 20 32 98 46 / (0) 609 20 25 20
Fax: (0) 3 20 32 98 46
mppitau@aol.com

Facilities: garden, pets not accepted, kitchen, babies welcome, free cot, 100% no smoking, interesting flora 4km, fishing 10km, golf course 20km, hiking 20km, cycling 30km, sea watersports 60km
Fluent English spoken

Price Structure – 1 Apartment
lounge, kitchen, shower room, wc, twin beds: €45

Reduction: 5 nights
Capacity: 2 people

Directions: From Lille take the A25 towards Dunkerque, exit 6 towards Béthune. N41 for 5km then take the exit for Wavrin and follow the arrows to 'Hôtel de Ville'. Rue Sadi Carnot is behind the town hall, on the left. At number 34, ring the bell at the back.

62.36 Arras

Residence of Outstanding Character

Isabelle & Franck SMAL
'La Corne d'Or', 1 place Guy Mollet, 62000 ARRAS
Tel: (0) 3 21 58 85 94 / (0) 609 40 72 49
famillesmal@wanadoo.fr
www.lamaisondhotes.com

Price Structure – 2 Bedrooms, 1 Suite and 2 Apartments
'Nature': lounge, television, kitchen, bathroom, wc, double bed, twin beds: €114 – 2 people
€158 – 4 people
'Loft': lounge, television, kitchen, shower room, wc, double bed, single bed: €104 – 2 people
€126 – 3 people
'Regina': lounge, television, bathroom, wc, twin beds. En-suite room, single bed: €151 – 3 people
'Baroque': television, shower room, wc, double bed: €89
plus 1 room

Reduction: 01/11–31/03, 3 nights, children
Capacity: 14 people

Location
ARRAS
in: Arras, station pick-up on arrival/departure
Railway station: 1km

In central Arras, this mansion house is architecturally 18th century even though parts of it date back to the 16th. Isabelle has preserved many of the original features during her renovations but being not quite finished at the time of our visit. We feel it will merit four 'suns' in time, as Isabelle has thought of everything. Opt for the romanticism of 'Anges' or 'Baroque', or 'Nature' with its spa bath. The vaulted cellar hides wartime graffiti and there are two sitting rooms to choose from, one with a piano. Artists exhibit here.

Facilities: private parking, garden, tv lounge, hosts have pets, dinner available, babies welcome, free cot, 100% no smoking, cycling, riversports 3km, golf course 5km, hiking 5km

Directions: Please contact your hosts in advance for detailed directions.

62.40 Arras

Private Home

Christophe DESAINTGHISLAIN
'Caribou', 105 rue Dégréaux,
62580 GIVENCHY-EN-GOHELLE
Tel: (0) 3 21 48 18 42 / (0) 615 84 60 31
Bdesaintghislain@aol.com
www.caribou-chambresdhotes.fr

Price Structure – 3 Bedrooms
first room: television, shower room, wc, twin beds: €65
second & third rooms: television, shower room, wc, double bed: €65

Extra Bed: €10
Capacity: 6 people

Location
12km N of ARRAS
in: Givenchy-en-Gohelle, station pick-up on arrival/departure
Railway station: 10km
Airport: Lille-Lesquin 25km
car essential

As we go to press this home has not yet been classified, but will be shortly. This old farmhouse is called 'Caribou' and they have a rabbit called 'Panpan'. This happy family like naming things, from the animals to the kids. The bedrooms are in the barn and you have the use of a large living room with a lounge corner. The atmosphere is very easy-going as is the décor, so expect a relaxing stay. If you are a football fan, the local team is Lens.

Facilities: private parking, garden, tv lounge, hosts have pets, pets not accepted, internet access, dinner available, babies welcome, free cot, 100% no smoking
Adequate English spoken

Directions: From the A26, exit 7 Arras, Lens. Then take the N17 towards Lens. Near Vimy take the third exit at the roundabout (D51 for Givenchy) and take the Rue Dégréaux on the right.

✻ ✻ ✻

Private Home

Nord-Pas-de-Calais – Arras, Béthune

Location
25km N W of ARRAS
in: Magnicourt-en-Comté, station
pick-up on arrival/departure
Railway station: 25km
Airport: Lille-Lesquin 70km
car essential

All roads from Calais, Holland and Belgium lead to the conveniently situated 'Maison de Campagne', which is located in the heart of a quiet little village. This large house in red brick is surrounded by a pleasant little garden which is impeccably tidy and has an attractive lounge with a large bay window. Jacqueline is a retired librarian and if you stay a few days she will be delighted to accompany you on trips to explore this region.

Facilities: private parking, garden, tv lounge, pets not accepted, dinner available, babies welcome, free cot, 100% no smoking, wheelchair access, 1 shared bathroom, 1 shared shower room, 2 wcs, hiking, cycling, gliding, golf course 7km, riversports 20km
Adequate English spoken

Directions: A26 Exit 5. D916 towards St-Pol. In Cauchy, at the tower, D341 on the left to Houdain. At the 'Stop' sign, D86 on the right. The house is reached via a private lane at number 6 Rue de l'Europe (the main road of the school and *la mairie*).

Jacqueline & Pierre GUILLEMANT
'La Maison de Campagne', 6 rue de l'Europe,
62127 MAGNICOURT-EN-COMTE
Tel: (0) 3 21 41 51 00 / (0) 676 65 04 07
Fax: (0) 3 21 41 51 00
jguillemant@gmail.com
www.lamaisondecampagne.com

Price Structure – 2 Bedrooms and 1 Suite
'Côte d'Opale': wheelchair access, television, shower room, wc, double bed: €44
'Côte d'Emeraude': lounge, television, bathroom, wc, double bed, cot. En-suite room, 3 single beds: €44 – 2 people €80 – 5 people
'Côte de Grenat': lounge, television, shower room, wc, double bed: €44

Extra Bed: €12
Reduction: 2 nights
Capacity: 9 people

✻ ✻ ✻

Private Home

Location
25km W of BETHUNE
in: Auchy-au-Bois, station pick-up
on arrival/departure

Here you are only 45 minutes from Calais. This restored farmhouse is full of flowers, which are Gina's great passion. She and her children guarantee you a kind, smiling welcome, and you will enjoy her traditional French cuisine. The British and Canadian military cemetery at Vimy is 20km away.

Facilities: extensive grounds, tv lounge, hosts have pets, dinner available, kitchen, babies welcome, free cot
Adequate English spoken

Directions: From the A26, take exit 4 (Thérouanne). At Thérouanne take the D341 towards Arras. 1km after Rely, turn right towards Auchy. Then take the first on the left (Rue des Pernes) and continue for 1km.

Gina BULOT
'Les Cohettes', 28 rue de Pernes,
62190 AUCHY-AU-BOIS
Tel: (0) 3 21 02 09 47 / (0) 607 06 65 42
Fax: (0) 3 21 02 81 68
temps-libre-evasion@wanadoo.fr
www.chambresdhotes-chezgina.com

Price Structure – 5 Bedrooms
and 1 Apartment
'Rose' & 'Verte': shower room, wc, double bed: €50
'Bleue': shower room, wc, double bed, 2 single beds: €50 – 2 people €76 – 4 people
'Jonquille': bathroom, wc, double bed: €50
'Lilas': bathroom, wc, double bed, 2 single beds: €50 – 2 people €76 – 4 people
'Châlet': kitchen, bathroom, wc, double bed, single bed: €50 – 2 people €62 – 3 people

Capacity: 17 people

62.26 Boulogne-sur-Mer

Private Home

Location
15km S E of BOULOGNE-SUR-MER
in: Samer
Railway station: 15km
Airport: Le Touquet 25km
car essential

Liliane and Bernard's house is located between Boulogne and Le Touquet, and they will welcome you like old friends, with great warmth. This detached house has an uninterrupted view over the countryside, and in each room there is a collection of French porcelain. It's only 10km from the beach.

Liliane & Bernard POCHET
150 chemin du Tournier, 62830 SAMER
Tel: (0) 3 21 33 52 46

Price Structure – 4 Bedrooms
1 room: along corridor bathroom, double bed: €42
'Rose': along corridor shower, double bed. Along corridor room, single bed: €42 – 1 person
€84 – 3 people
1 room: double bed: €30

Extra Bed: €12
Reduction: 5 nights
Capacity: 7 people

Facilities: off-street parking, garden, lounge, hosts have pets, 1 shared shower room, wc, 10 years old minimum age, hiking, fishing 2km, cycling 12km, golf course 12km, interesting flora 12km, sea watersports 12km, bird-watching 60km
Basic English spoken

Directions: From Boulogne-sur-Mer, take the N1 as far as Samer. In the village, turn right towards 'Le Stade' (sports ground) and go down Chemin du Tournier on the left. Number 150 is on the right.

62.27 Calais

Residence of Outstanding Character

Location
15km S E of CALAIS
in: Bois-en-Ardres
Ferry port: 19km
car essential

This *Maison de Maître*, dating from 1880, is about 15km from Calais and located in spacious grounds with ancient trees, a great favourite with many birds. Bernadette's enthusiasm is infectious, as she makes every effort to welcome you and to point you towards the main attractions of the coast (Cap Gris Nez) or the walks round the nearby lake. The 'Jaune' room is beautiful, with its own walk-in shower corner. You can even get British TV to make you feel at home!

Bernadette BALLOY
'Les Fuchsias', 292 rue du Général de St Just,
62610 BOIS-EN-ARDRES
Tel: (0) 3 21 82 05 25 Fax: (0) 3 21 82 05 25
lesfuchsias@aol.com
lesfuchsias-ardres.fr.fm

Price Structure – 2 Bedrooms and 1 Suite
'Bleue': shower, double bed, single bed:
€50 – 2 people €67 – 3 people
'Jaune': shower, washbasin, twin beds: €50
'Rose': shower room, wc, double bed. En-suite room, double bed: €46 – 2 people €92 – 4 people

Extra Bed: €17
Reduction: 3 nights
Capacity: 9 people

Facilities: private parking, extensive grounds, tv lounge, hosts have pets, babies welcome, free cot, 2 shared bathrooms, wc, 1 shared shower room, hiking, fishing, interesting flora, bird-watching, sea watersports, mushroom-picking 10km, golf course 15km
Fluent English spoken

Directions: From Calais take the N43 toward Ardres as far as Bois-en-Ardres, then take the second road on the left after the roundabout (turn at the shop 'Wine Collection'). The house is in this street on the right, near to the church.

Location
28km E of CALAIS
in: Bourbourg
Railway station: 25km
car essential

***

Private Home

Régine and Patrick will give you a warm welcome in their home, midway between Calais and Dunkerque in the centre of Bourbourg, a small town with a population of 7,000. There is a charming little wooded garden full of flowers, filled with birdsong from the aviary. Both bedrooms are spacious and quiet, decorated and furnished in different styles. The garden room with its flowery fabrics has a British feel to it, and the room on the street side, mainly in blue, has a flavour of the sea. Régine's speciality is regional cooking, so be sure to book for dinner.

Régine BEHAGUE
'Villa Blanc Marine', 25 rue des Martyrs de la Résistance, 59630 BOURBOURG
Tel: (0) 3 28 62 50 57 / (0) 685 21 06 15
villablancmarine@yahoo.fr
www.villablancmarine.com

Facilities: extensive grounds, tv lounge, pets not accepted, internet access, dinner available, babies welcome, free cot, 100% no smoking, cycling, hiking 2km, fishing 10km, lake watersports 10km, bird-watching 15km, golf course 30km
Basic English spoken

Price Structure – 2 Bedrooms
'Flandre' & 'Côte d'Opale': television, shower room, wc, double bed: €50

Extra Bed: €15
Capacity: 4 people

Directions: Take the A16 from Calais, then exit 23 and continue on the D11. In Bourbourg, follow signs to the *mairie*. The house is 50m down the street to the left of the *mairie* (town hall).

Location
27km S E of CALAIS
in: Audrehem
Railway station: 15km
Airport: 25km
car essential

***

Private Home

Your hosts are experts on the history of the Channel Tunnel and this friendly couple love to make friends. There are hiking (GR128) and mountain bike trails nearby. A washing machine and a tumble-drier are available for serious walkers. Here, you will find peace and quiet in the heart of the country. On sale: honey, foie gras, poultry, bread.

Thérèse de LAMARLIÈRE
693 rue du Parc, 62890 AUDREHEM
Tel: (0) 3 21 35 06 30

Facilities: private parking, garden, lounge, pets not accepted, dinner available, kitchen, babies welcome, free cot, 100% no smoking, wc, fishing, hiking 1km, cycling 1km, golf course 17km, bird-watching 20km, sea watersports 20km
Basic English spoken

Price Structure – 3 Bedrooms
first room: shower room, wc, double bed: €40
second & third rooms: shower, washbasin, double bed: €38

Extra Bed: €30
Capacity: 6 people

Directions: From the A26, exit 2 towards Licques. Then take the D217 towards Tournehem, as far as Clerques. Follow the signs 'Bed & Breakfast France'.

62.29 Calais

Private Home

Location
27km S E of CALAIS
in: Clerques, station pick-up on arrival/departure
Railway station: 26km
Airport: Calais 26km
car essential

Christiane loves to welcome guests. Her house is well placed if you are travelling via Calais, located as it is at the bottom of the Vallée de l'Hem. It is brand new and very spacious and thanks to numerous large windows has a magnificent view over the countryside, which is a mosaic of fields, woods and gently rolling hills. The inside is sparkling white, decorated by superb *biscuits* (unglazed white porcelain figurines) and a beautiful collection of Desvres. They do deserve three 'suns', despite there only being one bathroom.

Christiane DEVINES
27 route de Guémy, Le Hamel, 62890 CLERQUES
Tel: (0) 3 21 82 40 65 Fax: (0) 3 21 82 40 65
chrisdevines@aol.com
http://maisonhotes.free.fr

Price Structure – 3 Bedrooms
1 room: telephone, along corridor shower room, wc, twin beds: €39
1 room: along corridor shower room, wc, double bed. Along corridor room, double bed:
€39 – 2 people €78 – 4 people

Extra Bed: €15
Reduction: 01/12–30/03, 4 nights, groups
Capacity: 6 people

Facilities: private parking, extensive grounds, tv lounge, pets not accepted, kitchen, babies welcome, free cot, hiking, cycling, fishing, mushroom-picking 3km, sea watersports 10km, golf course 18km, bird-watching 25km
Adequate English spoken

Directions: On the A26 Calais-Paris, take exit 2 towards Licques and the D217 towards Clerques (8km). When you are facing the church, take the small road on the right towards La Chapelle St Louis for 500m. The house is on the left.

62.38 Calais

Residence of Outstanding Character

Location
15km S W of CALAIS
in: Escalles, station pick-up on arrival/departure
Railway station: 6km
car essential

In the 'Deux Caps' area, at the foot of the Cap Blanc-Nez, just five minutes from the Channel Tunnel, you will find Jacqueline's place. A great place to stay with a warm and attentive welcome, with its ancient beams, antique furniture and a pigeon loft dating from the 18th century. These farm buildings are typical of this area, quiet and in coastal countryside. The spacious bedrooms with their flowery bedspreads give a British touch. Take breakfast in the conservatory and admire the garden while breakfasting on home-made jam and fresh eggs.

Jacqueline & Marc BOUTROY
'La Grand' Maison', place Haute Escalles, 62179 ESCALLES
Tel: (0) 3 21 85 27 75 Fax: (0) 3 21 85 27 75
lagrandmaison@infonie.fr
http://lagrandmaison.chez-alice.fr

Price Structure – 4 Bedrooms
and 2 Apartments
2 rooms: shower room, wc, double bed, single bed, cot: €50 – 2 people €65 – 3 people
'Studio 1': kitchen, shower room, wc, double bed: €60
television, bathroom, wc, double bed, single bed:
€60 – 2 people €80 – 3 people
'Studio 2': television, kitchen, bathroom, wc, double bed: €60
television, bathroom, wc, 2 double beds, cot:
€60 – 2 people €95 – 4 people

Reduction: 3 nights
Capacity: 17 people

Facilities: private parking, garden, hosts have pets, pets not accepted, kitchen, babies welcome, free cot, 100% no smoking, hiking, cycling, interesting flora, bird-watching 1km, sea watersports 7km, golf course 25km
Fluent English spoken

Directions: Exit 39 or 40 from the A16 towards Cap Blanc-Nez and Peuplingues. Go through Peuplingues following signs to Escalles. Exit the village and continue for 2km then turn left after the first house. Signposted.

59.05 Calais

Château/Manor House

Location
35km E of CALAIS
in: St-Pierre-Brouck
Ferry port: Calais
Airport: Lille-Lesquin 80km
car essential

We have known Nathalie for many years. She is very welcoming and loves her home, which has plenty of charm and a large garden, 2 hectares in size. You are sure to appreciate the refined décor, the modern furnishings and the quality of service offered by Nathalie and her husband. The family lounge with a large veranda and a piano is wide open to you. The bedrooms are impeccable, with embroidered towels, quality bed linen, four-poster beds, porcelain china, silver cutlery and fresh cut flowers. A great address and excellent value.

Nathalie DUVIVIER
'Le Château', 287 route de la Bistade,
59630 ST-PIERRE-BROUCK
Tel: (0) 3 28 27 50 05 Fax: (0) 3 28 27 50 05
contact@lechateau.net
www.lechateau.net

Facilities: private parking, extensive grounds, lounge, hosts have pets, pets not accepted, dinner available, 100% no smoking, 5 years old minimum age, golf course 10km
Basic English spoken

Price Structure – 4 Bedrooms and 1 Suite
'Jonquille': shower room, wc, double bed. En-suite room, single bed: €90 – 2 people €100 – 3 people
'Myosotis': television, bathroom, wc, four-poster double bed (queen-size): €80
'Rose': television, shower room, wc, double bed (king-size): €80
'Tournesol': television, shower room, wc, double bed (king-size): €77
'Primevère': shower room, wc, double bed (king-size): €80

Extra Bed: €20
Capacity: 11 people

Directions: Please contact your host in advance for detailed directions.

62.39 Calais

Location
25km S E of CALAIS
in: Tournehem-sur-la-Hem, station pick-up on arrival/departure
Railway station: 10km
car essential

Private Home

Denise and Henri are charming and will do all they can to make you feel at home. Pick their brains on what to see in this area. The rooms are simply decorated, with comfortable beds, one of which is electrically adjustable by a remote control. The house is at your disposal, including the piano in the lounge if you fancy a sing-song. They also know a friend who has a wine cellar and Henri will just love to take you over for a tasting. The nearby Forest of Tournehem is great for long walks or cycle rides.

Denise & Henri LYSENSOONE
30 rue de Valenciennes,
62890 TOURNEHEM-SUR-LA-HEM
Tel: (0) 3 21 35 60 56 Fax: (0) 3 21 36 86 50
henri.lysensoone@orange.fr

Facilities: garden, tv lounge, hosts have pets, dinner available, hiking, cycling, vineyard 5km, sea water-sports 20km
Adequate English spoken

Price Structure – 1 Bedroom and 1 Suite
television, along corridor shower room, wc, double bed, single bed (child-size). En-suite room, wc, washbasin, double bed: €40 – 2 people
€70 – 5 people
television, shower room, wc, double bed: €40

Extra Bed: €8
Capacity: 7 people

Directions: Exit 2 from the A26 towards Tournehem-sur-la-Hem and Licques. In Tournehem follow signs to Licques. At the bank 'Crédit Agricole', turn left then right. The house is just on the corner, opposite the café 'La Taverne de Sarrasine'.

Nord-Pas-de-Calais – Calais

62.24 Calais

Residence of Outstanding Character

Sonia BENOIT
'La Bohème', 1947 rue de la Grasse Payelle,
62370 ZUTKERQUE
Tel: (0) 3 21 35 70 25 / (0) 616 18 71 22
sonia-benoit-la-boheme@wanadoo.fr
http://perso.wanadoo.fr/sonia.la.boheme/

Price Structure – 3 Bedrooms
'Eglantine' (our favourite room): bathroom, wc, shower, double bed: €53
'Primevère': wheelchair access, shower room, wc, double bed, single bed: €55 – 2 people
€70 – 3 people
'Camélia indépendante': lounge, bathroom, wc, double bed, 2 single beds: €58 – 2 people
€80 – 4 people

Extra Bed: €20
Capacity: 9 people

Location
15km S E of CALAIS
in: Zutkerque
Railway station: 25km
Airport: 100km
car essential

Bienvenue en France

Sonia is bubbling over with enthusiasm to do everything to ensure an unforgettable stay here. The house is full of character in the style typical of northern France. Her attention to detail is quite amazing. Her skills as a decorator are only surpassed by her skill as a cook, in which she has been professionally trained. Her other love is horses and she stables several on the premises. This delightful village is only a short drive from Calais or the Eurostar station at Frethun (25km).

Facilities: private parking, extensive grounds, tv lounge, hosts have pets, dinner available, wheelchair access, riding, hiking, cycling, fishing 2km, sea watersports 6km, golf course 7km, interesting flora 10km, mushroom-picking 10km, bird-watching 20km, riversports 50km
Adequate English spoken

Directions: From the A26 take exit 2. Cross the N43 and turn left onto the D226 direction Zutkerque, Château de Cocove. Go past the château and then, on the bend, it is the fourth house on the right.

62.06 Hesdin

Château/Manor House

Christiane & René AUGUSTIN
'Château de Drucas', Beauvoir-Wavans,
62390 AUXI-LE-CHATEAU
Tel: (0) 3 21 04 01 11
www.cheznous.com

Price Structure – 2 Bedrooms
and 1 Apartment
first room: double bed, single bed (child-size): €50
second room: double bed: €50
apartment: kitchen, bathroom, wc, double bed. En-suite room, double bed. En-suite room, single bed: €60 – 2 people €90 – 5 people

Capacity: 10 people

Location
22km S of HESDIN
in: Beauvoir-Wavans
Airport: Paris-Roissy 150km
car essential

Bienvenue en France

This small château is about 200 years old. It is reached via an avenue of lime trees, leading to magnificent grounds, through which a river flows. Madame's welcome is charming. The décor is simple, unpretentious rococo style.

Facilities: private parking, extensive grounds, lounge, hosts have pets, 1 shared bathroom, wc, hiking, cycling, mushroom-picking, interesting flora 2km, sea watersports 2km, bird-watching 25km, golf course 25km
Adequate English spoken

Directions: In Abbeville, take the D925 towards St Riquier and the D941 towards Auxi-le-Château. In Auxi, turn right onto the D938.

Location
15km S E of LE TOUQUET-PARIS-PLAGE
in: Marles-sur-Canche
Railway station: 20km
car essential

Château/Manor House

This is a genuine 16th-century manor, built entirely of chalk bricks. You enter through iron gates to a courtyard with a beautiful lawn and pond, where turkeys and peacocks do their thing. Ring the old bell at the front door and Dominique's welcome will guarantee you an unforgettable stay. Every room is decorated in the style of the period, in perfect taste, with great attention to detail and authenticity. It is a rare experience to stay in such a unique home.

Dominique LEROY
'Manoir Francis', 1 rue de l'Eglise,
62170 MARLES-SUR-CANCHE
Tel: (0) 3 21 81 38 80 Fax: (0) 3 21 81 38 80
manoir.francis@wanadoo.fr
manoirfrancis.com

Facilities: private parking, garden, hosts have pets, hiking, fishing 2km, cycling 4km, riversports 4km, golf course 20km, sea watersports 20km, gliding 20km
Fluent English spoken

Price Structure – 3 Bedrooms
'Rouge' & 'Bleue': lounge, bathroom, wc, shower, double bed: €65
'Family Suite': lounge, bathroom, wc, shower, double bed, 2 single beds: €65 – 2 people €105 – 4 people

Capacity: 8 people

Directions: At Montreuil-sur-Mer, head towards Neuville, D113 for 4km. When you see the sign for Marles-sur-Canche, pass a couple of buildings and then keep going until you reach the centre of the village. Look for the entrance with its large archway and metal gates, immediately after the phone box on the right.

62.20 Le Touquet-Paris-Plage

Location
13km E of LE TOUQUET-PARIS-PLAGE
in: Recques-sur-Course
Railway station: 5km
car essential

Private Home

Monique and Jean-Michel's front garden is full of flowers. Here you will be a part of the family and will admire Michel's dedication as he continues to improve the house for your comfort. This pretty *village fleuri* is convenient for Boulogne-sur-Mer, Le Touquet and Montreuil.

Monique MELCHIOR
'Les Yuccas', 49 rue de la Ballastière,
62170 RECQUES-SUR-COURSE
Tel: (0) 3 21 90 78 94 Fax: (0) 3 21 90 78 94
lesyuccas@hotmail.com

Facilities: off-street parking, garden, tv lounge, hosts have pets, pets not accepted, 100% no smoking, cycling 1km, hiking 5km, fishing 5km, riversports 5km, golf course 15km, sea watersports 15km, bird-watching 30km

Directions: From Montreuil on the N1 towards Boulogne, take the turning on the right after the factory, signposted Inxent and Estrelles La Vallée de la Course. Continue along this road until you reach Recques-sur-Course. No. 49 is the first white house in the village on the right.

Price Structure – 3 Bedrooms
shower room, wc, double bed: €50
shower room, wc, double bed, single bed:
€50 – 2 people €66 – 3 people
along corridor shower room, wc, double bed, single bed: €50 – 2 people €66 – 3 people

Extra Bed: €16
Capacity: 8 people

62.34 St-Omer

Residence of Outstanding Character

Marie-Christine & Dominique BOGAERT
'Chambres d'hôtes des Caps et Marais d'Opale',
11 quai du Commerce, 62500 ST-OMER
Tel: (0) 3 21 93 89 82 / (0) 630 26 83 03
mariec.bogaert@wanadoo.fr
www.bb-opale.fr

Price Structure – 2 Bedrooms and 1 Suite
'Fontinettes': television, along corridor shower room, wc, twin beds, single bed (child-size):
€55 – 2 people €74 – 3 people
'Mathurin': television, bathroom, wc, double bed, single bed: €55 – 2 people €74 – 3 people
'Romelaère': television, shower room, wc, double bed. En-suite room, twin beds, single bed (child-size): €94 – 2 people €126 – 5 people

Extra Bed: €17
Reduction: 7 nights
Capacity: 11 people

Location
ST-OMER
in: St-Omer, station pick-up on arrival/departure
Railway station: St-Omer
Airport: Lille-Lesquin 70km

Bienvenue en France

Close to the town centre, inside this brick 19th-century *Maison de Maître*, set by a river, is a delightful interior with parquet floors, rose windows, mouldings and collectables, including antique dolls. The vast dining room extends out to the veranda and quiet enclosed garden. Tailored breakfasts of homemade jams and cakes are served in the winter garden or by the marble fireplace. Comfortable bedrooms (with fridge and microwave) but with tired bathrooms. Very attentive, Marie-Christine knows all about St-Omer.

Facilities: private parking, garden, tv lounge, hosts have pets, babies welcome, free cot, 100% no smoking, hunting, fishing, mushroom-picking, bird-watching, hiking, cycling, interesting flora, riversports, golf course 15km
Fluent English spoken

Directions: From Calais, head to St-Omer via the A26 or the N43 (48km). Head for 'Centre Ville, la Gare'. The house is 300m from the station.

62.41 St-Omer

Residence of Outstanding Character

Marie & Maurice RONSIN
'Domaine des Araucarias', 35 boulevard de Paris,
62190 LILLERS
Tel: (0) 3 21 53 49 86 / (0) 608 85 52 02
Fax: (0) 3 21 53 49 86
mronsin@free.fr
www.ledomainedesaraucarias.com

Price Structure – 6 Bedrooms
'Aurore' & 'Hélène': television, shower room, wc, double bed: €50
'Coline': television, shower room, wc, double bed, single bed: €50 – 2 people €75 – 3 people
'Camélia': lounge, television, shower room, wc, washbasin, twin beds: €50
'Coquelicot': lounge, television, along corridor shower room, wc, washbasin, twin beds, single bed: €50 – 2 people €75 – 3 people
'Anémone': lounge, television, along corridor shower room, wc, double bed: €50
Extra Bed: €25 **Reduction:** groups
Capacity: 14 people

Location
25km S E of ST-OMER
in: Lillers
Railway station: St-Omer

As we go to press this host has not yet been classified, but will be shortly. This very beautiful 19th-century residence is very attractive, set in wooded grounds. The inside is cosy and Marie and Maurice have taken care of every detail. The work has been a labour of love so that their guests enjoy their stay fully, as a warm welcome is an *art de vivre* for them. Marie is chatty but you will never tire of her company, especially when you eat with these two retired restaurateurs. Have a great evening in good company.

Facilities: private parking, extensive grounds, tv lounge, hosts have pets, pets not accepted, dinner available, babies welcome, free cot, 100% no smoking
Basic English spoken

Directions: From the A26, exit 5 Lillers. Follow signs to Le Mensecq Centre-Ville.

Location
27km S E of SOISSONS
in: Fère-en-Tardenois, station pick-up on arrival/departure
Railway station: 4km
Airport: Paris-Orly 110km

Private Home

Nicolas and Stefan are two young thirtysomethings with hospitality training to their credit, which they have drawn on and put into practice here to welcome guests and create for you a relaxing and enjoyable place to stay. The house is full of plants and the location is calm and green with grounds full of trees. Enjoy the outdoor activities on offer which include cycling and *pétanque* (also known as *boules*). The guest bedrooms are in neutral colours and tastefully decorated.

Nicolas PERRAUD
'Au Fou du Roy', 45 route du Château,
02130 FERE-EN-TARDENOIS
Tel: (0) 3 23 82 64 54 Fax: (0) 3 23 82 64 54
info@aufouduroy.com
www.aufouduroy.com

Facilities: off-street parking, extensive grounds, tv lounge, hosts have pets, dinner available, babies welcome, free cot, 100% no smoking, wc, private swimming pool, hunting, fishing, mushroom-picking, bird-watching, hiking, cycling, interesting flora, lake watersports
Fluent English spoken

Price Structure – 5 Bedrooms
'Luxe' 3 rooms: bathroom, wc, double bed: €68
'Confort 1': shower, double bed: €55
'Confort 2': shower, double bed, single bed: €55 – 2 people €75 – 3 people

Extra Bed: €20
Capacity: 11 people

Directions: Motorway A4 Paris-Metz, exit 20 or 21 direction Fère-en-Tardenois. At the centre of the village take the D967 direction Fismes. The house is opposite the entrance to the château.

Location
11km S of BEAUVAIS
in: Abbecourt, station pick-up on arrival/departure
Railway station: 3km
car essential

Private Home

On the edge of Picardie and the Pays de Bray, this longhouse from 1816 is the family house of your hosts. They are very friendly; he is a designer and she is an ex-school teacher who have now taken to B&B. They love classical music and the violin, the piano and painting. It is in fact Keith who painted the pictures you see in the house. At your disposal is a pleasant reading room with bay windows that also serves as an independent entrance for you and it is through this room that you access the bathroom.

Catherine & Keith INGRAM
'Le Courtil', 15 rue du Courtil, 60430 ABBECOURT
Tel: (0) 3 44 89 28 53 / (0) 661 43 62 87
bandb.courtil@free.fr

Facilities: private parking, garden, lounge, pets not accepted, babies welcome, free cot, 100% no smoking, closed: 1/08–31/08
Fluent English spoken

Price Structure – 1 Bedroom
lounge, along corridor bathroom, wc, double bed: €55

Extra Bed: €25
Reduction: 3 nights, children
Capacity: 2 people

Directions: Please contact your hosts in advance for detailed directions.

Picardie – Soissons, Beauvais

60.12 Beauvais

Private Home

Location
30km S of BEAUVAIS
in: Fay-les-Etangs, station pick-up on arrival/departure
Railway station: 5km
Airport: Paris-Roissy 58km
car essential

Over 300 years old, this typical longhouse is in a tranquil village in picturesque Vexin. The bedrooms, in a wing of the house, have independent entrances. Exposed beams, stone walls and regional furniture add to its authenticity. A microwave and a fridge are modern extras. Your hosts love music and food, serving homemade *viennoiseries* and mouth-watering dishes like *poulet façon canard bourbon, sauce de kirsch et champagne*. There is a lovely garden, secure parking and a large orchard. Don't miss Monet's house at Giverny.

Facilities: private parking, garden, lounge, dinner available, mushroom-picking, hiking, cycling, fishing 3km, golf course 5km
Fluent English spoken

Chantal & Philippe VERMEIRE
'Chambres d'Hôtes du Clos', 3 rue du Chêne Noir,
60240 FAY-LES-ETANGS
Tel: (0) 3 44 49 92 38 / (0) 687 01 85 61
Fax: (0) 3 44 49 92 38
philippe.vermeire@wanadoo.fr
http://www.leclosdefay.com

Price Structure – 4 Bedrooms
room 1: lounge, television, shower room, wc, double bed, single bed: €56 – 2 people €68 – 3 people
room 2: television, shower room, wc, double bed: €56
room 3: lounge, television, shower room, wc, double bed, single bed: €56 – 2 people €68 – 3 people
room 4: television, shower room, wc, single bed: €40 – 1 person

Extra Bed: €18
Reduction: 5 nights
Capacity: 9 people

Directions: From Paris A15 towards Pontoise exit 10 direction Gisors D915 until Marines, then turn right D28 and D3 to Fleury (12km), then turn left D105 to Fay-les-Etangs. In the village head for the château. The Rue du Chêne Noir is off this road, on your left at the double bend.

60.13 Beauvais

Private Home

Location
33km S of BEAUVAIS
in: Liancourt-St-Pierre
Railway station: 2km
Airport: Paris-Roissy 60km
car essential

A place for lovers of modern architecture! This 18th-century house on a hillside in a traditional village has been extended by the talents of the architect A. Perret (1930). You'll love the huge space in the living and dining room with a long wooden table and a library. The bedrooms have reclining twin beds and the spacious 'Perret' suite has wood panelling and a terrace with a great view. The décor hints at your hosts' passion for horses. They can suggest routes across this beautiful region close to Giverny. Good value.

Facilities: private parking, garden, lounge, hosts have pets, dinner available, babies welcome, free cot, 100% no smoking, riding, fishing, hiking, cycling, golf course 4km
Fluent English spoken

Fiona & Luc GALLOT
'La Pointe', 10 rue du Donjon,
60240 LIANCOURT-ST-PIERRE
Tel: (0) 3 44 49 32 08 / (0) 680 14 67 56
Fax: (0) 3 44 49 32 08
lucgallot@wanadoo.fr
www.la-pointe.com

Price Structure – 3 Bedrooms
'Perret': bathroom, wc, twin beds, 2 single beds: €55 – 2 people €75 – 4 people
'Colette': shower room, wc, twin beds: €55
'Rose': shower room, wc, twin beds, single bed: €55 – 2 people €65 – 3 people

Extra Bed: €10
Capacity: 9 people

Directions: From the Paris A15 motorway towards Pontoise take exit 10, D915 direction Gisors to Marines then the D28 on the right. D3 to Fleury (12km) and left at Loconville to Liancourt-St-Pierre. In the centre of the village (by the 'Mairie, Ecole') turn down the cul-de-sac and continue to the end.

Picardie – Beauvais

Location
15km N of COMPIEGNE
in: Cambronne-lès-Ribécourt,
station pick-up on arrival/departure
Railway station: 2km
Airport: Paris-Roissy 50km
car essential

Residence of Outstanding Character

This old farmhouse near the autoroute A1 has been restored with great charm. It is on the edge of the forest and the rooms have a delightful view over the canal. Pauline is an excellent chef so be sure to book for dinner. She offers you the unique opportunity to discover the waterways of Picardie, has riverboats for hire by the day and also offers a 'B&B & Boat' package or a fitness programme using the sauna and gym.

Facilities: off-street parking, garden, tv lounge, hosts have pets, dinner available, 10 years old minimum age, hiking, cycling, fishing, hunting, interesting flora, mushroom-picking, golf course 5km, lake watersports 5km, riversports 5km
Fluent English spoken

Pauline BRUNGER
'Ferme-Hôtel de Bellerive', 492 rue de Bellerive,
60170 CAMBRONNE-LES-RIBECOURT
Tel: (0) 3 44 75 02 13 Fax: (0) 3 44 76 10 34
bellerive@bellerive.fr
www.bellerive.fr

Price Structure – 5 Bedrooms
2 rooms: shower room, wc, double bed: €55
shower room, wc, twin beds: €55
bathroom, wc, shower, twin beds: €55
bathroom, wc, shower, double bed: €55

Extra Bed: €20
Reduction: 4 nights
Capacity: 10 people

Directions: In Compiègne, take the N32 towards Noyon. In Ribécourt, turn right onto the D66. (From Calais: A1, exit 12 Roye, then follow directions for Noyon. Then take the N32 towards Compiègne. After Ribécourt turn left onto the D66.) Cross the canal, and the house is immediately on the right after the bridge.

Picardie – Compiègne

Location
6km S of COMPIEGNE
in: Jaux
Railway station: 7km
Airport: Paris-Roissy 70km
car essential

Private Home

The two guest rooms, full of character and with their own fireplaces, are in the old house. Your charming hostess, Françoise, a retired chemist, lives in the converted barn next door. Enjoy breakfast outside in the lovely, peaceful garden. Françoise will make you feel very welcome, as will her dogs.

Facilities: private parking, garden, hosts have pets, dinner available, babies welcome, free cot, wc, hiking 6km, cycling 6km, golf course 6km, mushroom-picking 6km, lake watersports 6km

Françoise GAXOTTE
'La Gaxottière', 363 rue du Champ du Mont,
Hameau de Varanval, 60880 JAUX
Tel: (0) 3 44 83 22 41 / (0) 687 77 28 05
Fax: (0) 3 44 83 22 41
lagaxottiere@tele2.fr

Price Structure – 3 Bedrooms
television, bathroom, wc, double bed: €60
television, shower, wc, twin beds: €60
television, shower room, wc, single bed: €40

Capacity: 5 people

Directions: Exit 10 on the A1 signposted to Compiègne (4km). Follow signs to Jaux (1.2km from the N31 turning). In Varanval, 'La Gaxottière' is on the right opposite an impressive metal gate.

80.16 Abbeville

Working Farm

Bienvenue
en
France

Location
6km N E of ABBEVILLE
in: Caours
Railway station: 6km
car essential

On this working farm, the bedrooms are in a separate building opposite the main house. They open directly on to the garden with the river at the bottom. It is a good place to relax or let off steam, with activities available such as a trampoline for the kids and the heated, covered pool. Hélène and Marc will give you a great welcome and be delighted to tell you more about the Bay of the Somme, so rich in wildlife. They will also let you use their beach hut at Le Crotoy in the summer.

Hélène & Marc de LAMARLIERE
2 rue de la Ferme, 80132 CAOURS
Tel: (0) 3 22 24 77 49 Fax: (0) 3 22 24 76 97
helene-marc@voila.fr
www.de-lamarlierem.com

Price Structure – 5 Bedrooms
and 1 Apartment
2 rooms: shower room, wc, double bed: €59
bathroom, wc, double bed: €59
shower room, wc, double bed, 2 single beds (child-size): €59 – 2 people €100 – 4 people
'Studio': kitchen, double bed (queen-size), single bed: €69 – 2 people €89 – 3 people
shower room, wc, 4 single beds: €100 – 4 people

Extra Bed: €20
Reduction: 3 nights
Capacity: 17 people

Facilities: private parking, garden, tv lounge, internet access, babies welcome, free cot, private swimming pool, cycling, bird-watching, gliding 4km, golf course 12km
Fluent English spoken

Directions: From the A16, exit 22. Continue on the D925 then turn left towards Caours. In the village follow signs to 'La Rivièrette'.

80.14 Abbeville

Residence of Outstanding Character

Location
22km N W of ABBEVILLE
in: Le Crotoy, station pick-up on arrival/departure
Railway station: 7km

A large blue and white *maison bourgeoise* in the centre of Le Crotoy, near to the beaches, the port and the beautiful Baie de Somme. Inside is a lovely courtyard with teak furniture, a marine-themed lounge, a relaxation room with a flat-screen TV and a cosy veranda full of plants and tropical flowers. The décor is inspired by the area and trips abroad: marine colours, solid wood from Brazil, a Persian carpet, a Slavic trunk. 'Verte' and 'Bois' have sloping ceilings. Rosana is Brazilian and her welcome is warm and attentive.

Rosana de PAULA-CESSAC
'La Maison Bleue en Baie', 12 rue de la Croix,
80550 LE CROTOY
Tel: (0) 3 22 27 73 86 Fax: (0) 3 22 27 73 86
la.maison.bleue@baie-de-somme.fr
www.baie-de-somme.fr

Price Structure – 3 Bedrooms
'Bleue': shower room, wc, double bed: €96
'Verte': lounge, shower room, wc, double bed, single bed (child-size): €85 – 2 people €100 – 3 people
'Bois': along corridor shower room, wc, double bed: €70

Extra Bed: €15
Reduction: 1/11–29/03
Capacity: 7 people

Facilities: tv lounge, hosts have pets, pets not accepted, 100% no smoking, bird-watching, hiking, cycling, sea watersports, fishing 1km, hunting 3km, interesting flora 3km, golf course 20km
Fluent English spoken

Directions: From Abbeville, A16 exit 23 (or exit 24 from Calais) to Le Crotoy. The house is situated in a perpendicular road to the main road Rue du Crotoy. Follow arrow signs to 'La Maison Bleue en Baie'.

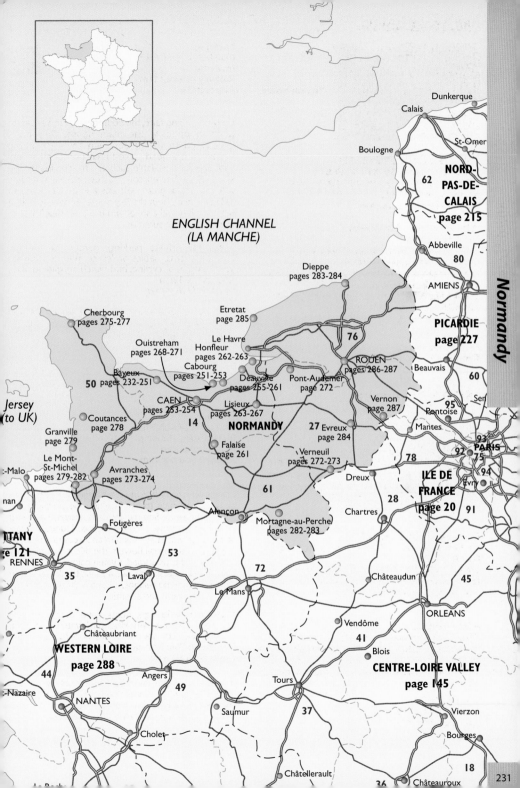

Dunkerque

Calais

Boulogne

St-Omer

NORD-
PAS-DE-
CALAIS
page 215

62

Abbeville

80

AMIENS

ENGLISH CHANNEL
(LA MANCHE)

Dieppe
pages 283–284

PICARDIE
page 227

76

Cherbourg
pages 275–277

Etretat
page 285

Beauvais

60

Ouistreham
pages 268–271

Le Havre
Honfleur
pages 262–263

ROUEN
pages 286–287

95

Sen

Bayeux
pages 232–251

50

Cabourg
pages 251–253

Deauville
pages 255–261

Pont-Audemer
page 272

Vernon
page 287

Pontoise

Jersey
(to UK)

Coutances
page 278

CAEN
pages 253–254

Lisieux
pages 263–267

Mantes

93

PARIS

92

75

14

NORMANDY

27 Evreux
page 284

94

Granville
page 279

Falaise
page 261

Verneuil
pages 272–273

78

Evry

Le Mont-
St-Michel
pages 279–282

Avranches
pages 273–274

Dreux

ILE DE
FRANCE
page 20

91

-Malo

61

28

Chartres

nan

Alençon

Mortagne-au-Perche
pages 282–283

TANY
e 121

RENNES

Fougères

53

72

Châteaudun

45

35

Laval

Le Mans

ORLEANS

Châteaubriant

Vendôme

WESTERN LOIRE
page 288

41

Blois

CENTRE-LOIRE VALLEY
page 145

44

Angers

49

Tours

Vierzon

-Nazaire

NANTES

Saumur

37

Bourges

Cholet

Châtellerault

18

231

Châteauroux

14.011 Bayeux

Private Home

Marie-Alice DUCHEMIN
'La Roseraie', 3 rue de Port en Bessin,
14400 BAYEUX
Tel: (0) 2 31 21 35 43 / (0) 682 83 14 29 / (0)
675 47 37 72

Price Structure – 4 Bedrooms
and 1 Apartment
television, shower, washbasin, double bed: €51
television, shower, washbasin, double bed: €47
television, bathroom, wc, washbasin, double bed:
€61
television, bathroom, wc, washbasin, double bed:
€57
'Pavillon dupleix': kitchen, bathroom, wc, 3 double
beds: €70 – 2 people €125 – 6 people

Extra Bed: €18
Reduction: 01/10–01/04
Capacity: 14 people

Location
BAYEUX
in: Bayeux
Railway station: 3km
Airport: Caen-Carpiquet 30km

The Normandy landings' museum, the Musée du Débarquement, is within easy reach of Marie-Alice's home. Everyone here has a house to themselves: the three B&B bedrooms are in one house, Marie-Alice lives in another and the third is a gîte. They are in a lovely garden with deckchairs at your disposal. The décor is fairly sober and the showers are in the bedrooms. Marie-Alice spends her days renovating a château that she has bought and hopes to open to her guests in the future!

Facilities: off-street parking, garden, hosts have pets, wc, interesting flora, golf course 8km, fishing 8km
Basic English spoken

Directions: Please contact your host in advance for detailed directions.

14.05 Bayeux

Private Home

Marie-Pierre & Pierre-Henri LEMESSIER
'Les Trois Pierre', 22 rue des Bouchers,
14400 BAYEUX
Tel: (0) 2 31 92 34 38 / (0) 616 44 68 09
Fax: (0) 2 31 92 34 38
mplemessier@wanadoo.fr
www.les3pierre.com

Price Structure – 3 Bedrooms and 1 Suite
'Champagne': shower room, wc, washbasin, double bed, single bed: €62 – 2 people €85 – 3 people
'Val de Loire': bathroom, wc, washbasin, double bed:
€60
'Bourgogne': shower, double bed: €56
'Alsace': bathroom, wc, double bed, 2 single beds.
En-suite room, single bed: €80 – 2 people
€120 – 5 people

Extra Bed: €12
Capacity: 12 people

Location
BAYEUX
in: Bayeux
Railway station: 1km
Airport: Caen-Carpiquet 20km

You can only be well received when staying with Pierre-Henri, who is not only a wine connoisseur but also a lover of blues and a bass guitarist. But there is not just one Pierre here, but a family of three: the father, the mother and the son are all called Pierre (unbelievably, even Marie is called Marie-Pierre!) so there are no excuses for forgetting their names. Here in their newly built house you can share with the family their passions for music, travel, literature, fine wines, and sport. Wonderful evenings with plenty to talk about!

Facilities: pets not accepted, babies welcome, free cot, 100% no smoking, wc, interesting flora, vineyard, cycling 2km, fishing 5km, golf course 7km, sea watersports 12km
Adequate English spoken

Directions: Please contact your hosts in advance for detailed directions.

Location
BAYEUX
in: Bayeux, station pick-up on arrival/departure
Railway station: Bayeux
Airport: Caen-Carpiquet 28km

Residence of Outstanding Character

In the centre of Bayeux in complete calm stands this charming 18th-century residence in white stone, with a terrace, a courtyard and a secure enclosed parking area. You will appreciate above all the delightful garden of trees, set out with different intimate spaces, as well as the independent maisonette which houses the guest bedrooms. There is a kitchen area and extra facilities for your convenience, including free WIFI access, a shoe-shiner, and an electric awning. Myriam and Christian are keen to share their region and organise sightseeing trips. An attentive and serene welcome.

Facilities: private parking, garden, tv lounge, hosts have pets, kitchen, babies welcome, free cot, 100% no smoking, wheelchair access, internet access, interesting flora 3km, gliding 6km, fishing 6km, hiking 6km, sea watersports 6km, golf course 10km
Fluent English spoken

Myriam & Christian MICHAUT
'Villa Aggarthi', 13 rue St-Exupère,
14400 BAYEUX
Tel: (0) 2 31 21 99 43 / (0) 662 67 81 92
sauvch@wanadoo.fr
www.chambresdhotesbayeux.com

Price Structure – 3 Bedrooms
'Sap': shower room, wc, double bed: €65
'Shon': shower room, wc, double bed: €70
'Kham': shower room, wc, double bed (queen-size): €75

Extra Bed: €15
Reduction: 21/08–13/07
Capacity: 6 people

Directions: From the N13 on arrival at Bayeux, turn right at the 2nd roundabout and then at the traffic lights, turn left. Continue for 300m and then turn left. Continue down for 500m and stop by the large white porch.

Location
BAYEUX
in: Bayeux
Railway station: 2km
Airport: Caen-Carpiquet 20km
car essential

Private Home

Bayeux is a small town, rich in history and well worth several days' stay. This place, a few minutes from the town centre in a quiet area, is the ideal base and is a spacious detached house with a warm welcome. You can easily visit the Cathedral of Notre-Dame, the famous Bayeux Tapestry of La Reine Mathilde, which is one of the most precious treasures from the Middle Ages, and, of course, the D-Day Museum.

Facilities: private parking, garden, tv lounge, pets not accepted, internet access, babies welcome, free cot, 2 nights minimum stay, riding, hiking, cycling, golf course 6km, sea watersports 12km, gliding 20km

Geneviève & Jean-Luc BRIANT
4 rue Eustache de Boulogne, 14400 BAYEUX
Tel: (0) 2 31 92 72 84 / (0) 673 50 85 28
Fax: (0) 2 31 92 72 84
genevieve.briant@free.fr
lagrandemaison.free.fr

Price Structure – 1 Bedroom and 1 Suite
suite: bathroom, wc, double bed. En-suite room, twin beds: €55 – 2 people €85 – 4 people
bathroom, wc, washbasin, double bed: €55

Capacity: 6 people

Directions: From the Bayeux bypass head towards Port-en-Bessin for 500m. Then take the second street on the right, go past a large lawn (500m) and then turn left into Rue Eustache de Boulogne.

Normandy – Bayeux

14.56 Bayeux

Private Home

Annick & Louis FAUVEL
'Les Glycines', 13 rue aux Coqs, 14400 BAYEUX
Tel: (0) 2 31 22 52 32 Fax: (0) 2 31 51 01 90

Price Structure – 3 Bedrooms
'Hortensias' & 'Rétro': shower room, wc, double bed:
€63
'Bleue': shower room, wc, double bed, single bed:
€63 – 2 people €81 – 3 people

Capacity: 7 people

Location
BAYEUX
in: Bayeux
Railway station: 1km
Airport: Caen-Carpiquet 25km
car essential

Annick and Louis sold their farm in Normandy to retire to the centre of the historic town of Bayeux. Once you enter via the gates and an arcade of wisteria, you will immediately feel at home, whether it be in the large living room with its unique, massive walk-through fireplace or in a corner of the delightful walled garden. Step outside and you are in the picturesque streets of this town, famous for its tapestry, old houses and its *hôtels particuliers*.

Facilities: off-street parking, garden, lounge, pets not accepted, 100% no smoking, cycling, golf course 10km, mushroom-picking 10km, gliding 10km, fishing 20km, interesting flora 20km, bird-watching 20km, sea watersports 20km

Directions: At Bayeux take the ring road (*boulevard circulaire*) towards the station and then take the street opposite the station leading to the town centre. After the second junction continue straight on into the Rue aux Coqs to number 13.

14.77 Bayeux

Private Home

Martine PICHONNIER
'La Pomme de Nuit', 6 rue du Moulin-Renard,
14400 BAYEUX
Tel: (0) 621 81 03 49
pommedenuit@yahoo.fr

Price Structure – 1 Bedroom
television, shower room, wc, four-poster double bed,
single bed: €50 – 2 people €60 – 3 people

Capacity: 3 people

Location
BAYEUX
in: Bayeux
Railway station: Bayeux
Airport: Caen-Carpiquet 30km

Close to the historic centre of Bayeux (accessible on foot), this house is in a quiet area with narrow streets by large stone buildings once used for roasting coffee. Independent from the white, newly built main house and its small walled garden is the maisonette. There is a mini-bar and a microwave on the ground floor. Breakfast is served here or on the terrace. The bedroom is on the first floor and is well presented with painted wood panelling and a large four-poster bed. Martine can uncover for you the 'real' Bayeux.

Facilities: private parking, garden, 3 years old minimum age, fishing 10km, sea watersports 10km, mushroom-picking 15km, golf course 18km, riversports 35km
Adequate English spoken

Directions: At Bayeux when arriving from Caen, at the 'Eisenhower' roundabout (large roundabout on the ring road with a statue in the centre) head for the Centre-Ville. Pass the traffic lights and then turn down the first road on the left. At the next set of traffic lights turn right. At the next crossroads, park in the small car park. Rue du Moulin-Renard is on the left.

Normandy – Bayeux

Location
BAYEUX
in: Bayeux, station pick-up on arrival/departure
Railway station: Bayeux
Airport: Caen-Carpiquet 27km

Top marks! four 'suns' for this 19th-century *Maison de Maître*. Within walking distance of the centre of Bayeux and its tapestry. Enjoy peace and quiet on the terrace and in the walled grounds. Carole and Jérôme care greatly about their home. They welcome you as a friend into their warm family atmosphere with four young children. The well-proportioned bedrooms are comfortable and attractive; the one in the old converted attic is more modest but still charming. Jérôme knows all about the Normandy D-Day landings and owns a restored bunker.

Facilities: private parking, extensive grounds, lounge, hosts have pets, pets not accepted, babies welcome, free cot, cycling, interesting flora, sea watersports 10km, golf course 15km, hunting 15km, fishing 15km, bird-watching 15km, hiking 15km, mushroom-picking 20km
Adequate English spoken

Directions: At Bayeux when arriving from Caen, at the 'Eisenhower' roundabout (large roundabout on the ring road with a statue in the centre) head for 'Centre-Ville, Gare' and then turn right immediately into Rue Bellefontaine. Be careful as the house numbers do not seem to follow any logical order! The number 6 is situated after the small crossroads on the left-hand side.

Residence of Outstanding Character

Carole & Jérôme MALLET
'Clos de Bellefontaine', 6 rue Bellefontaine,
14400 BAYEUX
Tel: / (0) 681 42 24 81
clos.bellefontaine@wanadoo.fr
http://clos.bellefontaine.monsite.wanadoo.fr/

Price Structure – 2 Bedrooms
'Elégance': lounge, bathroom, wc, shower, double bed (queen-size), single bed: €130 – 2 people €150 – 3 people
'Charme': bathroom, wc, shower, 2 single beds: €95

Capacity: 5 people

Location
BAYEUX
in: Bayeux, station pick-up on arrival/departure
Railway station: Bayeux
Airport: Caen-Carpiquet 25km

Residence of Outstanding Character

This charming 15th-century house is in a quiet street in the historic centre of Bayeux, 100m from the cathedral, the famous tapestry and the porcelain and lace museum. The rooms are tastefully decorated and are reached via a winding staircase in a tower. Note that the 'Bleuet' room has a shower unit that is not partitioned off from the room itself. You will find your hosts friendly and helpful. Breakfast and dinner (local specialities) are served in the dining room or in the lovely interior courtyard full of flowers and shrubs.

Facilities: off-street parking, garden, hosts have pets, pets not accepted, dinner available, babies welcome, free cot, 100% no smoking, 2 nights minimum stay: 1/07–31/08, cycling, fishing 5km, golf course 10km, hiking 10km, sea watersports 10km
Fluent English spoken

Directions: From the centre of Bayeux, head for 'Parvis de la Cathédrale' where you then turn down Rue de la Maîtrise followed by the first road on the right, Rue Quincangrogne. This road is pedestrianised. It is advisable to park on Place Charles de Gaulle which is 50m away.

Pascal & Antoine LEBRET-SOCHELEAU
'Le Petit Matin', 2 bis rue Quincangrogne,
14400 BAYEUX
Tel: (0) 2 31 10 09 27 / (0) 608 28 65 59
Fax: (0) 2 31 10 09 27
lepetitmatin@hotmail.com
www.lepetitmatin.com

Price Structure – 3 Bedrooms
'Rose': shower room, wc, double bed, single bed, cot: €65 – 2 people €80 – 3 people
'Lilas' & 'Bleuet': shower room, wc, double bed, cot: €65

Extra Bed: €15
Reduction: 13/11–30/03
Capacity: 7 people

Normandy – Bayeux

14.90 Bayeux

Private Home

Location
BAYEUX
in: Bayeux
Railway station: 1km
Airport: Caen-Carpiquet 35km

Christèle & François LECORNU
'Logis des Remparts', 4 rue Bourbesneur,
14400 BAYEUX
Tel: (0) 2 31 92 50 40 Fax: (0) 2 72 64 98 32
info@lecornu.fr
www.lecornu.fr

Price Structure – 2 Bedrooms and 1 Suite
'Bourbesneur': shower room, wc, double bed. En-suite room, double bed, single bed: €130 – 5 people
'Judaine': shower room, wc, double bed, single bed: €55 – 2 people €85 – 3 people
'Bajocasse': shower room, wc, double bed, single bed (child-size): €70

Extra Bed: €20
Capacity: 11 people

In the medieval historic centre of Bayeux is the home of Christèle and François which was rebuilt in the 18th century, but parts of which date back to medieval times. The three guest bedrooms (one of which is made up of two connecting rooms) are quiet and comfortable. You are close to the famous Bayeux Tapestry, the cathedral and museums. At approximately 30km from Bayeux, the American cemetery at Colleville-sur-Mer, the D-Day landing beaches, Pointe du Hoc and Arromanches are all within easy reach.

Facilities: hosts have pets, pets not accepted, 100% no smoking, closed: 15/12–01/02
Fluent English spoken

Directions: Follow signs to the 'Sous-Prefecture' which is an official building in the same street. If you get lost please call your hosts.

14.96 Bayeux

Residence of Outstanding Character

Location
BAYEUX
in: Bayeux
Railway station: Bayeux
Airport: Caen-Carpiquet 20km

Monique & Anthony VOIDIE
'Hotel Tardif', 16 rue de Nesmond, 14400 BAYEUX
Tel: (0) 2 31 92 67 72 / (0) 687 12 57 83
Fax: (0) 2 31 92 67 72
anthony.voidie@wanadoo.fr
www.hoteltardif.com

Price Structure – 5 Bedrooms
'Monseigneur de Nesmond': television, shower room, wc, double bed, single bed: €130 – 2 people €155 – 3 people
'Baron d'Ussel': shower room, wc, double bed, 2 single beds: €130 – 2 people €180 – 4 people
'Veuve Langlois': television, shower room, wc, double bed: €80
'Dodeman': shower room, wc, double bed, single bed: €185 – 2 people €210 – 3 people
'Maître Moisson de Vaux': shower room, wc, double bed, single bed: €160 – 2 people €185 – 3 people

Reduction: children
Capacity: 15 people

Monique and her son Anthony have bought this superb *hôtel particulier* right in the centre of Bayeux, a few steps away from the 'Tapisserie de la Reine Mathilde' and the cathedral, as well as a beautiful enclosed park (on the site of the former botanical gardens). We knew their former home where they welcomed guests for years with great warmth and charm and Monique has proved to us again her talent for interior decoration. She has created refined, comfortable, bright and spacious bedrooms with bathrooms boasting double basins.

Facilities: private parking, extensive grounds, hosts have pets, pets not accepted, babies welcome, free cot, 100% no smoking, interesting flora, vineyard 5km, golf course 8km, gliding 8km, fishing 8km, sea watersports 8km, hiking 20km
Fluent English spoken

Directions: From Bayeux, head for the Centre-Ville and follow the signs to the 'Parc d'Ornano' or 'Tapisserie'. The house is just opposite where you'll find the tapestry.

Normandy – Bayeux

Location
14km N W of BAYEUX
in: Asnières-en-Bessin
Railway station: 14km
Airport: Caen-Carpiquet 40km
car essential

Working Farm

A warm welcome here from Anne, a former hotelier, who missed meeting visitors to the region so much she recently decided to try her hand at being a bed and breakfast host when she moved with her family to this Normandy farmhouse. The guest bedrooms are in an independent wing of the farm and have been completely renovated and redecorated. Each bedroom has its own bathroom and a spa-jet shower. As you would expect from her experience in the hotel trade, she is a fountain of knowledge on the local area and will be happy to advise you.

Anne & Patrick FERON
'Ferme de Montigny',
14710 ASNIERES-EN-BESSIN
Tel: (0) 2 31 21 99 28 / (0) 620 93 46 66
anne.feron@wanadoo.fr
http://chambrealaferme.monsite.wanadoo.fr

Facilities: off-street parking, garden, lounge, hosts have pets, pets not accepted, kitchen, babies welcome, free cot, private tennis court, gliding 7km, golf course 14km
Adequate English spoken

Price Structure – 3 Bedrooms
3 rooms: shower room, wc, double bed: €46

Extra Bed: €10
Reduction: 3 nights
Capacity: 6 people

Directions: From Bayeux, take the N13 towards Trévières. Pass through Trévières and head for Formigny. At the junction turn left and head for Asnières-en-Bessin. At Asnières-en-Bessin, turn right at the crossroads. It is the first farm on the left.

Location
16km S W of BAYEUX
in: Balleroy
Railway station: 15km
Airport: Caen-Carpiquet 30km
car essential

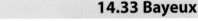

Residence of Outstanding Character

The long frontage of this character 17th-century home is hidden away behind rich vegetation, in parts wild, that descends to the grounds of the Forbes family château. Once home to the château's tutor, the interior is warm and intimate with period furniture, African tapestries and murals, and a stone fireplace and deep armchairs in the lounge. Renée and Alain are both teachers and music-lovers. Play the piano or enjoy a recital by one of the family's professional musicians. There is a hot-air balloon museum at the château.

Renée MALAVAL
Place du Château, 14490 BALLEROY
Tel: (0) 2 31 51 91 62 / (0) 603 39 77 38
Fax: (0) 2 31 51 91 62
reneemalaval@hotmail.fr

Facilities: off-street parking, garden, lounge, kitchen, mushroom-picking, hiking 2km, fishing 3km
Fluent English spoken

Price Structure – 1 Bedroom
along corridor bathroom, wc, double bed: €60

Extra Bed: €15
Reduction: 15/09–15/05, 2 nights
Capacity: 2 people

Directions: From Bayeux, D572 towards St-Lô for 16km, then the D13 on the left to Balleroy. The house is situated by the entrance to the château on the right behind the trees. Enter via the barrier on the road.

Normandy – Bayeux

14.24 Bayeux

Château/Manor House

Constance & Arnaud BROCHARD
Le lieu Vauquelin, 14230 CANCHY
Tel: (0) 2 31 92 46 15 / (0) 688 02 79 99
contact@entre-mer-et-marais.com
www.entre-mer-et-marais.com

Price Structure – 2 Bedrooms
'La Volière': bathroom, wc, double bed: €75
'La Rosière': twin beds, single bed: €75 – 2 people
€85 – 3 people

Extra Bed: €20
Reduction: 1/10–31/05, 3 nights
Capacity: 5 people

Location
24km W of BAYEUX
in: Canchy
Railway station: 25km
Airport: Caen-Carpiquet 50km
car essential

A manor farm from the 18th century in the Parc Naturel des Marais du Cotentin et du Bessin, a few minutes from the coast and historic sites. The interior, typically laid out in a long line, is completely open to you, and includes a spacious lounge, dining and television rooms as well as a fitness room with a sauna. The two comfortable bedrooms can be booked together as a suite but the bathroom is more basic. Constance is a talented porcelain painter and sporty Arnaud advises on local activities. A cheerful, pleasant welcome.

Facilities: private parking, extensive grounds, tv lounge, hosts have pets, babies welcome, free cot, bird-watching, hiking, fishing 1km, sea watersports 8km, interesting flora 10km, mushroom-picking 15km, golf course 20km, gliding 30km, riversports 30km
Fluent English spoken

Directions: Please contact your hosts for detailed directions.

14.93 Bayeux

Private Home

Chantal & Jean-Claude REAUBOURG
La Cour Blanche, 14490 CASTILLON
Tel: (0) 2 31 51 89 28 Fax: (0) 2 31 51 89 28
jc.reaubourg@wanadoo.fr
http://lacourblanche.monsite.wanadoo.fr

Price Structure – 3 Bedrooms
'Equestre' & 'Campagne': shower room, wc, double bed, 2 single beds: €50 – 2 people €100 – 4 people
'Herbier': shower room, wc, twin beds, single bed: €50 – 2 people €75 – 3 people

Extra Bed: €20
Reduction: 3 nights, groups, children
Capacity: 11 people

Location
12km S W of BAYEUX
in: Castillon, station pick-up on arrival/departure
Railway station: 11km
Airport: Caen-Carpiquet 35km
car essential

On the edge of Bayeux, amongst the Normandy battlefields and the heartlands of William the Conqueror, is this former farmhouse typical of the Bessin region. Take the time to unwind in this quiet, rural setting. Chantal and Jean-Claude have renovated the farm for their retirement and the benefit of their guests. The bedrooms retain a charming country feel, thanks to Chantal's artistic talents. The garden has an abundance of flowers and is surrounded by pastures and hedgerows where you can watch your hosts' goats and horses roam freely.

Facilities: off-street parking, garden, hosts have pets, pets not accepted, babies welcome, free cot, 100% no smoking, closed: 01/11–15/03, hiking, cycling, fishing 5km, vineyard 10km, interesting flora 11km, bird-watching 40km

Directions: From Bayeux, D572 towards St-Lô. 1km after Noron-la-Poterie (7km from Bayeux), D73 on the left until Castillon. Cross the village towards Balleroy. 'La Cour Blanche' is on the right opposite the exit sign to the village.

Location
15km N E of BAYEUX
in: Crepon, station pick-up on arrival/departure
Railway station: 25km
Airport: Caen-Carpiquet 21km
car essential

Private Home

René is a retired hotel/restaurant owner and provides a warm welcome at his place near the invasion beaches. He is a keen golfer and hiker and will be only too pleased to help you discover this area which he knows intimately and loves passionately. When you get back, relax in the bright guest lounge or in the garden with its boules pitch. There are also games for the children. Breakfast is plentiful, and the two rooms, on the first floor, are pleasant and spacious.

Françoise & René GOGUELET
'La Bessine', route de Creuilly, 14480 CREPON
Tel: (0) 2 31 21 07 79 / (0) 607 84 89 14
Fax: (0) 2 31 21 07 79
rene.goguelet@wanadoo.fr
www.bessine.fr

Facilities: private parking, garden, tv lounge, babies welcome, free cot, 1 shared shower room, wc, hiking, fishing 3km, sea watersports 3km, mushroom-picking 12km, golf course 19km

Price Structure – 2 Bedrooms
double bed: €50
double bed, 2 single beds (child-size): €50 – 2 people €70 – 4 people

Extra Bed: €10
Capacity: 6 people

Directions: At Bayeux take the D12 as far as Sommervieu, then the D112 as far as Crépon then the D65 towards Creully. 'La Bessine' is on this road, on the left.

Location
30km S of BAYEUX
in: Dampierre
Railway station: 30km
Airport: 50km
car essential

Château/Manor House

Conveniently placed between the Normandy beaches and Brittany, this 17th-century château, re-built in the 19th century, is completely surrounded by a water-filled moat. Choose between the 'Tour' or 'Nuptiale' (with exposed beams and turret windows) bedrooms. There are magnificent reception rooms, a listed dovecote and a walled garden. It deserves its rating just for the character of the château alone.

Jean-Claude JOUVIN
'Château de Dampierre', 14350 DAMPIERRE
Tel: (0) 2 31 67 31 81 Fax: (0) 2 31 67 02 06

Facilities: private parking, extensive grounds, pets not accepted, babies welcome, free cot, 100% no smoking, fishing, hiking 5km, cycling 5km, golf course 15km, interesting flora 15km, sea watersports 15km, riversports 15km, gliding 15km, bird-watching 20km

Price Structure – 4 Bedrooms and 1 Suite
'Nuptiale' & 'Tour': shower room, wc, double bed: €100
no 5: shower room, wc, double bed: €70
no 3: shower room, wc, twin beds: €70
suite: shower room, wc, double bed. En-suite room, twin beds: €140 – 4 people

Reduction: 3 nights
Capacity: 12 people

Directions: On the A84 between Avranches and Caen, exit 41 to St-Martin-des-Besases, then head towards Dampierre on the D185. The château is located just as you enter the village.

Normandy – Bayeux

14.14 Bayeux

Private Home

Location
16km N W of BAYEUX
in: Formigny
Railway station: 15km
Airport: Caen-Carpiquet 45km
car essential

On route to Omaha Beach is this 18th-century farm by a superb 12th-century church: an authentic image of Normandy. Sit in the rural garden and contemplate the pond, islet, ducks and the nine cats! Part of the house is just for you with a communal room, lounge, kitchen area, mini-bar and pleasant bedrooms. When Loïc is not out in Africa for work, see his collection of historical objects from WW2 (some for sale). Joëlle is attracted to antiques and the furniture in the house bears witness to this. Ground floor room with disabled facilities.

Joëlle & Loïc RIVOALLAN
'La Ferme aux Chats', L'Eglise, 14710 FORMIGNY
Tel: (0) 2 31 51 00 88 / (0) 661 71 10 99
Fax: (0) 2 31 51 00 88
fermeauxchats@wanadoo.fr
www.lafermeauxchats.com

Price Structure – 4 Bedrooms
shower room, wc, twin beds: €60
2 rooms: shower room, wc, double bed: €60
shower room, wc, double bed, twin beds:
€60 – 2 people €90 – 4 people

Reduction: children
Capacity: 10 people

Facilities: private parking, extensive grounds, lounge, hosts have pets, pets not accepted, kitchen, babies welcome, free cot, 100% no smoking, wheelchair access, closed: 15/11–31/12, private swimming pool, hiking 1km, sea watersports 5km, golf course 10km
Fluent English spoken

Directions: From Bayeux N13 towards Cherbourg for 15km to Formigny. Then head for St-Laurent-sur-Mer. The 'Ferme aux Chats' is opposite the church.

14.38 Bayeux

Château/Manor House

Location
25km W of BAYEUX
in: Géfosse-Fontenay
Railway station: 15km
Airport: 60km
car essential

This fortified farm and manor house dates back to medieval times and is situated in the Regional National Park, near to the invasion beaches. Ask for the guest bedroom in the square tower, complete with loopholes. Isabelle's warm welcome reflects the cosy atmosphere of this place. Also available to rent: a gîte for two people and an apartment for four people.

Isabelle & Gérard LEHARIVEL
'Manoir de la Rivière', Géfosse-Fontenay,
14230 ISIGNY-SUR-MER
Tel: (0) 2 31 22 64 45 / (0) 681 58 25 21
Fax: (0) 2 31 22 01 18
manoirdelariviere@wanadoo.fr
www.chez.com/manoirdelariviere

Price Structure – 3 Bedrooms
'Louis Philippe': shower room, wc, double bed, single bed (child-size): €65 – 2 people €85 – 3 people
'Louis XV': shower room, wc, double bed, single bed: €65 – 2 people €85 – 3 people
'Tour': shower room, wc, double bed: €65

Extra Bed: €20
Capacity: 8 people

Facilities: private parking, garden, lounge, hosts have pets, pets not accepted, dinner available, hiking, fishing, interesting flora, bird-watching, sea watersports 4km, cycling 5km, golf course 25km
Adequate English spoken

Directions: At Bayeux, take the N13 towards Cherbourg for 29km and turn off at Osmanville. Cross the village and at the roundabout, take the D514 towards Grandcamp-Maisy for 4km. Then turn left towards Géfosse-Fontenay. Continue for 800m and the manor is on the left, just before the church and the lake by the entrance.

Location
25km W of BAYEUX
in: La Cambe
Railway station: 20km
car essential

Private Home

Tucked away in the countryside of the Parc Naturel du Contentin is this farm outbuilding, typical of the Bessin region. Its stone walls and enclosed courtyard full of ancient machinery harks back to its agricultural past. Today, Yula and Brian, originally from Britain, have brought with them apart from the obvious comforts and touches of modernity a strong desire to really improve and enhance the property. Yula's savoir faire in matters of decoration and Brian's carpentry skills are indisputable. A beautiful backdrop for a very agreeable stay. Recommended.

Yula & Brian LAWRENCE
Le lieu Besnard, 14230 LA CAMBE
Tel: (0) 2 31 10 12 81
Lawrence.Brian@wanadoo.fr
www.lelieubesnard.com

Facilities: off-street parking, extensive grounds, lounge, hosts have pets, pets not accepted, dinner available, babies welcome, free cot, 100% no smoking, closed: 15/12–05/01, cycling, fishing 5km, bird-watching 5km, sea watersports 10km, golf course 15km
Fluent English spoken

Price Structure – 2 Bedrooms
'Géranium': along corridor bathroom, wc, twin beds: €65
'Lavande': shower room, wc, double bed: €65

Reduction: 3 nights
Capacity: 4 people

Directions: From Carentan towards Bayeux, fast road for 18km, exit at La Cambe. In the village take the road in front of the church by the post office, then the first road on the right towards La Vieille Place. Continue for 500m (B&B France sign).

Location
13km S W of BAYEUX
in: Le Molay-Littry
Railway station: 13km
car essential

Private Home

Enjoy the tranquillity of the countryside whilst staying in a bright, comfortable and welcoming home. René, a retired farmer, designed this house which is located on the edge of a *lotissement* with open views over fields. The guest rooms are on the first floor which is reserved for guests. Breakfast is served in a large bright living room, with a kitchen and seating area and bay windows looking out onto the garden. A footpath leads to the village and the Musée de la Mine. You are 15km from the sea and closer still to Bayeux.

Thérèse & René HENNEQUIN
La Moignerie, 4 rue des Mineurs,
14330 LE MOLAY-LITTRY
Tel: (0) 2 31 21 60 56 / (0) 682 21 19 01
Fax: (0) 2 31 21 60 56

Facilities: private parking, lounge, pets not accepted, dinner available, babies welcome, free cot, 1 shared bathroom, wc, hiking 4km, fishing 10km, sea watersports 15km

Price Structure – 2 Bedrooms
2 rooms: double bed: €40

Extra Bed: €15
Capacity: 4 people

Directions: From Bayeux D5 to Le Molay-Littry (14km). Enter the *lotissement* opposite the supermarket 'Super U'. Last road on the left.

Normandy – Bayeux

14.023 Bayeux

Private Home

Location
12km S W of BAYEUX
in: Le Tronquay
Railway station: 8km
Airport: Caen-Carpiquet 25km
car essential

You have the run of Carole's house, located in a residential area, and she is happy for you to relax in her lounge and use the kitchen. A home visitor by profession, she likes meeting people and is a warm and welcoming person and a good listener. Be sure to accept the invitation to have an *apéritif* on arrival with Carole and Michel. They may invite you to go walking with them or advise you on what to do in this area, which, being Normans, they know well. Breakfast is taken in the dazzlingly light conservatory.

Carole & Michel JOURDAN
La Tuilerie, 14490 LE TRONQUAY
Tel: (0) 2 31 21 37 72 / (0) 689 59 70 18
m.jourdan@infonie.fr

Price Structure – 1 Suite
lounge, along corridor shower room, wc, twin beds, single bed (child-size). En-suite room, double bed: €44 – 2 people €88 – 5 people

Capacity: 5 people

Facilities: private parking, garden, tv lounge, pets not accepted, babies welcome, free cot
Adequate English spoken

Directions: Please contact your host in advance for detailed directions.

14.26 Bayeux

Private Home

Location
12km S W of BAYEUX
in: Le Tronquay
Railway station: 9km
Airport: Caen-Carpiquet 25km
car essential

A well-preserved 19th-century house in Normandy's typical *bocage* landscape near to Bayeux, the landing beaches and Cerisy forest. At the turn of the last century it was the hotel for the station. Michel, son of a local farmer, can fill you in on the history. However, the house no longer hints at its past. Today, the spacious room on the ground floor has an independent entrance, a large bathroom and a sober contemporary feel (but with two 'Godin' stoves). Personalised breakfasts and a garden. A friendly welcome.

Michel ROBIN
'La Hoguette', route de Castillon,
14490 LE TRONQUAY
Tel: (0) 2 31 22 88 70 / (0) 670 65 24 96
michel.celia@wanadoo.fr

Price Structure – 1 Bedroom
shower room, wc, double bed: €48

Reduction: 3 nights
Capacity: 2 people

Facilities: private parking, garden, lounge, hosts have pets, babies welcome, free cot, hiking, cycling, fishing 5km, mushroom-picking 5km, interesting flora 9km, vineyard 9km, golf course 15km, sea watersports 15km, bird-watching 40km, riversports 40km
Fluent English spoken

Directions: From Bayeux take the D512 direction St-Lô for 9km to 'La Tuilerie' then the D73 on the left towards Castillon. It is the first old house on the right.

Location
9km N of BAYEUX
in: Manvieux
Railway station: 10km
Airport: Caen-Carpiquet 40km
car essential

✹✹✹

Private Home

The scent of perfumed candles that greets you on arrival is a sure sign that Patricia is into interior decorating. The bedrooms, in a separate building, are tasteful and the pleasant garden has ponds and a veranda. There is a kitchenette available with a small dining area and a terrace, but you should also try Patricia's cooking, as this was her profession, and her 'Turkey Escalope Surprise' and 'Chicken with Camembert' are not to be missed. She also knows a thing or two about looking after guests and advising them on their stay.

Facilities: private parking, garden, hosts have pets, dinner available
Adequate English spoken

Directions: Please contact your host in advance for detailed directions.

Patricia DUVAL
'La Magnanerie', 18 route de Port,
14117 MANVIEUX
Tel: (0) 2 31 92 84 54
patricia.duval6@wanadoo.fr

Price Structure – 2 Bedrooms and 1 Suite
'Mimosa': along corridor shower room, wc, double bed: €65
'Rose': along corridor bathroom, wc, double bed: €60
'Hortensia': lounge, shower room, wc, double bed. En-suite room, 2 single beds (child-size): €70 – 2 people €100 – 4 people

Extra Bed: €15
Capacity: 8 people

Location
11km S E of BAYEUX
in: Martragny
Railway station: 7km
Airport: Caen-Carpiquet 15km
car essential

✹✹

Residence of Outstanding Character

This *manoir* is in fact a superb fortified farm from the 17th and 18th centuries. Typical of the local architecture, it has a central courtyard framed by the main house and stone barns. Locals Yvette and Maurice are now retired and continue to maintain this piece of their local heritage. There is also a campsite but it is small, so you can take advantage of the facilities (buy food and wash clothes) without it encroaching on your peace and quiet. Avoid the overflow room in the campsite annex. The shower rooms are quite basic.

Facilities: off-street parking, garden, tv lounge, hosts have pets, babies welcome, free cot, hiking, fishing 10km, sea watersports 10km, golf course 20km
Adequate English spoken

Directions: From Caen take the N13 towards Bayeux for 18km. Exit at Martragny. Take the D82 towards Creully. 'Le Manoir' is on this road (signposted). Enter into the courtyard.

Yvette & Maurice GODFROY
'Manoir de l'Abbaye', 15 rue de Creully,
14740 MARTRAGNY
Tel: (0) 2 31 80 25 95 Fax: (0) 2 31 80 25 95
yvette.godfroy@libertysurf.fr
http://perso.wanadoo.fr/godfroy

Price Structure – 2 Bedrooms and 1 Suite
television, shower room, wc, washbasin, double bed: €50
'Suite': television, shower room, wc, washbasin, twin beds. En-suite room, television, double bed: €50 – 2 people €100 – 4 people
television, shower room, wc, twin beds: €50

Reduction: 7 nights
Capacity: 8 people

Normandy – Bayeux

14.30 Bayeux

Working Farm

Location
4km S E of BAYEUX
in: Nonant
Railway station: 6km
Airport: 20km
car essential

Let Chantal's exuberant joie de vivre sweep you into her farmhouse, full of character, in this quiet village close to the sea. On your return from sightseeing trips or swimming, try her local dishes cooked with local farm produce.

Chantal KLEIN
'Ferme de la Houlotte', 14400 NONANT
Tel: (0) 2 31 92 50 29 / (0) 613 13 58 97
kdamechantal@aol.com

Price Structure – 4 Bedrooms
'Orme': along corridor shower, wc, double bed: €50
'Hêtre' & 'Noyer': shower, double bed, single bed: €50 – 2 people €65 – 3 people
'Merisier': shower, double bed, 2 single beds: €50 – 2 people €80 – 4 people

Extra Bed: €16
Reduction: 3 nights, groups, children
Capacity: 12 people

Facilities: private parking, extensive grounds, lounge, hosts have pets, dinner available, babies welcome, free cot, 1 shared shower room, 2 wcs, cycling
Fluent English spoken

Directions: On the A13 exit 36 then head to Nonant. Turn right at the church and go under the bridge. The farm is situated 1.6km further down the road. Follow the signs.

14.32 Bayeux

Château/Manor House

Location
4km S E of BAYEUX
in: Nonant
Railway station: 6km
Airport: 20km
car essential

An 18th-century house with 6 hectares of grounds. Your hosts have completely transformed the interior, which is fantastic. Florence is an excellent cook, so be sure to try her cooking. On sale: cider, jam.

Florence MOREL
'Le Manoir du Chêne', 14400 NONANT
Tel: (0) 2 31 51 00 51/ 31 51 82 72 / (0) 630 34 77 85
manoirduchene@wanadoo.fr

Price Structure – 5 Bedrooms
'Ardoise': shower, wc, double bed (queen-size), 2 single beds: €90 – 2 people €112 – 4 people
'Le nid': shower, double bed: €56
'La plage': shower room, wc, double bed, single bed: €70 – 2 people €84 – 3 people
'Le verger': shower room, wc, twin beds: €56
'Les cerfs-volants': shower room, wc, double bed: €56

Extra Bed: €17
Capacity: 13 people

Facilities: private parking, extensive grounds, lounge, hosts have pets, dinner available, babies welcome, free cot, wc, private tennis court, hiking, hunting, cycling 10km, golf course 12km, bird-watching 12km, fishing 30km
Adequate English spoken

Directions: At Bayeux take the N13 towards Caen. As you leave Bayeux, at the roundabout (with the dairy opposite you) turn left towards Nonant. 'Le Manoir du Chêne' is 1.6km from Nonant at 'Les Maisons' on the left.

Location
9km N W of BAYEUX
in: Port-en-Bessin-Huppain
Railway station: 8km
Airport: Caen-Carpiquet 30km
car essential

✺ ✺ ✺
Private Home

As they are between Omaha and Gold Beaches, this is the ideal base for visiting the sites of the Normandy landings. Corinne has given up work now to devote herself to B&B full time. Her guests get a warm welcome in a nice large residence just next to her main home, all set in a wooded garden that you are free to enjoy. Each room has the latest gismos. This contrasts with the furniture that Corinne has restored and personalised herself to give an authentic touch. In the large lounge you are welcome to tinkle on the piano.

Corinne COLIN
'Normandy Omaha', 4 chemin du Sémaphore,
14520 PORT-EN-BESSIN-HUPPAIN
Tel: (0) 2 31 22 44 66 / (0) 662 22 83 39
Fax: (0) 2 31 22 44 66
normandy.omaha@orange.fr
www.normandy-omaha.fr

Facilities: private parking, garden, tv lounge, hosts have pets, internet access, babies welcome, free cot, 100% no smoking, golf course, hiking, cycling, sea watersports, fishing, gliding 30km
Adequate English spoken

Price Structure – 3 Bedrooms and 1 Suite
'Utah' & 'Gold': television, bathroom, wc, double bed (queen-size): €99
'Omaha': television, bathroom, wc, double bed (queen-size): €99
'June': television, bathroom, wc, shower, double bed (queen-size). En-suite room, television, double bed (queen-size): €79 – 2 people €140 – 4 people

Reduction: 01/10–30/04, 7 nights, groups
Capacity: 10 people

Directions: At Bayeux take the D6 as far as Port-en-Bessin-Huppain. Then head towards Gold Omaha Beach. As you exit Port-en-Bessin, turn right at the lights and follow signs to 'Port-Land' and then 'Normandy Omaha'.

Location
8km N E of BAYEUX
in: Ryès
Railway station: 10km
Airport: Caen-Carpiquet 30km
car essential

✺ ✺
Working Farm

Michel's working farm is 1km from the Arromanches beaches and 10km from Bayeux. The bright and spacious room is in a converted outhouse, which has been restored to a good standard of comfort. A hearty breakfast is served in the family dining room.

Michel GUILBERT
'Gîte du Petit Fontaine ', Le Petit Fontaine,
14400 RYES
Tel: (0) 2 31 22 32 92 / (0) 684 14 33 06
petitfontaine@wanadoo.fr
http://petitfontaine.monsite.wanadoo.fr/

Facilities: off-street parking, garden, pets not accepted, hiking, fishing 2km, golf course 8km

Price Structure – 1 Bedroom
television, bathroom, wc, washbasin, double bed: €47

Extra Bed: €20
Reduction: 01/09–30/06
Capacity: 2 people

Directions: From Bayeux go to Ryes and then follow signs to Arromanches. About 2km from Ryes it is the second farm on the right.

Normandy – Bayeux

14.68 Bayeux

Private Home

Location
8km N E of BAYEUX
in: Ryès
Railway station: 9km
Airport: Caen-Carpiquet 37km
car essential

Just a few kilometres from Marie-France and Michel's newly built home are the D-Day landing beaches, but be sure to explore the many other places of interest in the region: small winding tree-lined roads, old rural houses, a fortified manor and farmhouses, and historic churches. The charms of all these are echoed here in the village of Ryès with great hospitality to boot. They also make umbrellas in the area!

Marie-France & Michel BEAUREGARD
'Le Verger Fleuri', 3 chemin des Avenues,
14400 RYES
Tel: (0) 2 31 51 78 60 / (0) 687 18 87 53
mf.ryes@wanadoo.fr
www.verger-fleuri-vacances.com

Price Structure – 3 Bedrooms
'Coquelicots' & 'Bleue': television, double bed. Along corridor room, 2 single beds, cot: €46 – 2 people
€66 – 4 people

Extra Bed: €15
Capacity: 6 people

Facilities: off-street parking, garden, tv lounge, babies welcome, free cot, 100% no smoking, 1 shared shower room, wc, closed: 25/12, riding, hiking, sea watersports 4km, golf course 10km

Directions: From Bayeux, D12 direction Courseulles-sur-Mer. Pass Sommervieu and take the D205 to Ryès. In the centre of the village, head towards St-Cosme-de-Fresne. It is the second lane on the right (just after the doctor's surgery).

14.87 Bayeux

Private Home

Location
8km N E of BAYEUX
in: Ryès
Railway station: 8km
Airport: Caen-Carpiquet 30km
car essential

As is typical in this region steeped in heritage, it is the straightforward and discreet welcome from your host Henriette that will make a lasting impression. The lounge with a fireplace and the garden area of this half-timbered house are all available to you. For dinner they suggest the restaurant close by in the village.

Henriette & Roger LAINE
14400 RYES
Tel: (0) 2 31 21 38 65 / (0) 620 83 46 85
Fax: (0) 2 31 51 87 85
henriette.laine@wanadoo.fr

Facilities: private parking, garden, lounge, hosts have pets, pets not accepted, babies welcome, free cot, 100% no smoking, hiking, fishing 3km, golf course 10km, hunting 20km, mushroom-picking 20km
Adequate English spoken

Price Structure – 2 Bedrooms
2 rooms: television, shower room, wc, double bed: €42

Extra Bed: €12
Capacity: 4 people

Directions: From Bayeux, take the D12 towards Courseulles-sur-Mer. Pass through Sommervieu and take the D205 to Ryès. In the village head for Arromanches and then take the first road on the left after the restaurant.

Location
3km E of BAYEUX
in: Sommervieu
Railway station: 4km
Airport: Caen-Carpiquet 25km
car essential

Private Home

At first this young couple were apprehensive about retiring from farming to start up a B&B but they now open their doors to guests with pleasure and great kindness. Their typically traditional house is in a quiet cul-de-sac. The two guest bedrooms are only offered together as a suite. Nicole and Eric love gardening and you can't fail to miss the immaculate large hedge and impressive flower-bed by the house (Nicole knows the names of all her flowers off by heart!).

Nicole & Eric LEMARQUIER
2 impasse des Puits, 14400 SOMMERVIEU
Tel: (0) 2 31 51 88 15 / (0) 608 34 07 14
eric.lemarquier@orange.fr

Facilities: off-street parking, garden, lounge, hosts have pets, pets not accepted, 100% no smoking, 1 shared shower room, wc, gliding 7km, sea watersports 7km, golf course 12km, interesting flora 25km
Fluent English spoken

Price Structure – 2 Bedrooms
suite: television, double bed. En-suite room, television, double bed, single bed:
€45,80 – 2 people €82,00 – 5 people

Extra Bed: €12
Capacity: 5 people

Directions: From Bayeux take the D12 heading towards Courseulles for 3km until you reach the entrance to Sommervieu. At the water tower, turn left onto the D153. On the bend continue straight ahead down the cul-de-sac. The house is on the right after the sports ground.

Location
2km N of BAYEUX
in: St-Vigor-le-Grand
Railway station: 3km
Airport: Caen-Carpiquet 25km
car essential

Private Home

Near the centre of Bayeux and easily accessible is this contemporary house surrounded by a lawn on the edge of fields by the countryside. The guest bedroom is in the blue 'azure' colours of the sea and sky and has an adjustable reclining bed for your comfort. The interior of the house is impeccable, bright and decorated with Annie's delightful paintings. She is very easy to chat to and get along with and will share with you her love for the region.

Annie LETOURNEUR
40 route d'Arromanches,
14400 ST-VIGOR-LE-GRAND
Tel: (0) 2 31 92 83 04 Fax: (0) 2 31 21 77 38
thierry.letourneur2@wanadoo.fr

Facilities: off-street parking, garden, 100% no smoking
Basic English spoken

Price Structure – 1 Bedroom
television, shower room, wc, double bed: €50

Capacity: 2 people

Directions: On the Bayeux ring-road head for Arromanches. The house is 800m along on the right (signposted).

Normandy – Bayeux

14.47 Bayeux

Working Farm

Bienvenue
on
France

Location
14km N W of BAYEUX
in: Ste-Honorine-des-Pertes
Railway station: 13km
Airport: Caen-Carpiquet 20km
car essential

Pascal has a gentle, quiet and reserved manner. He works on site at the stables where he trains the horses and organises activities. Stables can even be rented for those travelling by horseback! The main farmhouse is located 800m from the beach. The spacious and pleasant guest bedrooms are in a separate building where there is also a seating area available for guests.

Fabienne & Pascal CHEMEL
'Ecurie St Siméon',
14520 STE-HONORINE-DES-PERTES
Tel: (0) 2 31 51 94 63 / (0) 670 06 99 34
fabienne.chemel@wanadoo.fr
www.ecuriestsimeon.com

Price Structure – 2 Bedrooms
2 rooms: shower room, wc, double bed, single bed:
€50 – 2 people €70 – 3 people

Extra Bed: €20
Capacity: 6 people

Facilities: private parking, garden, lounge, hosts have pets, babies welcome, free cot, 100% no smoking, hiking, sea watersports 1km, golf course 4km
Fluent English spoken

Directions: From Bayeux, D6 towards Port-en-Bessin. Take the D514 on the left. Cross Ste-Honorine, and 'Ecurie St Siméon' is on the left (signposted).

14.64 Bayeux

Private Home

Bienvenue
on
France

Location
14km N W of BAYEUX
in: Ste-Honorine-des-Pertes
Railway station: 11km

This British couple have been living in France for 13 years, first at Limoges, then the Somme and now in Normandy where Colin is a tourist guide (minibus tours to the Normandy landing beaches). Enjoy the family atmosphere in their newly built bungalow where they live with their three young children. The family guest rooms are simply furnished and have an independent entrance. The veranda is reserved for guests for relaxation.

Lisa & Colin GILLARD
'Omaha Heights', 2 rue des Bâteaux,
14520 STE-HONORINE-DES-PERTES
Tel: (0) 2 31 22 26 09 / (0) 680 08 68 63
Fax: (0) 2 31 22 26 09
colingillard@orange.fr
www.somme-normandy-tours.com

Price Structure – 2 Bedrooms
television, shower room, wc, washbasin, double bed, 2 single beds: €55 – 2 people €65 – 4 people
television, shower room, wc, washbasin, double bed, single bed: €55 – 2 people €65 – 3 people

Reduction: groups
Capacity: 7 people

Facilities: private parking, garden, tv lounge, hosts have pets, pets not accepted, babies welcome, free cot, 100% no smoking, closed: 23/12–03/01, vineyard 2km, golf course 3km, sea watersports 3km
Fluent English spoken

Directions: From Bayeux, D6 towards Port-en-Bessin. Take the D514 on the left for 3km then at the entrance to the village turn right into Rue des Bâteaux. The house is the first on the right.

Location
6km N of BAYEUX
in: Vaux-sur-Aure
Railway station: 6km
Airport: Caen-Carpiquet 40km
car essential

Private Home

Aptly named, this house is completely lost in the heart of the countryside, surrounded by fields and nature. The bedrooms, laid out around a square courtyard full of plants, are on the first floor. They all benefit from an independent entrance and have a comfortable, contemporary style with painted wood furniture, thick curtains and flowers from the garden. In summer, breakfast can be served in the large, heated veranda, as can good home-cooked dinners (*pot au feu*, regional cheeseboard). Marie-Christine is very personable and will happily chat to you about her experiences with the theatre and her travels.

Marie-Christine TEILLANT
'Côté Campagne', Le Lieu Aubin,
14400 VAUX-SUR-AURE
Tel: (0) 2 31 92 53 56 / 31 92 53 56
cote.campagne@wanadoo.fr
www.campagne-en-normandie.com

Facilities: off-street parking, garden, lounge, hosts have pets, pets not accepted, dinner available, babies welcome, free cot, golf course 5km, gliding 5km, hiking 6km, fishing 10km
Adequate English spoken

Price Structure – 2 Bedrooms and 1 Apartment
'Fleurs de Pommier' & 'Fleurs de Jardin': shower room, wc, 2 double beds: €48 – 2 people
€80 – 4 people
'Apartment l'Ecurie': lounge, kitchen, shower room, wc, double bed, single bed: €48 – 2 people
€65 – 3 people

Capacity: 11 people

Directions: Bayeux north ring-road, D104 towards Vaux-sur-Aure for 3km, then just before the small bridge at the entrance to the village, take the D135 on the left towards Maison for 3km.

Location
15km N E of BAYEUX
in: Ver-sur-Mer, station pick-up on arrival/departure
Railway station: 15km
Airport: Caen-Carpiquet 25km
car essential

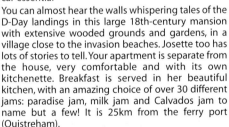

Residence of Outstanding Character

You can almost hear the walls whispering tales of the D-Day landings in this large 18th-century mansion with extensive wooded grounds and gardens, in a village close to the invasion beaches. Josette too has lots of stories to tell. Your apartment is separate from the house, very comfortable and with its own kitchenette. Breakfast is served in her beautiful kitchen, with an amazing choice of over 30 different jams: paradise jam, milk jam and Calvados jam to name but a few! It is 25km from the ferry port (Ouistreham).

Josette BOURRY
'Castel Provence', 7 rue de la Libération,
14114 VER-SUR-MER
Tel: (0) 2 31 22 22 19 / (0) 681 19 87 63
Fax: (0) 2 31 22 22 19
josette@castelprovence.fr
www.castelprovence.fr

Facilities: private parking, extensive grounds, lounge, hosts have pets, pets not accepted, kitchen, babies welcome, free cot, 100% no smoking, 2 nights minimum stay: 01/01–28/02, fishing 2km, sea watersports 2km, golf course 25km, bird-watching 25km
Fluent English spoken

Price Structure – 1 Apartment
Apartment: kitchen, shower room, wc, double bed: €60

Extra Bed: €20
Reduction: 01/10–31/03, 4 nights
Capacity: 2 people

Directions: At Bayeux, take the D12 for Sommervieu then Ver-sur-Mer. The house is just after the church, on the right. Look for the 'Bed & Breakfast France' sign.

Normandy – Bayeux

14.49 Bayeux

Private Home

Location
15km N E of BAYEUX
in: Ver-sur-Mer
Railway station: 15km
car essential

People stay with Marie-Rose because of her warm welcome and her stories. She landed here in 1945, a short time after the invasion, and she will tell you about the times when this place was a lively guesthouse which has now been transformed into a quieter and smaller B&B. She will tell you how to walk to Gold Beach, one of the D-Day invasion beaches. She is a master in the art of jam-making and is always ready to assist and help you with those little extras that make a stay so pleasant.

Marie-Rose LE DARD
'Chambres d'hôtes', 5 rue de la Libération,
14114 VER-SUR-MER
Tel: (0) 2 31 22 21 78

Price Structure – 4 Bedrooms
washbasin, double bed, single bed: €37 – 2 people
€46 – 3 people
3 rooms: washbasin, double bed: €37

Reduction: 7 nights, children
Capacity: 9 people

Facilities: garden, hosts have pets, kitchen, 100% no smoking, 1 shared shower room, wc
Adequate English spoken

Directions: At Bayeux take the D12 for Sommervieu and then Ver-sur-Mer. No. 5 is after the church on the right. Look for the blue shutters.

14.63 Bayeux

Château/Manor House

Location
15km N E of BAYEUX
in: Ver-sur-Mer
Railway station: 15km
Airport: Caen-Carpiquet 25km

Huguette and Richard are very welcoming and Huguette is very outgoing and loves to chat. Their passion is renovating their manor house dating back to the 12th and 14th centuries. It stands on wooded grounds crossed by the river 'La Provence' (for that touch of sunshine!), where ducks swim. Despite the renovations in hand, you benefit from excellent value for money and the assurance of a pleasant stay. Join your hosts visiting *brocantes*, cider farms or benefit from their knowledge of Bayeux. Homemade jams for breakfast.

Huguette & Richard ANDREAK
'Manoir de la Marefontaine', N°24,
14114 VER-SUR-MER
Tel: (0) 2 31 51 76 58 / (0) 667 83 26 51
Fax: (0) 2 31 51 76 58
marefontaine@wanadoo.fr
http://perso.wanadoo.fr/marefontaine

Price Structure – 2 Bedrooms
'Mathilde': television, shower room, wc, double bed: €70
'Polonaise': television, shower room, wc, 2 double beds: €70 – 2 people €120 – 4 people

Extra Bed: €25
Capacity: 6 people

Facilities: private parking, extensive grounds, tv lounge, hosts have pets, pets not accepted, babies welcome, free cot, 100% no smoking, hiking, cycling, fishing 2km, sea watersports 2km, golf course 15km, riversports 25km
Basic English spoken

Directions: From Caen, ring road North, exit 5 direction Douvres-la-Délivrande and go to Courseulles-sur-Mer then Ver-sur-Mer. In the village, go towards Crépon and turn left into the sixth road (after the church).

Location

11km E of BAYEUX
in: Villiers-le-Sec, station pick-up on arrival/departure
Railway station: 11km
Airport: Caen-Carpiquet 15km
car essential

Residence of Outstanding Character

Fall under the spell of this part of Normandy, easily done when staying in this former residence of a justice official from the 17th century; a unique and authentic site. Typical of the manor houses and fortress farms of the Bessin are the large walled courtyard and beautiful undulating garden and pond. It is located just a few steps from the large bell tower in the centre of the village. The décor in the comfortable bedrooms, reached via a restored staircase, evoke a warm and restful ambience. Geneviève is a doctor.

Geneviève COQUET
'La Maison du Bailli', 2 route de Courseulles,
14480 VILLIERS-LE-SEC
Tel: (0) 2 31 37 61 70 / (0) 615 04 87 50
lamaisondubailli@yahoo.fr
www.maison-du-bailli.com

Facilities: private parking, garden, lounge, pets not accepted, babies welcome, free cot, 100% no smoking, closed: 5/01–31/01, bird-watching, hiking, sea watersports 7km, interesting flora 10km, golf course 20km
Adequate English spoken

Price Structure – 1 Bedroom and 1 Suite
'Ce soir ou jamais': television, bathroom, wc, twin beds: €70
'Petite Chérie': television, shower room, wc, double bed (king-size). En-suite room, television, twin beds: €70 – 2 people €110 – 4 people

Extra Bed: €10
Reduction: 01/12–31/03, 2 nights
Capacity: 6 people

Directions: From Bayeux take the D12 to Villiers-le-Sec (11km). The house is on this road in the centre of the village on the right.

Location

CABOURG
in: Cabourg, station pick-up on arrival/departure
Railway station: 20km
Airport: Caen-Carpiquet 20km

Private Home

The sea and the Promenade Marcel Proust are only 300m away from these spacious rooms, pleasantly furnished and with WIFI access. Anne provides a warm welcome in this typically Norman-style house. She goes out of her way to ensure that you have a pleasant stay. Each bedroom has its own private space in the garden where you can relax in peace. In the winter, Anne organises foie gras courses, which include both traditional and modern recipes, and also painting courses.

Anne DELBAC
'Villa Aurore', 5 boulevard des Diablotins,
14390 CABOURG
Tel: (0) 2 31 24 41 87 / (0) 673 84 69 79
aurore.calvados@free.fr
http://aurore.calvados.free.fr

Facilities: garden, lounge, hosts have pets, internet access, dinner available, babies welcome, free cot, 100% no smoking, closed: 15/12–15/02, fishing, hiking, sea watersports, golf course 2km
Fluent English spoken

Price Structure – 4 Bedrooms
'Bleue': television, shower room, wc, double bed: €56,50
'Les Fleurs', 'Belle Epoque' & 'Istanbul': television, shower room, wc, twin beds: €56,50

Extra Bed: €50,75
Reduction: 3 nights
Capacity: 8 people

Directions: As you enter Cabourg on the A13, turn left towards Caen by the church. Then go towards Ouistreham for about 300m. Cross the junction and the house in on the left, towards the sea.

Normandy – Bayeux, Cabourg

14.022 Cabourg

Private Home

Colette DELETRAZ
'La Raspelière', 2 rue du Commerce,
14390 CABOURG
Tel: (0) 2 31 91 40 59 / (0) 617 22 43 63
raspeliere@free.fr
http://raspeliere.free.fr

Price Structure – 5 Bedrooms
'Rivebelle': television, bathroom, wc, shower, double bed (queen-size): €80
'Cambremer': television, bathroom, wc, double bed (queen-size): €80
'Oriane' & 'Guermantes': television, bathroom, wc, shower, double bed (queen-size): €90
'Villeparisis': lounge, television, bathroom, wc, shower, double bed (queen-size): €120

Extra Bed: €20
Capacity: 10 people

Location
CABOURG
in: Cabourg
Railway station: Cabourg
Airport: Caen-Carpiquet 19km

Really warm, welcoming, talkative. . . in fact 'the perfect hostess' is how we would describe Colette. She lives in the heart of Cabourg, a short walk from the beach. She is just retired and has had the wonderful idea of doing B&B. The house has just been refurbished, with new bedrooms with lots of space, and is well organised with WIFI access, trendily decorated and very 'zen'. Enjoy breakfast overlooking the garden from the large bay windows. You will like the combination of friendliness and comfort here.

Facilities: garden, tv lounge, pets not accepted, internet access, babies welcome, free cot, 100% no smoking, closed: 1/01–15/02
Adequate English spoken

Directions: Please contact your host in advance for detailed directions.

14.23 Cabourg

Residence of Outstanding Character

Evelyne & Olivier PAZ
'Domaine de la Londe', chemin de l'Anguille,
14860 ROBEHOMME
Tel: (0) 2 31 78 28 69 / (0) 616 34 10 72
pazoliv@aol.com
www.lalonde.netavoo.com

Price Structure – 2 Bedrooms and 2 Apartments
'Verte': television, bathroom, wc, double bed (queen-size), single bed: €60 – 2 people
€80 – 3 people
'Cigogne': television, shower room, wc, double bed, single bed: €60 – 2 people €80 – 3 people
'Héron' & 'Furet': lounge, television, kitchen, shower room, wc, double bed: €75

Extra Bed: €20
Reduction: 7 nights
Capacity: 10 people

Location
9km S of CABOURG
in: Robehomme
Ferry port: 12km
Airport: Caen-Carpiquet 20km
car essential

Between Ouistreham and Cabourg, a few minutes from the beaches of the Côte Fleurie, is this comfortable, charming property in a beautiful setting. Former cider producers, they now rear horses, with a dozen grazing in over 30 hectares. The bedrooms are in the 18th-century *Maison de Maître* or the outbuildings. Quiet, with period furniture and independent entrances, some have equipped kitchens (fridge, washing machine) and a lounge. Olivier is the mayor of the neighbouring village, so an excellent source of advice!

Facilities: off-street parking, garden, hosts have pets, pets not accepted, dinner available, babies welcome, free cot, bird-watching, hiking, interesting flora, fishing 5km, golf course 10km, sea watersports 10km
Adequate English spoken

Directions: From Caen, A13 motorway direction Paris exit 29 or 29b. At Dozulé D400 towards Cabourg for 4km to the roundabout then turn left towards Varaville for 2km. Turn left into the winding Chemin de l'Anguille. The 'Domaine de la Londe' is on the right after 2.5km.

Location
22km S E of CABOURG
in: St-Laurent-du-Mont, station pick-up
on arrival/departure
Railway station: 12km
Airport: 28km
car essential

✳ ✳ ✳

**Residence of
Outstanding
Character**

Just 20 minutes from Deauville is this comfortable 18th-century house furnished with exquisite taste. From the garden there is a panoramic view over the valley and La Suisse Normande. Local excursions, delicious homemade jam, and relaxed hours spent at the table with Michel and Dany will add to your enjoyment (the *poulet au cidre* is a masterpiece!).

Facilities: off-street parking, extensive grounds, tv lounge, hosts have pets, pets not accepted, dinner available, 100% no smoking, 2 nights minimum stay: 01/07–31/08, golf course 25km, sea watersports 25km
Adequate English spoken

Directions: Exit Cabourg, on the A13. Take the D49 towards Carrefour-St-Jean (N13) where you turn left onto the D50 towards Cambremer. The house is on the bend as you go up the hill, on the right.

Dany & Michel BERNARD
'Le Clos de St-Laurent', St-Laurent-du-Mont,
14340 CAMBREMER
Tel: (0) 2 31 63 47 04 / (0) 603 46 32 26
mikdan@wanadoo.fr
http://clos.stlaurent.free.fr

Price Structure – 4 Bedrooms and 1 Suite
'La Maison de José' (our favourite room): lounge, television, shower room, wc, double bed. En-suite room, twin beds. En-suite room, single bed: €98 – 2 people €125 – 5 people
'Orange': television, along corridor bathroom, wc, double bed: €56
'Rose': shower room, wc, double bed, single bed: €56 – 2 people €75 – 3 people
'Jaune': television, bathroom, wc, double bed: €56
'Bleuet': television, shower room, wc, double bed: €56

Extra Bed: €18   **Reduction:** 2 nights
Capacity: 14 people

Location
18km S of CAEN
in: Cauvicourt
Railway station: 20km
car essential

✳ ✳ ✳

Private Home

Large pastures, forests and meadows surround this typical family farmhouse with a large courtyard. A fairly steep stairway leads to the entrance of the autonomous duplex-style bedroom. Under a sloping ceiling, with large Velux windows, it is well furnished and equipped with a kitchenette (and multi-jet shower). On the rustic terrace by the garden and the vegetable plot is an astonishing 9m long pool, to delight adults and children alike! Horses can be put out to grass and stabled here. A friendly welcome from Philippe, a doctor.

Facilities: private parking, extensive grounds, lounge, hosts have pets, pets not accepted, dinner available, babies welcome, free cot, hiking, cycling, interesting flora, golf course 5km, mushroom-picking 6km, gliding 15km, riversports 15km, sea watersports 30km
Basic English spoken

Directions: Exit 13 on the Caen south ring-road: périphérique Sud de Caen. Then the N158 towards Alençon, Falaise for 15km until Cauvicourt. When facing the church, take the lane 'Haussé' on the right. Continue to the end.

Isabelle & Philippe CAYÉ
'Ferme de la Ruette', 5 chemin Haussé,
14190 CAUVICOURT
Tel: (0) 2 31 78 11 82 / (0) 684 60 15 91
Fax: (0) 2 31 78 00 62
edouard612@hotmail.com

Price Structure – 1 Apartment
Television, kitchen, shower room, wc, double bed, single bed: €50 – 2 people €60 – 3 people

Extra Bed: €10
Capacity: 3 people

Normandy – Cabourg, Caen

14.007 Caen

Residence of Outstanding Character

Jacques LARSON
'Le Cottage', 2 rue de Langrais, 14930 MALTOT
Tel: (0) 2 31 26 96 10 / (0) 678 99 31 46
jack.larson@wanadoo.fr

Price Structure – 4 Bedrooms
'Hermes': shower room, wc, double bed, 2 single beds: €42 – 2 people €67 – 4 people
'Dior': television, along corridor bathroom, wc, double bed, single bed: €42 – 2 people
€57 – 3 people
'Chanel' & 'Cardin': shower room, wc, double bed: €42

Capacity: 11 people

Location
7km S W of CAEN
in: Maltot
Railway station: 7km
Airport: Caen-Carpiquet 6km
car essential

This is a newly built house in a quiet location with large, shady and well-maintained grounds with a play area for the children. The guest bedrooms are named after inspirational fashion houses: 'Chanel', 'Dior', 'Hermes'. . . You are located in the centre of Caen with a notable history all the way back to William the Conqueror! From here be sure to visit and take in the Peace Memorial, the coastline, the cider farms, the typical farming *bocage* countryside, Bayeux. . . the list goes on. . .

Facilities: off-street parking, extensive grounds, pets not accepted, 100% no smoking, hiking 3km, cycling 3km, golf course 12km, bird-watching 13km, sea watersports 20km
Basic English spoken

Directions: From the centre of Caen, at the Zenith roundabout, head in the direction of Louvigny. At the following roundabout, head for direction Maltot via the D212. The house is on the right.

14.42 Caen

Private Home

Ginette & Gérard CHAPEL
'La Bruyère', route du Val de May,
14320 MAY-SUR-ORNE
Tel: (0) 2 31 79 68 01 / (0) 630 68 41 16
Fax: (0) 2 31 79 68 01
chapel@aol.com

Price Structure – 2 Bedrooms, 1 Suite and 1 Apartment
'Tilleul-Mezzanine' (our favourite room): television, bathroom, wc, double bed, twin beds:
€75 – 2 people €90 – 4 people
'Soleil-Mezzanine': shower room, wc, double bed, twin beds: €65 – 2 people €90 – 4 people
'Arome': shower room, wc, double bed: €65
en-suite room 'Marine': shower room, wc, double bed: €55
apartment: television, kitchen, shower room, wc, double bed. En-suite room, shower room, wc, twin beds: €75 – 2 people €110 – 4 people

Extra Bed: €17   **Capacity:** 16 people

Location
10km S of CAEN
in: May-sur-Orne, station pick-up on arrival/departure
Ferry port: 12km
Airport: Caen-Carpiquet 15km
car essential

This house is perched high up, between a meander in the River Orne, in the heart of the countryside. It is a beautiful house with lakes and tennis courts, yet only five minutes from Caen and 15 minutes from the War Memorial. The bedrooms have been redecorated with great care. 'Tilleul' has a balcony and a superb view of the Orne Valley. There are also two bedrooms with mini-bedlofts for the children. Ginette and Gérard are ex-hoteliers and their skill as hosts is evident. Take care to supervise your children at the water's edge.

Facilities: private parking, extensive grounds, tv lounge, hosts have pets, kitchen, babies welcome, free cot, 100% no smoking, private tennis court, hiking, cycling, fishing, mushroom-picking, riversports, golf course 8km, sea watersports 20km
Basic English spoken

Directions: At Caen, on the southern ring road, exit 11 towards Laval on the D562 and continue for 5km. At the traffic lights at May-sur-Orne, turn right and take the first on the left, then the third on the right. Follow signs for 'Le Val de May', then look for the 'Bed & Breakfast France' sign.

Location
DEAUVILLE
in: Deauville
Railway station: 1km
Airport: Deauville St-Gatien 4km

Bienvenue en France

✹ ✹ ✹

Private Home

You are in the centre of Deauville close to the port, so once you have arrived, park your car and soak up the charms of Deauville on foot. Isabelle has bought the house next door to hers to be better able to receive guests. A sunny terrace separates the two houses. Everything is new inside and you have a complete house at your disposal with a lounge (TV & DVD) and a kitchen at your disposal. Isabelle is quiet and gentle and paints during her spare time. She also has a predilection for chickens!

Facilities: tv lounge, hosts have pets, babies welcome, free cot, fishing, hiking, cycling, sea watersports, golf course 2km, vineyard 10km, riversports 15km
Fluent English spoken

Directions: Head down the Quai de la Marine opposite the train station, pass in front of the IBIS hotel. At the next roundabout decorated with flowers, take the road in the middle. The house is 50m further on.

Isabelle LARATTE
'La Cerisée', 15 rue du Général Leclerc,
14800 DEAUVILLE
Tel: (0) 2 31 81 18 29 / (0) 683 16 51 19
Fax: (0) 2 31 81 18 29
la.cerisee@wanadoo.fr

Price Structure – 1 Apartment
lounge, television, kitchen, shower room, wc, double bed (queen-size), 2 single beds (child-size):
€100 – 2 people €120 – 4 people

Extra Bed: €20
Reduction: 2 nights
Capacity: 4 people

Location
DEAUVILLE
in: Deauville
Railway station: 1km
Airport: Deauville St-Gatien 9km

Bienvenue en France

✹ ✹ ✹ ✹

Apartment

This is what you would expect at Deauville: comfort, a warm welcome and a touch of class. This flat is in the heart of the town, a few steps from the casino and the beach with its famous boardwalk. Michèle and Lionel have pulled out all the stops to make sure you have a wonderful stay and nothing has been overlooked; there is as a well stocked mini-bar, tea and coffee, flat-screen TV. . . in fact all you would expect in a big hotel, but with the charm of a B&B, where you are received as a friend.

Facilities: tv lounge, pets not accepted, 100% no smoking, cycling, sea watersports, golf course 3km
Adequate English spoken

Directions: At Deauville follow signs to the Centre-Ville and La Plage. The residence is in the pedestrian street, opposite the casino entrance.

Michèle & Lionel PRUVOT
'Nuit à Deauville', Résidence Dosia, place du Casino, 14800 DEAUVILLE
Tel: (0) 2 31 14 96 11 Fax: (0) 2 31 14 96 11
contact@nuitadeauville.com
www.nuitadeauville.com

Price Structure – 1 Bedroom
television, shower room, wc, double bed: €160

Reduction: 1/10–30/04
Capacity: 2 people

Normandy – Deauville

14.44 Deauville

Private Home

Laurence CHAPUIS
'La Cabane à Flot', 4 avenue Hocquart de Turtot,
14800 DEAUVILLE
Tel: / (0) 620 98 37 48
lacabaneaflot@wanadoo.fr
http://perso.orange.fr/lacabaneaflot

Price Structure – 2 Bedrooms
television, bathroom, wc, double bed: €50
television, shower room, wc, double bed, single bed
(child-size): €50 – 2 people €60 – 3 people

Capacity: 5 people

Location
DEAUVILLE
in: Deauville
Railway station: Deauville
Airport: Deauville St-Gatien 10km

Laurence offers simple hospitality in this little maisonette, perfumed with incense and set amongst the houses that once lodged stable-boys servicing the grand houses for which Deauville is known. An alley of plants lead to your room which is independent and behind the house. 'La Cabane' is cosy with subtle oriental décor and an extra futon bed (the bathroom and wc are separated off). Horse-riding, polo, the beaches and the casino are less than 500m away. Laurence can advise you on all the best places to eat and where to go out.

Facilities: tv lounge, pets not accepted, 100% no smoking, fishing, hiking, cycling, sea watersports
Adequate English spoken

Directions: From the A13 on arrival at Deauville, head towards the hippodrome, continue ahead and pass in front of the hippodrome. When you can no longer continue straight ahead, turn right into Avenue Hocquart de Turtot.

14.28 Deauville

Private Home

François VOISIN
'Villa Janine', 159 avenue Michel d'Ornano,
14910 BLONVILLE-SUR-MER
Tel: (0) 2 31 81 39 79 / (0) 677 11 77 17
Fax: (0) 2 31 14 04 76
contact@villajanine.com
www.villajanine.com

Price Structure – 2 Bedrooms and 1 Suite
suite 'Le Pressoir': 'Pommeau': lounge, along corridor
shower room, wc, double bed. En-suite room,
double bed: €127 – 4 people
'Calvados' & 'Poiré': shower room, wc, twin beds: €75

Extra Bed: €20
Reduction: 2 nights
Capacity: 8 people

Location
4km S W of DEAUVILLE
in: Blonville-sur-Mer, station pick-up
on arrival/departure
Railway station: 5km
Airport: Deauville St-Gatien 12km

An enviable location. right by the sea and near to Deauville. This typical Anglo-Norman house has been renovated by François and Yvette, former *traiteurs*. Their comfortable home offers a range of facilities: a safe, welcome trays, games. The carefully decorated bedrooms on two floors look out to sea just 50m away! 'Le Pressoir' is ideal for a family. There is a sitting room, a garden, a terrace and a private path to the beach. Breakfast (or even brunch) can be served on the veranda. An enthusiastic, sincere welcome.

Facilities: private parking, garden, tv lounge, pets not accepted, babies welcome, free cot, 100% no smoking, 2 nights minimum stay, closed: 1/01–31/01, fishing, bird-watching, hiking, cycling, interesting flora, sea watersports, golf course 3km
Basic English spoken

Directions: Blonville-sur-Mer is on the coast between Deauville and Cabourg. The house is on the coastal road on the side of Villiers-sur-Mer.

Location
4km S W of DEAUVILLE
in: Blonville-sur-Mer
Railway station: 4km
Airport: Deauville St-Gatien 10km

Bienvenue en France

Private Home

This place deserves three 'suns' just for the location alone! On a coast covered with flowers by captivating, lively seaside resorts is this impressive house overlooking the pier and beach. It oozes the romantic style of the area that has inspired so many artists and writers. We liked the 'Poisson' bedroom, which is spacious and opens out onto the sea. The walled garden has tables and chairs and games – plus another bonus if you have children: Catherine will be delighted to babysit, so you can dine out with complete peace of mind. Charge for pets: €4 per day.

**Catherine DE PREAUMONT
50 avenue d'Ornano,
14910 BLONVILLE-SUR-MER
Tel: (0) 2 31 98 18 32 Fax: (0) 2 31 98 18 32
cathome@free.fr
http://cathome.free.fr**

Facilities: private parking, garden, lounge, wheelchair access, hiking, cycling, fishing, bird-watching, sea watersports, golf course 8km
Adequate English spoken

Price Structure – 3 Bedrooms and 1 Suite
'Poisson' (our favourite room): bathroom, wc, twin beds, 2 single beds (child-size): €85 – 2 people €115 – 4 people
'Ecossaise': wheelchair access, along corridor shower room, wc, washbasin, double bed: €58
'Fleurie': shower room, wc, double bed: €72
suite 'Montgolfière': shower room, wc, twin beds, 2 single beds. En-suite room, 3 single beds: €65 – 2 people €140 – 7 people

Directions: At Deauville, take the D513 towards Houlgate. When you reach Blonville, the house is on this road, number 50.

Extra Bed: €15   **Reduction:** groups
Capacity: 15 people

Location
17km S of DEAUVILLE
in: Clarbec, station pick-up on arrival/departure
Railway station: 9km
Airport: Deauville St-Gatien 25km
car essential

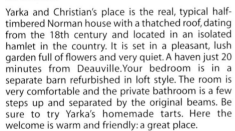

Bienvenue en France

**Residence of
Outstanding
Character**

Yarka and Christian's place is the real, typical half-timbered Norman house with a thatched roof, dating from the 18th century and located in an isolated hamlet in the country. It is set in a pleasant, lush garden full of flowers and very quiet. A haven just 20 minutes from Deauville. Your bedroom is in a separate barn refurbished in loft style. The room is very comfortable and the private bathroom is a few steps up and separated by the original beams. Be sure to try Yarka's homemade tarts. Here the welcome is warm and friendly: a great place.

**Yarka & Christian DAVY
'La Maison de Yarka', Le Lieu Cardine,
14130 CLARBEC
Tel: (0) 610 50 16 74
yarka4@gmail.com
yarka4.googlepages.com**

Facilities: off-street parking, garden, pets not accepted, 100% no smoking, 2 nights minimum stay, closed: 15/11–31/03, hiking, cycling, riversports 9km, vineyard 10km, golf course 16km, sea watersports 20km
Fluent English spoken

Price Structure – 1 Bedroom
lounge, television, bathroom, wc, shower, double bed (queen-size): €80

Extra Bed: €60
Reduction: 4 nights
Capacity: 2 people

Directions: On the A13, exit 29a La Haie Tondue. Then take the D16 towards Falaise then the D45 on the left towards Lisieux. After the junction with the D280 for Clarbec, take the next lane on the left. It is the second house on the left.

Normandy – Deauville

14.55 Deauville

Residence of Outstanding Character

Hannah & Cyril LE PAGE
'Domaine du Clos Joli', route de Honfleur,
14130 ST-GATIEN-DES-BOIS
Tel: (0) 2 31 64 68 89

Price Structure – 4 Bedrooms and 1 Apartment
'Dorée': bathroom, wc, double bed: €65
'Rouge': shower room, wc, double bed: €60
'Bleue': shower room, wc, washbasin, twin beds: €50
'Jaune': double bed: €45
'Beige': lounge, television, kitchen, shower room, wc, double bed: €80

Extra Bed: €15
Capacity: 10 people

Location
11km E of DEAUVILLE
in: St-Gatien-des-Bois, station pick-up on arrival/departure
Railway station: 13km
Airport: Deauville St-Gatien 7km
car essential

Bienvenue en France

This place is on the D114 between the famous resort of Deauville and Honfleur, one of the prettiest Normandy ports, whose old buildings and their façades have enthralled many artists. Hannah's villa, which dates from the 19th century and is typical of the splendid past of this town, reflects her unique style with its collection of objects from her native land, Kenya. Her husband has complemented this with many other souvenirs from his travels. The house has extensive wooded grounds.

Facilities: private parking, extensive grounds, lounge, pets not accepted, 100% no smoking, 1 shared shower room, wc, golf course 4km, sea watersports 10km, riversports 10km, vineyard 10km
Fluent English spoken

Directions: From the A29 exit 2, then take the D144 towards Pont-l'Evêque for 4km. The house is on the left of this road, just after the junction with the D579 which goes towards Honfleur.

14.78 Deauville

Private Home

Brigitte & Jacky BERTHAULT
'Millenium', Le Clos des Haras, 4 rue des Herbages, 14130 ST-GATIEN-DES-BOIS
Tel: (0) 2 31 64 13 30 / (0) 607 77 21 29
laura.ludivine@wanadoo.fr
milleniumhote.free.fr

Price Structure – 2 Bedrooms
'Terres Lointaines': television, shower room, wc, double bed (queen-size): €65
'Plages du Nord': shower room, wc, double bed: €55

Extra Bed: €15
Reduction: 1/10–30/03, children
Capacity: 4 people

Location
11km E of DEAUVILLE
in: St-Gatien-des-Bois, station pick-up on arrival/departure
Railway station: 8km
Airport: Deauville St-Gatien 3km
car essential

Near to Deauville, Honfleur and the beaches is this newly built house in a residential area surrounded by greenery. The house is well laid out with a bright communal room where breakfast is served by the large bay windows. The two lovely neutral-coloured bedrooms are brightened up with embroidery and patchwork by the talented Brigitte. Each bedroom is equipped with hydro-jet showers and there is a microwave and a fridge in the more spacious 'Terres Lointaines' room.

Facilities: off-street parking, garden, tv lounge, hosts have pets, babies welcome, free cot, cycling, golf course 1km, mushroom-picking 1km, hiking 1km, interesting flora 1km, gliding 3km, vineyard 4km, sea watersports 7km
Adequate English spoken

Directions: On the A29, exit 2 south of Honfleur. D144 then D579 direction Pont-l'Evêque for 8km then D74 on the right towards St-Gatien-des-Bois. Turn left opposite the hotel 'Le Clos St-Gatien', then take the second turn on the left and it is the second house on the right.

Location
15km S E of DEAUVILLE
in: St-Hymer
Railway station: 5km
Airport: Deauville St-Gatien 15km
car essential

✸ ✸ ✸

Residence of Outstanding Character

The countryside here, known as *bocage*, is full of wonderful villages with half-timbered houses and old farms where you can taste cider and other local produce. It is one of the prettiest parts of Normandy and it's where, in a green corner of the countryside, Isabelle has two bedrooms for her guests. Visit Deauville and the Côte Fleurie which are just 20 minutes' drive away.

Isabelle & Bruno MEZERAY
'La Cour du Four', chemin de la Chancellerie,
14130 ST-HYMER
Tel: (0) 2 31 64 34 63 / (0) 682 34 34 24
isabelle.mezeray@wanadoo.fr
www.locations-lacourdufour.com

Facilities: off-street parking, garden, tv lounge, hosts have pets, pets not accepted, dinner available, 100% no smoking, hiking, sea watersports 4km, cycling 5km, fishing 5km, golf course 8km
Adequate English spoken

Price Structure – 2 Bedrooms
2 rooms: shower room, wc, double bed, single bed:
€50 – 2 people €62 – 3 people

Extra Bed: €12
Capacity: 6 people

Directions: On the A13, exit Pont-l'Evêque. In the town head towards Caen on the N175. Turn left onto the D48 towards Lisieux. Go under the autoroute, take the first on the right (D101) towards Cambremer. At the next crossroads continue straight on for 900m. Chemin de la Chancellerie is on the left. Continue right to the very end.

Location
25km S E of DEAUVILLE
in: St-Philbert-des-Champs
car essential

Private Home

As we go to press, this host has not yet been classified, but will be shortly. This is how you imagine Normandy. It is green, there are deck chairs, Deauville is close by with its casinos, boardwalks, film festival, half-timbered buildings and camembert. There is something for everyone, whether they come for the yearling sales, as punters at the races, or pilgrims to pray at the shrine of Ste Thérèse at Lisieux. Chez Aaron the bedrooms are pleasant, the breakfast copious and it is quiet. You cannot go far wrong here.

Aaron LEDERFAJN
'La Bergerie', Le Bourg,
14130 ST-PHILBERT-DES-CHAMPS
Tel: (0) 2 31 64 33 60
contact@chambresdhotes-labergerie.com
www.chambresdhotes-labergerie.com

Facilities: off-street parking, extensive grounds, tv lounge, pets not accepted, dinner available, 100% no smoking, wheelchair access

Price Structure – 4 Bedrooms
'Cannelle': television, shower room, wc, double bed (queen-size), single bed: €100 – 2 people
€130 – 3 people
'Lavande': wheelchair access, television, shower room, wc, double bed, single bed: €100 – 2 people
€130 – 3 people
'Safran': television, shower room, wc, double bed (queen-size): €100
'Vanille': television, shower room, wc, double bed: €100

Extra Bed: €30
Capacity: 10 people

Directions: From the A13, exit Deauville and take the spur for Lisieux for about 9km. Then turn left for Le Breuil-en-Auge and at the first set of lights, in front of the post office (*La Poste*), turn left for St-Philbert-des-Champs. In front of the church, head towards Moyaux and it is the sixth house on the right.

Normandy – Deauville

14.08 Deauville

Château/Manor House

Location
10km S E of DEAUVILLE
in: Toutlaville
Railway station: 3km
Airport: Caen-Carpiquet 50km
car essential

Near Deauville and Honfleur is this beautiful château in vast grounds with age-old trees. Once belonging to painters it will certainly move you too. It is characteristic of the region with its strata of black and white flint, but is uniquely adorned with baroque features. The interior has been overhauled (work still ongoing) and the impressive dining and living rooms are open to you. Isabelle, warm-hearted and dynamic, has boldly mixed different styles. The bedrooms with canopies, fabrics and period furniture also boast multi-jet showers.

Isabelle **LEVIEILS**
'Château de Toutlaville', Toutlaville,
14130 ST-MARTIN-AUX-CHARTRAINS
Tel: / (0) 673 86 90 27
Fax:(0) 2 31 98 84 67
info@chateau-deauville.com
www.chateau-deauville.com

Price Structure – 6 Bedrooms
'21' & '30': shower room, wc, double bed (queen-size): €120
'22': shower room, wc, double bed (queen-size): €110
'31': bathroom, wc, double bed: €100
'33': bathroom, wc, double bed (queen-size): €110
'19': shower room, wc, double bed (queen-size), single bed: €130 – 2 people €200 – 3 people

Extra Bed: €25
Reduction: 15/10–15/04, groups
Capacity: 13 people

Facilities: private parking, extensive grounds, tv lounge, hosts have pets, babies welcome, free cot, hiking, cycling, riversports 3km, golf course 7km, hunting 7km, sea watersports 7km
Adequate English spoken

Directions: From the A13 exit Pont-l'Evêque and take the N177 towards Deauville for 3.5km. Then take the D58 on the right towards Toutlaville for 400m. Just after the bridge, turn right.

14.39 Deauville

Private Home

Location
1km N of DEAUVILLE
in: Trouville-sur-Mer, station pick-up on arrival/departure
Railway station: Trouville-sur-Mer
Airport: Deauville St-Gatien 2km

On a hillside, in the centre of Trouville, is this *Maison de Maître* from the early 1900s. From the terrace or your bedroom window is a view of the port, the casino and at night, the lights of the fishing boats heading out to sea. A romantic and a touch old-fashioned family home with floral wallpaper, wrought-iron beds and tables, and flowers. '*Mignon*', says Annick. There is a blockhouse buried in the garden area and stairs lead down to the fishing port, the fish market, casino and restaurants. A charming and discreet welcome.

Annick **LANNOY**
'Le Vieux Logis', 28 avenue d'Eylau,
14360 TROUVILLE-SUR-MER
Tel: (0) 2 31 98 96 88 / (0) 684 77 37 13
annick.lannoy@wanadoo.fr

Price Structure – 2 Bedrooms
television, shower room, wc, washbasin, double bed: €112
bathroom, wc, shower, double bed: €112

Reduction: 1/10–15/04, 3 nights
Capacity: 4 people

Facilities: garden, sea watersports, golf course 2km, vineyard 5km

Directions: At the A13 exit head in the direction of Trouville-Deauville, then Trouville. Pass over the small bridge that separates the two towns and follow in the direction of Honfleur. Head up the hill and after passing in front of the church 'Notre Dame', take the second road on the right into Avenue D'Eylau.

Location
4km S W of DEAUVILLE
in: Vauville, station pick-up on arrival/departure
Railway station: 4km
Airport: Deauville St-Gatien 7km car essential

Residence of Outstanding Character

Your hostess has succeeded in creating a relaxed atmosphere where conversation flows freely in a wonderfully fragrant setting from the flora all around. 'Conducive to relaxing body and soul to melt away the stresses of daily life,' as your hostess would say. The house is newly built but in the typical Normandy architectural tradition and this style follows through to the prettily decorated bedrooms. Each one has an independent entrance and a small corner of garden. Breakfasts with homemade bread are completely organic.

FLORE
'L'Angelerie', chemin du Petit Vauville,
14800 VAUVILLE
Tel: (0) 2 31 87 10 97 / (0) 662 62 49 98
langelerie@wanadoo.fr

Facilities: private parking, extensive grounds, hosts have pets, 100% no smoking, gliding, cycling, golf course 2km, sea watersports 4km
Fluent English spoken

Price Structure – 1 Bedroom and 1 Apartment
'Coeur d'Artichaud': television, bathroom, wc, twin beds: €130
'Butterfly': lounge, television, kitchen, bathroom, wc, shower, twin beds, single bed: €150 – 2 people €170 – 3 people

Directions: A13 exit Deauville-Trouville. Then take the D27 direction Cean-Dozuléé-Tourgeville.

Extra Bed: €20
Reduction: 01/10–31/03, 2 nights
Capacity: 5 people

Location
25km W of FALAISE
in: Clécy
Ferry port: 45km
Airport: Caen-Carpiquet 45km

Private Home

In Suisse Normande, Clécy is a very pretty spot in the Orne Valley. On the river bank by steep wooded slopes and rocky escarpments is this family house. Handed down through generations it used to be a hotel-restaurant, but is now a B&B since Marie-Thérèse's retirement. The pull here is the backdrop and the garden. The bedrooms are fairly standard but for romantics, we recommend the maisonette by the river. An ideal base for boating, walks and rock-climbing and for dancing and feasting at the *guinguettes* down the river.

Facilities: private parking, garden, lounge, hosts have pets, 100% no smoking, wc, closed: 01/11–31/03, fishing, hiking, cycling, riversports, vineyard, golf course 3km
Fluent English spoken

Marie-Thérèse & Jackie BRION
'Le Pont du Vey', 14570 CLECY
Tel: (0) 2 31 69 72 90

Price Structure – 5 Bedrooms
shower room, wc, washbasin, 2 double beds: €46 – 2 people €64 – 4 people
shower, washbasin, double bed: €40
bathroom, wc, washbasin, double bed: €46
shower room, wc, washbasin, double bed, single bed: €46 – 2 people €58 – 3 people
shower room, wc, washbasin, double bed: €46

Directions: From the Caen ring-road, take exit 11 towards Flers. D562 to Clécy (30km). In the village, head towards Le Vey. The house is on the right by the bridge.

Extra Bed: €11,50
Capacity: 13 people

Normandy – Deauville, Falaise

14.018 Honfleur

Château/Manor House

Nathalie & François DESALOS
'Le Manoir du Petit St Pierre', chemin du Petit St Pierre, 14600 HONFLEUR
Tel: (0) 2 31 88 91 94 / (0) 615 94 64 12
contact@manoirsaintpierre.com
www.manoirsaintpierre.com

Price Structure – 5 Bedrooms
'Arum' & 'Coquelicot': shower room, wc, double bed (queen-size): €70
'Bleu Azur': bathroom, wc, 2 single beds: €85
'Coloniale': bathroom, wc, double bed (queen-size): €105
'Romantique': lounge, bathroom, wc, double bed (queen-size): €130

Extra Bed: €15
Reduction: 3 nights, groups
Capacity: 10 people

Location
HONFLEUR
in: Honfleur, station pick-up on arrival/departure
Railway station: 17km
Airport: Deauville St-Gatien 10km
car essential

Nathalie and François' place is on the heights of Honfleur, a haven of tranquillity in the country, just five minutes from the old port. Their welcome is warm in this former Norman cider-making house dating from the 18th century, which has now been transformed into a manor house in the local style. All the bedrooms, with separate entrance and access to the garden, are decorated and furnished in perfect harmony with the style of the house. This is a great place from which to discover Honfleur and the area, and your hosts can organise tours, including a picnic.

Facilities: private parking, garden, lounge, pets not accepted, internet access, babies welcome, free cot, 100% no smoking, 2 nights minimum stay: 01/05–31/08, hiking, cycling, sea watersports 2km, golf course 8km, riversports 15km, vineyard 15km
Fluent English spoken

Directions: Exit 3 from the A29 to the D580 towards Honfleur-Centre. Just after the fourth roundabout (by the 'Gare Routière'), left in front of the Etap Hotel. Go along the Rue Vannier and at the second crossroads (speed limit 30km) go straight on up the Côte Vassal. Follow 'Manoir du Desert' signs for 1km. Right onto the Avenue d'Yberville. At the 'Stop' sign, right into the Avenue Terre Neuve. It is the first house by the 'Stop' sign on the right.

14.52 Honfleur

Residence of Outstanding Character

Jean-Louis CABARÉ & Sophie CHAP
'Villa Ariane', 29-31route Emile Renouf, 14600 HONFLEUR
Tel: (0) 2 31 81 11 88 / (0) 670 30 87 86
Fax: (0) 2 31 81 35 12
sophie.chap@laposte.net
www.villaariane.com

Price Structure – 4 Bedrooms and 1 Suite
first room: shower room, wc, double bed (queen-size): €100
second room: shower room, wc, double bed: €95
third room: bathroom, wc, shower, double bed (super king-size): €120
fourth room: shower room, wc, double bed (super king-size), single bed: €100 – 2 people €115 – 3 people
suite: shower room, wc, double bed. En-suite room, 3 single beds: €120 – 2 people €150 – 5 people

Extra Bed: €15   **Reduction:** 1/09–30/06, 3 nights
Capacity: 14 people

Location
HONFLEUR
in: Honfleur, station pick-up on arrival/departure
Railway station: 12km
Airport: Deauville St-Gatien 10km

An 1850s *maison bourgeoise* in the upper parts of Honfleur from which to visit the old town but with plenty of space: 4000m of grounds and private parking. A good level of comfort in the bedrooms with very large 2x2m beds. The contemporary feel sits well with the old woodwork, floors and solid wood doors. The bathrooms are bright and spacious. Breakfast with homemade jams and cakes is served in the large, bright dining room with bay windows and views of the impressive Pont de Normandie. A good location with character.

Facilities: private parking, garden, pets not accepted, 100% no smoking, hiking, cycling, sea watersports, hunting 2km, fishing 2km, mushroom-picking 2km, bird-watching 2km, vineyard 2km, interesting flora 3km, golf course 7km
Fluent English spoken

Directions: On the A29, exit 3 towards Honfleur. At the second roundabout, D144 towards Pont-L'Evêque for about 150m and then turn right at the traffic lights for 800m. The house is on the right.

Location
HONFLEUR
in: Honfleur, station pick-up on arrival/departure
Railway station: 8km
Airport: Deauville St-Gatien 8km

Residence of Outstanding Character

This former convent is right in the centre of one of the most beautiful Normandy harbours. You are a short walk from the old port and the unbelievable Eglise Ste. Catherine, with its wooden roof in the form of an upturned boat. The town is exceptional and so is this house, which has a beautiful interior courtyard with spacious, comfortable rooms and the kindly welcome of Liliane and Antoine. Some of the bedrooms are reached by a narrow staircase, but this place is still worth a detour.

Facilities: private parking, garden, tv lounge, hosts have pets, babies welcome, free cot, hiking, cycling, golf course 8km, sea watersports 8km
Fluent English spoken

Directions: In Honfleur, follow the quayside of the old port as far as the Eglise Ste. Catherine. You will then come to the Rue des Capucins on your right and then take the second turning on the left and then left again. You should then be in Rue du Puits which is a one-way street, and the house is immediately on your left.

Liliane & Antoine GIAGLIS
'La Cour Sainte Catherine', 74 rue du Puits,
14600 HONFLEUR
Tel: (0) 2 31 89 42 40 / (0) 6 22 34 78 94
giaglis@wanadoo.fr
www.giaglis.com

Price Structure – 6 Bedrooms
2 rooms: lounge, television, bathroom, wc, double bed: €70
lounge, television, bathroom, wc, double bed (queen-size), single bed: €90 – 2 people
€110 – 3 people
television, shower room, wc, double bed (queen-size): €90
shower room, wc, double bed, twin beds: €90 – 2 people €130 – 4 people
shower room, wc, double bed (queen-size): €90

Extra Bed: €20
Capacity: 15 people

Location
LISIEUX
in: Lisieux, station pick-up on arrival/departure
Railway station: 2km
Airport: Deauville St-Gatien 30km

Private Home

For the creative among you, this is an artist's studio. Nathalie's lounge is her studio and her craft is needlework. She sells her many creations and also organises creative courses. You are in the centre of Lisieux and the town centre is easily accessible on foot.

Facilities: garden, lounge, 100% no smoking, 1 shared shower room, wc
Adequate English spoken

Nathalie DARMAYAN
23 rue Guizot, 14100 LISIEUX
Tel: (0) 2 31 62 98 25
lesateliersdamalthee@orange.fr
lesateliersdamalthee.com

Price Structure – 1 Bedroom
double bed, single bed: €42 – 2 people
€50 – 3 people

Capacity: 3 people

Directions: In Lisieux, from the town centre, go towards Caen then take the D45 (Rue Guizot) towards Cabourg.

Normandy – Honfleur, Lisieux

14.012 Lisieux

Residence of Outstanding Character

Location
17km W of LISIEUX
in: Crevecoeur-en-Auge
Railway station: 18km
Airport: Deauville St-Gatien 35km
car essential

In the heart of the Pays d'Auge, this is the sort of B&B that you love to find. Chez Françoise it is open house with a warm, family atmosphere. The simply furnished but comfortable rooms are on the first floor. The breakfast is served at the family table, by the fire in winter, in the old converted stables. Françoise is a *cordon bleu* cook and serves local Normandy specialities for dinner or a barbecue in summer.

Françoise DECONINCK
'Au relais du pressoir', 4 route de Cambremer,
14340 CREVECOEUR-EN-AUGE
Tel: (0) 2 31 63 08 03 / (0) 611 50 81 55
Fax: (0) 2 31 63 08 03
elodie-deconinck@orange.fr

Facilities: private parking, garden, tv lounge, pets not accepted, dinner available, babies welcome, free cot, 100% no smoking, fishing 1km, vineyard 5km, golf course 25km
Basic English spoken

Price Structure – 1 Suite
double bed, single bed (child-size). En-suite room, bathroom, wc, twin beds: €53 – 2 people
€117 – 5 people

Extra Bed: €32
Capacity: 5 people

Directions: On the D16 from Lisieux, as you enter Crevecoeur, take the first on the left. 'Le Relais' is 100m on the right.

14.021 Lisieux

Private Home

Location
8km S E of LISIEUX
in: Le Mesnil-Guillaume
car essential

Sue and Henry are originally from England, which they left to settle in this place, in the heart of the Normandy countryside. When visiting this area they fell in love with it and found the perfect house to start their new life. They have renovated the old barn into a B&B. Tall guests should watch their heads on the sloping ceilings – a small price to pay for the natural style of this comfortable suite with its beautifully restored beams. It is ideal for couples with children, as Sue has thought of providing a cot, high chair and toys.

Sue & Henry WESTON
Chemin de Cesnes,
14100 LE MESNIL-GUILLAUME
Tel: (0) 2 31 61 93 52 / (0) 615 48 82 71
susubeedoo@yahoo.co.uk
www.chambredelavande.co.uk

Facilities: private parking, garden, hosts have pets, pets not accepted, babies welcome, free cot, 100% no smoking, 2 nights minimum stay: 01/07–30/09, closed: 01/11–28/02, hiking, cycling, fishing 15km, golf course 20km, sea watersports 25km
Fluent English spoken

Price Structure – 1 Suite
shower room, wc, washbasin, double bed. En-suite room, 2 single beds: €75 – 2 people €115 – 4 people

Reduction: 3 nights
Capacity: 4 people

Directions: In Lisieux take the D519 towards Orbec and go through Beuvilliers. At Glos take the second road on the left towards Chambray for 1.5km, then the first on the right. After 100m take the first alley on the left.

Normandy – Lisieux

Location
3km S W of LISIEUX
in: Les Authieux-Papion, station
pick-up on arrival/departure
Railway station: 3km
Airport: Deauville St-Gatien 50km
car essential

Private Home

Here, Lucette welcomes you to the countryside and to peace and tranquillity. When the weather is fine, you can enjoy her garden and make use of the barbecue, or stay inside and sit by the fireplace on wintry days. There is plenty to do in the area including visits to the beach at Cabourg, 20 minutes away, and a trip to Caen and the memorial. You can also uncover Suisse Normande and follow the 'Cider Route'.

Facilities: off-street parking, garden, tv lounge, hosts have pets, pets not accepted, dinner available, kitchen, babies welcome, free cot, 100% no smoking, closed: 01/12–31/03, hiking 1km, cycling 1km, fishing 2km, vineyard 10km, golf course 12km

Lucette MARQUISE
'La Tuilerie', 14140 LES AUTHIEUX-PAPION
Tel: (0) 2 31 62 84 99 / (0) 660 91 52 59
lucette.marquise@aliceadsl.fr

Price Structure – 3 Bedrooms
'Pivoine': shower room, wc, double bed: €59
'Etoile de Mer' & 'Coccinelle': shower room, wc, double bed: €48

Directions: A13, exit Chauffour and N13 to Lisieux. Take the ring-road towards Caen and exit at St-Désir, St-Julien-le-Faucon. Turn right and cross the village for 1km. Then D47 on the right towards Mézidon-Canon. The house is 200m ahead on the left.

Extra Bed: €15
Reduction: 01/03–30/06, 15 nights
Capacity: 6 people

Location
27km S of LISIEUX
in: Livarot
Railway station: 27km
car essential

Château/Manor House

British Jane and Tim have settled here with their four children. They fell in love with this 19th-century manor, overlooking the valley, 5km from Livarot. The odours of this delicious cheese don't quite waft this far, but your hosts do not hesitate to serve traditional Normandy fare for dinner! The Pays d'Auge is also known for its cider. The décor is sober and the second floor rooms have sloping ceilings, so watch your head! The bathrooms are large and the living rooms, including a lounge with an imposing fireplace, are comfortable.

Facilities: private parking, garden, tv lounge, hosts have pets, dinner available, babies welcome, free cot, 100% no smoking, mushroom-picking, bird-watching, hiking, interesting flora, vineyard, fishing 2km, riversports 27km, golf course 50km
Fluent English spoken

Jane & Tim ROCKE
'Les Tourneurs', La Chapelle-Haute-Grue,
14140 LIVAROT
Tel: (0) 2 31 31 63 50 / (0) 611 67 36 98
tim.rocke@wanadoo.fr
www.lestourneurs.com

Price Structure – 4 Bedrooms
'Noyer' & 'Cèdre': along corridor bathroom, wc, double bed: €75
'Pommier': bathroom, wc, double bed: €60
'Figuier': bathroom, wc, twin beds: €60

Directions: From Lisieux, D579 to Livarot and continue in the direction of Vimoutiers for about 4km. D110 on the right for La Chapelle-Haute-Grue which you pass. D155 direction Les Autels-St-B. and follow the signs for 'Les Tourneurs'.

Extra Bed: €15
Reduction: 2 nights, children
Capacity: 8 people

Normandy – Lisieux

14.21 Lisieux

Residence of Outstanding Character

Bienvenue en France

Marie-Josette & Germain LAMBERT
'Diner-Dormir', Aux Pommiers de Livaye,
14340 NOTRE-DAME-DE-LIVAYE
Tel: (0) 2 31 63 01 28 / (0) 614 72 21 28
bandb.normandy@wanadoo.fr
http://bandb.normandy.free.fr

Price Structure – 4 Bedrooms and 1 Suite
'Reine des champs' (our favourite room): lounge, television, bathroom, wc, double bed (queen-size): €89
'Rose des prés': television, bathroom, wc, twin beds: €76
'Famille-Tendresse': television, bathroom, wc, double bed (queen-size), single bed: €110 – 3 people
'Haut du pommier': television, bathroom, wc, double bed (queen-size), 2 single beds: €118 – 4 people
'Les Lauriers': lounge, bathroom, wc, double bed. En-suite room, twin beds: €140 – 4 people

Reduction: 4 nights
Capacity: 15 people

Location
15km W of LISIEUX
in: Notre-Dame-de-Livaye
Railway station: 15km
Airport: Deauville St-Gatien 30km
car essential

Don't be anxious when you see the entrance to this former farm so close to the motorway! The rumbling noise of the *autoroute* is absorbed and muffled by the grounds between the house and the road. An extensive lawn and fruit trees outside, and a charming collection of plates, antiques, a large fireplace and shelves brimming with homemade jam inside. There are comfortable romantic bedrooms and a lovely veranda with views of the fields. Marie-Josette was born here and shares her love and enthusiasm for the area.

Facilities: off-street parking, extensive grounds, lounge, hosts have pets, pets not accepted, dinner available, babies welcome, free cot, closed: 15/11–15/03, hiking, vineyard 3km, fishing 5km, golf course 10km, sea watersports 20km, riversports 30km
Adequate English spoken

Directions: At Lisieux take the N13 towards Caen for 15km. At Notre-Dame-de-Livaye, look for the sign on the right for 'Aux Pommiers de Livaye'.

14.25 Lisieux

Private Home

Véronique & Georges LORETTE
'Côté Jardin', 62 rue Grande,
14290 ORBEC-EN-AUGE
Tel: (0) 2 31 32 77 99 Fax: (0) 2 31 32 77 99
georges.lorette@wanadoo.fr
www.cotejardin-france.be

Price Structure – 4 Bedrooms and 1 Suite
'Africaine', 'Chasse' & 'Orbecquoise': lounge, shower room, wc, double bed, single bed: €70 – 2 people €90 – 3 people
'Printemps': lounge, shower room, wc, double bed, 2 single beds: €70 – 2 people €110 – 4 people
'Suite Marine': lounge, along corridor shower room, wc, double bed. En-suite room, single bed: €70 – 2 people €90 – 3 people

Extra Bed: €20
Capacity: 16 people

Location
20km S E of LISIEUX
in: Orbec-en-Auge
Railway station: 20km
Airport: Caen-Carpiquet 70km
car essential

This large *maison bourgeoise* is in the town centre with a quiet garden of flowers and a lovely little stream. The bedrooms are on different levels in overlapping outbuildings. The 'Orbecquoise' room is in the local style whereas 'Africaine' – the most spacious – is inspired by visits to Africa. The 'Chasse' is up a narrow staircase. Delicious breakfasts are served on the veranda or the terrace. Your Belgian hosts impart good cheer, a good sense of humour and an enthusiastic welcome. On sale: regional souvenirs, cider.

Facilities: private parking, garden, hosts have pets, pets not accepted, dinner available, babies welcome, free cot, hiking, fishing 2km
Fluent English spoken

Directions: From Lisieux sud, D519 to Orbec (19km). The house is on the main road (Rue Grande) that cuts across town.

Location
31km S of LISIEUX
in: St-Aubin-de-Bonneval, station
pick-up on arrival/departure
Railway station: 25km
Airport: Deauville St-Gatien 50km
car essential

✳ ✳ ✳
Residence of Outstanding Character

Your hosts are the sixth generation to live in this manor and seignory dating back to the 16th century. They welcome you by the fireplace which is used to flambé dishes with cider and Calvados. The suite in the pigeon loft is reached via a period staircase and has an unusual water feature in the bathroom. There is also a gîte opposite in a large red-brick building which has been modernised. It retains a certain originality, housing unique period furniture and genuine Portuguese hand-painted *azulejos* tiles. True hospitality!

Facilities: private parking, garden, tv lounge, hosts have pets, pets not accepted, dinner available, babies welcome, free cot, hiking, cycling, golf course 40km, sea watersports 55km
Adequate English spoken

Directions: From Lisieux, D519 to Orbec, take the bypass road direction l'Aigle then turn right straight away onto the D130 towards Le Sap for 7km and then turn left and follow the signs to 'La Hérissonnière' for about 1.4km.

Marie-Françoise & Denis TUEL
'Hérissonnière et Compagnie', La Hérissonnière,
61470 ST-AUBIN-DE-BONNEVAL
Tel: (0) 2 33 39 48 55 / (0) 603 91 60 88
Fax: (0) 2 33 39 55 56
dtuel@terre-net.fr
www.herissonniere.fr

Price Structure – 6 Bedrooms
'Hydrangea': along corridor shower room, wc, double bed: €40
'Pigeonnier': along corridor shower room, wc, four-poster double bed (queen-size): €50
'Découverte': bathroom, wc, twin beds: €60
'Beauvoir': shower room, wc, twin beds: €60
'Tulipes': shower room, wc, double bed (queen-size): €55
'Orient': shower room, wc, double bed (queen-size): €55

Extra Bed: €10 **Reduction:** 5 nights, groups
Capacity: 12 people

Location
14km S W of LISIEUX
in: St-Julien-le-Faucon
Railway station: 14km
Airport: Deauville St-Gatien 45km
car essential

✳ ✳ ✳
Private Home

Yvette, who is well travelled and enjoys cultural exchanges, is now retired after a career in the air transport business during which time she lived abroad. Today, she is always on hand and has the time, know-how and spontaneity to provide you with a warm welcome. From her village, typical of the Pays d'Auge and its half-timbered houses, she offers to guide you around the region's manors, châteaux, cheese producers and cider cellars.

Facilities: private parking, garden, tv lounge, pets not accepted, babies welcome, free cot, 100% no smoking, closed: 15/11–15/03, hiking, cycling, interesting flora, golf course 30km, sea watersports 40km
Fluent English spoken

Directions: Please contact your host in advance for detailed directions.

Yvette PECOT
'La Baronnie', 2 route de Livarot,
14140 ST-JULIEN-LE-FAUCON
Tel: (0) 2 31 31 30 61
pirosset@wanadoo.fr

Price Structure – 1 Bedroom and 1 Suite
'Pivoine': along corridor bathroom, wc, double bed. En-suite room, washbasin, single bed. En-suite room, washbasin, double bed: €58 – 2 people €130 – 5 people
'Camélia': bathroom, wc, double bed: €65

Extra Bed: €15
Capacity: 7 people

Normandy – Lisieux

14.008 Ouistreham

Private Home

Location
OUISTREHAM
in: Ouistreham
Railway station: 12km
Airport: Caen-Carpiquet 20km
car essential

Hélène used to work in the restaurant business during the holiday seasons in Ouistreham. She loves to chat and is very warm and welcoming. There is a little gîte in the garden for four people and the door to her home is always open for guests to come in and enjoy her lounge. Her whole house is open to you for that matter! The 'Le Phare' bedroom has a lovely bathroom and the 'Moussaillon' room is spacious with everything you need to accommodate a baby plus the possibility of adding an extra bed.

Facilities: garden, tv lounge, pets not accepted, babies welcome, free cot, 100% no smoking, fishing 1km, riversports 1km, sea watersports 1km, cycling 2km, golf course 10km
Basic English spoken

Hélène & Christian VIOLET
55 rue Gambetta, 14150 OUISTREHAM
Tel: (0) 2 31 96 18 43 / (0) 682 57 63 56
violet.helene@aliceadsl.fr

Price Structure – 2 Bedrooms
'Le Phare': television, along corridor shower room, wc, double bed: €50
'Moussaillon': television, shower, double bed, cot: €60

Extra Bed: €18
Reduction: children
Capacity: 4 people

Directions: In Ouistreham, follow the direction 'Centre-Ville'. After the town hall ('mairie'), straight on and the house is just after the shop 'fleuriste'.

14.09 Ouistreham

Private Home

Location
OUISTREHAM
in: Ouistreham
Ferry port: Ouistreham
Airport: Caen-Carpiquet 20km

Close to the shops, the marina and the car ferry, which is less than 500m away, this charming little house is perfectly peaceful. The guest room on the ground floor is set back at the end of the courtyard. The bedroom is comfortable, well decorated and has its own entrance and private patio. Breakfast is served on the veranda or on the terrace, weather permitting. Secure parking is possible if requested. Françoise is a keen gardener and the fruits of her labour can be seen all around the house. She is also a keen walker.

Facilities: garden, hosts have pets, pets not accepted, babies welcome, free cot, 100% no smoking, fishing, hiking, cycling, sea watersports, bird-watching 3km
Basic English spoken

Françoise BOUQUET
'Villa Désirée', 103 avenue de la Redoute, 14150 OUISTREHAM
Tel: (0) 2 31 97 39 15 / (0) 623 18 09 32
francoise.bouquet@tiscali.fr

Price Structure – 1 Bedroom
television, shower room, wc, 2 double beds:
€65 – 2 people €95 – 4 people

Extra Bed: €16
Reduction: 4 nights
Capacity: 4 people

Directions: Ouistreham is 15km north of Caen. On arrival at Ouistreham head for 'Le Port, Ferry', then from the port head for Courseul, Avenue du Mal. The supermarket 'Leclerc' is 500m further on and then take the second road on the right.

Location
OUISTREHAM
in: Ouistreham
Railway station: 12km
Airport: Caen-Carpiquet 20km

Private Home

In an ideal location in the centre of Ouistreham, near the listed church and by the busy shopping streets, you will find this tastefully decorated newly built house. You are also just 500m from the port which serves as a yachting harbour, fishing and car ferry port. If possible choose the 'Mauve' room as the bed in the 'Bleue' room is a bit small.

Evelyne MAILLOT
5 rue de l'Union, 14150 OUISTREHAM
Tel: (0) 2 31 97 75 74

Facilities: private parking, garden, tv lounge, babies welcome, free cot, 1 shared bathroom, wc, hiking 1km, cycling 1km, fishing 1km, bird-watching 1km, sea watersports 1km
Basic English spoken

Price Structure – 2 Bedrooms
'Mauve' & Bleue': double bed: €54

Extra Bed: €13
Reduction: 5 nights
Capacity: 4 people

Directions: At Ouistreham, head to 'Le Ferry, Le Port'. After the second roundabout, turn left at the traffic lights into Rue du Bief, then take the third road on the right.

Location
18km N W of OUISTREHAM
in: Courseulles-sur-Mer
Ferry port: 15km
Airport: Caen-Carpiquet 15km
car essential

Private Home

This is a farmhouse building from the 1800s with a large enclosed walled courtyard where tables are set out for you. The bedrooms are spacious, simply decorated, bright and contain a television, fridge and a microwave. There is even an iron available in the lounge! Simon's house is meticulously clean and he welcomes you with kindness and simple hospitality.

Simon BENYAICHE
26 rue de l'Amiral Robert,
14470 COURSEULLES-SUR-MER
Tel: (0) 2 31 74 88 43 / (0) 668 57 33 66
Fax: (0) 2 31 74 88 43
kadosch.tswika@wanadoo.fr
http://simonchambresdhotes.ifrance.com

Facilities: lounge, pets not accepted, babies welcome, free cot, 100% no smoking, hiking, cycling, fishing, sea watersports, golf course 10km
Adequate English spoken

Price Structure – 4 Bedrooms and 1 Suite
3 rooms: television, shower room, wc, double bed, single bed: €50 – 2 people €75 – 3 people
television, bathroom, wc, twin beds: €50
bathroom, wc, twin beds. En-suite room, 2 single beds: €50 – 2 people €90 – 4 people

Extra Bed: €25
Reduction: children
Capacity: 15 people

Directions: Please contact your host in advance for detailed directions.

14.69 Ouistreham

Private Home

Location
18km N W of OUISTREHAM
in: Courseulles-sur-Mer
Railway station: 15km
Airport: Caen-Carpiquet 15km

Béatrice DI ROSA
'A Marée Hôtes', 24 rue de l'Amiral Robert,
14470 COURSEULLES-SUR-MER
Tel: (0) 2 31 97 35 68 / (0) 663 46 06 97
Fax: (0) 2 31 97 35 68
amareehotes@tele2.fr
http://amareehotes.free.fr

An old renovated farmhouse in a quiet street in the centre of Courseulles-sur-Mer, a lovely little seaside town with all the usual local amenities that you would come to expect, restaurants and shops, etc. Close to the D-Day landing beaches; it is here that Winston Churchill and Général de Gaulle disembarked. The bedrooms, with original stone walls, lead onto a patio where you can sit out and enjoy breakfast. Restaurant nearby.

Price Structure – 5 Bedrooms
television, shower room, wc, double bed: €50
television, shower room, wc, twin beds: €50
television, shower room, wc, double bed, single bed: €50 – 2 people €80 – 3 people
television, shower room, wc, double bed, 2 single beds: €50 – 2 people €90 – 4 people
'Suite': television, shower room, wc, 2 double beds: €50 – 2 people €90 – 4 people

Reduction: groups, children
Capacity: 15 people

Facilities: off-street parking, lounge, pets not accepted, kitchen, babies welcome, free cot, 100% no smoking, wheelchair access, hiking, cycling, fishing, sea watersports, golf course 10km

Directions: At Ouistreham, head to Courseulles via the D514, towards Lion-sur-Mer until Courseulles-sur-Mer. The house is opposite the church in Rue de l'Amiral Robert which is a one-way street.

14.15 Ouistreham

Private Home

Location
10km N W of OUISTREHAM
in: Douvres-La-Délivrande
Ferry port: 10km
Airport: Caen-Carpiquet 15km

Pascale & Vincent MENUDE
'Les Marguerites', 19 route de Caen,
14440 DOUVRES-LA-DELIVRANDE
Tel: (0) 2 31 23 06 28 / (0) 633 32 29 37
Fax: (0) 2 31 23 06 28
lesmarguerites14@wanadoo.fr

This young couple (seasonal sweet sellers) have recently renovated their home. Each bedroom has a theme and is well-equipped with a mini-bar and reclining beds, some with garden views. 'La Palmeraie' comes complete with an amusing Inca totem. Enjoy a drink in the enclosed garden behind the house. Local Vincent is passionate about the history of the landing beaches. He can advise on all the cemeteries and places of interest. A cycling lane away from busy roads leads to the beaches. Old motorbike and 2CV enthusiasts especially welcome!

Price Structure – 4 Bedrooms
'La Palmeraie' (our favourite room): television, shower room, wc, double bed: €60
'Vent du large': television, shower room, wc, double bed: €60
'La Marquise': television, bathroom, wc, double bed: €60
'La Fleur des Champs': television, shower room, wc, four-poster double bed: €60

Extra Bed: €16
Capacity: 8 people

Facilities: private parking, garden, hosts have pets, pets not accepted, babies welcome, free cot, 100% no smoking, wheelchair access, hiking, cycling, sea watersports 2km, fishing 5km, golf course 9km, bird-watching 15km
Adequate English spoken

Directions: From Caen, ring road North, exit 5 direction Douvres-la-Délivrande. Continue straight ahead towards the town centre. The house is just after the first roundabout and the British Military Cemetery (just before the second roundabout), on the right.

Location
5km W of OUISTREHAM
in: Hermanville-sur-Mer
Ferry port: 5km
Airport: Caen-Carpiquet 15km
car essential

Private Home

This 19th-century farmhouse is built of Caen stone and is just 2km from the sea and the ferry port of Ouistreham. It is also close to the nature reserve of the Baie de l'Orne. The house is totally dedicated to the sea and throughout the house are superb models of fishing boats and some, in the bedrooms, are larger than the bed. Be sure to see the very beautiful model in the first bedroom!

Françoise & Jean-Pierre GIRAUD
'La Guillaumière', 766 Grande Rue, 14880
HERMANVILLE-SUR-MER
Tel: (0) 2 31 96 41 30 / (0) 689 58 64 32
francoise.giraud14@wanadoo.fr

Facilities: private parking, garden, hosts have pets, pets not accepted, babies welcome, free cot, 100% no smoking, hiking, fishing, sea watersports 2km, golf course 3km, cycling 5km, interesting flora 10km, bird-watching 10km
Adequate English spoken

Price Structure – 3 Bedrooms
No 1: television, shower room, wc, double bed: €65
No 2: television, along corridor shower room, wc, double bed: €65
No 3: lounge, television, bathroom, wc, washbasin, double bed: €70

Extra Bed: €20
Reduction: 5 nights
Capacity: 6 people

Directions: From Ouistreham, follow the coast towards Lion-sur-Mer on the D514 and at the second set of traffic lights, turn left as far as Hermanville-sur-Mer. Go through this village to number 766.

Location
14km N W of OUISTREHAM
in: St-Aubin-sur-Mer
Railway station: 15km
Airport: Caen-Carpiquet 18km
car essential

Private Home

A warm and uncomplicated welcome from Sophie and Thierry who have recently bought this little town-house in April 2006. They are undertaking B&B for the first time and you can benefit from their great enthusiasm. Thierry has good relations with the local village shops and can offer good advice. What is more the road opposite the house leads directly to the beach (ten minutes on foot). The guest bedroom is on the first floor and has an en-suite lounge area with an extra sofa-bed.

Sophie & Thierry DEPOILLY
'Le Relais du Cap Romain', 16 rue du Maréchal
Joffre, 14750 ST-AUBIN-SUR-MER
Tel: (0) 2 31 97 41 02 / (0) 672 79 01 11
sophie.uteza@wanadoo.fr
www.relaisducapromain.com

Facilities: tv lounge, hosts have pets, 100% no smoking

Price Structure – 1 Bedroom
'Guillaume': lounge, bathroom, wc, double bed: €55

Extra Bed: €10
Capacity: 2 people

Directions: Please contact your hosts in advance for detailed directions.

Normandy – Ouistreham

27.17 Pont-Audemer

Residence of Outstanding Character

Martine & Eric BEELE
'Vallée du Moulin de Grainville', 1096 rue de Grainville, 27450 ST-ETIENNE-L'ALLIER
Tel: (0) 2 32 41 73 15 / (0) 633 11 12 61
valleedumoulin@free.fr
http://valleedumoulin.free.fr

Price Structure – 3 Bedrooms
'Jaune': wheelchair access, lounge, shower room, wc, double bed, 2 single beds (child-size):
€58 – 2 people €85 – 4 people
'Bleue': bathroom, wc, double bed (queen-size): €58
'Chambre du Meunier': bathroom, wc, double bed (queen-size), 2 single beds: €58 – 2 people
€85 – 4 people

Extra Bed: €10
Reduction: 4 nights
Capacity: 10 people

Location
12km S of PONT-AUDEMER
in: St-Etienne-l'Allier, station pick-up on arrival/departure
Railway station: 20km
car essential

Bienvenue en France

Two half-timbered houses, in a pretty spot, surrounded by a vast garden overhanging a beautiful valley and a tennis court. One is for guests, with a terrace, lounge, fireplace, and kitchen area. Breakfast can be served on the terrace and for dinner, feast on charcuterie, Normandy cheeses and seasonal starters. The 'Bleue' room has a sloping ceiling and a large futon bed, more 'zen' than the 'Jaune' room with wood panelling. Bucolic charm and a courteous and positive welcome from Martine and Eric, who also organise trips.

Facilities: private parking, extensive grounds, lounge, hosts have pets, pets not accepted, dinner available, kitchen, babies welcome, free cot, wheelchair access, private tennis court, mushroom-picking, hiking, cycling, riversports 18km, golf course 25km, sea watersports 30km
Fluent English spoken

Directions: From Rouen, A13 towards Caen, exit 26, Pont-Audemer. D810 towards Bernay. At St-Siméon turn left towards St-Martin, St-Firmin for 1.5km. At the T-junction, turn right. The property is 200m further up, on the left.

27.13 Verneuil-sur-Avre

Private Home

Margaret & Michael EDWARDS
5 rue de Francheville, 27580 BOURTH
Tel: (0) 2 32 30 44 69 / (0) 613 15 54 53
Fax: (0) 2 32 30 44 69
bourth-bab@club-internet.fr
www.bourth-bab.com

Price Structure – 3 Bedrooms
television, along corridor bathroom, wc, twin beds, 2 single beds: €48 – 2 people €73 – 4 people
television, shower room, wc, double bed: €53
television, shower room, wc, double bed: €48

Extra Bed: €15
Reduction: 4 nights
Capacity: 8 people

Location
10km W of VERNEUIL-SUR-AVRE
in: Bourth
Railway station: 10km
Airport: Rouen-Boos 80km
car essential

Bienvenue en France

You will be warmly welcomed by your English hosts, Margaret and Michael, in this small, pretty village full of flowers (your hosts won a prize for theirs), beside the River Iton on the edge of a large forest. Keen fishing enthusiasts, there is even an enormous aquarium in their dining room! Margaret is continually complimented on her fine cooking, using fresh vegetables from the garden and local farm produce. A relaxing stay here, in tune with village life, apart from Sky TV.

Facilities: private parking, garden, tv lounge, pets not accepted, dinner available, babies welcome, free cot, 100% no smoking, fishing, cycling
Fluent English spoken

Directions: At Verneuil-sur-Avre, take the N26 towards L'Aigle for 7km. Then take the D54 on the right to Bourth.

27.15 Verneuil-sur-Avre

Location
11km E of VERNEUIL-SUR-AVRE
in: Tillières-sur-Avre, station pick-up
on arrival/departure
Railway station: 9km
car essential

✺ ✺ ✺
Private Home

Find peace and quiet in the upper parts of the village in this charming renovated former farmhouse. We loved the landscaped grounds with an abundance of interesting aromatic planting, water features with aquatic plants, plus arbours, pergolas – and all lit up at night! Period furniture to be found in the 'Napoléon' suite, which is spacious with a well-equipped bathroom. In addition to a warm welcome, Michel and Alexandra offer original cuisine inspired by their Slavic origins. A large barbecue is at your disposal.

Alexandra & Michel LIBIS
'Le Clos Fontaines', 4 place des Ecoles,
27570 TILLIERES-SUR-AVRE
Tel: (0) 2 32 60 30 85 / (0) 681 70 55 05
Fax: (0) 2 32 60 30 85
libis@clos-fontaines.com
www.clos-fontaines.com

Facilities: private parking, extensive grounds, tv lounge, hosts have pets, dinner available, cycling, hiking 5km, fishing 30km, golf course 40km
Fluent English spoken

Price Structure – 1 Bedroom and 1 Suite
'Napoléon': television, shower room, wc, double bed.
En-suite room, single bed: €65 – 2 people
€89 – 3 people
television, shower, washbasin, double bed: €34

Extra Bed: €10
Reduction: 3 nights
Capacity: 5 people

Directions: From Paris, N12 towards Dreux et Verneuil-sur-Avre. Tillières-sur-Avre is on this road 10km after Nonancourt. Head for the centre and turn right towards 'la Poste, les écoles'. Head up the hill to Place des Ecoles.

50.11 Avranches-Mont-St-Michel

Location
8km E of AVRANCHES-MONT-ST-MICHEL
in: Bas Courtils
Railway station: 35km
Airport: 70km
car essential

Bienvenue en **France**

✺ ✺
Working Farm

We love Marie-Pierre, a lady with a kind, strong character who runs a classic, Normandy stone farmhouse on a working farm specialising in rearing *agneaux de pré salé* (sought-after lambs that graze on the plant life by the sea giving their meat a distinctive taste). The bedrooms are decorated with pinewood panelling and a few are a little narrow due to the shower. Ideal for families on a budget. Members of a local cycling club. On sale: cider. One self-catering apartment for six people available to rent by the week.

Marie-Pierre LEMOULAND
'La Ferme de la Ruette', 50220 COURTILS
Tel: (0) 2 33 70 95 90 / (0) 666 57 26 22
Fax: (0) 2 33 70 95 90
lemouland.marie-pierre@club-internet.fr
http://site.voila.fr/fermedelaruette

Facilities: off-street parking, garden, tv lounge, pets not accepted, kitchen, babies welcome, free cot, 2 wcs, cycling, sea watersports 1km

Price Structure – 5 Bedrooms
first floor – 2 rooms: shower room, wc, double bed: €46,50
second floor – extra room: television, shower room, wc, washbasin, 2 double beds, single bed: €46,50 – 2 people €77,00 – 5 people
second floor – 'Mansardées' 2 rooms: shower room, wc, washbasin, 2 double beds: €46,50 – 2 people €66,00 – 4 people

Extra Bed: €10
Capacity: 17 people

Directions: Leaving Le Mont-St-Michel, turn left onto the D275 towards Courtils. In Bas Courtils, take the D288 towards Roche-Torin for 200m. The farm is on the right.

50.06 Avranches-Mont-St-Michel

Private Home

Location
10km E of AVRANCHES-MONT-ST-MICHEL
in: Ceaux
Railway station: 10km
Airport: 65km
car essential

Marie-Thérèse & Michel GUESDON
'Au Jardin Fleuri', route de Servon, 2 La
Mottaiserie, 50220 CEAUX
Tel: (0) 2 33 70 97 29 / (0) 684 10 13 77
aujardin@club-internet.fr
http://site.voila.fr/aujardin

Price Structure – 5 Bedrooms
first floor – first room & second floor – fifth room:
shower room, wc, double bed: €50
first floor – second room: bathroom, wc, double bed:
€50
second floor – fourth room: shower room, wc,
double bed, single bed: €50 – 2 people €60 – 3
people
third room: shower room, wc, double bed, twin
beds: €50 – 2 people €70 – 4 people

Extra Bed: €10
Capacity: 13 people

Your charming hostess will make you want to spend
several nights here, in her stone-built house. Near to
Le Mont-St-Michel and Avranches, and with a
restaurant 100m away, the surroundings are relaxing
with a beautiful view. On sale: cider, Pommeau,
Calvados and *gâteaux*.

Facilities: off-street parking, garden, tv lounge,
kitchen, babies welcome, free cot, 100% no smoking,
2 nights minimum stay: 14/07–15/08, closed:
1/10–15/10, hiking, cycling, mushroom-picking, sea
watersports, fishing 3km, bird-watching 5km
Adequate English spoken

Directions: Leaving Le Mont-St-Michel, turn left onto
the D275 towards Courtils, then Ceaux. Opposite the
'Hôtel du Petit Quinquin', continue in the direction of
Servon for 50m. First entrance on the right.

50.49 Avranches-Mont-St-Michel

Private Home

Location
2km S E of AVRANCHES-MONT-ST-MICHEL
in: St-Martin-des-Champs, station
pick-up on arrival/departure
Railway station: 3km
Airport: Rennes St-Jacques 70km
car essential

Jocelyne & Henri BERNARD
'Le Quesnoy', 50300 ST-MARTIN-DES-CHAMPS
Tel: (0) 2 33 58 30 72 / (0) 680 20 85 90
bhenri@wanadoo.fr
http://chambres.lequesnoy.free.fr

Price Structure – 4 Bedrooms
'Gypaète': shower room, wc, double bed (king-size):
€50
'Lagopède': shower room, wc, twin beds: €50
'Cerise': shower room, wc, double bed: €50
'Prune': shower room, wc, double bed, single bed:
€50 – 2 people €65 – 3 people

Extra Bed: €15
Reduction: 15/09–31/05, 3 nights
Capacity: 9 people

Stay with Jocelyne and Henri in their pleasant and
bright home, tucked away on the south side of a
hillside deep in the countryside near Avranches.
From the balconies of the two bedrooms with fairly
basic décor and furnishings, you have a panoramic
view onto the Mont-St-Michel and the bay. Relax and
enjoy the beautiful swimming pool which is a real
find in this region. There is also an outdoor summer
kitchen with cooking rings and a barbecue. Excellent
value for money.

Facilities: off-street parking, extensive grounds, tv
lounge, kitchen, babies welcome, free cot, closed:
01/01–01/03, private swimming pool, hiking 3km,
bird-watching 6km, gliding 8km, fishing 9km, sea
watersports 16km, golf course 26km
Adequate English spoken

Directions: At the centre of Avranches, at Place
Patton, take the D78 towards St-Quentin-sur-l'Homme for 1.4km. The house is on the right after a
bend (signposted).

Location
37km S of CHERBOURG
in: Barneville-Carteret
Ferry port: 30km
Airport: Caen-Carpiquet 110km
car essential

**Château/Manor
House**

Close to the resort of Carteret is this 18th-century manor, full of character, where General Eisenhower visited in July 1994! Today, Catherine, Eric and their three children offer a suite of two large rooms with notable Louis XV panelling, a harmonium, period fireplaces and contemporary paintings. For a more modest budget, consider 'Sercq', a small mezzanine studio, or 'Aurigny' on the ground floor, off the courtyard. A lounge area, snooker room, heated swimming pool, terrace and floral garden top it all off.

Facilities: off-street parking, extensive grounds, lounge, pets not accepted, babies welcome, free cot, 100% no smoking, private swimming pool, fishing 2km, hiking 2km, cycling 2km, sea watersports 4km, interesting flora 20km
Adequate English spoken

Directions: From Cherbourg, D904 to Barneville-Carteret (37km) and then take the third road on the left (D132) signed for St-Maurice-en-Cotentin. The 'Manoir' is 500m further on, on the left.

Catherine & Eric FOUCHE
'Manoir de Caillemont', St-Georges-de-la-Rivière,
50270 BARNEVILLE-CARTERET
Tel: (0) 2 33 53 25 66 Fax: (0) 2 33 53 25 66
manoircaillemont@aol.com
www.manoircaillemont.com

Price Structure – 4 Bedrooms and 1 Apartment
'Jersey': lounge, bathroom, wc, double bed (queen-size). Along corridor room 'Ecrehous': twin beds:
€139 – 2 people €189 – 4 people
'Guernesey': lounge, shower room, wc, twin beds: €119
'Aurigny': wheelchair access, shower room, wc, double bed (queen-size), single bed: €99 – 2 people
€119 – 3 people
'Sercq': kitchen, shower room, wc, 2 double beds:
€65 – 2 people €100 – 4 people

Extra Bed: €25
Capacity: 13 people

Location
41km S E of CHERBOURG
in: Foucarville-Plage
Railway station: 20km
Airport: Caen-Carpiquet 40km
car essential

Private Home

A modern house facing the beach between two German bunkers. Near to Ste-Mère-Eglise and between the salt marshes of Marais Cotentin and the Utah Normandy landing beach. The comfortable, if slightly old-fashioned bedrooms have sloping ceilings and a sea view. Homemade produce is served at breakfast and local specialities are served for dinner. Numerous services are offered including use of a washing machine and picnics can be prepared. This is a great area for walkers and one of the routes leading to St-Jacques-de-Compostelle passes by here.

Facilities: private parking, garden, lounge, hosts have pets, pets not accepted, babies welcome, free cot, fishing, hiking, sea watersports, golf course 5km, bird-watching 5km, interesting flora 10km
Basic English spoken

Directions: From Carentan, take the N13 towards Cherbourg for 2km, then the D913 on the right towards Utah Beach and then follow the D421 by the sea towards Quineville for 5km. The house is near to a German blockhaus.

Catherine & René LECARPENTIER
5 St-Hubert, 50480 FOUCARVILLE-PLAGE
Tel: (0) 2 33 40 03 92 / (0) 684 63 61 78
renelecarpentier@aol.com
www.ifrance.fr/hotes-normandie/

Price Structure – 2 Bedrooms
'Jaune': double bed: €45
'Saumon': twin beds: €45

Extra Bed: €15
Reduction: 4 nights
Capacity: 4 people

Normandy – Cherbourg

50.38 Cherbourg

Château/Manor House

Regula & Denis COEPEL
'Château des Poteries', 50310 FRESVILLE
Tel: (0) 2 33 95 02 03 Fax: (0) 2 33 95 02 03
Regula.Coepel@wanadoo.fr
http://bandb_lespoteries.monsite.wanadoo.fr/

Price Structure – 3 Bedrooms
'Bleue': shower room, wc, twin beds: €64
'Jaune': shower room, wc, twin beds, single bed:
€64 – 2 people €73 – 3 people
'Verte': shower room, wc, twin beds: €64

Extra Bed: €9
Capacity: 7 people

Location
30km S E of CHERBOURG
in: Fresville
Railway station: 12km
Airport: Cherbourg-Maupertus 30km
car essential

This 19th-century château has magnificent grounds which you should not miss visiting, with little bridges and a large pond beside the ancient moat. It is situated in the Parc National des Marais du Cotentin et du Bessin, just 8km from the sea and 5km from Ste-Mère-Eglise. You are welcome to use the barbecue. Golf and riding can be arranged locally.

Facilities: off-street parking, extensive grounds, lounge, hosts have pets, pets not accepted, babies welcome, free cot, hiking, cycling, fishing, bird-watching 8km, sea watersports 8km, golf course 10km
Fluent English spoken

Directions: On the N13 Caen–Cherbourg road, turn off at Fresville. Turn right at the church, and after 800m turn left and continue for 200m.

50.32 Cherbourg

Château/Manor House

Laurence & Gilles LE COUTOUR
'Le Valciot', 14 chemin des Costils,
50340 SIOUVILLE-HAGUE
Tel: (0) 2 33 52 93 15
valciot@wanadoo.fr

Price Structure – 1 Bedroom
and 3 Apartments
'Tourelle': bathroom, wc, double bed: €48
'Bureau': kitchen, bathroom, wc, double bed: €50
'Les Meurtrières': kitchen, shower room, wc, double bed, single bed: €40 – 2 people €48 – 3 people
'La Mansarde': lounge, kitchen, bathroom, wc, double bed: €50

Extra Bed: €8
Reduction: 4 nights
Capacity: 9 people

Location
25km S W of CHERBOURG
in: Siouville-Hague
Ferry port: 25km
Airport: Cherbourg-Maupertus 40km
car essential

A charming family manor house, on a hillside, only 300m from the sea. Over generations the house has been continually updated. A communal room with a seating area is where breakfast is served and there are three new bedrooms. The older bedrooms with views over the garden and the sea are still available. More spacious and rustic they are reached via an impressive stone stairway. The garden and a games area are available and the ferry to the Channel Islands is just 2km away. A kind welcome and excellent value for money.

Facilities: off-street parking, garden, hosts have pets, dinner available, kitchen, babies welcome, free cot, hiking, cycling, fishing, sea watersports, interesting flora 15km, gliding 15km, golf course 22km
Basic English spoken

Directions: From Cherbourg take the D904 as far as Les Pieux, and then the D23 towards Siouville. In the village, facing the cemetery, turn left and then turn right at the 'Stop' sign. Then take the first on the right. The house is 500m further on, on the right.

Location
25km S W of CHERBOURG
in: St-Germain-le-Gaillard
Ferry port: 25km
Airport: Cherbourg-Maupertus 25km
car essential

Château/Manor
House

The location on its own is worth three 'suns'! Situated in the countryside but close to the coast, several buildings dating from the 14th and 17th centuries make up this manor, surrounded by a magical garden where each plant is listed and labelled. The apartment integrates beautifully with the style of the place. Odile is a charming science teacher and goes out of her way to make your stay as pleasant as possible. Boats leave for excursions to Jersey and Guernsey only 10km away.

Facilities: off-street parking, extensive grounds, pets not accepted, kitchen, babies welcome, free cot, 100% no smoking, wheelchair access, hiking, cycling 5km, sea watersports 5km, gliding 16km, interesting flora 20km
Basic English spoken

Odile & Didier VIEJO
'Manoir de Bunehou',
50340 ST-GERMAIN-LE-GAILLARD
Tel: (0) 2 33 93 54 48
didier.viejo@wanadoo.fr
www.manoir-de-bunehou.com

Price Structure – 1 Apartment
wheelchair access, television, telephone, kitchen, shower room, wc, double bed: €53

Capacity: 2 people

Directions: From Cherbourg take the D940 towards Le Carteret. 5km after Les Pieux, turn left onto the D131 for St-Germain-le-Gaillard. Continue towards Le Vrétôt as far as the manor, which is on the left.

Location
55km S E of CHERBOURG
in: St-Pellerin, station pick-up on arrival/departure
Railway station: 4km
car essential

Château/Manor
House

This 17th-century manor house is typical of the style of the reign of Louis XIII. Its origins are in the 14th century and it owes its name to the two 300-year-old oak trees in the grounds. Isabelle and Gilles provide a warm welcome. They organise weekends around relaxing themes. Whether you are on a romantic weekend or in a large party, they have rooms to suit. Two charming rooms in the main house, are reached by a 500-year-old stone staircase. All the rooms are spacious and decorated with good taste.

Facilities: private parking, garden, tv lounge, hosts have pets, pets not accepted, internet access, kitchen, babies welcome, free cot, 100% no smoking, 3 nights minimum stay: 1/07–31/08, closed: 3/01–8/02, hiking, cycling, sea watersports 15km, golf course 20km
Fluent English spoken

Gilles LEMONNIER & Isabelle DLUBEK
'Manoir du Vieux Chêne', Le Bois,
50500 ST-PELLERIN
Tel: (0) 2 33 71 91 38 / (0) 616 09 78 05
lemonnier.gilles@club.fr
www.manoirduvieuxchene.com

Price Structure – 5 Bedrooms
'Framboise': shower room, wc, double bed (queen-size): €65
'Bleue': shower room, wc, twin beds: €65
'Avec Jardin': shower room, wc, double bed (queen-size): €65
'Melon': shower room, wc, double bed (queen-size), single bed: €55 – 2 people €75 – 3 people
'Chocolat': shower room, wc, double bed (queen-size), 2 single beds (child-size): €55 – 2 people €95 – 4 people

Extra Bed: €15
Reduction: 15/10–30/04
Capacity: 13 people

Directions: From St-Lô take the N174 towards Carentan for 22km. When you reach the sign that indicates St-Pellerin at 0.5km to the right, take the lane opposite on the left. The house is 800m down at the end of this lane.

Normandy – Cherbourg

50.46 Coutances

Private Home

Location
10km W of COUTANCES
in: Blainville-sur-Mer, station pick-up
on arrival/departure
Railway station: 12km
car essential

Jeanne & Maurice POSLOUX
6 rue du Château d'Eau,
50560 BLAINVILLE-SUR-MER
Tel: (0) 2 33 45 34 13 / (0) 667 62 12 46
Fax: (0) 2 33 45 34 13

This little house with blue shutters has a panoramic view over the bay which contains one of the largest oyster beds in Europe. Maurice, a former baker, frequently exercises his craft and produces wonderful homemade cakes, baked in the old bread oven. Since retiring, he is involved with the Blainville tourist office and you will therefore not find a better guide for boat trips to the surrounding resorts, along the sand dunes or on land to the surprising hinterland. You will certainly not be bored here!

Price Structure – 2 Bedrooms
'Angèle': television, shower room, wc, double bed: €45
'Baptiste': television, shower room, wc, twin beds: €45

Extra Bed: €10
Reduction: 7 nights
Capacity: 4 people

Facilities: private parking, garden, tv lounge, pets not accepted, babies welcome, free cot, 100% no smoking, hiking, golf course, fishing, bird-watching, cycling 2km, sea watersports 2km, riversports 5km

Directions: From Coutances, take the D44 towards Agon-Coutainville. At Tourville-sur-Sienne take the D650 as far as Blainville-sur-Mer. In the village, cross the main square towards 'Cabanor, Le Senequet', then take the first on the right and the house is opposite a small water tower.

50.62 Coutances

Private Home

Location
16km S E of COUTANCES
in: Hambye
car essential

Lavinia & John BEVINGTON
'Maison Quesnel', 7 place Jeanne Painel,
50450 HAMBYE
Tel: (0) 2 33 50 89 25
j-l.bevington@wanadoo.fr
www.maisonquesnel.com

In true English style, you will probably find John in his garage and Lavinia, a retired caterer, in her kitchen. If you appreciate vintage and classic cars, you will admire John's two MGs, which he is currently restoring. The welcome is warm and friendly and you have the run of the house. The bedrooms are spacious and decorated with style. There is a large garden, with a croquet lawn. Lavinia's dinners combine English and French cuisines and her breakfast is served in the room with an impressive fireplace. Let them show you the area, it will be great fun.

Price Structure – 2 Bedrooms and 1 Suite
2 rooms: television, shower room, wc, double bed: €58
television, shower room, wc, twin beds. En-suite room, television, washbasin, double bed: €50 – 2 people €95 – 4 people

Extra Bed: €13
Reduction: 3 nights
Capacity: 8 people

Facilities: private parking, garden, lounge, pets not accepted, dinner available, babies welcome, free cot, 100% no smoking
Fluent English spoken

Directions: Please contact your hosts for detailed directions.

Location

GRANVILLE
in: Granville, station pick-up on arrival/departure
car essential

✴ ✴ ✴

Residence of Outstanding Character

A ship owner's home from the 18th century, standing on the ramparts of Granville's old town, which dominate the port with fine views of the sea and the Iles de Chausey. Inside are many maritime objects collected over the years and a pleasant, relaxed atmosphere. The bedrooms are on several floors but the third floor room, reached via a narrow staircase, has the best views of the port and the beach. In the garden, with a courtyard (great in summer), is a self-contained apartment that can be booked on a B&B basis. Secure parking.

Facilities: private parking, garden, lounge, babies welcome, free cot, gliding, fishing, hiking, cycling, sea watersports, golf course 4km
Adequate English spoken

Directions: At Granville head for the 'Centre-Ville' then the 'Haute Ville'. Head up to the ramparts and pass through the Grand' Porte to the Place Forte. Take the first road on the right and then the fourth road on the right (the only one viable by car) and then right again.

Annette & Philippe BOUGLIER DESFONTAINES
33 rue Lecarpentier, 50400 GRANVILLE
Tel: (0) 2 33 90 61 14 / (0) 674 54 34 52

Price Structure – 1 Bedroom, 1 Suite and 1 Apartment
suite: bathroom, wc, double bed. En-suite room, television, 2 single beds: €60 – 2 people €90 – 4 people
room: shower room, wc, double bed: €60
apartment: lounge, television, kitchen, shower room, wc, 2 double beds, twin beds: €60 – 2 people €150 – 6 people

Extra Bed: €15
Capacity: 12 people

Location

2km S of LE MONT-ST-MICHEL
in: Ardevon
Railway station: 7km
Airport: Rennes St-Jacques 50km
car essential

✴ ✴ ✴

Working Farm

This majestic, impressive house is on a farm behind fields of carrots and potatoes. It has an uninterrupted view of Le Mont-St-Michel from the garden, which is separated from the road by a thick hedge. Everything runs professionally and is well organised.

Facilities: off-street parking, garden, lounge, hosts have pets, babies welcome, free cot, 100% no smoking, wheelchair access, closed: 15/11–08/02, hiking, fishing, hunting, bird-watching, cycling 5km
Adequate English spoken

Directions: When you are on the D976, Pontorson to Le Mont-St-Michel road, 7km from Pontorson turn right onto the D275. Continue for 300m and the farm is on the left.

Claudine BRAULT
'La Jacotière', Ardevon, 50170 PONTORSON
Tel: (0) 2 33 60 22 94 Fax: (0) 2 33 60 20 48
la.jacotiere@wanadoo.fr

Price Structure – 5 Bedrooms and 1 Apartment
'Marine': wheelchair access, television, shower room, wc, double bed: €60
'Familiale': television, shower room, wc, 2 double beds, single bed: €62 – 2 people €108 – 5 people
'Romantique': television, shower room, wc, double bed: €60
'Rétro': wheelchair access, television, shower room, wc, double bed, single bed: €76,50 – 3 people
'Campagne': television, shower room, wc, double bed, 2 single beds: €92 – 4 people. Plus 1 apart.

Reduction: 3 nights
Capacity: 19 people

50.59 Le Mont-St-Michel

Private Home

Juliette HALLAIS
7 La Rive, Ardevon, 50170 PONTORSON
Tel: (0) 2 33 60 80 30 / (0) 687 29 64 63
juliette.hallais@wanadoo.fr
juliette.ifrance.com

Price Structure – 2 Bedrooms and 1 Suite
2 rooms: television, shower room, wc, double bed: €36
television, shower room, wc, double bed. En-suite room, twin beds: €36 – 2 people €60 – 4 people

Extra Bed: €10
Capacity: 8 people

Location
2km S of LE MONT-ST-MICHEL
in: Ardevon
Railway station: 7km
car essential

On the edge of an isolated hamlet, Juliette lives in a newly built house surrounded by fields in a unique spot. From the end of the road are panoramic views of the Mont-St-Michel and its flocks of *pré-salé* sheep, a view worthy of the best postcards of the region! The independent guest rooms are on the first floor and are spotlessly clean, and there is a communal room reserved for guests. There is a restaurant nearby and a GR route all the way to the bay.

Facilities: off-street parking, garden, hosts have pets, pets not accepted, kitchen, babies welcome, free cot, 2 nights minimum stay, hiking, cycling, riversports 5km, golf course 20km, gliding 30km

Directions: From Avranches take the fast road to St-Malo for 8km then turn right towards the Mont-St-Michel via the coast. D43, D75 for 12km. After the 'Auberge de la Baie', turn left towards Ardevon for 500m. The house is on the right just after exiting the hamlet.

50.40 Le Mont-St-Michel

Private Home

Danielle VOISIN TCHEN
'Les Vieilles Digues', route du Mont-St-Michel, 50170 BEAUVOIR
Tel: (0) 2 33 58 55 30 / (0) 624 79 27 38
Fax: (0) 2 33 58 83 09
danielle.tchen@wanadoo.fr
www.bnb-normandy.com

Price Structure – 6 Bedrooms
4 rooms: wheelchair access, shower room, wc, double bed: €65
shower room, wc, double bed, 2 single beds: €101 – 4 people
'Vue sur le Mont': shower room, wc, double bed, single bed: €83 – 3 people

Extra Bed: €18
Reduction: 15/10–01/04, groups
Capacity: 15 people

Location
3km S of LE MONT-ST-MICHEL
in: Beauvoir
Railway station: 5km
Airport: Rennes St-Jacques 45km
car essential

Danielle and Kim are a Franco-Vietnamese couple who are completely trilingual. They have combined their skills and cultures with great effect to restore this large family home with a warm welcome. The décor is elegant, the garden well tended and there is a bar in the guests' lounge. The Couesnon River is a stone's throw from the house and there is a lovely walk along its banks for 3km as far as the Mont-St-Michel.

Facilities: private parking, garden, tv lounge, hosts have pets, pets not accepted, kitchen, wheelchair access, closed: 01/01–31/01, hiking, cycling, fishing, bird-watching, mushroom-picking 15km, interesting flora 25km, riversports 25km, golf course 30km
Fluent English spoken

Directions: From Pontorson, take the D976 towards Le Mont-St-Michel. It is the first house on the right as you leave Beauvoir. The house is set back from the main road.

Location
15km S of LE MONT-ST-MICHEL
in: Pleine-Fougères
Railway station: 3km
Airport: Rennes St-Jacques 60km
car essential

Residence of Outstanding Character

Just 10 kilometres from the Mont-St-Michel, in green and tranquil farmland, is this house dating back to the late 16th century. Inside is a large living room with an impressive fireplace and a double wooden staircase leading up to nautical guest rooms with attractive, exposed beams. Games are available on the first floor in a room that also serves as Evelyne's art studio. The grounds are being landscaped and extend down to a river where donkeys and horses can also be stabled. On sale: wine, homemade bread and painting courses.

Evelyne HARCHIN
'Entre Terre et Mer', La Touche,
35610 PLEINE-FOUGERES
Tel: (0) 2 99 48 65 39 / (0) 682 45 20 85
mer.terre@wanadoo.fr

Facilities: off-street parking, extensive grounds, tv lounge, hosts have pets, babies welcome, free cot, fishing, hunting, hiking, cycling, mushroom-picking 3km, riversports 3km, bird-watching 5km, gliding 8km, sea watersports 15km, golf course 20km
Adequate English spoken

Price Structure – 3 Bedrooms
'Cabine 3': bathroom, wc, double bed, single bed:
€48 – 2 people €61 – 3 people
'Automne': bathroom, wc, double bed: €48
'Capitaine': bathroom, wc, double bed, 2 single beds
(child-size): €48 – 2 people €74 – 4 people

Extra Bed: €13
Reduction: 1/11–31/03, 5 nights
Capacity: 9 people

Directions: At Pontorson centre, D576 direction Dol-de-Bretagne for 2km then D4 on the left towards Pleine-Fougères. After the railway line (1km), take the second road on the left (signposted).

Location
15km S of LE MONT-ST-MICHEL
in: Sains
Railway station: 7km
Airport: Rennes St-Jacques 70km
car essential

Private Home

Near to the Mont-St-Michel, in a new residential area, is this house in stone in a garden of flowers with a lawn and a miniature mill that looks out over the countryside. The first floor is for guests, with a kitchen and a lounge. There are two bedrooms, one classic and the other a family room in sea colours. In view of the price range and the facilities on offer (dressing gowns, secure private parking) they are more than satisfactory. A natural and spontaneous welcome but watch out for their potent cider! Françoise is a keen walker.

Françoise & Maurice BAZIN
32 rue de Bellevue, 35610 SAINS
Tel: (0) 2 99 48 54 41 / (0) 672 80 75 36

Facilities: off-street parking, garden, lounge, hosts have pets, kitchen, babies welcome, free cot, 100% no smoking, hiking, cycling, fishing 2km, bird-watching 4km, mushroom-picking 5km, golf course 15km, sea watersports 20km

Price Structure – 1 Bedroom and 1 Suite
'Suite Nature': television, along corridor bathroom, wc, double bed. En-suite room, television, twin beds:
€37,20 – 2 people €58,40 – 4 people
'La Mer': television, along corridor bathroom, wc, 3 single beds: €37,20 – 2 people €47,80 – 3 people

Extra Bed: €10,60
Reduction: 7 nights
Capacity: 7 people

Directions: On the fast road between St-Malo (32km) and Avranches (27km), exit at Sains. Pass in front of the church and head towards Pleine-Fougères and take the second road on the right into Rue de Bellevue.

Normandy – Le Mont-St-Michel

35.81 Le Mont-St-Michel

Private Home

Christiane COQUELIN
La Mahommerie, 35460 TREMBLAY
Tel: (0) 2 99 98 27 21 / (0) 662 75 05 44
christiane.coquelin@orange.fr

Price Structure – 2 Bedrooms
2 rooms: shower room, wc, double bed, 2 single beds: €55 – 2 people €70 – 4 people

Extra Bed: €15
Reduction: groups
Capacity: 8 people

Location
25km S of LE MONT-ST-MICHEL
in: Tremblay
Railway station: 40km
Airport: Rennes St-Jacques 40km
car essential

Just outside the village, in a spot of green, you will find Christiane's restored stone farmhouse. It is quiet here, and there is a beautiful panorama over the Couesnon valley. There are two family rooms which are spacious and comfortable. You reach them via the 300-year-old wooden staircase which has been retained to preserve the style of the place. The lounge and dining room are available to you, with a fireplace in the cooler months, where Christiane serves dinner. Breakfast is plentiful with lots of different homemade jams, served either indoors or on the terrace.

Facilities: off-street parking, lounge, dinner available, 2 nights minimum stay, closed: 30/11–31/03, hunting, fishing, mushroom-picking, hiking, cycling

Directions: From the Mont-St-Michel take the N175 towards Rennes. In Tremblay, on the church square follow signs to the hotel-restaurant 'Rockland', and when you have passed it, take the first road on the left to the hamlet of La Mahommerie and follow the signs.

61.13 Mortagne-au-Perche

Residence of Outstanding Character

Frédérique & Emmanuel VALENTIN
'Lauseraie', Lauseraie,
61130 BELLOU-LE-TRICHARD
Tel: (0) 2 37 91 00 94 / (0) 683 38 09 85
evalentin@club-internet.fr
http://lauseraie.free.fr

Price Structure – 4 Bedrooms
'Au Bouquet': shower room, wc, double bed (queen-size): €65
'Bibliothèque': shower room, wc, 2 double beds (queen-size): €70 – 2 people €110 – 4 people
'Mansardée': bathroom, wc, double bed (king-size): €70
'Au Colombage': bathroom, wc, double bed (queen-size): €80

Extra Bed: €25
Reduction: 3 nights, children
Capacity: 10 people

Location
32km S of MORTAGNE-AU-PERCHE
in: Bellou-le-Trichard, station pick-up on arrival/departure
Railway station: 12km
car essential

She is a journalist and he is a photographer. They left Paris to settle in the Parc Naturel Régional du Perche. Frédérique and Emmanuel's 18th-century farm with five outbuildings is isolated in the heart of the countryside where aside from wild animals, only cows and Jacques, their donkey mascot, are around for company. Everything is authentic here, in keeping with local traditions. The welcome is sincere and your hosts' love for the region is infectious. Comfortable bedrooms and a lounge with a piano for an impromptu recital.

Facilities: off-street parking, extensive grounds, tv lounge, pets not accepted, kitchen, babies welcome, free cot, hiking, cycling, fishing 2km, mushroom-picking 10km, golf course 12km, lake watersports 12km
Fluent English spoken

Directions: Motorway A11 Paris-Le Mans, exit La Ferté-Bernard. At La Ferté-Bernard, D36 direction Bellême. At St-Germain-de-la-Coudre turn right to Bellou-le-Trichard for 4km. Before Bellou-le-Trichard, turn left towards Lauzeraie for 600m. When the road bends to the right, take the lane that is straight ahead. It is straight away on the left.

61.03 Mortagne-au-Perche

Location
10km S of MORTAGNE-AU-PERCHE
in: Le Pin-la-Garenne
Railway station: 30km
Airport: Paris-Orly 130km
car essential

✳ ✳ ✳

Working Farm

Madame du Plessis is charming. You will stay in a little house within this working farm. It has a lot of class and has been furnished with great taste and character. In September there is a programme of cultural events. A region with beautiful forests.

Joseph Le MOTHEUX du PLESSIS
'La Miotière', 61400 LE PIN-LA-GARENNE
Tel: (0) 2 33 83 84 01 Fax: (0) 2 33 83 81 24
joseph.du-plessis@tele2.fr

Facilities: off-street parking, extensive grounds, lounge, hosts have pets, pets not accepted, dinner available, babies welcome, free cot, wheelchair access, hiking, mushroom-picking, golf course 10km
Basic English spoken

Price Structure – 1 Suite and 2 Apartments
House 1: shower room, wc, double bed. En-suite room, lounge, 2 single beds: €80 – 2 people €120 – 4 people
House 2 : lounge, kitchen, bathroom, wc, double bed. En-suite room, twin beds: €80 – 2 people €120 – 4 people
House 3: lounge, kitchen, bathroom, wc, double bed. En-suite room, 2 single beds. En-suite room, single bed: €80 – 2 people €120 – 5 people

Extra Bed: €12
Reduction: 3 nights, groups
Capacity: 13 people

Directions: In Mortagne, take the D938 towards Le Pin-la-Garenne. In the village, turn right onto the D256 towards St-Jouin-de-Blavou for about 1km. It is the first lane on the left.

76.39 Dieppe

Location
7km E of DIEPPE
in: Derchigny
Railway station: 7km
car essential

Residence of Outstanding Character

As we go to press, this host has not yet been classified, but will be shortly. At Dieppe the sea is bracing and this place is 3km from it. Anne-Lise and Philippe invite you to share the atmosphere of this authentic family home (they have brought up four children here), which is also a manor house dating from the 18th and 19th centuries. Comfort is guaranteed here and there is plenty to do: a putting green, sophrology sessions and cultural visits. Or why not admire the changing light by the sea after a parachuting lesson? They also arrange babysitters.

Anne-Lise & Philippe BARON
'Manoir de Graincourt', 10 place Ludovic Panel,
76370 DERCHIGNY
Tel: (0) 2 35 84 12 88 / (0) 617 21 36 16
Fax: (0) 2 35 84 12 88
contact@manoir-de-graincourt.com
www.manoir-de-graincourt.com

Facilities: off-street parking, extensive grounds, tv lounge, pets not accepted, internet access, dinner available, babies welcome, free cot
Fluent English spoken

Price Structure – 4 Bedrooms and 1 Suite
'Auguste Renoir': bathroom, wc, double bed (queen-size), single bed: €100 – 2 people €117 – 3 people
'Cidre et Pommiers': shower room, wc, 2 single beds: €84
'Papillons': bathroom, wc, double bed (queen-size), single bed (child-size): €84 – 2 people €97 – 3 people
'Arlequin': shower room, wc, double bed (queen-size), single bed: €95 – 3 people
'Suite Fleurie': lounge, shower room, wc, double bed (queen-size). En-suite room, twin beds: €119 – 2 people €135 – 4 people

Capacity: 15 people

Directions: From Dieppe take the D925 towards Eu and Le Tréport. The village is about 10km further on on the right, and the manor is next to the church.

76.37 Dieppe

Château/Manor House

Marika GEZIC-ROULIN
'Vieux Manoir Neuville-les-Dieppe', 32 rue du Général de Gaulle, 76370 NEUVILLE-LES-DIEPPE
Tel: (0) 662 57 72 86
Fax: (0) 2 35 83 51 86
marika@manoirdeneuville.fr
www.manoirdeneuville.fr

Price Structure – 4 Bedrooms
'Nuptiale': bathroom, wc, shower, four-poster double bed: €100
'Henri IV': bathroom, wc, shower, double bed: €90
'Romantique': lounge, shower room, wc, double bed: €74
'Normande': along corridor shower, wc, washbasin, double bed: €49

Extra Bed: €25
Reduction: 1/10–1/05, 3 nights
Capacity: 8 people

Location
DIEPPE
in: Neuville-lès-Dieppe, station pick-up on arrival/departure
Railway station: Dieppe
Airport: Dieppe 4km

Marika and François charm you with their love for this 16th-century residence where Henri IV stayed during the battle at Arques. Marika's strong sense of hospitality from her Serbo-Croat roots is spontaneous and genuine. Stroll in the grounds, play billiards or relax in the sitting room by an open fire. The bedrooms with exposed beams are well decorated. The modest 'Normande' room should be considered as an extra room only. A copious breakfast is served in this open, friendly, characterful house, five minutes from the beaches and Dieppe.

Facilities: private parking, extensive grounds, tv lounge, hosts have pets, dinner available, kitchen, babies welcome, free cot, 2 nights minimum stay: 1/07-31/08, golf course, hiking, cycling, sea watersports, fishing 4km, riversports 4km, interesting flora 8km
Adequate English spoken

Directions: Head for Dieppe Centre-Ville and signs for the 'Office de Tourisme' then head for Le Tréport. Cross over the two bridges and head up the hill. At the fifth set of traffic lights, turn right and head to the 'Eglise St Aubin', then take the second road on the left.

76.26 Dieppe

Residence of Outstanding Character

Jacqueline CAILLOUET
**'L'Ermitage', rue Jacob Bontemps,
76730 OMONVILLE**
Tel: (0) 2 35 83 20 82 / (0) 610 57 38 69

Price Structure – 3 Bedrooms
ground floor 'Verte': bathroom, wc, twin beds: €77
first floor 'Bleue': shower, wc, double bed: €75
first floor 'Rouge': twin beds, single bed:
€68 – 2 people €88 – 3 people

Extra Bed: €15
Reduction: 3 nights
Capacity: 7 people

Location
15km S of DIEPPE
in: Omonville
Ferry port: 15km
Airport: Rouen-Boos 50km
car essential

Jacqueline and Yves have kept this place as a treasure house, devoted to several generations of their family. Nothing much has changed and the place is like a small family museum, full of mementoes and serious nostalgia. The house is set in its own grounds, in a lovely little village within easy reach of Dieppe and the coast. Although we found the odd cobweb, this does not detract from this authentic experience of a genuine French family home.

Facilities: off-street parking, extensive grounds, lounge, pets not accepted, dinner available, hiking, golf course 15km, interesting flora 15km, sea watersports 15km
Adequate English spoken

Directions: From the *autoroute*, take the exit Omonville and, when you are in the village on the main road, follow the sign to 'Centre Bourg', on the left. 'L'Ermitage' is opposite the church on the left before you reach the first road.

Residence of Outstanding Character

Location
ETRETAT
in: Etretat
Railway station: 20km
Airport: Le Havre 25km

As we go to press this home has not yet been classified, but will be shortly. You are not dreaming! Jon has turned this 19th-century manor house into a real jewel, just 50m from the beach. He has restored it with class and meticulous decoration, both in the main building and also in the 'friends' house'. The attention to detail is remarkable, and once installed you will not want to leave. Even though it is in the centre of Etretat, the garden is quiet and relaxing.

Facilities: garden, tv lounge, hosts have pets, pets not accepted, internet access, babies welcome, free cot, 100% no smoking, 2 nights minimum stay, closed: 2/01–31/01
Fluent English spoken

Directions: In Etretat, follow signs to the beach ('La Plage'). The Rue Boissaye is the last street before the beach.

Jon COOPER
'Jardin Gorbeau', 27 rue Boissaye, 76790 ETRETAT
Tel: (0) 2 35 27 16 72 / (0) 684 32 45 05
Fax: (0) 2 72 68 55 19
info@gorbeau.com
www.gorbeau.com

Price Structure – 5 Bedrooms
'Cosette', 'Fanine' & 'Laigle': lounge, television, shower room, wc, double bed (queen-size): €130
'Gavroche' & 'Enjolras': lounge, television, shower room, wc, double bed (queen-size): €130

Extra Bed: €15
Reduction: 7 nights
Capacity: 10 people

Location
8km S E of ETRETAT
in: Criquetot-l'Esneval, station pick-up on arrival/departure
Railway station: 15km
Airport: Le Havre 12km
car essential

Bienvenue en France

✸ ✸ ✸
Château/Manor House

Just 8km from the famous cliffs of Etretat, Brigitte and Serge, a couple of retired farmers, have settled in the manor house of their dreams. At the heart of this charming little town, the large meadows have that idyllic, pastoral look, with flocks of sheep grazing under the trees. Brigitte will offer you a glass of cider and you will probably leave with a whole bottle, another souvenir of *la douce France*. There is a see-saw for the children and Calvados for the grown-ups! On sale: cider.

Facilities: private parking, extensive grounds, tv lounge, hosts have pets, pets not accepted, dinner available, wheelchair access, hiking, cycling, mushroom-picking 2km, fishing 3km, golf course 8km, sea watersports 8km
Basic English spoken

Directions: From Etretat, take the D39 towards Criquetot-l'Esneval. The manor house is on the square leading to the church.

Brigitte & Serge QUEVILLY
'Le Manoir', 5 place des Anciens Elèves, route d'Etretat, 76280 CRIQUETOT-L'ESNEVAL
Tel: (0) 2 35 29 31 90 / (0) 630 46 54 07
Fax: (0) 2 35 29 31 90
serge.quevilly@wanadoo.fr
www.quevillyserge.com

Price Structure – 5 Bedrooms
first floor 'Cardinal': shower room, wc, bathroom, double bed, single bed: €66 – 2 people €75 – 3 people
first floor 'Bleue': shower room, wc, double bed, single bed: €66 – 2 people €75 – 3 people
first floor 'Mme Maugean': shower room, wc, bathroom, 2 double beds: €66 – 2 people €85 – 4 people
second floor 'Vitrée' & 'Fond': shower room, wc, double bed, single bed: €64 – 2 people €70 – 3 people

Extra Bed: €10
Capacity: 16 people

Normandy – Etretat

76.36 Rouen

Residence of Outstanding Character

Christiane & Sophie LOUIS DE PAS
'Les Vallées', 76750 BOIS-GUILBERT
Tel: (0) 2 35 34 41 23
jeromejum@wanadoo.fr

Price Structure – 2 Bedrooms
first room: lounge, bathroom, wc, twin beds, single bed: €66 – 2 people €86 – 3 people
second room: bathroom, wc, twin beds, single bed: €66 – 2 people €86 – 3 people

Extra Bed: €25
Reduction: 3 nights, groups
Capacity: 6 people

Location
36km N E of ROUEN
in: Bois-Guilbert, station pick-up on arrival/departure
Railway station: 10km
Airport: Rouen-Boos 30km
car essential

A winding dirt track leads through woods to this half-timbered Normandy farmhouse, hidden away in a charming pastoral valley. The bedrooms with sloping ceilings sit under the rafters, where the stairs are narrow and the windows are small, evoking the warm feel of a cosy cottage (but the bathrooms are cramped and impractical). A lovely spot, home to many ponies with a club for children and where horses are accommodated. The pool has views over the rolling hills and there is a friendly welcome from Christiane and her daughter Sophie.

Facilities: off-street parking, extensive grounds, lounge, hosts have pets, pets not accepted, dinner available, babies welcome, free cot, 100% no smoking, private swimming pool, riding, hiking, interesting flora, vineyard, fishing 5km, cycling 7km, golf course 17km
Fluent English spoken

Directions: From Rouen take the A28 towards Abbeville for 16km then exit heading to Buchy on the D919. At Buchy take the D41 to Bois-Guilbert then the D261 towards Héronchelles for 3km. Follow the signs in the wood on the unsurfaced track; 'Les Vallées' is on the left.

76.31 Rouen

Private Home

Françoise & Daniel COURTENS
'La Ferme du Colombier', chemin du Catelier, 76350 OISSEL-SUR-SEINE
Tel: (0) 2 35 66 23 06 / (0) 622 60 15 11
francoisecourtens@yahoo.fr
f.courtens.free.fr

Price Structure – 2 Bedrooms
'Bleue' & 'Verte': shower room, wc, twin beds, single bed (child-size): €50

Extra Bed: €12
Reduction: 2 nights
Capacity: 6 people

Location
6km S of ROUEN
in: Oissel-sur-Seine, station pick-up on arrival/departure
Railway station: 2km
Airport: 10km
car essential

This former farm once served a château and is in an outstanding rural setting on the edge of a forest, overlooking the Vallée de la Seine. Of note is the imposing dovecote in the large garden, which dates back to the 16th century and is currently undergoing restoration. The living and breakfast rooms are full of interesting old trinkets and artefacts such as an old creamer! You receive a warm and attentive welcome from Françoise who serves homemade *pâtisseries* and bread. She also supplies all sorts of information on the area.

Facilities: private parking, extensive grounds, lounge, babies welcome, free cot, 100% no smoking
Fluent English spoken

Directions: South of Rouen on the A13, take exit 22 towards Rouen-Centre and Oissel. Then turn right to Oissel-Centre and then right and right again onto the Route des Roches along the River Seine. Pass under the *autoroute* and then turn right into Chemin du Catelier. Follow the signs until you reach 'La Ferme du Colombier'.

Location
7km N W of ROUEN
in: St-Jean-du-Cardonnay
Railway station: 8km
Airport: Rouen-Boos 20km
car essential

Working Farm

This is a 17th-century half-timbered Normandy farmhouse in the heart of the country, with a duck pond. You could visit the abbeys in the region, but you are more likely to decide to stay and be enthralled by the warm smile and welcome of Marie-Cécile.

Marie-Cécile LAMBERT
'La Ferme de Vivier', 88 route de Duclair,
76150 ST-JEAN-DU-CARDONNAY
Tel: (0) 2 35 33 80 42 Fax: (0) 2 35 33 80 42
lambert76150@yahoo.fr
http://membres.lycos.fr/lambert76150

Facilities: off-street parking, garden, lounge, pets not accepted, kitchen, 100% no smoking, wheelchair access, riversports 4km, golf course 15km, sea watersports 45km
Basic English spoken

Price Structure – 5 Bedrooms
'Rose': television, shower room, wc, double bed: €45
'Bleue': television, shower room, wc, twin beds: €45
'Iris': television, shower room, wc, double bed, single bed: €45 – 2 people €67 – 3 people
'Palmiers': television, shower room, wc, double bed, 2 single beds: €45 – 2 people €89 – 4 people
'Rhododendron': television, shower room, wc, washbasin, double bed: €45

Extra Bed: €22
Reduction: children
Capacity: 13 people

Directions: At Rouen, take the A15 towards Dieppe, Le Havre for 4km. Take the second exit to St-Jean-du-Cardonnay. On the second roundabout take the D43 towards Duclair. Continue for 2km, and the house is on the right.

Location
24km E of ROUEN
in: Vascoeuil
Railway station: 23km
Airport: Rouen-Boos 22km

Private Home

Close to the magnificent forest of Lyon and Rouen, tucked away on a sleepy road in the village, is this former 19th-century *café-épicerie*. The guest room is very pleasant with a wooden floor, 1900s-style bathtub and objects acquired here and there by your hosts. Enjoy the flowers and trees in the garden and the village tennis courts (free of charge), plus the many châteaux, art exhibitions and botanical gardens in the area that are worthy of your attention. Karine teaches dance and François is a school teacher.

Karine & François SEDARD
'L'Epicerie du Pape', 5 rue de la Ferme,
27910 VASCOEUIL
Tel: (0) 2 35 23 64 37 / (0) 681 29 02 41
lepiceriedupape@club-internet.fr
http://perso.club-internet.fr/sedard/

Facilities: private parking, garden, lounge, hosts have pets, babies welcome, free cot, hunting, fishing, mushroom-picking, hiking, cycling, interesting flora, riversports 20km, gliding 22km, golf course 23km, sea watersports 75km
Fluent English spoken

Price Structure – 1 Bedroom
bathroom, wc, double bed, single bed, cot:
€60 – 2 people €75 – 3 people

Reduction: 4 nights
Capacity: 3 people

Directions: From Rouen, N131 towards Gournay-en-Bray for 22km until Vascoeuil. Pass in front of the château and follow signs to 'L'Epicerie du Pape'.

Normandy – Rouen

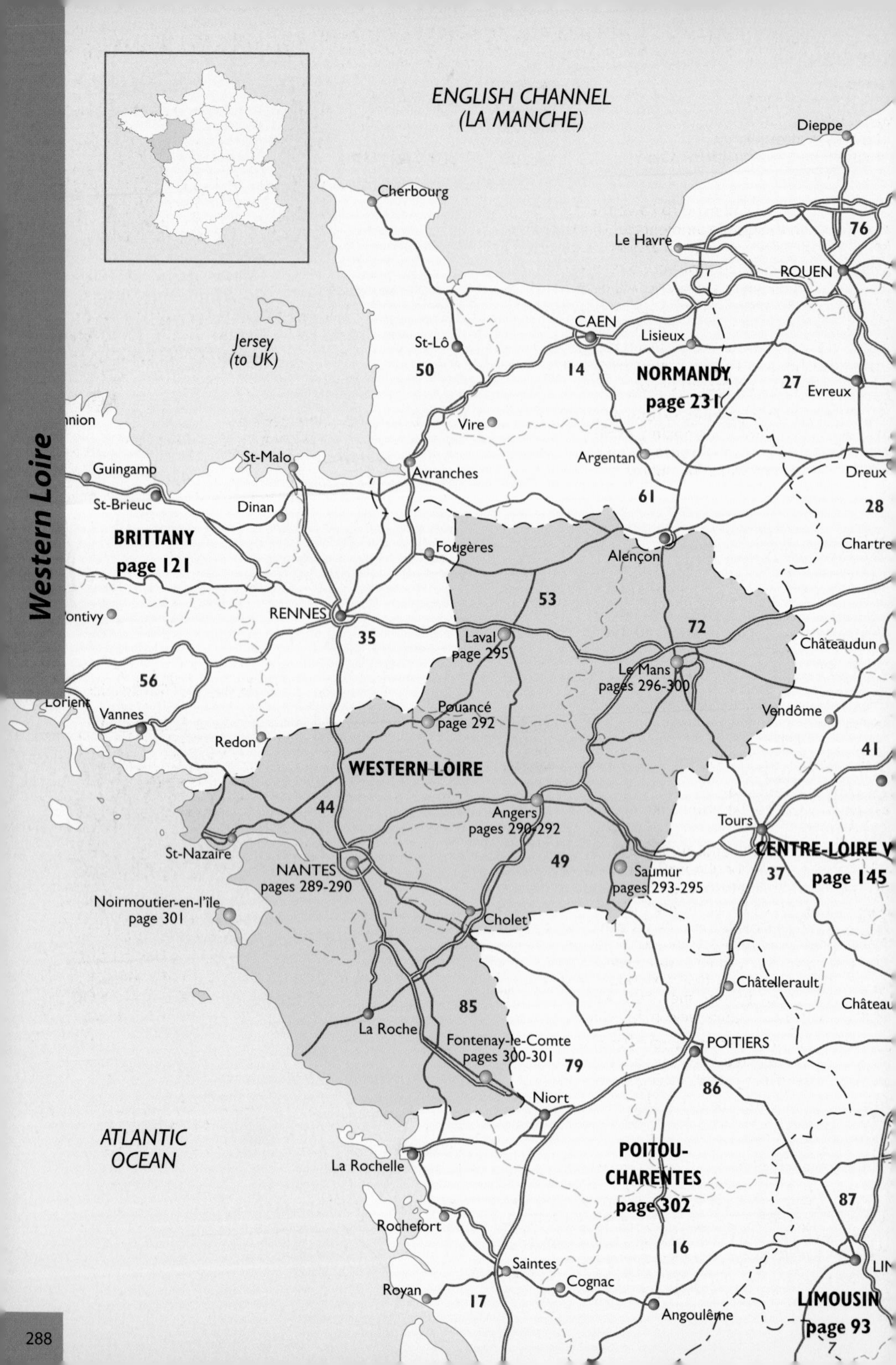

ENGLISH CHANNEL
(LA MANCHE)

Dieppe

Cherbourg

Le Havre

76

ROUEN

St-Lô

CAEN

Lisieux

NORMANDY
page 231

27

Evreux

50

14

Vire

Argentan

61

Dreux

28

Jersey
(to UK)

St-Malo

Avranches

Chartre

Guingamp

Dinan

Fougères

Alençon

nnion

St-Brieuc

BRITTANY
page 121

53

72

Châteaudun

ontivy

RENNES

Laval
page 295

Le Mans
pages 296-300

35

Vendôme

56

Pouancé
page 292

41

Lorient

Vannes

Redon

WESTERN LOIRE

St-Nazaire

44

Angers
pages 290-292

Tours

CENTRE-LOIRE V
page 145

NANTES
pages 289-290

49

Saumur
pages 293-295

37

Noirmoutier-en-l'île
page 301

Cholet

Châtellerault

Château

85

La Roche

Fontenay-le-Comte
pages 300-301

79

POITIERS

86

Niort

ATLANTIC
OCEAN

La Rochelle

POITOU-
CHARENTES
page 302

87

Rochefort

16

LIN

Saintes

Royan

17

Cognac

Angoulême

LIMOUSIN
page 93

Western Loire – Nantes

Location
40km S of NANTES
in: Legé
Railway station: 45km
Airport: Nantes-Atlantique 40km
car essential

Château/Manor House

To find this place you need to leave the main roads. Then relax in the gentle ambience of this large 17th-century mansion, typical of La Vendée. Françoise and Alain are retired, and punctilious respecters of tradition. They love this area and will be delighted to introduce you to it. At breakfast you will also be impressed by Françoise's decoration skills, as she has painted the china and the table linen, using her own special technique. This charming personal touch is also found in the bathroom décor.

Françoise & Alain de TERNAY
'Logis de Richebonne', 44650 LEGE
Tel: (0) 2 40 04 90 41 / (0) 661 78 90 41
Fax: (0) 2 40 04 90 41
adeternay@wanadoo.fr

Facilities: private parking, extensive grounds, pets not accepted, 100% no smoking, fishing, hiking, sea watersports 9km, mushroom-picking 10km, golf course 30km, bird-watching 30km
Basic English spoken

Price Structure – 3 Bedrooms
'Suite': bathroom, wc, double bed, 2 single beds:
€70 – 2 people €118 – 4 people
'Ciel de Lit': shower room, wc, double bed: €70
'Oiseaux': bathroom, wc, double bed: €70

Extra Bed: €18
Capacity: 8 people

Directions: From the A83, exit 4 Montaigu, south of Nantes. Head towards Nantes and right onto D753 towards Rocheservière and Legé. Head towards 'Legé-Centre' and go through the town towards Challans, Machecoul. After the last house in the village (which is a bar/restaurant), turn left towards the small château.

Location
40km S of NANTES
in: Paulx, station pick-up on arrival/departure
Railway station: 5km
Airport: Nantes-Atlantique 39km
car essential

Private Home

Near the beaches of Pornic and St-Jean-de-Mont is this 18th-century stone longhouse, on route to La Vendée. The bright and colourful bedrooms are credit to Jérôme, a painter-decorator by trade. Breakfast, from organic and fair-trade produce, is served in the communal room. Nature is at the forefront in the large garden with chickens, ducks, ponies and games. Sylvia, a graphologist, is writing her next book; polyglot and passionate about history, she offers with Jérôme an enlightened and attentive welcome. Restaurant 200m.

Sylvia & Jérôme SCHMIDT
'Chambre d'Hôtes la Cartroussière', 17 la Cartroussière, 44270 PAULX
Tel: (0) 2 40 26 02 93 / (0) 661 10 85 95
chambres.hotes.sylvia@tiscali.fr

Facilities: off-street parking, garden, lounge, hosts have pets, pets not accepted, babies welcome, free cot, 100% no smoking, gliding 3km, fishing 3km, hiking 3km, cycling 5km, riversports 6km, bird-watching 10km, golf course 18km, sea watersports 20km
Fluent English spoken

Price Structure – 3 Bedrooms
first room: shower room, wc, double bed (queen-size): €60
second room: bathroom, wc, four-poster double bed, single bed: €60 – 2 people €70 – 3 people
third room: bathroom, wc, four-poster double bed: €52

Capacity: 7 people

Directions: From Nantes, A83 towards Bordeaux, exit 1 for Challans until you reach Machecoul (32km), then at the roundabout take the D13 on the left until the first 'Stop' sign at Paulx. Then turn left and right onto the D73 towards Bois-de-Cené until the roundabout 'Des 5 routes' (3.5km). Head for St-Etienne-de-Mer-Morte for 200m then turn left when facing the water tower. Continue until you reach the house with the blue shutters.

44.05 Nantes

✵ ✵ ✵ ✵

Château/Manor House

Bienvenue en France

Antonio FALANGA
'Château de St-Thomas',
44360 ST-ETIENNE-DE-MONTLUC
Tel: (0) 2 40 85 90 60 Fax: (0) 2 40 86 97 62
chateaudesaintthomas@hotmail.com

Location
25km N W of NANTES
in: St-Etienne-de-Montluc
Railway station: 2km
Airport: Nantes-Atlantique 20km
car essential

A peaceful 19th-century château with wooded grounds and a remarkable lake, this is one of the most beautiful romantic gardens of the Loire estuary. You will be captivated by the charms of this Italian host and his French wife. There are stables and archery in the grounds. An ideal place for playing golf and discovering the marshlands.

Price Structure – 5 Bedrooms
'Saumon': television, bathroom, wc, double bed:
€130
'Verte': bathroom, wc, twin beds. Along corridor room 'Bleue': bathroom, wc, double bed:
€130 – 2 people €260 – 4 people
'Rouge' & 'Romantique': bathroom, wc, double bed:
€130

Extra Bed: €20
Reduction: 01/10–31/05
Capacity: 10 people

Facilities: private parking, extensive grounds, tv lounge, hosts have pets, pets not accepted, dinner available, babies welcome, free cot, riding, hiking, cycling, fishing, golf course 8km, bird-watching 30km

Directions: At Nantes, take the N165 towards Vannes and leave it at St-Etienne-de-Montluc. In the village, after the large square in front of the town hall (*la mairie*), take the second road on the left.

49.24 Angers

Residence of Outstanding Character

Bienvenue en France

Marie-Claire & Bernard BOMPAS
'Domaine Etangs de Bois Robert', route de Candé, 49370 BECON-LES-GRANITS
Tel: (0) 2 41 77 32 85 / (0) 615 40 06 05
Fax: (0) 2 41 77 31 00
mc.bompas@libertysurf.fr
www.anjou-vacances.com

Location
20km W of ANGERS
in: Bécon-les-Granits, station pick-up on arrival/departure
Railway station: 20km
Airport: Angers-Marcé 28km
car essential

This pleasant property is on the châteaux route, situated in the middle of a 6-hectare estate, with several lakes. Breakfast is served in a bright room overlooking the countryside or in the garden beside the lake, home of Napoléon the black swan and his family.

Price Structure – 3 Bedrooms and 1 Suite
'Tour Louis XIII': bathroom, wc, twin beds. En-suite room, lounge, twin beds: €78 – 2 people
€110 – 4 people
'Tropicale': lounge, bathroom, wc, double bed, 2 single beds (child-size): €78 – 2 people
€110 – 4 people
'Bleu' & 'Rose': double bed: €62

Extra Bed: €16
Capacity: 12 people

Facilities: private parking, extensive grounds, tv lounge, hosts have pets, babies welcome, free cot, 1 shared bathroom, wc, cycling, fishing, hiking 1km, golf course 20km, bird-watching 20km, lake watersports 20km, hunting 25km
Fluent English spoken

Directions: From the A11, exit 18. Then take the D963 towards Châteaubriant, as far as Bécon-les-Granits. The property is on the right as you leave the village.

Location
45km N W of ANGERS
in: Chatelais
Railway station: 45km
car essential

This is a really tempting stop between Brittany and the châteaux of the Loire Valley, in an old village that has grown up on a Merovingian archaeological site. This beautiful bourgeois house is enhanced by many superb watercolours, painted by Florence, who also gives lessons. There is a delightful view over the countryside. Richard loves reading, but also plays the bagpipes, which will liven up your evenings. You can just soak up the atmosphere of la vieille France, and the relaxed way of life, typical of this area near Angers. On sale: watercolours, painting lessons.

Facilities: off-street parking, garden, lounge, dinner available, babies welcome, free cot, hiking, cycling, fishing, riversports
Fluent English spoken

Directions: At Angers, take the D129 towards Lion d'Angers, then the D863 for Segré. Take the D923 towards Château-Gonthier for 3km, and then turn left onto the D863 to Craon. At 'L'Hôtellerie de Flée', take the D180 on the left as far as the centre of Chatelais and then take the first street on the left in the village.

Residence of Outstanding Character

Florence & Richard SENCE
'Le Frêne', 22 rue St Sauveur, 49520 CHATELAIS
Tel: (0) 2 41 61 16 45 / (0) 689 41 62 55
Fax: (0) 2 41 61 16 45
lefrene@free.fr
http://lefrene.online.fr

Price Structure – 3 Bedrooms and 1 Suite
'Bleue': shower room, wc, double bed: €55
'Rouge': shower room, wc, twin beds: €55
'Papillons': bathroom, wc, twin beds: €55
suite: lounge, shower room, wc, twin beds. En-suite room, twin beds: €90 – 4 people

Extra Bed: €15
Capacity: 10 people

Location
45km N E of ANGERS
in: Crosmières
Railway station: 18km
Airport: Angers-Marcé 20km
car essential

This dynamic couple have 17 rooms available in this large house, all of which are equally comfortable and pleasant. 'Le Haras de la Potardière' is also ideal for wedding receptions or special events, etc. It is near the châteaux of the Loire Valley, with the mild Anjou weather as a bonus.

Facilities: off-street parking, extensive grounds, lounge, hosts have pets, kitchen, babies welcome, free cot, wheelchair access, private swimming pool, private tennis court, hiking, cycling, fishing 3km, lake watersports 9km
Fluent English spoken

Directions: At Angers on the A11 towards Le Mans, exit Durtal. Head towards Le Mans. In Bazouges turn left towards Crosmières for 3km. The château is on the left.

Château/Manor House

François & Marie BENOIST
'Haras de la Potardière', route de Bazouges, 72200 CROSMIERES
Tel: (0) 2 43 45 83 47 / (0) 685 02 46 15
Fax: (0) 2 43 45 81 06
haras-de-la-potardiere@wanadoo.fr
www.potardiere.com

Price Structure – 16 Bedrooms and 1 Suite
Château
3 rooms: television, telephone, bathroom, wc, double bed (queen-size) or twin beds: €150
'Verte': television, telephone, bathroom, shower, wc, double bed (queen-size): €150
'Saumon': television, telephone, bathroom, shower, wc, double bed, single bed: €180 – 3 people
plus 2 Suites
Haras
1 Suite, 9 rooms from €110 – 2 people to €170 – 4 people

Extra Bed: €23   **Reduction:** groups
Capacity: 43 people

49.41 Angers

Private Home

Bienvenue en France

Location
8km W of ANGERS
in: St-Lambert-la-Potherie, station pick-up on arrival/departure
Railway station: 8km
car essential

In the heart of the countryside, just 8km from Angers is this family home, surrounded by fields and paddocks. This is a training centre for racing horses and Béatrice's husband is a trainer. It is also possible to stop and stable horses here if travelling on horseback. Béatrice is lovely and loves cultural outings and can advise you on the numerous festivals held at Angers or on the *châteaux de la Loire*. The suite here is original and modern, and the lounge space is pleasant and bright. From the bay window is a beautiful view of the horses.

Facilities: off-street parking, garden, tv lounge, hosts have pets, dinner available, kitchen, babies welcome, free cot, riding, hiking, golf course 6km, riversports 10km
Adequate English spoken

Béatrice CHEVALIER DU FAU
'Le Grand Mainguet',
49070 ST-LAMBERT-LA-POTHERIE
Tel: / (0) 680 71 97 32
Fax: (0) 2 41 77 56 38
lemainguet@orange.fr

Price Structure – 1 Suite
'Acacias': television, along corridor shower room, wc, twin beds, single bed. En-suite room, double bed (queen-size): €70 – 2 people €135 – 5 people

Extra Bed: €15
Reduction: 3 nights
Capacity: 5 people

Directions: From Angers, head for Nantes for 5km, then exit at Beaucouzé, Laval. Continue for 1.3km keeping on the left and take the D56 direction St-Clément-de-la-Place for 4.5km. At the crossroads, D105 on the right direction La Meignanne for 600m, then first road on the right. Parking on the right at the end of the lane, it is the house at the end.

49.32 Pouancé

Private Home

Bienvenue en France

Location
3km S of POUANCE
in: La Prévière
Railway station: 16km
Airport: Nantes-Atlantique 60km
car essential

You are right in the centre of this idyllic little village on the church square. Roses grow up the stone walls and Florence and Nicolas welcome you to their 200-year-old house, which has been completely restored, and which they think was formerly the town hall. 'Jardin' is a quiet, separate bedroom on the ground floor which leads directly onto the garden. Your hosts also run a restaurant on the other side of the square where Florence serves simple, quality dishes, which gourmets should not miss.

Facilities: off-street parking, garden, tv lounge, babies welcome, free cot, wheelchair access, closed: 01/02–27/02 & 01/09–04/09, hiking, fishing, mushroom-picking, cycling 3km, lake watersports 3km, gliding 3km
Adequate English spoken

Florence & Nicolas PETITJEAN
7 place de l'Eglise, 49420 LA PREVIERE
Tel: (0) 2 41 92 44 44 / (0) 680 02 94 40 / (0) 633 42 44 70
Fax: (0) 2 41 94 36 54
http://lefourneau.free.fr/

Price Structure – 2 Bedrooms
'Bleue': television, shower room, wc, double bed, single bed: €50
'Jardin': wheelchair access, television, shower room, wc, twin beds: €50

Extra Bed: €20
Reduction: 3 nights
Capacity: 5 people

Directions: Take the N171, the Rennes to Nantes road, as far as Pouancé, then the D878 towards La Prévière for about 3km. In the centre of this village it is number 7 on the church square (Place de l'Eglise).

Location
10km S W of SAUMUR
in: Doué-la-Fontaine
Railway station: 10km
car essential

Private Home

Let Françoise show you her hidden treasures! As she opens the pantry door and you enter her cool cellar full of vintage bottles, you just know that you must stay for dinner. Her welcome is simply genuine, and you have the run of the house. The rooms are comfortable with nice bed linen and electrically adjustable beds. There is a large rose garden next to the house and ducks, geese, chickens and cats roam freely in the garden. Be sure to visit the majestic church at Puy Notre Dame and the vineyards of Saumur and Bellay.

Françoise DOUET
'Les Roses roses', 34 rue de Soulanger,
49700 DOUE-LA-FONTAINE
Tel: (0) 2 41 59 21 43 / (0) 671 63 02 03
Fax: (0) 2 41 50 65 20
douet.F@wanadoo.fr
www.lesrosesroses.com

Facilities: private parking, garden, lounge, hosts have pets, pets not accepted, dinner available, kitchen, babies welcome, free cot, 100% no smoking, hiking, cycling, fishing, vineyard, interesting flora, golf course 10km, riversports 10km
Adequate English spoken

Price Structure – 2 Bedrooms and 1 Suite
'Verte': television, bathroom, wc, double bed (queen-size): €45
'Pavillon': television, shower room, wc, washbasin, double bed (queen-size), single bed: €45 – 2 people €55 – 3 people
'Rose': television, shower room, wc, double bed, single bed. En-suite room, television, washbasin, 2 single beds: €45 – 2 people €75 – 5 people

Directions: Exit 3 Saumur from the A85. Then take the D347 towards Saumur and after Saumur continue on the D960 towards Cholet as far as Doué-la-Fontaine, where you continue towards Cholet, 'Le Jardin des Roses' and 'Parc Zoologique'. The house is next to the rose garden.

Capacity: 10 people

Location
22km S W of SAUMUR
in: Le Puy-Notre-Dame
Railway station: 20km
Airport: Nantes-Atlantique 105km
car essential

Château/Manor House

You will only marvel at your good fortune if, after 'doing' the *châteaux de la Loire*, you take this road which leads you to some of the best wines of Saumur. 'Le Relais', overlooked by its 12th-century collegiate church, contains two spacious bedrooms and a third in the authentically converted wine cellar, with its own kitchen. After a hearty breakfast, there are some wonderful walks on the vine-covered slopes or amongst the walnut trees.

Caroline & Philippe WADOUX
'Relais du Bien-Etre', Château la Paleine, 10 place
Jules Raimbault, 49260 LE PUY-NOTRE-DAME
Tel: (0) 2 41 38 28 25 / (0) 678 51 47 12
Fax: (0) 2 41 38 42 38
lapaleine@wanadoo.fr
www.relais-du-bien-etre.com

Facilities: private parking, extensive grounds, lounge, pets not accepted, kitchen, babies welcome, free cot, 100% no smoking, wheelchair access, closed: 10/01–25/01, hiking, vineyard, fishing 7km, lake watersports 7km
Adequate English spoken

Price Structure – 8 Bedrooms and 1 Apartment
'Glycine': wheelchair access, television, kitchen, shower room, wc, double bed (queen-size), single bed: €79 – 2 people €99 – 3 people
'Foudre': television, bathroom, wc, double bed: €79
'Tilleul': television, shower room, wc, double bed, 3 single beds: €119 – 5 people
'Noyer': television, shower room, wc, twin beds: €68
'Sauvignon': television, shower room, wc, double bed (queen-size): €75
plus 4 rooms

Directions: From Saumur, take the N147 (towards the south) as far as Montreuil-Bellay and then the D77 as far as Le Puy-Notre-Dame. In this village, head towards Doué-la-Fontaine. You will reach the 'Château la Paleine' when you get to the 'Stop' sign, having passed the square. Look for their sign.

Extra Bed: €15   **Reduction:** 01/11–30/04, 3 nights
Capacity: 24 people

49.27 Saumur

Residence of Outstanding Character

Marie BOUILLARD
7 rue des Courances, Les Basses Fontaines,
49700 LES VERCHERS-SUR-LAYON
Tel: (0) 2 41 50 56 80 Fax: (0) 2 41 50 56 80
mariebouillard@loire-fontaines.com
www.loire-fontaines.com

Price Structure – 4 Bedrooms
'Rouge': shower room, wc, double bed: €61
'Verte': bathroom, wc, double bed: €61
'Jaune': bathroom, wc, shower, double bed: €61
'Bleue': shower room, wc, twin beds: €61

Extra Bed: €15
Capacity: 8 people

Location
20km S W of SAUMUR
in: Les Verchers-sur-Layon
Railway station: 22km
Airport: Angers-Marcé 60km
car essential

Marie and Jean-Claude have worked wonders in their conversion of this beautiful old house, typical of the area around Saumur. Their perfect taste and brilliant decorating skills ensure that every room is full of its own distinct character, all in keeping with the style of this old building. As Jean-Claude works for a famous Saumur wine-maker, he knows all the best places to eat and may even be able to get you a table when they are fully booked!

Facilities: private parking, garden, lounge, hosts have pets, pets not accepted, babies welcome, free cot, hiking, cycling, vineyard, fishing 1km, interesting flora 5km, mushroom-picking 8km, golf course 15km, riversports 22km
Adequate English spoken

Directions: From Saumur, D960 to Doué-la-Fontaine. On Place du Champs de Foire, take Avenue du Gl Leclerc and right into Rue d'Argentan. At the crossroads (traffic lights) continue straight on the D69 to Verchers. There, take the first road on the left for 1km, signed Les Fontaines. Cross Les Hautes-Fontaines and take Rue des Courances on the right to Basses-Fontaines. The back of no. 7 is on the left.

49.42 Saumur

Château/Manor House

Chantal & Yves PADOVANI
'Château de Boissimon',
49490 LINIERES-BOUTON
Tel: (0) 2 41 82 30 86 / (0) 682 32 78 35
Fax: (0) 2 41 82 23 86
contact@chateaudeboissimon.com
chateaudeboissimon.com

Price Structure – 3 Bedrooms and 2 Suites
'Baroque': television, bathroom, wc, double bed (king-size). En-suite room, 2 single beds:
€220 – 2 people €280 – 4 people
'Blanche': television, bathroom, wc, shower, double bed (queen-size). En-suite room, 2 single beds:
€190 – 2 people €250 – 4 people
'Nature': television, bathroom, wc, four-poster double bed (queen-size): €160
'Victorienne': television, bathroom, wc, double bed (queen-size), single bed: €220 – 3 people
plus 1 room

Capacity: 15 people

Location
25km N of SAUMUR
in: Linières-Bouton
Railway station: 25km
car essential

We fell in love with the really warm welcome of Chantal and Yves and the charm of this Renaissance château. At night, the ancient trees in the 47-hectare grounds are illuminated to emphasise the beauty of its natural setting. It took them three years to completely restore the château and landscape the grounds. The result is outstanding: comfort, charm and excellent taste and a natural feel. The rooms and bathrooms are bright and spacious. Wherever you look, you will be impressed by the attention to detail and everything is perfect. The prices are more than justified.

Facilities: off-street parking, extensive grounds, tv lounge, pets not accepted, internet access, babies welcome, free cot, 100% no smoking, closed: 1/11–15/04, private swimming pool, hiking, cycling, golf course 15km, lake watersports 15km, vineyard 20km, riversports 25km
Adequate English spoken

Directions: Exit 3 Saumur from the A85. Then take the D767 as far as Linières-Bouton. Go through the village to reach the château.

✹ ✹ ✹

**Residence of
Outstanding
Character**

Location
20km S of SAUMUR
in: Vaudelnay
Railway station: 20km
Airport: Angers-Marcé 60km
car essential

A warm family welcome awaits from Pascale and Olivier in their 17th-century house. The bedrooms are neat and comfortable with attractive stone walls. Olivier is a restaurateur who prepares dinner with produce from the market, notably fresh fish. He also runs cookery courses and wine tours (minimum stays of two nights). They accompany you to the market in the morning and then dinner is prepared in their professionally equipped kitchen. A very pleasant and educational stay.

Facilities: off-street parking, garden, lounge, hosts have pets, dinner available, babies welcome, free cot, closed: 24/12–1/01 & 10/02–26/02, private swimming pool, hiking, cycling, vineyard, fishing 5km, riversports 5km, golf course 20km
Fluent English spoken

Directions: Please contact your hosts in advance for detailed directions.

Pascale & Olivier SCHVIRTZ
'La Pinsonnière', 225 rue du Château, Sanziers,
49260 VAUDELNAY
Tel: (0) 2 41 59 12 95 Fax: (0) 2 41 59 12 95
pascale@la-pinsonniere.fr
www.la-pinsonniere.fr

Price Structure – 3 Bedrooms and 1 Suite
'Oyat': bathroom, wc, shower, double bed (king-size), twin beds: €72 – 2 people €102 – 4 people
'Zanzibar': bathroom, wc, shower, four-poster double bed (queen-size), single bed. En-suite room, 2 single beds: €72 – 2 people €117 – 5 people
'Garance': shower room, wc, double bed: €60
'Shamroch': shower room, wc, double bed (queen-size): €64

Extra Bed: €15
Reduction: 3 nights
Capacity: 13 people

✹ ✹ ✹

Working Farm

Location
29km S W of LAVAL
in: Livré-la-Touche, station pick-up on arrival/departure
Railway station: 30km
Airport: Nantes-Atlantique 100km
car essential

This former farm lives up to its name, in beautiful countryside where cider is produced. Set apart from the main house, the outbuilding has its own living and kitchen area for your use. The attractive bedrooms are decorated in spring colours. One ground floor room opens onto a terrace. Brigitte organises themed weekends on photography and nature. A nurse by profession, she is happy to welcome and assist elderly guests needing extra care and attention. Mountain bike through the orchards to a nature reserve for migrating birds.

Facilities: off-street parking, extensive grounds, lounge, hosts have pets, pets not accepted, kitchen, babies welcome, free cot, 100% no smoking, wheelchair access, hunting, mushroom-picking, hiking, cycling, riversports, fishing 6km, bird-watching 6km, golf course 25km
Adequate English spoken

Directions: From Laval, take the N171 towards Châteaubriant to Craon, then the D25 towards Vitré for 6km and then the C2 on the right towards Livré. Second lane on the left (signposted).

Brigitte & Pierre GILLET
'La Symphonie des Vergers',
53400 LIVRE-LA-TOUCHE
Tel: (0) 2 43 07 46 89 / (0) 618 04 30 19
Fax: (0) 2 43 06 16 54
franlottell@wanadoo.fr
http://persowanadoofrlasymphonieduverger

Price Structure – 4 Bedrooms
'Printemps': television, shower room, wc, twin beds, single bed: €47 – 2 people €60 – 3 people
'Eté': television, shower room, wc, double bed: €47
'Automne': television, shower room, wc, twin beds: €47
'Hiver': television, shower room, wc, double bed, 2 single beds: €55 – 2 people €70 – 4 people

Extra Bed: €15
Reduction: 3 nights
Capacity: 11 people

72.35 Le Mans

Residence of Outstanding Character

Madeleine & Jacques LERET
'Green Lane', 176 avenue Nationale,
72230 ARNAGE
Tel: (0) 2 43 21 29 27
jacques.leret2@wanadoo.fr

Price Structure – 3 Bedrooms
and 1 Apartment
'Arnage': shower room, wc, double bed: €52
'Mulsanne': twin beds, single bed, cot:
€52 – 2 people €64 – 3 people
'Aline': along corridor bathroom, wc, 2 single beds:
€52
'Pavillon': kitchen, shower room, wc, 2 double beds:
€52 – 2 people €74 – 4 people

Extra Bed: €12
Capacity: 11 people

Location
9km S of LE MANS
in: Arnage, station pick-up on arrival/departure
Railway station: 8km
Airport: Le Mans-Arnage 3km

Who would expect to see an English street sign on a house in France? Madeleine and Jacques, a wonderful French couple who lived in Britain for many years, are one of our favourite hosts. Their classic French house, formerly the home of a doctor who was summoned from his fishing by a bell on the roof, extends from the main street of the town down to the river bank. The 'Old Town' of Le Mans, the racing circuit and museum are well worth a visit all year round. Arnage Corner is well known to motor-racing fans throughout the world.

Facilities: private parking, extensive grounds, tv lounge, hosts have pets, babies welcome, free cot, 1 shared shower room, wc, hiking, fishing, cycling 5km, golf course 5km
Fluent English spoken

Directions: When you reach Le Mans, follow signs to Angers. When you enter Arnage pass the petrol station on your right, continue along the main street and when the shops begin to fizzle out, it is on the right just after the last roundabout. Look for 'B&B France' sign.

72.40 Le Mans

Private Home

Bérangère ZARAMELLA
14 rue du Collège, 72150 COURDEMANCHE
Tel: (0) 2 43 44 91 27 Fax: (0) 2 43 44 91 27

Price Structure – 2 Suites
shower room, wc, double bed. En-suite room,
double bed: €50 – 2 people €120 – 4 people
shower room, wc, double bed. En-suite room,
lounge, single bed: €50 – 2 people €90 – 3 people

Extra Bed: €25
Reduction: 7 nights, children
Capacity: 7 people

Location
38km S E of LE MANS
in: Courdemanche
Railway station: 40km
Airport: Tours 50km
car essential

This house is on the scenic wine trail by the banks of the River Loir, a wooded, undulating landscape. The house is spacious and sparsely furnished but the layout of the bedrooms is particularly suitable for large families. Bérangère, a wardrobe mistress, is slowly retiring from the stresses and strains of the Parisian theatre scene to concentrate on looking after this village house by herself. Supplement payable during the 24-hour Le Mans race.

Facilities: private parking, tv lounge, hosts have pets, dinner available, babies welcome, free cot, fishing, mushroom-picking, hiking, cycling, riversports, vineyard 10km
Basic English spoken

Directions: From Le Mans take the D304 towards La Chartre-sur-le-Loir for 35km to St-Pierre-du-Lorouër, then turn left onto the D63 to Courdemanche. The house is practically opposite the town hall (*la mairie*).

Location
32km W of LE MANS
in: Joué-en-Charnie, station pick-up on arrival/departure
Railway station: 25km
car essential

Private Home

After a career in air-navigation, Linda and Christopher settled here. Easy to reach from the main N road (which passes by their land), this typical longhouse is all on one level. It houses new bedrooms, a common room and a kitchen area. A lake with a little island is surrounded by weeping willows. Perfect for walks and for fishing enthusiasts with carp and bream aplenty (equipment available). Opt for a cooked breakfast if you fancy it and enjoy the raised swimming pool. The welcome and the lake are worthy of three 'suns'.

Linda & Christopher ELLIOTT
'La Lune Lake', route de Sille,
72540 JOUE-EN-CHARNIE
Tel: (0) 2 43 21 66 75 / 0044 (0)794 127 8672
lalunebandb@wanadoo.fr
lalunelake.co.uk

Facilities: private parking, garden, hosts have pets, pets not accepted, dinner available, babies welcome, free cot, fishing, hiking, lake watersports 6km, cycling 6km
Fluent English spoken

Price Structure – 4 Bedrooms
television, shower room, wc, double bed: €60
television, along corridor shower room, wc, twin beds: €60
television, along corridor shower room, wc, double bed, single bed: €60 – 2 people €70 – 3 people
television, shower room, wc, double bed, twin beds: €60 – 2 people €80 – 4 people

Reduction: 1/09–30/06, 5 nights, children
Capacity: 11 people

Directions: From Le Mans D357 towards Laval for 31km to the crossroads just 2km after Joué-en-Charnie. D4 on the right. The house is straight away on the left (at the crossroads).

Location
30km S of LE MANS
in: Le Lude
Railway station: 10km
Airport: Le Mans-Arnage 30km
car essential

Bienvenue en France

Private Home

Eliane and Jean-Louis are teachers and adore conversation. There is a family atmosphere here and you will certainly feel at home. Their cooking is refined and of a high quality and they serve a plentiful breakfast. There is a comfortable spacious bedroom on the ground floor with a school table and plenty of rustic charm. There are many trails for hikers and mountain-bikers in the Vallée du Loir, and the Château de Lude should not be missed!

Eliane & Jean-Louis BRAZILIER
'Les 14 Boisselées', route de Château-du-Loir,
72800 LE LUDE
Tel: (0) 2 43 94 90 65 / (0) 661 87 66 38
jl.brazilier@wanadoo.fr

Facilities: private parking, extensive grounds, lounge, pets not accepted, dinner available, babies welcome, free cot, 100% no smoking, hiking, fishing, mushroom-picking, cycling 2km, golf course 30km
Adequate English spoken

Price Structure – 2 Bedrooms
ground floor: along corridor shower room, wc, twin beds, single bed: €47 – 2 people €67 – 3 people
first floor: along corridor bathroom, wc, twin beds: €47

Extra Bed: €20
Capacity: 5 people

Directions: From Le Mans D307 towards Arnage, Pontvallain and Le Lude. Then take the D305 towards Château-du-Loir for 2km.

72.45 Le Mans

Private Home

Claudine & Joël GOBILLE
La Grande Perraudière, 72230 MULSANNE
Tel: (0) 2 43 42 43 59 / (0) 685 18 41 59
Fax: (0) 8 25 23 76 91
gobille56@hotmail.com
http://banb.mulsanne.chez-alice.fr/

Price Structure – 2 Suites
'Suite 1': television, shower room, wc, double bed.
En-suite room, washbasin, 2 double beds:
€60 – 2 people €150 – 6 people
'Suite sous-toit': shower room, wc, 2 double beds.
En-suite room, twin beds: €60 – 2 people
€150 – 6 people

Extra Bed: €15
Capacity: 12 people

Location
11km S of LE MANS
in: Mulsanne, station pick-up on
arrival/departure
Railway station: 13km
car essential

At the end of the famous Hunaudières straight, on
the 24-hour Le Mans circuit, is Mulsanne Corner.
Continue a little further on and you are chez
Claudine and Joël. The interior is open plan with a
large living and dining area with large bay windows
looking out to the garden. There is an inviting terrace
and a lovely swimming pool framed with flowers and
shrubs. Claudine is an accomplished artist as the
beautiful paintings inspired by her travels testify. A
warm and kind welcome in an unpretentious,
relaxed atmosphere.

Facilities: private parking, extensive grounds, tv
lounge, hosts have pets, 100% no smoking, private
swimming pool, golf course, hiking, gliding 10km,
lake watersports 10km, vineyard 40km
Adequate English spoken

Directions: From Le Mans, N138 towards Tours. Cross
through Mulsanne and turn down the first road on
the right just after leaving Mulsanne, by the sign. It is
the first house on the right.

72.39 Le Mans

Private Home

Marion DE BORTOLI
'La Petite Rigannerie', 72150 PRUILLE-L'EGUILLE
Tel: (0) 2 43 40 88 72 Fax: (0) 2 43 40 88 72
marion.debortoli@orange.fr

Price Structure – 2 Bedrooms
wheelchair access, shower room, wc, double bed:
€49
bathroom, wc, twin beds: €49

Extra Bed: €15
Capacity: 4 people

Location
32km S E of LE MANS
in: Pruillé-l'Eguillé
Railway station: 30km
Airport: Tours 70km
car essential

Bienvenue en France

On the edge of the superb forest of Bercé renowned
for its majestic oak trees, is this small village
farmhouse set in charming landscaped gardens.
Marion left her Berlin restaurant for this peaceful
haven. Inside, the house is crammed with an eclectic
array of miscellaneous objects including a collection
of signet stamps, glass candlesticks and cooking
utensils! A bedroom and its bathroom is located in the
chalet in the garden; the other bedroom is smaller
with a sloping ceiling and is not recommended for tall
people. A very good two 'suns' host.

Facilities: private parking, extensive grounds, tv
lounge, pets not accepted, dinner available, babies
welcome, free cot, 100% no smoking, hunting,
fishing, mushroom-picking, hiking, cycling,
interesting flora, vineyard 10km, bird-watching
20km, riversports 20km, golf course 25km
Adequate English spoken

Directions: From Le Mans take the D304 towards La
Chartre-sur-le-Loir for 27km to Grand-Lucé. Then turn
right onto the D13 to Pruillé-l'Eguillé. In the village
head for Ecommoy and then turn right towards St-
Mars-d'Outillé. It is the third house on the left.

Location
35km N of LE MANS
in: St-Germain-sur-Sarthe
Railway station: 2km
Airport: Paris-Roissy 180km
car essential

Working Farm

A convenient stop en route from Normandy to the Loire Valley and near to Fresnay-sur-Sarthe, a town of great character in the heart of the Alpes Mancelles, a green and verdant region of northwest France. The rooms in the main house are comfortable and your hosts run a dairy herd of 50 cows. This is a relaxing area, ideal for many sports and countryside pursuits. The famous *rillettes* are served for breakfast.

Chantal & Pierre GOIDEAU
'Les Ruettes', 72130 ST-GERMAIN-SUR-SARTHE
Tel: (0) 2 43 97 50 87
chantalpierregoideau@yahoo.fr
goideau.free.fr

Facilities: private parking, garden, tv lounge, hosts have pets, babies welcome, free cot, hiking, cycling, fishing, interesting flora, mushroom-picking, golf course 4km, riversports 4km, gliding 4km, lake watersports 15km
Basic English spoken

Price Structure – 3 Bedrooms
and 1 Apartment
'Balcon': lounge, kitchen, shower room, wc, double bed: €48
'Bleue': shower room, wc, four-poster double bed, cot: €43
'Rose': shower room, wc, double bed, cot. Along corridor room 'Blanche': shower room, wc, twin beds, cot: €43 – 2 people €75 – 4 people

Directions: From Le Mans, take the N138 towards Alençon as far as La Hutte. Turn left onto the D130 towards Fresnay-sur-Sarthe, continue for about 2km and follow the signs.

Extra Bed: €12
Reduction: 1/10–31/03
Capacity: 8 people

Location
7km W of LE MANS
in: Yvré-l'Evêque
Railway station: 12km
car essential

Private Home

Deep in the countryside, this house in landscaped grounds is just 7km from Le Mans. Plenty of space and facilities include a terrace, garden, swimming pool, and badminton and volleyball courts. Although you have to share the bathroom here, weigh that against the relaxed welcome, social ambience and the quality facilities that would otherwise be worthy of a three 'sun' rating. Plus a hearty breakfast and dinner prepared largely with organic produce from the garden and you have a place where you would gladly return. On sale: honey, jam.

Anne-Marie & Jacky POTTIER
'Les Elendennes', 178 chemin de la Jugannerie, 72530 YVRE-L'EVEQUE
Tel: (0) 2 43 89 63 54 / (0) 632 01 16 40
pottier.j.am@wanadoo.fr
http://perso.wanadoo.fr/pottier.j.am/

Facilities: private parking, garden, lounge, hosts have pets, dinner available, babies welcome, free cot, 100% no smoking, 2 shared shower rooms, wc, closed: 01/02–29/02, private swimming pool, hiking, cycling, golf course 4km, riversports 12km
Adequate English spoken

Price Structure – 3 Bedrooms
'Marine', 'Florale' & 'Québécoise': lounge, double bed: €48

Extra Bed: €18
Reduction: groups
Capacity: 6 people

Directions: From Le Mans take the N157 towards Paris for 5km to Yvré-l'Evêque. In the village, take the D91 towards Parence for 2.3km and then turn left after 'Château de Vaux' into Route de la Croix and follow the 'Chambres d'Hôtes' signs.

72.46 Le Mans

Château/Manor House

Chantal & Michel METAIS
'Château des Arches', 72530 YVRE-L'EVEQUE
Tel: (0) 2 43 89 49 92 Fax: (0) 2 43 89 49 92
michel.metais@neuf.fr
www.chateaudesarches.org

Price Structure – 5 Bedrooms
first room: bathroom, wc, shower, double bed
(queen-size), twin beds: €100 – 2 people €120 – 4
people
second room: shower room, wc, twin beds: €80
third room: bathroom, wc, shower, twin beds: €90
fourth room: bathroom, wc, shower, 4 single beds:
€100 – 2 people €120 – 4 people
fifth room: shower room, wc, double bed (queen-
size): €60

Capacity: 14 people

Location
7km E of LE MANS
in: Yvré-l'Evêque
Railway station: 6km
car essential

Just 15 minutes by car from the racing circuit,
surrounded by vast forested grounds and a river, the
restoration of this château, dating from the
Napoléon Bonaparte era, is finished. The bedrooms
are reached by a grand staircase decorated with a
mural on a pastoral theme. They are bright and
spacious, and combine a modern touch with stylish
decoration and antiques. For riders there is a training
area and, of course, stables for the horses. Your hosts
used to raise ostriches, amongst other things, and
provide a passionate and pleasant welcome in a
calm and relaxing way.

Facilities: off-street parking, extensive grounds, tv
lounge, hosts have pets, pets not accepted, babies
welcome, free cot, fishing, mushroom-picking, hiking,
golf course 6km, gliding 6km

Directions: From Le Mans, D314, N157 towards Paris.
Do not take Yvré-l'Evêque on your left but head
towards Changé on your right. Pass under the bridge.
The château is 200m along on the right.

85.12 Fontenay-le-Comte

Private Home

Monique FAVRE
'La Pérotine', 23 rue Jean Moulin,
85770 LE POIRE-SUR-VELLUIRE
Tel: (0) 2 51 52 35 00 / (0) 676 37 42 80

Price Structure – 3 Bedrooms and 1 Suite
'Lavande': bathroom, wc, double bed, four-poster
double bed, single bed: €68 – 2 people
€158 – 5 people
'Rose' & 'Lilas': wc, washbasin, double bed: €68
'Muguet': shower room, wc, double bed. En-suite
room, double bed: €68 – 2 people €136 – 4 people

Extra Bed: €22
Reduction: children
Capacity: 13 people

Location
9km S W of FONTENAY-LE-COMTE
in: Le Poiré-sur-Velluire
Railway station: 1km
Airport: La Rochelle 35km
car essential

Monique's house is warm and friendly, and tastefully
decorated. She welcomes you to this house, typical of
La Vendée, in the heart of the Marais Poitevin. She
has her own fishing boat and can take you on a boat
trip through the Venise Verte and the nearby wildlife
reserve or lend you bicycles for a cycle ride. Monique
is an antique dealer and antiques are on sale.

Facilities: garden, tv lounge, hosts have pets, pets
not accepted, hunting, fishing, mushroom-picking,
bird-watching, hiking, cycling, interesting flora,
riversports, vineyard 3km, gliding 10km
Basic English spoken

Directions: From the A83 or Fontenay-le-Comte,
head towards La Rochelle via the D938. After 7km
turn right to Velluire, Le-Poiré-sur-Velluire. The house
is in the centre of the village.

Location
17km S E of FONTENAY-LE-COMTE
in: Oulmes
Railway station: 17km
Airport: Nantes-Atlantique 120km
car essential

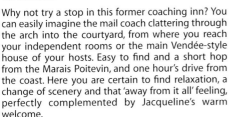

Residence of Outstanding Character

Why not try a stop in this former coaching inn? You can easily imagine the mail coach clattering through the arch into the courtyard, from where you reach your independent rooms or the main Vendée-style house of your hosts. Easy to find and a short hop from the Marais Poitevin, and one hour's drive from the coast. Here you are certain to find relaxation, a change of scenery and that 'away from it all' feeling, perfectly complemented by Jacqueline's warm welcome.

Jacqueline DUMOULIN
'Relais de l'Autize', 14 route de Fontenay,
85420 OULMES
Tel: (0) 2 51 52 45 94 / (0) 681 68 27 54
Fax: (0) 2 51 50 48 27
relais-autize@wanadoo.fr
www.relaisdelautize.com

Facilities: private parking, garden, hosts have pets, pets not accepted, babies welcome, free cot, 100% no smoking, private swimming pool, hiking, cycling, fishing, interesting flora 2km, bird-watching 2km, riversports 10km, golf course 25km, sea watersports 50km
Adequate English spoken

Price Structure – 5 Bedrooms
4 rooms: wheelchair access, television, shower, wc, double bed, single bed: €55 – 2 people
€67 – 3 people
'Nieul sur l'Autize': wheelchair access, television, shower, wc, double bed, twin beds: €55 – 2 people
€85 – 4 people

Extra Bed: €12
Capacity: 16 people

Directions: From Fontenay-le-Comte, take the N148 towards Oulmes. Go through Oulmes and the 'Relais de l'Autize' is on the left on the main road.

Location
NOIRMOUTIER-EN-L'ILE
in: Noirmoutier-en-l'île
Airport: Nantes-Atlantique 70km

Private Home

Véronique and Jean's house is at Noirmoutier-en-l'île, five minutes from the town centre and the beach. Enjoy their large garden or relax beside the pool. There is also a hot-tub under a pergola with a Chinese wisteria. Each room has its own separate entrance and its own private terrace with teak garden furniture. The rooms have large, typical Vendéenne beds and one Moroccan, very comfortable, with TV and a small fridge. A gourmet breakfast includes the homemade jam and be sure to try dinner which includes local produce and the famous Noirmoutier potatoes.

Véronique & Jean DALRIC
'Blanc Marine', 1bis rue de l'Acquenette,
85330 NOIRMOUTIER-EN-L'ILE
Tel: (0) 2 51 39 99 11 / (0) 607 05 21 24
Fax: (0) 2 51 39 99 11
contact@blanc-marine.net
www.blanc-marine.net

Facilities: private parking, garden, tv lounge, internet access, dinner available, 100% no smoking, 2 nights minimum stay, private swimming pool, fishing, bird-watching, hiking, cycling, interesting flora, sea watersports, golf course 25km
Fluent English spoken

Price Structure – 4 Bedrooms
and 1 Apartment
'Luzeronde' & 'La Clère': television, telephone, shower room, wc, double bed (queen-size): €125
'L'Anse Rouge': television, telephone, shower room, wc, twin beds: €135
'Les Souzeaux': television, telephone, shower room, wc, double bed (queen-size): €135
'Les Dames': lounge, television, telephone, kitchen, shower room, wc, double bed (queen-size), 2 single beds: €255 – 2 people €255 – 4 people

Extra Bed: €25   **Reduction:** 1/11–31/03, groups
Capacity: 12 people

Directions: Please contact your host in advance for detailed directions.

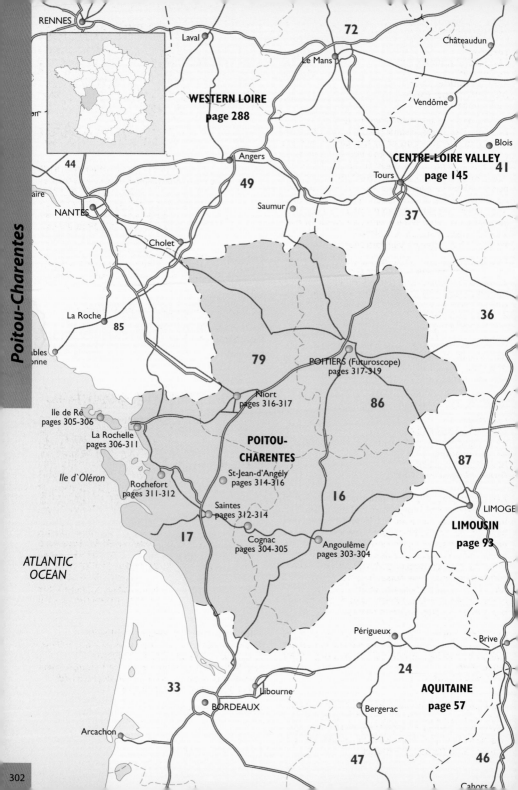

RENNES

Laval

72

Châteaudun

Le Mans

Vendôme

WESTERN LOIRE
page 288

Blois

Angers

CENTRE-LOIRE VALLEY
page 145

41

Tours

49

44

Saumur

37

NANTES

Cholet

36

La Roche

85

79

POITIERS (Futuroscope)
pages 317-319

Ile de Ré
pages 305-306

Niort
pages 316-317

86

La Rochelle
pages 306-311

POITOU-
CHARENTES

87

Ile d'Oléron

St-Jean-d'Angély
pages 314-316

Rochefort
pages 311-312

LIMOGE

16

Saintes
pages 312-314

LIMOUSIN
page 93

ATLANTIC
OCEAN

17

Cognac
pages 304-305

Angoulême
pages 303-304

Périgueux

Brive

24

33

Libourne

AQUITAINE
page 57

BORDEAUX

Bergerac

Arcachon

47

46

Cahors

Poitou-Charentes

Location
43km N E of ANGOULEME
in: St-Claud
Railway station: 12km
Airport: Limoges 64km
car essential

Château/Manor House

An imposing Charentaise *Maison de Maître* in 90 hectares of grounds, in some parts wooded. Whether it be on the tennis court or by the large swimming pool, the overwhelming feeling you get here is of space and being in the great outdoors. The house itself, with its grand proportioned rooms, marble floors and colonnades is also very open towards the countryside. The guest bedrooms are on the first floor and have been decorated with care. They have access to a covered terrace with panoramic bucolic views. Penelope and John welcome you with great kindness. They organise vineyard trips.

Facilities: private parking, extensive grounds, lounge, hosts have pets, pets not accepted, 100% no smoking, 10 years old minimum age, 2 nights minimum stay: 1/07–31/08, private swimming pool, private tennis court, hiking, vineyard, riversports 21km, golf course 24km
Fluent English spoken

Penelope & John HITCHINGS
'Manoir la Betoulle', route de Grand Madieu
(D28), 16450 ST-CLAUD
Tel: (0) 5 45 30 23 10 / (0) 624 25 72 39
ph@manoir-la-betoulle.com
www.manoir-la-betoulle.com

Price Structure – 4 Bedrooms
'Hortensia': bathroom, wc, shower, double bed: €66
'Tournesol': bathroom, wc, shower, twin beds: €66
'Magnolia': bathroom, wc, shower, double bed (queen-size): €76
'Lotus': bathroom, wc, shower, double bed: €76

Reduction: 3 nights, groups
Capacity: 8 people

Directions: From Angoulême, N141 towards Limoges for 30km to Chasseneuil then the D951 to St-Claud. In the village, D28 for 1km towards Champagne-Mouton. The house is on the left just after the fire station.

Location
43km N E of ANGOULEME
in: St-Claud, station pick-up on arrival/departure
Railway station: 6km
Airport: Angoulême 40km

Château/Manor House

As we go to press, this host has not yet been classified, but will be shortly. History, charm and quality sums up this place. After six centuries, history hangs heavy here, but do not be intimidated, simply admire and enjoy the Aubusson tapestries, the French ceilings, the mullioned windows in the hexagonal tower and the stone staircase, all combined with quality and modern comfort. They now raise horses here but it was once a winegrowing property as the vaulted cellars and the old wine vats prove. As Sylviane says, 'Push open the heavy door and step back into history'.

Facilities: private parking, extensive grounds, tv lounge, hosts have pets, babies welcome, free cot, 100% no smoking, private swimming pool, private tennis court
Adequate English spoken

Sylviane CASPER
'Logis de la Broue', rue Abbé Rousselot,
16450 ST-CLAUD
Tel: (0) 5 45 71 43 96 / (0) 672 14 68 94
Fax: (0) 5 45 63 06 41
sylviane.casper@wanadoo.fr
www.logisdelabroue.com

Price Structure – 1 Bedroom and 1 Suite
'Les Matins Céladon': bathroom, wc, shower, 3 single beds: €90 – 2 people €120 – 3 people
'Val de Jour Cyan': along corridor bathroom, wc, twin beds. En-suite room, shower room, wc, twin beds: €90 – 2 people €150 – 4 people

Capacity: 7 people

Directions: From Angoulême, N141 to Limoges for 30km as far as Chasseneuil then D951 to St-Claud. In the village, continue towards Mansles. As soon as you reach the Rue Victor Hugo, you will immediately see the Rue Abbé Rousselot on the left.

16.15 Angoulême

Residence of Outstanding Character

Danièle & Alain BARBOU
'Le Couvent des Cordeliers', 8 rue du Dr Deux-Deprés, 16510 VERTEUIL-SUR-CHARENTE
Tel: (0) 5 45 31 01 19 / (0) 608 88 88 91
Fax: (0) 5 45 31 01 19
barbou@lecouventdescordeliers.com
www.lecouventdescordeliers.com

Price Structure – 6 Bedrooms
'François VI': bathroom, wc, shower, twin beds: €95
'Anne de Polignac': shower room, wc, double bed: €95
'Le Prieur' & 'Le Chapelain': bathroom, wc, double bed: €95
'Les Abbesses': bathroom, wc, twin beds: €95
'André de Vivonne': shower room, wc, double bed (queen-size): €95

Extra Bed: €20
Capacity: 12 people

Location
41km N of ANGOULEME
in: Verteuil-sur-Charente, station pick-up on arrival/departure
Railway station: 5km
Airport: Bordeaux-Mérignac 150km
car essential

A truly exceptional B&B in a charming medieval village! The *couvent* was taken from the Franciscans and partially destroyed by the revolutionaries in 1793. Now carefully and authentically restored, you can meditate by the fountain and the formal garden or enjoy the pool and the concerts and exhibitions held in the church. The former sacristy and dining hall still house a monumental fireplace and original religious murals. The bedrooms, decorated with real insight and taste, are superb! A generous and attentive welcome.

Facilities: private parking, extensive grounds, tv lounge, hosts have pets, dinner available, babies welcome, free cot, 100% no smoking, closed: 01/01–31/01, private swimming pool, fishing, hiking, cycling, riversports, vineyard 25km, golf course 35km
Fluent English spoken

Directions: N10 between Poitiers (63km) and Angoulême (40km). Exit south of Ruffec and head to Verteuil-sur-Charente. In the village, cross the bridge over the Charente River heading towards Poursac. The 'Couvent' is on the right just before the second bridge over the river.

16.11 Cognac

Residence of Outstanding Character

Nicole JACQUES
'Le Moulin du Breuil', 16300 ST-PALAIS-DU-NE
Tel: (0) 5 45 78 72 95 Fax: (0) 5 45 79 07 41
nicole.jacques@tele2.fr

Price Structure – 4 Bedrooms
'Chèvrefeuille' (our favourite room): bathroom, wc, washbasin, double bed (queen-size): €48
'Tournesol': shower, wc, washbasin, twin beds: €48
'Rose': bathroom, wc, washbasin, double bed: €48
'Bleuet': shower, wc, washbasin, double bed: €48

Extra Bed: €12
Capacity: 8 people

Location
17km S of COGNAC
in: St-Palais-du-Né, station pick-up on arrival/departure
Railway station: 18km
Airport: Angoulême 26km
car essential

Between Cognac and Bordelais, this old Charentaise farmhouse is in the middle of large grounds crossed by the lazy River Né, which meanders between poplar trees, fields and orchards. The large rooms have plenty of space and charm. For breakfast in the conservatory, Nicole will spoil you with her delicious homemade *pâtisseries* and give suggestions for excursions to vineyards and other interesting places in the region. On sale: Cognac, Pineau.

Facilities: private parking, extensive grounds, lounge, hosts have pets, pets not accepted, dinner available, babies welcome, free cot, 100% no smoking, wc, closed: 01/11–31/03, hiking, cycling, fishing, vineyard, lake watersports 3km, golf course 12km
Adequate English spoken

Directions: At Cognac, take the D731 towards Barbezieux as far as St-Fort-le-Né, then take the D151 towards St-Palais-du-Né. At St-Palais-du-Né, turn left and follow signs to 'Moulin du Breuil'.

Location
18km S E of COGNAC
in: St-Preuil, station pick-up on arrival/departure
Railway station: 30km
Airport: Bordeaux-Mérignac 110km
car essential

Residence of Outstanding Character

Tucked away by the hillsides of a Cognac Premier Cru is this coaching inn from the 17th and 18th centuries, with meticulously restored pale stonework and a backdrop of green vines. The bedrooms are stylish and we loved the chinese-style bed in 'Palanquin'. Lots of extras including bathrobes, safes, radios, internet access, newspapers and Cognac are made available. There is a kitchen area for guests, a lovely heated swimming pool (7x14m) with a terrace, plus games for children and a tennis court. A professional yet relaxed welcome.

Facilities: private parking, extensive grounds, tv lounge, hosts have pets, pets not accepted, internet access, dinner available, kitchen, babies welcome, free cot, 100% no smoking, private swimming pool, private tennis court, hiking, cycling, vineyard, golf course 19km
Fluent English spoken

Directions: From Cognac-Sud, D24 to Segonzac then the D1 and left to St-Preuil. In the village head for Boutteville and 'Le Relais de St-Preuil' (signposted).

Jean-Luc MONTEMBAULT
'Le Relais de St-Preuil', Lieu-dit Chez Rivière,
16130 ST-PREUIL
Tel: (0) 5 45 80 80 08 Fax: (0) 5 45 80 80 09
contact@relais-de-saint-preuil.com
www.relais-de-saint-preuil.com

Price Structure – 5 Bedrooms and 1 Suite
'Palanquin' (our favourite room): bathroom, wc, four-poster double bed (queen-size): €159
'Postillon': bathroom, wc, twin beds: €119
'Patachon': bathroom, wc, four-poster double bed (queen-size): €159
'Cocher' & 'Messager': bathroom, wc, double bed (queen-size): €139
'Calèche': bathroom, wc, double bed (queen-size). En-suite room, twin beds, single bed: €139 – 2 people €175 – 5 people

Extra Bed: €20
Reduction: 1/10–30/04, 3 nights, groups
Capacity: 15 people

Location
ILE DE RE
in: La Couarde-sur-Mer
Railway station: 18km
Airport: La Rochelle 14km

Private Home

On the Ile de Ré, La Couarde is a little preserved village between the *marais* and the beaches. It is a good starting base for walks and cycle rides as Bénédicte, a sailing instructor, well knows, being from the island herself. The independent bedrooms, like the village with its little alleyways dotted with flowers, are well laid out. The room on the first floor has a kitchenette where breakfast is served. There is not a communal dining room here. Breakfasts are copious and refined. Authentic surroundings and a reliable welcome.

Facilities: babies welcome, free cot, 100% no smoking, fishing, mushroom-picking, bird-watching, hiking, cycling, interesting flora, sea watersports, vineyard 4km, golf course 12km
Adequate English spoken

Directions: At Ile de Ré take direction Itinéraire Nord/Saint-Martin then La Couarde-sur-Mer. On arrival at the village follow Ars-Phare des Baleines. At the roundabout by the 'Credit Agricole' bank, continue in the direction of La Couarde, Les Plages & Marché d'été and then at the roundabout by the shop 'Shopi' follow signs to Centre, Office du Tourisme. The Petite Rue de la Plage is at the end of the market (*Marché d'été*).

Bénédicte CONTAL
8 Petite Rue de la Plage,
17670 LA COUARDE-SUR-MER
Tel: (0) 5 46 29 93 69 / (0) 668 94 24 89
info@bcontal.com
www.bcontal.com

Price Structure – 1 Bedroom and 1 Apartment
ground floor: shower room, wc, double bed, single bed: €61 – 2 people €64 – 3 people
first floor: television, kitchen, shower room, wc, washbasin, double bed: €61

Reduction: 1/10–30/03, 15 nights
Capacity: 5 people

Poitou-Charentes – Cognac, Ile de Ré

17.46 Ile de Ré

Private Home

Location
ILE DE RE
in: La Flotte-en-Ré
Railway station: 25km
Airport: La Rochelle 14km

Close to the pedestrianised centre of a fishing village with a marina and character buildings in small narrow streets, is the door into an 18th-century house. The interior has been completely transformed by the multitude of Jean-Pierre's exotic, creative design ideas. He is particularly proud of his pebble-encrusted bathrooms. . . The lovely garden-patio full of plant pots and a small fountain is Christian's creation. Two artists with their own but not overpowering styles. An enjoyable stay with a relaxed welcome is to be had here.

Christian NAUD & Jean-Pierre QUINTARD
'Le Château de Sable', 16 rue Volcy-Fèvre,
17630 LA FLOTTE-EN-RE
Tel: (0) 5 46 01 75 60
www.lechateaudesable.net

Price Structure – 4 Bedrooms and 1 Suite
first room: wheelchair access, shower room, wc, double bed: €98
second room: wheelchair access, shower room, wc, double bed: €98
third room: shower room, wc, twin beds: €108
fourth room: shower room, wc, double bed: €108
suite: shower, wc, washbasin, double bed. En-suite room, single bed: €117 – 2 people €126 – 3 people

Capacity: 11 people

Facilities: garden, lounge, pets not accepted, 100% no smoking, 5 years old minimum age, 2 nights minimum stay: 21/06–21/09, closed: 01/11–20/12 & 03/01–01/04, fishing, hiking, cycling, sea watersports, vineyard 5km, bird-watching 10km, golf course 12km
Adequate English spoken

Directions: From La Rochelle, D735 heading to l'Ile de Ré, until La Flotte-en-Ré. The house is in the centre of the village opposite the church; Rue Volcy-Fèvre is off Rue de l'Eglise.

17.32 La Rochelle

Residence of Outstanding Character

Location
LA ROCHELLE
in: La Rochelle
Railway station: 1km
Airport: La Rochelle 4km

In the historic, animated centre of La Rochelle, not far from the fortified harbour, old streets and arcades, is this 17th-century half-timbered house: a good example of the aristocratic townhouses making this city one of the most enchanting on the Atlantic coast. Odile and Marc are watchmakers with a shop on the ground floor, so unsurprisingly the house has a collection of clocks. The two small Louis-Philippe-style bedrooms are on the second floor and one has a piano. The croissants at breakfast are superb. *Bon appétit!*

Odile & Marc PARSY
2 rue Bujaud, 17000 LA ROCHELLE
Tel: (0) 666 81 86 53
Fax: (0) 5 46 41 09 35

Price Structure – 3 Bedrooms
2nd floor – first room: television, shower room, wc, double bed: €65
3rd floor – second room: television, shower room, wc, double bed: €80
3rd floor – third room: television, along corridor shower room, wc, double bed, single bed: €65 – 2 people €80 – 3 people

Extra Bed: €15
Capacity: 7 people

Facilities: lounge, pets not accepted, 100% no smoking, 1 shared shower room, wc, closed: 30/11–31/01, hiking, cycling, fishing, hunting, sea watersports, riversports, vineyard, golf course 7km, bird-watching 15km, gliding 60km
Basic English spoken

Directions: In the centre of La Rochelle at Place de Verdun, turn left by the side of the cathedral, Rue Fleuriau (towards 'Musée du Nouveau Monde'), then right onto Rue St Yon. The house is on the corner of the first road on the right, Rue Bujaud, a one-way-street.

Location
5km S of LA ROCHELLE
in: Aytré, station pick-up on arrival/departure
Railway station: 6km
Airport: La Rochelle 12km
car essential

Private Home

In the centre of a protected natural area is this modern house just 400m from the beach. All the bedrooms have electronic shutters and a quiet private terrace. Also open to you is a living room with a kitchenette that links the two parts of the building together and a garden with a lovely swimming pool. From here you can even walk to La Rochelle, 3km away via the many footpaths. Thomas is German and is fluent in several languages.

Thomas & Chantal KOENITZER
'Locatlantique', 6 route du Pontreau,
17440 AYTRE
Tel: (0) 5 46 31 02 41 / (0) 662 16 43 64
Fax: (0) 5 46 31 02 41
tom.koenitzer@wanadoo.fr
www.locatlantique.info

Facilities: private parking, garden, tv lounge, hosts have pets, pets not accepted, kitchen, babies welcome, free cot, 100% no smoking, private swimming pool, hiking, cycling, sea watersports, golf course 12km
Fluent English spoken

Price Structure – 6 Bedrooms
2 rooms: television, shower room, wc, twin beds: €74
4 rooms: television, shower room, wc, double bed: €68

Extra Bed: €12,80
Reduction: 15/09–30/03, 7 nights, groups, children
Capacity: 12 people

Directions: From La Rochelle on the fast road towards Rochefort, exit Aytré, and head towards 'La Plage'. When you reach the sea, turn left just before the level-crossing. Continue along this one-way street to no. 6.

Location
15km N of LA ROCHELLE
in: Charron, station pick-up on arrival/departure
Railway station: 17km
Airport: La Rochelle 15km
car essential

Residence of Outstanding Character

This old fisherman's longhouse, 15 minutes from La Rochelle, is full of interest: the brightly decorated bedrooms, the beautiful dining room, the swimming pool – and, of course, a really wonderful welcome from Nicole and Raphaël. Allow time for them to arrange one of their interesting excursions to the Baie de l'Aiguillon on a fishing boat. Fantastic.

Nicole & Raphaël PUNTI
'L' Avocette', 23 rue des Groies, 17230 CHARRON
Tel: (0) 5 46 01 69 44 / (0) 613 13 84 01
lavocette@orange.fr
http://perso.libertysurf.fr/lavocette

Facilities: private parking, garden, tv lounge, hosts have pets, pets not accepted, kitchen, 100% no smoking, closed: 30/10–01/04, private swimming pool, interesting flora, hiking 2km, fishing 2km, golf course 5km, sea watersports 15km
Adequate English spoken

Price Structure – 4 Bedrooms
and 1 Apartment
'Ocre' & 'Lavande': shower room, wc, double bed: €65
'Bleu' & 'Jaune': shower room, wc, twin beds: €65
studio: kitchen, shower room, wc, double bed, twin beds: €82,50 – 2 people €117,00 – 4 people

Extra Bed: €13
Reduction: 7 nights, groups
Capacity: 12 people

Directions: From La Rochelle, take the D105 for 16km as far as Charron. Then turn right after the church, left after the school and left again after the post office. (From the A83, exit 7, then take the N137 towards La Rochelle. At Marans, take the D105 on the right towards Charron.)

Poitou-Charentes – La Rochelle

17.59 La Rochelle

Private Home

Tamar & Michel SOUID
11 rue Pierre Mendès France, 17137 ESNANDES
Tel: (0) 5 46 00 48 26 / (0) 613 20 60 36
tamar.souid@wanadoo.fr
oliviersetcoquillages.com

Price Structure – 2 Bedrooms
2 rooms: television, shower room, wc, double bed
(queen-size): €70

Reduction: 15/09–31/05, 5 nights
Capacity: 4 people

Location
2km N of LA ROCHELLE
in: Esnandes, station pick-up on
arrival/departure
Railway station: 8km
Airport: La Rochelle 8km
car essential

Only ten minutes from La Rochelle and the Ile de Ré, at the gateway to the Marais Poitevin, Tamar and Michel will give you a warm welcome in this quiet, typical village. You are only 2km from the sea, where they recommend you try the coastal path, on foot or by bike. The two comfortable rooms, completely restored, are in a separate building beside the pool, ideal for that early morning swim. Both are equipped with flat screen digital TV and WIFI access. Breakfast is served under the veranda beside the pool. Tamar makes excellent wholemeal bread.

Facilities: private parking, garden, pets not accepted, babies welcome, free cot, 100% no smoking, private swimming pool, hiking, cycling, bird-watching, golf course 2km, sea watersports 8km
Fluent English spoken

Directions: At La Rochelle, follow signs to Ile de Ré and on to the bypass. Exit Lagord and take the D105 towards Esnandes. In the village, after the small shopping centre, take the first on the right which is Rue Pierre Mendès France.

17.16 La Rochelle

Private Home

Françoise SENAN
'Le Chalet du Treuil', 53 rue de la Fée au Bois,
17450 FOURAS
Tel: (0) 5 46 84 28 80 Fax: (0) 5 46 84 28 80
chalet.du.treuil@wanadoo.fr
www.chaletdutreuil.com

Price Structure – 5 Bedrooms
'Boyard' & ' Ré': television, shower room, wc, double bed: €65
'Aix' & 'Loti': shower, washbasin, double bed: €58
'Passerose': shower, washbasin, twin beds: €59

Extra Bed: €15
Reduction: 01/09–30/06, 4 nights
Capacity: 10 people

Location
27km S of LA ROCHELLE
in: Fouras, station pick-up on
arrival/departure
Railway station: 20km
Airport: La Rochelle 20km

Opposite Fort Boyard of TV fame, 'Le Chalet du Treuil' is situated in the heart of the town, 300 metres from the beaches, in a leafy location. With its bird reserves and oyster farms, Fouras is a lively resort. Françoise, president of the local radio station, knows her region very well.

Facilities: private parking, garden, kitchen, 2 wcs, hiking, cycling, fishing, interesting flora, mushroom-picking, sea watersports, golf course 6km
Fluent English spoken

Directions: From La Rochelle, take the N137 and head towards Fouras. On entering the town, take the Ile d'Aix and La Fumée exit off the first roundabout. At the second roundabout, take the Le Chalet du Treuil and Le Cimetière exit. Go straight on for 400m.

Location
27km S W of LA ROCHELLE
in: Fouras
Railway station: 24km
Airport: La Rochelle 25km

✳ ✳
Private Home

In the centre of Fouras, a lively seaside resort, 300m from the sea is Catherine's Charentaise family home. Enjoy the peace and quiet by the raised swimming pool shaded by oak trees. Prunelle the donkey may come by as you enjoy breakfast looking out over the garden of flowers. Watch out for the low doors under the main beam on the first floor. The comfortable, well-presented bedrooms have sloping ceilings. Inspired by her voyages as a skipper she serves unusual breakfasts. In winter, an open fire awaits you in the lounge.

Catherine CHOGNOT
'Le Clos des Rosiers', 5 bis rue Paul Behu,
17450 FOURAS
Tel: (0) 5 46 84 17 81 / (0) 672 71 85 04
Fax: (0) 5 46 84 17 81
reservation@leclosdesrosiers.com
www.leclosdesrosiers.com

Facilities: private parking, extensive grounds, tv lounge, hosts have pets, babies welcome, free cot, 100% no smoking, fishing, bird-watching, hiking, cycling, sea watersports, golf course 5km, interesting flora 12km
Adequate English spoken

Price Structure – 3 Bedrooms
'Fleurie' & 'Bambou': shower room, wc, double bed: €63
'Bateau': bathroom, wc, double bed, single bed: €63 – 2 people €73 – 3 people

Extra Bed: €10
Reduction: 1/10–30/03, 15 nights, groups, children
Capacity: 7 people

Directions: From the dual carriageway La Rochelle-Rochefort, exit Fouras direction 'Fouras centre' or 'Fouras sud'. Pass in front of the water tower and take the first turn on the right (Bed & Breakfast France sign).

Location
2km N of LA ROCHELLE
in: Lagord
Railway station: 2km
Airport: La Rochelle 2km
car essential

✳ ✳ ✳
Private Home

This Charentaise house with dove grey shutters is just five minutes from the old port at La Rochelle. The house has been built quite recently and is in a quiet residential area of detached houses. The room is air-conditioned, large and comfortable. Françoise is very keen on interior decoration and for the household linen has combined toile de Jouy and old lace with modern towels. The individual soaps are coordinated with the room colours. Not surprisingly she runs a little shop on the premises. The same attention to detail goes into the breakfast crockery.

Françoise & Christian MAUBLANC
'Le Clos des Oliviers', 2 rue Edwige Feuillère,
17140 LAGORD
Tel: (0) 5 46 34 90 68 / (0) 670 24 98 61
surcouf1735@club-internet.fr

Facilities: off-street parking, garden, babies welcome, free cot, 100% no smoking, hiking, cycling, sea watersports 2km, golf course 7km
Fluent English spoken

Price Structure – 1 Bedroom
television, shower room, wc, double bed: €70

Extra Bed: €12
Reduction: 4 nights
Capacity: 2 people

Directions: At La Rochelle, follow signs to Ile de Ré and on to the bypass. Exit at Lagord and at the large roundabout take 'Lagord Centre'. At the second set of lights turn left and keep going straight on as far as the roundabout adorned with a wine press. Take the road directly on the opposite side of the roundabout (at 12 o'clock) and it is the first house on the right.

Poitou-Charentes – La Rochelle

17.56 La Rochelle

Private Home

Bienvenue en France

Location
34km W of LA ROCHELLE
in: Surgères, station pick-up on arrival/departure
Railway station: 1km
Airport: La Rochelle 30km

Odile & Dominique QUETTE
'Le Logis des Oiseaux', 4 rue Neuve,
17700 SURGERES
Tel: (0) 5 46 31 38 10 / (0) 613 43 72 43
Fax: (0) 5 46 31 38 10
doquette@wanadoo.fr
www.lelogisdesoiseaux.fr

Odile and Dominique are kind and welcoming in their beautiful property with blue shutters and its own spinney where you can relax in the shade in the summer. Yet they are in the centre of the town, so handy for shops, restaurants etc, in a quiet street with little traffic, so a quiet night's sleep is guaranteed. Surgères is famous for the quality of its butter as well as the historic centre with its medieval ramparts. The rooms are comfortable but not extravagantly furnished. You feel good and well looked after here.

Price Structure – 2 Bedrooms and 1 Suite
'Mésanges bleues': shower room, wc, double bed.
En-suite room, 2 single beds: €55 – 2 people
€95 – 4 people
'Colibri': shower room, wc, double bed: €55
'Hirondelles': shower room, wc, double bed (queen-size): €55

Extra Bed: €15
Reduction: 1/10–31/03, 4 nights
Capacity: 8 people

Facilities: private parking, garden, tv lounge, pets not accepted, internet access, babies welcome, free cot, 100% no smoking, private swimming pool, hiking, cycling, fishing 15km, bird-watching 20km, golf course 25km, sea watersports 30km
Adequate English spoken

Directions: At La Rochelle take the bypass towards Rochefort then the D939 as far as Surgères. Then follow signs to 'Centre-Ville' and 'Parking des Huguenots', then signs to the Logis des Oiseaux.

17.60 La Rochelle

Private Home

Location
13km E of LA ROCHELLE
in: Ste-Soulle
Railway station: 10km
Airport: La Rochelle 10km
car essential

Eric COLIN
'La Rochelle Lodge', 26 rue de l'Aquitaine,
Usseau, 17220 STE-SOULLE
Tel: (0) 689 90 61 35
eric.colin@larochellelodge.fr
www.larochellelodge.fr

As we go to press, this host has not yet been classified, but will be shortly. This is an authentic old Charentaise residence, with comfortable rooms, pool and generous breakfast. La Rochelle is well known to be a magical place, close to the beaches, but why not also discover the Marais Poitevin which is close by, full of surprising treasures? Ask Eric about his favourite places. Internet access in the rooms.

Price Structure – 5 Bedrooms
'Nature': wheelchair access, television, shower room, wc, double bed (queen-size), single bed:
€89 – 2 people €106 – 3 people
'Lin' & 'Art Déco': television, shower room, wc, twin beds, single bed: €89 – 2 people €106 – 3 people
'Noir, Blanc' & 'Exochic': television, shower room, wc, double bed (queen-size): €79

Extra Bed: €17
Reduction: 1/09–30/06
Capacity: 13 people

Facilities: private parking, garden, pets not accepted, internet access, 100% no smoking, wheelchair access, private swimming pool
Adequate English spoken

Directions: When you are on the N11 La Rochelle to Niort road, at the junction with the N137 go towards Nantes and then the first street on the left (Rue des Hirondelles).

Location
22km E of LA ROCHELLE
in: Virson
Railway station: 6km
Airport: La Rochelle 25km
car essential

✳ ✳ ✳

Private Home

Tamara and Didier have completely restored this 18th-century farmhouse in the peaceful Charentaise countryside. The welcome is warm as they open their house to you. Located between La Rochelle, Rochefort and the Marais Poitevin, this is the ideal base for exploring this area. The rooms are pleasant, bright and quite spacious. There are lots of activities for the children, not to mention the animals they rear: sheep, rabbits, ducks and chickens. Didier is a trained cook, and his dinners use seasonal produce, beginning with the local *apéritif* of Pineau des Charentes.

Tamara & Didier CHAUVIN
'Fief du Préneau', 5 chemin des Fontaines,
17290 VIRSON
Tel: (0) 5 46 67 34 45
fiefdupreneau@wanadoo.fr
www.fiefdupreneau.com

Facilities: private parking, extensive grounds, lounge, hosts have pets, pets not accepted, dinner available, babies welcome, free cot, 100% no smoking, closed: 22/12–3/01, private swimming pool, hiking, cycling, golf course 15km, sea watersports 20km
Fluent English spoken

Price Structure – 2 Bedrooms
and 1 Apartment
'Royal': bathroom, wc, double bed (queen-size), single bed: €55 – 2 people €70 – 3 people
'Romantique': bathroom, wc, four-poster double bed (queen-size): €55
'La suite': lounge, kitchen, bathroom, wc, twin beds, 2 single beds (child-size): €100 – 2 people €100 – 4 people

Capacity: 9 people

Directions: At La Rochelle, take the bypass towards Rochefort then the D108. After Virson, take the D205 on the right, towards Chambon, for 2km. Le Préneau is indicated on the right.

17.24 Rochefort

Location
ROCHEFORT
in: Rochefort, station pick-up on arrival/departure
Railway station: 2km
Airport: La Rochelle 35km

✳ ✳ ✳

Residence of Outstanding Character

Elisabeth and Patrick live with their four children in this beautiful townhouse from the 19th century, in the most charming cobbled street in Rochefort. Elisabeth is a teacher and makes homemade bread and jams for breakfast and Patrick is an engineer. We have awarded three 'suns' for the 'Hermione' bedroom alone! The family provides a warm and friendly welcome and excellent advice on places to visit and the history of this charming town, made famous in the film *Les Demoiselles de Rochefort*.

Elisabeth & Patrick FORESTIER
'Au Jardin du Roy', 4 rue Amiral Courbet,
17300 ROCHEFORT
Tel: (0) 5 46 87 01 80
ElisaFORES@aol.com
www.aujardinduroy.com

Facilities: garden, lounge, pets not accepted, dinner available, babies welcome, free cot, 100% no smoking, closed: 20/12–10/01, hiking, bird-watching, fishing 2km, golf course 5km, hunting 5km, riversports 5km, sea watersports 13km, vineyard 50km
Fluent English spoken

Price Structure – 3 Bedrooms, 1 Suite
and 1 Apartment
television, double bed (queen-size) in each room
'L'Hermione' (our favourite room): bathroom, wc, cot: €75
'Diane' (our other favourite room): bathroom, wc, single bed: €93 – 3 people
apt 'La Belle Poule': telephone, kitchen, bathroom, wc, cot: €77
'Syrène': shower room, wc, cot: €59
'Aurore': bathroom, wc, 3 single beds (child-size). En-suite room, 2 single beds: €148,80 – 7 people

Extra Bed: €18
Capacity: 16 people

Directions: Head for Place Colbert in the Centre-Ville. Rue A. Courbet is a small cobbled street leading off the square, right next to the main pedestrian street (between the 'Hôtel de la Marine' and Place Colbert).

17.47 Rochefort

Residence of Outstanding Character

Bienvenue en France

Jane & Dany CONIL
Lieu-dit St-Pierre, 438 route Impériale,
17450 ST-LAURENT-DE-LA-PREE
Tel: (0) 5 46 82 47 99 Fax: (0) 5 46 82 47 99
jane.conil@wanadoo.fr
http://monsite.wanadoo.fr/chambreschezjane

Price Structure – 3 Suites
'Phare Haon': shower room, wc, double bed. En-suite room, twin beds: €50 – 2 people €90 – 4 people
'Atmos Phare': bathroom, wc, twin beds. En-suite room, double bed: €50 – 2 people €90 – 4 people
'Phare Ouest': shower room, wc, single bed. En-suite room, double bed, single bed: €50 – 2 people €90 – 4 people

Extra Bed: €15
Reduction: 7 nights, groups
Capacity: 12 people

Location
5km N W of ROCHEFORT
in: St-Laurent-de-la-Prée, station pick-up on arrival/departure
Railway station: 5km
Airport: La Rochelle 20km
car essential

By a village, salt marshes, a golf course and sandy beaches is this ideal place to recharge your batteries. This large *Maison de Maître* in beautiful wooded grounds, half-wild, is sought after by artists and nature lovers. Jane practises and teaches sculpture and exhibits her work and that of other artists. The bedrooms, with playful names, can be booked as suites. Enjoy her homemade *viennoiseries* for breakfast in the garden by the cacti. At dinner she spoils you with seafood and garden produce. Boat trips possible.

Facilities: private parking, garden, tv lounge, hosts have pets, dinner available, babies welcome, free cot, closed: 01/12–30/03, golf course, bird-watching, hiking, cycling, sea watersports 5km
Adequate English spoken

Directions: On the fast road between Rochefort and La Rochelle take the exit for Fouras and then immediately head for St-Pierre, Golf. Do NOT enter the village St-Laurent-de-la-Prée. The house is on the right on the main road of the hamlet St-Pierre.

17.23 Saintes

Private Home

Bienvenue en France

Renata VEDANA
'La Bribaudonnière de Renata', Bribaudon,
17800 ST-PALAIS-DE-PHIOLIN
Tel: (0) 5 46 49 02 91 Fax: (0) 5 46 49 02 91
info@labribaudonniere.com
www.labribaudonniere.com

Price Structure – 2 Bedrooms
2 rooms: shower room, wc, twin beds: €77,50

Extra Bed: €31
Reduction: 3 nights
Capacity: 4 people

Location
30km S of SAINTES
in: Bribaudon
Railway station: 10km
Airport: Bordeaux-Mérignac 80km
car essential

Renata and her sister Anna-Maria are from Venice, and have brought with them unlimited enthusiasm and warmth. They have painstakingly restored this house, which is typical of the Saintonge area, and have excellent taste for displaying beautiful objects. Over a real espresso they can advise you on visiting the Côte de Blaye and the Roman churches. There is also a small campsite on the property and a chalet for weekly rentals. On sale: wine, Cognac.

Facilities: private parking, extensive grounds, lounge, hosts have pets, babies welcome, free cot, 100% no smoking, closed: 02/01–31/03, hiking, cycling, mushroom-picking, fishing 5km, vineyard 7km
Basic English spoken

Directions: On the A10, exit 36 to Pons or exit 37 to Mirambeau. Then take the N137 towards St-Genis-de-Saintonge. If you are coming from the south, it is the first country lane on the left, after St-Genis, towards St-Palais-de-Phiolin. The house is on the right, after 1km.

Location
20km E of SAINTES
in: Burie, station pick-up on arrival/departure
Railway station: 14km
Airport: La Rochelle 100km
car essential

✹ ✹ ✹
Private Home

Poitou-Charentes – Saintes

You can feel a little touch of Britishness that is hard to put your finger on, here in this former farmhouse from 1802! This charming British couple are striving to improve their French as they live out their life in this peaceful hamlet with views over the vines. The guest bedrooms are comfortable and simply decorated with taste. Original fireplaces, exposed beams and floors have been restored true to the style of the house. Steve can accompany you to play golf whilst Lynne prepares dinner. She can even accommodate a gluten-free diet specially for you if warned in advance!

Facilities: off-street parking, garden, tv lounge, pets not accepted, dinner available, 100% no smoking, closed: 15/11–15/03, hiking, vineyard, hunting 1km, fishing 5km, golf course 12km, riversports 20km
Fluent English spoken

Lynne & Steve ADAMS
'Le Chêne Vert', Chez Primo, 34 rue des Abatis,
17770 BURIE
Tel: (0) 5 46 90 66 96
lynneadams34@hotmail.com
www.lechenevert.eu.com

Price Structure – 4 Bedrooms
3 rooms: shower room, wc, double bed: €60
shower room, wc, twin beds: €60

Extra Bed: €12
Capacity: 8 people

Directions: Please contact your hosts in advance for detailed directions.

Location
20km S of SAINTES
in: St-André-de-Lidon, station pick-up on arrival/departure
Railway station: 20km
Airport: La Rochelle 60km
car essential

✹ ✹ ✹
Private Home

Practical and accessible at the meeting of the Royan beaches, Charente, Cognac and Bordeaux, this little farm lives again thanks to your hosts' devotion and hard work. The garden includes fruit trees, where you might spot a deer. The bedrooms have independent entrances and there is a guest lounge. John and Christina appreciate and serve good food and are full of advice if you plan to settle here to enjoy the micro-climate and gentle way of life.

Facilities: off-street parking, garden, lounge, pets not accepted, dinner available, 100% no smoking, wc, closed: 01–30/03, private swimming pool, hiking, vineyard, sea watersports 10km, gliding 15km, golf course 20km
Fluent English spoken

Christina & John LAMPERD
6 rue de la Bertauderie,
17260 ST-ANDRE-DE-LIDON
Tel: (0) 5 46 98 68 46 / (0) 699 04 91 53
Fax: (0) 5 46 98 68 46
j-clamperd@orange.fr

Price Structure – 1 Bedroom and 1 Suite
bathroom, wc, double bed. En-suite room, double bed: €55 – 2 people €100 – 4 people
shower room, wc, double bed, single bed:
€55 – 2 people €70 – 3 people

Extra Bed: €15
Reduction: 3 nights
Capacity: 7 people

Directions: A10 exit 36, D732 towards Royan. 8km after Gémozac and then at La Merletterie, take the D129 on the right towards St-André-de-Lidon for 1.5km, then turn left towards 'Chez Ménard'. Next take the first right turn followed by the first left turn, following signs to 'La Bertauderie'.

17.53 Saintes

Working Farm

Location
10km N W of SAINTES
in: Venerand
Railway station: 8km
Airport: La Rochelle 80km
car essential

Martine and Thierry, producers of Pineau and Cognac, are a down-to-earth couple and their welcome is sincere. On the farm they grow vines and cereals. You stay in an annex 80m from the main farmhouse, with a lounge area. Martine is on hand to spend time with her guests who more often than not leave with a bottle of their Cognac! They also offer guided tours to the famous Cognac house Martell. The bedrooms are all spacious family rooms but the two rooms on the second floor are best avoided if you are tall.

Martine & Thierry TEXIER
'Le Petit Talvard', 17 rue du Château,
17100 VENERAND
Tel: (0) 5 46 97 71 21
lepetittalvard@club-internet.fr
www.chambre-petit-talvard.com

Price Structure – 4 Bedrooms
'Bleue': shower room, wc, double bed, 2 single beds: €50 – 2 people €84 – 4 people
'Rose' & 'Fleurie': shower room, wc, double bed, single bed: €50 – 2 people €66 – 3 people
'Jaune': shower room, wc, double bed, single bed: €50 – 2 people €66 – 3 people

Extra Bed: €17
Reduction: 2 nights
Capacity: 13 people

Facilities: off-street parking, garden, lounge, pets not accepted, dinner available, babies welcome, free cot, 100% no smoking, hiking, cycling, vineyard, golf course 5km, fishing 10km, riversports 10km
Adequate English spoken

Directions: Please contact your hosts in advance for detailed directions.

17.27 St-Jean-d'Angély

Residence of Outstanding Character

Location
7km S of ST-JEAN-D'ANGELY
in: Asnières-la-Giraud
Railway station: 5km
Airport: La Rochelle 80km
car essential

This house stands proud and noble, planted amongst the vines in this wine-producing domain in Cognac. Henriette and Aart are a well-travelled Dutch couple and have completely restored the outbuildings to provide several spacious apartments well equipped to a high standard of comfort. There is the traditional bread oven, a gargantuan cooking pot, and a cauldron. The internal walls, with their exposed stone, add a really original regional flavour to some of the bedrooms.

Henriette & Aart ZOETBROOD
'Domaine de la Laigne', 17 rue Louis Audoin Dubreuil, 17400 ASNIERES-LA-GIRAUD
Tel: (0) 5 46 58 72 11 Fax: (0) 5 46 58 57 57
info@domainedelalaigne.com
www.domainedelalaigne.com

Price Structure – 4 Apartments
'Four à Pain' & 'Le Chai': lounge, television, kitchen, shower room, wc, double bed, 3 single beds (1 child-size): €70 – 2 people €90 – 5 people
'Cargouilles': lounge, television, kitchen, shower room, wc, washbasin, double bed, 4 single beds (2 child-size): €70 – 2 people €90 – 6 people
'Cyprès': lounge, television, kitchen, shower room, wc, washbasin, double bed, 5 single beds (1 child-size): €70 – 2 people €110 – 7 people

Capacity: 23 people

Facilities: off-street parking, extensive grounds, tv lounge, hosts have pets, pets not accepted, babies welcome, free cot, private swimming pool, hiking, cycling, vineyard 3km, fishing 5km, riversports 5km, golf course 20km
Fluent English spoken

Directions: From the A10, exit 34. Go through St-Jean-d'Angély and take the N150 towards Saintes for 2km, then turn right as far as Véron and La Laigné. The 'Domaine' is on the left as you enter the hamlet.

Location
29km E of ST-JEAN-D'ANGELY
in: Gourvillette
Railway station: 27km
Airport: Angoulême 44km
car essential

Château/Manor House

A lovely manor house in a tranquil spot. Relax and enjoy the garden and enjoy the pool (table tennis and snooker too) or enjoy walks and trips to the Cognac distilleries. Liz and Will are British with B&B experience. Liz loves to chat about gardening and cooking and you would do well to sample her cuisine at her elegantly laid table. With Will the conversation turns more readily to golf and he can help you to book a round. Beautiful, comfortable, spacious rooms with thoughtful touches. A spa and sauna are also at your disposal.

Liz & Will WEEKS
'Le Manoir Souhait', 7 rue du Château d'Eau,
17490 GOURVILLETTE
Tel: (0) 5 46 26 18 41
weeks@manoirsouhait.com
www.manoirsouhait.com

Facilities: private parking, extensive grounds, tv lounge, hosts have pets, pets not accepted, dinner available, babies welcome, free cot, 100% no smoking, private swimming pool, hiking, cycling, vineyard 3km, lake watersports 15km, golf course 27km
Fluent English spoken

Directions: Please contact your hosts in advance for detailed directions.

Price Structure – 1 Bedroom and 3 Suites
'Grande Champagne': bathroom, wc, double bed. En-suite room, 2 single beds: €70 – 2 people
€100 – 4 people
'Petite Champagne': bathroom, wc, double bed. En-suite room, twin beds: €65 – 2 people
€100 – 4 people
'Studio suite': shower room, wc, double bed. En-suite room, single bed: €65 – 2 people €85 – 3 people
'Pommereau': shower room, wc, double bed: €65

Capacity: 13 people

Location
23km N W of ST-JEAN-D'ANGELY
in: St-Mard, station pick-up on arrival/departure
Railway station: 7km
Airport: La Rochelle 38km
car essential

Private Home

A warm reception from Véronique and Virgile who left Picardie over a year ago to come and settle here in these former 19th-century stables. You are surrounded by fields and near to La Rochelle and Marais Poitevin. To the delight of young and old, the farm animals kept here include a horse, three sheep, chickens, rabbits and cats and dogs! Children can help to feed the animals with Virgile. The bedrooms and the breakfast room are spacious and modestly furnished. 'Rétro' with its preserved bathroom is a must for all 70s fans!

Virgile BIRGENTZLE
'La Clergerie', 120 rue des Acacias, Charentenay,
17700 ST-MARD
Tel: (0) 5 46 35 39 33 / (0) 674 37 64 48
contact@laclergerie.net
www.laclergerie.net

Facilities: off-street parking, extensive grounds, tv lounge, hosts have pets, dinner available, babies welcome, free cot, 100% no smoking, private swimming pool, hunting, fishing, hiking 5km, cycling 5km, sea watersports 30km, golf course 40km
Fluent English spoken

Directions: A10, exit 34, St-Jean-d'Angély, direction Surgères, La Rochelle. After about 20km, at Château d'Eau Charentenay, second on the left.

Price Structure – 2 Bedrooms and 1 Suite
'Romance': along corridor bathroom, wc, shower, 2 double beds: €65 – 2 people €75 – 4 people
'Rétro': bathroom, wc, double bed: €65
'La suite': shower room, wc, double bed. En-suite room, 2 single beds: €65 – 2 people €85 – 4 people

Extra Bed: €12
Reduction: 4 nights
Capacity: 10 people

Poitou-Charentes – St-Jean-d'Angély

17.06 St-Jean-d'Angély

Residence of Outstanding Character

Jenny & John ELMES
'Le Moulin de la Quine', 17350 ST-SAVINIEN
Tel: (0) 5 46 90 19 31 Fax: (0) 5 46 90 19 31
elmes@club-internet.fr
www.laquine.co.uk

Price Structure – 1 Bedroom
'Parc': shower, bathroom, double bed, single bed:
€52 – 2 people €62 – 3 people

Extra Bed: €10
Reduction: 2 nights
Capacity: 3 people

Location
15km S W of ST-JEAN-D'ANGELY
in: St-Savinien
Railway station: 3km
Airport: 50km
car essential

Bienvenue en France

Jenny and John, a friendly English couple, have created a really cosy atmosphere with a strong feel-good factor. The bedroom leads on to an attractive and beautifully landscaped garden. You feel as if you are in the depths of the countryside, but can also smell the salt in the air from the ocean. One spare room also available.

Facilities: off-street parking, extensive grounds, hosts have pets, pets not accepted, dinner available, 100% no smoking, closed: 25/12, hiking, cycling, fishing 3km, golf course 25km, sea watersports 35km
Fluent English spoken

Directions: Take exit N34 from A10. Head towards St-Jean-d'Angély, following hospital signs, and turn right onto the D18 as far as St-Savinien. At the traffic lights, turn right and under the railway bridge. Turn left onto the D124 towards Bords. After 2km take the second on the left after the 'Le Pontreau' village sign. The house is 200m on the right.

79.11 Niort

Private Home

Richard BARTER & Ianthe ROPER
'Chez Freddie', Le Bourg, 79170 CHERIGNE
Tel: (0) 5 49 07 82 35
info@chezfreddie.com
www.chezfreddie.com

Price Structure – 4 Bedrooms and 1 Suite
first room: shower room, wc, twin beds: €49,50
second room: shower room, wc, double bed: €49,50
third room: shower, wc, double bed: €49,50
fourth room: shower room, wc, double bed, single bed: €49,50 – 2 people €60,50 – 3 people
suite: shower, wc, double bed. En-suite room, twin beds: €49,50 – 2 people €88,00 – 4 people

Reduction: 7 nights, groups
Capacity: 13 people

Location
35km S E of NIORT
in: Chérigné
Railway station: 35km
Airport: Poitiers 70km
car essential

Bienvenue en France

A royal welcome here 'Chez Freddie', Freddie being the resident cat. British like his owners, together they welcome you to this large family home located in a quiet village. A tranquil location with grounds measuring 5000m^2, bordered by a river. ideal for relaxation and fishing (category 1). The large salt-water swimming pool and the spacious, equipped terrace offer everything you need for lounging around in the sun. There are plenty of games available too including table tennis, *pétanque*, *baby-foot* and darts. A good atmosphere and up-to-date facilities.

Facilities: off-street parking, garden, tv lounge, hosts have pets, pets not accepted, dinner available, babies welcome, free cot, private swimming pool, fishing, hiking, cycling, riversports 10km, interesting flora 15km, hunting 17km, lake watersports 20km, golf course 35km
Fluent English spoken

Directions: From Niort D948 to Mielle and then the D950 towards St-Jean-d'Angély. After Brioux-sur-Boutonne take the D104 on the left and then the first road on the left to Chérigné. When there, pass the chapel on your right and take the first road on the left and continue to the end.

Location
26km E of NIORT
in: Souvigné
Airport: Poitiers 40km
car essential

Private Home

This polite British couple welcome you to their renovated former convent. The pretty garden full of flowers is well maintained with a swimming pool and a barbecue for your use. The comfortable bedrooms have a British flavour. There is also a well-equipped gîte with a fireplace and a private garden that can be rented on a daily basis. Sue and Paul know their region very well and are a good source of local information. They have free entry passes to visit the production site at Cognac Martell. Dinner can be served on the terrace.

Sue & Paul WOODS
'Maison Bois Fleurie', Le Bourg, 79800 SOUVIGNE
Tel: (0) 5 49 76 03 42 / (0) 609 68 02 50
Fax: (0) 5 49 76 03 42
info@maisonboisfleurie.com
www.maisonboisfleurie.com

Facilities: private parking, garden, lounge, hosts have pets, pets not accepted, dinner available, babies welcome, free cot, 100% no smoking, private swimming pool, riding, mushroom-picking 1km, fishing 5km, riversports 5km, golf course 15km, sea watersports 45km
Fluent English spoken

Price Structure – 3 Bedrooms
and 1 Apartment
3 rooms: bathroom, wc, double bed: €60
lounge, television, kitchen, bathroom, wc, double bed: €90

Extra Bed: €10
Capacity: 8 people

Directions: Please contact your hosts in advance for detailed directions.

Location
8km N E of POITIERS
(FUTUROSCOPE)
in: Beaumont
Railway station: 15km
Airport: Poitiers 15km
car essential

Bienvenue en France

Château/Manor House

You will be charmed by this 15th-century hunting lodge on the Poitou wine trail (Henri IV had an affair with his cousin here!). It has now been totally refurbished, and Jean-Noël is adept at combining traditional features with modern comfort, a demonstration of all that is best in the area. You will be torn between the châteaux or Futuroscope!

Annick & Jean-Noël CURNIS
'Manoir de Beaumont', 12 rue des Portes Rouges,
86490 BEAUMONT
Tel: (0) 5 49 85 05 29 / (0) 625 79 06 79
Fax: (0) 5 49 85 05 29
jncurnis@aol.com
www.manoir-de-beaumont.com

Facilities: off-street parking, extensive grounds, tv lounge, hosts have pets, pets not accepted, babies welcome, free cot, 100% no smoking, mushroom-picking, vineyard, hiking 5km, cycling 5km, golf course 5km, fishing 5km, lake watersports 5km
Basic English spoken

Price Structure – 4 Bedrooms and 1 Suite
'Louis XV', 'Régence' & '1900': shower room, wc, double bed: €65
'Louis XVI': shower room, wc, double bed (queen-size): €70
'Suite Duplex Directoire': bathroom, wc, shower, double bed. En-suite room, 3 single beds: €80 – 2 people €155 – 5 people

Extra Bed: €20
Reduction: 3 nights
Capacity: 13 people

Directions: From the A10 (between Poitiers and Châtellerault), exit 27. Take the N10 towards Poitiers for 5km. In La Tricherie, take the D82 towards Beaumont. In the town centre, continue onto the D82 towards Marigny-Brizay (Rue des Portes Rouges) for 300m. The manor is number 12.

86.25 Poitiers (Futuroscope)

Private Home

Chantal NEVEUX
'La Closerie du Rocher', 1 le Rocher, 86340
NIEUIL-L'ESPOIR
Tel: (0) 618 62 23 52
Fax: (0) 5 49 53 00 51
closeriedurocher@a4.cernet.fr
www.closeriedurocher.com

Price Structure – 5 Bedrooms
No 2: along corridor bathroom, wc, double bed: €50
No 3 & No 4: along corridor shower room, wc,
double bed, single bed: €50 – 2 people €60 – 3
people
No 9: along corridor shower room, wc, four-poster
double bed: €42 – 2 people
No 10: along corridor bathroom, wc, 2 double beds:
€50 – 2 people €77 – 4 people

Extra Bed: €10   **Reduction:** 1/10–30/04, 7 nights,
groups   **Capacity:** 14 people

Location
18km S E of POITIERS
(FUTUROSCOPE)
in: Nieuil-l'Espoir, station pick-up on
arrival/departure
Railway station: 16km
Airport: Poitiers 20km

What was once a hotel by a small lake has been
enthusiastically resurrected by Chantal into a B&B, so
keen is she to see this building live again. The
bedrooms, decorated with objects from around the
world, have their own terrace and views over the
garden, down the gentle slope to the lake. The
bathrooms are fairly standard. The very large lounge,
with wooden wardrobes and central fireplace in the
form of a well, has a rustic feel. Chantal adds an
original touch to her copious, delicious breakfast. An
honest and genuine welcome.

Facilities: private parking, garden, hosts have pets,
babies welcome, free cot, fishing, mushroom-picking,
hiking, cycling, golf course 5km, riversports 12km,
gliding 15km, vineyard 25km
Fluent English spoken

Directions: Exit Poitiers via the N147 towards
Limoges for 7km then turn right onto the D1 to
Nieuil-l'Espoir. At the village church, take the road by
the bar called 'Le Solitaire' heading for Le Rocher and
then follow the signs.

86.15 Poitiers (Futuroscope)

**Château/Manor
House**

Claude & Alain GAIL
'Château de Masseuil', 86190 QUINÇAY
Tel: (0) 5 49 60 42 15 Fax: (0) 5 49 60 70 15

Price Structure – 2 Bedrooms
'Empire': shower room, wc, double bed: €65
'Louis XVI': shower room, wc, twin beds: €65

Extra Bed: €15
Reduction: 3 nights
Capacity: 4 people

Location
10km W of POITIERS
(FUTUROSCOPE)
in: Quinçay, station pick-up on
arrival/departure
Railway station: 12km
Airport: Poitiers 10km
car essential

Alain and Claude will receive you in their magnificent
15th-century château. Their kindness and warmth
will ensure that you have an unforgettable stay with
this family. A great feature of this region is the
contrast between the Futuroscope Science Park,
dedicated to advanced technology, and the remains
of ancient civilisations and architectural treasures, of
which the châteaux are the main examples.

Facilities: private parking, extensive grounds, tv
lounge, hosts have pets, kitchen, babies welcome,
free cot, 100% no smoking, 2 wcs, private tennis
court, hiking, cycling, fishing, riversports, mushroom-
picking 4km, lake watersports 6km, golf course 15km

Directions: On the A10 exit Poitiers-Nord. Follow
signs to Nantes for 12km. At the bottom of the small
descent before Vouillé, turn left. Château de Masseuil
is 1.5km further on.

Location
41km S of POITIERS (FUTUROSCOPE)
in: Romagne, station pick-up on arrival/departure
Railway station: 40km
Airport: Poitiers 45km
car essential

Residence of Outstanding Character

A 19th-century flour mill by the Clain River, in a beautifully preserved setting. One of the region's oldest, built on an historic ford dating back to the 12th century. Downstairs the exposed beams, fireplaces and original mechanisms and gears are on show. The bedrooms too are appealing; either rustic chic or Louis-Philippe. The 'Coquillage' has its own small terrace. Philippe is like a fish in water, so if you love nature and appreciate a sincere and good-humoured welcome, then this is for you. Horses can be accommodated; boat trips.

Facilities: off-street parking, extensive grounds, tv lounge, hosts have pets, pets not accepted, dinner available, wheelchair access, riding, fishing, mushroom-picking, bird-watching, hiking, cycling, interesting flora, riversports
Basic English spoken

Directions: From Poitiers, N10 towards Angoulême to Couhé (25km), then the D158 on the left via Vaux and the D27 to Romagne. Take the D25 towards Sommières-du-Clain for 2.5km. The 'Moulin de la Cueille' is on the left.

Philippe COPIN
'Moulin de la Cueille', 86700 ROMAGNE
Tel: (0) 5 49 87 68 64 / (0) 637 08 23 45
Fax: (0) 5 49 87 68 64
moulindelacueille@gmail.com
www.moulindelacueille.com

Price Structure – 4 Bedrooms
'Sapin': shower room, wc, double bed: €59
'Clain': bathroom, wc, shower, double bed (queen-size): €85
'Coquillage': shower room, wc, double bed: €59
'Gîte': shower room, wc, double bed, twin beds: €65
– 2 people €95 – 4 people

Extra Bed: €19
Reduction: 3 nights
Capacity: 10 people

Location
17km E of POITIERS (FUTUROSCOPE)
in: Vouneuil-sur-Vienne
Railway station: 15km
car essential

Private Home

This charming, old restored farmhouse on the edge of the forest and the Pinail Nature Reserve is a great place to unwind in a tranquil setting. If you want excitement, Futuroscope is only 18km away. Florence has been welcoming guests for ten years and in true B&B tradition gives you the run of all the house. This includes the charming family lounge with its tasteful décor. Her family has been in this area for five generations, so the Poitou holds no secrets for Florence and her relatives. Breakfast is plentiful and home-made jam is de rigueur.

Facilities: off-street parking, garden, lounge, hosts have pets, dinner available, babies welcome, free cot, closed: 15/11–1/03, mushroom-picking, bird-watching, hiking, cycling, interesting flora, riversports 4km, golf course 9km, lake watersports 9km, vineyard 15km
Adequate English spoken

Directions: On the N10, midway between Poitiers and Châtellerault, take the D15 towards Vouneuil-sur-Vienne and follow the 'Chambres d'hôtes' signs.

Florence PENOT
'Les Hauts de Chabonne', Chabonne,
86210 VOUNEUIL-SUR-VIENNE
Tel: (0) 5 49 85 28 25
penot.antoine@wanadoo.fr
www.chabonne.com

Price Structure – 3 Bedrooms
3 rooms: bathroom, wc, double bed, single bed: €58
– 2 people €78 – 3 people

Extra Bed: €20
Capacity: 9 people

SWITZERLAND

Bourg

01

74

Chamonix

Annecy

Aix-les-Bains

Albertville

Chambéry

73

42

Vienne

St-Etienne

St-Jean

38 Grenoble

ITALY

07

RHONE-ALPES
page 374

Valence

Privas

26

05

Gap
page 323

Valréas
pages 372-373

Vaison-la-Romaine
pages 371-372

Sisteron
page 323

04

Digne

LANGUEDOC-ROUSSILLON
page 186

84 Carpentras
page 370

06

30

Avignon
pages 362-369 Cavaillon
page 371

Apt

PROVENCE-ALPES-COTE D'AZUR

MONACO
pages 328-329

Nîmes

Les Baux-de-Provence
page 349

Manosque
page 322

Grand Canyon
du Verdon page 321

Grasse
pages
327-328

Nice
pages 329-33

13 Salon-de-Provence
page 350

Draguignan
pages 354-355

Cannes
pages 324-327

Aix-en-Provence
pages 334-346

83

St-Maximin-la-Ste-Baume
pages 357-358

Brignoles
pages 351-353

St-Raphaël
pages 358-360

MARSEILLE

St-Tropez
pages 360-361

Cassis
pages 346-348

Bandol
page
350

Hyères-les-Palmiers
pages 355-356

Toulon
page 362

MEDITERRANEAN SEA

04.18 Grand Canyon du Verdon

Location
GRAND CANYON DU VERDON
in: St-Laurent-du-Verdon, station
pick-up on arrival/departure
Railway station: 15km
Airport: Marseille-Provence 100km
car essential

Private Home

Remember those restoration projects you have seen on TV? Véronique and Paul have restored this old farmhouse with a charming dovecote in the tower, parts of which date back to around 700 AD! This is authentically rustic, with wooden ceilings and beams, and thick stone walls. The bedrooms are simple, cool and bright. Walk on the high plateaus, amid the lavender fields, or enjoy rock-climbing and kayaking in the Gorges du Verdon and the Lac de Ste-Croix. In the evenings just enjoy the quality of the silence.

Facilities: off-street parking, garden, tv lounge, hosts have pets, dinner available, kitchen, babies welcome, free cot, closed: 01/01–31/01, riding, fishing, mushroom-picking, bird-watching, hiking, interesting flora, riversports, lake watersports, vineyard 20km, winter sports 80km
Fluent English spoken

Véronique & Paul TEISSEIRE
'La Colombière', route de Riez,
04500 ST-LAURENT-DU-VERDON
Tel: (0) 4 92 74 06 32 / (0) 674 70 05 59
colombiere.chateau@wanadoo.fr
www.colombiereduchateau.com

Price Structure – 3 Bedrooms
and 1 Apartment
'Dindouleto' & 'Machoto': shower room, wc, four-poster double bed, single bed: €76 – 2 people
€90 – 3 people
'Agasso': shower room, wc, double bed (queen-size):
€66
'Colombetto': lounge, kitchen, shower room, wc,
2 double beds (queen-size): €76 – 2 people
€96 – 4 people

Extra Bed: €15
Reduction: 01/10–30/04, 6 nights, groups
Capacity: 12 people

Directions: When in the village of St-Laurent-du-Verdon pass the château on your left and take the first unmade track on your left. Go gently, and you should end up in the farmyard with your exhaust intact!

83.18 Grand Canyon du Verdon

Location
GRAND CANYON DU VERDON
in: Aiguines, station pick-up on
arrival/departure
Railway station: 60km
Airport: 100km
car essential

Private Home

A quiet authentic village very close to the lake of Ste-Croix and the amazing Gorges du Verdon. There's a fantastic view over the lake from the swimming pool or the terrace. Your hosts run a restaurant in the village.

Facilities: private parking, garden, tv lounge, dinner available, 100% no smoking, wheelchair access, closed: 15/11–01/04, private swimming pool, hiking, cycling, hunting, fishing 4km, mushroom-picking 4km, sea watersports 4km, riversports 4km
Basic English spoken

Jean-Pierre BAGARRE
'Le Bosquet', Quartier le Bosquet,
83630 AIGUINES
Tel: (0) 4 94 70 22 09 Fax: (0) 4 94 70 21 02
contact@verdon-lebosquet.com
www.verdon-lebosquet.com

Price Structure – 6 Bedrooms
4 rooms: television, shower room, wc, double bed:
€55
2 rooms: television, shower room, wc, double bed,
single bed: €55 – 2 people €65 – 3 people

Extra Bed: €8
Reduction: groups, children
Capacity: 14 people

Directions: At Moustiers, take the D952 towards Castellane. Turn right onto the D957 towards Aups and then left onto the D19 towards Aiguines ('Corniche Sublime'). The house is just at the end of the village on the right.

04.14 Manosque

Private Home

Marie-Paule & Leopold de MEESTER
'La Guérine', 04210 VALENSOLE
Tel: (0) 4 92 74 97 38 Fax: (0) 4 92 74 97 38
laguerine@wanadoo.fr

Price Structure – 5 Bedrooms
'Sauge','Coquelicot','Tournesol' & 'Lavande': shower room, wc, twin beds: €70
'Iris': bathroom, wc, double bed, twin beds:
€70 – 2 people €130 – 4 people

Reduction: 2 nights
Capacity: 12 people

Location
17km E of MANOSQUE
in: Valensole
Railway station: 60km
Airport: Marseille-Provence 65km
car essential

Bienvenue en France

This 17th-century farmhouse is typical of the Plateau de Valensole in the Verdon Regional Park. There are a thousand reasons to come to this beautiful part of Provence, in particular the scent of lavender and the peace and quiet. Activities available nearby are canoeing, gliding, riding, tennis and golf, or visit Les Gorges du Verdon or the historic places of interest such as Riez, Moustiers and Ganagobie.

Facilities: off-street parking, garden, hosts have pets, pets not accepted, 100% no smoking, 2 nights minimum stay: 01/07–31/08, private swimming pool
Fluent English spoken

Directions: Please contact your hosts in advance for detailed directions.

04.19 Manosque

Château/Manor House

Alia & Jacques GLORY
'Château du Grand Jardin', 1 chemin de l'Amiral de Villeneuve, 04210 VALENSOLE
Tel: (0) 4 92 74 96 40
info@lechateau-valensole.com
www.lechateau-valensole.com

Price Structure – 5 Bedrooms
'Louise de Savoie': lounge, shower room, wc, twin beds: €110
'Eugénie': lounge, shower room, wc, double bed (queen-size): €98
'Marie-Antoinette': shower room, wc, double bed (queen-size), single bed (child-size): €85 – 2 people €110 – 3 people
'Joséphine': shower room, wc, twin beds, single bed (child-size): €85 – 2 people €110 – 3 people
'Belle Epoque': bathroom, wc, shower, twin beds: €75

Extra Bed: €25
Reduction: 3 nights
Capacity: 12 people

Location
17km E of MANOSQUE
in: Valensole
Railway station: 20km
car essential

You are at the gateway to the Grand Canyon du Verdon, in the heart of the lavender fields, near to Giono country. Your hosts are hidden behind the public wash-house in this beautiful Provence village. Here you combine the tranquillity of Haute Provence, the perfumes of the Midi, the thrill of steep cliffs, the peacefulness of a lake and Alia's welcome. Her cosy little château is out of the ordinary with its tasteful décor, its gastronomic dinners... Everything is vertical, with the bedrooms on the upper floors. Two rooms have their little bathrooms fitted into the tower.

Facilities: private parking, garden, lounge, pets not accepted, dinner available, babies welcome, free cot, 100% no smoking, hiking, cycling, fishing 20km, golf course 25km, gliding 30km, riversports 30km, lake watersports 30km
Fluent English spoken

Directions: From the A51 Aix-Sisteron *autoroute*, exit 18 Manosque. Cross the river Durance towards Gréoux-les-Bains then D6 towards Valensole. The château is this side of the village, just outside, on the road that leads to Gréoux. It is near the chapel and the war memorial, behind the fountain that adjoins the public wash-house.

Location
20km S of SISTERON
in: Cruis, station pick-up on arrival/departure
Railway station: 25km
Airport: Marseille-Provence 110km
car essential

Private Home

In the shade of age-old trees, this authentic provençal *mas* is like an oasis of peace and quiet where you can relax in cool, lush surroundings. Last season, Béatrice and Peter took over this property which has always been popular with those in search of beautiful landscapes and rest and relaxation. It is possible to bathe in the stone pool in the water from the fountain of the Montagne de Lure. This is authentic Haute Provence as described by French writer Jean Giono.

Facilities: off-street parking, extensive grounds, hosts have pets, dinner available, babies welcome, free cot, hiking, cycling, interesting flora, mushroom-picking, winter sports 20km, gliding 20km, golf course 40km, vineyard 40km, lake watersports 70km, riversports 75km
Adequate English spoken

Beatrice & Peter GRUBER
'Vitaverde', Le Claus, 04230 CRUIS
Tel: (0) 4 92 77 00 89 Fax: (0) 4 92 77 02 33
p.l.gruber@wanadoo.fr
www.vitaverde-provence.com

Price Structure – 4 Bedrooms
and 1 Apartment
'Ganagobie': shower room, wc, double bed (queen-size): €55
'Coquelicot': lounge, kitchen, shower room, wc, double bed: €50
'Valensole': bathroom, wc, double bed (king-size), single bed: €55,00 – 2 people €72,50 – 3 people
'La Fontaine': shower room, wc, double bed: €55
'Lure': shower room, wc, twin beds, single bed: €55 – 2 people €70 – 3 people

Extra Bed: €15
Reduction: 3 nights
Capacity: 12 people

Directions: On the A51 take exit Peyruis and continue towards the D951 for St-Etienne-les-Orgues and Cruis. 300m from the Cruis exit turn right down a private lane (signposted).

Location
15km N of GAP
in: St-Bonnet, station pick-up on arrival/departure
Railway station: 15km
Airport: Grenoble-St Geoirs 90km

Bienvenue en **France**

Private Home

This place is on the Grenoble–Gap road, but forget about your car. Here, you are at the gateway to the Parc National des Ecrins, where you can walk, ski, breathe the fresh air and recharge your batteries. Tourism operates here all the year round, with ski resorts, wonderful countryside, mountains and many outdoor activities and sports. Wander through the tempting markets, full of local produce, and ideal for unusual souvenirs.

Facilities: off-street parking, garden, lounge, dinner available, babies welcome, free cot, hiking, cycling, fishing, riversports, winter sports
Fluent English spoken

Agnès & Donald CLARK
'La Combe Fleurie', route de Chaillol,
05500 ST-BONNET-EN-CHAMPSAUR
Tel: (0) 4 92 50 53 97 / (0) 670 21 40 66
Fax: (0) 4 92 50 18 28
clark@lacombefleurie.com
www.lacombefleurie.com

Price Structure – 6 Bedrooms
'Mazurka': television, shower room, wc, double bed: €42
3 rooms: television, shower room, wc, double bed, single bed: €42,00 – 2 people €52,50 – 3 people
'Ronde': television, bathroom, wc, double bed, single bed: €42,00 – 2 people €52,50 – 3 people
'Rigodon': television, shower room, wc, double bed, 3 single beds: €42 – 2 people €63 – 5 people

Extra Bed: €8
Reduction: groups, children
Capacity: 19 people

Directions: In Gap, take the N85 towards Grenoble. Turn right to St-Bonnet. The house is just after the village.

06.70 Cannes

Apartment

Simone & Jean-Louis PASCAL
'Villa Francesca A21', 538 chemin des Hautes
Bregnières, 06600 ANTIBES
Tel: (0) 674 23 54 16
Fax: (0) 4 97 21 93 86
jl.pascal@tele2.fr

Price Structure – 2 Bedrooms
along corridor shower room, wc, 2 single beds
(child-size): €60
shower room, wc, 2 single beds (child-size): €60

Capacity: 4 people

Location
10km E of CANNES
in: Antibes, station pick-up on
arrival/departure
Railway station: 2km
Airport: Nice Côte-d'Azur 16km

If you like the idea of relaxing with some thalas-satherapy, do not hesitate to come and stay with Simone and Jean-Louis as they are walking distance from a thalassatherapy spa. You are just ten minutes from the centre of Antibes, 20 minutes from the airport and your host is used to showing people around the region so make the most of his expe-rience! The apartment has small rooms but a large terrace full of flowers. It is in a small newly built build-ing with a garden and a swimming pool in a quiet and green part of town.

Facilities: private parking, tv lounge, hosts have pets, pets not accepted, dinner available, babies welcome, free cot, 100% no smoking, closed: 20/12–15/01, private swimming pool, hiking, sea watersports, golf course 2km, fishing 2km, mushroom-picking 10km
Fluent English spoken

Directions: A8 exit Antibes. Pass in front of the shop 'Carrefour', then straight ahead on Chemin St-Claude. At the bottom, take Route Jules Grec on the left and then at the second roundabout, turn right and then first left.

06.40 Cannes

**Residence of
Outstanding
Character**

Ghislaine & René POULIN
'Maison Louijane', 3225 boulevard des Horizons,
06220 GOLFE JUAN
Tel: (0) 4 93 63 75 79 / (0) 609 83 67 60
maison.louijane@wanadoo.fr
www.maisonlouijane.fr.st

Price Structure – 3 Bedrooms
'Louis': shower room, wc, double bed, single bed:
€100 – 2 people €120 – 3 people
'Jeanne': bathroom, wc, double bed (queen-size):
€100
'Blanche': shower room, wc, double bed: €90

Extra Bed: €20
Reduction: 01/10–30/04, 3 nights, children
Capacity: 7 people

Location
2km E of CANNES
in: Golfe Juan
Railway station: 4km
Airport: Nice Côte-d'Azur 25km
car essential

Bienvenue en France

Ghislaine and René welcome you to their family home perched high above Golfe Juan. Your accommodation is in a separate small house in the grounds, near to the main house, with an attractive flower garden. High above the madding crowd, you can easily while away many hours beside the pool, or enjoy the solarium with its panoramic view towards Cap d'Antibes. If you walk down, there is a small creek by the sea, really only known to the locals. There is also a secure car parking space. What more could one ask?

Facilities: private parking, garden, pets not accepted, babies welcome, free cot, 100% no smoking, private swimming pool, hiking, fishing, sea watersports 1km, interesting flora 4km, golf course 6km, mushroom-picking 15km, gliding 25km
Basic English spoken

Directions: From the A8, exit 44 towards Vallauris, then Golfe Juan. As you leave Vallauris take the Boulevard des Horizons and then the first on the right off the large roundabout.

Location
10km E of CANNES
in: Juan-les-Pins, station pick-up on arrival/departure
Railway station
Airport: Nice Côte-d'Azur 25km

Private Home

Bernadette knows a thing or two about hospitality. She has given up her 3-star hotel in the north of France and is now ready to receive guests in her house that she has completely renovated. The rooms are spacious and this is an ideal spot: a villa in Juan-les-Pins near to the beach!

Bernadette RAMBAUD
'Le Bellagio', 105 boulevard Wilson,
06160 JUAN-LES-PINS
Tel: (0) 4 93 61 84 16 / (0) 660 44 27 47

Facilities: private parking, garden, tv lounge, wheelchair access, 2 years old minimum age, fishing, sea watersports, hiking 2km, interesting flora 2km, golf course 10km, riversports 10km, gliding 30km, winter sports 60km, vineyard 60km
Adequate English spoken

Price Structure – 3 Bedrooms
first room: television, telephone, bathroom, wc, four-poster double bed: €84
second room: television, telephone, shower room, wc, four-poster double bed: €74
third room: television, telephone, bathroom, wc, four-poster double bed: €74

Extra Bed: €15
Reduction: 15/10–15/04
Capacity: 6 people

Directions: From the A8, exit Antibes, head towards Juan-les-Pins, follow the main boulevard (Boulevard Wilson). The villa is on the left, at the end of the boulevard.

Location
4km W of CANNES
in: Mandelieu, station pick-up on arrival/departure
Railway station: 2km
Airport: Nice Côte-d'Azur 35km
car essential

Private Home

This is a great place to stay for a holiday and Monique and Michel are a friendly couple who welcome you to their provençal house in private grounds where you can play tennis and make use of the swimming pool. The two bedrooms are comfortable and plentiful breakfasts are served on the terrace with a view over the Estérel mountains. The living area is decorated with attractive artworks and paintings. To reach the beach you simply have to pass through the village of La Napoule.

Monique & Michel GINISTY
'Domaine de Sénanque', Villa No 35,
06210 MANDELIEU
Tel: (0) 4 93 49 02 91 / (0) 612 78 59 73
mig-mog@wanadoo.fr
www.mandchou.com/clients/mandelieu

Facilities: off-street parking, garden, tv lounge, hosts have pets, pets not accepted, dinner available, babies welcome, free cot, 2 nights minimum stay, private swimming pool, private tennis court, golf course 1km, fishing 2km, sea watersports 2km
Basic English spoken

Price Structure – 2 Bedrooms
'Champagne': television, bathroom, wc, double bed: €75
'Bleue': television, along corridor bathroom, wc, twin beds: €65

Reduction: 2 nights, children
Capacity: 4 people

Directions: A8, exit 40, Mandelieu. Head towards Fréjus, cross the town and pass under the A8. At the 2nd roundabout, turn right at the BP petrol station. 50m from the traffic lights, turn right. Go up Avenue Carbon for 800m. Go along by the side of the 'Domaine' until you reach the 2nd entrance. The villa is at the end.

Provence – Cannes

83.95 Cannes

Private Home

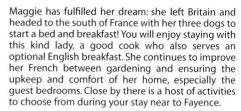

Location
33km N W of CANNES
in: Montauroux, station pick-up on arrival/departure
Railway station: 25km
Airport: Nice Côte-d'Azur 50km
car essential

Maggie has fulfilled her dream: she left Britain and headed to the south of France with her three dogs to start a bed and breakfast! You will enjoy staying with this kind lady, a good cook who also serves an optional English breakfast. She continues to improve her French between gardening and ensuring the upkeep and comfort of her home, especially the guest bedrooms. Close by there is a host of activities to choose from during your stay near to Fayence.

Maggie & Martin PAYNE
'M&M's B&B', La Gineste, chemin des Adrechs de Valcros, 83440 MONTAUROUX
Tel: (0) 4 94 70 48 15 / (0) 668 39 98 79
Fax: (0) 4 94 70 48 15
info@magsinfrance.com
www.magsinfrance.com

Price Structure – 3 Bedrooms
'Verte' & 'Rouge': television, shower room, wc, double bed: €65
'Twin': television, along corridor bathroom, wc, along corridor shower, twin beds: €65

Reduction: 1/11–28/02
Capacity: 6 people

Facilities: off-street parking, garden, hosts have pets, dinner available, 100% no smoking, closed: 25/12–26/12 & 31/12–01/01, private swimming pool, hiking, cycling, fishing 4km, sea watersports 4km, golf course 6km, gliding 6km, interesting flora 30km
Fluent English spoken

Directions: A8, exit 39 Fayence. Head for Montauroux. After the first roundabout, take the second turning on the right, a hairpin bend, and continue along Chemin des Adrechs de Valcros for about 3km.

06.41 Cannes

Residence of Outstanding Character

Location
5km N of CANNES
in: Mougins
Railway station: 7km
Airport: Nice Côte-d'Azur 25km

Set high up on the ramparts of a medieval village with an exceptional position and view over the countryside is this very pleasant home with a small terrace, a pool and reclining chairs. There is also a shaded, terraced walled garden. For cooler mornings there is the living room with a panoramic bay window which ensures you do not miss out on the view. The village is lively in the summer with many gastronomic restaurants and art galleries but without any traffic noise as the village is pedestrianised. Chez Sara and Stuart, peace and quiet is guaranteed.

Sara & Stuart PARKES
'La Vallée', 21 rue du Vallat, 06250 MOUGINS
Tel: (0) 4 93 75 60 33 / (0) 678 17 07 82
stuart.parkes@wanadoo.fr
www.gocannes.com

Price Structure – 1 Bedroom
bathroom, wc, shower, double bed: €85

Extra Bed: €15
Reduction: 30/10–30/03, 3 nights
Capacity: 2 people

Facilities: garden, tv lounge, pets not accepted, 100% no smoking, closed: 15/11–15/03, private swimming pool, hiking 2km, golf course 2km, sea watersports 7km
Fluent English spoken

Directions: On the A8 take exit 42 Cannes-Mougins. The house is situated in the centre of the old village in the pedestrian zone. Park in one of the free car parks. Rue du Vallat is off Place du Commandant Lamy (easy to find).

Location
6km N of CANNES
in: Valbonne
Railway station: 12km
Airport: Nice Côte-d'Azur 30km
car essential

Private Home

The superb medieval village of Valbonne is very popular with tourists and can easily be reached on foot from this place. This is in fact a small motel, spotlessly clean and with a private car park, which is very rare in Valbonne. Sylvain knows this region well and he will happily advise on what is new to do, the excursions to take and the interesting places to visit. You could spend hours browsing in the small streets of Valbonne and then relax on the terrace of a café on the village square.

Sylvain GILARDONI
'Résidence La Cigale', 287 route de Nice, Quartier la Baïsse, 06560 VALBONNE
Tel: (0) 4 93 12 24 43 / (0) 661 98 96 73
Fax: (0) 4 93 12 32 42
cigalevsa@free.fr
http://cigalevsa.free.fr

Facilities: off-street parking, hosts have pets, pets not accepted, babies welcome, free cot, 3 nights minimum stay, hiking, cycling, interesting flora, golf course 5km, mushroom-picking 10km, sea watersports 10km
Fluent English spoken

Price Structure – 3 Bedrooms
No 10: television, telephone, bathroom, wc, twin beds: €56
No 12B: television, telephone, bathroom, wc, double bed: €65
No 14: television, telephone, bathroom, wc, double bed (queen-size): €56

Reduction: 1/11–28/02
Capacity: 6 people

Directions: From the A8 exit 44 towards Antibes/Grasse/Mougins then Sophia-Antipolis. At the Les Bouillides crossroads, head for Valbonne on the D103. The motel is at the top of the village.

Location
5km N E of GRASSE
in: Magagnosc
Railway station: 3km
Airport: Nice Côte-d'Azur 30km
car essential

Bienvenue en France

Private Home

The kind, elegant and discreet welcome of Judith and Rolf makes you feel like staying and then coming back as soon as possible. They know how to look after you and make you feel at home in their 18th-century *bastide*. The panoramic view is wonderful and Judith ensures that calm reigns so you can relax. The plentiful breakfast is served in a cosy room. By staying inland you benefit from the southern climate and Grasse, yet are near to Cannes and the hustle and bustle of the coast.

Judith & Rolf RITTELMANN
'La Bastide des Anges', 2 chemin du Camp de la Besse, 06520 MAGAGNOSC
Tel: (0) 4 93 36 47 16 / (0) 679 85 87 95
Fax: (0) 4 93 36 47 16
azur@bastidedesanges.com
www.bastidedesanges.com

Facilities: private parking, garden, tv lounge, hosts have pets, pets not accepted, internet access, babies welcome, free cot, 100% no smoking, private swimming pool, golf course 4km, hiking 10km, sea watersports 15km, winter sports 30km, vineyard 30km
Fluent English spoken

Price Structure – 2 Bedrooms
'Jasmin': lounge, television, bathroom, wc, shower, 2 single beds: €100
'Lavande': lounge, television, shower room, wc, double bed: €100

Extra Bed: €25
Reduction: 01/01–31/03 & 01/10–30/11, 2 nights
Capacity: 4 people

Directions: Head for the centre of Grasse and follow signs to Magagnosc, towards Nice. Just after entering Magagnosc you will see the Chemin du Camp de la Besse on the left.

06.36 Grasse

Private Home

Location
5km S W of GRASSE
in: Peymeinade, station pick-up on arrival/departure
Railway station: 15km
Airport: Nice Côte-d'Azur 35km
car essential

You head up into the foothills of the Alpes de Provence to reach Grasse, the perfume town and its surrounding villages perched on the hillsides, perfectly designed to blend in with the landscape. This property is in its own grounds, surrounded by hedges and with many attractive spots in which to relax, such as under the arbour, the veranda or on the terrace. They also have lots of extra facilities such as a lift, jacuzzi, fish-pond, kitchenettes and some rooms with air-conditioning.

Facilities: private parking, extensive grounds, hosts have pets, pets not accepted, dinner available, kitchen, babies welcome, free cot, 100% no smoking, wheelchair access, private swimming pool, hiking, cycling, golf course 10km, sea watersports 10km, riversports 15km, vineyard 15km
Fluent English spoken

Martine & Pierre MARCOUX-GENTY
'Bastide des Jaïsous', 67 avenue des Jaïsous, 06530 PEYMEINADE
Tel: (0) 4 93 66 28 74 Fax: (0) 4 93 66 28 74
pierre.marcoux@wanadoo.fr
www.hotegenty.com

Price Structure – 2 Bedrooms and 1 Suite
'Mimosas': television, along corridor bathroom, wc, 2 single beds: €60
'Iris': television, shower room, wc, washbasin, double bed: €70
suite 'Lavande': television, shower room, wc, washbasin, double bed. En-suite room, double bed: €80 – 2 people €100 – 4 people

Extra Bed: €15
Reduction: 01/10–15/05
Capacity: 8 people

Directions: From Grasse take the D562 towards Draguignan for about 5km as far as Peymeinade. Continue on this road, through this village and as you are leaving the village, 300 metres past the 'Garage Fiat Iveco', turn right and follow signs to 'Les Jaïsous'.

06.46 Monaco

Residence of Outstanding Character

Location
1km N E of MONACO
in: Roquebrune-Cap-Martin
Railway station: 2km
Airport: Nice Côte-d'Azur 20km
car essential

Here, between Roquebrune and Monaco, you are in an area full of notorious residences belonging to stars, princes and football managers. This charming white villa is worth a stay, just to experience its prestigious location. There is a little terrace and a swimming pool surrounded by lemon trees and ponds and the comfortable rooms have their own private balcony with a superb view over the bay. Your hosts are charming and attentive to your every whim. Ideal for the Monaco Grand Prix (expect to pay double the normal tariff).

Facilities: garden, tv lounge, hosts have pets, pets not accepted, babies welcome, free cot, private swimming pool, sea watersports, golf course 8km
Fluent English spoken

Nicole & Christian REY
'Les Mouettes', 39 avenue Jean-Jaurès, 06190 ROQUEBRUNE-CAP-MARTIN
Tel: (0) 4 93 35 08 21 / (0) 680 86 20 39
nicolechristian.Rey@wanadoo.fr

Price Structure – 4 Bedrooms
'Suite Pivoine': television, bathroom, wc, double bed (super king-size): €195
'Celadon', 'Citronelle' & 'Myosotis': television, shower room, wc, double bed: €195

Capacity: 8 people

Directions: This house is situated on Basse Corniche (N98) between Monaco (1km) and Roquebrune in the direction of Menton.

Location
1km N E of MONACO
in: Roquebrune-Cap-Martin
Airport: Nice Côte-d'Azur 25km
car essential

Private Home

Seen from the road, do not let the frontage put you off! The location is superb; on the lower coastal road between Monte Carlo and Menton, overhanging the Golfe Bleu. Your three charming hostesses will win you over in their super *Maison d'Hôtes* converted from a well-known restaurant where Patricia was one of the few women to be star-rated by the Michelin guide! You must try a *bourride* or a *bouillabaisse*. There is a bar, modern rooms with a terrace, a sea view and a path that leads down to the beach. Magical!

Facilities: off-street parking, tv lounge, hosts have pets, internet access, dinner available, babies welcome, free cot, wheelchair access, gliding, hiking, sea watersports 3km, interesting flora 3km, cycling 5km, riversports 10km, golf course 15km
Fluent English spoken

Directions: A8 between Nice and Menton, exit 57, La Turbie, towards Menton. Continue down the coastal roads via the large and then the smaller *corniche* (N7), always in the direction of Menton and Monaco. On arriving on *la basse corniche* turn right to Monaco (N98). You arrive at Avenue Jean Jaurès. 'Le Roquebrune' is straight away on your left. Large sign 'Chambre d'hôtes'.

Patricia & Marine MARINOVICH
'Le Roquebrune', 100 avenue Jean Jaurès, 06190
ROQUEBRUNE-CAP-MARTIN
Tel: (0) 4 93 35 00 16 Fax: (0) 4 93 28 98 36
leroquebrune@wanadoo.fr
www.leroquebrune.com

Price Structure – 5 Bedrooms
'Golfe Bleu': wheelchair access, television, shower room, wc, double bed (super king-size), single bed: €195 – 2 people €215 – 3 people
'Bougainvillier': television, shower room, wc, double bed: €135
'Ciel et Mer': television, bathroom, shower, wc, double bed: €125
'Olivier': television, bathroom, shower, wc, double bed (super king-size): €135
plus 1 room

Reduction: 10/01–06/04 & 01/11–22/12, 3 nights
Capacity: 12 people

Provence – Monaco, Nice

Location
NICE
in: Nice
Railway station: 14km
Airport: Nice Côte-d'Azur 14km

Private Home

Here with Nathalie and her family, you are in the upper parts of Nice, just 20 minutes from the centre of town but completely away from all the hustle and bustle. Enjoy the lovely view over the undulating valleys of Bellet and its AOC vineyard and set off to discover from here the château, the *villages perchés*, the Mercantour peaks. . . or simply just enjoy her garden of fruit trees, the infinity swimming pool and make use of the outdoor summer kitchen. Nathalie makes her own jams and she can also offer an evening meal if booked in advance.

Facilities: private parking, garden, tv lounge, hosts have pets, pets not accepted, dinner available, kitchen, babies welcome, free cot, 100% no smoking, private swimming pool, hiking, vineyard, fishing 7km, sea watersports 12km, golf course 25km
Fluent English spoken

Directions: Please contact your host in advance for detailed directions.

Nathalie MOUROT-GRAFFAGNINO
'Villa Kilauea', 6 chemin du Candeu, 06200 NICE
Tel: (0) 4 93 37 84 90 / (0) 625 37 21 44
villakilauea@orange.fr
www.villakilauea.com

Price Structure – 3 Bedrooms
'Lavande': bathroom, wc, twin beds, cot: €110
'Marina': shower room, wc, double bed (queen-size), cot: €105
'Agapanthe': shower room, wc, double bed: €95

Extra Bed: €25
Reduction: 1/10–31/03
Capacity: 6 people

06.69 Nice

Private Home

Location
NICE
in: Nice
Railway station: Nice
Airport: Nice Côte-d'Azur 7km

This is a wonderful 19th-century house. All the exterior friezes have been restored by the Beaux-Arts as the house is classified. Large rooms with high ceilings are furnished with antiques and the odd touch of exoticism. It is in a quiet residential area, high up, with an exceptional view of the port of Nice and the hills behind, just five minutes from both the state forest and the town centre. There is a good bus service if you wish to leave your car behind. An excellent three 'sun' host that we heartily recommend.

Noëlle & Gérard PIERI
'Villa Vermorel', 59 bis boulevard du Mont Boron, 06300 NICE
Tel: (0) 4 93 89 21 91 / (0) 621 16 88 99
Fax: (0) 4 93 89 21 91
harmony@mail.pf
www.harmony-cotedazur.com

Facilities: garden, pets not accepted, babies welcome, free cot, 100% no smoking, fishing, mushroom-picking, hiking, cycling, interesting flora, sea watersports, vineyard, golf course 20km, riversports 25km, winter sports 50km
Adequate English spoken

Price Structure – 2 Bedrooms
'Baie des Anges': shower room, wc, double bed (queen-size): €110
'L'Oranger': bathroom, wc, twin beds: €90

Extra Bed: €25
Reduction: 7 nights
Capacity: 4 people

Directions: Head for the port, then direction Monaco which is straight ahead (church on your left and the sea on your right). Head up as far as the estate agency 'Century 21' and the supermarket 'Champion' on the left. At the lights before 'Champion', turn left into Boulevard du Mont Boron.

06.71 Nice

Apartment

Location
NICE
in: Nice
Railway station: Nice
Airport: Nice Côte-d'Azur 10km

Bienvenue en **France**

You must visit Nice, and you will be captivated by this very beautiful flat, typical of Nice, dating from the 19th century. Rare antiques, beautiful china, top quality linen and above all Josiane's very warm welcome will make you instantly forget the two floors of stairs that you have just climbed. Take our advice and be sure to take dinner here, as Josiane is a Master of Wine and was formerly the number three chef at the legendary Hôtel Negresco. She also gives cooking classes. When the new tramway is finished you will be five minutes from the beach.

Josiane FINANCE-MAURICE
44 avenue Borriglione, 06100 NICE
Tel: (0) 4 93 52 61 88 / (0) 609 55 65 37
gritin@clubinternet.fr
www.byzancecotebalcon.com

Facilities: private parking, tv lounge, pets not accepted, internet access, dinner available, babies welcome, free cot, 100% no smoking, 1 shared bathroom, wc, 2 nights minimum stay, hiking 2km, sea watersports 2km, interesting flora 4km, vineyard 8km
Basic English spoken

Price Structure – 2 Bedrooms
'Byzance': television, double bed: €75
'Louis-Philippe': television, single bed: €65 – 1 person

Capacity: 3 people

Directions: Please contact your host in advance for detailed directions.

Location
12km W of NICE
in: Cagnes-sur-Mer, station pick-up
on arrival/departure
Railway station: 2km
Airport: Nice Côte-d'Azur 6km

Residence of Outstanding Character

This beautiful residence from the 1920s is full of charm. The décor has a personal touch with warm Mediterranean paintings, a pool and a pleasant garden where you can cut yourself off from the outside world, yet be only ten minutes from the centre of Cagnes and 20 minutes from Nice airport. The bedrooms are spacious, and although the bathrooms are a bit small they have been completely modernised. You will enjoy the family atmosphere and the generous breakfasts, and as Marie-Paule is Belgian it all has an international flavour.

Marie-Paule MOMBEEK
'Jardins Fragonard', 12 rue Fragonard,
06800 CAGNES-SUR-MER
Tel: (0) 4 93 20 07 72 / (0) 683 93 67 93
Fax: (0) 4 93 20 07 72
jardinsfragonard@hotmail.com
www.babazur.com

Facilities: private parking, extensive grounds, tv lounge, hosts have pets, pets not accepted, kitchen, babies welcome, free cot, 100% no smoking, 2 nights minimum stay: 01/05–30/09, private swimming pool, sea watersports 3km, golf course 6km, hiking 10km
Fluent English spoken

Price Structure – 5 Bedrooms
'Fragonard': television, shower room, wc, double bed (king-size), single bed (child-size): €95 – 2 people
€110 – 3 people
'De Staël', 'Dufy' & 'Renoir': television, shower room, wc, double bed (queen-size): €80
'Bonnard': television, kitchen, shower room, wc, double bed: €90

Extra Bed: €15
Capacity: 11 people

Directions: Go to Cagnes-sur-Mer and follow signs to the Musée Renoir. The Rue Fragonard is parallel to the street where the museum is situated (Chemin des Colettes). DO NOT TAKE the museum street, but carry straight on and take the second street on the left.

Provence – Nice

Location
35km N W of NICE
in: Gilette
Railway station: 35km
Airport: Nice Côte-d'Azur 30km
car essential

Private Home

The windows of Nicole and Patrick's imposing house are dressed with lovely window boxes, a good sign of the warm welcome you will receive here. From the garden, there is an uninterrupted view over the mountains, the valley and the ruins of a 12th-century château. In season, no guest is allowed to leave without a basket of cherries.

Nicole & Patrick FAVERE
'Au Relais Fleuri', rue des Laves, 06830 GILETTE
Tel: (0) 4 93 08 56 45 / (0) 615 35 21 01
Fax: (0) 4 93 08 56 45

Facilities: off-street parking, garden, tv lounge, pets not accepted, dinner available, babies welcome, free cot, 100% no smoking, 4 shared bathrooms, wc, private tennis court, hiking, riversports 6km, golf course 20km
Adequate English spoken

Price Structure – 6 Bedrooms
4 rooms: double bed: €59
'Coquelicot': single bed: €52 – 1 person
'Bouquet': twin beds: €59

Extra Bed: €20
Reduction: 7 nights
Capacity: 11 people

Directions: From Nice airport, take the N202 towards Digne for about 20km, then turn left onto the D17 towards Roquesteron, as far as Gilette. In the village, go under an archway, down the road and take a sharp left turn, which will bring you to the car park 'Ste-Anne'. The house is in front of you.

06.10 Nice

Private Home

Location
17km W of NICE
in: La Colle-sur-Loup
Railway station: 16km
Airport: Nice Côte-d'Azur 12km
car essential

It is with great joy that we introduce you again to Béatrice, so very French and elegant! Notwithstanding the fact that you are at the foot of St-Paul-de-Vence, you will be tempted to while away the hours in the very pleasant garden or in the equally enticing swimming pool. A refrigerator and a picnic table are also at your disposal. The guest bedrooms, although a touch small, represent excellent value.

Béatrice RONIN PILLET
'Le Clos de St Paul', 71 chemin de la Rouguière,
06480 LA COLLE SUR LOUP
Tel: (0) 4 93 32 56 81 Fax: (0) 4 93 32 56 81
leclossaintpaul@hotmail.com
www.stpaulweb.com/closstpaul

Price Structure – 3 Bedrooms
'Madras': wheelchair access, television, bathroom, wc, twin beds: €75
'Sable': shower room, wc, double bed: €75
'Tropique': bathroom, wc, twin beds: €85

Extra Bed: €15
Reduction: 2 nights
Capacity: 6 people

Facilities: garden, hosts have pets, kitchen, 100% no smoking, wheelchair access, 12 years old minimum age, private swimming pool
Fluent English spoken

Directions: From the A8 exit 48 (coming from Nice) or exit 47 (coming from Marseille). Head for Vence. On the D7 (Avenue de Verdun), in La Colle-sur-Loup, after the cemetery, turn right down Chemin de la Souquée, and then left into Boulevard J. B. Layet and then first left.

06.57 Nice

Private Home

Location
17km W of NICE
in: La Colle-sur-Loup
Railway station: 7km
Airport: Nice Côte-d'Azur 14km
car essential

Martine and Bernard will welcome you to this large *bastide* (a provençal country house), with a swimming pool overlooking a quiet wooded valley. All the bedrooms face south, are air-conditioned and equipped with a fridge, television and DVD player. A great location, 3km from St-Paul-de-Vence and 7km from the beaches.

Martine & Bernard DELOUPY
'Un Ange passe. . .', 419 avenue Jean Leonardi,
06480 LA COLLE-SUR-LOUP
Tel: (0) 4 93 32 60 39 / (0) 660 51 61 72
Fax: (0) 4 93 32 63 64
contact@unangepasse.fr
www.unangepasse.fr

Price Structure – 6 Bedrooms
'Savane' & 'Soleil': lounge, television, bathroom, wc, shower, twin beds, 2 single beds (child-size): €105 – 2 people €150 – 4 people
'Touareg' & 'Yang': television, shower room, wc, double bed, single bed (child-size): €90 – 2 people €105 – 3 people
'Bambou': television, bathroom, wc, shower, double bed (queen-size): €95
'Yin': television, shower room, wc, twin beds: €90

Extra Bed: €25
Reduction: 01/10–30/04, 10 nights
Capacity: 18 people

Facilities: off-street parking, extensive grounds, lounge, hosts have pets, pets not accepted, kitchen, 100% no smoking, private swimming pool, hiking, cycling, interesting flora, fishing 1km, riversports 1km, golf course 7km, sea watersports 7km, winter sports 40km
Fluent English spoken

Directions: A8 exit Cagnes-sur-Mer. At the roundabout head for Vence, La Colle-sur-Loup. At the third roundabout, head towards La Colle-sur-Loup. At the fourth roundabout, take the road that heads up to Bar-sur-Loup. At the top of the hill, turn right. Finally at the fifth roundabout head towards Pont-du-Loup. After 200m, after the pharmacy, turn right, pass around the pharmacy and follow the small winding road for 1km (Signed 'Chambre d'Hôtes').

Location
5km W of NICE
in: St-Laurent-du-Var, station pick-up
on arrival/departure
Railway station: 1km
Airport: Nice Côte-d'Azur 2km

Private Home

This provençal villa is in a quiet location, at the centre of St-Laurent, ten minutes from the centre of Nice and five minutes from the airport and beaches. There are supermarkets, a yacht harbour and restaurants nearby. This is the ideal base from which to visit the Côte d'Azur, St-Tropez, Menton, Monaco, Nice, Antibes, Cannes, the Estérel, Fréjus and the hinterland, including St-Paul-de-Vence. Windsurfing available. A warm welcome awaits, plus many tips on what to see.

Monique & Pierre ALLIEZ
89 boulevard Louis Roux,
06700 ST-LAURENT-DU-VAR
Tel: (0) 4 93 31 74 35
alliez@club-internet.fr
www.superriviera.com

Facilities: private parking, garden, tv lounge, pets not accepted, babies welcome, free cot, 100% no smoking, fishing, sea watersports
Adequate English spoken

Price Structure – 1 Suite
suite: bathroom, wc, shower, double bed. En-suite room, 2 single beds: €75 – 2 people
€105 – 4 people

Extra Bed: €15
Capacity: 4 people

Directions: From Nice, on the A8, exit 49, St-Laurent-du-Var. Follow the River Var and, at the third roundabout, follow 'Centre-Ville, Toutes Directions' and at the traffic lights turn right and then immediately left, after the post office.

Provence – Nice

Location
20km E of NICE
in: St-Paul-de-Vence
Railway station: 5km
Airport: Nice Côte-d'Azur 14km
car essential

Bienvenue
en
France

Private Home

On the road where villages cling to the hillside, two minutes from St-Paul-de-Vence, this villa, typical of the region, is built on an elevated site and blends in perfectly with the surrounding countryside of wooded hillsides dotted with beautiful villas. The bedrooms are comfortable and lead onto a lovely lounge with a vaulted ceiling and full of plants. Enjoy the seductive scents of lavender, lemon and rosemary wafting from the garden. The apartment boasts a large bay window with an impressive view over the hillside and the sea. Elvira serves a copious German-style breakfast.

Elvira BARCHET-BEIERL
'Villa Bel Air', 1238 chemin des Espinets,
06570 ST-PAUL-DE-VENCE
Tel: (0) 4 93 24 28 62 Fax: (0) 4 93 24 28 62
ebarchetbeierl@gmx.de
www.stpaulweb.com/belair

Facilities: off-street parking, garden, lounge, pets not accepted, wheelchair access, 5 years old minimum age, hiking 5km, sea watersports 5km, golf course 10km, interesting flora 14km, riversports 35km, vineyard 65km
Fluent English spoken

Price Structure – 3 Bedrooms
and 1 Apartment
'Blanc': shower room, wc, double bed: €115
'Bleue': bathroom, wc, twin beds: €115
'Jaune': shower room, wc, twin beds: €115
'Apartment': kitchen, shower room, wc, double bed: €125

Extra Bed: €15
Capacity: 8 people

Directions: From the A8 exit 48 Cagnes-sur-Mer, head for Vence via the D36 and D336. On the D336 at the second roundabout, take the first right, Chemin des Espinets.

13.13 Aix-en-Provence

Château/Manor House

Marie & François GREGOIRE
'Pavillon de la Torse', 69 cours Gambetta,
13100 AIX-EN-PROVENCE
Tel: (0) 4 42 26 10 52
contact@latorse.com
www.latorse.com

Price Structure – 5 Bedrooms
'Pomerol': bathroom, wc, double bed (queen-size):
€140
'St Emilion': shower room, wc, double bed (queen-size): €130
'St Estèphe': along corridor shower room, wc, double bed (queen-size): €120
'Pauillac': bathroom, wc, double bed (king-size), single bed: €150 – 2 people €190 – 3 people
'Margaux': bathroom, wc, double bed (queen-size), single bed: €140 – 2 people €180 – 3 people

Extra Bed: €20
Reduction: 15/04–31/05 & 1/09–31/10, 3 nights
Capacity: 12 people

Location
AIX-EN-PROVENCE
in: Aix-en-Provence
Railway station: 15km
Airport: Marseille-Provence 25km

The gate opens to reveal a long avenue of age-old plane trees that lead to this beautiful *bastide* from the 18th century. François has returned to Aix-en-Provence with his wife from New York after 20 years of living in San Francisco. They now spend six months of the year here and then return to visit their children for six months. The large grounds are a part of the countryside within the lovely town of Aix, where you'll find beautiful, comfortable bedrooms. We particularly loved the 'Margaux' room and the original pigeon loft.

Facilities: off-street parking, extensive grounds, tv lounge, pets not accepted, 100% no smoking, 10 years old minimum age, 2 nights minimum stay, closed: 1/11–15/04, hiking, cycling, vineyard 5km, golf course 10km
Fluent English spoken

Directions: A8 exit 31 Aix-3 Sautets. At the first roundabout, turn right and then at the second roundabout, turn left. Follow the signs to the 'Centre-Ville'. At the second set of traffic lights, spot the sign 'Age d'Or' and the green parapet. Turn right just after the bridge and the black gate.

13.20 Aix-en-Provence

Private Home

Tinou & Guy BOONEN
'Leï Faveloun', 85 chemin des Cruyes,
13090 AIX-EN-PROVENCE
Tel: (0) 4 42 92 14 74 / (0) 677 11 14 78
leifaveloun@aol.com
france-balades.fr/lei-faveloun.html

Price Structure – 2 Bedrooms
'Les Roses': shower room, wc, double bed: €98
'Les Lavandes': bathroom, wc, shower, double bed, single bed: €108 – 2 people €153 – 3 people

Extra Bed: €45
Reduction: 1/10–31/03, 2 nights
Capacity: 5 people

Location
AIX-EN-PROVENCE
in: Aix-en-Provence
Railway station: 15km
Airport: Marseille-Provence 28km
car essential

A very provençal and exquisitely furnished little *mas* at Aix-en-Provence yet in the countryside. Set in grounds measuring 5000m², there is also a pool with an oak tree forest serving as the backdrop. Guy is retired and dedicates himself to serving you an excellent breakfast. This is a truly Euro family with Belgian, Dutch, Spanish and German members, and as such your nationality will be acknowledged on arrival with the hoisting of your flag!

Facilities: off-street parking, extensive grounds, pets not accepted, 100% no smoking, private swimming pool, hiking, vineyard, golf course 12km
Fluent English spoken

Directions: A51 towards Gap, take exit D14 Aix, Puyricard. At the roundabout head for Puyricard. After about 700m take the first road on the left, Chemin des Cruyes. 85m after this fork in the road, at the level of the bus stop, is an electric pole on the left with a small sign saying 'No 85'. Head down the unsurfaced lane (not very good). It is the first entrance on the left, the 'Leï Faveloun'. Follow the signs 'Boonen'.

13.25 Aix-en-Provence

Private Home

Location
AIX-EN-PROVENCE
in: Aix-en-Provence, station pick-up
on arrival/departure
Railway station: 20km
Airport: Marseille-Provence 35km

This is an authentic, restored provençal house only five minutes from the centre of Aix. It is quietly located in the middle of 6000 square metres of pine woods. You will sleep well here. The rooms are large and soberly furnished. Catherine has travelled the world as a humanitarian aid worker, so if you join her for dinner you are sure to spend an interesting evening.

Facilities: off-street parking, extensive grounds, tv lounge, internet access, dinner available, babies welcome, free cot, 100% no smoking, private swimming pool, mushroom-picking, hiking, sea watersports 40km
Fluent English spoken

Directions: From the centre of Aix, follow the Boulevard du Roi René, the Boulevard Carnot and the Cours des Arts et Metiers on the right, towards Vauvenargues, then straight on. At the lights by the aqueduct, turn left into the Chemin de Bibernus and continue for 1km. The lane is on the right.

Catherine & Bernard SARRADE
'Le Bosquet des Esquirous', 370 chemin
d'Escracho-Pevou, 13100 AIX-EN-PROVENCE
Tel: (0) 620 28 78 34
le-bosquet@soleil.org
www.esquirous.fr

Price Structure – 1 Bedroom, 1 Suite and 1 Apartment
'Estelle': television, bathroom, wc, double bed (queen-size), single bed: €100 – 2 people
€115 – 3 people
'Hillette': along corridor bathroom, wc, double bed.
En-suite room : 2 single beds:
€70 – 2 people €110 – 4 people
'Solea': kitchen, shower room, wc, single bed:
€60 – 1 people

Extra Bed: €10
Reduction: 6 nights
Capacity: 8 people

13.27 Aix-en-Provence

Working Farm

Location
AIX-EN-PROVENCE
in: Aix-en-Provence
Railway station: 20km
Airport: Marseille-Provence 30km
car essential

Surrounded by vines, this large vineyard awaits and you are welcomed with a bottle of wine in your room on arrival. The pleasant and comfortable guest bedrooms are in a wing of the building and have all been renovated. It would be tempting to stay put and just relax, enjoying the peace and quiet, but Aix-en-Provence is tantalisingly close by.

Facilities: off-street parking, extensive grounds, hosts have pets, pets not accepted, wheelchair access, bird-watching, hiking, cycling, vineyard, golf course 15km
Fluent English spoken

Directions: On the A8 take the exit towards A51 Gap, Sisteron until the N296. On the N296, exit 12 'Aix les Platanes' and then straight away on the left follow 'St-Canadet, Le Puy-Ste-Réparade'. Continue for 3.4km after the bridge on the D13 that straddles the motorway. Turn left towards 'Couteron' and follow the sign to the 'Domaine'.

Rupert BIRCH & Mary MERTENS
'Domaine de la Brillane', 195 route de Couteron,
13100 AIX-EN-PROVENCE
Tel: (0) 4 42 54 21 44 / (0) 674 77 01 20
Fax: (0) 4 42 54 31 25
domaine@labrillane.com
www.labrillane.com

Price Structure – 5 Bedrooms
'Cabernet': wheelchair access, television, bathroom, wc, double bed: €145
'Syrah': television, shower room, wc, double bed: €135
'Grenache' & 'Mourvèdre': television, shower room, wc, double bed: €115
'Carignan': television, shower room, wc, 2 single beds: €95

Extra Bed: €15
Reduction: 1/11–1/04, 4 nights
Capacity: 10 people

13.89 Aix-en-Provence

Residence of Outstanding Character

Huguette & Marcel MOME
'Bastide de Puycouvert', avenue Montfleuri,
13090 AIX-EN-PROVENCE
Tel: (0) 4 42 21 65 52 / (0) 609 54 36 55
Fax: (0) 4 42 21 65 52
p.mome@worldonline.fr

Price Structure – 4 Bedrooms
'Mistral': bathroom, wc, double bed: €105
'Calendal': shower room, wc, double bed: €95
'Mireille': along corridor bathroom, wc, twin beds: €80
'Merto': shower room, wc, double bed: €90

Capacity: 8 people

Location
AIX-EN-PROVENCE
in: Aix-en-Provence
Railway station: 20km
Airport: Marseille-Provence 30km

In a small lane high up in Aix-en-Provence, just ten minutes from the cathedral and the old town, the *bastide* is a beautiful old bourgeois mansion house where you will find comfortable, tastefully decorated bedrooms with air-conditioning. You will receive a warm welcome from Marcel who will be happy to organise themed visits for you in the area. He is passionate about archaeology and has an impressive collection of ammonites. Unwind in the grounds full of trees, a swimming pool and romantic nooks and crannies.

Facilities: private parking, extensive grounds, hosts have pets, 100% no smoking, 18 years old minimum age, 2 nights minimum stay: 01/07–31/08, private swimming pool, hiking, cycling, vineyard 5km, golf course 10km, sea watersports 30km
Fluent English spoken

Directions: A8 exit 29 to Aix-Centre. Head for *autoroute* Gap, Sisteron. On the dual carriageway take exit Puyricard towards Aix-Centre. Turn right at the second set of traffic lights. You are in Avenue Montfleuri, a small lane. It is the second house on the left.

13.91 Aix-en-Provence

Private Home

Evelyne VERDU
'La Petite Maison de Carla', 7 rue du Puits Neuf,
13100 AIX-EN-PROVENCE
Tel: (0) 4 42 21 20 73 / (0) 674 18 60 98
Fax: (0) 4 42 21 20 73
maison-de-carla@wanadoo.fr
guideweb.com/provence/bb/maison-carla/index.html

Price Structure – 6 Bedrooms
3 rooms: television, bathroom, wc, double bed: €85
'Garrigue' & 'Mistral': television, bathroom, wc, twin beds: €85
'Suite Manuella': lounge, television, bathroom, wc, double bed: €140

Extra Bed: €25
Reduction: 01/10–28/02, 6 nights, groups, children
Capacity: 12 people

Location
AIX-EN-PROVENCE
in: Aix-en-Provence
Railway station: 20km
Airport: Marseille-Provence 25km

You are in the centre of Aix-en-Provence and can therefore take full advantage of all that this beautiful provençal town has to offer, notably its internationally renowned music festival. Chez Evelyne, you have a comfortable, friendly place to stay full of charm and authenticity yet with facilities including mini-bars, satellite TV and air-conditioning for one of the suites. The Bellegarde car park is 200m away.

Facilities: lounge, pets not accepted, babies welcome, free cot, hiking 3km, cycling 3km, golf course 5km, vineyard 5km, riversports 20km, fishing 30km, interesting flora 30km, sea watersports 30km, bird-watching 80km
Adequate English spoken

Directions: On the A8, take exit and head for 'Aix-Centre'. Continue along Avenue des Belges. At the 'Rotonde', turn into Avenue Victor Hugo then Boulevard du Roi René, followed by Boulevard Carnot and finally Cours Saint Louis to then rejoin Place Bellegarde. You can park in the Bellegarde car park. Rue du Puits Neuf is 200m behind the car park.

13.93 Aix-en-Provence

Location
AIX-EN-PROVENCE
in: Aix-en-Provence
Railway station: 15km
Airport: Marseille-Provence 20km
car essential

Residence of Outstanding Character

Right out in the country, yet only five minutes drive from the centre of Aix, Corinne and Alain have taken over this beautiful 18th-century *bastide* and retained all its original charm. Corinne has done the decoration with excellent taste and the rooms are comfortable and spacious. The shade of the old chestnut tree gives an air of tranquillity and the pool is a pleasant spot to relax. You may be lucky enough to view exhibitions of paintings, sculpture and photography as Corinne has an art gallery in Aix that she plans to move to the *bastide*. An excellent address.

Corinne & Alain LAUBIN
'Bastide de la Pierre de Feu', 1523 chemin de la Pierre de Feu, 13090 AIX-EN-PROVENCE
Tel: (0) 611 75 63 36
reservation.pierredefeu@wanadoo.fr
www.bastidepierredefeu.com

Facilities: off-street parking, extensive grounds, hosts have pets, pets not accepted, internet access, babies welcome, free cot, 100% no smoking, 2 nights minimum stay: 01/05–30/09, private swimming pool, golf course 3km, vineyard 10km, sea watersports 30km
Adequate English spoken

Price Structure – 4 Bedrooms
'Platane': shower room, wc, double bed (queen-size): €100
'Tilleuls': bathroom, wc, double bed (queen-size): €100
'Marronnier-balnéo': bathroom, wc, shower, double bed (queen-size), 2 single beds (child-size): €140 – 2 people €180 – 4 people
'Fontaine': bathroom, wc, shower, double bed (queen-size): €90

Directions: East of Aix-en-Provence, take the D17, Route d'Eguilles for 4km. After the sign for St-Mitre, go straight over the roundabout, continue for 80m and then turn right into Chemin de la Pierre de Feu and follow the signs.

Extra Bed: €20
Reduction: 01/10–30/04, groups
Capacity: 10 people

13.22 Aix-en-Provence

Location
15km S of AIX-EN-PROVENCE
in: Cabriès
Railway station: 8km
Airport: Marseille-Provence 15km
car essential

Private Home

A village house that most French people would love to inherit from their grandmothers. . . a belfry on one side and an uninterrupted view of the valley on the other. This lovely couple's home, comfortable and in good taste, has a large lounge with a fireplace, mezzanine beds and a large, modern bathroom. Béatrice, a keen gardener with no garden, puts her talents to good use on the balcony where she keeps a baobab tree. She brought it back from Mali where she met her husband Dabou, who makes superb traditional *bogolans* bedspreads.

Béatrice BOURGUIGNON-THERA
'Le Toit du Piton', rue St-Roch, 13480 CABRIES
Tel: (0) 4 42 22 26 14 / (0) 666 16 13 06
le-toit-du-piton@wanadoo.fr
www.le-toit-du-piton.com

Facilities: off-street parking, lounge, hosts have pets, dinner available, kitchen, babies welcome, free cot, 1 shared shower room, wc, golf course 8km
Fluent English spoken

Price Structure – 2 Apartments
'Duplex': lounge, television, kitchen, double bed, single bed: €75 – 2 people €90 – 3 people
'Blanche': kitchen, double bed: €60

Extra Bed: €15
Reduction: groups
Capacity: 5 people

Directions: Please contact your host in advance for detailed directions.

Provence – Aix-en-Provence

13.39 Aix-en-Provence

Private Home

Location
8km W of AIX-EN-PROVENCE
in: Eguilles, station pick-up on
arrival/departure
Railway station: 20km
Airport: Marseille-Provence 25km

Annick & Thomas LE METAYER-JOUSTRA
'Plein Sud', 1110 route des Milles-Pierredou,
13510 EGUILLES
Tel: (0) 4 42 92 56 75 / (0) 686 64 17 58
annick.lemetayer@neuf.fr

Eguille is a delightful little village, 15km from Aix-en-Provence. Here they have a separate studio that can take two adults plus two children on the mezzanine. As the pool is close to your front door it is preferable if your children can swim. 'So So' is very welcoming and speaks good English, so you should get on well with her and Thomas and their three small children. It is quiet here, so you should sleep well after a day's serious sightseeing.

Price Structure – 1 Apartment
kitchen, shower room, wc, washbasin, double bed,
single bed: €80 – 2 people €90 – 3 people

Extra Bed: €10
Capacity: 3 people

Facilities: private parking, garden, pets not accepted, kitchen, babies welcome, free cot, 100% no smoking, hiking, interesting flora, golf course 8km, cycling 10km
Adequate English spoken

Directions: From Aix, D17 ('Route d'Eguilles') for about 1.5km. Left into Avenue Brédasque then right into Avenue de Bagatelle. Turn right (D10 'Route de Berre') for about 3.3km. At the second roundabout take the D18 'Route des Milles'. The house is on the left.

13.44 Aix-en-Provence

Private Home

Location
28km N E of AIX-EN-PROVENCE
in: Jouques
car essential

Pascale & Jean-Denis LACASSIE
'Mas Petite Borie', D 11, La Tour, 13490 JOUQUES
Tel: (0) 4 42 67 65 93 / (0) 616 72 04 21
petiteborie@free.fr
http://petiteborie.free.fr

Pascale, a former top flight volleyball player and retired English teacher welcomes you with a lovely smile. She will advise on the best places in this area, which is much sought after by tourists. She has been receiving guests for several years, but work is still going on as she is doing it herself. An interesting, intelligent and lovely lady. You will also feel close to nature here.

Price Structure – 1 Bedroom and 1 Suite
'Bleue': shower room, wc, double bed: €54
'Orange': bathroom, wc, double bed (queen-size).
En-suite room, 3 single beds (child-size):
€54 – 2 people €108 – 5 people

Extra Bed: €18
Reduction: 4 nights
Capacity: 7 people

Facilities: off-street parking, garden, hosts have pets, pets not accepted, dinner available, 100% no smoking, 2 nights minimum stay: 01/07–31/08, mushroom-picking, bird-watching, hiking, cycling, interesting flora, riversports 15km, golf course 30km
Fluent English spoken

Directions: At Aix, head towards Gap (A51 and N296). Exit 14 and then N96. Go through Meyrargues and Peyrolles, then the D561 and go through Jouques. Turn right towards Rians, then right again towards Sambuc and Vauvenargues. After la Tour, keep left to the 'Petite Borie'.

Location
24km W of AIX-EN-PROVENCE
in: La Fare-les-Oliviers
car essential

Private Home

It was in Britain that Jeannine and Joseph discovered B&B. They liked it so much that as soon as they retired they decided to open one! The interior reflects their 20 years spent in Indonesia and Saudi Arabia. They are kind and helpful, and will advise on your trips with pleasure. Breakfast is very continental, with Jeannine's homemade jam. Very close to the *autoroute*, this is a good overnight stop and Aix is very close.

Jeannine & Joseph RUBIOLO
'L'Oasis', 5 Clos de la Treille, Route des Oliviers,
13580 LA FARE-LES-OLIVIERS
Tel: (0) 4 90 45 43 92 / (0) 685 03 72 38
jeannine.rubiolo@wanadoo.fr

Facilities: private parking, garden, pets not accepted, 100% no smoking, 14 years old minimum age, closed: 01/11–30/03, private swimming pool, hiking, vineyard, golf course 15km, sea watersports 25km
Fluent English spoken

Price Structure – 3 Bedrooms
'L'Orientale': along corridor bathroom, wc, double bed (queen-size): €80
'L'Asiatique': television, bathroom, wc, double bed (queen-size). Along corridor room, 2 single beds: €50 – 2 people €130 – 4 people

Capacity: 6 people

Directions: Exit 28 Berre-Marignane from the A8. Head for La Fare-les-Oliviers and take the D19 then the D10. Take the Chemin des Barrales on the right to the Route des Oliviers.

Location
22km N W of AIX-EN-PROVENCE
in: Lambesc
Railway station: 30km
Airport: Marseille-Provence 50km
car essential

Working Farm

A real oasis for rest and relaxation. The charming and dynamic Claudette left her demanding job to dedicate herself to looking after her guests. Her houses with barbecues and fridges are completely at your disposal. You will find yourself reluctant to leave, rested and refreshed after enjoying the use of the interior swimming pools (one is 25x6m in size), jacuzzi, sauna and hammam. If you can turn a blind eye to the surroundings that are not quite finished, you will feel like you are staying in a four 'sun' property. Be sure to make the most of the facilities.

Claudette DAIMAY
'A la Claudy', Campagne Janet, chemin de la Tour
de Janet, 13410 LAMBESC
Tel: (0) 4 42 92 96 65 / (0) 618 67 71 47
Fax: (0) 4 42 92 96 65
claudette.daimay@wanadoo.fr
www.a-la-claudy.com

Facilities: off-street parking, extensive grounds, tv lounge, hosts have pets, pets not accepted, kitchen, 100% no smoking, wheelchair access, 10 years old minimum age, 2 nights minimum stay: 1/07–31/08, closed: 25/02–5/03, private swimming pool, hiking, vineyard
Basic English spoken

Price Structure – 3 Bedrooms and 1 Suite
'L'Evasion': wheelchair access, shower room, wc, twin beds, single bed: €102 – 2 people €128 – 3 people
'La Charmante': bathroom, wc, shower, double bed (queen-size), single bed: €128 – 3 people
'La Rêveuse': bathroom, wc, double bed (queen-size), single bed: €128 – 3 people
'La Douce': lounge, bathroom, wc, shower, double bed (queen-size). En-suite room, bathroom, wc, double bed (queen-size), single bed: €230 – 5 people

Extra Bed: €26
Reduction: 4 nights, groups
Capacity: 14 people

Directions: At Aix-en-Provence, head for 'Celony' via the N7, continue for 12km. At Lambesc centre-ville, follow signs for 'Les Béates'. At the 'Poste', take the D66 direction 'Caire Val', continue for 4km. Pass the hamlet Janet on your left. Continue for 500m and take the rural lane with 30 km/h, signs, then the second lane on the left that is surfaced, signed 'Chemin de la Tour de Janet'. Continue along the olive grove for 500m. It is on the right.

13.62 Aix-en-Provence

Private Home

Location
22km N W of AIX-EN-PROVENCE
in: Lambesc
car essential

Roselyne FOGLIA
'Le Gallatras', route de Caire-Val,
13410 LAMBESC
Tel: (0) 4 42 92 75 70 / (0) 687 39 43 38
Fax: (0) 4 42 92 75 92

Our faithful readers may remember Roselyne for her kindness and helpfulness. She is now back in her cosy house, all in stone, with its inspired interior décor in the best possible taste. The size of her lounge will impress you and you will enjoy the calm and feeling of wellbeing as you take a dip in the large pool. The surrounding countryside is delightful, as are the towns of Aix and Salon. She has only two rooms so its never crowded.

Price Structure – 2 Bedrooms
bathroom, wc, twin beds: €100
along corridor shower room, wc, double bed: €95

Capacity: 4 people

Facilities: off-street parking, garden, hosts have pets, pets not accepted, 10 years old minimum age, private swimming pool, mushroom-picking, hiking, cycling, interesting flora, vineyard, golf course 9km

Directions: Exit Salon from the A7 and take the N7 to Lambesc. Head for 'Lambesc-Centre'. At the post office, head towards Caireval and after 1.5km turn left to 'Le Gallatras'.

13.09 Aix-en-Provence

Private Home

Location
5km E of AIX-EN-PROVENCE
in: Le Tholonet
Railway station: 15km
Airport: Marseille-Provence 25km
car essential

Sophie HUET-LEGRAND
'La Bruissanne', 283 chemin du Vallon des Gardes
Bas, Le Tholonet, 13100 AIX-EN-PROVENCE
Tel: (0) 4 42 21 16 76 / (0) 620 94 16 43
sophieaix@wanadoo.fr

An ideal location for a holiday in this little green oasis, not least because Sophie is very charming. She lived all her childhood in Québec, which she loves, which we completely understand! She has also lived in Asia but it is here, just five minutes away from the centre of Aix-en-Provence, that she has decided to live with her little family and raise her two adorable young daughters. The large garden and grounds are defined areas with a swimming pool, a bowling area and an area for breakfast surrounded by flowers. The provençal-style bedrooms are very pretty.

Price Structure – 2 Bedrooms
'Marius': lounge, television, bathroom, wc, shower, double bed (queen-size): €120
'Fanny': shower room, wc, double bed (queen-size): €100

Capacity: 4 people

Facilities: private parking, extensive grounds, hosts have pets, 100% no smoking, 16 years old minimum age, closed: 01/11–01/05, private swimming pool, cycling, hiking 5km, mushroom-picking 5km, vineyard 5km, golf course 18km
Fluent English spoken

Directions: A8 exit 31 Aix-les-3-Sautets. Follow signs to 'Centre-Ville' then Le Tholonet. Continue on the Route de Cézanne (Avenue Général Préaud) and take the first right turn (lower Chemin du Vallon des Gardes). It is the fifth gate on the left.

Location
6km S W of AIX-EN-PROVENCE
in: Luynes
Railway station: 15km
Airport: Marseille-Provence 25km
car essential

Private Home

You will like Marie-Renée, a Corsican with long blonde hair, a much travelled, retired university professor, who was once a cultural attachée in Egypt. Her house is pretty and pleasantly decorated with objects she has collected on her travels. There is a large garden with a pool. Peace and calm in relaxing surroundings, just seven minutes by car from Aix. When we visited her, she had just finished taking students so there was some tidying up to be done, which is why she has only two 'suns' at present.

Facilities: private parking, garden, hosts have pets, pets not accepted, dinner available, 100% no smoking, 2 shared shower rooms, wc, 2 nights minimum stay, private swimming pool, golf course, fishing, mushroom-picking, interesting flora, *Adequate English spoken*

Marie-Renée FRAYSSINET
380 chemin de la Blaque, 13080 LUYNES
Tel: (0) 4 42 60 94 34 / (0) 685 02 49 41

Price Structure – 6 Bedrooms
1 room: shower room, wc, double bed: €60
'Suite Madame': bathroom, wc, double bed: €80
2 rooms: double bed: €60
2 rooms: single bed: €50 – 1 person

Capacity: 10 people

Directions: At Aix, take the N8 towards Marseille. Slow down as you approach the name sign for Luynes, and before the railway bridge, turn right into the Chemin de la Blaque by the bus shelter.

Location
2km S of AIX-EN-PROVENCE
in: Meyreuil
Railway station: 15km
Airport: Marseille-Provence 30km
car essential

Residence of Outstanding Character

This haven of peace is only ten minutes from the centre of Aix. Cécile has created this place for her guests and the interior is straight out of a glossy magazine. All is discreet and colour coordinated. The rooms are very large and comfortable. With its beautiful pool, calm location and Cécile's warm welcome, you have all you need for a great stay near Aix.

Facilities: private parking, garden, tv lounge, pets not accepted, babies welcome, free cot, 100% no smoking, private swimming pool, hiking, cycling, vineyard, golf course 7km, sea watersports 30km

Cécile WILHELM
'Mas du Grivoton', 860 chemin de la Plaine
Montaiguet, 13590 MEYREUIL
Tel: (0) 4 42 50 39 53
www.masdugrivoton.com

Price Structure – 4 Bedrooms
'Frère & Soeur': television, bathroom, wc, double bed (queen-size): €150
'Herbiers' & 'Les grands Hommes': television, shower room, wc, double bed (queen-size): €120
'Architecte': television, bathroom, wc, twin beds: €150

Reduction: 01/10–30/04, 3 nights
Capacity: 8 people

Directions: Exit 31 from the A8 and then take the N7 towards Fréjus and St-Raphaël. Turn right at the third set of lights, and after the Pont des Trois Sautets (bridge) turn left towards Meyreuil. Climb upwards for 3.5km and take the lane on the right for 800m.

13.78 Aix-en-Provence

Private Home

Julie & Dave FULLER
'Mas des Micocouliers', 3800 chemin la Plaine du Montaiguet, Pont-des-Trois-Sautets, 13590 MEYREUIL
Tel: (0) 4 42 26 23 39 / (0) 633 84 02 09
Fax: (0) 4 42 26 23 39
contact@aix-masdesmicocouliers.com
www.aix-masdesmicocouliers.com

Price Structure – 5 Apartments
2 rooms: television, kitchen, shower room, wc, double bed: €71
duplex: television, kitchen, shower room, wc, double bed: €77
'Loft': lounge, television, kitchen, shower room, wc, 2 double beds: €101 – 2 people €141 – 4 people
'Old Style Apartment': lounge, television, kitchen, shower room, wc, double bed, 2 single beds: €101

Extra Bed: €20
Reduction: 01/10–31/03
Capacity: 14 people

Location
2km S of AIX-EN-PROVENCE
in: Meyreuil
Railway station: 18km
Airport: Marseille-Provence 30km

Julie and Dave left Britain and their three children behind to take over from Albane and Guy after having spent so much time in the region on holiday. This *mas*, dating from the 19th century, has been completely restored and is in a desirable location between town and country, in the heart of the National Park of the Massif du Montaiguet. The bedrooms are in fact self-contained studio flats. From here, discover the cultural attractions of Aix-en-Provence, or explore the countryside from the footpath leading from the house.

Facilities: private parking, garden, pets not accepted, kitchen, babies welcome, free cot, 100% no smoking, wheelchair access, 2 nights minimum stay: 01/07–31/08, private swimming pool, hiking, vineyard, golf course 10km, sea watersports 30km
Fluent English spoken

Directions: From Aix-en-Provence, take the *autoroute* A8 towards Toulon, exit 31. Then take the N7 towards Fréjus, St-Raphaël for 1km. At the third set of traffic lights, turn right, go over the bridge (Le Pont des Trois Sautets), and then turn right immediately. The house is 100m further on, on the left.

84.02 Aix-en-Provence

Château/Manor House

Nathalie SOUZAN
'Château Grand Callamand', route de la Loubière, 84120 PERTUIS
Tel: (0) 4 90 09 61 00 / (0) 625 12 38 82
Fax: (0) 4 90 09 61 00
contact@chateaugrandcallamand.fr
www.chateaugrandcallamand.fr

Price Structure – 3 Bedrooms
'L'Arche': television, telephone, shower room, wc, bathroom, 2 double beds (queen-size): €190 – 2 people €250 – 4 people
'Les Mariés': television, telephone, shower room, wc, bathroom, double bed (queen-size), 2 single beds: €190 – 2 people €250 – 4 people
'Insolite': television, telephone, shower room, wc, bathroom, double bed (queen-size): €160

Extra Bed: €30
Reduction: 1/11–31/03, 7 nights
Capacity: 10 people

Location
20km N of AIX-EN-PROVENCE
in: Pertuis
Railway station: 2km
Airport: Marseille-Provence 55km
car essential

A magnificently restored 16th-century château in the heart of the Luberon. The beautiful guest bedrooms have vaulted ceilings and look out to an ancient forest, perfect for walks. Here, you will find quiet, serenity and comfort (air-conditioning, internet access), class, good taste and a touch of magic. . .We urge you to come and stay with Nathalie, a passionate vinegrower who will share with you her know-how and enthusiasm, and enjoy this historic lieu. Dinner is also available and prepared for you by an accomplished chef.

Facilities: off-street parking, extensive grounds, hosts have pets, pets not accepted, internet access, babies welcome, free cot, 100% no smoking, private swimming pool, cycling, vineyard, fishing 1km, hiking 1km, lake watersports 10km, golf course 45km
Fluent English spoken

Directions: From Aix, direction A51 Gap, Sisteron then to Pertuis. Pass La Durance, pass over four roundabouts and at the end of the industrial zone, before the railway bridge, turn right towards St-Martin, Route de la Bastidonne. Continue along the railway line for 1.8km then turn left, cross the railway line and follow the signs for 700m.

Private Home

Location
10km N of AIX-EN-PROVENCE
in: Puyricard
Railway station: 20km
Airport: Marseille-Provence 30km
car essential

Fifteen minutes from the centre of Aix-en-Provence, in the countryside, is the small, provençal village of Puyricard with views of Cézanne's Montagne Ste-Victoire. Sandra dedicates herself to making your stay as enjoyable as possible. Enjoy the swimming pool and her homemade *croquants*. The spacious bedrooms and a large guest lounge are on the first floor of the house. From October to March you can rent this whole area by the week. Sandra also organises creative activities for children and relaxing weekends for adults!

Facilities: off-street parking, garden, lounge, hosts have pets, pets not accepted, dinner available, babies welcome, free cot, hiking, vineyard, cycling, golf course 10km
Fluent English spoken

Directions: From Aix-en-Provence, D14 towards Le Puy-Ste-Réparade. At Ferronnier Bonnefoy, turn left straight away into Chemin de Tascel. It is at the end of the lane on the left.

Sandra LUMBROSO
'La Cerisaie', chemin de Tascel,
13540 PUYRICARD
Tel: (0) 661 19 44 46
lacerisaiedaix@wanadoo.fr
www.lacerisaiedaix.com

Price Structure – 4 Bedrooms
'de Staël': shower, wc, washbasin, double bed (queen-size): €90
'Cézanne': bathroom, double bed: €70
'Masson': bathroom, 2 single beds: €70
'Suite': bathroom, wc, double bed (king-size): €70

Reduction: 7 nights
Capacity: 8 people

Private Home

Location
15km N W of AIX-EN-PROVENCE
in: Rognes, station pick-up on arrival/departure
Railway station: 20km
Airport: Marseille-Provence 50km
car essential

In the middle of the *garrigue* you will find this typical stone provençal house amid holm oaks and pine trees. You are lodged either in a bright guest bedroom on the ground floor with a small terrace area or alternatively in a small gîte in a little hut with an equipped open-plan kitchen. Hearty breakfasts are served on the terrace. Listen to the song of nightingales and chat with Michel who will be happy to tell you all about his truffle-hunting dogs. A relaxed family atmosphere where you will feel at ease and at home with friends.

Facilities: private parking, extensive grounds, tv lounge, hosts have pets, pets not accepted, babies welcome, free cot, 100% no smoking, wheelchair access, private swimming pool, mushroom-picking, hiking, cycling, golf course 20km, gliding 30km, sea watersports 50km
Basic English spoken

Directions: From Aix-en-Provence, N7 towards Avignon for 8km then turn right at the roundabout onto the D543 to Rognes. In the village, head towards Lambesc on the D15. The house is 1.2km from Rognes, on the left.

Rolande & Michel PARISSE
'Le Mas de Laurisa', route de Lambesc,
13840 ROGNES
Tel: (0) 4 42 50 18 87 / (0) 607 06 78 30
Fax: (0) 4 42 50 14 99
micpariss@aol.com
www.lemasdelaurisa.com

Price Structure – 2 Bedrooms
and 1 Apartment
'La Cerisaie': wheelchair access, shower room, wc, twin beds: €70
'L'Olivade': lounge, television, shower room, wc, twin beds: €80
'Gîte': television, kitchen, shower room, wc, double bed (queen-size), 2 single beds (1 child-size): €80 – 2 people €110 – 4 people

Extra Bed: €15
Reduction: 01/10–15/04
Capacity: 8 people

13.47 Aix-en-Provence

Private Home

Nadine & Jérôme CLEMENT
'La Tangana', chemin du Jas Blanc,
13840 ROGNES
Tel: (0) 4 42 50 12 91 / (0) 666 16 45 58

Price Structure – 1 Bedroom
television, bathroom, wc, shower, twin beds: €90

Reduction: 1/10–31/05, 7 nights
Capacity: 2 people

Location
15km N W of AIX-EN-PROVENCE
in: Rognes, station pick-up on arrival/departure
Railway station: 20km
Airport: Marseille-Provence 40km
car essential

Jérôme comes from Aix so is well placed to advise you on the town. He is also a tennis coach. Nadine is well up on all the sporting and cultural events in the area so pick their brains if this is of interest. If you climb the mound behind the house there is a great view over the Durance valley. The house is in a pine wood, with a large pool and in an area much sought after by walkers. The bedroom is large and the bathrooms spacious, bright and spotless. A quiet place for a few nights, relaxation.

Facilities: off-street parking, extensive grounds, tv lounge, hosts have pets, 100% no smoking, closed: 1/08–31/08, private swimming pool, mushroom-picking, bird-watching, hiking, cycling, vineyard, lake watersports 20km, golf course 25km
Adequate English spoken

Directions: From Aix, N7 towards Avignon for 6km. At the second roundabout, D543 on the right towards Rognes for 10.8km. D66 towards Le Puy-Ste-Réparade for 1.4km then right on to the D14c for 1.5km. Take the Chemin du Jas Blanc on the left and continue on the hard road as far as the 'Hameau du Jas Blanc'. Take the second unmade road on the left, before the house with the blue shutters.

13.57 Aix-en-Provence

Private Home

Marie-Hélène & Jean-Pierre FLOREMONT
'Le Mas des Chênes', chemin des Mauvares,
13840 ROGNES
Tel: (0) 4 42 50 16 60 / (0) 610 25 32 15
Fax: (0) 4 42 50 16 60
lemasdeschenes@wanadoo.fr
www.masdeschenes.com

Price Structure – 3 Bedrooms and 1 Suite
'Lavande': television, shower room, wc, double bed, single bed, cot: €87 – 2 people €102 – 3 people
'Safran': television, bathroom, wc, twin beds, cot: €87
'Maisonnette': television, shower room, wc, double bed, single bed, cot: €87 – 2 people €102 – 3 people
suite 'Orientale': along corridor bathroom, wc, double bed, cot. En-suite room, 2 single beds: €87 – 2 people €133 – 4 people

Extra Bed: €15
Reduction: 16/09–14/06, 8 nights
Capacity: 12 people

Location
15km N W of AIX-EN-PROVENCE
in: Rognes, station pick-up on arrival/departure
Railway station: 20km
Airport: Marseille-Provence 35km
car essential

At the foot of the Luberon, 'Le Mas des Chênes' is a provençal house in Rognes stone, set back in the middle of an oasis of pine and oak trees, pervaded by the scent of thyme. You will happily laze on your own private terrace beside the swimming pool. For the more energetic, there is a *boules* pitch. Marie-Hélène and Jean-Pierre will be delighted to advise you on a choice of excursions to the heart of Provence and its pretty villages. Bicycles available.

Facilities: off-street parking, extensive grounds, tv lounge, hosts have pets, babies welcome, free cot, 100% no smoking, wheelchair access, private swimming pool, hiking, cycling, mushroom-picking, vineyard, golf course 15km, sea watersports 40km, riversports 40km
Adequate English spoken

Directions: From Aix-en-Provence, take the N7 towards Avignon for 6km, then at the second roundabout turn right on to the D543 towards Rognes. 1km before Rognes, on a straight stretch of road, take Chemin de Mauvares on the left, then follow the signs 'Chambres d'Hôtes'.

Location
16km E of AIX-EN-PROVENCE
in: Rousset
Railway station: 35km
Airport: Marseille-Provence 40km
car essential

Residence of Outstanding Character

Henriette has stopped working to look after her two young boys in their beautiful 19th-century *bastide* near to Aix-en-Provence. At your disposal are two rooms on the ground floor. They are well laid out with a small kitchenette. In summer, you can take advantage of the 15m-long swimming pool. Granted, the motorway is not far away but the sound barrier measures due to be installed should be in place by the time of your visit.

Henriette & Yann GUILLY
'Les Terres Rouges', chemin de la Montaurone,
13790 ROUSSET
Tel: (0) 4 42 29 06 53 / (0) 629 43 88 77
Fax: (0) 4 42 29 05 86
auxterresrouges@free.fr
http://auxterresrouges.free.fr

Facilities: off-street parking, garden, tv lounge, hosts have pets, pets not accepted, babies welcome, free cot, 100% no smoking, 2 nights minimum stay, private swimming pool, interesting flora, hiking, cycling, golf course 2km, vineyard 3km
Adequate English spoken

Price Structure – 2 Apartments
lounge, television, kitchen, shower room, wc, double bed: €58
television, kitchen, bathroom, wc, double bed, single bed: €58 – 2 people €68 – 3 people

Reduction: 5 nights
Capacity: 5 people

Directions: A52 or A8 exit 32. Rejoin the N7 heading towards St-Maximin, Fréjus. Rousset is on the right, after Châteauneuf.

Location
13km E of AIX-EN-PROVENCE
in: Vauvenargues
Railway station: 13km
Airport: Marseille-Provence 39km
car essential

Private Home

At the foot of the steep slopes of the Montagne Ste-Victoire, on one of the most touristic roads in the region is Jacqueline's home. A former hotelier in Aix, she will happily recount to you her encounters with French artists, writers and stars – from the 'shameless wink' of Picasso to the 'wild young days' of Johnny Hallyday during the swinging sixties – all backed up by her visitor book. The Château de Vauvenargues where Picasso is buried is nearby. Jacqueline's personality compensates for the simplicity of the rooms.

Jacqueline THERY
'La Jacquière', chemin des Mattes,
13126 VAUVENARGUES
Tel: (0) 4 42 66 01 79

Facilities: off-street parking, garden, lounge, hosts have pets, pets not accepted, wc, 3 nights minimum stay, closed: 15/10–15/02, hiking
Basic English spoken

Price Structure – 3 Bedrooms
'Bleue': shower, washbasin, double bed: €45
'Beige': shower room, wc, double bed: €45
'Verte': shower, twin beds: €45

Extra Bed: €10
Capacity: 6 people

Directions: At Aix-en-Provence take the D10 towards the Montagne Ste. Victoire and Vauvenargues. Pass through the village avoiding entering the centre, then turn down the first lane on the right just after exiting the village. Follow the arrow signs.

Provence – Aix-en-Provence

13.08 Aix-en-Provence

Private Home

Location
16km W of AIX-EN-PROVENCE
in: Ventabren
Railway station: 12km
Airport: Marseille-Provence 15km
car essential

This is the sort of village where they shoot TV footage: bijou, chic and immaculate. You would expect it to have a top B&B and it does! This gem was setup by an American and when Marie-Christine and Pierre gave up their restaurant, they polished it to perfection. The rooms are a blaze of provençal colours and breakfast is taken on the rooftop terrace with views to the Alpilles and the Etang de Berre. Who cares about stairs and headroom? This couple exude enthusiasm, professionalism and count singers and *artistes* as guests.

Pierre GATEAU & Marie-Christine DUSSAUD
'Le Mistral', 8 rue Frédéric Mistral,
13122 VENTABREN
Tel: (0) 4 42 28 94 69 / (0) 686 89 72 75
Fax: (0) 4 42 28 94 69
contact@lemistral.com
www.lemistral.com

Price Structure – 4 Bedrooms
'Lavande': television, bathroom, wc, shower, double bed (queen-size): €85
'Olivier': television, bathroom, wc, shower, double bed (queen-size): €95
'Tournesol': television, bathroom, wc, shower, double bed (super king-size): €95
'Coquelicot': television, bathroom, wc, shower, twin beds: €75

Reduction: 1/10–30/04, 3 nights
Capacity: 8 people

Facilities: off-street parking, tv lounge, hosts have pets, dinner available, kitchen, babies welcome, free cot, closed: 15/01–30/01, hiking, cycling, interesting flora, golf course 10km, sea watersports 25km
Fluent English spoken

Directions: Take the road that climbs up to the village and follow signs to 'L'Eglise', turning sharp left at one point. Park in the Place de l'Eglise. Head for the 'Table de Ventabren' restaurant and then take Rue Frederic Mistral. On the right up the steps.

13.04 Cassis

Private Home

Location
CASSIS
in: Cassis, station pick-up on arrival/departure
Railway station: 3km
Airport: Marseille-Provence 45km

Having only just stepped over the threshold, you'll know you've made the right choice! Firstly, the impressive view over one of the highest cliffs in the world that drops steeply into the sea will lift your spirits. Your charming hosts have travelled the world for some of the most prestigious brands of French perfume and here too every detail has been considered to ensure a memorable stay, including air-conditioning, thoughtful little touches and tasteful décor.

Laurent AIELLO
'L'Escale', 3 avenue Jean-Jacques Garcin,
13260 CASSIS
Tel: (0) 4 42 01 27 69
contact@escalecassis.com
www.escalecassis.com

Price Structure – 4 Bedrooms
'Mansarde': lounge, bathroom, wc, double bed, single bed: €105 – 2 people €145 – 3 people
'Belvedère': lounge, bathroom, wc, double bed (queen-size), single bed: €150 – 2 people €200 – 3 people
'Arcades': lounge, bathroom, wc, double bed (queen-size): €200
'Colonel': lounge, shower room, wc, double bed (super king-size): €200

Extra Bed: €50
Reduction: 01/10–31/03
Capacity: 10 people

Facilities: garden, hosts have pets, 12 years old minimum age, 2 nights minimum stay, fishing, hiking, cycling, sea watersports, vineyard 1km
Fluent English spoken

Directions: A50 Marseille-Toulon, exit 8, Cassis. Once in the village, head for La Presqu'île.

Location
CASSIS
in: Cassis, station pick-up on arrival/departure
Railway station: 6km
Airport: Marseille-Provence 40km
car essential

Private Home

A lovely *Maison de Maître* in several hectares of pine forest. From the large terrace, you overlook the forest and the bay of Cassis. The sunsets here are often magical! The bedrooms are refreshingly cool, typical of these large houses with thick walls and Suzanne ensures you enjoy your stay. Her daughter offers riding lessons. Access is tricky and therefore we would advise a 4x4 car.

Suzanne MASSARDO
'Le Mas du Pas d'Ouillier', chemin des Cuettes,
Quartiers des Janots, 13260 CASSIS
Tel: (0) 4 42 01 74 47 / (0) 612 44 23 25
chambre.du.mas@free.fr
http://chambre.du.mas.free.fr

Facilities: off-street parking, extensive grounds, lounge, hosts have pets, mushroom-picking, hiking, cycling, fishing 6km, interesting flora 6km, sea watersports 6km, vineyard 6km, golf course 30km

Price Structure – 5 Bedrooms
'Bartavelle' & 'Tourne': shower room, wc, double bed: €90
'Fanny': bathroom, wc, double bed: €90
'Pichonnets': bathroom, wc, 3 single beds: €90 – 2 people €120 – 3 people
'Pitalogne': shower room, wc, twin beds: €90

Extra Bed: €20
Reduction: 1/09–31/05, 6 nights
Capacity: 11 people

Directions: A50 Marseille-Toulon, exit 7 La Bédoule. Follow signs to 'Maison de Retraite' and then after you pass the actual sign for the retirement home on the Chemin de la Source, there is a barrier opposite that closes off the road. If it is closed, please call Suzanne on the phone. Continue for 1km on a difficult unsurfaced track.

Location
CASSIS
in: Cassis
Railway station: 4km
Airport: Marseille-Provence 55km
car essential

Private Home

An exceptional location by the *calanques*: the rocky inlets loved by walkers and sunbathers. Here, along a *calanque* and its yachts, this house with a garden is in a superb tranquil spot just 100m from the sea at the end of the Port-Miou peninsula.

Martine & Alain ESNAULT
'La Villa des 4 Vents', 39 avenue Notre-Dame,
13260 CASSIS
Tel: (0) 4 42 01 35 04 / (0) 676 18 13 58
Fax: (0) 4 42 01 35 04
alain.esnault@wanadoo.fr

Facilities: private parking, garden, pets not accepted, 100% no smoking, 16 years old minimum age, 2 nights minimum stay, fishing, hiking, sea watersports, vineyard 2km, golf course 15km
Adequate English spoken

Price Structure – 1 Suite
along corridor bathroom, wc, double bed. En-suite room, double bed: €90 – 2 people €170 – 4 people

Reduction: 1/09–30/04, 7 nights
Capacity: 4 people

Directions: A50 Marseille-Toulon, exit 8 to Cassis. In Cassis, head towards 'Calanque' et 'Presqu'île'. The house is situated at the end of the peninsula.

Provence – Cassis

13.31 Cassis

Private Home

Location
CASSIS
in: Cassis, station pick-up on arrival/departure
Railway station: 2km
Airport: Marseille-Provence 40km
car essential

Anne-Marie & Joseph GIACALONE
'Le Cap', 24 montée de la Chapelle, 13260 CASSIS
Tel: (0) 4 42 03 33 01 Fax: (0) 4 42 03 33 01

Price Structure – 4 Bedrooms
lounge, television, shower room, wc, double bed (queen-size): €140
lounge, television, shower room, wc, washbasin, twin beds: €140
television, shower room, wc, washbasin, twin beds: €140
television, shower room, wc, washbasin, double bed (queen-size): €110

Extra Bed: €35
Reduction: 12/11–20/12 & 5/01–28/02, 7 nights, children
Capacity: 8 people

Joseph is still a restaurateur in Aix-en-Provence but Anne-Marie, for her part, has sold her well-known restaurant on the Cours Mirabeau at Aix to devote herself to her guests. Passionate, enthusiastic and joyful, she welcomes you to her house in the upper parts of Cassis, opposite the Cap Canaille and with a beautiful view. The house is peaceful and tranquil and comes complete with a swimming pool and palm trees. The guest bedrooms have been tastefully decorated with flair, making this a delightful place to stay and enjoy your holidays.

Facilities: private parking, garden, hosts have pets, pets not accepted, babies welcome, free cot, 2 nights minimum stay, private swimming pool, vineyard, fishing 2km, cycling 2km, sea watersports 2km, golf course 20km
Basic English spoken

Directions: Please contact your hosts in advance for detailed directions.

13.64 Cassis

Private Home

Location
19km N of CASSIS
in: Roquevaire
Railway station: 10km
Airport: Marseille-Provence 50km
car essential

Hélène & André VERDY
'Villa Blanca Verde', 372 chemin la Caou, 13360 ROQUEVAIRE
Tel: (0) 4 42 01 94 26 / (0) 607 08 37 42
villablancaverde@orange.fr
www.villablancaverde.com

Price Structure – 1 Bedroom
shower room, wc, double bed (queen-size): €100

Capacity: 2 people

This is the first time that Hélène and André, who are retired, have done B&B. They are full of enthusiasm and only too pleased to help with whatever you need. The breakfast pastries are homemade. Although you are only 15km from the beach, midway between Marseilles and Aix-en-Provence, this place is quiet, with a large garden at the foot of the Sainte Baume, a wonderful area for walking.

Facilities: private parking, garden, lounge, 100% no smoking, 18 years old minimum age, 3 nights minimum stay, closed: 20/12–28/02, private swimming pool, hiking, cycling, vineyard, golf course 15km, sea watersports 15km
Fluent English spoken

Directions: On the A8, then A52 to Aubagne-Toulon, exit at Pont-de-l'Etoile, taking the first right on to the D43g.

13.33 Les Baux-de-Provence

Location
5km S W of LES BAUX-DE-PROVENCE
in: Fontvieille
Railway station: 30km
Airport: Marseille-Provence 70km
car essential

Residence of Outstanding Character

A real find: 5000m of landscaped garden with nooks and crannies and a spring that runs down the terraces. A haven of peace amid the pines and cypress trees, just 250m from the 'Moulin de Daudet', so popular with tourists. Choose between 'Arlésienne' on two levels with its lovely bathroom up a level, or the 'Oliveraie' with a child's bed on a mezzanine. The 'Camarguaise' is smaller, on the ground floor but just as charming. A communal lounge is available. Discover the beautiful Alpilles, Les-Baux-de-Provence, Roman Glanum.

Facilities: private parking, extensive grounds, pets not accepted, 100% no smoking, 2 nights minimum stay: 1/05–30/09, closed: 1/11–1/04, private swimming pool, mushroom-picking, hiking, cycling, vineyard, sea watersports, golf course 10km, gliding 25km, birdwatching 40km
Adequate English spoken

Directions: Fontvieille is on the main road between St-Rémy-de-Provence and Arles, via Les Baux-de-Provence. At Fontvieille, head for the Moulin de Daudet. The house is signposted from the village.

Mireille & Jacques ROUY
'Le Clos', allée des Pins, 13990 FONTVIEILLE
Tel: (0) 4 90 54 76 07
leclos.fontvieille@wanadoo.fr
www.leclos-fontvieille.com

Price Structure – 3 Bedrooms
'Arlésienne-Mezzanine': bathroom, wc, double bed (queen-size), single bed: €120 – 2 people
€150 – 3 people
'Oliveraie-Mezzanine': shower room, wc, double bed (queen-size), single bed: €120 – 2 people
€150 – 3 people
'Camarguaise': shower room, wc, double bed (queen-size): €120

Extra Bed: €20
Reduction: 1/10–30/04, 3 nights
Capacity: 8 people

13.77 Les Baux-de-Provence

Location
5km S of LES BAUX-DE-PROVENCE
in: Maussane-les-Alpilles
Railway station: 35km
Airport: Marseille-Provence 70km
car essential

Bienvenue en France

Private Home

This old *mas*, which has been extended, is below Les Baux-de-Provence in the charming little village of Maussane. The tastefully furnished bedrooms are comfortable and have bright provençal décor with their own private terrace and access to the garden and swimming pool. Cécile is the perfect hostess and from time to time, she also organises artistic and cultural events such as classical *apéritifs concerts*.

Facilities: private parking, garden, tv lounge, pets not accepted, kitchen, babies welcome, free cot, wheelchair access, private swimming pool, hiking, cycling, golf course 1km, vineyard 5km
Adequate English spoken

Directions: From Les Baux-de-Provence, head for Maussane. As you leave this village heading towards Fontvieille and Arles, at the intersection turn left into Chemin de la Pinède and continue for about 600m.

Cécile & Guy MARGUERITE
'Mas des Marguerites', chemin de la Pinède, 13520 MAUSSANE-LES-ALPILLES
Tel: (0) 4 90 54 20 48 / (0) 661 79 02 10
Fax: (0) 4 90 54 20 48
contact@mas-des-marguerites.com
www.masdesmarguerites.com

Price Structure – 5 Bedrooms
'Arlésienne-Mezzanine': shower room, wc, double bed (queen-size), 2 single beds: €110 – 2 people
€160 – 4 people
'Cigale-Mezzanine': bathroom, wc, double bed (queen-size), 2 single beds: €110 – 2 people €160 – 4 people
'Cézanne-Mezzanine': shower room, wc, double bed (queen-size), single bed: €110 – 2 people
€135 – 3 people
'Van Gogh': bathroom, wc, twin beds: €100
'Lavande': wheelchair access, shower, twin beds: €100

Extra Bed: €25   **Reduction:** 01/10–31/03
Capacity: 15 people

13.16 Salon-de-Provence

Private Home

Annie RABATTU
'Domaine de Méjeans', Quartier les Méjeans,
Route Départementale 71B, 13980 ALLEINS
Tel: (0) 4 90 57 31 74 / (0) 623 25 29 16
Fax: (0) 4 90 57 31 74
info@domainedemejeans.com
www.domainedemejeans.com

Price Structure – 4 Bedrooms and 1 Suite
'Calisson', 'Nougat', 'Berlingot' & 'Amande': television, bathroom, wc, shower, double bed (queen-size): €150
'Praline': television, bathroom, wc, shower, double bed (king-size). En-suite room, single bed: €170 – 2 people €200 – 3 people

Extra Bed: €30
Reduction: 1/10–30/04, 7 nights
Capacity: 11 people

Location
20km N of SALON-DE-PROVENCE
in: Alleins
Railway station: 20km
Airport: Marseille-Provence 45km
car essential

Chez Annie and her two daughters, you find yourself in a lovely old provençal house which rivals even the most prestigious hotels. Refined décor as you would expect to see in glossy magazines and a discreet and warm welcome to boot. You are not the only guests here as the lake hosts geese and ducks amongst other birds. Be sure to make the most of this lovely area, not forgetting that the village of Alleins dates back to the 15th century and you are by Salon and St-Rémy-de-Provence as well as Aix-en-Provence at 30km.

Facilities: private parking, extensive grounds, lounge, pets not accepted, dinner available, 100% no smoking, hiking, cycling
Adequate English spoken

Directions: From Salon-de-Provence, take the N538 for 5km via Lamanon. At the roundabout, head for Alleins-Mallemort (D71b). A bit further ahead turn right towards Alleins (D17d), then turn left after about 500 metres (there is a small sign showing 'Sylvestres'). Continue along the canal for 1km. You will see on the right a large avenue of poplar trees and a sign 'Domaine de Méjeans'.

83.92 Bandol

Private Home

Didier MARCHAL & Patrice DARRAS
'Les Quatre Saisons', 370 montée des Oliviers,
route du Brûlat, 83330 LE CASTELLET
Tel: (0) 4 94 25 24 90 / (0) 684 20 81 83
reservation@lesquatresaisons.org
www.lesquatresaisons.org

Price Structure – 4 Bedrooms and 1 Apartment
'Méditerranée' & 'Midi': bathroom, wc, double bed (queen-size): €100
'Oliviers': shower room, wc, twin beds: €90
'Restanques': lounge, kitchen, bathroom, wc, double bed (queen-size): €110
'Tropezienne': lounge, television, shower room, wc, twin beds: €110

Reduction: 15/10–15/03
Capacity: 10 people

Location
10km N of BANDOL
in: Le Castellet, station pick-up on arrival/departure
Railway station: 20km
Airport: Toulon-Hyères 45km
car essential

Patrice and Didier have left behind their restaurant in Paris and we can say for sure that they 'ne regrettent rien'! And neither will you when you come to stay in their superb B&B. Whether you come for a weekend, in summer or in winter, whenever you like in fact, you must go! A convivial atmosphere prevails whether sitting by the fireplace, or on the large terrace with an uninterrupted view whilst tucking into a gastronomic meal, or perhaps just a salad by the swimming pool.

Facilities: private parking, extensive grounds, tv lounge, hosts have pets, pets not accepted, dinner available, wheelchair access, 16 years old minimum age, 2 nights minimum stay: 01/07–31/08, private swimming pool, vineyard 2km, golf course 10km, sea watersports 10km
Fluent English spoken

Directions: A50 Marseille-Toulon, exit 11. Head for Le Beausset and then at the large roundabout, take the D26 towards Le Brûlat, Le Castellet for 1.5km.

Location
BRIGNOLES
in: Brignoles
Railway station: 50km
Airport: Toulon-Hyères 60km
car essential

Private Home

A warm and cheerful welcome in the heart of the Var chez Nelly and Bruno. Three hectares of pine forest and provençal heathland, never far from the coast or the wild and picturesque interior. Your hosts are young and full of energy but above all charming. Bruno will welcome you with one of his *apéritifs* to sip by the pool on arrival whilst Nelly, for her part, will serve her jams at breakfast time to ensure you have a good start to the day whilst you contemplate the view from under the bower in the shade.

Nelly MULLER
'La Bastide de Messine', chemin de Cante-Perdrix, 83170 BRIGNOLES
Tel: (0) 4 94 72 09 06 / (0) 603 15 82 68
Fax: (0) 4 94 72 09 06
info@bastide-messine.com
www.bastide-messine.com

Facilities: off-street parking, extensive grounds, tv lounge, hosts have pets, pets not accepted, dinner available, babies welcome, free cot, wheelchair access, 2 nights minimum stay: 1/07–31/08, private swimming pool, hiking, cycling, vineyard, golf course 10km
Fluent English spoken

Price Structure – 5 Bedrooms
'Jasmin': lounge, bathroom, wc, double bed (queen-size), 2 single beds: €101 – 2 people €132 – 4 people
'Tournesol': bathroom, wc, double bed: €76
'Lavande': bathroom, wc, twin beds: €76
'Terra-Cotta': along corridor shower room, wc, double bed: €76
'Basilic': shower room, wc, 2 sets of twin beds: €76 – 2 people €91,50 – 4 people

Directions: A8 exit 35 for Brignoles. After the first *péage*, at the roundabout, continue straight on towards Aix-en-Provence/St-Maximin. At the second roundabout, take the first right turn and then first right again. Next, turn left and follow the signs to the 'Bastide' for 1km.

Extra Bed: €15 **Reduction:** 10 nights
Capacity: 14 people

83.26 Brignoles

Location
15km S E of BRIGNOLES
in: Besse-sur-Issole, station pick-up on arrival/departure
Railway station: 40km
Airport: Toulon-Hyères 40km
car essential

Private Home

Pierre has decorated this house, on three floors, with great taste and charm. Everything is designed for your wellbeing. The atmosphere is friendly and the location is quiet, in the heart of this 17th-century listed village. The ideal spot from which to explore Provence and enjoy its festivals.

Pierre ROGER
'Chez Pierre', 9 rue Montenard, 83890 BESSE-SUR-ISSOLE
Tel: (0) 4 94 69 79 84 / (0) 662 66 46 54
info@chezpierre.net
www.chezpierre.net

Facilities: garden, tv lounge, 10 years old minimum age, closed: 30/11–15/01
Adequate English spoken

Price Structure – 4 Bedrooms
'Jaune' & 'Grise': shower room, wc, double bed: €65
'Fleurs' & 'Ciel': bathroom, wc, twin beds: €65

Directions: On the A8, exit Brignoles. Take the N7 towards Le Luc for 13km. Turn right to Besse-sur-Issole. When in the village, go as far as the fountain and the statue, and then take Rue Montenard.

Extra Bed: €15
Reduction: 7 nights
Capacity: 8 people

Provence – Brignoles

83.89 Brignoles

Private Home

Anne & Jean-Paul LIAUMOND
'Le Mas de Maupassets', Pont de l'Issole, route du
Luc, 83340 CABASSE
Tel: (0) 4 94 80 27 92 / (0) 608 43 64 47
Fax: (0) 4 94 80 27 92
abecle@aol.com
www.masdemaupassets.com

Price Structure – 5 Bedrooms
'Lavande': bathroom, wc, twin beds: €65
'Amaryllis': shower room, wc, twin beds: €65
'Figues': shower room, wc, double bed, 2 single beds:
€65 – 2 people €105 – 4 people
'Olivier': shower room, wc, twin beds, 3 single beds:
€65 – 2 people €145 – 5 people
'Cigale': wheelchair access, shower room, wc, twin
beds: €65

Extra Bed: €20
Reduction: 01/10–30/04, 7 nights, groups, children
Capacity: 15 people

Location
15km E of BRIGNOLES
in: Cabasse
Railway station: 20km
Airport: Nice Côte-d'Azur 100km
car essential

On the edge of a picturesque medieval town, on the banks of the river, is this renovated former *magnanerie* (silkworm farm) from the 19th century. The stone walls and the large dining room cupboard stuffed full of delicious jams point to how Anne and Jean-Paul insist on preserving its charm and rustic feel. This magnificent region has so much to see but return to sit out in the shade by the swimming pool or by an open fire in winter. Jean-Paul is a jazz musician so you may be lucky to hear a demonstration of his talents.

Facilities: off-street parking, extensive grounds, lounge, hosts have pets, pets not accepted, dinner available, babies welcome, free cot, 100% no smoking, wheelchair access, private swimming pool, fishing, hiking, cycling, vineyard, golf course 5km, riversports 15km
Fluent English spoken

Directions: A8 between Cannes and Aix-en-Provence, exit 35 to Brignoles and then the N7 towards Le Luc for 12km. At the roundabout, take the D13 on the left to Cabasse. In the village head for the D33 towards Le Luc. The property is just after the bridge on the right.

83.96 Brignoles

Private Home

Marie-Thé & Thierry BONNICHON
'Bastide Notre-Dame', Adrech de Ste-Anne,
83570 ENTRECASTEAUX
Tel: (0) 4 94 04 45 63 / (0) 611 42 12 09
Fax: (0) 4 94 04 45 63
mariethevalentin@aol.com
www.bastidenotredame.free.fr

Price Structure – 4 Bedrooms
'Jaune', 'Bleue' & 'Rouge': shower room, wc, double
bed (queen-size): €80
'Verte': bathroom, wc, twin beds: €80

Extra Bed: €20
Reduction: 2 nights
Capacity: 8 people

Location
27km N E of BRIGNOLES
in: Entrecasteaux
Railway station: 30km
Airport: Toulon-Hyères 80km
car essential

A former *bastide*, pleasantly renovated, with views over vines and olive groves. There is so much to see and taste in the region that you will not know where to start. Choose from local pottery, earthenware, truffles and wine, to visiting the nearby lake, waterfall, abbey, château and the Gorges du Verdon for example. Or if that all sounds too taxing, opt for the shade in the garden and enjoy the large swimming pool.

Facilities: private parking, extensive grounds, hosts have pets, pets not accepted, dinner available, babies welcome, free cot, 100% no smoking, closed: 1/12–31/01, private swimming pool, hunting, fishing, mushroom-picking, hiking, vineyard, riversports 9km, golf course 30km
Adequate English spoken

Directions: A8 exit 35 Brignoles. Take the D554 towards Barjols to Val or turn right and take the D562 to Carcès. Then the D31 on the left towards Entrecasteaux. The 'Bastide' is between the chapel and the cemetery.

Location
10km N of BRIGNOLES
in: Montfort-sur-Argens
Railway station: 60km
Airport: Nice Côte-d'Azur 125km
car essential

Residence of Outstanding Character

Pierre welcomes you to his substantial residence dating from the 19th century, in this medieval village dominated by the château of the Knights' Templar dating from the 12th century. The house is spacious and its walls are thick, keeping it delightfully cool in the summer. Breakfast and dinner are taken in the unusual and unique setting of the vaulted dining room. Your host is a music lover (even the cat is an instrument maker!) and also a great traveller (do you want to see his collection of transport tickets?).

Facilities: private parking, tv lounge, hosts have pets, dinner available, babies welcome, free cot, hiking, cycling, fishing, hunting, mushroom-picking, vineyard, riversports 1km, golf course 20km, gliding 30km, sea watersports 35km
Fluent English spoken

Directions: From the A8 exit 35 towards Brignoles, then head towards Le Val and Montfort-sur-Argens (on the D562 and the D22). In the village, when the street turns at right angles take the Rue du Barri, which is the little road that goes up between the fountain and the plane tree.

Pierre MITRANO
'Le Chat Luthier', 4 rue du Barri,
83570 MONTFORT-SUR-ARGENS
Tel: (0) 4 94 59 51 01 Fax: (0) 4 94 59 51 01
le.chat.luthier@wanadoo.fr
http://perso.wanadoo.fr/le.chat.luthier/

Price Structure – 3 Bedrooms
'Récamier': bathroom, wc, double bed, single bed: €55 – 2 people €70 – 3 people
'Pompadour': shower room, wc, double bed: €55
'Astrolabe': along corridor shower room, wc, double bed: €40

Extra Bed: €15
Capacity: 7 people

Location
16km S of BRIGNOLES
in: Rocbaron
Railway station: 30km
Airport: Toulon-Hyères 25km

Private Home

This sleepy village is north of Toulon, about 45 minutes from the coast. Jeanne and Guy's house is a former *bergerie* dating from the 19th century, with creaky wooden floors and lots of old furniture, decorated in style. Whether you are outside in the cool garden with a pool, or dining at the long teak table inside, you will feel at home here. Jeanne is from Luxembourg and multi-lingual and Guy has left his native Paris. Do not miss the dresser in the dining room, full of quality local products that you can buy. Large secure car park.

Facilities: private parking, extensive grounds, lounge, hosts have pets, pets not accepted, dinner available, babies welcome, free cot, 100% no smoking, private swimming pool, hiking, cycling, vineyard 5km, fishing 6km, golf course 15km, riversports 20km
Fluent English spoken

Directions: In the centre of the village, opposite the town hall (*la mairie*).

Jeanne & Guy LAGUILHEMIE
'La Maison de Rocbaron', 3 rue St Sauveur,
83136 ROCBARON
Tel: (0) 4 94 04 24 03 / (0) 687 31 77 61
maison.de.rocbaron@wanadoo.fr
www.maisonderocbaron.com

Price Structure – 5 Bedrooms
'Amicale': shower room, wc, double bed (queen-size): €90
'Bourgeoise': bathroom, wc, shower, double bed (queen-size): €90
'Honorine' & Eugénie': shower room, wc, 2 double beds: €98 – 2 people €158 – 4 people
'Caline': bathroom, wc, shower, double bed: €78

Extra Bed: €25
Reduction: 5 nights, children
Capacity: 14 people

Provence – Brignoles

83.23 Draguignan

Private Home

Location
10km N of DRAGUIGNAN
in: Figanières
Railway station: 20km
Airport: Nice Côte-d'Azur 95km
car essential

Take in the lovely open views of the area, with its park, woods and orchard, as you enjoy breakfast on the terrace. Laurence and Michael made the right decision in leaving Britain and have created the ideal environment in which to relax, with Laurence attending to all the little extras that will make your stay so memorable. On sale: regional products.

Laurence & Michael ALTMAN
'Mas de l'Hermitage', St Pons, 83830 FIGANIERES
Tel: (0) 4 94 67 94 94 / (0) 686 56 63 29
Fax: (0) 4 94 67 83 88
mail@masdelhermitage.com
www.masdelhermitage.com

Price Structure – 3 Bedrooms and 3 Apartments
'Menthe': lounge, kitchen, bathroom, wc, shower, twin beds: €90
'Olive': kitchen, shower room, wc, double bed: €90
'Bergamote': lounge, kitchen, shower room, wc, twin beds, 2 single beds (child-size): €105 – 2 people
€135 – 4 people
'Thym': lounge, bathroom, wc, shower, double bed: €90
'Anis': lounge, shower room, wc, twin beds: €67,50
'Safran': lounge, shower room, wc, twin beds: €75

Extra Bed: €20
Reduction: 19/10–15/04, 7 nights
Capacity: 14 people

Facilities: off-street parking, extensive grounds, hosts have pets, pets not accepted, dinner available, babies welcome, free cot, 2 nights minimum stay: 1/07–31/08, private swimming pool, hiking, cycling, interesting flora, golf course 12km, sea watersports 28km, riversports 38km
Fluent English spoken

Directions: On the A8 exit 36, Le Muy, and head towards Draguignan. At the second roundabout take the D54 towards Figanières for 17km. Carry straight on at the junction with the road to Grasse, and the house is 150m along on the left (signposted).

83.33 Draguignan

Private Home

Location
25km S W of DRAGUIGNAN
in: Le Thoronet
Railway station: 20km
Airport: Toulon-Hyères 55km
car essential

On a wooded estate of 12 hectares with trees three centuries old, is this lovely *bastide* in stone from the 19th century, often featured in many interior design magazines! The guest bedrooms and the bathrooms are original, large, comfortable and with an Italian style. After a delicious dinner prepared by Antoine, the chef, you may wish to head for the fitness room, the swimming pool or the billiards table. We cannot dream of a better place from which to comfortably visit *la Provence Verte* and the coast.

Catherine & Antoine DEBRAY
'Bastide des Hautes Moures ', Lieu-dit les Moures, 83340 LE THORONET
Tel: (0) 4 94 60 13 36 / (0) 610 14 67 21
Fax: (0) 4 94 60 13 36
infos@bastidedesmoures.com
www.bastidedesmoures.com

Price Structure – 4 Bedrooms
'Les Moures' (our favourite room): lounge, television, bathroom, wc, shower, double bed (king-size): €150
'Oasis': lounge, television, bathroom, wc, shower, double bed (queen-size): €110
'Lavandin': television, bathroom, wc, double bed (queen-size), single bed: €120 – 2 people
€140 – 3 people
'Arlequin': television, shower room, wc, double bed: €110

Reduction: 15/10–31/03
Capacity: 9 people

Facilities: off-street parking, garden, lounge, hosts have pets, pets not accepted, dinner available, 100% no smoking, private swimming pool, hiking, sea watersports 55km
Fluent English spoken

Directions: On the A8, exit Le Luc or Le Cannet des Maures and take direction Le Thoronet. On the D17, before Le Thoronet, take the D84 on the right towards Vidauban. After 4.7km, at the sign for Les Moures, take the road on the right that ends with 800m of cobbled road.

Location
10km S W of DRAGUIGNAN
in: Taradeau, station pick-up on arrival/departure
Railway station: 5km
Airport: Nice Côte-d'Azur 85km
car essential

Private Home

This former *bergerie* has been delightfully transformed into a private house, a *Maison d'Hôtes* by Jeanine, who guarantees a sincere welcome for her guests. Located midway between the sea and the mountains, it is the ideal spot for visiting Les Gorges du Verdon, L'Abbaye du Thoronet and St-Tropez. For your comfort all the bedrooms are air-conditioned and equipped with a mini-bar.

Facilities: private parking, garden, tv lounge, pets not accepted, babies welcome, free cot, 100% no smoking, 3 nights minimum stay: 01/07–31/08, private swimming pool, hiking 2km, vineyard 2km, cycling 5km, fishing 5km, riversports 5km, golf course 15km
Adequate English spoken

Jeanine & Richard GUILLOT
'La Bergerie du Moulin', chemin du Vieux Moulin,
83460 TARADEAU
Tel: (0) 4 94 99 91 51 Fax: (0) 4 94 99 98 98
bergerie.moulin@wanadoo.fr
www.bergeriedumoulin.com

Price Structure – 5 Bedrooms
suite: television, bathroom, wc, double bed (king-size), single bed: €110 – 2 people €140 – 3 people
'La Campagnarde': double bed (king-size): €100
'Les Lavandes': television, bathroom, wc, shower, double bed (king-size): €110
'Lune de Miel (Honeymoon)': television, shower room, wc, four-poster double bed (queen-size): €120
'Le Grenier': television, shower room, wc, double bed (king-size): €90

Capacity: 11 people

Directions: From the A8, exit 34, Le Muy, Draguignan. Then take the N7 towards Vidauban, Brignoles for about 6.5km, then turn right onto the D10 as far as Taradeau. 'La Bergerie du Moulin' is signposted from the village.

Location
HYERES-LES-PALMIERS
in: Hyères-les-Palmiers, station pick-up on arrival/departure
Railway station: 18km
Airport: Toulon-Hyères 6km

Private Home

Hyères-les-Palmiers lives up to its name. It is one of those small towns full of palm trees, which has kept its charming style, typical of the coastal resorts of the Var. It is a favourite spot for retired people and Pierre is no exception. He is a retired engineer who loves playing bridge and doing DIY. The house is set high up above the town and offers a splendid view of Toulon and the Faron mountain.

Facilities: private parking, garden, tv lounge, hosts have pets, pets not accepted, dinner available, kitchen, private swimming pool, sea watersports
Fluent English spoken

Jacqueline & Pierre BRUNET
'Li Rouvre', chemin du Vieux Château,
83400 HYERES-LES-PALMIERS
Tel: (0) 4 94 35 43 44 Fax: (0) 4 94 35 43 44

Price Structure – 2 Bedrooms
'Rez jardin': lounge, shower room, wc, double bed, 2 single beds: €60 – 2 people €120 – 4 people
'Rez piscine': bathroom, wc, double bed: €60

Capacity: 6 people

Directions: At Toulon, take the A57 towards Hyères, Nice, then the A570 towards Hyères. At the roundabout, where the railway station is signposted to the right, go in the opposite direction, towards the north. At this point, you are advised to telephone your host for detailed directions.

83.77 Hyères-les-Palmiers

Private Home

Location
15km E of HYERES-LES-PALMIERS
in: Bormes-les-Mimosas
Railway station: 45km
Airport: Toulon-Hyères 25km
car essential

Discover this guest house hidden deep in the forest whilst touring along the road to St-Tropez. Even if you happen across 20-odd people on your way to the swimming pool and tennis court you will not feel overrun. The bedrooms have been tastefully redecorated, each one with its own colour scheme. Take in the sights and smells of Provence on a fishing trip out to sea or simply from the aromas of Laura's cooking. Bormes is pleasant at quieter times of the year but if you cannot avoid the summer months be sure to book in advance.

Laura DEVOS
'Villa Naïs', 1568 route de Martegasse,
83230 BORMES-LES-MIMOSAS
Tel: (0) 4 94 71 28 57 / (0) 684 53 34 15
Fax: (0) 4 94 71 28 57
villanais@wanadoo.fr
www.villanais.com

Price Structure – 9 Bedrooms
'Clémence', 'Nathalie', 'Gisèle', 'Anis' & 'Lavande': shower room, wc, double bed: €89,70
'Anaïs': bathroom, wc, double bed, single bed:
€126,60 – 3 people
'Amandine': shower room, wc, double bed, single bed:
€126,60 – 3 people
'Laura': bathroom, wc, double bed, twin beds: €89,70
– 2 people €166,80 – 4 people
'Angèle': television, shower room, wc, double bed, twin beds: €166,80 – 4 people

Extra Bed: €39,50
Reduction: 01/10–31/03, 4 nights, groups, children
Capacity: 24 people

Facilities: private parking, extensive grounds, tv lounge, hosts have pets, dinner available, kitchen, babies welcome, free cot, wheelchair access, private swimming pool, private tennis court, hiking, cycling 2km, golf course 6km, sea watersports 6km, vineyard 6km
Adequate English spoken

Directions: At Hyères take the N98 towards St-Tropez. At the fork, continue straight on towards St-Tropez, Cogolin for about five minutes. There is a big yellow sign on the right.

83.97 Hyères-les-Palmiers

Residence of Outstanding Character

Location
8km W of HYERES-LES-PALMIERS
in: Le Pradet
Railway station: 10km
Airport: Toulon-Hyères 9km
car essential

This old winegrower's house from 1870 is set back on peaceful slopes, less than 1km from the sea. After 40 years abroad, Rosy has returned to her roots with her English husband. The charming refurbished bedrooms are air-conditioned and three have sea views. A pool is available and John advises on local timetables, the famous Toulon market, St-Tropez and the Ile de Porquerolles. In spring and autumn the Haut Var villages are at their best: antique fairs and flower, chestnut, truffle and wine festivals. Classic cars welcome.

Rosy & John ETTE
'Mas de la Tourette', 505 chemin des Bernard,
83220 LE PRADET
Tel: (0) 4 94 08 15 91
masdelatourette@bedbreak.com
www.masdelatourette.iowners.net

Price Structure – 4 Bedrooms
'Cool Coquelicot': bathroom, wc, double bed: €75
'Bellevue Balcony': bathroom, wc, twin beds (€95 –
2 people). Along corridor room 'Monet Marine':
washbasin, double bed: €65 – 2 people
€145 – 4 people
'Brigitte Bardot': shower, washbasin, wc, single bed:
€55 – 1 person

Extra Bed: €22
Reduction: 15/09–1/06
Capacity: 7 people

Facilities: private parking, garden, pets not accepted, 100% no smoking, 14 years old minimum age, 2 nights minimum stay: 31/05–12/09, private swimming pool, interesting flora, hiking, cycling, sea watersports 1km, vineyard 2km, golf course 6km
Fluent English spoken

Directions: In the centre of Le Pradet, head east along the main street through the town. Pass the main square on your right and at the lights turn right by the fishing shop 'L'Escale' on the corner into Blvd. Jean Jaurès, sign to 'La Garonne, Oursinières'. Continue for about 800m. After a bend on the descent, left at the red sign 'Sables d'Or' (Chemin du Traversier). At the T-junction right into the Chemin des Bernard for 400m (pink house on the left).

Location
ST-MAXIMIN-LA-STE-BAUME
in: St-Maximin-la-Ste-Baume
Railway station: 45km
Airport: Marseille-Provence 65km
car essential

Private Home

Of the six daughters of this discreet couple, only the youngest is still at home. Monsieur is a doctor and Madame is a plastic surgeon. This is a delightful and unusual option. Françoise is very pleasant and has organised for you two traditional, comfortable and authentically decorated Camargue caravans, known as *roulottes*! If you prefer a more conventional room, there is also a large bedroom available in the house. This is a beautiful, green part of Provence where nature, watersports and medieval sites are among the highlights. Of note to visit: the Basilique Ste-Marie-Madeleine de St-Maximin.

Facilities: private parking, extensive grounds, hosts have pets, pets not accepted, dinner available, 100% no smoking, 12 years old minimum age, private swimming pool, vineyard, golf course 10km, hiking 10km, sea watersports 50km, riversports 50km

Françoise SUR
route de Nice,
83470 ST-MAXIMIN-LA-STE-BAUME
Tel: (0) 672 40 16 25
Fax: (0) 4 94 78 02 54
francoise.sur@wanadoo.fr

Price Structure – 2 Bedrooms and 1 Suite
Suite: along corridor shower room, wc, double bed.
En-suite lounge, television, single bed.
2 'Gypsies roulottes', double bed (queen-size): €120 – 2 people €300 – 7 people

Capacity: 7 people

Directions: A8 exit 34 St-Maximin-la-Ste-Baume. N7 direction St-Maximin. After the building materials on the right and after the large cedar tree, it is the gate in dark wood.

Location
20km N E of ST-MAXIMIN-LA-STE-BAUME
in: Tavernes
car essential

Residence of Outstanding Character

You will certainly thank your hosts, Sylvie and Gilles, for taking you to the olive oil press and the wine cooperative. Olive oil, wine, and pottery are typical of the Midi and well worth bringing back. On sale: Olive oil, wine.

Facilities: private parking, garden, dinner available, private swimming pool, cycling, sea watersports 16km
Adequate English spoken

Gilles & Sylvie BARREME
1 chemin de Braou, 83670 TAVERNES
Tel: (0) 4 94 72 31 04 / (0) 688 25 30 95
gilles.barreme@orange.fr
www.provenceweb.fr/barreme.htm

Price Structure – 2 Bedrooms
'Grenache': shower room, wc, double bed: €52,60
'Provençale': shower room, wc, twin beds: €52,60

Extra Bed: €17
Reduction: 7 nights
Capacity: 4 people

Directions: On the A8, take the exit to St-Maximin where you take the D560 towards Tavernes and Riez. The house is at the crossroads with the D554 towards Ginarsservis.

83.58 St-Maximin-la-Ste-Baume

Private Home

Ginette & René SWEENS
'La Calade des Candoux', 83170 TOURVES
Tel: (0) 4 94 78 94 55 / (0) 689 19 59 05
lacalade@hotmail.com
www.la-calade-des-candoux.com

Price Structure – 2 Bedrooms
'Le Pigeonnier': wheelchair access, lounge, shower room, wc, washbasin, double bed: €69
'Au Coeur du Mas': shower, wc, washbasin, double bed: €54

Reduction: 15/09–01/04, 4 nights
Capacity: 4 people

Location
7km S E of ST-MAXIMIN-LA-STE-BAUME
in: Tourves, station pick-up on arrival/departure
Railway station: 45km
Airport: Marseille-Provence 50km
car essential

Ginette and René left Belgium for this wonderful spot and as they say, 'We could not imagine living anywhere else'. This provençal *mas* is hidden away midway between the coastal plain and the high pine covered slopes. The largest bedroom is very unusual, located in an ornamental *pigeonnier* and has a small music room in the loft. René is a retired chemist and can advise on the health-giving properties of the local plants and Ginette, who is a nurse, will take good care of you.

Facilities: private parking, garden, lounge, hosts have pets, pets not accepted, dinner available, babies welcome, free cot, 100% no smoking, wheelchair access, wc, 2 nights minimum stay: 1/04–30/09, private swimming pool, hiking, cycling, vineyard 2km, golf course 10km
Fluent English spoken

Directions: From the A8 exit 34 St-Maximin. N7 towards Brignoles. When you are in the village (Tourves), continue to Place de l'Hôtel de Ville and phone your hosts. They will then come to fetch you.

83.99 St-Raphaël

Private Home

Martine VION
'Le Clos des Vignes', Chemin de la Lauve,
83700 ST-RAPHAEL
Tel: (0) 4 94 95 00 31 / (0) 685 48 04 85
m.vion@wanadoo.fr
www.bnb-chambredhotes83.com

Price Structure – 6 Bedrooms
and 1 Apartment
'Verte': bathroom, wc, double bed (queen-size): €100
'Rose' & 'Blanche': bathroom, wc, twin beds: €100
'Orange': bathroom, wc, twin beds, 2 single beds:
€100 – 2 people €160 – 4 people
'Jaune': along corridor bathroom, wc, double bed (queen-size). Along corridor room: twin beds:
€100 – 2 people €160 – 4 people
apartment: kitchen, shower room, wc, 2 double beds, 2 single beds: €200 – 6 people

Extra Bed: €20
Reduction: 1/10–31/05, 7 nights, groups
Capacity: 20 people

Location
ST-RAPHAEL
in: St-Raphaël, station pick-up on arrival/departure
Railway station: St-Raphaël
Airport: Nice Côte-d'Azur 60km

Martine is welcoming and will even come to meet you at the bus stop. Her guest bedrooms and the bathrooms are a touch on the small side, quite modest, but you are just ten minutes away from the town centre and the beaches. You can also picnic in her garden and there is a refrigerator and a microwave oven available for you to use.

Facilities: off-street parking, garden, tv lounge, dinner available, kitchen, babies welcome, free cot, 100% no smoking, fishing, cycling, sea watersports, golf course 1km, hiking 1km, interesting flora 1km, riversports 1km
Fluent English spoken

Directions: A8 exit 37 and rejoin St-Raphaël. Head for the hospital 'Hôpital' and head down on the right, Avenue Valescure. At the 'Prado' bar turn left into Avenue du XVème Corps. Then at the roundabout turn left into Chemin de la Lauve.

Private Home

Location
15km W of ST-RAPHAEL
in: Roquebrune-sur-Argens
Railway station: 12km
Airport: Nice Côte-d'Azur 80km
car essential

This small holiday complex of B&B accommodation and gîtes is in a beautiful, quiet setting among the pine and oak trees. Ideal for young families, choose either the self-contained gîte with a kitchenette or the bed and breakfast rooms with air-conditioning. Béatrice and Luc are a very organised and friendly couple who left Paris three years ago to live out their dream. Easy access from the motorway and also an ideal location for a short stay out of the main holiday season. Roquebrune is a classified medieval village at the foot of the famous rock.

Facilities: private parking, extensive grounds, tv lounge, hosts have pets, pets not accepted, kitchen, 100% no smoking, 3 nights minimum stay: 1/07–31/08, private swimming pool, vineyard 3km, cycling 4km, riversports 4km, golf course 6km, sea watersports 12km
Basic English spoken

Directions: A8 exit 37 Fréjus-St-Raphaël. At the second roundabout turn right just before the 'Formule 1' hotel and continue on this one-way street for 1.5km up to the tunnel under the motorway. Turn left, and continue to the end of the road that runs along the motorway. Green gate.

Béatrice & Luc MESNIL
'Les Mayombes', chemin de la Combe au Blavet,
83520 ROQUEBRUNE-SUR-ARGENS
Tel: (0) 4 94 81 66 89 / (0) 621 13 53 72
Fax: (0) 4 94 81 66 89
lesmayombes@wanadoo.fr
www.lesmayombes.com

Price Structure – 2 Bedrooms and 5 Apartments
'Orchidée' & 'Nymphéa': television, shower room, wc, double bed (queen-size): €75
apart. 'Datura': television, kitchen, shower room, wc, double bed (queen-size): €95
apart. 'Canelle': television, kitchen, shower room, wc, double bed, single bed: €110 – 2 people
€110 – 3 people
apart. 'Amaryllis': lounge, television, kitchen, shower room, wc, 2 double beds, single bed: €125 – 2 people
€125 – 5 people
plus 2 apart.

Extra Bed: €15   **Reduction:** 1/10–31/05
Capacity: 22 people

Location
15km W of ST-RAPHAEL
in: Roquebrune-sur-Argens
Railway station: 15km
Airport: Nice Côte-d'Azur 50km
car essential

Private Home

Top-notch quality, plenty of charm and good taste and the Midi sun as well. Armand and Maurice live in the beautiful listed village of Roquebrune, are experts on antiques and will be delighted to advise you on what to look for in this region. The house is set back a little from the village in a quiet wooded area. A place not to be missed and only 10km from the coast.

Facilities: private parking, garden, tv lounge, pets not accepted, 100% no smoking, 18 years old minimum age, 2 nights minimum stay, closed: 01/10–30/04, private swimming pool, hiking, cycling, riversports, vineyard, golf course 3km, sea watersports 10km
Adequate English spoken

Directions: At St-Raphaël, follow the N98 coast road towards St-Tropez. At St-Aygulf, take the D7 on the right as far as Roquebrune. In Roquebrune at the traffic lights follow the signs and take the first road on the left and then the first on the right. 'La Bergerie' is 200m ahead on the right.

Armand PETIT
'La Bergerie', rue du Jas de Callian,
83520 ROQUEBRUNE-SUR-ARGENS
Tel: (0) 4 94 45 73 67 / (0) 613 80 16 58
Fax: (0) 4 94 45 73 67
petit.armand@wanadoo.fr

Price Structure – 2 Bedrooms
'Olivier': television, shower room, wc, washbasin, double bed: €80
'Moutons': television, bathroom, wc, shower, washbasin, double bed: €90

Capacity: 4 people

Provence – St-Raphaël

83.20 St-Raphaël

Private Home

Location
20km N of ST-RAPHAEL
in: St-Paul-en-Forêt
Railway station: 20km
Airport: Nice Côte-d'Azur 70km
car essential

This charming English lady knows only too well how to give her guests a great welcome. She has discovered a wonderful place in Provence that is the envy of all those who wish they had discovered it first. This magnificent village is full of character. You will feel at home here.

Jennifer PRESTON
Les Bas Baudissets, 83440 ST-PAUL-EN-FORET
Tel: (0) 4 94 76 37 58 / (0) 633 57 86 38
Fax: (0) 4 94 76 32 82

Price Structure – 2 Bedrooms
television, bathroom, wc, twin beds. Along corridor
room: single bed: €30,50 – 1 person
€107 – 3 people

Extra Bed: €20
Capacity: 3 people

Facilities: off-street parking, garden, tv lounge, hosts have pets, pets not accepted, dinner available, 6 years old minimum age, 2 nights minimum stay, closed: 31/10–31/03, private swimming pool, hiking, cycling, golf course 4km, sea watersports 15km
Fluent English spoken

Directions: On the A8, exit Les Adrets. Take the D37 to join up with the D562 (Grasse–Draguignan). Turn left towards Draguignan. At the 'Lou Pascouren' auberge on the D4, turn left towards Fréjus. In St-Paul, stay on this road and phone so that your host can come and fetch you.

83.10 St-Tropez

Private Home

Location
12km S of ST-TROPEZ
in: La Croix-Valmer
Railway station: 40km
Airport: Toulon-Hyères 40km
car essential

Caroline and Olivier's very large and pleasant provençal house, set in beautiful grounds, is only five minutes' walk from a very beautiful beach. Caroline is a retired restaurateur so knows about looking after clients. The rooms are spacious, comfortable, practical and modern and decorated in good taste. Each one has its own private terrace overlooking the grounds. An ideal place for a holiday.

Caroline & Olivier WATINE
'Cante Cigalo', Quartier du Vergeron – Rond-point de Sylvabelle, route de Gigaro,
83420 LA CROIX-VALMER
Tel: (0) 680 21 05 85
Fax: (0) 4 94 79 79 09
info@cantecigalo.com
www.cantecigalo.com
Price Structure – 4 Bedrooms and 1 Suite
suite: television, bathroom, wc, shower, double bed (queen-size). En-suite room, twin beds:
€140 – 2 people €180 – 4 people
room 1: television, shower room, wc, double bed (queen-size), single bed (child-size):
€110 – 2 people €130 – 3 people
room 2: shower room, wc, double bed (queen-size), single bed (child-size): €110 – 2 people €130 – 3 people
rooms 4 & 5: shower room, wc, double bed (queen-size): €110

Extra Bed: €20
Reduction: 15/09–14/06
Capacity: 14 people

Facilities: off-street parking, extensive grounds, hosts have pets, babies welcome, free cot, 5 nights minimum stay: 15/06–2/08, closed: 8/11–31/03 & 2/08–30/08, fishing, hiking, cycling, interesting flora 2km, sea watersports 2km, vineyard 2km, golf course 10km
Adequate English spoken

Directions: On the A8 exit 36 Le Muy, then head towards Ste-Maxime, then St-Tropez. Then go towards La Croix-Valmer and the 'Plage de Gigaro' and it is just before the Sylvabelle roundabout.

Location
15km N of ST-TROPEZ
in: Plan-de-la-Tour
Railway station: 35km
Airport: Nice Côte-d'Azur 90km
car essential

✹ ✹ ✹

Private Home

This is a small corner of paradise, bathing in the sun of the Gulf of St-Tropez, located in a verdant site amongst cork oaks, pines and other Mediterranean shrubs. Michèle and Georges open the doors of their home and share with you the charm of this provençal house, with its own swimming pool and a restful and relaxing atmosphere.

Facilities: private parking, garden, hosts have pets, pets not accepted, 3 nights minimum stay: 01/07–31/08, private swimming pool
Adequate English spoken

Michèle & Georges PONSELET
'Le Petit Magnan', Quartier St-Sébastien, Golfe de St-Tropez, 83120 PLAN-DE-LA-TOUR
Tel: (0) 4 94 43 72 00 Fax: (0) 4 94 43 72 00
lepetitmagnan@worldonline.fr
www.lepetitmagnan.fr.st

Price Structure – 2 Bedrooms
shower room, wc, double bed: €80
bathroom, wc, double bed: €80

Capacity: 4 people

Directions: From A8, exit Le Muy and head towards Ste-Maxime, St-Tropez. Before Ste-Maxime, turn right on the D74 towards Plan-de-la-Tour and Centre-Ville. When you are in the town centre, take the D44 towards Grimaud. Go past the hotel 'Mas des Brugassières' and take the second left to Prat Bourdin. Follow signs to 'Le Petit Magnan'.

Location
14km N of ST-TROPEZ
in: Ste-Maxime, station pick-up on arrival/departure
Railway station: 25km
Airport: Nice Côte-d'Azur 80km

✹ ✹ ✹

Private Home

Luce's villa is between the Gulf of St-Tropez and the Estérel mountains, in a residential area surrounded by hills and parasol pines. It is ideally located just 900m from the centre of a charming little resort with excellent beaches. Each studio is simply furnished but comfortable, and has a well-equipped kitchenette as well as its own private terrace. Luce proposes many tempting local specialities: *bouillabaisse, moules, couscous, croquets aux amandes*. We really loved this place. On site: French language courses. Reductions 10-20% out of season.

Facilities: off-street parking, garden, pets not accepted, dinner available, babies welcome, free cot, 7 nights minimum stay: 07/07–26/08, private swimming pool, fishing, sea watersports, golf course 1km, hiking 1km, interesting flora 10km
Adequate English spoken

Luce CORTES
'Villa Siledelune', 2 impasse Bouscarlo, Angle rue Jean Corona, 83120 STE-MAXIME
Tel: (0) 4 94 43 82 13 / (0) 611 71 28 15
contact@siledelune.com
www.siledelune.com

Price Structure – 4 Apartments
'Sylbleu': television, kitchen, shower room, wc, double bed, 2 single beds: €97 – 2 people €135 – 4 people
'Agneshia': television, kitchen, bathroom, wc, double bed, 2 single beds: €95 – 2 people €135 – 4 people
'Luche': television, kitchen, bathroom, wc, double bed: €87
'Rocaille': television, kitchen, shower room, wc, double bed, 2 single beds: €87 – 2 people €127 – 4 people

Extra Bed: €20
Reduction: 01/02–30/04 & 15/10–20/12, 7 nights, groups, children
Capacity: 14 people

Directions: A8 exit 6 Le Muy. D25 to Ste-Maxime for 20km. Follow signs to Centre-Ville, then 'Golf de Ste-Maxime' via Route du Plan-de-la-Tour and Avenue du Débarquement. Go right around the roundabout by the golf course in order to go down the Rue J. Corona for about 800m. The house is in the second road on the right, on the corner of Rue J. Corona and the Impasse Bouscarlo.

Provence – St-Tropez

83.61 Toulon

Residence of Outstanding Character

Bienvenue en France

Location
5km W of TOULON
in: Tamaris, station pick-up on arrival/departure
Railway station: 2km
Airport: Toulon-Hyères 15km

Isabelle BERTSCH
'Villa Héliotropes', avenue de la Grande Maison,
Tamaris, 83500 LA SEYNE-SUR-MER
Tel: (0) 4 94 87 86 26 / (0) 622 22 35 19
heliotropes@villa-heliotropes.com
www.villa-heliotropes.com

Our inspector fell in love with this place, so it has four 'suns' and a *coup de cœur*. This *Maison de Maître* is full of old-world charm and the class of the grand bourgeois houses of the Côte d'Azur. The garden is typically Mediterranean, with a view of the mussel beds of Tamaris. The décor has been carefully considered by your hosts to preserve the atmosphere of this house. Isabelle is discreet and charming and Philippe just loves to chat. The dog may look impressive but is very docile. You will feel good here.

Price Structure – 5 Bedrooms
'Terre de Provence': television, bathroom, wc, double bed: €100
'Glycine' & 'Camille': television, bathroom, wc, double bed: €90
'Eucalyptus' & 'Pacha': television, bathroom, wc, double bed: €85

Extra Bed: €20
Reduction: 15/09-30/04, groups, children
Capacity: 10 people

Facilities: private parking, extensive grounds, tv lounge, hosts have pets, dinner available, babies welcome, free cot, private swimming pool, cycling, fishing, interesting flora, sea watersports, vineyard, hiking 2km, golf course 8km
Adequate English spoken

Directions: From the A50 exit La Seyne-sur-Mer. Head towards the Centre-Ville and follow signs 'La Villa Tamaris Pacha'. The gate of the villa leads off the car park of the very impressive 'Musée Villa Tamaris'.

84.03 Avignon

Working Farm

Bienvenue en France

Location
10km E of AVIGNON
in: Châteauneuf-de-Gadagne
Railway station: 15km
Airport: Avignon 7km
car essential

Caroline & Vincent CORNILLE
'Les Vertes Rives', chemin des Magues,
84470 CHATEAUNEUF-DE-GADAGNE
Tel: (0) 4 90 22 37 10 Fax: (0) 4 90 22 03 31
mvr2@tiscali.fr
www.mas-des-vertes-rives.com

We fell in love with Caroline which has earned her four 'suns' and a *coup de cœur*. Her welcome proves how warm the welcome from the Midi people can be. You will be surrounded by geese, ducks, donkeys and pigs. There is an inn that is part of the premises where they also organise seminars. Only ten minutes from Avignon.

Price Structure – 4 Bedrooms and 1 Suite
'Colline': shower room, wc, 2 single beds: €66
'Ventoux': shower room, wc, double bed, twin beds: €66 – 2 people €93 – 4 people
'Village' & 'Lubéron': shower room, wc, double bed: €66
'Côté Cour': shower room, wc, double bed, single bed. En-suite room, shower room, wc, 2 single beds: €120 – 5 people

Reduction: 2 nights
Capacity: 15 people

Facilities: private parking, extensive grounds, tv lounge, hosts have pets, dinner available, babies welcome, free cot, 100% no smoking, 2 nights minimum stay: 01/07–31/08, closed: 24/12–7/01, hiking, cycling, golf course 5km, riversports 15km, winter sports 35km
Fluent English spoken

Directions: At Avignon, take the N100 towards Morières, L'Isle-sur-la-Sorgue and Apt. At Châteauneuf-de-Gadagne, turn right onto the D6 towards Caumont for 300m. Turn left and continue for 800m. The property is on the right.

Location
9km S of AVIGNON
in: Châteaurenard-de-Provence
Railway station: 10km
Airport: Avignon 8km
car essential

Private Home

From your bedroom window, in the evening, there is a wonderful view of the illuminated feudal château. Leave your bags with Marie-José and go off to visit the pleasant little provençal town of Châteaurenard with its Sunday market. Your hostess is a qualified guide, so is a great help with advice and organising visits to Avignon if you wish. The pool is there to revive you on your return. The plentiful breakfast is served on the patio. Enjoy.

Facilities: off-street parking, garden, tv lounge, pets not accepted, internet access, babies welcome, free cot, 100% no smoking, private swimming pool, hiking, cycling, golf course 10km, vineyard 20km
Adequate English spoken

Marie-José NICOLAS
'Mas des Beaumes', 51 avenue du Baron de Coubertin,
13160 CHATEAURENARD-DE-PROVENCE
Tel: (0) 9 51 13 17 47 / (0) 626 86 03 60
masdesbeaumes@free.fr
http://masdesbeaumes.free.fr

Price Structure – 2 Bedrooms
'Bleue': television, shower room, wc, washbasin, double bed: €60
'Jaune': television, shower room, wc, double bed, 2 single beds: €75 – 2 people €105 – 4 people

Reduction: 01/10–31/03
Capacity: 6 people

Directions: On the A7 exit 24, Avignon-Sud. As you enter Châteaurenard, at the roundabout turn left to 'complexe sportif'. At the next roundabout, turn left and continue for 50m.

Location
9km S of AVIGNON
in: Châteaurenard-de-Provence,
station pick-up on arrival/departure
Railway station: 10km
Airport: Marseille-Provence 90km

Private Home

Maryse and Raphaël provide a very warm welcome to their house, set into the hillside and surrounded by flowers. This is the ideal location for visiting the numerous tourist attractions within a radius of 50km, such as Avignon and its Papal Palace, Arles with its Roman arena, Tarascon with the château of the Roi René and La Camargue with its nature reserve and Les Saintes-Maries-de-la-Mer (famous gypsy festival in May).

Facilities: private parking, garden, tv lounge, dinner available, kitchen, babies welcome, free cot, 100% no smoking, cycling, hiking 1km, golf course 8km, vineyard 20km, lake watersports 25km, riversports 30km
Basic English spoken

Maryse & Raphaël TRIBO
'La Sousto', 54 avenue 1ère D-F-L, 13160
CHATEAURENARD-DE-PROVENCE
Tel: (0) 4 90 94 48 41 / (0) 620 90 24 01
tribo-bb-provence@wanadoo.fr
www.lasousto.com

Price Structure – 3 Bedrooms
2 rooms: television, shower room, wc, double bed, cot: €50
television, shower room, wc, twin beds, cot: €50

Extra Bed: €15
Reduction: 01/11–15/03, 8 nights, children
Capacity: 6 people

Directions: From Avignon, take the N570 towards Arles for 2km. Take the D571 on the left, as far as Châteaurenard. At the post office, head towards St-Rémy for 800m, then turn left towards 'Parcours Sportif'. Then take the Avenue 1ère D-F-L. 'La Sousto' is 900m along on the left (signposted).

Provence – Avignon

84.82 Avignon

Residence of Outstanding Character

Patrick MELIS
'Domaine du Grand Causeran', 60 allée du Grand Causeran, 84320 ENTRAIGUES-SUR-LA-SORGUE
Tel: (0) 870 44 44 60 / (0) 633 78 44 71
Fax: (0) 4 90 01 39 36
patrick@grandcauseran.com
www.grandcauseran.com

Price Structure – 1 Bedroom and 4 Apartments
'Arum', 'Bruyère' & 'Dauphinelle': lounge, television, kitchen, bathroom, wc, double bed: €95
'Cranson': wheelchair access, lounge, television, kitchen, bathroom, wc, double bed, 2 single beds: €150 – 2 people €180 – 4 people
'Epilobes': wheelchair access, television, bathroom, wc, shower, double bed: €85

Extra Bed: €15
Reduction: 01/10–31/05, 4 nights, groups, children
Capacity: 12 people

Location
12km N E of AVIGNON
in: Entraigues-sur-la-Sorgue, station pick-up on arrival/departure
Railway station: 15km
Airport: Avignon 20km
car essential

In very little time, Patrick and Anne have given a new lease of life to their provençal *bastide*. You'll find plenty of space, comfort, coolness and quiet: perfect for long stays! Patrick is Belgian and well travelled but is now on hand and at your disposal. Anne, for her part, is a trained nurse. If over the years you find it harder and harder to get about, then this is the place for you; everything has been thought through to make things easier for you, even the swimming pool. The apartments, also rented weekly, are spacious with sober décor.

Facilities: off-street parking, extensive grounds, tv lounge, hosts have pets, babies welcome, free cot, 100% no smoking, wheelchair access, 1 shared bathroom, wc, private swimming pool, vineyard 2km, hiking 3km, riversports 10km, gliding 10km
Fluent English spoken

Directions: From the A7, exit Avignon-Nord. Take the D952 towards Carpentras. Exit D53-Vedène and take the D53 towards Vedène. The Chemin de Causeran is ahead, in front of you and then first on the left.

84.98 Avignon

Private Home

Marie-Paule CARPANEDO
'Mas de la Dragonette', 260 chemin André Massager, 84320 ENTRAIGUES-SUR-LA-SORGUE
Tel: (0) 4 90 39 20 77 Fax: (0) 4 90 39 08 35
info@masdeladragonette.com
www.masdeladragonette.com

Price Structure – 5 Bedrooms
'Africaine': bathroom, wc, double bed (queen-size): €85
'Petit Paradis': along corridor shower room, wc, bathroom, twin beds: €85
'Champêtre': shower room, wc, twin beds: €85
'Levant': double bed: €85
'Couchant': twin beds: €85

Extra Bed: €23
Reduction: groups
Capacity: 10 people

Location
12km N E of AVIGNON
in: Entraigues-sur-la-Sorgue, station pick-up on arrival/departure
Railway station: 15km
Airport: Avignon 15km
car essential

It is well worth a detour to Entraigues to come and stay with Marie-Paule. It is rare to meet such an interesting person and together with her little family they ensure for you a pleasant and memorable stay. This *mas* has been restored and dates back to the 18th century. It boasts a spacious living room, beautiful bathrooms and large guest bedrooms with attractive décor. The swimming pool is large and there is plenty of space here and an abundance of fresh air. The gastronomic restaurant here champions organic produce so be sure to book a table.

Facilities: off-street parking, extensive grounds, tv lounge, hosts have pets, dinner available, babies welcome, free cot, 1 shared shower room, wc, 3 nights minimum stay: 01/07–31/08, private swimming pool, cycling, vineyard 3km, golf course 6km
Adequate English spoken

Directions: Please contact your host in advance for detailed directions.

Location
25km E of AVIGNON
in: L'Isle-sur-la-Sorgue, station pick-up
on arrival/departure
Railway station: 3km
Airport: Avignon 20km
car essential

**Residence of
Outstanding
Character**

This 17th-century *mas* is surrounded by an enormous estate. L'Isle-sur-la-Sorgue is famous for its antiques and Fontaine de Vaucluse is very close. This place is known for its food.

Josette & Jean-Marie SECCHI
'Château du Domaine des Costières',
1634 route de Carpentras D938,
84800 L'ISLE-SUR-LA-SORGUE
Tel: (0) 4 90 38 39 19 Fax: (0) 4 90 38 39 19

Facilities: private parking, extensive grounds, tv lounge, hosts have pets, babies welcome, free cot, 100% no smoking, hiking, golf course 1km
Adequate English spoken

Directions: In Avignon, take the N100 towards Morières, L'Isle-sur-la- Sorgue and Apt. The property is 1km from L'Isle-sur-la-Sorgue, on the D938 towards Carpentras (signposted).

Price Structure – 4 Bedrooms and 1 Suite
3 rooms: shower room, wc, double bed: €65
bathroom, wc, twin beds: €75
suite: shower room, wc, double bed. En-suite room, single bed: €75 – 2 people €100 – 3 people

Extra Bed: €15
Capacity: 11 people

Location
25km E of AVIGNON
in: Lagnes, station pick-up on
arrival/departure
Railway station: 20km
Airport: Marseille-Provence 70km

Bienvenue en France

Private Home

This charming renovated former silkworm farm has bright, comfortable bedrooms facing 2 hectares of idyllic orchard and a swimming pool. Each bedroom, all decorated with provençal fabrics, is different. In summer, hearty breakfasts and dinner are served under a majestic chestnut tree or otherwise inside by the fireplace. Thomas, a chef, prepares specialities (*bœuf braisé à la marseillaise, souris d'agneau à la provençale*) from local market produce. He gladly shares cooking tips as you prepare dinner together. Golfing days available.

Ina & Thomas FICHTEL
'Mas du Grand Jonquier', R.D. 22, 84800 LAGNES
Tel: (0) 4 90 20 90 13 Fax: (0) 4 90 20 91 18
masgrandjonquier@wanadoo.fr
www.grandjonquier.com

Facilities: private parking, extensive grounds, lounge, hosts have pets, dinner available, 100% no smoking, wheelchair access, private swimming pool, hiking, cycling, golf course 5km, fishing 5km, riversports 5km, vineyard 8km
Fluent English spoken

Directions: Exit 24 on the A7 to Avignon-Sud and then head for Apt, Sisteron on the D973 and then the D22. At the 'Petit-Palais', continue straight on for 1.8km. The house is on this road on the left and is signposted (16km from the *autoroute*).

Price Structure – 6 Bedrooms
4 rooms: television, telephone, shower room, wc, twin beds: €93
'Amandier': television, telephone, shower room, wc, twin beds, single bed: €93 – 2 people
€102 – 3 people
'Figuier': television, telephone, shower room, wc, twin beds, single bed: €93 – 2 people
€102 – 3 people

Extra Bed: €12
Capacity: 14 people

Provence – Avignon

84.12 Avignon

Residence of Outstanding Character

Chantal & Régis SANGLIER
'La Garance en Provence', 4010 route de St-Saturnin, 84250 LE THOR
Tel: (0) 4 90 33 72 78 / (0) 607 56 06 23
Fax: (0) 4 90 33 72 78
contact@garance-provence.com
www.garance-provence.com

Price Structure – 4 Bedrooms and 1 Suite
'La Calade' & 'Le Pigeonnier': shower room, wc, double bed (queen-size): €95
'Les Ocres': shower room, wc, double bed (queen-size): €110
'Les Roses': shower room, wc, 2 single beds: €95
'La Fenière': shower room, wc, double bed (queen-size). En-suite room, single bed: €110 – 2 people €130 – 3 people

Extra Bed: €20
Capacity: 11 people

Location
17km E of AVIGNON
in: Le Thor
Railway station: 14km
Airport: Avignon 8km
car essential

Bienvenue en France

This former 17th-century coaching inn has been restored with passion and it shows. Compared to other places we have visited, it is clear that Chantal and Régis are true professionals. They are also very nice and love antiques and cooking. The view from the house is outstanding with lots of space. The rooms are also spacious with a minimalist décor, in excellent taste using quality materials. Here you are near Avignon and Isle-sur-la-Sorgue, a charming village renowned for its antique fairs.

Facilities: private parking, extensive grounds, lounge, pets not accepted, internet access, dinner available, 100% no smoking, private swimming pool, hiking, cycling, fishing 4km, vineyard 4km, golf course 5km, riversports 5km
Fluent English spoken

Directions: Exit 23 Avignon-Nord from the A7. Then take the D942 towards Carpentras and the D6 on the right towards Vedène and Châteauneuf-de-Gadagne. At St-Saturnin-lès-Avignon, take the D28 Route de Pernes on the left for 2.5km. Then the D98 on the right towards Le Thor for 800m.

84.77 Avignon

Private Home

Sylvie & Yves GUEGUEN
'Le Mas de l'Estiou', 2362 route de Bédarrides, 84170 MONTEUX
Tel: (0) 4 90 66 91 83 / (0) 619 89 15 23
lestiou@wanadoo.fr
www.lestiou.com

Price Structure – 4 Bedrooms and 1 Suite
'Cigales': shower room, wc, double bed (queen-size): €80
'Amandier': lounge, bathroom, wc, double bed (queen-size), single bed: €80 – 2 people €95 – 3 people
'Dentelle': shower room, wc, twin beds: €78
'Mimosa': shower room, wc, double bed (queen-size): €78
'Suite Ventoux': lounge, shower room, wc, bathroom, double bed. En-suite room, 2 single beds: €130 – 4 people

Extra Bed: €15   **Reduction:** 01/09–30/06, 4 nights, groups   **Capacity:** 13 people

Location
20km N E of AVIGNON
in: Monteux
Railway station: 30km
Airport: Avignon 30km
car essential

In a rural location with easy access to Avignon, Orange and Carpentras, this beautiful renovated residence was once where silkworms were farmed in the 17th century. The rooms on the first floor are accessed by a large exterior staircase. Each room is pleasantly decorated and furnished with pieces in wrought iron. Breakfast is served under the age-old plane trees or in the provençal dining room. Sylvie and Yves are keen walkers and will be pleased to suggest circuit routes you can take towards Le Mont Ventoux or Les Dentelles de Montmirail.

Facilities: private parking, garden, tv lounge, hosts have pets, pets not accepted, dinner available, babies welcome, free cot, 100% no smoking, private swimming pool
Adequate English spoken

Directions: From the A7, take exit Avignon Nord towards Carpentras. Then take the D942, exit Monteux Nord. Head for Monteux Centre and then after 500m take the D87 on the right towards Bédarrides for 2km. The 'Mas' is on the right.

Location
9km E of AVIGNON
in: Morières-lès-Avignon
Airport: Avignon 5km
car essential

Private Home

Everything is spotless chez Lisa, so do not be surprised to be asked to take off your shoes to reach the bedroom. This is a little house 10km from Avignon. Lisa is very sporty and keen on hiking, and may invite you to come with her. It is amazing what you can get up to between the Mont Ventoux and the Luberon. To help you recover from that, she also organises themed stays on Asian, Alsatian and provençal cuisine.

Facilities: private parking, garden, lounge, hosts have pets, pets not accepted, 100% no smoking, hiking, cycling, interesting flora, riversports, golf course 1km, fishing 20km
Adequate English spoken

Lisa LUCASSON
'Le Clos de Morières', 11 rue Henri Manguin,
84310 MORIERES-LES-AVIGNON
Tel: (0) 4 90 33 50 29 Fax: (0) 4 90 33 50 29

Price Structure – 2 Bedrooms
along corridor shower room, wc, double bed: €60
television, along corridor shower room, wc, twin beds: €60

Capacity: 4 people

Directions: Exit 23 Avignon-Nord from the A7. Take the D942 on the right towards Carpentras and then the D6 on the right to Vedène. Go through Vedène and turn right towards Morières-lès-Avignon (Avenue d'Eguilles then the D53). When you reach Morières, at the roundabout go right towards Avignon (Route de Réalpanier). The Rue Henri Manguin is on the left.

Location
9km E of AVIGNON
in: Morières-lès-Avignon
Railway station: 5km
Airport: Avignon 5km
car essential

Private Home

At close proximity to the former city of popes stands this modern provençal-style house on a brand new *lotissement*. The guest bedroom is on the ground floor and has its own independent entrance. Here you enjoy a traditional B&B experience with a warm and friendly welcome from smiling couple Sylvie and Patrick. The living room (a little sober) with a reading corner is open to you, as is the garden.

Facilities: off-street parking, garden, tv lounge, pets not accepted, 100% no smoking, golf course, hiking, cycling, vineyard
Adequate English spoken

Patrick LE BLAY & Sylvie KIRAT
'Les Jardins du Comtat', 15 rue Daniel Sorano,
84310 MORIERES-LES-AVIGNON
Tel: (0) 4 90 22 00 34 / (0) 685 07 64 75
lesjardinsducomtat@free.fr
http://lesjardinsducomtat.free.fr

Price Structure – 1 Bedroom
shower, wc, double bed: €55

Capacity: 2 people

Directions: A7 exit Avignon Nord and head for Avignon, Morières-lès-Avignon. When opposite the 'Intermarché' supermarket, enter into the development with the entrance just on the left. Continue straight on to the roundabout and then take the second exit on the right into Rue Daniel Sorano.

Provence – Avignon

30.55 Avignon

Residence of Outstanding Character

Tehila & Jean-Victor CHERRIER
'Les Soleils', 10 place de la République,
30490 MONTFRIN
Tel: (0) 4 66 20 96 58 / (0) 608 17 18 29
Fax: (0) 4 66 58 05 90
lessoleils-montfrin@wanadoo.fr
www.lessoleils-montfrin.camargue.fr

Price Structure – 3 Bedrooms and 2 Suites
'Santa Fe' & 'Gitane': television, shower room, wc, double bed (king-size): €90
'Marrakech': television, shower room, wc, twin beds: €90
'Suite Blanche': lounge, television, telephone, bathroom, wc, shower, double bed (king-size). En-suite room, twin beds: €150 – 4 people
'Suite Andalouse': lounge, television, telephone, shower room, wc, double bed (king-size). En-suite room, double bed: €150 – 4 people

Extra Bed: €25
Reduction: 15/10–15/03, 7 nights, groups
Capacity: 14 people

Location
22km S W of AVIGNON
in: Montfrin, station pick-up on arrival/departure
Railway station: 20km
Airport: Montpellier-Méditerranée 50km

Bienvenue en France

On a historic village square, close to Avignon and the Pont du Gard, is this 19th-century *maison bourgeoise*. With a real grasp of colour, Tehila and Jean-Victor have brought the bedrooms to life. Voyage through scorching lands: from 'Gitane' (solid wood panelling) to 'Santa Fé' (ochre walls, Navarro Indian style, an amazing shower room) to Andalusia and southern Morocco (*moucharabieh*, arabesques and Moorish arches). Somewhere for everyone! Relax by the Mexican pool, in the Cuban lounge or sip cocktails at the bar.

Facilities: private parking, garden, tv lounge, pets not accepted, dinner available, closed: 1/01–31/01, private swimming pool, hunting, fishing, mushroom-picking, bird-watching, hiking, vineyard, riversports 15km, gliding 20km, golf course 25km, interesting flora 30km
Fluent English spoken

Directions: A9 exit 23 to Remoulins. Then the D986 towards Beaucaire to Montfrin and it is on the main square.

30.53 Avignon

Residence of Outstanding Character

Pierre DUCRUET
'Bize de la Tour', 2 place du Portail,
30210 REMOULINS
Tel: (0) 4 66 22 39 33 / (0) 664 96 19 54
Fax: (0) 4 66 63 97 25
2.dupartet@wanadoo.fr
www.bizedelatour.com

Price Structure – 3 Bedrooms
'Louis XIII': television, telephone, bathroom, wc, shower, four-poster double bed: €75
'Aux Dais': television, telephone, shower room, wc, twin beds: €75
'Grand-Mère': television, telephone, bathroom, wc, twin beds: €75

Extra Bed: €15
Reduction: 7 nights
Capacity: 6 people

Location
22km W of AVIGNON
in: Remoulins, station pick-up on arrival/departure
Railway station: 20km
Airport: Nîmes-Arles-Camargue 30km

Bienvenue en France

In the historic heart of Remoulins, 3km from the Pont du Gard, is a 19th-century bourgeois house by a 12th-century monument. There are two living areas; one is more intimate with 19th-century décor. A stone stairway (Napoleon III) leads to the 'Louis XIII' room with a luxurious canopy over the bed. Admire the fireplace with Aubagne tiles, period furniture and a spacious bathroom. Continue up to the 1900s 'Grand-Mère' room, after passing remnants of a medieval tower and terrace. A quality service from the serenely efficient Pierre.

Facilities: private parking, lounge, pets not accepted, fishing, hiking, cycling, interesting flora, riversports, vineyard, golf course 10km, interesting flora 30km, lake watersports 50km
Fluent English spoken

Directions: A9 exit 23 Remoulins and head for Pont du Gard. The house is in the centre of the village, opposite the church.

Location
19km N W of AVIGNON
in: St-Laurent-des-Arbres
Railway station: 18km
Airport: Avignon 20km
car essential

Private Home

An easy house to find, on the edge of a little village and a pine forest close to vineyards and popular tourist spots. Modest, but a respectable size and pleasant, offering a ground-floor room which leads out to a pretty rose garden. Breakfast is served on the terrace or inside in the family lounge. Over a welcome drink – fruit juice from the monastery – Claire will happily enlighten you about her region and share her passion for classical and Celtic music. Simplicity, comfort and quiet at very reasonable prices for the area.

Claire VERMEE
'Au Jardin de Claire', impasse du Nizon, chemin
de la Cabanette,
30126 ST-LAURENT-DES-ARBRES
Tel: (0) 4 66 82 67 53

Facilities: private parking, garden, tv lounge, pets not accepted, dinner available, babies welcome, free cot, 100% no smoking, wheelchair access, hiking, vineyard, riversports 15km
Basic English spoken

Price Structure – 1 Suite
wheelchair access, bathroom, wc, double bed. En-suite room, single bed: €60 – 2 people
€90 – 3 people

Directions: A9 between Orange and Nîmes, exit 22 towards Bagnols-sur-Cèze. N580, for 5km to the roundabout towards St-Laurent-des-Arbres. Turn left here and then left again down the Chemin de la Lauze opposite 'La Maison des Vins'. Continue for 800m then turn left and straight away right into Chemin de la Cabanette. The Impasse du Nizon is 300m on the right. Second house on the left.

Reduction: 3 nights, children
Capacity: 3 people

Location
4km N E of AVIGNON
in: Villeneuve-lez-Avignon
Railway station: 6km
Airport: Nîmes-Arles-Camargue 20km

Bienvenue en France

Private Home

Clinging to the hillside, this newly built house overhangs Villeneuve-lez-Avignon with a magnificent view of Le Mont Ventoux, Le Fort St. André and Les Dentelles de Montmirail. The bedrooms are on the ground floor with their own access onto the terrace in the garden with a barbecue and swimming pool. Very convenient for visiting Avignon and the surrounding area.

Dominique HANOT
93 bis avenue Paul Ravoux,
30400 VILLENEUVE-LEZ-AVIGNON
Tel: (0) 4 32 70 22 45 / (0) 609 56 12 68
Fax: (0) 4 32 70 22 45
dominiquehanot@hotmail.fr

Facilities: private parking, garden, lounge, hosts have pets, kitchen, babies welcome, free cot, wheelchair access, 1 shared shower room, wc, closed: 01/08–15/08, private swimming pool, vineyard 6km, hiking 10km, golf course 10km, riversports 20km
Fluent English spoken

Price Structure – 3 Bedrooms
3 rooms: double bed: €50

Directions: From Avignon, cross the Daladier bridge in the left lane, head to l'Ile-de-la-Barthelasse, Villeneuve-lez-Avignon, then Les Angles. At the top of the hill (fourth set of lights), turn right into Avenue Pasteur.

Extra Bed: €10
Reduction: 5 nights
Capacity: 6 people

Provence – Avignon

84.11 Carpentras

Private Home

Marie-Luce & Valérie RICQUART
'Moulin d'Antelon', 84410 CRILLON-LE-BRAVE
Tel: (0) 4 90 62 44 89 / (0) 632 27 55 86
Fax: (0) 4 90 62 44 90
moulin-dantelon@wanadoo.fr
www.moulin-dantelon.com

Price Structure – 5 Bedrooms and 1 Suite
'Le Tilleul' & 'La Terrasse': television, bathroom, wc,
double bed (queen-size): €67
'La Bergerie': television, bathroom, wc, double bed
(queen-size), single bed: €88 – 3 people
'Le Paroir': television, shower room, wc, double bed,
single bed: €88 – 3 people
'Le Foulon': television, shower room, wc, double bed
(queen-size), 3 single beds: €145 – 5 people
'Foin chaude': bathroom, wc, double bed (queen-size).
En-suite room, washbasin, twin beds: €120 – 4 people

Extra Bed: €25   **Capacity:** 19 people

Location
13km N E of CARPENTRAS
in: Crillon-le-Brave
car essential

We have total confidence in Valérie who is taking over from her mum, Marie-Luce, who is still around to give her the benefit of her long experience of doing B&B. This is God's Own Country: at the foot of the Mont Ventoux (great cycling country with some fantastic hiking routes); lots of typical villages; famous wines such as Beaumes de Venise and famous towns like Avignon and Vaison-la-Romaine. Les Gorges de la Nesque are a must. This place is ideal for children, with big rooms and a large pool. Excellent value for this area.

Facilities: private parking, garden, tv lounge, pets not accepted, dinner available, babies welcome, free cot, closed: 1/12–1/03, private swimming pool, hiking, cycling, interesting flora, golf course 25km
Adequate English spoken

Directions: Exit 22 from the A7. Head for Carpentras and the D974 towards Bedoin. DO NOT GO TO CRILLON, but follow the Bedoin road and the signs to the 'Moulin'.

84.47 Carpentras

Private Home

Marianne MYIN
'Siloé', Le Canadel, 84570 MORMOIRON
Tel: (0) 4 90 61 87 67 / (0) 608 43 39 70
jmyin@club-internet.fr
http://perso.club-internet.fr/jmyin

Price Structure – 3 Bedrooms
2 rooms: shower room, wc, double bed: €65
third room: shower room, wc, twin beds, single bed:
€65 – 2 people €80 – 3 people

Extra Bed: €10
Capacity: 7 people

Location
11km E of CARPENTRAS
in: Mormoiron
Railway station: 30km
Airport: Avignon 30km
car essential

Bienvenue en **France**

If you choose Marianne and Jacques' place, you will get a warm welcome, peace and quiet, wonderful countryside and a view over Mont Ventoux, as well as use of the swimming pool. A great place to unwind and recharge your batteries. They organise weekly *Conversation Française* packages, which include excursions throughout Provence. An excellent way to improve your French and to get to know this area.

Facilities: off-street parking, extensive grounds, tv lounge, hosts have pets, pets not accepted, dinner available, babies welcome, free cot, closed: 15/12–15/01, private swimming pool, hiking, cycling, fishing, mushroom-picking, lake watersports, golf course 20km, riversports 20km
Adequate English spoken

Directions: At Carpentras, take the D942 towards Mormoiron, Sault. When you reach Mormoiron, continue towards Sault for 300m. Turn right at the sign 'Domaine des Anges' and go towards Le Canadel for 2km. At fire hydrant 21, the sign to 'Siloé' is on the right.

Provence – Carpentras

Location
18km N E of CAVAILLON
in: Gordes
Railway station: 45km
Airport: Marseille-Provence 50km
car essential

Bienvenue en France

⭐ ⭐

Residence of Outstanding Character

Escape the 'war of the walls' in Gordes and ironically, take the road to Murs. This old farm complex houses family members, with guests accommodated in the middle part. Lovely Christine is a mine of local information. The rooms are comfortable with access to a living room (and kitchen for 4+ nights). Gastronomes should avoid Wednesdays, as most listed restaurants are closed, except Le Crillon which is fantastic. You walk to Christine and Robert's house for breakfast via their garden. Robert is a landscape gardener and it shows!

Facilities: off-street parking, extensive grounds, lounge, pets not accepted, kitchen, 100% no smoking, 2 nights minimum stay: 01/01–01/04, mushroom-picking, hiking, cycling, vineyard 6km, fishing 15km, riversports 15km, golf course 20km
Adequate English spoken

Directions: In Gordes, D15 towards Murs. After 5km the entrance is up the drive on the left. On arrival continue to the reception (follow sign) at the main house to get your key.

Christine & Robert GUILLEN
'La Guillone', Murs, 84220 GORDES
Tel: (0) 4 90 72 06 43 Fax: (0) 4 90 72 06 43
laguillone@free.fr
www.guillone-luberon.com

Price Structure – 3 Apartments
'Genêt': lounge, kitchen, shower room, wc, four-poster double bed, single bed: €72 – 2 people €94 – 3 people
'Garance': lounge, kitchen, shower room, wc, double bed (queen-size): €72
'Suite Bergerie': lounge, kitchen, shower room, wc, double bed. En-suite room, 2 single beds: €75 – 2 people €150 – 4 people

Extra Bed: €25
Reduction: 16/11–31/03
Capacity: 9 people

Location
20km N E of VAISON-LA-ROMAINE
in: Buis-les-Baronnies, station pick-up on arrival/departure
Railway station: 64km
Airport: Avignon 64km
car essential

2008

Bienvenue en France

⭐ ⭐ ⭐ ⭐

Residence of Outstanding Character

'L'Ancienne Cure' formerly belonged to the bishopric of Valence and dates from the 16th century. It is squeezed into the heart of the village and exudes charm, with its small priest's garden, a haven of quiet, ideal for meditation, relaxation or dining in the shade of the old lime tree. There is a hot tub outside under the palm trees, and a sunny terrace next to a very rare rose bush. The stylish bedrooms with their luxury bathrooms are very romantic, and will tempt you to stay longer. On sale: olive oil from Nyons, apricot nectar and honey.

Facilities: private parking, garden, tv lounge, hosts have pets, dinner available, babies welcome, free cot, 100% no smoking, closed: 05/12–28/03, hiking, cycling, fishing 1km, lake watersports 1km, vineyard 2km, gliding 69km
Adequate English spoken

Directions: At Vaison-la-Romaine, take the D938 towards Carpentras for 3km. Then turn left onto the D54 to Entrechaux, Mollans-sur-Ouvèze and Buis-les-Baronnies. The house is in the centre of the village, near the church.

Martine & Eric FRAIPONT
'L'Ancienne Cure', 2 rue du Paroir,
26170 BUIS-LES-BARONNIES
Tel: (0) 4 75 28 22 08 Fax: (0) 4 75 28 22 08
contact@ancienne-cure.com
www.ancienne-cure.com

Price Structure – 6 Bedrooms
'Papillon': television, shower room, wc, double bed (queen-size): €67
'Petites Fleurs': television, shower room, wc, four-poster double bed: €80
'Peintre': television, shower room, wc, twin beds: €87
'Montagne-Mezzanine': television, shower room, wc, 2 double beds, single bed: €142 – 5 people
'l'Orientale': lounge, television, kitchen, shower room, wc, double bed (king-size): €95
plus 1 room

Extra Bed: €20
Reduction: 15/09–04/12, 6 nights, groups
Capacity: 15 people

Provence – Cavaillon, Vaison-la-Romaine

26.44 Vaison-la-Romaine

Private Home

Location
28km N E of VAISON-LA-ROMAINE
in: Vercoiran
Railway station: 8km
Airport: Marseille-Provence 160km
car essential

Bienvenue en France

This is a former sheep pen, nestling on the hillside amongst the lavender fields and apricot orchards. There is a fantastic view over the surrounding countryside from the terrace and swimming pool. Nicole is a dietician, so knows all about a healthy lifestyle to make you feel good, and you can sense it here. This place represents excellent value for money, given the location and the service provided.

Facilities: off-street parking, garden, pets not accepted, kitchen, babies welcome, free cot, 100% no smoking, closed: 01/11–31/03, private swimming pool, hiking, cycling, fishing, interesting flora 7km, riversports 7km, vineyard 10km, gliding 15km, winter sports 30km
Adequate English spoken

Nicole GIROD
'La Bergerie du Lou', L'Hubac, Vercoiran,
26170 BUIS-LES-BARONNIES
Tel: (0) 4 75 28 16 95 / (0) 685 40 83 36
girodnicole@aol.com
www.bergerie-du-lou.com

Price Structure – 3 Bedrooms
and 1 Apartment
'Suite': shower room, wc, double bed, cot. Along corridor room, wc, twin beds: €55 – 2 people
€95 – 4 people
room: shower room, wc, double bed: €50
apartment: kitchen, shower room, wc, double bed:
€55

Extra Bed: €16
Reduction: 2 nights
Capacity: 8 people

Directions: At Vaison-la-Romaine, take the D938 towards Carpentras for 3km. Then turn left onto the D54 to Entrechaux, Mollans-sur-Ouvèze and Buis-les-Baronnies. Continue on the D546 towards Séderon, as far as Le Moulin-Vercoiran. Cross the River Ouvèze on the right, and follow signs to 'La Bergerie du Lou'.

84.64 Valréas

Private Home

Location
VALREAS
in: Valréas
car essential

Bienvenue en France

Colette and Patrick will be delighted to welcome you to their pleasant house with a swimming pool. It is located within the 'Enclave des Papes', at the crossroads of Nyons, Vaison-la-Romaine, Orange and Avignon, and is the perfect base for exploring the Drôme, Provence or even the Ardèche. This region is full of festivals and artistic events, a feast for lovers of music and theatre. There are fields of lavender, olive groves and vineyards with famous names. Explore them on foot or by bike.

Colette & Patrick LORION
'Diamantina', route de Richerenches,
84600 VALREAS
Tel: (0) 4 90 35 53 21 Fax: (0) 4 90 35 53 21
diamantina.pc@wanadoo.fr
http://diamantina.free.fr

Price Structure – 2 Bedrooms
'Daffodil': shower room, wc, double bed: €72,20
'Abricot': shower room, wc, double bed: €72,20

Extra Bed: €38,89
Reduction: 8 nights
Capacity: 4 people

Facilities: off-street parking, garden, tv lounge, hosts have pets, 100% no smoking, private swimming pool
Fluent English spoken

Directions: From Valréas, head west on the D18, and turn left towards Richerenches. 'Diamantina' is on the left.

Location
5km W of VALREAS
in: Grillon
car essential

Private Home

This is more a holiday centre than a B&B and has 17 rooms, but Jacques' personality swung it for us. It is great for a group of friends or large families. There is a pool, a large 6000 square metre orchard and sleepy countryside. Grignan, with its links to Madame de Sévigné is nearby. Jacques is a yoga teacher, has led a very varied and full life and is a great host. The rooms are basically furnished and inexpensive.

Jacques FOREST
'Le Mas du Sillot', Les Plans, 84600 GRILLON
Tel: (0) 4 90 28 44 00 Fax: (0) 4 90 28 44 19
lemasdusillot@wanadoo.fr
www.giteprovence.net

Facilities: off-street parking, extensive grounds, tv lounge, dinner available, wheelchair access, private swimming pool, mushroom-picking, hiking, cycling, golf course 12km

Price Structure – 17 Bedrooms
3 rooms: shower room, wc, twin beds: €58
3 rooms: shower room, wc, double bed, single bed: €58 – 2 people €87 – 3 people
4 rooms: shower room, wc, 3 single beds (child-size): €58 – 2 people €87 – 3 people
2 rooms: shower room, wc, 4 single beds (2 child-size): €58 – 2 people €116 – 4 people
1 room: shower room, wc, 6 single beds (4 child-size): €58 – 2 people €174 – 6 people
1 room: shower room, wc, 3 single beds: €58 – 2 people €87 – 3 people
plus 3 rooms

Directions: Exit 18 Montélimar-Sud from the A7. Continue south and take the D541 on the left towards Nyons. Between Grignan and Valréas, after Grillon, turn left to Les Plans.

Reduction: groups   **Capacity:** 55 people

Location
9km S of VALREAS
in: Visan, station pick-up on arrival/departure

Bienvenue en France

Private Home

Bernard seduces the ladies with his smile and his cooking and with his wife Bernadette, they make a lovely couple. Their house is in the heart of the countryside and you can look at the uninterrupted view from the terrace for hours. The small room is quaint and has its own fridge. This area is known as the 'Popes' Enclave'. No fools they, with the olives from the Drôme Provençal, the vines of the Comtat Venaissin producing the famous Rasteau wine and the sublime Beaumes de Venise. There are also Roman ruins to visit.

Bernadette & Bernard MARKOVICOVA
'Les Oliviers de Claron', Quartier Claron,
84820 VISAN
Tel: (0) 4 90 41 93 40

Facilities: off-street parking, garden, tv lounge, hosts have pets, dinner available, babies welcome, free cot, 100% no smoking, hiking, cycling, golf course 25km

Price Structure – 1 Bedroom
television, shower room, wc, double bed: €60

Extra Bed: €20
Capacity: 2 people

Directions: Exit 19 Bollène from the A7 towards Nyons. After Tulette on the D94, take the D576 on the left. Bernard will come and meet you in Visan if you give him a call.

Provence – Valréas

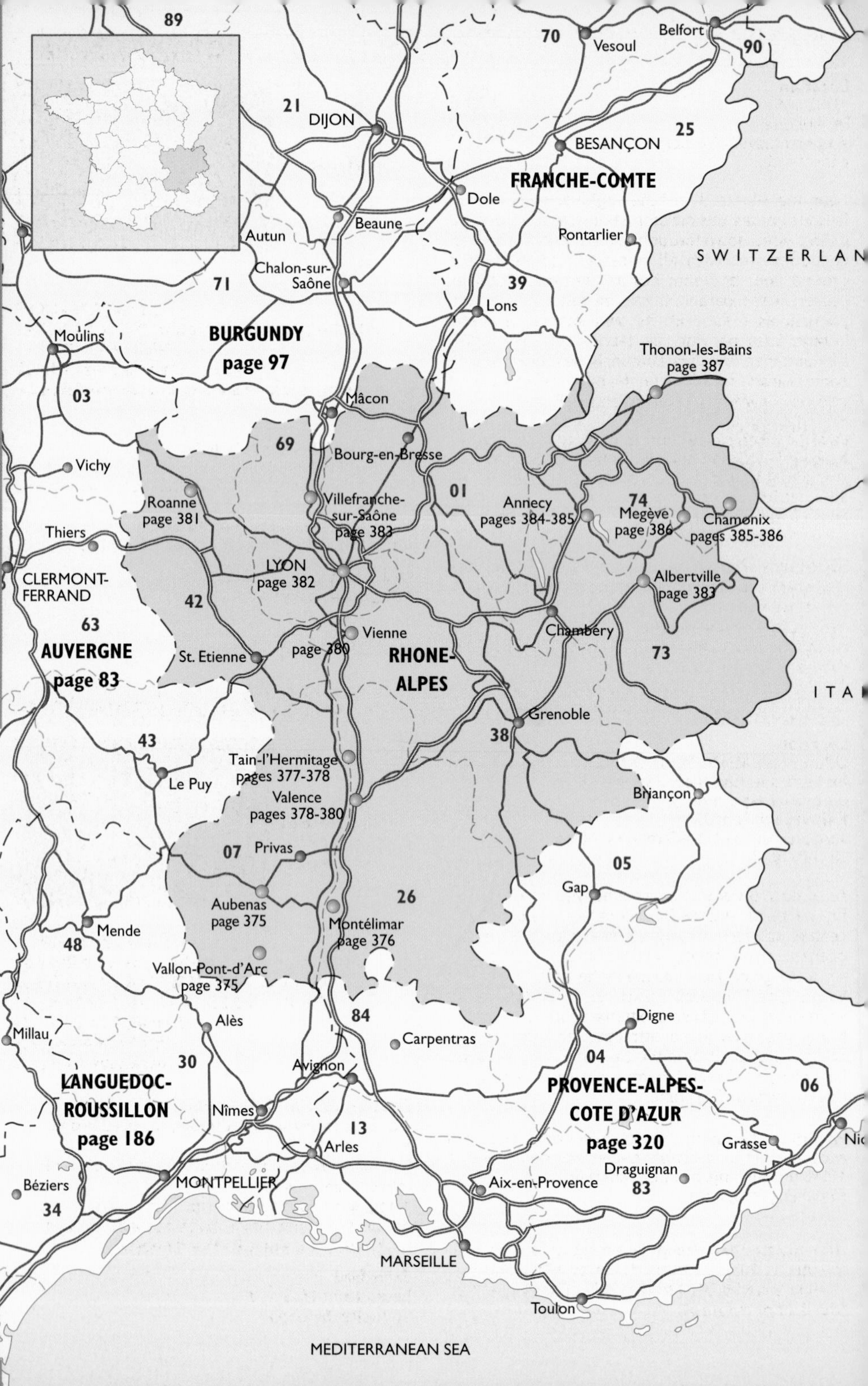

89

21 DIJON

70 Vesoul

Belfort

90

Autun

Beaune

Dole

BESANÇON

25

FRANCHE-COMTE

Pontarlier

SWITZERLAN

Moulins

71

Chalon-sur-Saône

39

Lons

Thonon-les-Bains
page 387

03

BURGUNDY
page 97

Mâcon

Vichy

69

Bourg-en-Bresse

01

74

Thiers

Roanne
page 381

Villefranche-
sur-Saône
page 383

Annecy
pages 384-385

Megève
page 386

Chamonix
pages 385-386

CLERMONT-
FERRAND

42

LYON
page 382

Albertville
page 383

63

**AUVERGNE
page 83**

St. Etienne

page 380

Vienne

**RHONE-
ALPES**

Chambéry

73

43

Tain-l'Hermitage
pages 377-378

38

Grenoble

Le Puy

Valence
pages 378-380

Briançon

48

07 Privas

26

05

Gap

Mende

Aubenas
page 375

Montélimar
page 376

Vallon-Pont-d'Arc
page 375

84

Digne

04

Millau

30

Alès

Carpentras

**PROVENCE-ALPES-
COTE D'AZUR
page 320**

06

**LANGUEDOC-
ROUSSILLON
page 186**

Avignon

Nîmes

13

Arles

Grasse

Ni

Béziers

MONTPELLIER

Aix-en-Provence

Draguignan

83

34

MARSEILLE

ITA

DIJON

Beaune

Moulins

Toulon

MEDITERRANEAN SEA

Location
AUBENAS
in: Aubenas
Airport: Lyon-St Exupéry 170km
car essential

Private Home

Near the Monts d'Ardèche regional park and its famous gorges, this old stone house in the vines has been passed down through generations. The interior is modest yet with all necessary comforts. The ground floor bedroom has its own entrance with access to the garden. It can be rented for a supplement as a flat with its own kitchen area and lounge. Suzanne, who has taught and undertaken humanitarian missions abroad, is delighted to welcome visitors and advise on the outdoor activities on offer: rock-climbing, kayaking and walks.

Suzanne DELAUCHE
Le Moulon, chemin du Moulin, 07200 AUBENAS
Tel: (0) 687 13 87 33
suzanne.delauche@wanadoo.fr
http://perso.wanadoo.fr/suzanne.delauche

Facilities: private parking, garden, tv lounge, hosts have pets, kitchen, babies welcome, free cot, 100% no smoking, 1 shared shower room, wc, vineyard, hiking 3km, cycling 5km, riversports 15km
Fluent English spoken

Price Structure – 3 Bedrooms and 1 Apartment
lounge, television, kitchen, shower room, wc, twin beds: €65
2 rooms: single bed: €35 – 1 person
television, shower room, wc, twin beds: €45

Reduction: 01/09–15/06
Capacity: 6 people

Directions: From Montélimar N102 to just before Aubenas. Just after St-Didier, at the roundabout, head to Aubenas, and then at the next roundabout, take exit ZA Ponson-Moulon. Again at a further roundabout take the second exit on the right. The house is the first one on the right.

Location
20km W of VALLON-PONT-D-ARC
in: Berrias-et-Casteljau, station pick-up on arrival/departure
Railway station: 35km
Airport: Nîmes-Arles-Camargue 60km
car essential

Residence of Outstanding Character

As we go to press this home has not yet been classified, but will be shortly. For Sabrina, in her converted 17th-century silkworm factory, the keywords are: a smile, peace of mind, family, holidays, welcome, respect. . . we could go on. Here you are in the Ardèche, close to Vallon-Pont-d'Arc, well known to all enthusiasts of whitewater sports. Even if extreme sports are not your thing, this river is so attractive and pretty well undisturbed, apart from the canoeists. The bedrooms have style, comfort and charm and you will be happy in this very welcoming home.

Sabrina & Cyril GARCIA
'La Mais'Ange', route des Vans, Le Village de Berrias, 07460 BERRIAS-ET-CASTELJAU
Tel: (0) 4 75 39 84 21 / (0) 609 34 03 02
Fax: (0) 4 75 39 84 21
info@lamaisange.fr
www.lamaisange.fr

Facilities: tv lounge, hosts have pets, pets not accepted, dinner available, babies welcome, free cot, 100% no smoking, private swimming pool
Fluent English spoken

Price Structure – 2 Bedrooms and 1 Suite
'Soleiado': television, bathroom, wc, double bed (queen-size): €90
'Romance': television, bathroom, wc, double bed (queen-size): €90
'Campagne': lounge, television, shower room, wc, double bed (queen-size). En-suite room, 2 single beds: €95 – 2 people €135 – 4 people

Extra Bed: €20
Reduction: 1/10–1/05
Capacity: 8 people

Directions: From Vallon-Pont-d'Arc go to Aubenas on the D579 then turn left on to the D111 and continue on the D104 towards Alès. The village is on the right of this road.

26.49 Montélimar

Private Home

Location
23km E of MONTELIMAR
in: Le Poët-Laval
Railway station: 25km
Airport: Lyon-St Exupéry 150km
car essential

Marie-Elise & Vincent BETTON
'Au Jardin des Jeanne', Combe Reynaud,
26160 LE POET-LAVAL
Tel: (0) 4 75 91 01 68
aujardindesjeanne@wanadoo.fr
http://perso.orange.fr/aujardindesjeanne/

Price Structure – 2 Bedrooms
'Ancolie': wheelchair access, twin beds: €49
'Valériane': wheelchair access, shower room, wc,
double bed: €49

Extra Bed: €10
Reduction: 7 nights
Capacity: 4 people

On a slope, with views over wooded hills stretching all the way to the foothills of the Alps, is this contemporary house. The modest guest bedrooms are in a wooden-framed extension and have been decorated with care. Both rooms have an independent entrance and air-conditioning. An extra special regional breakfast can be served on request (supplement payable). You are deep in the countryside but close to the village of Poët-Laval, considered to be one of the most beautiful in France.

Facilities: off-street parking, garden, lounge, hosts have pets, dinner available, wheelchair access, hunting, fishing, hiking, interesting flora, cycling 5km, golf course 20km, gliding 30km, vineyard 30km, riversports 40km, winter sports 60km
Fluent English spoken

Directions: From Montélimar D540 towards Dieulefit for 15km. Pass La Bégude-de-Mazenc and the place called 'Labry'. Continue for 1km and turn left towards Serre Crue. The house is 10m along on the right (signposted).

Helpline

You are not on your own.

When in France our **HELPLINE** is available to you if you have a problem with a reservation.

Dial 01 34 19 90 00

From your mobile phone or outside of France: **+33 1 34 19 90 00**

Office hours only.

Residence of Outstanding Character

Rhône-Alpes – Tain-l'Hermitage

Location
4km E of TAIN-L'HERMITAGE
in: Chanos-Curson
Railway station: 13km
Airport: Lyon-St Exupéry 90km
car essential

On the Route des Vins, in the centre of a sleepy village opposite the church, this much-travelled couple have created an oasis of cool, culture and comfort inside this former 18th-century silkworm factory passed down through the family. Enter through the enormous porch, worn away by centuries of passing cart-loads of hay and emerge into the courtyard with its swimming pool, spring and shady plane trees. After an *apéritif* in the wine cellar you must stay for dinner.

Marie-Françoise & Claude MERLE
'Domaine des Mirabiaux', chemin du Facteur,
Chanos-Curson, 26600 TAIN L'HERMITAGE
Tel: (0) 4 75 07 36 36 / (0) 676 81 12 80
mfmerle@club-internet.fr
madeinchanos.com

Facilities: private parking, garden, tv lounge, pets not accepted, dinner available, 100% no smoking, wc, 16 years old minimum age, closed: 15/12–15/01, private swimming pool, vineyard
Fluent English spoken

Price Structure – 3 Bedrooms
1 room: telephone, along corridor bathroom, single bed: €45 – 1 person
1 room: along corridor shower, double bed: €55
'Loft': lounge, television, shower room, wc, double bed, twin beds: €85 – 2 people €120 – 4 people

Extra Bed: €20
Reduction: 7 nights
Capacity: 7 people

Directions: A7, exit 13 Tain-l'Hermitage. Join the D532 and turn right and continue to Chanos-Curson. Opposite the church, take Rue du Rioux for 40m and then the small lane on the right (Chemin du Facteur).

Private Home

Location
7km N of TAIN-L'HERMITAGE
in: Chantemerle-les-Blés
Railway station: 6km
Airport: Lyon-St Exupéry 100km
car essential

Bienvenue en France

This former flourmill is situated in grounds crossed by a small canal and a trout-fishing lake. Odile has just retired from teaching English and her only desire now is to enjoy her passion for making friends and meeting other nationalities in the relaxed atmosphere of her home. There is a kitchenette in the studio or a snack-bar on the property (outside in summer and inside the mill in winter). A four-person gîte is also available to rent weekly.

Odile BOUYON
'Le Vieux Moulin', Quartier Grenouillet,
26600 CHANTEMERLE-LES-BLES
Tel: (0) 4 75 07 46 31 Fax: (0) 4 75 07 46 31
odile.bouyon@wanadoo.fr

Facilities: private parking, extensive grounds, pets not accepted, 100% no smoking, 16 years old minimum age, hiking, cycling, fishing, bird-watching 6km, golf course 10km, lake watersports 10km, mushroom-picking 30km, interesting flora 50km, riversports 60km
Fluent English spoken

Price Structure – 1 Apartment
studio: lounge, television, kitchen, shower room, wc, washbasin, twin beds: €47

Capacity: 2 people

Directions: From the A7, exit 13, Tain-l'Hermitage. Head towards Tain and after about 1km, turn right onto the D109 towards Chantemerle-les-Blés. 'Le Vieux Moulin' is on this road before you enter the village on the right, opposite a campsite. The large car park is a little further on, on the right.

07.29 Tain-l'Hermitage

Private Home

Bienvenue en France

Location
7km N of TAIN-L'HERMITAGE
in: Vernolet, station pick-up on arrival/departure
Railway station: 10km
Airport: Valence 35km
car essential

From the Rhone Valley head up between the vineyards of St-Joseph to arrive at this vast, impressive contemporary property. The breathtaking view from the house will leave you stunned. There is a large communal room and a terrace with a pool. The bedrooms, each different and with a terrace, offer a good level of comfort and extra facilities: fridge, microwave, safe, internet access. Mathias is at your service and a keen advocate of the local wines.

Mathias SERERO
'Les Terrasses du Vernolet', Vernolet, 07610 VION
Tel: (0) 4 75 06 50 66 / (0) 681 73 71 29
Fax: (0) 4 75 06 50 67
levernolet@orange.fr
www.levernolet.com

Price Structure – 3 Bedrooms
'Le Cheval': television, bathroom, wc, double bed (queen-size): €120
'L'Eléphant': television, along corridor bathroom, wc, double bed: €100
'La Gazelle': television, along corridor bathroom, wc, shower, double bed: €100

Capacity: 6 people

Facilities: off-street parking, extensive grounds, tv lounge, internet access, dinner available, 2 years old minimum age, private swimming pool, mushroom-picking, hiking, cycling, vineyard, fishing 10km, riversports 10km, golf course 23km
Fluent English spoken

Directions: On the A7 Valence-Lyon, exit 13 towards Tournon then the N86 towards Vienne for 7km to Vion. On the main village square, head up the road that lies between the bakery and the post office towards Vernolet for 4km. At the junction with Vernolet signed in both directions, take the right one and continue for 400m. The house is on the left.

07.24 Valence

Private Home

Bienvenue en France

Location
18km W of VALENCE
in: Boffres, station pick-up on arrival/departure
Railway station: 22km

At the gateway to the Parc Regional des Monts d'Ardèche, high up on the hillside amid chestnut trees, is this completely renovated former farm. Here, is everything you need for a revitalising stay, so take advantage of the countryside that lends itself to walks and mountain-biking, or enjoy the peace and quiet and just relax. Be impressed by the enthusiasm and motivation of your hosts for organising all sorts of activities for you, and how the local produce is enhanced by Jean-Luc's culinary skills. Horses can be accommodated!

Sandrine & Jean-Luc BROTTES
'Domaine de Reiller', Reiller, 07440 BOFFRES
Tel: (0) 4 75 58 15 14 / (0) 675 36 86 21
domaine.reiller@wanadoo.fr
www.reiller.com

Facilities: private parking, extensive grounds, tv lounge, hosts have pets, dinner available, kitchen, babies welcome, free cot, wheelchair access, private swimming pool, private tennis court, hiking, cycling, fishing, hunting, interesting flora, mushroom-picking, vineyard 10km, riversports 15km
Fluent English spoken

Price Structure – 4 Bedrooms and 1 Suite
'Lucie': wheelchair access, shower room, wc, washbasin, double bed: €60
'Matis','Flora' & 'Rosalie': wheelchair access, lounge, shower room, wc, washbasin, double bed, 2 single beds (child-size): €60 – 2 people €84 – 4 people
suite 'Léa': lounge, shower room, wc, double bed. En-suite room 2 sets of twin beds: €60 – 2 people €108 – 6 people

Extra Bed: €12
Capacity: 20 people

Directions: From Valence, D533 direction Le Puy-en-Velay for 12km to the crossroads of Leyrisse then the D14 on the left towards Vernoux-en-Vivarais for 6km. By the kilometre marker stone turn right and follow the signs until you reach the 'Domaine de Reiller'.

Location
10km S of VALENCE
in: Charmes-sur-Rhône, station pick-up
on arrival/departure
Railway station: 10km
Airport: Lyon-St Exupéry 110km
car essential

Private Home

High up in the picturesque village of Charmes-sur-Rhône, tranquil amongst vineyards and orchards, is this contemporary modern-style house. The white communal room is decorated with splashes of colour and bathed in sunlight from the large bay windows open onto the garden. Breakfast can be served here or on the terrace under the plane trees. The two bedrooms are independent, spacious and set out on different levels with a cosy mini-mezzanine. Comfortable bathrooms with chequered coloured tiles. Their cuisine is based on produce from the garden.

Christine & Jean-Marc HOTOLEAN
'Les Charmes', 966 route des Ménafauries,
07800 CHARMES-SUR-RHONE
Tel: (0) 4 75 60 90 69 / (0) 661 48 73 21
jean-marc.hotolean@wanadoo.fr
www.les-charmes.com

Facilities: private parking, garden, lounge, dinner available, babies welcome, free cot, 100% no smoking, closed: 01–31/01, private swimming pool, hiking, cycling, bird-watching 6km, vineyard 8km, golf course 15km, riversports 60km
Adequate English spoken

Price Structure – 2 Bedrooms
2 rooms: shower room, wc, washbasin, double bed, 2 single beds: €70 – 2 people €110 – 4 people

Extra Bed: €20
Reduction: 7 nights
Capacity: 8 people

Directions: Charmes-sur-Rhône is on the N86. At Valence cross the River Rhône and take the N86 towards Privas, Aubenas. As you enter Charmes, at the traffic lights right on to D379 then on to the Route des Crêtes and then left on to the Route des Ménafauries.

Location
16km E of VALENCE
in: Châteaudouble
Railway station: 18km
Airport: Valence 6km
car essential

Bienvenue
en
France

Private Home

Stop at Josette's place in this village house and you are on the doorstep of the beautiful Vercors. Josette is retired and loves travel, reading, music and singing.

Josette DUCOIN
'Place de la Fontaine', 26120 CHATEAUDOUBLE
Tel: (0) 4 75 59 80 26 / (0) 674 79 96 64
josette.ducoin@freesbee.fr
http://josette.ducoin.free.fr

Facilities: private parking, pets not accepted, babies welcome, free cot, 100% no smoking, wc, hiking, cycling, fishing, mushroom-picking, interesting flora 8km, gliding 10km, golf course 20km, hunting 20km, winter sports 20km, riversports 30km

Price Structure – 1 Bedroom
shower, double bed, single bed: €45 – 2 people
€55 – 3 people

Reduction: 2 nights
Capacity: 3 people

Directions: From the A7 take exit Valence-Sud towards Grenoble. After 5km turn right onto D68 towards Chabeuil. On entering the town turn left towards Romans and take the D68 again on the right, continuing towards Le Vercors for 5km. Châteaudouble is on the right.

Rhône-Alpes – Valence

07.30 Valence

Private Home

Bienvenue en France

Nathalie RICHERAND
**'La Ferme de Prémaure', route de Lamastre,
07240 VERNOUX-EN-VIVARAIS**
Tel: (0) 4 75 58 63 97 Fax: (0) 4 75 58 63 97
accueil@premaure.com
www.premaure.com

Price Structure – 4 Bedrooms and 1 Suite
'Campanules', 'Rosier' & 'Genet': shower room, wc,
double bed: €68
'Tilleul': shower room, wc, double bed, twin beds:
€68 – 2 people €99 – 4 people
'Moissonneurs': shower room, wc, double bed, single
bed. En-suite room, shower room, wc, twin beds:
€68 – 2 people €99 – 5 people

Reduction: 4 nights, groups
Capacity: 15 people

Location
30km W of VALENCE
in: Vernoux-en-Vivarais, station pick-up
on arrival/departure
Railway station: 35km
car essential

By the Monts d'Ardèche regional park, revitalise
yourself on this isolated property of woodland and
meadows. A farmhouse in local stone, it offers modest-
sized rooms, some with mezzanine floors. The attraction is the great outdoors and breakfasts (organic rustic
bread and homemade *brioche*) served on the terrace.
The pool has an exceptional backdrop of the Monts du
Vercors. There is a play area and donkeys and horses for
the children. Nathalie offers delicious regional dishes
and runs keep fit classes. Massages and shiatsu.

Facilities: off-street parking, extensive grounds, tv
lounge, hosts have pets, pets not accepted, dinner
available, babies welcome, free cot, 100% no smoking,
private swimming pool, riding, mushroom-picking,
hiking, cycling, interesting flora, lake watersports 10km,
riversports 20km
Basic English spoken

Directions: From Valence take the D533 towards Le
Puy-en-Velay for 12km then the D14 on the right to
Vernoux-en-Vivarais. At Vernoux, take the D2 towards
Lamastre for 7km. The 'Ferme de Prémaure' is on the
right.

38.21 Vienne

Château/Manor House

Bienvenue en France

Danielle & Michel PLAS
**'Au Manoir des Forges', 22 rue Francisque
Cartallier, 38780 PONT-EVEQUE**
Tel: (0) 4 74 16 05 68
manoirdesforges@wanadoo.fr
www.manoirdesforges.com

Price Structure – 5 Bedrooms
'Baraton' & 'Valèze': bathroom, wc, twin beds: €95,60
'Gère' & 'Suze': bathroom, wc, double bed: €119,60
'Vezonne': bathroom, wc, double bed: €95,60

Extra Bed: €30
Reduction: 7 nights, groups
Capacity: 10 people

Location
3km E of VIENNE
in: Pont-Evèque
Railway station: 5km
Airport: Lyon-St Exupéry 35km
car essential

Near the Rhone Valley vineyards and Lyon, this
attractive, restored 19th-century residence offers
superb facilities: grounds, tennis court, water features
and a covered pool with a sauna and a gym. Inside, the
same standards apply to the spacious, comfortable
bedrooms, the lounge, library, billiards room. Sociable Danielle and Michel strive to offer an impeccable
service. Literature on the region is provided, as well as
themed activities. Home-cooking based on homegrown and local produce. VISA accepted.

Facilities: private parking, extensive grounds, lounge,
hosts have pets, dinner available, 100% no smoking,
closed: 1/08–31/08, private swimming pool, private
tennis court, cycling, fishing 1km, hiking 1km, vineyard
8km, interesting flora 10km, golf course 20km
Fluent English spoken

Directions: From Lyon exit A7 to Vienne. On the
quays head for L'Isle d'Abeau then Pont-Evèque
Centre. Pass in front of the church, then after the
traffic light take the first road on the right. 'Le Manoir'
is on the right.

Location
12km N of ROANNE
in: Noailly, station pick-up on arrival/departure
Railway station: 12km
Airport: St-Etienne 80km

Bienvenue en France

✹ ✹ ✹ ✹
Château/Manor House

Stroll to the lake and island pavilion from this 18th- and 19th-century château. The décor inside is refined with antiques, fireplaces and large mirrors. Certain rooms have seating in the turret whilst others like 'Victor Hugo' have superb bathrooms. There is a touch of modernity in 'Lamartine', with a round bath set into the tower! Dinner prepared from farm produce is served at the large dining table. A swimming pool, pool-house, fitness room and a Finnish sauna are on site. An attentive welcome from hosts who are always on hand.

Facilities: private parking, extensive grounds, tv lounge, hosts have pets, dinner available, babies welcome, free cot, private swimming pool, fishing, mushroom-picking, hiking, cycling, vineyard 5km, gliding 10km, riversports 10km, golf course 15km, winter sports 20km
Adequate English spoken

Directions: From Roanne, N7 towards Moulins to St-Germain-Lespinasse (12km), then the D4 on the right to Noailly. The château is 500m from the village, D4 direction Pouilly.

Anny & Alain FROUMAJOU
'Château de la Motte', La Motte, 42640 NOAILLY
Tel: (0) 4 77 66 64 60 Fax: (0) 4 77 66 68 10
chateaudelamotte@wanadoo.fr
www.chateaudelamotte.net

Price Structure – 5 Bedrooms and 1 Suite
'Victor Hugo' (our favourite room): bathroom, wc, double bed (queen-size): €105
'George Sand': lounge, bathroom, wc, double bed. En-suite room, twin beds: €97 – 2 people
€145 – 4 people
'Marcel Proust': bathroom, wc, twin beds: €97
'Sévigné': lounge, telephone, bathroom, wc, double bed: €97
'Lamartine': telephone, bathroom, wc, four-poster double bed (queen-size): €97
'Apollinaire': telephone, bathroom, wc, double bed: €74

Extra Bed: €18   **Reduction:** 7 nights
Capacity: 14 people

Location
13km S W of ROANNE
in: St-Jean-St-Maurice-sur-Loire, station pick-up on arrival/departure
Railway station: 15km
Airport: Clermont-Ferrand 100km
car essential

✹ ✹ ✹
Private Home

This restored farmhouse overlooks the Villerest Lake where they have created an outstanding environment, and we are not just talking about the view. Each room has its private area beside the lake with sun-loungers. It is also ideal for fishing. If you are to discover this area, Anne-Marie and Charles are experts, and when you return there is a jacuzzi and a hammam to enjoy. They can also call in a private masseur from the village. . . but you may prefer fishing! If you are tired on your first evening, they can provide dinner for you.

Facilities: private parking, extensive grounds, tv lounge, hosts have pets, babies welcome, free cot, 100% no smoking, 2 nights minimum stay, closed: 15/01–15/02, fishing, mushroom-picking, hiking, cycling, riversports, vineyard 3km, golf course 7km
Adequate English spoken

Directions: A72 exit 5 St-Germain-Laval. Take the D8 towards Roanne for about 10 km and then follow the signs 'La Ferme de la Source'.

Anne-Marie & Charles FRENEA
'La Ferme de la Source', Lupé,
42155 ST-JEAN-ST-MAURICE-SUR-LOIRE
Tel: (0) 4 77 63 77 63 / (0) 676 22 17 76
contact@lafermedelasource.com
www.lafermedelasource.com

Price Structure – 4 Bedrooms
'Tilleul' & 'Lotus': shower room, wc, double bed: €80
'Raphaël': shower room, wc, double bed, single bed: €80 – 2 people €90 – 3 people
'Grain d'orge': shower room, wc, double bed: €65

Extra Bed: €10
Capacity: 9 people

Rhône-Alpes – Roanne

69.17 Lyon

Residence of Outstanding Character

Véronique MAIRE
7 ter rue Chevalier, 69390 VOURLES
Tel: (0) 4 72 31 60 45
maire.vourles@wanadoo.fr
www.chambresdhotesvourles.com

Price Structure – 2 Bedrooms
television, shower, double bed: €50
television, shower room, wc, double bed: €50

Extra Bed: €12
Capacity: 4 people

Location
17Km S of LYON
in: Vourles
Airport: Lyon-St Exupéry 17km
car essential

This place is reminiscent of the TV series *The Little House on the Prairie*, but in modern style. So if you are over 30, do not expect to meet Charles Ingalls, but rather Véronique and her five adolescent children. The family is very extrovert, welcoming and with a great sense of sharing. Lots of French windows open on to the grounds with its pool. The beautiful house has a lot of charm

Facilities: extensive grounds, lounge, pets not accepted, babies welcome, free cot, 100% no smoking, closed: 1/08–25/08, private swimming pool
Fluent English spoken

Directions: Please contact your hosts for detailed directions.

01.08 Lyon

Private Home

Christine & Jean CABARDI
'La Villa du Rhône', 58 chemin de la Lune,
01700 MIRIBEL
Tel: (0) 4 78 55 54 16
contact@lavilladurhone.com
www.lavilladurhone.com

Price Structure – 3 Bedrooms and 1 Suite
'Cèdres' (our favourite room): lounge, television, bathroom, wc, double bed (queen-size): €110
'Palmiers': television, shower room, wc, double bed: €110
'Les Mûriers': lounge, television, shower room, wc, double bed: €90
'Les Cyprès': television, shower room, wc, double bed. En-suite room, television, double bed, single bed: €90 – 2 people €150 – 5 people

Extra Bed: €15
Reduction: groups, children
Capacity: 11 people

Location
12km N E of LYON
in: Miribel, station pick-up on arrival/departure
Railway station: 2km
Airport: Lyon-St Exupéry 20km

Christine and Jean's modern villa is close to Lyon, on the slopes of a wooded hillside. It is well placed for visiting the region and particularly the European Bird Sanctuary at Les Dombes. Bedrooms have a private terrace overlooking the swimming pool, and an uninterrupted view over the Rhône Valley and the Alps. Breakfast and dinner are served in a large room open onto the flower garden.

Facilities: private parking, extensive grounds, hosts have pets, dinner available, private swimming pool, hiking, cycling 3km, lake watersports 3km, riversports 3km, golf course 5km, interesting flora 5km, bird-watching 10km, winter sports 70km
Fluent English spoken

Directions: Follow the ring road round Lyon to the east, exit at Rillieux and then follow signs to 'Le Mas Riller'. In the village, turn right towards Miribel. As you go down the hill, you will come to a bend and a statue of the Virgin Mary. Turn right after the statue into Chemin de la Lune.

69.16 Villefranche-sur-Saône

Location
12km S W of VILLEFRANCHE-SUR-SAONE
in: Theizé
Railway station: 12km
Airport: Lyon-St Exupéry 50km
car essential

Bienvenue en France

✸✸✸

Residence of Outstanding Character

Amid the vines, this former winemaker's abode from 1790 is in typical golden Beaujolais stone. The cellars and vats have been preserved. The comfortable bedrooms are well decorated, have a warm feel and are in an independent wing. A drawing room with literature and tea/coffee making facilities is available. The sitting room (in summer) is really quite beautiful with paintings and wood panelling. Christine advises on visits and tastings; she loves to cook and serves dinner, with wine of course! She also enjoys gardening.

Facilities: private parking, garden, lounge, hosts have pets, pets not accepted, dinner available, babies welcome, free cot, 10 years old minimum age, closed: 15/01–01/03, private swimming pool, hiking, cycling, vineyard, lake watersports, golf course 12km
Fluent English spoken

Christine LACK
'Le Clos des Pierres Dorées', Le Boitier,
69620 THEIZE
Tel: (0) 4 74 71 26 38 / (0) 619 29 40 97
closdespierresdorees@wanadoo.fr
http://perso.wanadoo.fr/closdespierresdorees/

Price Structure – 3 Bedrooms
'Tilleul': shower room, wc, four-poster double bed (queen-size): €105
'Acacia': shower room, wc, double bed: €95
'Cèdre': shower room, wc, twin beds: €110

Capacity: 6 people

Directions: From the A6 motorway, exit Villefranche then head for direction Roanne. On the D38, after 'Le Grand Passeloup', at the crossroads at Alix, turn right and follow the signs, the ones with a green background.

73.17 Albertville

Location
23km S W of ALBERTVILLE
in: St-Pierre-d'Albigny, station pick-up on arrival/departure
Railway station: 3km
Airport: Lyon-St Exupéry 120km
car essential

Bienvenue en France

✸✸

Private Home

Amongst the vines, against the crenellated silhouette of the imposing Château de Miolans (the Marquis de Sade stayed here), is the home of Marie-Reine and Serge. It is in the barn of this former village farm, adjoining the house, where they have created a sort of small apartment with mod cons (fridge, microwave) whilst maintaining the character of the stone walls and wooden beams. There is a lounge area, a kitchenette and a mini-mezzanine for the children. A keen walker, Marie-Reine can advise on the paths in this beautiful area.

Facilities: off-street parking, garden, lounge, babies welcome, free cot, hiking, vineyard, gliding 25km, winter sports 40km
Basic English spoken

Marie-Reine & Serge LIMARE
'Le Bourget', 73250 ST-PIERRE-D'ALBIGNY
Tel: (0) 4 79 71 17 32 / (0) 621 20 76 11
slimare@club-internet.fr

Price Structure – 1 Apartment
studio: lounge, kitchen, along corridor shower room, wc, double bed, twin beds: €55 – 2 people
€80 – 4 people

Extra Bed: €15
Reduction: 6 nights
Capacity: 4 people

Directions: A43, exit 23. N6 towards Albertville for 3km then at the Pont Royal crossroads, turn left onto the D32, a small road heading towards Château de Miolans, Le Bourget. Pass the level-crossing and keep to the right and then at the next crossroads (in front of the cross) turn right towards Fréterive and then straight away turn left into a small road that passes in front of a fountain. The house is immediately on your left just behind some ruins.

74.34 Annecy

Private Home

Location
34km E of ANNECY
in: Entremont, station pick-up on arrival/departure
car essential

Bienvenue en France

Stéphanie POLLET-VILLARD
'Les Sapins', Le Pont Nord, 74130 ENTREMONT
Tel: (0) 4 50 25 97 05 / (0) 668 43 67 96
Fax: (0) 4 50 25 88 47
spollet_villard@club-internet.fr
www.giteentremont.com

Price Structure – 8 Bedrooms and 1 Suite
suite: television, bathroom, shower, wc, double bed.
En-suite room, washbasin, 2 single beds:
€90 – 2 people €160 – 4 people
2 rooms: television, bathroom, wc, twin beds (or double bed), single bed: €120 – 3 people
1 room: television, bathroom, wc, double bed: €90
4 rooms: television, bathroom, wc, double bed (queen-size): €90
1 room: wheelchair access, television, bathroom, wc, double bed (queen-size): €90

Reduction: 4 nights, groups
Capacity: 22 people

You cannot miss this large Savoyard house, next to the sawmill between the road and the river that runs at the bottom of the garden. As you park your car, take a deep breath of clean mountain air. Stéphanie is new to B&B and is bubbling over with enthusiasm to make her guests welcome. The spacious guest bedrooms are all sparkling new and cosy, with pine-panelled walls and despite there being just two floors, she has even installed a lift. You will sleep well here, lulled in your slumber by the goat's bells and the rushing river.

Facilities: off-street parking, extensive grounds, tv lounge, hosts have pets, dinner available, wheelchair access, fishing, mushroom-picking, hiking, cycling, interesting flora, golf course 5km, winter sports 5km, riversports 10km, lake watersports 30km
Fluent English spoken

Directions: Please contact your host in advance for detailed directions.

74.25 Annecy

Private Home

Location
20km S of ANNECY
in: Lathuile
Railway station: 15km
Airport: Geneva 60km
car essential

Bienvenue en France

Sylvie & Jean-François CERCELET
'La Grange de Julie', 450 route de Chevilly, 74210 LATHUILE
Tel: (0) 4 50 44 38 87 Fax: (0) 4 50 44 38 81
lagrangedejulie@wanadoo.fr
www.homestead.com/lagrangedeJulie

Price Structure – 4 Bedrooms and 1 Suite
first room: bathroom, wc, double bed: €85
second room: bathroom, wc, double bed, single bed: €85 – 2 people €105 – 3 people
third room: bathroom, wc, 2 single beds: €85
fourth room: bathroom, wc, twin beds, single bed (child-size): €85 – 2 people €105 – 3 people
suite: television, bathroom, wc, twin beds. En-suite room, double bed: €100 – 2 people
€140 – 4 people

Extra Bed: €20
Reduction: 1/09–30/06, 7 nights, children
Capacity: 14 people

Situated on the western slopes facing the Lac d'Annecy, this pretty barn has been completely transformed by the talents of interior designer Jean-François. You will marvel at the large living room with its enormous wooden staircase. You can easily walk from here to the lakeside and the beaches. The air is pure and there is an almost Swiss quality about the cleanliness. Another bonus is the beautiful view of Les Dents de Lanfon and its wooded peaks which overlook the lake.

Facilities: off-street parking, garden, lounge, hosts have pets, dinner available, babies welcome, free cot, hiking, cycling, interesting flora, mushroom-picking, riversports, fishing 1km, lake watersports 1km, golf course 4km, winter sports 15km
Fluent English spoken

Directions: Follow the lake on the N508 towards Albertville. At Le Bout-du-Lac, bear right towards Lathuile as far as the roundabout. Then take Route de Chevilly on the right and continue for about 450m.

Location
15km N of ANNECY
in: Thorens-Glières, station pick-up
on arrival/departure
Airport: Geneva 30km
car essential

Private Home

This large restored Savoy farmhouse is buried amongst the trees overlooking the nature reserve 'Sous-Dine' famous for its flora and wildlife. Totally immersed in the forest, you will sleep well after wonderful hikes and the traditional dishes served around the fire in the large dining room. Yann, who is a ski instructor, takes really good care of his guests and organises many activities and themed evenings throughout the season.

Yann & Claude MUFFAT
'Domaine de la Sapinière', La Borne,
74570 THORENS-GLIERES
Tel: (0) 4 50 22 85 92 / (0) 685 02 55 68
Fax: (0) 4 50 22 85 93
sapinere@aol.com
www.domaine-sapiniere.com

Facilities: private parking, extensive grounds, lounge, hosts have pets, dinner available, babies welcome, free cot, riding, hiking, cycling, hunting, interesting flora, mushroom-picking, fishing 1km, riversports 5km, winter sports 5km, lake watersports 20km
Fluent English spoken

Directions: From Annecy N203 towards Cluses for 12km as far as Le Plot. Right onto D2 as far as Thorens-Glières then continue onto the D22 towards La Roche-sur-Foron for 5km. Left into the little road and follow signs to 'Domaine de la Sapinière'.

Price Structure – 9 Bedrooms
3 rooms: television, bathroom, wc, double bed, 2 single beds: €72 – 2 people €140 – 4 people
rooms 2 & 3: television, telephone, shower room, wc, double bed, single bed: €72 – 2 people
€100 – 3 people
1 room: television, telephone, bathroom, wc, double bed, 5 single beds: €230 – 7 people
1 room: television, telephone, bathroom, wc, double bed, 3 single beds: €175 – 5 people
rooms 7 & 8: television, telephone, shower room, wc, 2 double beds, single bed: €175 – 5 people

Capacity: 40 people

Location
30km S W of CHAMONIX
in: Les Contamines-Montjoie,
station pick-up on arrival/departure
Railway station: 15km
Airport: Geneva 80km

Private Home

At the foot of glaciers, opposite Mont Blanc, is this contemporary chalet run by a Scottish couple. The bedrooms are not large but they are comfortable and have a safe, CD player, a canopy over the bed and some have a balcony. The hot tub offers a fabulous view of the stars, and there is a sauna and a fitness room. In winter, with the panoramic backdrop of the Alps, enjoy dinner prepared by an experienced chef. In summer, innumerable activities are on offer. The warm family atmosphere and the exemplary facilities earns a deserved four 'suns'.

Fiona & Christopher HOPKINSON
'Chalet Chovettaz', 30 chemin la Chovettaz d'en
haut, 74170 LES CONTAMINES-MONTJOIE
Tel: (0) 4 50 47 73 05 / (0) 627 39 02 70
Fax: (0) 4 50 90 30 81
enquiries@skicontamines.com
www.skicontamines.com

Facilities: off-street parking, garden, tv lounge, hosts have pets, dinner available, babies welcome, free cot, 100% no smoking, closed: 24/04–4/06 & 22/10–16/12, fishing, hiking, cycling, interesting flora, winter sports, golf course 20km, riversports 20km
Fluent English spoken

Directions: A40, exit at Sallanches and head for Megève and then take the exit for St-Gervais-les-Bains. Next take the D902 towards Les Contamines-Montjoie. Before arriving at the village, take the road Plan du Moulin on the right signed 'Accès au piste, téléphérique'. Cross the bridge and the chalet is on the fourth road on the right.

Price Structure – 6 Bedrooms
first room: bathroom, wc, shower, double bed: €100
second room: bathroom, wc, shower, twin beds, 2 single beds: €100 – 2 people €180 – 4 people
third room: bathroom, wc, shower, double bed (king-size): €100
fourth room: bathroom, wc, shower, four-poster double bed: €100
fifth room: bathroom, wc, shower, twin beds: €100
sixth room: shower room, wc, twin beds: €75

Extra Bed: €15
Reduction: 4 nights, children
Capacity: 14 people

74.16 Chamonix

Private Home

Location
3km S W of CHAMONIX
in: Les Houches
Railway station: Taconnaz
Airport: Geneva 70km

This chalet, typical of the Chamonix Valley, is covered with masses of hanging baskets. There is a wonderful view of Mont Blanc from the balcony. Marcel is a blacksmith who knows this area in depth and Danièle is a wonderful cook, famous for her local dishes. This place is well worth a visit at any time of the year and if you are going to Chamonix, you must be sure to go and see Danièle! Half-board available.

Danièle & Marcel FRASSERAND
'Chalet à l'Orée du Bois', Fond de Taconnaz,
74310 LES HOUCHES
Tel: (0) 4 50 54 46 80 / (0) 4 50 55 53 14 Fax: (0)
4 50 54 54 73
chalet@oreedubois.net
www.oreedubois.net

Price Structure – 5 Bedrooms
'Amis': television, shower room, wc, bathroom, double bed, 2 single beds: €74 – 2 people
€90 – 4 people
'Alain': television, bathroom, wc, double bed: €57
'Drus' & 'Merlet': television, shower room, wc, double bed, single bed: €57 – 2 people €74 – 3 people
'Brevent': television, shower room, wc, double bed: €51

Extra Bed: €17
Reduction: children
Capacity: 14 people

Facilities: private parking, garden, hosts have pets, pets not accepted, dinner available, babies welcome, free cot, 100% no smoking, wheelchair access, 3 nights minimum stay: 01/07-31/08, hiking, cycling, fishing, riversports, winter sports 2km, golf course 5km
Adequate English spoken

Directions: From the A40, take the N205 towards Chamonix. Go through Les Houches and 1km after the petrol station turn left towards Les Bossons for 400m and then left under the bridge.

74.31 Megève

Private Home

Location
3km N of MEGEVE
in: Demi-Quartier, station pick-up on arrival/departure
Railway station: 2km
Airport: Geneva 70km

This renovated farm, done with taste by a British couple, is close to Megève, a small medieval town transformed by Mme de Rothschild in the 60s into a chic ski resort. Enjoy 300km of slopes and ski right up to the chalet. The interior is just as good, with a long lounge and a traditional fireplace supported by massive beams. Charming bedrooms with solid wood doors, terracotta tiles and stone bathrooms. After skiing or walking tuck into a copious home-cooked meal. Impeccably well-kept and social. Excellent, pushing four 'suns' in winter!

Claudia & Simon BLUNDELL
'Ferme Le Petit Bois', 1478 route de Sallanches,
74120 DEMI-QUARTIER
Tel: (0) 4 50 90 13 06 Fax: (0) 4 50 90 13 06
info@skifarm.com
www.skifarm.com

Price Structure – 5 Bedrooms
2 rooms: bathroom, double bed, single bed (child-size): €100 – 2 people €100 – 3 people
3 rooms: shower, double bed: €100

Extra Bed: €10
Capacity: 12 people

Facilities: off-street parking, garden, tv lounge, hosts have pets, pets not accepted, dinner available, babies welcome, free cot, 100% no smoking, hiking, cycling, winter sports, golf course 2km
Fluent English spoken

Directions: A40, exit at Sallanches and head for Megève on the N212. The hamlet Demi-Lune is on this road 2km before Megève. The house is on the left just after the 'Hôtel Demi Lune'.

Location
17km S E of THONON-LES-BAINS
in: La Baume
Railway station: 17km
Airport: Geneva 50km
car essential

**Residence of
Outstanding
Character**

A charming restored 19th-century *Savoyarde* farm, redecorated by Catherine. She offers four spacious, comfortable bedrooms, prettily decorated with traditional regional furniture. The 'Célestin' room with a sloping ceiling has a beautiful panoramic view whilst the other bedrooms benefit from a large balcony. A sloping, lush garden is crossed by a mountain stream. The *livre d'Or* here is full of praise for Catherine's cooking! All year the welcome is warm and attentive. NB. In winter your vehicle must be well-equipped.

**Catherine COULAIS
'La Ferme aux Ours', La Voagère,
74430 LA BAUME
Tel: (0) 4 50 72 19 88 / (0) 607 29 73 44
catherine.coulais@wanadoo.fr
www.lafermeauxours.com**

Facilities: off-street parking, garden, lounge, hosts have pets, pets not accepted, dinner available, kitchen, babies welcome, free cot, 100% no smoking, closed: 10/11–30/11, hiking, fishing 4km, cycling 5km, winter sports 5km, riversports 5km, golf course 21km
Fluent English spoken

Price Structure – 4 Bedrooms
'Anatole': bathroom, wc, double bed: €95
'Barnabé': bathroom, wc, double bed: €95
'Basile': shower room, wc, twin beds: €85
'Célestin': twin beds, 2 single beds: €95 – 2 people
€130 – 4 people

Directions: From Thonon-les-Bains, take the D902 towards Morzine for 18km, then head for La Baume on the right. Continue a little bit further on, passing in front of the church, then follow the signs for about 1km.

Reduction: 01/05–30/11, 7 nights
Capacity: 10 people

Rhône-Alpes – Thonon-les-Bains

Index of towns

Index of towns

Index of towns

Le Feedback

Please tell us what you think of the places at which you stayed, taking into account VALUE FOR MONEY, COMFORT, WELCOME, LOCATION, FOOD and SPECIAL INTERESTS. It is our policy to pass on all guests' comments to our hosts. If you do not wish us to do this, tick the box below.

☐ I do not wish for my comments to be passed on to the hosts.

☐ I booked direct or ☐ My reservation number is: _____

Please indicate the Host Reference Number for each place.

_____

_____

_____

_____

_____

_____

_____

_____

_____

_____

_____

_____

Name: _____

Address: _____

Town: _____ Post Code: _____ Country: _____

Telephone: _____ Fax: _____

E-mail: _____

Please return to:
Customer Service, Bed & Breakfast France, PO Box 47085, London, SW18 9AB, UK or E-mail bookings@bedbreak.com; Fax 0871 781 0835 – UK Only – Outside UK +33 1 39 94 89 72

BED AND BREAKFAST FRANCE

Arrive as a guest... leave as a friend!

To book direct with your host
either telephone or complete this letter and post, e-mail or fax it.
Be sure to mention Bed & Breakfast France.

Date:

Madame, Monsieur,

Nous avons trouvé vos coordonnées dans le guide *Bed & Breakfast FRANCE* de Thomas Cook Publishing. Nous souhaiterions séjourner chez vous. Vous trouverez ci-dessous les informations concernant notre demande de réservation. Voulez-vous nous dire très rapidement si les dates souhaitées vous conviennent et ce que nous devons faire pour confirmer cette réservation. Dans l'attente du plaisir de vous rencontrer, nous vous prions d'agréer, Madame, Monsieur, nos salutations distinguées.

Signature: _____

Number of Adults: _____ Number of Children (with Ages): _____

Room Arrangement: _____

Date of Arrival: _____ Date of Departure: _____

Number of Nights: _____

Train station pick up (with contribution towards car expenses) from: _____ station requested.

Dinner Requested Yes/No: _____ Time of arrival: _____

Mr / Mrs / Ms   First Name – Family Name

_____

Address: _____

_____

Town: _____ Post Code: _____ Country: _____

Telephone: _____ Fax: _____

E-mail: _____